A Question Bank on Veterinary Science for Competitive Exams

ABOUT THE AUTHORS

Dr. Ajay Kumar Upadhyay born at District Azamgarh and did his pre-graduation schooling at Prestigious S.K. Inter College, popularly known as 'Khatri Pathshala' of Alalhabad that has a very rich galaxy of alumni.

He did his graduation in the year 1986 from College of Veterinary Sciences, G.B. Pant University of Agriculture and Technology, Post graduation from Indian Veterinary Research Institute, Bareilly and Ph.D. work back from the graduating institute.

He served the Department of Animal Husbandry during the year 1990 & 1991 and joined as Assistant Professor in December 1991 at the Department of Medicine, College of Veterinary Sciences, Pantnagar. He became Associate Professor in the Department of Epidemiology and Preventive Medicine in the year 2001. Now working as Associate Professor, Veterinary Public Health and Epidemiology and In-charge of the department. He is member of 11 professional societies and authored more than 5 books and 6 manuals. He has earned several honours and awards related with professional work and fellow of Academy of Sciences for Animal Welfare.

Dr. S. C. Tripathi, MVSc, Ph.D, is working as Professor in the Department of Veterinary and Animal Husbandry Extension Education, College of Veterinary & Animal Sciences, Pantnagar. He is having over 25 years of experience in teaching, research, extension and administration. Dr. Tripathi has published over 40 research and semi research papers in journals of national & international repute. He has contributed number of policy papers and chapters in books and authored 8 proceedings. His proceedings "Food Safety Quality Assurance and Global Trade: Concerns & Strategies" published by IBDC Lucknow, fetch special attention of readers and policy planners. Dr Tripathi worked as technical advisor to Minister for Animal Husbandry & Fisheries, Uttar Pradesh as well as UP Poultry & Livestock Specialities Ltd., UP while working as Scientific Officer, U P Council of Agricultural Research (UP). Various awards and honours conferred to Dr. Tripathi include Late G.V. Narayana Khedkar Memorial Award-2002, Vigyan Bharti Appreciation Award-2000 and Pashu Mitra Award-1999.

Dr. R.J. Sharma born on July 5, 1948 in village Rampur of Aligarh district in U.P. He began his professional Journey in Veterinary Sciences in 1966 to earn B. V.Sc. & A.H. degree he obtained M.V.Sc. and Ph.D. degrees in Animal Genetics and Breeding in 1972 and 1983, respectively. He joined as Veterinary Assistant Surgeon from January 1970 to July 1970 in Animal Husbandry Department, U.P. He served G.B. Pant University of Agriculture & Technology from February 1972 to March 1974 as Assistant Extension Specialist from March 1974 to March 1986 as Subject Matter' Specialist and from March 1986 to October 1996 as Associate Professor and then as Professor and Head of the department of LPM from August 2002 to July 2005. He remained as Joint Director, IDF and IPF. He was adorned as Dean, College of Veterinary and Animal Sciences from August, 2005 to July, 2008 and rendered matchless leadership. He handled 26 research projects and successfully guided 8 Post Graduate and 3 Ph. D. students. He has published more than 40 research papers and 120 Hindi articles in national and international journals of repute. He authored 5 books, 6 booklets, 10 chapters, 60 leaflets and folders and 7 laboratory manuals. He was awarded Dr. Rajendra Prasad Award in 1985 and 1987 for his popular books, which are frequently referred by the students and researchers.

A Question Bank on Veterinary Science for Competitive Exams

Dr. A.K. Upadhyay
Dr. S.C. Tripathi
Dr. R.J. Sharma

2015

Educationist Press

A Division of

Write & Print Publications

New Delhi-110 015

ISBN: 978-93-84649-17-3

Published by : Hitesh Mittal
For Write & Print Publications
H-13, Bali Nagar
New Delhi-110 015
Phone: 011-45635684
E-mail: info@writeandprint.com
Website: www.writeandprint.com

Laser Typesetting : Rajender Vashist
Delhi - 110 059

Printed at : Salasar Imaging Systems
Delhi - 110 035,
Phone: 011-27185653

Preface

Lot many of our graduating as well as graduate students felt need of a good book containing all the relevant information of various subjects of Veterinary sciences in a concise form that can be helpful in their preparation of various competitive examinations like JRF and Civil Services. We tried at our level best to provide all such informations in this book needed by students who are preparing for their life shaping competitions. This is one of the unique books of its type which included comprehensive knowledge of all works of Veterinary Science. The entire book has been divided in thirteen chapters and the first three chapters are unique in way that it covers all the general aspects of veterinary sciences. It also includes historical background of development of veterinary sciences and some very pertinent information of the subject. Chapter four to thirteen covers multiple type questions of all the subjects of veterinary sciences. Contents of the book are presented in a way so that students may get maximum benefit out of it. Multiple type questions of a particular subject have covered all the related aspects.

We are thankful to all the authors of different kind of veterinary sciences books because visiting of those books only can provide materials for preparation of this book.

Dr. A.K. Upadhyay
Dr. S.C. Tripathi
Dr. R.J. Sharma

Contents

1 History of Veterinary Science

- A special branch of Indian medicine was devoted to the treatment of elephants was called Hastyayurveda.
- Brothers of King Yudhisthir (Pandav Emperor) namely Nakula and Sahdeva were considered as foremost practitioner of Veterinary Science. They had expertise in equine husbandry.
- Charaka, the great Ayurvedic physician of the 1st Century AD, had written Charaka Samhita, the first scientific medical text. Charaka's work consisted of eight chapters devoted to pharmacology, diet and treatment of major diseases like fever, diarrhoea, consumption, leprosy and tumour among others. He also wrote on specialized subjects such as pathology, embryology and anatomy.
- In third fourth century B.C., in the Ashoka's times, there were great advances in veterinary science. For treatment of elephants, "Palkapya Samhita" and for treatment of horses, "Shalihotra Samhita" was written. We find in his edicts, mention of hospitals established by him for men and animals even in far off places in south India.
- In the fourth century, came Sushruta, who is considered the father of surgery. In his treatise Sushruta Samhita, he lists about 125 surgical instruments used by him in his surgeries, details methods of operations among other subjects. In his time he is believed to have performed Caesarean sections, done plastic surgeries and set compound fractures.
- First veterinary school was opened in India by English people in Puna in later half of 19th century.
- The history of domesticated elephants in India goes to about 6000 B.C. Seals of the Indus Valley Civilization (2500-1500 B.C.) also suggest the presence of domesticated elephants in India at that time. Aryans, who are believed to have entered India about 1500 B.C., picked up the art of domesticating elephants in the process of assimilating the culture of the country they had adopted. Ancient literature, such as the *Rig Veda* (1500-1000 B.C.) and the *Upanishads* (900-500 B.C.), which is associated with the Aryans, contains many references to trained elephants. Vedic literature also confirms that by the Sixth Century B.C., the taming and catching of elephants had become quite a refined art.
- Knowledge about elephants was considered as a part of '*Arthasastra*', the science of statecraft. In Kautilya's *Arthasastra* (300 B.C. to 300 A.D.) there is a reference to the duty of the overseer of elephants to take care of training. It prescribes the setting up of elephant sanctuaries on the periphery of the kingdom that were to be patrolled by guards. Anyone killing an elephant within the sanctuary was to be put to death. It also prohibits the capturing of elephant calves, tusker bulls or those with small tusks, diseased elephants and cows with suckling calves. During the regime of Emperor Ashoka (273-232 B.C.) the elephant became the symbol of Buddhism. The Ashokan edicts refer to setting up of hospitals for the treatment of elephants and other animals.
- The 'Pit Method' of capturing was popular in southern India until recently. The *Khedda* (*i.e.* Stockade Method), with many variations, has been prevalent in different parts of the country and has also been recorded by Megasthanese, the Greek envoy to the court of the Emperor Chandra Gupta Maurya (third century B.C.). It was introduced to the

Mysore Plateau in Southern India by Sanderson in 1874. *Mela Shikar* (*i.e.* noosing from the back of a trained elephant) is popular in the North-eastern part of the country. Sanskrit literature describes two more methods of capturing elephants: the use of female elephants as decoys and the use of nooses concealed on the ground. Indian experts have also gone to other Asian countries to teach the art of capturing and training elephants.

- The sage Palakapya (fifth or sixth century B.C.) is reputed to be the author of *Hasti ayurveda*, a treatise on the medical treatment of elephants and *Matanglila*, which is a treatise on the physical and mental characteristics of elephants, their capture and care. *Hastividyarnava*, the famous Assamese treatise on the medical treatment of elephants was authored in the 18th Century by Sukumar Borkayat on instructions from the then Ahom queen.
- First written record of veterinary medicine from ancient Egypt was provided by Kahun Papyrus (1900 B.C.)
- First mention of rabies was reported in Eshuna code of 2300 B.C.
- Ashoka (269 – 232 B.C.) made compulsory provision of Charitable animal hospitals.
- First Veterinary School at Lyon in France in 1762 and the second veterinary school at Alfort near Paris in 1776 were established.
- Royal charter (1844) recognized the Veterinary Art as a profession.
- First Army Veterinary School of India was opened at Poona 1862.
- First Veterinary College of India was set in 1877 at Babugarh.
- Imperial Bacteriological Laboratory in 1889 was established at Mukteswar Uttarakhand (then U.P.).
- According to Chamber's English Dictionary;

Veterinary means:

i. as Adjective; concerned with diseases of animals

ii. as Noun; one skilled in disease of domestic animals and

HERMITAGES IN BHARHUT SCULPTURES (c. second century B.C.)

iii. Originated from Latin word *Veterinarius* (veterinae), means cattle, Beasts of Burden.

The ascetic, clad in birch bark, with matted hair bound up into a knot, leaning and grieving over his dead pet antelope.

2 Did You Know That.....

- *Ablation* refers to excision or amputation.
- *Abstem* is citrated Calcium carbimide.
- *Acholia* means absence of bile.
- *Acrodynia* is painful reddening of extremities.
- *Actinobiology* is the study of effects of radiation on livery organisms.
- *Kynology* is study of dogs.
- Congenital absence of bladder is *acystia*.
- Inflammation of a gland or lymph nodc is *adenitis*.
- *Hilar adenitis* is inflammation of bronchial lymph nodes.
- *Ametria* refers to congenital absence of uterus.
- *Anastomosis* is establishment of intercommunication between two hollow organs, vessels or nerves.
- *Atavism* is reappearance of a hereditary trait, which was disappeared in one or more generations.
- *Athlete's foot* is a fungal disease caused by *Tinea podia*.
- *BIPP* is pasty mixture of bismuth subnitrate, iodoform, liquid paraffin.
- *Bulimia* refers to excessive appetite.
- *Callosity* is local hardening of skin, caused by Pressure or friction.
- *Canicola fever* is leptospirosis in man by species of Leptospira from rats, dogs, pigs, (*Leptospira canicola*) foxes, mice, voles.
- Chromicised catgut and iodized catgut holds for 20-40 days, after suturing.
- *Cheilitis* is inflammation of lip.
- *Chemosis* is swelling of bulbar conjunctiva.
- *Chyme* is partially digested food while chyle is digested fats.
- Enlargement of a vein is known as *cirsoid*.
- Clavicle is also known as ***Collar bone***.
- *Colpitis* is inflammation of vagina.
- *Demulcent* is a slippery, mucilaginous fluid which allays invitation and soothes inflammation.
- **Hydropic degeneration** is usually associated with epithelial lesions.
- Hydropic degeneration with inclusion bodies in urinary tract epithelium of dogs indicates **distemper** disease.

- Most common location of fatty degeneration is **liver**, followed by kidney and heart.
- Liver is considered the **nutritional guardian** of the body.
- **Fatty liver** is seen in diabetes (dogs) and Ketosis (cows).
- Periacinar distribution of lipids is the most common distribution of fatty liver.
- **Fatty liver** has yellow colour and greasy texture on cut surface.
- **Steatosis** is fatty infiltration resulting mottled colour of muscle.
- **Hyaline droplets** are small ionisaphlic structure in cytoplasm of cells.
- **Fibrinoid** is eosinophilic material in blood vessel common in Arthus reaction, mast cell tumors.
- **Amyloid** is the best known primary cause of uremia.
- Without meiosis, sexual reproduction is not possible.
- First meiotic division during spermatogenesis occurs in primary spermatocyte to form secondary spermatocyte.
- During spermatogenesis, second meiotic division occurs between secondary spermatocyte and spermatic.
- 4n condition appears in primary oocyte and is condition in ovum.
- Two polar bodies are formed during oogenesis in farm animals.
- First polar body has diploid chromosome number while second polar body has haploid chromosome number.
- Diameter of a chromosome is approximately 0.2 m.
- **Allelomorphs** usually affect a trait in contrasting manners.
- Deletions never mutate back to normal.
- **Andalusian** poultry is example of blending inheritance or in complete dominance.
- 9: 3: 3: 1 ratio is obtained in F_2 generation of dihybrid inheritance.
- $2\ p\ q = 2 \times p^2\ q^2$ is known as **Hardy Weinberg Equation**.
- Deaf mutism is a case of epistasis. This is also called duplicate recessive epistasis.
- Hardy Weinberg principle determines frequency of a particular recessive allele in a population.
- Baldness in men is sex linked trait.
- Hen feathered condition in poultry is an example of a sex limited trait.
- A woman with Turner's syndrome has one X-chromosome and no Barr body.
- Male with **Klinefelter syndrome** has one Barr body.
- Black and white spotted condition in Holstein cattle occurs due to single pair of recessive genes. This is an example of Modifying genes.
- Muton is the smallest genetic unit capable of mutation.
- Recon is smallest individual unit of DNA capable of recombination.
- Muton and recon are single bases in a nucleotide.
- Cistron is the unit of DNA carrying information for formation of one polypeptide chain in protein formation.
- mRNA carries genetic code.
- **Cytoplasmic RNA** is also known as tRNA.
- Only two amino acids have single genetic code.
- All the 64 triplets do not code for amino acids.
- PMCG and FSH are most commonly used to induce superovulation.
- Animal husbandry contributes about 24% to the India's agriculture output.
- India is the largest producer of milk in world (100.9 mmt in 2007 -08).
- Per capita availability of milk in India is 245 gm per day. (2007-08).
- India ranks fifth in egg production in the world.
- India has 27 indigenous cattle and 7 buffalo breeds.
- Central frozen semen production and training Institute (CFSPTI) is situated in Hessarghatta (Karnataka).
- IgG is **heterocytotropic** antibody.
- Chromosome 6 in human has major histocompatibility complex.
- Sequence of appearance of complements in classic pathway is: C1-C4-C2-C3-C5-C6-C9.
- Cellular immunity was evolved before humoral immunity.

- T and B lymphocytes are first seen in amphibian during evolution.
- IgM Antigen interaction is most important initiating stimulus for the classic complement pathway.
- Monocytes are largest white blood cells.
- Monocyte has kidney shaped nucleus.
- Presence of macrophage indicates non-antigenic irritant.
- Presence of mural cardiac thrombi is pathognomic lesion of black quarter.
- H. N. Ray gave stilbamidine test for trypanosma.
- P. G. Pandey discovered *Stephanofilaria assamensis*.
- Alfred Lingard was first director of IVRI.
- Hoogstral is known as Master of Ticks.
- Fasciola was discovered by Rinhow.
- *Fasciolopsis buski* is a true zoonotic.
- Moneizia is most common tapeworm of ruminants.
- White spots in liver, caused by *Ascaris suum*, are known as Milk spots.
- IgG is found in highest concentration in serum as compared to other Ig.
- Ig M has highest sedimentation coefficient (19).
- Heaviest Ig is IgM (900, 000 mol. Wt.).
- Only IgG crosses placenta.
- Ig G is lightest immunoglobulin (mol. Wt. 140,000).
- Ig G is most common serum antibody.
- Ig G opsonise virus and bacterial toxins.
- Ig A is also called as Secretory or coproantibody.
- Ig M is first antibody formed as compared to other Ig.
- Ig M is the most efficient class of Ig in fixing complement.
- Ig A is a part of first line of defence.
- Ig M is the only antibody found in shark.
- Salmonella infection triggers IgM production.
- IgA is principal antibody in human colostrum.
- Ig G is principal antibody in animal colostrum.
- Ig E is homocytotropic.
- Metastrongylus, also known as lungworm of pig, carries Swine Influenza Virus.
- Husk or Hoose Disease is caused by Dictyocaulus.
- Trichostrongylloidea members are also known as Geohelminths.
- Dewclaw sore is caused by *Stephanofilaria kaili*.
- Asuntol is drug of choice for Stephonofilaria.
- Indian Kalazar is not a zoonotic disease.
- Kalazar is also known as Dum Dum fever.

Animal diseases and their nicknames

Diseases	Nick name/s
Anaplasmosis	Gall sickness
Hemobartenellosis	Feline infectious anaemia
Schistosomiasis	Bilharzia
Trypanosoma cruzi infection	Chagas disease
Trypanosoma evansi infection	Surra
Trypanosoma equipardum	Dourine
Congenital intrinsic Platelet function disorder	Chediak higashi syndrome
Congenital Extrinsic Platelet Function Disorder	Von will brand's disease
Cutaneous asthenia	Ehlers danlos syndrome Rubber puppy disease
Streptococcal lymphadenitis in pigs	Jowl abscess
Dirofilariasis	Heart worm disease
High mountain disease	Brisket disease; Pulmonary hypertensive heart disease.
Clostridium piliforme disease	Tyzzer's disease
Brachygnathia	Parrot mouth (in horse)
Prognathia .	Sow mouth (in horses)
Ankyloglossia	Bird tongue (abnormal incomplete tongue)
Epitheliogenesis imperfecta	Smooth tongue (incomplete development of lingual filiform papillae)
Segmented aplasia	Rectal agenesis
Epulis	Gingival hyperplasia or Fibromatosis gingivae
Lipomatosis	Abnormal fat necrosis
Bloat	Ruminal tympany
Lactic acidosis	Grain overload
Hardware disease	Traumatic gastritis or Traumatic reticulo-peritonitis
Fasciolocides magna infection	Giant liver fluke infection
Dicrocoelium dendriticum infection	Lancet fluke infection
Eurytrema infection	Pancreatic fluke infection
Paramphistome infection	Rumen fluke infection or Conical fluke infection
Trichostrongylus axei infection	Hair worm infection
Theiler's disease	Serum hepatitis Idiopathic Acute Hepatitis
Black disease	Infectious necrotic hepatitis (by *Clostridium novyi* B)
Equine ehrlichial colitis	Potomac horse fever
Escherichia coli enterotoxemia	Edema disease
Porcine proliferative enteritis	Ileitis or Porcine intestinal adenomatosis
Slavery mouth / Slavers / Rattle Belly	Watery mouth disease (lambs) by E. coli
Vincent's stomatitis or Trenchmouth	Necrotizing Ulcerative gingivostomatitis
Spirocerca lupi infection	Esophageal worm infection
Trichuris infection	Whipworms infection
Ancylostoma caninum infection	Hookworm infection
Acanthocephalus infection	Thorny headed worm infection
Blepheritis	Eyelid inflammation
Dacrocystitis	Lacrimal sac inflammation
Pink eye	Infectious ophthalmia
Cushing's disease	Hyperadrenocorticism
Addison's disease	Hypoadrenocorticism
Actinobacillus lignieresii infection	Wooden tongue
Actinomyces bovis infection	Lumpy jaw
Splenic fever or charbon or Milzbrand	Anthrax
Borreliosis	Lyme disease
Redwater disease	Bacillary hemoglobinunis
Clostridium chauvoei infection	Black leg disease

Diseases	Nick name/s
Clostridium novyi infection	Big head disease
Lamziekte	Botulism
Pulpy kidney disease	Type D enterotoxemia
Akabane disease	Akabane virus infection
Hairy shaker disease	Border disease (Pestivirus)
Leptospirosis	Redwater disease of calves
Circling disease	Listeriosis or Listerellosis
Plague	Yersiniosis
Tularemia	Francisella tularemia
Swamp fever	Equine infectious Anemia
Equine typhoid / Rotalaufseuche	Equine viral arteritis
Farcy	Glanders
Swine fever	Hog cholera
Glasser's disease	Infectious polyarthritis
San Mignel sea lion virus disease	Vesicular exanthema of swine
Coronaviral encephalomyelitis	Vomiting and washing disease
Ondiri disease	Bovine petechial fever
Three day sickness	Ephemeral fever
Thrombotic menigoencephalitis	Haemophilus somnus disease
Cowdriosis	Heartwater disease
Snotsiektte	Catarrhal fever or gangrenous coryza
Johne's disease	Paratuberculosis
Cattle plague	Rinderpest
Hardpad disease	Canine distemper
Feline distemper	Feline panleucopenia

3 Third Eye Openers

- 100 c.c. blood has 20 ml oxygen.
- Camelidae family members have nucleated red blood corpuscles (RBCs).
- Amphibians have largest RBCs.
- Smallest RBCs are found in mammals.
- Spleen is store house of dead RBCs & is also known as **Graveyard of RBCs.**
- Life of RBCs is calculated by radioactive chromium method.
- Cu is responsible for blue color of blood.
- Hales discovered blood pressure.
- Sphygmomanometer is used to measure blood pressure.
- Average life of WBC is 10 days.
- Kendiv and Piutrz proposed the structure of hemoglobin.
- Blood group 'O' is **universal blood** donor group.
- Person with blood group "AB" can accept all types of blood groups.**(universal acceptor)**
- Land Steiner discovered blood groups in year 1900.
- Smallest RBCs are found in musk deer.
- William Harvey discovered blood circulation.
- Thrombocytes are found only in mammals.
- Minimata disease is caused by toxicity of mercury.
- Itai-Itai disease occurs due to toxicity of cadmium.
- India has about 53% of buffalo, 20% of goat and 15 % of cattle population of the world.
- Contribution of milk is higher than combined contribution of wheat and sugarcane.
- Meat has 16% of total output of livestock products in India.
- Community development programme was started on 2nd October 1952.
- **Lab to land programme** was started in 1979.
- NATP was started in 1997.
- Institutional Village Linkage Programme was started 1n 1995.
- Mixed farming refers to crop production with livestock farming, having contribution of minimum 10% and maximum 49% from livestock.

- TRYSEM is abbreviation of Training of Rural Youth for Self Employment, started in 1979.
- DWCRA is abbreviation of Development of Women and Children in Rural Areas.
- Jawahar Rozgar Yojna was started in 1989 for rural employment.
- High yielding variety (HYV) programme was initiated in 1966.
- Key Village Scheme (KVS) was started in 1952. It was first systematic approach for livestock improvement.
- Pratopterus is also known as lungfish.
- Anavas is called as climbing perch.
- 34000 species of fishes are found in India.
- Fishes have Mesonephric kidney.
- Aristotle is founder of fishery history.
- V C Jhingaran is father of Indian Fishery Science.
- Central Inland Fisheries Research Institute is situated in Bairakpur (West Bengal).
- Phycomycetes fungus causes gill sloughing in fishes.
- Air bladder of fishes is used for commercial production of icing glass.
- Central Institute of Fishery Education is situated in Bombay.
- Largest Aquarium of India is located in Bombay.
- Blue eye condition in dog is resulted after vaccination with live canine adenovirus (CAV) vaccine.
- Granulomatous reaction is a variant of delayed hypersensitivity found in leprosy, tuberculosis, parasitic, fungal infection and syphilis.
- 1 HA unit is highest dilution at which agglutination of erythrocytes occurs.
- Myeloma patients excrete light chain of Ig in urine.
- IgM does not have hinge region.
- C_3 is most abundant and most pivotal complement present in plasma.
- IgM is **longest living antibody** (70 days $T_{1/2}$).
- Ig E is also known as **Reagin.**
- **MMPO** (Milk and Milk Product Order) was issued in **1992.**
- Fowl is most resistant to warfarin toxicity.
- Byssinosis is caused by exposure to cotton dust/ lint.
- Iron dust results Siderosis.
- Corn feed result niacin deficiency in pigs.
- DCP is most common way of expressing the protein value of feed for ruminants.
- Among food borne toxins, botulinum toxin is most toxic.
- 1 mg Penicillin G Sodium is equivalent to 1667 unit.
- 1 kg TDN is equivalent 0.869 starch equivalent.
- Blood cells are also known as corpuscles.
- Life on earth was originated before 3.7×10^9 years.
- India has 390 species of wild mammals.
- India has 1232 species of wild birds.
- India has 665 species of reptiles and amphibians.

- 2546 species of arthropods are found in India.
- Jim Carbett National Park is situated in Uttarakhand. **(First NP of India)**
- Denis Tito is **the first space tourist.**
- Louis Pasteur produced Rabies vaccine.
- **Param Padma** is a super computer.
- Book "The Hindu view of life" is written by **Dr. S. Radhakrishnan**.
- **Dr. B. P. Pal** was **first Director General of recognized ICAR**.
- Wildlife Institute of India is situated in Dehradun.
- ICAR was established on **16 July 1929**.
- Musk deer is state wild animal of Uttarakhand.
- Brahma Kamal (*Saussurea obvullata*) is state flower of Uttarakhand.
- Rhododendron arboretum (Buraaus) is state tree of Uttarakhand.
- Monal pheasant (*Lopophorus impejanus*) is state bird of Uttarakhand.
- Ashok (*Saraca indica*) is the state tree of Uttar Pradesh.
- **First KVK of India** was established **in Pondichery**.
- Madhya Pradesh is also known as **Tiger state.**
- **Eucalyptus** is also known as **Environmental Terrorist**.
- Methane is only green house gas produced by ruminants.
- **Arrhenium** gave **term "green house gas" is 1890.**
- Green house gas absorbs infrared rays.
- CFC is the only man made green house gas.
- PCR technique was developed by **Kary Mullis (1983).**
- Humming bird is the smallest bird and also known as **natural helicopter**.
- Glucagon is made up of 29 amino acids.
- Haemoglobin is made up of 574 amino acids.
- Ribosome is molecular machine for protein formation.
- Plasmid is extra chromosomal DNA of cell.
- **Dominant gene mel is responsible for melanin synthesis.**
- **No. of chromosomes in Ascaris is 24.**
- C. Mc Claung discovered sex determining chromosome.
- H. Mullu proved first of all the notating effect of X- rays in first fly.
- Beadle & Tatum first proposed **one gene one enzyme theory**.
- S. Ochoo was first scientist to synthesize RNA artificially.
- DNA was first synthesized artificially by **A. Conberg**.
- J. Beckwidth **first isolated the gene.**
- H. G. Khorana was first scientist to synthesize **artificial gene.**
- A. Munay and J. Szostak were first to form **artificial chromosome.**
- **A. Jeffrick** developed DNA finger printing technique.
- Robert Winston is father of test tube baby.

- Griffith was first to propose DNA as a genetic material.
- National Institute of Animal Nutrition and Physiology is situated in Hyderabad
- Cornea and lens are blood less parts.
- Red dog is a byproduct of milling spring wheat. It has 17 -20 % protein with 2-4 % crude fibre.
- Rice bran has 14% protein and less than 14% crude fibre.
- Rice bran is laxative in action.

4 Anatomy

Salient Points

- A rod of bone can be elongated only about 1/ 200 part of its length before breaking.
- Adductor muscles move limb towards the medium plane.
- Amphiarthrosis is found in spinal column.
- Anal atresia results when dorsal membrane separating the rectum and anus fails to rupture.
- Bodies of Hassell are found in thymic medulla.
- Bony pelvis consists of sacrum, Coccygeal vertebrae and coaxae.
- Bull and ram have helmet shaped glans – *galea glandis.*
- Bursa of Fabriscius, lymphoid organ of poultry epithelial out growth of cloaca.
- Cardiac muscle is striated with centrally located nuclei.
- Cat has 6 incisors.
- Cow, sheep and goat have 32 teeth.
- Ectopic heart is most common in cattle.
- Flexor muscles decrease angle between bones.
- Fore stomach of ruminants consists of reticulum, rumen and Omasum.
- Fornix is the angle formed by cervical projection into vagina.
- Fovea capitis is found on the head of femur.
- Galvayne's groove is a longitudinal groove on the upper corner incisor in horses.
- Glans is spiral twist anti-clock wise in boars.
- Gluteal muscle is an abductor muscle.
- In Ebstein's anomaly, tricuspid valve is displaced toward the cardiac apex.
- Neck of uterus is known as cervix.
- Patella is the largest sessamoid bone in body.
- Pectineus muscle in inguinal region is an adductor muscle.
- Pituitary gland is located at the base of brain is sella tursica of sphenoid bone.
- Resistance of bone to tension is 10 kg / mm^2 and to compression is 16.86 kg / mm^2.
- Rigor mortis is absent in smooth muscle.
- Sigmoid flexure is not present in stallion.
- Study of visceral organs related structures is known as splanchnology.
- Tendons are fibrous tissue, connecting bones to muscle.
- Testicle, ovary, pancreas have both endocrine and exocrine function.
- Thyroid follicles are formed by single layer of cuboidal epithelium.
- Tricuspid dysplasia is common in Labradors, Retrievers and German shepherd dogs.

Important Terms

- **Callus** is a mass of osteoid tissue.
- **Cancellous bone -** Composed of plates (Spicules) arranged to form a porous network. Also known as **spongy bone.**
- **Diarthroses -** Freely movable joints. They are true

joints. They are also called synovial joints.

- **Endosteum** - Fibrous membrane that lines marrow cavity of bone.
- **Epiphysis** - Either extremity of a bone.
- **Asthesiology** - Study of sensory system eye, ear.
- **Facet** - Flat articular surface as found between adjacent carpal bones.
- **Fovea** - Small non-articular depression.
- **Gomphosis** - Articulation of teeth in their sockets in mandible and maxillae.
- **Holocrine gland** - Fully filled cells with secretary material is discharged.
- **Merocrine gland** - Pass their secretion through call wall without any loss to architecture.
- **Osteoclastoma** - Tumor of osteoclasts. Also known as Giant cell tumor.
- **Osteoma** - is tumour of bone.
- **Plantar** - Caudal surface of hind limb below the hocks.
- **Prone** - Position in which dorsal aspect of body is uppermost.
- **Proximal** - Closer to given part usually vertebral column.
- **Serum** - Fluid portion of blood after clotting.
- **Sessamoid bone** - Resembles sesame seed and is developed along the course of tendons to reduce friction.
- **Splanchnology** - Study of visceral organs.
- **Supine** - Position in which ventral aspect of the body is uppermost.
- **Synostosis** - Joint in which uniting medium is bone.
- **Volar** - Flexion or caudal surface of forelimb distal to the elbow.

Questions

1. Branch of Anatomy in which structure of particular organ is studied is -
   (a) Systemic anatomy
   (b) Radiological anatomy
   (c) Topographic anatomy
   (d) Comparative anatomy
2. Branch of Anatomy in which principal structures of any part of body are described in relations a definite & united area of surface is-
   (a) Systematic anatomy
   (b) Radiological anatomy
   (c) Topographic anatomy
   (d) Comparative anatomy
3. Branch of Anatomy in which analogous structures of different species of animals are studies is -
   (a) Systemic anatomy
   (b) Radiological anatomy
   (c) Pseudo anatomy
   (d) Specific anatomy
4. Branch of Anatomy in which structure of particular organ is studied is -
   (a) Systemic anatomy
   (b) Specific anatomy
   (c) Species anatomy
   (d) Comparative anatomy
5. Position away from median place is known as -
   (a) Anterior (b) Posterior
   (c) Lateral (d) Medial
6. Surface of forelimbs that contacts the ground in standing sanitation is-
   (a) Palmar (b) Planter
   (c) Axial (d) Abaxial
7. Surface of hind limb that contacts the ground in standing condition is-
   (a) Palmar (b) Planter
   (c) Axial (d) Abaxial
8. Study of organs of special senses is-
   (a) Angiology (b) Neurology
   (c) Splanchnology (d) Aesthesiology
9. Skeleton which compresses of bones of skull, vertebral column ribs & sternum is-
   (a) Axial (b) Abaxial
   (c) Appendicular (d) None
10. Skeleton which comprises of bones of limbs is-
    (a) Axial (b) Abaxial
    (c) Appendicular (d) None
11. Which of the following is a sesamoid bone-?
    (a) Phalanges (b) Patella
    (c) Oscardis (d) Ospenis
12. Intervertebral discs are formed by which type of cartilage-
    (a) Hyaline (b) Fibrocartilage
    (c) Elastic cartilage (d) All

13. Which cartilages do not posses pericondrium-
(a) Hyalme (b) Fibrocartilage
(c) Elastic cartilage (d) All

14. Bulk of small bones & ends of long bones are made by-
(a) Spongy bone (b) Cancellous bone
(c) Both (d) None

15. Which of the following are mature bone cells-?
(a) Osteoblasts (b) Osteoclasts
(c) Both a & b (d) Osteocytes

16. The fold which is invested around the wall of the intestine and attaches the intestine to the dorsal wall of the abdomen is known as:-
(a) Mesentery (b) Greater omentum
(c) Omentum (d) Lesser omentum

17. Osteocytes are derived from-
(a) Osteoblasts
(b) Osteoclasts
(c) Mesenchymal tissue
(d) All

18. Two caeca are seen in-
(a) Bird (b) Mammal
(c) Reptile (d) Fishes

19. Which cells are responsible for resorption of bone salts?
(a) Osteocytes (b) Osteoclasts
(c) Ostcoblasts (d) All

20. Periosteum is absent from which surface of bone-
(a) Shaft (b) Articular surface
(c) Tuberosities (d) Crests

21. Bones of cranial cavity & face ossify by- ossification-
(a) Intramembranous (b) Intracartilaginous
(c) Both (d) None

22. Which stage of Intra-cartilaginous ossification is the stage of true ossification-?
(a) Stage I (b) Stage II
(c) Stage III (d) All

23. An articular surface in the form of very small pit is-
(a) Fovea (b) Condyle
(c) Epicondyle (d) Trochlea

24. Knucle shaped paired auricular surfaces are called-
(a) Fovea (b) Condyle
(c) Epicondyle (d) Trochlea

25. A pully like grooved articular surface is-
(a) Fovea (b) Condyle
(c) Epicondyle (d) Trochlea

26. How many visceral bones are present in case of horse-?
(a) 1 (b) 2
(c) 3 (d) 0

27. *Os cardis* is present in case of-
(a) Ox (b) Horse
(c) Dog (d) Pig

28. *Os penis* is present in case of-
(a) Ox (b) Horse
(c) Dog (d) Pig

29. *Os rastrale* is present in case of-
(a) Ox (b) Horse
(c) Dog (d) Pig

30. Total number of bones in case of Ox is-
(a) 208 (b) 200
(c) 291 (d) 274

31. Total number of bones in case of Horse is-
(a) 208 (b) 200
(c) 291 (d) 274

32. Total number of bones in case of Pig is-
(a) 208 (b) 200
(c) 291 (d) 274

33. Total no. of bones in case of Dog is-
(a) 208 (b) 200
(c) 291 (d) 274

34. Total number of bones in case of Fowl is-
(a) 200 (b) 208
(c) 274 (d) 167

35. Bone of forelimb that extends from 3rd to 4th thoracic spine to the distil end of first rib is-
(a) Scapula (b) Humerus
(c) Radius (d) Ulna

36. Acromion process of scapula is absent in case of-
(a) Horse (b) Dog
(c) Ox (d) Pig

37. Deltoid tuberosity is in the form of a ridge in case of-
(a) Ox (b) Horse
(c) Dog (d) Pig

38. Interrosseus space extends throughout the length of radius & ulna in case of-

(a) Ox (b) Horse
(c) Dog (d) Pig

39. Which of the following carpals is also known as Scaphoid?
(a) Radial (b) Intermediate
(c) Ulnar (d) Accessory

40. Which carpal is also known as Semiular carpal-
(a) Radial (b) Intermediate
(c) Ulhar (d) Accessory

41. Which carpal is also known as Cuneiform carpal?
(a) Radial (b) Intermediate
(c) Ulnar (d) Accessory

42. Which carpal is also known as Pisiform carpal?
(a) Radial (b) Intermediate
(c) Ulnar (d) Accessory

43. Which carpal is also known as Os magnus?
(a) I & IV fused (b) I & II fused
(c) II & III fused (d) None

44. Which carpal is also known as Unciform carpal?
(a) I (b) II
(c) II & III fused (d) IV

45. Radial & intermediate carpals are fused in case of-
(a) Ox (b) Horse
(c) Dog (d) Pig

46. Which sesamoid bones are also known as navicular bones?
(a) Proximal (b) Destal
(c) Both (d) None

47. Which of the following in the largest bone in the skeleton -
(a) Humerus (b) Femur
(c) Tibia (d) Scapula

48. In which of the following pubic bone doesn't take part in the formation of acetabulum-
(a) Dog (b) Pig
(c) Dog (d) Rabbit

49. Ilioischiatic foramen is present in case of-
(a) Ox (b) Horse
(c) Dog (d) Fowl

50. Fovea capitis of femur is notched in case of-
(a) Ox (b) Horse
(c) Dog (d) Pig

51. Fibula reaches the entire length of tibia in case of-
(a) Ox (b) Dog
(c) Horse (d) Poultry

52. Which tarsal bone is common known as Talus-
(a) Tibial (b) Fibular
(c) C+4 (d) I[st]

53. Which Tarsal bone is commonly known as Caleaneous?
(a) Tibial (b) Fibular
(c) C+4 (d) Ulner

54. Which of the following cranial bones is not paired?
(a) Interparietal (b) Sphenoid
(c) Parietal (d) Frontal

55. Which of the following cranial bones is not single?
(a) Occpital (b) Sphenoid
(c) Ethmoid (d) Frontal

56. Which of the only facial bone found singly?
(a) Lacrimal (b) Pterygoid
(c) Mahar (d) Vomar

57. Maxillary sinus is formed by which of the following bones-
(a) Maxilla, Lacrimal, malar
(b) Maxilla, Nasal, Turbinate
(c) Lacrimal, Maxilla, Nasal
(d) Palatine, Maxilla, Nasal

58. Which of the following sinus is extended inside cornual process?
(a) Frontal (b) Maxillary
(c) Sphenoid (d) Palatine

59. How many thoracic vertebrae are present in dog?
(a) 7 (b) 13
(c) 14 (d) 18

60. How many thoracic vertebrae are present in Horse?
(a) 7 (b) 13
(c) 14 (d) 18

61. How many thoracic vertebrae are present in Ox?
(a) 7 (b) 13
(c) 14 (d) 18

62. How many thoracic vertebrae are present in pig?
(a) 13 (b) 14
(c) 12 (d) 18

63. How many cervical vertebrae are present in fowl?
(a) 7 (b) 13
(c) 14 (d) 18

64. How many lumbar vertebrae are present in ox-
(a) 6 (b) 7
(c) 14 (d) 18

65. How many lumbar vertebrae are present in dog-
(a) 6 (b) 7
(c) 14 (d) 18

66. How many lumbar vertebrae are present in fowl-
(a) 6 (b) 7
(c) 14 (d) 18

67. Sacrum is formed by how many vertebrae in ox-
(a) 3 (b) 4
(c) 5 (d) 2

68. Sacrum is formed by how many vertebrae in dog-
(a) 3 (b) 4
(c) 5 (d) 2

69. Sacrum is formed by how many vertebrae in pig-
(a) 3 (b) 4
(c) 5 (d) 2

70. Breast bone is composed of how many segments in case of ox-
(a) 6 (b) 7
(c) 8 (d) 9

71. Breast bone is composed of how many segments in case of dog-
(a) 6 (b) 7
(c) 8 (d) 9

72. Breast bone is composed of how many segments in case of pig-
(a) 6 (b) 7
(c) 8 (d) 9

73. Clavicle bone is present in case of-
(a) Ox (b) Horse
(c) Dog (d) All

74. Coracoid bone is present in case of-
a. Ox b. Horse
c. Dog d. Fowl

75. How many pair of ribs is sternal in ox-
a. 8 b. 5
c. 6 d. 7

76. How many pair of ribs are sternal in ox.-
a. 8 b. 5
c. 6 d. 7

77. Which joints are known as Diarthrodial?
a. Synovial b. Fibrous
c. Cartilagenous d. All

78. Which joints are known as Synarthrodial?
a. Synovial b. Fibrous
c. Cartelagenous d. All

79. Which joints are known as Amphiarthrodial?
a. Synovial b. Fibrous
c. Cartilagenous d. All

80. Which of the following joints show free movement?
a. Synovial b. Fibrous
c. Cartilagenous d. All

81. Which of the following joints show restricted movement?
a. Synovial b. Fibrous
c. Cartilagenous d. All

82. Which of the following joints are unmovable?
a. Synovial b. Fibrous
c. Cartilagenous d. All

83. Which ligaments are the fibrous bands situated on either side of the joint-
a. Collateral b. Intra-articular
c. Interosseous d. Annular

84. Which ligaments are the connecting bands remaining within the joint cavity?
a. Collateral b. Intra-articular
c. Interosseous d. Annular

85. Which ligaments connect apposed surface of bones-
a. Collateral b. Intro-articular
c. Interosseous d. Annular

86. Which ligaments are present over or near the joints for passage of protection of tendons?
a. Collateral b. Intro-articular
c. Interosseous d. Annular

87. On the basis of movements which of the following joints are uniaxial-
a. Temporomandibular joint
b. Interphalangeal articulations
c. Ball & socket joint
d. None

88. On the basis of movements which of the following joints are biaxial-
a. Temporomandibular joint
b. Interphalangeal articulations

c. Ball & socket joint
d. None

89. On the basis of movements which of the following joints are multiaxial-
a. Temporomandibular joint
b. Interphalangeal articulations
c. Ball & socket joint
d. None

90. Fibrous joints in which the borders of adjacent bones united by fibrous connective tissue are-
a. Sutures b. Syndesmosis
c. Schindylesis d. Gomphosis

91. Fibrous joints in which the uniting medium of the articulations is white fibrous tissue is-
a. Sutures b. Syndesmosis
c. Schindylesis d. Gomphosis

92. In a fibrous joint when a bone is fitted into the groove of another bone, it is called-
a. Sutures b. Syndesmosis
c. Schindylesis d. Gomphosis

93. The articulation between roots of the teeth in the alveolar sockets is known as-
a. Sutures b. Syndesmosis
c. Schindylesis d. Gomphosis

94. In young elbow joint is -
a. Amphiarthrosis b. Synarthrosis
c. Both d. None

95. In adult elbow joint is -
a. Amphiarthrosis b. Synarthrosis
c. Both d. None

96. Which of the following joints are examples of hinge joint?
a. Humero-radial joint
b. Knee joint
c. Fetlock joint
d. All

97. Which of the following sesamoidean ligament is known as suspensory ligamenta?
a. Superior b. Inferior
c. Intersesamoidean d. Collateral

98. Muscles in which the fibres are short & are oblique to the line of pull-
a. Pennate b. Spiral
c. Cruciate d. All

99. Muscles which help in rotational movements-
a. Pennate b. Spiral
c. Cruciate d. All

100. Muscles in which the fibres are arranged in superficial & deep plane, crossing like X is -
a. Pennate b. Spiral
c. Cruciate d. All

101. Which of the following muscles provide acceleration motion to a joint?
a. Spurt muscles b. Shunt muscles
c. Both d. None

102. Which muscles provide stabilizing centripetal force on a joint?
a. Spurt muscles b. Shunt muscles
c. Both d. None

103. A thin walled bag containing synovial fluid interposed at the point of pressure between muscles-
a. Bursa b. Sheath
c. Both d. None

104. A synovial bag encircling a tendon is known as-
a. Bursa b. Sheath
c. Both d. None

105. Which of the following muscles inserts at the scapular spine?
a. Trapezius b. Rhomboideus
c. Brachiocephalicus d. All

106. Which of the following muscles originated the wing of atlas & insert at the spine of scapula?
a. Serratus Thoracus
b. Omo Transversarious
c. Serratus cervices
d. None

107. Which of the following muscles insert at the Deltoid tuberosity-
a. Teres major b. Teres minor
c. Subscapular d. Brachialis

108. Which of the following muscles insert at the olecranon process of ulna?
a. Triceps brochi
b. Anconeus
c. Tensor fascia antibrachia
d. All

109. Which of the following muscles inserts at Tuber calcis?

a. Soleus b. Extersor brevis
c. Gastrocnemius d. peroneus longus

110. Popliteus muscle originates at
a. Medial condyle b. Lateral condyle
c. Trochanter d. Trochanter minor

111. Which of the following muscles from the prepubic tendon?
a. Transverse abdominis
b. Obliques abdominis Internus
c. Obliques abdominis externus
d. Rectus abdominis

112. *Psoas major* inserts at-
a. Trochanter minor of femur
b. Psoas tubercle
c. Trochanter major
d. None

113. *Psoas minor* inserts at-
a. Trochanter minor of femur
b. Trochanter major
c. Psoas tubercle
d. None

114. Which of the following layers line the lumen of digestive system?
a. Mucosa
b. Submucosa
c. Tunica muscularis
d. All

115. Outermost layer of the digestive system is-
a. T. muscularis b. T. Serosa
c. T. adventitia d. both b & c

116. A wide fold of mucous membranes connecting the floor of mouth & ventral surface of tongue is-
a. Tonue philtrum
b. Franulum linguae
c. Sublingual caruncle
d. All

117. Which of the following is a large pepilla opening behind the 3rd inceror?
a. Frenulum linguae
b. Philtrum
c. Sublingual caruncle
d. All

118. Planum nasoliabiale is horse bears a groove in horse which is known as-
a. Franulum linguae
b. Philtrum
c. Sublingual caruncle
d. All

119. Planum nasoliabiale is not keratinous but bears a groove known as philtrum in case of-
a. Ox b. Horse
c. Dog d. Pig

120. Papilla salevalis in horse is placed opposite to-
a. I[st] peremolar b. 2nd premolar
c. Last premolar d. I[st] molar

121. Dental pads are absent in case of-
a. Ox b. Horse
c. Dog d. None

122. Gland which open circumrallet papillae of tongue are known as-
a. Lingual glands b. Gastatory glands
c. Lingual tonsils d. All

123. Aggrregations of lymphoid follicles of the root of tongue are known as-
a. Lingual glands b. Gastatory glands
c. Lingual tonsils d. All

124. Torus linguae is absent in case of -
a. Horse b. Pig
c. Both d. None

125. A thick fibromuscular cord situated at the ventral surface of the tip of tongue known as lyssa is present in case of-
a. Horse b. Dog
c. Pig d. Ox

126. Two frenum linguae are present in case of-
a. Horse b. Dog
c. Pig d. Ox

127. A horizontal ridge on the crown of tooth close to the root & known as cingulum is found in-
a. Horse b. Ox
c. Dog d. Pig

128. Beside which of the following tooth, all are replaced by permanent teeth?
a. Incissors b. Canines
c. Premolars d. Molars

129. Cavity of pharynx communicates with other structures by how many openings-
a. 4 b. 5
c. 7 d. 10

130. Guttural pouches are found only in case of -
a. Canines b. Borines
c. Equines d. Caprines

131. Downward deverticulum from the auditory tube are known as-
a. Cingulum b. Frenumlinguae
c. Guttural pouch d. None

132. Visceral & parietal layer of peretoneum communicate with each other through-
a. Epiploic foramen
b. Foramen of Winslow
c. Both
d. None

133. Rumen is placed in the abdominal cavity from-
a: 4th rib to pelvic inlet
b. 5th rib to pelvic inlet
c. 6th rib to pelvic inlet
d. 8th rib to pelvic inlet

134. Cartilagenous compartment farmed at the point of bifurcation of trachea into two primary bronchi is-
a. Larynx b. Pharynx
c. Cingulum d. Syrinx

135. Which of the airsacs in the chicken are not paired?
a. Cranial thoracic b. Caudal thoracic
c. Abdominal d. None

136. Which of the airsaces in chicken are paired?
a. Cerical b. Clavicular
c. Abdominal d. All

137. Which of the following has 'J' shaped stomach?
a. Horse b. Dog
c. Pig d. All

138. Which of the following has pyriform shaped stomach-
a. Horse b. Dog
c. Pig d. All

139. Shape of stomach resembles a human embryo in-
a. Horse b. Dog
c. Pig d. All

140. Central; flexure is a part of which loop of ascending colon-
a. Proximal b. Spiral
c. Distil d. None

141. Which of the following is more in length?
a. Small intestine b. Large intestine
c. Both are equal d. any

142. Hepatopancreatic ampula is present in which of intestine?
a. Duodenum b. Jejunum
c. Caecum d. Colon

143. Peyer's patches are present in which part of intestine?
a. Duodenum b. Jejunum
c. Caecum d. Colon

144. Which part of intestine reaches beyond the peritoneal cavity?
a. Small colon b. Great colon
c. Caecum d. Rectum

145. Ducts of the anal sacs open in which part of intestine?
a. Caecum b. Colon
c. Rectum d. Duodenum

146. Vermiform appendix is present in which part of intestine?
a. Ileum b. Caecum
c. Colon d. Duodenum

147. Sacculus rotund is present in which part of intestine?
a. Ileum b. Caecum
c. Colon d. Duodenum

148. Mackel's diverticulum is present in which part of intestine?
a. Duodenum b. Jejunum
c. Ileum d. Caecum

149. Bursa of Fibrosus is present in which part of cloaca of fowl?
a. Coprodeum b. Urodeum
c. Proctodeum d. All

150. Brunner's glands are present in which part of intestine?
a. Duodenum b. Jejunum
c. Ileum d. Caecum

151. Papillae salivalis is the opening of which salivary gland?
a. Parotid b. Mandibular
c. Sublingual d. All

152. Stensen's duct belongs to which salivary gland?
a. Parotid b. Mandibular
c. Sublingual d. All

153. *Papilla salivalis* in ox opens opposite to
a. II upper molar b. III upper molar
c. III lower molar d. II lower molar

154. *Caruncula sublingualis* is the opening of which salivary?
a. Parotid b. Mandibular
c. Sublingual d. All gland

155. Wharton's duct belongs to which salivary gland?
a. Paroted b. Mandibular
c. Sublingual d. All

156. Papillae salivalis in horse opens opposite to
a. II upper molar b. III upper premolar
c. III upper molar d. II upper premolar

157. Which salivary gland is single in horse?
a. Paroted b. Mandibular
c. Sublingual d. All

158. An extra zygomatic salivary gland is present in-
a. Ox b. Horse
c. Dog d. Pig

159. Zygomatic salivary glands opens at the level of-
a. II upper molar b. II upper premolar
c. III upper molar d. III upper premolar

160. Infraorbital salivary glands are presnet in-
a. Pig b. Fowl
c. Rabbit d. Cats

161. Which glands are absent in case of rabbit?
a. Parotid b. Mandibular
c. Sublingual d. None

162. Which salivary glands in fowl are monstomatic?
a. Maxillary b. Palatine
c. Laryngeal d. Submandibular

163. Which salivary glands in fowl is not monstormatic?
a. Maxillary b. Angular
c. Palatine d. None

164. Duct of which salivary gland in fowl open into the mouth?
a. Maxillary b. Submandibular
c. Palatine d. All

165. Duct of which salivary gland in fowl opens into the cavity of pharynx?
a. Sphenopterygoid b. Laryngeal
c. Ceudal lingual d. All

166. Liver in ox extends from lumbocostal angle to the level of which rib-
a. 7th-8th b. 8th-9th
c. 6th-7th d. 4th-5th

167. Which ligament attaches liver with the diaphragm?
a. Round ligament b. Falciform ligament
c. Caudate ligament d. Lesser omentum

168. Which ligament connects the unibilical fissure of liver of the unibilicus?
a. Round ligament b. Falciform ligament
c. Caudate ligament d. Lesser omentum

169. Caudate lobe of liver is attached with kidney & pancreas by-
a. Round ligament b. Falciform ligament
c. Caudate ligament d. Lesser omentum

170. Liver is attached with omesum & lesser curvature of abomasum by-
a. Falciform ligament
b. Round ligament
c. Lesser omentum
d. Caudate ligament

171. Kupffer cells are related to-
a. Lung b. Liver
c. Brain d. Spleen

172. Gall bladder is absent is-
a. Dog b. Ox
c. Horse d. Pig

173. An extra left lateral ligament of liver is present in case of-
a. Dog b. Ox
c. Horse d. Pig

174. Caudate lobe of liver is divided into caudate process & papillary process in-
a. Ox b. Dog
c. Horse d. Pig

175. How many lobes are present in liver of fowl-
a. 2 b. 3
c. 4 d. 5

176. Pancreatic duct opens into-
a. Duodenum b. Jejunum
c. Caecum d. Colon

177. Two pancreatic ducts are present in case of-
a. Horse b. Dog

c. Fowl d. All

178. Arteries of spleen when became surrounded by reticular tissue & lymphocytes constitute-
a. Red pulp b. White pulp
c. Both d. None

179. The splenic tissue containing splenic senusoids & splenic cords infiltrated with circulating blood is known as-
a. Red pulp b. White pulp
c. Both d. None

180. Main functions of spleen include-
a. Phagocytosis b. Haemopoiesis
c. Immune response d. All

181. Spleen of which of the following is elliptical in outline
a. Ox b. Horse
c. Dog d. Pig

182. Spleen of which of the following is triangular in shape?
a. Ox b. Horse
c. Dog d. All

183. Spleen of which of the following is a human foot print shaped structure?
a. Ox b. Horse
c. Dog d. All

184. Spleen of which of following is spatula shaped?
a. Ox b. Horse
c. Dog d. Rabbit

185. Alar cartilages are related to-
a. Turbinate bones b. Frontal sinus
c. Maxillary sinus d. Nostrils

186. Organ of Jacobson is related to which system of body?
a. Digestive b. Respiratory
c. Genital d. Nervous

187. Which one is the largest cartilage of larynx?
a. Thyroid b. Cricoid
c. Arytenoid d. Epiglottis

188. Which cartilage of larynx is a signet ring shaped structure?
a. Thyroid b. Cricoid
c. Arytenoid d. Epriglottis

189. Which of the following represent space between vocal cords?
a. Vestible
b. Rima glottidis
c. Caudal compartment
d. None

190. An extra bronchus for apical lobe of lung is given at the level of which intercostal space?
a. 3rd b. 5th
c. 7th d. 1st

191. Cupula refers to the apex to-
a. Heart b. Lung
c. Pleural sac d. Peritoneal sec

192. Which lobe of the lung of ox is largest?
a. Apical b. Cardiac
c. Diaphragmatic d. Accessory

193. Right lung of ox possesses how many lobes?
a. 1 b. 2
c. 3 d. 4

194. Left lung of ox possesses how many lobes?
a. 1 b. 2
c. 3 d. 4

195. Which lobe is not present in left lung of ox?
a. Apical b. Cardiac
c. Diaphragmatic d. Accessory

196. Lobar bronchus refers to which bronchus?
a. Primary b. Secondary
c. Tertiary d. All

197. Which artery serves as functional blood supply of the bronchial tree?
a. Pulmonary artery b. Bronchial artery
c. Both d. None

198. Which artery serves as nutritional blood supply of the bronchial tree?
a. Pulmonary artery b. Bronchial artery
c. Both d. None

199. Apical bronchus is present in which lung?
a. Right b. Left
c. Both d. None

200. Which lung is larger?
a. Right b. Left
c. Both are equal d. Any

201. Cardiac impression is deeper in which lung?
a. Right b. Left
c. Both are equal d. Any

202. Which lung has larger apical lobe?
a. Right b. Left
c. Both are equal d. Any

203. Apical bronchus is absent in case of-
a. Horse b. Dog
c. Both d. None

204. Left lung has only 2 lobes in case of-
a. Pig b. Rabbit
c. Both d. None

205. Which air sacs of fowl are not paired?
a. Cranial thoracic b. Caudal thoracic
c. Abdominal d. Cervical

206. Which air sac of fowl is paired?
a. Cervical b. Clavicular
c. Both d. None

207. How many lobes are present in left lung of pig?
a. 1 b. 2
c. 3 d. 4

208. 'Snout' is related to which of the following species?
a. Horse b. Dog
c. Pig d. Cow

209. Apical bronchus is present in which lung?
a. Right b. Left
c. Both d. None

210. Which organ extends from proximal end of last rib to first 2 or 3 lumber vertebrae cow?
a. Lung b. Liver
c. Stomach d. Kidney

211. Shape of kidney of cow is-
a. Bean b. Oval
c. Irregular d. Star

212. Hilus is present on which surface of kidney?
a. Dorsal b. Ventral
c. Lateral d. Ruminal

213. Which of the following has been shaped kidney?
a. Cow b. Sheep
c. Goat d. All

214. The outer pale area of a cut surface of kidney is-
a. Cortex b. Medulla
c. Renal pyramid d. None

215. The inner darker area of kidney is-
a. Cortex b. Medulla
c. Renal pyramid d. None

216. Funnel shaped end of ureter is known as-
a. Renal sinus b. Renal pelvis
c. Renal pyramids d. All

217. Hilus of the kidney opens into-
a. Renal senus b. Renal pelvis
c. Renal pyramids d. All

218. Red dot like points distributed throughout the cortex of kidney are known as-
a. Malphagean cirpuscles
b. Renal pyramides
c. Uriniferous tubules
d. Renal papillae

219. Connective tissue lymphatics & blood vessels of kidney constitute-
a. Malphagian corpuscles
b. Renal pyramids
c. Uriniferous tubules
d. Renal papillae

220. Nephron is ______ unit of kidney
a. Structural b. Functional
c. Both d. None

221. Henle's loop belongs to which organ?
a. Kidney b. Intestine
c. Lymphaties d. Heart

222. Which part of the nephron is longest?
a. PCT b. DCT
c. Henle's loop d. Collecting duct

223. Duct of Bellini belongs to-
a. PCT b. DCT
c. Henle's loop d. Collecting duct

224. Right kidney of horse is ______ shaped-
a. Heart b. Bean
c. Horse-shoe d. Oval

225. Left kidney of horse is ________ shaped-
a. Heart b. Bean
c. Horse-shoe d. Oval

226. Surface of the kidney are not lobulated in-
a. Horse b. Dog
c. Both d. None

227. Area cribrosa belongs to the kidney of-
a. Ox b. Horse
c. Dog d. Pig

228. Which ligament of the urinary bladder presents the remnants of cembilical arteries?

a. Ventral b. Lateral
c. Collateral d. Round

229. Urinary Bladder is absent in case of-
a. Rabbit b. Mice
c. Fowl d. Hamsters

230. Scrotum of ox derives it's blood supply from-
a. External pudendal artery
b. Internal pudendal artery
c. Obturator artery
d. Umbilical artery

231. Which of the following arteries do not supply blood to the urinary bladder of ox?
a. External pudendal artery
b. Internal pudendal artery
c. Obturator artery
d. Combitical artery

232. Outermost tunic of testes is-
a. Tunica vagenalis b. Tunica vasculosa
c. Tunica albugenia d. None

233. Which side of testes are bigger in animals?
a. Right b. Left
c. Both d. Any

234. Average weight of an adult testis in ox is about-
a. 150 gm b. 250 gms
c. 350 gms d. 500 gms

235. A mediastinum testis is derived from-
a. Tunica vagenalis b. Tunica vasculosa
c. Tunica albugenia d. None

236. Tunica vaginalis is derived from-
a. Mediastinum testes
b. Peritoneum
c. Tunica albugenia
d. Tunica vasculosa

237. Rete testis is formed by-
a. Tubuli contorti b. Tubuli recti
c. Both d. None

238. Duct of epididymis is formed by-
a. Vasa efferentia b. Tubuli contorti
c. Tubuli recti d. Rete testes

239. Testosterone is secreted in testes by which cells?
a. Sertoli cells b. Interstitial cells
c. Chief cells d. All

240. Elonged supporting cells found in outer layer of seminiferous tubules are-
a. Sertole cells b. Interstitial cells
c. Chief cells d. All

241. Pampiniform plexus belongs to which system?
a. Digestive b. Skeleton
c. Respiratory d. Genital

242. Vas deferens is included in which bundle of spermatic cord?
a. Cranial b. Caudal
c. Both d. None

243. Caudal bundle of spermatic cord includes only
a. Cremaster muscle b. Vas deferens
c. Arteries d. Veins

244. Sigmoid flexure of Penis is absent in case of-
a. Ox b. Horse
c. Dog d. b & c

245. How many seminal vesicles are present in case of ox
a. 1 b. 2
c. 5 d. many

246. Main bulk of spermatic cord is formed by
a. Spermatic artery b. Crenester muscle
c. Spermatic vein d. Pampiniform plexus

247. Cowper's gland is a synonym for-
a. Prestal
b. Seminal vesicle
c. Bulbo urethral gland
d. All

248. Which of the following is absent in case of dogs-
a. Seminal vesicles
b. Bulbo urethral glands
c. Segnioid flexure
d. All

249. Prepucial diverticulum is present in case of-
a. Ox b. Horse
c. Boar d. Dog

250. Bulbous glandis is present in case of-
a. Ox b. Horse
c. Boar d. Dog

251. Os penis is related to-
a. Ox b. Horse
c. Boar d. Dog

252. Fold of peritoneum which attaches ovaries to broad ligament is-

a. Mesenterm b. Round ligament
c. Mesovarium d. All

253. Remnants of ruptured ovarian follicles are known as-
a. Graffian follicles b. Corpus luteum
c. Progloffids d. Ovarian bursa

254. Which cells of ovary secrete estrogen?
a. Sertoli cells b. Interstitial cells
c. Chief cells d. None

255. Interstitial cells of ovary secrets-
a. Estrogen b. Progesteion
c. Testosteron d. All

256. Interstitial cells are ______ in shape.
a. Circular b. Oval
c. Hexagonal d. Polyhedral

257. In one estrus cycle how many ovum are discharged in cow?
a. 1 b. 2
c. 10 d. Many

258. In one estrus cycle how many ovum are desiccated in rabbit?
a. 1 b. 2
c. 10 d. Many

259. Liquor follicle is-
a. Cavity in ovarian follicle
b. Cavity in hair follicle
c. Fluid of ovarian follicle
d. Fluid of hair follicle

260. Ovulation fossa is present in case of-
a. Mare b. Bitch
c. Fowl d. Cow

261. Ovarian bursa is present in case of-
a. Mare b. Bitch
c. Rat d. Cow

262. How many oviduct are present in case of hen?
a. 1 b. 2
c. Many d. None

263. Ovary is present in form of a bunch of grapes in case of-
a. Cow b. Bitch
c. Mare d. Hen

264. Uterine portion of oviduct in known as-
a. Isthmus b. Ampulla
c. Infundebulum d. All

265. A little dilated part of an oviduct is known as-
a. Isthmus b. Ampulla
c. Infundibulum d. All

266. Funnel shaped structure which receives ova in oviduct is known as-
a. Isthmus b. Ampulla
c. Infundibulum d. All

267. Which part of oviduct of hen secretes albumin-
a. Infundibulum b. Magnum
c. Isthmus d. Uterus

268. Which part of oviduct of hen secretes shell membrane-
a. Infundibulum b. Magnum
c. Isthmus d. Uterus

269. Which part of oviduct of hen is also known as shell gland-
a. Infundibulam b. Magnum
c. Isthmus d. Uterus

270. Broad ligament is related to-
a. Lung b. Liver
c. Uterus d. Stomach

271. Which statement is correct?
a. Broad ligament originates from round ligament
b. Round ligament originates from board ligament
c. Both originate from each other
d. both are unrelated

272. Uterus is covered as a whole by-
a. Perimetrium b. Endometrium
c. Myometrium d. All

273. Which layer of citreous acts as a sphincter?
a. Parametrium b. Endometium
c. Myometrium d. All

274. Which layer of uterus consists of surface epithelium & tunica propria?
a. Perimetrium b. Endometrium
c. Myometrium d. All

275. Which type of epithelium is found in horns of uterus?
a. Ciliated b. Columnar
c. Stratified d. None

276. Which type of epithelium is found in body & neck of uterus?

a. Ciliated b. Columnar
c. Stratified d. Cuboidal

277. Which type of epithelium is found in external os of uterus?
a. Ciliated b. Columnar
c. Stratified d. None

278. Caruncles are found in which layer of uterus?
a. Endometrium b. Myometrium
c. Perimetrium d. All

279. Cotyledons of uterus are absent in-
a. Mare b. Bitch
c. Both d. None

280. Fallopian tube & apical part of horn of uterus get blood supply from-
a. Utero-ovarian artery
b. Caudal uterine artery
c. Middle uterine artery
d. All

281. Which artery supplies caudal part of horn& adjacent part of body of uterus?
a. Utero-ovarian artery
b. Caudal uterine
c. Middle uterine
d. All

282. Caudal part of uterus & cranial part of vagina is supplied by-
a. Utero-ovarian artery
b. Caudal uterine artery
c. Middle uterine artery
d. All

283. The whole structure of uterus appears as a large V in case of-
a. Mare b. Bitch
c. Cow d. Hew

284. The luminal space of the cranial end around the vaginal part of cervix is-
a. Gartner's duct b. Fornix vaginae
c. Wolffian duct d. Infundibulum

285. Gartner's ducts are remnant of-
a. Mesonephric ducts
b. Paramesonephric ducts
c. Umbilical arteries
d. Spermatic cord

286. Enlargement of mammary glands occur under the influence of-
a. Estrogen b. Progesterone
c. Both d. None

287. which epithelium is present in case of vagina?
a. Stratified squamous
b. Ciliated
c. Stratified columnar
d. Cuboidal

288. Gartner's ducts are generally absent in-
a. Cow b. Mare
c. Bitch d. None

289. Vulvar cleft is a slat like aperture between-
a. Two vulvar lips b. Urelhra & vagina
c. Vagina & vulva d. Uterus & vagina

290. External urethral orifice is a slit like aperture between-
a. 2 vulvar lips b. Urethra & vagina
c. Vagina & vulva d. Uterus & vagina

291. Miniature penis present in female animals-
a. Cow clitoris b. Diverticulum
c. Fornix vaginai d. None

292. Suburethral diverticulum is absent in-
a. Cow b. Mare
c. Bitch d. None

293. Clitoris is flat in case of-
a. Cow b. Mare
c. Bitch d. None

294. Mature ovary is lobulated in case of
a. Cow b. Sow
c. Bitch d. Mare

295. A number of U shaped coils are characteristic of uterus of-
a. Cow b. Sow
c. Bitch d. Mare

296. Fold in the cervix are longitudinal in case of-
a. Cow b. Mare
c. Both d. None

297. Folds in cervix are transverse in case of
a. Cow b. Mare
c. Both d. None

298. Vulvar lips are pointed downwards in
a. Cow b. Mare
c. Sow d. Rabbit

299. Which of the following in an accessory organ of reproductive system?

a. Uterus b. Vagina
c. Oviduct d. Mammary gland

300. Suspensory apparatus is related to-
a. Uterus b. Vagina
c. Mammary gland d. Liver

301. How many mammary glands are present in case of mare?
a. 2 b. 4
c. 8 d. 10

302. How many mammary glands are present in case of mare?
a. 2 b. 5-6
c. 8 d. 10

303. How many mammary glands are present in case of bitch?
a. 2 b. 5-6
c. 8 d. 10

304. How many pairs of mammary glands are present in case of pig?
a. 2 b. 5-6
c. 8 d. 10

305. How many pairs of mammary glands are present in case of rabbit?
a. 2 b. 3-4
c. 4-5 d. 5-6

306. Lactiferous sinus is absent in-
a. Bitch b. Mare
c. Cow d. sow

307. How many lactiferous ducts are present in each teat of bitch?
a. 1 b. 8-12
c. Many d. 20

308. How many lactiferous ducts are present in each teat of pig?
a. 1 b. 2
c. 8-12 d. 4-5

309. What is the function of yolk sac in mammals?
a. Protection b. Immunity
c. Nutrition d. All

310. Outermost membranes enveloping the embryo is-
a. Chorion b. Amnion
c. Allantois d. Yolk Sac

311. What is the function of Amnion towards embryo-
a. Nutrition b. Protection
c. Immunity d. All

312. Allantois develops from-
a. Foregut b. Midgut
c. Hindgut d. All

313. Which layer of embryo helps in the formation of umbilical cord & placenta?
a. Yolk sac b. Amnion
c. Chorion d. Allantois

314. Which of the following belongs to maternal membranes?
a. Caruncles b. Chorionic villi
c. Cotyledons d. Both a & c

315. Which of the following belongs to foetal membrane?
a. Caruncles b. Cotyledons
c. Chorionic villi d. All

316. Which node is known as Pace maker of heart?
a. S.A. b. A.V.
c. Both d. None

317. Cardiac impulse initiates at which node?
a. S.A. b. A.V.
c. Both d. None

318. Weight of an adult heart is about how much % of the body weight
a. 0.1 % b. 5 %
c. 0.5 % d. 10 %

319. The shape of Os Cordis is -
a. Circular b. Triangular
c. Irregular d. Hexagonal

320. Which pericardium is known as epicardium?
a. Parietal b. Visceral
c. Both d. None

321. What is the function of pericardium?
a. Keeps heart in position
b. Prevents over dilation of heart
c. Protection d. All

322. What is the location of pericardium?
a. 3rd-5th rib b. 2nd-4th rib
c. 3rd-6th rib d. 3rd-4th rib

323. Maximum portion of heart lies in which part of the body?
a. Right b. Left
c. Any d. Equally

324. Heart lies in left of body because of the placement of-

a. Liver b. Lung
c. Diaphragm d. Ribs

325. Sinus venosus is possessed by-
a. Right atrium b. Right ventricle
c. Left atrium d. Left ventricle

326. Fossa ovalis belongs to-
a. Right atrium b. Left atrium
c. Right ventricle d. Left ventricle

327. Fossa ovalis works the sets of which foramen of foetal life?
a. Ovale b. Orbitorotendum
c. Both d. None

328. Muscular redges, known as pectenate muscles are present in heart of-
a. Right atrium b. Right ventricle
c. Left atrium d. All

329. Appendix belongs to which chamber of heart?
a. Right atrium b. Left atrium
c. Both d. None

330. The right atrioventricular opening is guarded by-
a. Tricuspid valve b. Bicuspid valve
c. Both d. None

331. Right atrium discharges blood into-
a. Left atrium b. Left ventricle
c. Right ventricle d. Aorta

332. Right ventricle discharges blood into-
a. Left atrium b. Aorta
c. Left ventricle d. Pulmonary trunk

333. Conus arteriosus belongs to-
a. Right atrium b. Left atrium
c. Right ventricle d. None

334. Papillary muscles belong to-
a. Right atrium b. Right ventricle
c. Both d. None

335. Moderator band is present in the cavity of-
a. Right atrium b. Right ventricle
c. Left atrium d. None

336. Exit of pulmonary artery is guarded by-
a. Tricuspid valves b. Bicuspid valve
c. Semilunar valve d. All

337. Which valves prevent in the re-entry of blood in the right ventricle?
a. Tricuspid b. Bicuspid
c. Semilunar d. All

338. Which atrium is larger?
a. Left b. Right
c. Any d. both are equal

339. Left atrium receives oxygenated blood from-
a. Aorta b. Right atrium
c. Pulmmary veins d. None

340. Wall of which chamber of heart is thickest?
a. Left atrium b. Left ventricle
c. Right atrium d. Right ventricle

341. Apex of heart is formed by-
a. Left atrium b. Left ventricle
c. Right atrium d. Right ventricle

342. Left auriculo ventricular opening is guarded by-
a. Tricuspid valve b. Bicuspid valve
c. Both d. None

343. Mitral valves are synonym for-
a. Tricuspid valves b. Bicuspid valves
c. Semilunar valves d. All

344. Cavities of heart are lined by-
a. Epicardium b. Myocardium
c. Endocardium d. All

345. Conduction system of heart is formed by which cells?
a. Nodal b. Transitional
c. Purkinje d. All

346. Which fibers are present in pacemaker of heart?
a. Nodal b. Transitional
c. Purkinje d. All

347. Heart of ox is situated at the level of II intercostals space to which rib?
a. 3rd b. 4th
c. 5th d. 6th

348. Ligamentum arteriosum is the remnant of-
a. Umbilical arteriosus
b. Ductus arteriosus
c. Umbilical cord
d. None

349. Which tunic consist of the endothelial lining of the lumen of blood vessel?
a. Tunica intima b. Tunica media
c. Tunica adventitiald. All

350. Which tunic of heart consists of smooth muscle cells?
a. Tunica intima b. Tunica media

c. Tunica adventitia d. All

351. Which type of epithelium is present in blood vessel?
a. Squamous b. Cuboidal
c. Columnar d. Ciliated

352. Which type of gland is salivary gland?
a. Serous b. Mucous
c. Mixed d. None

353. Mandibular gland is -
a. Serous b. Mucus
c. Mixed d. None

354. Parotid salivary gland is a example of -
a. Merocrine b. Apocrine
c. Holocrine d. None

355. Which of the two is apocrine gland-
a. Mammary gland b. Sweat gland
c. Both d. None

356. Type of sebaceous gland is -
a. Merocine b. Apocerine
c. Holocrine d. None

357. Spongy bones lack-
a. Osteoblasts b. Osteocytes
c. Ostesclast d. Haversian system

358. Which of the following is not a gustatory lingual papilla?
a. Filiform b. Lenticular
c. Fungiform d. Foliate

359. Which of the following is a gustatory lingual papilla?
a. Cercumvalate b. Foliate
c. Both d. None

360. Which lingual papilla are absent in equines?
a. Filliform b. Fungiform
c. Lenticular d. Foliate

361. Which lingual papilla are absent in ruminants?
a. Filliform b. Fungiform
c. Lenticular d. Foliate

362. Lyssa is present in case of-
a. Ox b. Horse
c. Dog d. Pig

363. Which of the following cells secrete Enamel?
a. Amyloblast b. Odontoblast
c. Cementocytes d. All

364. Dentin is secreted by-
a. Amyloblast b. Odontoblast
c. Cementocyte d. All

365. Aorta originates at the base of-
a. Right atrium b. Left Atrium
c. Right ventricle d. Left ventricle

366. Which of the following is a branch of occipital artery-
a. Palatene b. Stylemastord
c. Condyloid d. All

367. Careted sinus act at-
a. Neuro receptor b. Baro receptor
c. Valve d. None

368. Cornual artery is a branch of which artery-
a. External carotid b. Internal carotid
c. Maxillary d. None

370. Which of the following is the synonym for subclavian artery-
a. Maxillary b. Axillary
c. Palatine d. Condyloid

371. Nerve fibers which carry impulse from CNS to-
a. Efferent b. Affarent
c. Both d. None

372. Nerve fibers which carry impulse from periphery to CNS-
a. Efferent b. Afferent
c. Both d. None

373. Afferent fibers are-
a. Sensory b. Motor
c. Both d. None

374. Efferent fibers are-
a. Sensory b. Motor
c. Both d. None

375. Which of the following nerve cells are stellate shaped?
a. Astrocytes b. Oligodendroglia
c. Microglia d. All

376. Junction of one neuron with one another neuron is known as-
a. Synapse b. Ganglion
c. Both d. None

377. A nerve tissue where a number of nerve cell bodies are
a. Synapse b. Ganglion
c. Both d. None

378. Outermost meninges of brain is-
a. Duramater b. Piamater
c. Arachnoid d. None

379. Which of the following is the vertical fold of Duramater?
a. Falx. cerebri b. Tentorium cerebelli
c. Both d. None

380. Which one is the transverse partition between the cerebral hemispheres & cerebellum?
a. Falx cerrebri
b. Tentorium cerebellis
c. Both
d. None

381. Space between spinal canal & duramater is-
a. Epidural space b. Subdural space
c. Venous sinus d. None

382. Space between Duramater & Arachnoid is-
a. Epidural space b. Subdural space
c. Venous sines d. None

384. Lamina splendens belongs to-
a. Duramater b. Piamater
c. Arachnoid d. All

385. Denticulate ligament is produced by-
a. Duramator b. Piamater
c. Arachnoid d. All

386. Prosencephalon represents-
a. Fore brain b. Mid brain
c. Hind brain d. All

387. Rhobencephalon represents-
a. Fore brain b. Mid brain
c. Hind brain d. All

388. Pineal & pituitary bodies are included under-
a. Telencephalon b. Diencephalon
c. Metencephalon d. None

389. Mylencephalon involves-
a. Cerebellum b. Pens
c. Crurocerebri d. Medulla oblangata

390. Telencephalon includes-
a. Cerebral hemisphere
b. Lateral ventricles
c. Anterior part of III ventricle
d. All

391. Corona radiata includes which fibers of brain-
a. Grey matter b. White matter
c. Both d. None

392. Which of the following are non-striated muscles-
a. Skeletal muscles b. Cardiac muscles
c. Smooth muscles d. All

393. Sarcomere is the segment between two-
a. A bands b. I bands
c. Muscles d. Z-lines

394. Intercalated discs are present in case of which muscles?
a. Skeletal b. Smooth
c. Cardiac d. All

395. Spindle shaped muscle fibres are present in which type of muscles?
a. Skeletal b. Smooth
c. Cardiac d. All

396. Which of the following are slow twitch muscle?
a. Red b. White
c. Both d. None

397. Which of the following muscles derive energy from oxidative pathway?
a. Red muscles b. White muscles
c. Both d. None

398. Which muscle derive energy from anaerobic pathway?
a. Red muscles b. White muscles
c. Both d. None

399. Myoglobin is present in which type of muscles?
a. Red b. White
c. Both d. None

400. Which cells exist in ventricles of brain & central canal of spinal card?
a. Ependymal cells b. Microglia
c. Astrocytes d. None

401. Which cells form blood brain barrier?
a. Ependymal cells b. Astrocytes
c. Microglia d. Schwann cells

402. Which cells form myelin sheath across a neuron?
a. Oligodendroglial cells
b. Schwann cells
c. Both
d. None

403. Which cells form covering over ganglion in PNS?
a. Microglia b. Astrocytes
c. Amphicytes d. Schwann cells

404. Which brain cells are phagocytic in nature?
a. Microglia b. Astrocytes
c. Amphicytes d. None

405. Paccenian corpuscles are present for perception of-
a. Pressure b. Cold
c. Warmth d. Touch

406. End bulb of krause is present for perception of-
a. Pressure b. Cold
c. Warmth d. Touch

407. Raffinan corpuscles are present for perception of-
a. Pressure b. Cold
c. Warmth d. Touch

408. Meisinner corpuscles are present for perception of-
a. Pressure b. Cold
c. Warmth d. Touch

409. Which cells of lungs are phagocytic-
a. Duct cell b. Septal cells
c. Both d. None

410. Urease & mucous is secreted by which cells-
a. Neck cells b. Chief cell
c. Parietal cell d. Endocrine cell

411. Which for the following are enzyme secreting cells?
a. Neck cells b. Chief cell
b. Parietal cells c. Endocrine cells

412. Which cells secrete HCl & intrinsic factors-
a. Neck cell b. Chief cell
c. Parietal cell d. Endocrine cell

413. Which one is the serotonin secreting all-
a. Neck cell b. Chief cell
c. Parietal cell d. Endocrine cell

414. Paneth cells are present in-
a. Large intestine b. Small intestine
c. Both d. None

415. Brunner's glands are present in-
a. Duodenum b. Jejunum
c. Ileum d. Caecum

416. Meissner's plexus is present in which Tunic-
a. T. Submucosa b. T. mucosa
c. T. Serosa d. T. muscularis

417. Auerbach's plexus is present in which Tunic-
a. T. Submucosa b. T. mucosa
c. T. Serosa d. T. muscularis

418. Lunia anorectalis is the junction between-
a. Anus & rectum b. Caecum & colon
c. Colon & rectum d. part beyond rectum

419. Glisson's capsule is the connective sheath cover-
a. Lung b. Liver
c. Kidney d. Spleen

420. Endocrine function of liver is performed by-
a. Kupffer cells b. Hepatocytes
c. Both d. None

421. Phagocytosis in liver is done by-
a. Kupffer cells. b. Hepatocytes
c. Both d. None

422. Gall bladder is absent in-
a. Horse b. Camel
c. Both d. None

423. Pancreas is a which type of gland?
a. Mucus b. Serous
c. Mixed d. None

424. Acinar cells perform which function of pancreas?
a. Exocrine b. Endocrine
c. Both d. None

425. Islets of langerhans perform which function of pancreas?
a. Exocrine b. Endocrine
c. Both d. None

426. Which cells of Islets of langerhans secrete glucagon?
a. a b. b
c. d d. e

427. Which cells of Islets of Langerhans secrete somatostatin?
a. a b. b
c. d d. e

428. Which cells of Islets of Langerhans secrete insulin?
a. a b. b
c. d d. e

429. Which cells give rise to different types of cells of Islets of langerhans?
a. a b. b
c. d d. e

430. Which cells off Islets of langerhans secrete pancreatic polypeptides?

a. a b. b
c. d d. f cells

431. Which types of epithelium are present in the papillary duct of kidney?
a. Columnar b. Ciliated
c. Cuboidal d. Transitional

432. Which type of epitheliums is present in renal pelvis?
a. Columnar b. Ciliated
c. Cuboidal d. Transitional

433. Renal pelvis is absent in case of-
a. Horse b. Dog
c. Pig d. Ruminants

434. Which cells produce testosterone in testes-
a. Leydig cells b. Sertoli cells
c. Both d. None

435. A connective tissue are containing channels of rate testes & large blood vessels-
a. Mediastinum testes
b. Septula testes
c. Both
d. None

436. Seminiferous tubules are lined by which epithelium-
a. Stratified b. Pseudostratified
c. Both d. None

437. Epididymis is lined by which epithelium-
a. Stratified b. Pseudostratified
b. Both c. None

438. Which of the following sex glands is present in Dog-
a. Cowper's b. Prostat
c. Vesicular d. None

439. Which cells of Thyroid glands product calcitonin-
a. Follicular b. Parafollicular
c. Parenchymal d. All

440. Which cells are responsible for vision in dim light-
a. Rods b. Cones
c. Both d. None

441. Which cells are responsible for vision in bright light-
a. Rods b. Cones
c. Both d. None

442. Rods contain which pigment-
a. Rhodepsin b. Indopsin
c. Both d. None

443. Cones contain which pigment
a. Rhodepsin b. Indopsin
c. Both d. None

444. Endometrial proliferations in ovary occur in-
a. Proestrus b. Estrus
c. Metestrous d. Diestrus

445. Ovulation occurs in cow in-
a. Proestrus b. Estrus
c. Metestrous d. Diestrus

446. Corpus luteum development occurs in-
a. Proestrus b. Estrus
c. Metestrous d. Diestrus

447. Mammary gland is a -
a. Sweat b. Sebacous
c. Modified sweat d. Mixed

448. Mammary gland follows which mode of secretion-
a. Holocrine b. Merocine
c. Apocrine d. All

449. Complete development history of an individual-
a. Ontogeny b. Phylogeny
c. Both d. None

450. Complete developmental history of a race or group of organizers-
a. Ontogeny b. Phylogeny
c. Both d. None

451. Alecithal eggs are found in case of-
a. Man b. Reptiles
c. Mammals d. Asthropods

452. Telolecethal eggs are found in case of-
a. Reptiles b. Amphibians
c. Fish d. All

453. Centro lecithal eggs are found in case of-
a. Reptiles b. Amphibians
c. Fish d. Arthropods

454. Process in which female gamete grows into a whole individual at a stimulus from male gamete
a. Parthenogenesis b. Superfoetation
c. Polyspermy d. Super facendation

455. Phenomenon of entry of mere than one sperm into ovum-
a. Parthenogeneses b. Superfoetation

c. Polyspermy d. Super facendation

456. Ineposing of pregnancy on an existing pregnancy is known as-
a. Parthenogenesis b. Superfoetation
c. Polyspermy d. Super facendation

457. Impregnation of 2 or more ova that were released at same time-
a. Parthenogenesis b. Superfoetation
c. Polyspermy d. Super facendation

458. Which of the following is a complete cleavage of cells-
a. Holoblastic b. Mesoblastic
c. Discoidal d. All

459. Which one is an incomplete cleavage of cells-
a. Holoblastic b. Meroblastic
c. Discoidal d. All

459. Which one is an incomplete cleavage of cells-
a. Parthenogenesis b. Superfoetation
c. Polyspermy d. Super facendation

460. Which cell cleavage is only superficial-
a. Holoblastic b. Meroblastic
c. Discoidal d. All

461. Function of trophoblast layer of embryo-
a. Protection b. Nutrition
c. Immunity d. All

462. A cavety within the primitive gut in gastrula is-
a. Gastrocoel b. Archenteron
c. Blastopored d. None

463. Which one is not derived from Ectoderm-
a. Hair b. Mouth
c. Blood d. Glands of skin

465. Which one is not derived from endoderm
a. Nose b. Digestive tract
c. Uninary bladder d. All

466. Excretory function of embryo is carried by-
a. Yolk sac b. Amnion
c. Chorion d. Allantois

467. Epitheleochorial placenta is found in case of-
a. Cow b. Goat
c. Bitch d. Sheep

468. Endotheleochorial placenta is found in-
a. Cow b. Goat
c. Sow d. Bitch

469. Syndesmochorial placenta is found in-
a. Cow b. Goat
c. Sow d. Bitch

470. Which somite take part in formation of axial skeleton-
a. Selerotome b. Dermatome
c. Myotome d. All

471. Which somite form the connective tissue layer of integument-
a. Selerotome b. Dermatome
c. Myotome d. All

472. Which somite forms the major part of skeleton musculature-
a. Selerortome b. Dermatome
c. Myotome d. All

473. Development of eye in embryo is completed in-
a. 24 hours b. 48 hours
c. 72 hours d. 112 hours

474. Thickening occurring prior to development of a sense organ-
a. Placode b. Pouch
c. Ridge d. Cleft

475. Seessel's pockets represent dorsal blind end of endodermal-
a. Foregut b. Midgut
c. Hind gut d. All

476. Eustachian tube is formed by which pharyngeal pouch-
a. Ist b. 2nd
c. 3rd d. 4th

477. Palatine tonsils are formed by which pharyngeal pouches-
a. Ist b. 2nd
c. 3rd d. 4th

478. 3rd & 4th pharyngeal pouch form which glands-
a. Thymus b. Parathyroid
c. Both d. None

479. Which pharyngeal pouch is rudimentary
a. Ist b. 2nd
c. 3rd d. 5th

480. Meconium is-
a. Ist faeces b. Last faeces
c. Infective faeces d. Diarrhoeic faeces

481. Aorta is which type of artery-
a. Elastic b. Muscular

c. Mixed d. None

482. Which type of epithelium is found in intestine-
a. Celeated b. Columnar
c. Cuboidal d. Transitional

483. Which of the following are specific gastric glands
a. Fundic b. Pyloric
c. Cardiac d. All

484. Which of the following are non specific gastric gland-
a. Fundic b. Pyloric
c. Cardiac d. both b & c

485. Which type of epithelium is found in vestibule of nasal cavity-
a. Stratified b. Pseudostratified
c. Both d. None

486. Which epithelium is found in tertiary bronchi-
a. Columnar b. Cuboidal
c. Both d. None

487. Which epithelium is found in tertiary bronchiole-
a. Columnar b. Cuboidal
c. Both d. None

488. Which one of the thick myofilament-
a. Actin b. Myosin
c. Both d. None

489. Which one is the thin myofilament
a. Actin b. Myosin
c. Both d. None

490. Calcium in muscles is essential for
a. Contraction b. Relaxation
c. Both d. None

491. Which type protein is found in myosine-
a. Troponin b. Tropomysin
c. Both d. None

492. Which muscles form the contractile portion of walls of vesseles-
a. Smooth b. Cardiac
c. Skelatal d. All

493. Which muscles originate & end at the bones-
a. Smooth b. Cardiac
c. Skeletal d. All

494. Which muscles are present in the wall of heart-
a. Smooth b. Cardiac
c. Skeletal d. All

495. Which muscles are rich in mitochondria-
a. Red b. White
c. Both d. None

496. Skeletal muscles fibers are long in case of which muscles-
a. Red b. White
c. Both d. None

497. Nodes of Ranvier are present in which type of neurons-
a. Myelinated b. Non myelinated
c. Both d. None

498. Saltatory conduction takes place in which type of nerve fibers-
a. Myelinated b. Unmyelinated
c. Both d. None

499. Which of the following has thicker wall-
a. Artery b. Vein
c. Both d. any

500. Which of the following are deep in location-
a. Artery b. Vein
c. Both d. Any

501. Axial skeleton consists of:
A. Rib B. Sternum
C. Vertebral column D. All of these

502. Os penis is found in:
a. Dog b. Bull
c. Human d. None

503. Snout of pig consists:
a. Os cardis b. Os rostrale
c. Os penis d. None

504. Os cardis is present in heart of:
a. Cow b. Dog
c. Women d. Fish

505. Elastic cartilage is found in:
a. External ear b. Internal ear
c. Arm d. Leg

506. Which one is not intended to be function of skeleton:
a. Support b. Locomotion
c. Protection d. Reproduction

507. Parietal layer of Bowmans's capsule is made up of:
a. Simple squamous epithelium
b. Simple cuboidal epithelium

c. Simple columnar epithelium
d. Stratified epithelium

508. Simple cuboidal epithelium is present in:
a. Testes b. Oviduct
c. Glands d. None

509. Gastrointestinal tract, excretory ducts of gland, gall bladder are made up of:
a. Simple columnar epithelium
b Simple cuboidal
c. Stratified epithelium
d. All of above

510. Which one supports head:
a. Ligamentum nuchae
b. Ligamentum flava
c. Abdominal tunic
d. Arteries

511. Choose yellow elastic connective tissue:
a. Ligamentum flava
b. Tendon
c. Collagen
d. Areolar tissue

512. Which one cartilage is located in intervertebral discs
a. Elastic b. Fibrocartilage
c. Hyaline d. None

513. Choose the exocrine gland
a. Gonads b. Adrenal
c. Thyroid d. Liver

514. Which one of the following is ductless gland:
a. Adrenal b. Pituitary
c. Thyroid d. All of above

515. Choose the right sequence
a. Cell – tissue – organ - body
b. Cell – organ – tissue – body
c. Cell – organ – body – tissue
d. Cell – tissue – body – organ

516. Which one is not a characteristic of a living cell?
a. Irritability b. Reproduction
c. Movement d. All of above

517. Type of articulation present in spinal column:
a. Synarthrosis b. Diarthrosis
c. Amphiathrosis d. All of above

518. Striated muscle with centrally located nuclei is characteristic of muscle found in:
a. Lungs b. Heart
c. Uterus d. Mammary glands

519. Foetal median ligament of the bladder contains:
A. Urachus B. Umbilical veins
C. Umbilical arteries D. Both A and C

520. In foetus, yolk sac is attached to:
A. Lungs B. Small intestine
C. Stomach D. None

521. Extrabdominal part of gubernaculum forms ligament of.
a. Tail of epididymis
b. Testis
c. Fore limb
d. All of above

522. Mullerian duct forms:
a. Pulmonary artery b. Cervix
c. Vagina d. Both b and c

523. Occipital myotomes are the origin of muscles of:
a. Tongue b. Eye
c. Leg d. Abdomen

524. Paramesonephric duct is also known as:
A. Kuhne's duct B. Epinephric duct
C. Mullerian duct D. Darwin duct

525. Urogenital sinus gives rise to:
A. Cervix B. Vagina
C. Kidney D. Liver

526. Bones having alveoli for teeth development in ruminant are:
A. Maxilla B. Mandible
C. Incisive bones D. Both A and B

527. Surface of teeth frequently used to determine age is ruminants is:
A. Occlusal B. Buccal surface
C. Liquid surface D. None

528. Blood vessel supplying teeth of lower dental arcade in ruminants is:
A. Infraorbital artery B. Inferior alveolar artery
C. Femoral artery D. Palatine artery

529. Nerve supplying the teeth of upper dental arcade in ruminants is:
A. Infraorbital B. Lingual
C. Supraorbital D. Alveolar

530. In ruminants, alveolar nerve supplies to:
A. Lower dental arcade
B. Upper dental arcade

C. Both 1 & 2
D. None

531. Which one is present in ox but absent in sheep:
A. Sphenoid sinus B. Lacrimal sinus
C. Maxillary sinus D. Palatine

532. Major nerve supplied to bovine horn is derived from the:
A. Frontal sinus branch
B. Cornual nerve
C. Infratrochlear nerve
D. Supraorbital nerve

533. Cornual artery is a branch of:
A. Superficial temporal artery
B. Supraorbital artery
C. External carotid artery
D. None

534. In oxen, anaesthetic, for Petersons's eye block, is deposited around:
A. Optic foramen
B. Ethmoid foramen
C. Maxillary foramen
D. Orbito-rotundum foramen

535. Which one is present in ox but absent in sheep and goat:
A. Facial artery
B. Caudal auricular artery
C. Transverse facial artery
D. Caudal ophthalmic artery

536. Prepared site for thoraco-centesis in oxen in:
A. 6th or 7th intercostals space
B. 4th Intercostal space
C. 5th Intercostal space
D. None

537. Widest and most accessible ribs for bone marrow aspiration are:
A. 11th to 13th ribs B. 1st to 3rd ribs
C. 6th to 8th ribs D. 9th to 10th ribs

538. Which one does not form a part of fore-stomach?
A. Rumen B. Abomasum
C. Omasum D. Reticulum

539. Which one is true or glandular stomach in ruminants?
A. Rumen B. Reticulum
C. Omasum D. None of above

540. Most cranial cardiac valve in ruminants in:
A. Pulmonary valve
B. Aortic valve
C. Pulmono-aortic valve
D. None

541. Longest artery that supplies the distal regions of the pelvic limb of ruminants arise from the:
A. Femoral artery
B. Popliteal artery
C. Caudal glutted artery
D. None

542. 'Hard milker' condition involves:
A. Lactiferous duct B. Lactiferous sinus
C. Papillary duct D.. None of above

543. Choose the least accurate statement:
A. A hilus is present in all ruminants kidney
B. Renal pelvis is absent in ox, sheep and goat.
C. Renal calices are present in ox
D. External contour of kidney is smooth in all ruminants.

544. During semen ejaculation and urination, which muscle is mostly helpful:
A. Bulbo- spongiosus muscle
B. Urethralis muscle
C. Retractor penis muscle
D. None

545. For amputation of cows udder, which nerve is anesthetized:
A. L_1 and L_2 nerves B. Pelvic nerves
C. Epigastric nerves D. Supramammary nerve

546. Which one is absent in swine liver:
A. Gall bladder
B. Common bile duct
C. Papillary process of caudate lobe and caudate ligament
D. Lateral lobes

547. Teeth used as defensive weapons in boar are:
A. Incisors B. Canines
C. Molars D. Wolf teeth

548. Which one is absent in pigs:
A. Pharyngeal tonsil B. Lingual tonsil
C. Palatine tonsil D. All of above

549. Which hepatic ligament is absent in pigs:
A. Right triangular ligament

B. Caudate ligament
C. Coronary ligament
D. Falciform ligament

550. Which one is not a natural orifice in the wall of abdomen?
A. Deep inguinal ring
B. Epiploic foramen
C. Umbilicus
D. Pelvic inlet

551. Which one does not act by binding calcium?
A. Na citrate B. K oxalate
C. Heparin D. None

552. Heparin accelerates the activity of:
A. Antithrombin III B. Antithrombin X
C. Antithrombin IV D. None

553. Dicoumarol toxicosis affects clotting factors II, VII, IX, X because of:
A. Inhibition of Vitamin K
B. Inhibition of Vitamin A
C. Inhibition of Vitamin E
D. None

554. RBC with no central pallor and much smaller than normal:
A. Schistocyte B. Spherocyte
C. Kurloff body D. Russell body

555. Ig producing cell is:
A. Schistocyte B. Spherocyte
C. Plasma cell D. Lymphocyte

556. Eosinophillic inclusion body normally present in lymphoid cells of guinea: pigs
A. Schistocyte B. Spherocyte
C. Kurloff body D. Plasma cell

557. Which one is RBC fragment?
A. Schistocyte B. Russell body
C. Plasma cell D. Lmphocyte

558. Ig filled vacuole in cytoplasm of plasma cells:
A. Schistocyte B. Spherocyte
C. Kurloff body D. Russell body

559. Leukocyte predominant in peripheral blood of adult cow and weanling pig:
A. Schistocyte B. Spherocyte
C. Kurloff body D. Lymphocyte

560. Linear distribution of cells seen in fluids of high viscosity is known as:
A. Windrowing B. Castellation
C. Both D. None of above

561. Smallest erythrocytes are present in:
A. Cats B. Pigs
C. Goats D. Both A and B

562. Choose the only source of endogenous heparin:
A. Basophil B. Mast cell
C. RBC D. Both A and B

563. Plasma protein of large animals used to detect internal inflammatory lesions:
A. Kalliekrinin B. Thrombin
C. Serotonin D. Fibrinogen

564. Which of the following can not be counted with a haemocytometer?
a. Reticulocytes b. RBC
c. Leukocytes d. None

565. Species with natural sickle celled RBCs are:
A. Rats B. Deer
C. Birds D. Elephant

566. Iron supplement is specially required by:
A. Pigs B. Birds
C. Goats D. Horses

567. Intervenous crest is present in:
a. Right atrium b. Left atrium
c. Right ventricle d. Left ventricle

568. Right a/v opening is slit like in:
a. Ox b. Horse
c. Dog d. Fowl

569. Inherted dislocation of patella of dog occurs in:
a. Bostan b. Boxer
c. Bull terior d. All of the above

570. *Os penis* is present in:
a. Ox b. Horse
c. Dog d. Pig

571. *Os rostrale* is present in:
a. Ox b. Horse
c. Dog d. Pig

572. Pulmonary artery is related cranially with:
a. Right auricle b. Left auricle
c. None of the above d. All of the above

573. The dorsal sessamoid bones per leg in dog are:
a. 1 b. 2
c. 3 d. 4

574. Diploe is a:
a. Spongy substance in short bones
b. Spongy substance in flat bones
c. Spongy substance in long bones
d. None of the above

575. Adductor muscle is attached on the surface of the femur:
a. Posterior b. Anterior
c. Lateral d. Medial

576. *Fovia capitis* is well developed in:
a. Ox b. Horse
c. Dog d. Fowl

577. Crest of tibia is formed by:
a. Anterior border b. Posterior border
c. Lateral border d. Medial border

578. The typical cervical vertebrae are dorsoventrally compressed in:
a. Ox b. Dog
c. Horse d. Fowl

579. Occipital condyle is single in:
a. Ox b. Dog
c. Horse d. Fowl

580. Nasal bone fits in to frontal bone of:
a. Ox b. Dog
c. Horse d. Fowl

581. Alar canal is present in:
a. Ox b. Dog
c. Horse d. Fowl

582. Patellar ligament in dog are:
a. Medial b. Lateral
c. Middle d. Ligamentum patellae

583. Interparietal forms roof of cranium in:
a. Ox b. Horse
c. All of above d. None of the above

584. Alar notch is present in atlas of:
a. Ox b. Dog
c. Horse d. Fowl

585. Vertical diameter of pelvic inlet is distance between:
a. Promontary and pubis
b. Two psoas tubercles
c. Ischial arch and sacrum
d. Pubis and third/fourth sacral vertebrae

586. Transverse diameter of pelvic out let is measured between
a. First coccygeal and ischial arch
b. Two tuber ischii
c. Ischial arch and tuber ischii
d. Two psoas tubercles

587. The jugular lymph sac in the pig embryo arise at:
a. 12 mm stage b. 14 mm stage
c. 16 mm stage d. None of above

588. Annulus fibrosus of the bicuspid & tricuspid valves are associated with:
a. Inter ventricular septum
b. Endocardial cushion
c. Atrial foramen
d. None of above

589. The lateral lingual angles largely arise at the level of:
a. I branchial arch b. II branchial arch
c. III branchial arch d. None of above

590. Middle cervical nerve is absent in:
a. Ox b. Horse
c. Dog d. Fowl

591. Abducent nerve supply to:
a. Rectus lateralis b. Rectus medialis
c. All of the above d. None of the above

592. Trochlear nerve is:
a. Smallest sensory b. Smallest motor
c. Smallest mixed d. None of the above

593. Upper lip is supplied by:
a. Superior labial artery
b. Inferior labial
c. All of the above
d. None of the above

594. Prescapular lymph gland is supplied by:
a. Inferior cervical artery
b. Superior cervical artery
c. All of the above
d. None of the above

595. Reticulum is supplied by:
a. Right ruminal artery
b. Left ruminal artery
c. Omasoabomasal artery
d. All of the above

596. The connective tissue of lung develops from:

a. Ectoderm b. Mesoderm
c. Endoderm d. None of the above

597. Gall bladder is lined with:
a. Simple columnar epithelium
b. Simple cuboidal epithelium
c. Transitional epithelium
d. Simple squamous epithelium

598. Pancreatic duct is lined by:
a. Simple columnar epithelium
b. Simple cuboidal epithelium
c. Transitional epithelium
d. Simple squamous epithelium

599. Oesophagous is lined with:
a. Stratified squamous epithelium
b. Stratified columnar epithelium
c. Psudostratified columnar epithelium
d. Cuboidal epithelium

600. Trachea is lined by:
a. Stratified squamous epithelium
b. Stratified columnar epithelium
c. Psudostratified columnar epithelium
d. Cuboidal epithelium

601. Internal carotid is absent in:
a. Ox b. Horse
c. Dog d. None of the above

602. Pelvic floor is formed by:
a. Ilium and pubis b. Ischium and pubis
c. Ilium and ischium d. Ilium, ischium and pubis

603. Ischium ventrally gives attachment to:
a. Adductor muscle
b. Deep gluteal muscle
c. Iliacus muscle
d. Psoas major muscle

604. Tubercoxae is found in:
a. Horse b. Cow
c. Bitch d. Cat

605. Gluteal surface is depressed in:
a. Cow b. Horse
c. Cat d. Goat

606. 50% of acetabular cavity is formed by:
a. Sacrum b. Pubis
c. Ileum d. Ischium

607. Gluteal line starts from middle of lateral border and runs towards the tuber coxae in:
a. Cow b. Mare
c. Goat d. Bitch

608. Left coronary artery arise from:
a. Anterior aortic sinus
b. Posterior aortic sinus
c. None of the above
d. All of the above

609. Sterno-pericardiac ligament is present in:
a. Dog b. Ox
c. Horse d. Fowl

610. Falsiform ligament is present in:
a. Ox b. Horse
c. Dog d. Fowl

611. Two venacave are present in:
a. Ox b. Horse
c. Dog d. Fowl

612. Chordae tendinae are attached with:
a. Ventricular surface of the valve
b. Atrial surface of the valve
c. All of the above
d. None of the above

613. Angiology is the study of:
a. Organs of circulation of blood
b. Organs of circulation of lymph
c. All of the above
d. None of the above

614. Pes includes;
a. Tarsus b. Metatarsus
c. Digits d. All of the above

615. Long axis of ischium is directed obliquely:
a. Upward backward
b. Upward downward
c. Dorsal caudad
d. None of the above

616. Ischium has:
a. 3 surfaces, 3 borders and 3 angles
b. 2 surfaces, 4 borders and 4 angles
c. 4 surfaces, 4 borders and 4 angles
4. None of the above

617. Tuber sacral in dog is:
a. Prominent b. Truncated
c. Thickened d. None of the above

618. The Vertical diameter is distance between pectin pubis and:
a. 3rd and 4th sacral segment

b. 3rd sacral segment
c. 4th sacral segment
d. 4th and 5th sacral segment

619. Calcium phosphate in the bones is:
a. 33% b. 57.33%
c. 3.85% d. 2.05%

620. 2nd and 3rd tarsals are fused in:
a. Ox b. Horse
c. Dog d. Fowl

621. Carpal joint is:
a. Diarthrosis b. Ginglimus
c. Arthrodial d. All of the above

622. Lateral malliolus articulates with stentaculum teli in:
a. Ox b. Horse
c. Dog d. Fowl

623. The join with out collateral ligament is:
a. Stifle b. Carple
c. Elbow d. Shoulder joint

624. Cuboid shaped tarsal bone in horse is:
a. First b. Second
c. Third d. Fourth

625. Colateral ligament in fetlock joint of ox are:
a. 1 in no. b. 2 in no.
c. 3 in no. d. 4 in no.

626. Transverse process of cervical has 3 branches in:
a. Ox b. Dog
c. Horse d. Fowl

627. Foramen transversarium is absent in:
a. 6th cervical of horse
b. 6th cervical of ox
c. 7th cervical of ox
d. None of the above

628. Notarium is found in:
a. Ox b. Dog
c. Horse d. Fowl

629. Synsacrum is present in:
a. Ox b. Dog
c. Horse d. Fowl

630. Promonatory is found in:
a. Cervical vertebrae
b. Thoracic vertebrae
c. Lumber vertebrae
d. 1st segment of sacrum

631. Floating ribs are present in:
a. Ox b. Dog
c. Horse d. Fowl

632. The course of collateral vessel is:
a. Parallel to the parent vessel
b. Opposite to the parent vessel
c. All of the above
d. None of the above

633. Innermost membrane of the embryo is-
a. Chorion b. Amnion
c. Allantois d. Yolk sac

634. Intertransversus joints between last lumber and wing of sacrum are present in:
a. Ox b. Dog
c. Horse d. Buffalo

635. On rectal and vaginal palpation it can be easily detected:
a. Pelvic surface of ilium
b. Gluteal surface of ilium
c. Iliac surface of ilium facing forward
d. Antero lateral angle of ilium

636. Forms the angle of haunch:
a. Tuber coxae b. Tuber sacrale
c. Tuber ischii d. Pectin pubis

637. The angle of croup is formed by:
a. Tuber coxae b. Tuber sacrale
c. Tuber ischii d. Pectin pubis

638. Psoas tubercle is very prominent in:
a. Cow b. Mare
c. Sheep d. Sow

639. Ischial arch is rounded or acute in:
a. Sow b. Buffalo
c. Mare d. Goat

640. Pelvic inlet is:
a. Entirely bony
b. Bilateral
c. Continuous with thoracic cavity
d. Separated from abdominal cavity by diaphragm

641. Roof of pelvic cavity is less arched in:
a. Cow b. Buffalo
c. Mare d. Bitch

642. The recurrent vessel runs:
a. Parallel to parent vessel

b. Opposite to parent vessel
c. All of the above
d. None of the above

643. Bronchial groove-I gives rise to:
a. External auditory meatus
b. Ear drum
c. Ear tunic
d. None of the above

644. Spleen develops from mesenchyme in:
a. Dorsal mesentery
b. Dorsal mesogastrium
c. Ventral mesogastrium
d. None of the above

645. Cloaca is divided in to its lateral constituent parts by means of:
a. Urorectal fold b. Cloacal membrane
c. Cloacal sinus d. None of the above

646. The islets of langerhans arise:
a. From the acini
b. As out growths of ductular system
c. Independently
d. None of the above

647. Thalamus develops from:
a. Mesencephalon b. Metencephalon
c. Diencephalon d. None of the above

648. The rumen arises from the curvature of original saculation of:
a. Dorsal curvature
b. Ventral curvature
c. None of the above
d. All of the above

649. Sternal lymph gland is absent in:
a. Ox b. Horse
c. Fowl d. Dog

650. Ear ossicles are present in:
a. Middle ear b. External ear
c. Internal ear d. None of the above

651. Intermediate lobe is present in:
a. Right lung b. Left lung
c. All of the above d. None of the above

652. Last pair of lumbar artery arises from:
a. External iliac artery
b. Internal iliac artery
c. All of the above
d. None of the above

653. Scrotum is supplied by:
a. External pubic artery
b. Internal pubic artery
c. All of the above
d. None of the above

654. Brain of horse is supplied by:
a. External carotid artery
b. Internal carotid artery
c. All of the above
d. None of the above

655. Axillary lymph gland is supplied by:
a. External thoracic artery
b. Internal thoracic artery
c. All of the above
d. None of the above

656. RBC is nucleated in:
a. Ox b. Horse
c. Fowl d. Dog

657. Ovary is covered by bursa in:
a. Cow b. Mare
c. Bitch d. Hen

658. Granulocytes are:
a. Monocytes b. Lymphocytes
c. All of the above d. None of the above

659. Urinary bladder is lined by:
a. Psudostratified epithelium
b. Stratified epithelium
c. Transitional epithelium
d. Cuboidal epithelium

660. Costocervical Lymph gland is present in:
a. Ox b. Horse
c. Dog d. Fowl

661. Lymph vessel is in appearance:
a. Coiled b. Tubular
c. Beaded d. All of the above

662. Penis is musclovascular in:
a. Ox b. Horse
c. Dog d. Fowl

663. Primitive streak in chick appears at:
a. 7-8 hour b. 10-12 hour
c. 1-2 hour d. 3-4 hour

664. Primary ovarian follicle has:
a. Large antrium b. Small antrium

c. No antrium d. All of the above

665. Secondary spermatocytes have:
a. Haploid set of chromosomes
b. Diploid set of chromosomes
c. Triploid set of chromosomes
d. All of the above

666. Hyaluranidase is concentrated at:
a. Sperm head b. Sperm tail
c. All of the above d. None of the above

667. Ovary appears like bunch of grapes in:
a. Cow b. Mare
c. Bitch d. Hen

668. Mesencephalon represents-
a. Fore brain b. Mid brain
c. Hind brain d. All

669. Anvil shaped bone in ear is:
(a) Malleus (b) Incus
(c) Stepes (d) None

670. Optio nerve pierces the sclera at.
(a) Optic dise (b) Blind spot
(c) Both (d) None

671. The sinus with in the selero corneal junction is known as
(a) Canal of schlemam
(b) Sinus venosus
(c) Both
(d) None

672. The three cartilages present in external ear are
(a) Sentiform cartilage
(b) Conchal cartilage
(c) Annular cartilage
(d) All

673. The projected rim of scleral tissue behind the canal of schlemam is known as
(a) Scleral spur (b) Blood spot
(c) Optic disc (d) Sinous venous

674. The contents of membranous labyrinth.
(a) Cochlear duct
(b) Saccule & ubricle
(c) Three ducts of Semicircular canals
(d) All

675. Ear wax or cerumen is secreted by.
(a) Cochlear duct
(b) Saccule
(c) External acoustic meatus
(d) All

676. Band which surrounds the coronory border of hoof is
(a) Periople (b) White line
(c) Frog (d) none

677. Pneumatic bones are characteristic of.
(a) Poultry (b) Swine
(c) Equine (d) Canine

678. 3rd trochanter tessier is present in
(a) Horse (b) Swine
(c) Dog (d) Camel

679. Which of these is/are the functions of periosteum?
(a) Protect the bone
(b) Growth and repair of bone
(c) Supply nutrition of bone
(d) All of these

680. Bone of ox possess the highest quantity of which salt?
(a) Calcium phosphate
(b) Calcium chloride
(c) Calcium carbonate
(d) None of these

681. Which of the following muscle is an example of pennate muscle?
(a) Biceps brachi (b) Peroneus tertius
(c) Brachialis (d) Massater

682. The viscocity of synovial fluid depends on
(a) Albumin (b) Mucin
(c) Water (d) Hyaluronic acid

683. Which of the following skull bones are paired in number?
(a) Vomar (b) Occipital
(c) Sphenoid (d) Inter parietal

684. Which of the following is not a branch of thoracic aorta?
(a) Bronchial artery (b) Esophageal artery
(c) Phrenic arteries (d) Splenic artery

685. Among the following muscles, which muscle is not present on medial aspect of shoulder:
(a) Sub scapular (b) Deltoideus
(c) Teres major (d) Coracobrachialis

686. The muscle which extends from sternum to pubis along the floor of abdominal cavity is:

(a) Psoas major
(b) Levator costarum
(c) Rectus abdominis
(d) Transverse abdominis

687. Which of the following nerve is not sensory in nature?
(a) Olfactory (b) Facial
(c) Optic (d) Cochleo-vestibular

689. Number of thorasic vertebrae in horse:
(a) 18 (b) 12
(c) 13 (d) 14

690. Hoof is related with:
(a) I phalanx (b) II phalanx
(c) III phalanx (d) none

691. Percentage of hoof in bone composition of ox:
(a) 5.02% (b) 5.22%
(c) 5.20% (d) None of these

692. Ox containing total number of bone is the body except visceral bone:
(a) 206 (b) 207
(c) 208 (d) 210

693. Name of foramen which is used for desensitization of mandible:
(a) Mandible (b) Mental foramen
(c) Both (d) None

694. Horn is the progression of
(a) Bone (b) Cornual process
(c) Both (d) None

695. Distal inter phalangeal joint is called as:
(a) Pastern (b) Coggin
(c) Both (d) None

696. Nerves at abdominal regions are:
(a) 6 pairs (b) 3 is pair
(c) 4 is pair (d) None of these

697. Right kidney is heart shaped in which species:
(a) Cow (b) Horses
(c) Goat (d) Swine

698. In the horse shoe which part we say shock absorber:
(a) Bulb of heel (b) Fetlock bone
(c) Pastern bone (d) All

699. Brain is divided into:
(a) Prosencephalon
(b) Mesocephalon
(c) Rhombencephalon
(d) All

700. Acromion process of scapula is absent:
(a) Ox (b) Horse
(c) Dog (d) Poultry

701. Hip bone comprises of:
(a) Ilium (b) Ischium
(c) Pubis (d) All of these

702. Acetabulum is perforated in which of the species:
(a) Ox (b) Horse
(c) Pig (d) Fowl

703. Cornual process present in:
(a) Human (b) Horse
(c) Ox (d) Fowl

704. *Ossa opticus* in the eye is present in:
(a) Ox (b) Horse
(c) Fowl (d) Dog

705. Ball & socket type of joint is found in:
(a) Shoulder joint (b) Elbow joint
(c) Knee joint (d) Fetlock joint

706. Functional unit of muscle is:
(a) Nephron (b) Neuron
(c) Muscle fibre (d) Sarconere

707. The following is not a flexor muscle:
(a) Unlaris lateralis
(b) Pronator teres
(c) Extensor carpi radialis
(d) None of the above

708. Uterus is 'V' sharped in:
(a) Bitch (b) Mayer
(c) Sow (d) doe

709. The terminal part of spinal cord is known as:
(a) Couda medularis (b) Filum terminal
(c) Cardia equina (d) All of the above

710. The weight of an adult heart is:
(a) 0.4-0.5% (b) 0.5-0.6%
(c) 0.6-0.7% (d) 0.7-0.8%

711. Hinge joint type is seen in:
(a) Humero-radial joint
(b) Shoulder joint
(c) Temporo-mandibular joint
(d) Hip joint

712. Trapezius is a muscle found in:
(a) Shoulder girdle (b) Arm

(c) Forearm (d) Thigh

713. Snout is characteristic month of:
(a) Pig (b) Horse
(c) Cattle (d) Elephant

714. In mare following part of dentition is absent:
(a) Canine (b) Incisor
(c) Premolars (d) Molars

715. At the age of 8 weeks in cattle:
(a) (Rumen + Reticulum) × 2 = Abomasum
(b) (Rument+Reticulum)= Abomasum
(c) (Rumen + Reticulum) × ½ = Abomasum
(d) None of these

716. Zygomatic salivary gland is found in:
(a) Dog (b) Cat
(c) Horse (d) Pig

717. This bone of middle ear is hammer shaped:
(a) Malleus (b) Incus
(c) Stepes (d) None of the above

718. Foramen - winslow is found in-part of the body:
(a) Peritonium (b) Pleura
(c) Pericardium (d) Meninges

719. Which of the following are the membranes bones?
(a) Lacrymal (b) Frontal
(c) Nasal (d) All the above

720. Horns of deer are compound of which of following:
(a) Bone (b) Keratin
(c) Cartilage (d) Epidermis

721. Strongest vertebra is:
(a) Cervical (b) Lumbar
(c) Thoracic (d) Sacral

722. Thickest epidermis part is:
(a) Sole (b) Cornea
(c) Lip (d) None

723. Median atlanto-axial joint is which of the following:
(a) Ball & Socket (b) Hinge
(c) Pivot (d) Saddle

724. Teeth originate from:
(a) Ecoderm (b) Endoderm
(c) Mesoderm (d) Ecto-mesoderm

725. Essential vitamins for keratogenesis are:
(a) A & B (b) A & E
(c) A & E (d) A & K

726. The hyaline cartilage is found in:
(a) Bone (b) Trachea
(c) Bronchi (d) All above

727. Acromion process of scapula is absent in:
(a) Horse (b) Cattle
(c) Dog (d) Pig

728. Coracoid process of scapula is absent in:
(a) Ox (b) Dog
(c) Horse (d) Pig

729. Supratrochlear foramen in humerus is present in:
(a) Horse (b) Ox
(c) Dog (d) Pig

730. Only one interosseous space in Radius and ulna is found in:
(a) Dog (b) Horse
(c) Ox (d) Pig

731. Boat shaped Navicular bone is present in:
(a) Cat (b) Dog
(c) Horse (d) Ox

732. Seven thoracic vertebrae found in:
(a) Fowl (b) Dog
(c) Pig (d) Ox

733. Odentoid process of axis is more prominent in which species:
(a) Horse (b) Dog
(c) Ox (d) Pig

734. Keel bone found in which species:
(a) Ox (b) Horse
(c) Pig (d) Fowl

735. Ilioschiatic foramen in hip bone is found in:
(a) Fow (b) Horse
(c) Ox (d) Pig

736. In which species capoular ligament absent at shoulder joint:
(a) Dog (b) Sheep
(c) Horse (d) Cattle

737. Which one is not the muscle of abdomen?
(a) Oblique abdomins externus
(b) Oblique abdominis internus
(c) Transverse externus
(d) Rectus abdominis

738. Sacrum of dog form by fusion of how many vertebrae:
(a) 3 (b) 4
(c) 5 (d) 2

739. Splint bone is present at metacarpel of:
(a) Dog (b) Horse
(c) Cattle (d) Fowl

740. Supra condyloid fossa is absent in femur of:
(a) Dog (b) Pig
(c) Horse (d) Cattle

741. Torsal bone is not found in:
(a) Pig (b) Dog
(c) Horse (d) Fowl

742. Torus linguae (raised structure at posterior part of tongue) are absent in:
(a) Pig (b) Dog
(c) Horse (d) Fowl

743. In which species spleen is human foot print shape:
(a) Dog (b) Horse
(c) Cattle (d) Buffalo

744. Point of hip in animal is formed by:
(a) Lateral angle of ilium
(b) Medial angle of ilium
(c) External angle of ischium
(d) Internal angle of ischium

745. Rudimentary bone in ox is?
(a) Radius (b) Patella
(c) Fibula (d) Femer

746. Synovial joint is also known as?
(a) Amphiarthroidal (b) Synarthroidal
(c) Diarthroidal (d) Both a & b

747. Guttural pouch is found in?
(a) Cow (b) Fowl
(c) Dog (d) Horse

748. Soft palate is absent in:
(a) Cow (b) Fowl
(c) Dog (d) Horse

749. In humerus spiral groove is present at?
(a) Posterior surface (b) Medial surface
(c) Lateral surface (d) Anterior surface

750. Ulnar carpal bone is also known as?
(a) Pissiform (b) Semilunar
(c) Cuniform (d) Scaphoid

751. Falciform ligament attaches liner to:
(a) Kidney (b) Stomach
(c) Diaphragm (d) Intestine

752. No. of lobes in horse liver
(a) 2 (b) 3
(c) 4 (d) 5

753 The process of the neuran other than axon is called:
(a) Axine (b) Axis
(c) Dendrite (d) Dendron

754. Out of 2 myofilaments, _______ filaments occur only inside the 'I' bands & _______ filaments occur in both 'A' & 'I' bands:
(a) Actin, myosin (b) Actin, Actin
(c) Myosin, Actin (d) Myosin, Myosin

755. The surface of gastric mucosa is lined by:
(a) Simple columnar (b) Stratified squamous
(c) Transitional, (d) None

756. Trigeminal nerve is:
(a) Sensory (b) Motor
(c) Mixed (d) None

757. Smallest bone is:
(a) Malleus (b) Incus
(c) Stapes (d) None

758. Colunella is a bone present in ear of:
(a) Ox (b) Dog
(c) Horse (d) Poultry

759. Nervous layer of eyeball is:
(a) Choroid (b) Sclera
(c) Retina (d) None

760. Margo-plicatus is seen in stomach of:
(a) Horse (b) Dog
(c) Ox (d) Poultry

761. In fowl, non-functional ovary is:
(a) Left (b) Right
(c) Both (d) None

762. Renal Pyramids are not distinct in:
(a) Cat, dog (b) Horse, sheep, Goat
(c) Both of above (d) Ox & boar

763. Fluid in chamber of eye:
(a) Lacrimal fluid
(b) Aqueous humor
(c) Corebrospinal fluid
(d) Endolymph

764. Osseous labyrinth is filled by:
(a) Endolymph (b) Perilymph
(c) Both above (d) None of above

765. Medial head of triceps originates from medial surface of the shaft of:

(a) Femer (b) Scapula
(c) Tibia (d) Humerus

766. Maxillary nerve passes through foramen:
(a) Oval (b) Magnum
(c) Both above (d) Orbitorotundum

767. Phrenic artery supply blood to:
(a) Liver (b) stomach
(c) Kidney (d) Diaphragm

768. Fovea is a:
(a) Non articular eminence
(b) Articular eminence
(c) Non articular depression
(d) Articular depression

769. No of ribs in fowl:
(a) 18 pair (b) 13 pair
(c) 11 pair (d) 7 pair

770. The corona gtandis is present in the penis of:
(a) Ox (b) Dog
(c) Horse (d) Pig

771. Ischiatic tubes is trifid in:
(a) Ox (b) Horse
(c) Dog (d) Fowl

772. *Os penis* not is present in
(a) Ox (b) Dog
(c) Fowl (d) Both a & c

773. The central & fourth tarsal bones are fused to form a large bone in:
(a) Ox (b) Horse
(c) Dog (d) Fowl

774. The middle ear is located in:
(a) Ethmoid bone (b) Occipital bone
(c) Temporal bone (d) Conchal cartilage

775. The spleen is roughly triangular in:
(a) Horse (b) Dog
(c) Cow (d) Fowl

776. The number of ribs in horse:
(a) 26 (b) 28-30
(c) 36 (d) None of the above

777. Herring bodies are the structures found in
(a) Neurohypaphysis (b) Liver
(c) Thymus (d) None of the above

778. Chromophil cells of adrenal cortex are derived from:
(a) Mesoderm (b) Endoderm
(c) Neural crest cells (d) None of the above

779. Larynx is not the sound producing organ in:
(a) Fowl (b) Horse
(c) Dog (d) Ox

780. Which is sensory nerve?
(a) Olfactory (b) Optic
(c) Acoustic (d) All of above

781. Which is mixed cranial nerve?
(a) Oculomotor (b) Trochlear
(c) Abducent (d) None

782. Nerve supply to retractor oculi muscle is accomplished by:
(a) Optic nerve (b) Oculomotor nerve
(c) Trochlear nerve (d) Abducent nerve

783. Origin of olfactory nerve is:
(a) Behind corpora quadrigemina
(b) Lateral aspect of pons
(c) From optic commisure
(d) Olfactory bulb

784 Mixed longest nerve is:
(a) Trigeminal (b) Facial
(c) Glossophoryngeal (d) Vagus

785. Which nerve is also called as pneumogastric nerve?
(a) Trigeminal (b) Facial
(c) Glossopharyngeal (d) Vagus

786. Number of sacral vertebrae in cow is:
(a) 5 (b) 7
(c) 3 (d) 9

787. Most compact part of tooth is:
(a) Enamel (b) Dentine
(c) Cement (d) All of the above

788. Which is ivary like part of teeth?
(a) Enamel (b) Dentine
(c) Cement (d) All of the above

789. Which is dental formula for camel?
(a) I 0/4, C 0/0, P 3/3, M 3/3
(b) I 3/3, C 1/1, P 3/3, M 3/3
(c) I 3/3, C 1/1, P 4/4, M 2/3
(d) I 2/6, C 1/1, W 1/1, P 6/4, M 6/6

790. The musculospiral groove is present on which surface of humerus?
(a) Lateral (b) Lateral
(c) Medial (d) Non above

791. The glenoid cavity of scapula is oval in:
(a) Camel (b) Goat
(c) Horse (d) None above

792. Number of heads in muscle sartorius:
(a) 1 (b) 2
(c) 3 (d) 4

793. Supra-trochlear foramen is present in humerus of:
(a) Ox (b) Horse
(c) Fowl (d) Dog

794. Diaphragm is of rudimentary muscle in:
(a) Ox (b) Dog
(c) Fowl (d) Horse

795. Angular process is present in the mandible of:
(a) Dog (b) Ox
(c) Horse (d) Fowl

796. Quadrate bone is present in skull of:
(a) Horse (b) Dog
(c) Fowl (d) Ox

797. Accessory ligament is present in the hip joint of:
(a) Ox (b) Horse
(c) Pig (d) Dog

798. Auditory tube is part of which of the following
(a) Inter ear (b) External ear
(c) Middle ear (d) None of the above

799. The two part of the stomach fowl are:
(a) Crop & proventriculus
(b) Gizzard & Proventriculus
(c) Crop & gizzard
(d) All of the above

800. In dog a large supratrochlear foramen is present in
(a) Mandible (b) Femur
(c) Humerus (d) None of the above

801. Brunner's gland present in:
(a) Esophagus (b) Stomach
(c) Duodenum (d) All of these

802. The Epithelial lining of urinary bladder is:
(a) Cuboidal (b) Stratified squamous
(c) Columnar (d) None

803. The intestinal endocrine cells are also called as:
(a) Sertolis cells (b) Leydigs cells
(c) Purkinge cells (d) Parital cells

804. Agranulocyte of blood is:
(a) Neutrophil (b) Basophile
(c) Monocyte (d) Eosinophil

805. Parietal cells are present in
(a) Oesophagus (b) Stomach
(c) Ileum (d) Colon

806. Tracheal rings are mode up of:
(a) Elastic Cartilage (b) Fibrocartilage
(c) Hyaline cartilage (d) None of the above

807. The largest cell among the leucocyte is:
(a) Lymphocyte (b) Eositophill
(c) Basophill (d) Monocyte

808. The spine of the scapula divides the lateral surface in almost two equal half in:
(a) Camel (b) Horse
(c) Dog (d) Ox

809. Sper is present on which bone of male cock:
(a) Humerus (b) Metacarpal
(c) Metatarsal (d) Femur

810. The flat bones of the skull contain variable amount of spongy bone called as:
(a) Bone fat (b) Medulla adipose
(c) Both above (d) None

811. The most commonly used blood stain is:
(a) Leichmann (b) Eosin
(c) Xylene (d) All

812. Ideal Example of pivot joint is:
(a) Allanto-axial (b) Allanto-occipital
(c) Fetlock (d) None

813. Ischiatic tubere is trifid in:
(a) Ox (b) Horse
(c) Dog (d) Fowl

814. Amnion is embryo is formed by-
a. Mesoderm b. Ectoderm
c. Both d. None

815. In case of dog the left lung comprised of:
(a) 3 (b) 2
(c) 4 (d) 4

816. Gall baladder is absent in:
(a) Ox (b) Dog
(c) Horse (d) Pig

817. Lyssa is present in the tongue of:
(a) Horse (b) Dog
(c) Ox (d) Pig

818. The corona glandis's is presents the penis of:
(a) Pig (b) Dog

(c) Horse (d) Ox

819. The cylindrical articular eminence is called as-
(a) Epicendyle (b) Facet
(c) Condyle (d) Hiatus

820. Obturator foramen is situated between ileum and:
(a) Pubic (b) Ischeum
(c) Both above (d) Non above

821. Largest and most massive bone of the body:
(a) Femur (b) Humerus
(c) Radius (d) Ulna

822. Rudimentary bone in ox is:
(a) Radius (b) Fibula
(c) Patella (d) Femur

823. Adrenal cortex develop from-
(a) Ectoderm (b) Nesoderm
(c) Endoderm (d) Neuro ectoderm

824. Smallest metacarpal of ox is:
(a) III (b) IV
(c) V (d) None

825. Os ungulare is name of following:
(a) 1st phalynx (b) II phalynx
(c) III phalynx (d) I & II phalynx

826. The inter parietal bones are absent in:
(a) Ox (b) Horse
(c) Dog (d) Fowl

827. Accessary carpal bone of horse articulates with:
(a) Radius & ulnar carpal
(b) Radius only
(c) Ulnar only
(d) None

828. The sebaceous glands of skin are:
(a) Halocrine (b) Mesocrine
(c) aspocrine (d) Cylocrine

829. The central and 4th tarsal bones are fused to form a large bone in:
(a) Ox (b) Dog
(c) Horse (d) Fowl

830. Branchial artery is a branch of:
(a) Common carotid artery
(b) Thoracic arota
(c) Brachio-cephalic artery
(d) Brachial artery

831. CSF is produced by:
(a) Thalamus (b) Choroid plexus
(c) IV ventricle (d) None

832. Heart is situated in which:
(a) Cranial mediastinum
(b) Middle mediastinum
(c) Caudal mediastinum
(d) None

833. Which nerve is largest cranial nerve?
(a) Vagus (b) Trigeminal
(c) Trochlear (d) None

834. The cremaster internus muscle is consists of which fibre?
(a) Striped (b) Unstriped
(c) Both (d) None

835. Among cervical vetebrae the foramen transversarium is absent in:
(a) VII (b) VI
(c) V (d) IV

836. Lumbar vertebrae are characterized by size & form of their:
(a) Body (b) Spine
(c) Process (d) All

837. Foramen transversarium in horse is -
(a) Zero (b) One
(c) Two (d) Three

838. In fowl, the ox coxae has following two foramen:
(a) Sciatic, Pneumatic
(b) Obturator, sciatic
(c) Sciatic, Ovale
(d) Obturator, Ovale

839. The coracoid process present in-
(a) Scapula (b) Humerus
(c) Femur (d) Radius

840. The no of tarsal bones in ox & dogs respectively are:
(a) 6, 6 (b) 7, 5
(c) 5, 7 (d) 6, 7

841. The type of elbow joint comprised of lateral & medial ligament may be called as:
(a) Bell & socket (b) Ginglymus
(c) Both (d) None

842. The shoulder girdle is fully developed in:
(a) Ox (b) Dog
(c) Horse (d) Fowl

843. The alveolar border of mandible does not contain

alveoli for canine teeth in:
(a) Pig (b) Horse
(c) Ox (d) Dog

844. Which one not an ideal pivot joint:
(a) Atlanto-axial (b) Fotlock
(c) Both (d) None

845. Apex of heart is formed by:
(a) Left ventricle
(b) Left & right ventricle
(c) Right ventricle
(d) None

846. The middle ear is located in:
(a) Ethmoid bone (b) occipital bone
(c) Peterous temporal (d) None

847. Renal pyramid is distinct in:
(a) Cat/dog (b) Horse/Sheep/Goat
(c) Pig (d) None

848. The fluid in eye chambers is called:
(a) Lacrimal fluid (b) LSF
(c) Endolymph (d) Aqueous humour

849. The mandible of ________ is characterized by the angular process:
(a) Dog (b) Ox
(c) Horse (d) Fowl

850. Number of ribs in ox:
(a) 18 pair (b) 13 pair
(c) 11 pair (d) 7 pair

851. The types of movement between carpals is:
(a) Flexion (b) Extension
(c) Both (d) None

852. Supratrochlear foramen is round in which bone?
(a) Femur of Horse (b) Femur of Dog
(c) Humerus of Dog (d) None

853. Pneumatic foramen is found in:
(a) Humerus of Dog (b) Humerus of Fowl
(c) Femur of Fowl (d) Femur of Dog

854. Stomach is attached with which fold in abdominal cavity?
(a) Mesentry (b) Omentum
(c) Peritoneum (d) None

855. Fovea capitis is round in head of which bone?
(a) Femur (b) Humerus
(c) Radio-ulna (d) Scapula

856. Supra spinatous and infra spinatous process is equal in ratio (1: 1) in?
(a) Dog (b) Horse
(c) Cat (d) Fowl

857. How many cervical bones are there in Giraffe?
(a) 14 (b) 8
(c) 7 (d) 28

858. An animal having analogous segments in stomach known as Psudoruminant is?
(a) Horse (b) Ox
(c) Goat (d) Camel

859. Why horse does not sit?
(a) Due to anatomical disturbance
(b) Due to it's own nature
(c) Due to stay apparatus
(d) None

860. Which wall of heart is thickest?
(a) Left ventricle (b) Right ventricle
(c) Left auricle (d) Right auricle

861. Caudal extension called as uncirate process is present in ribs of which species:
(a) Pig (b) Fowl
(c) Rabbis (d) Canine

862. A small flat bony structure embaded in nasal septal cartilage is called as:
(a) Os cordis (b) Os rostrale
(c) Os opticus (d) None of the above

863. Dome shaped area between the dorsal sac of rumen & reticulum where esophagus opens is:
(a) Margo plicatus
(b) Atrium ventriculi
(c) Pubo vesicle pouch
(d) None of the above

864. Which of the following does not form part of the skull?
(a) Cresta galli (b) Thyroid cornea
(c) Darsal turbinate (d) Cribriform plate

865. Number of bones on sacrum of pig is:
(a) 3 (b) 4
(c) 5 (d) 6

866. Pastern joint is which type of joint?
(a) Amphi-arthrosis (b) Hinge
(c) Ball & socket type (d) None of the above

867. Which one of the following is not a branch of occipital arteries?

(a) Palatine (b) Molar
(c) Caudal meningeal (d) Stylomastoid

868. Type & number of spinal accessory nerve is:
(a) Sensery VIII (b) Motor XI
(c) Mixed VII (d) Motor IV

869. Hammer shaped bone in middle ear is:
(a) Incus (b) Malleus
(c) Stapes (d) All

870. Sacrum of dog form by the fusion of how many vertebrae:
(a) 3 (b) 4
(c) 5 (d) 2

871. Which is/are muscles of abdomen?
(a) Oblique abdominis externus
(b) Obliqus abdominis internus
(c) Transverse externus
(d) Both a & b

872. Tarsal bone not found in which species
(a) Pig (b) Horse
(c) Dog (d) Fowl

873. Bone of the ear is/are
(a) Incus (b) Malleus
(c) Stapes (d) All

874. Branch of occipital artery is/are
(a) Palatine (b) Stylomastoid
(c) Caudal menegeal (d) All

875. Origin of oral cavity-
(a) Ectodermal (b) Endodermal
(c) Mesodermal (d) Ecto+Mesodermal

876. Filiform papillae are cone shaped in:
(a) Dog (b) Cat
(c) Ruminant (d) Horse

877. Bulbourethral gland absent in:
(a) Cat (b) Cattle
(c) Horse (d) Dog

878. Skeletal muscle is:
(a) Mononucleate (b) Multinucleate
(c) Both (d) None

879. Myostellate cells absent in which muscle:
(a) Smooth (b) Skeletal
(c) Cardiac (d) (a) & (c)

880. Spectrin protein found in:
(a) Erythrocyte (b) Leucocyte
(c) Platlets (d) None

881. Spleen capsule is thickest in:
(a) Horse (b) Pig
(c) Ruminant (d) Dog

882. Molar is:
(a) Paired bone (b) Unpaired
(c) Three (d) Four bones

883. Malaris muscle found in which region-
(a) Palpebral (b) Hyoid
(c) Maxillary (d) Auricular

884. Aesthesiology is the study of:
(a) Nervous system (b) Visceral organs
(c) Sense organs (d) Muscular organs

885. Which among the following is an example of Pneumatic bone?
(a) Radius & ulna of fowl
(b) Femur of fowl
(c) Humerus of fowl
(d) Radius & ulna of ox

886. What is the name given to the "Bone producing cells"?
(a) Osteocytes (b) Osteoblast
(c) Osteoclast (d) None of the above

887. The intervening spong tissue in the bones of cranial vault is known as
(a) Diploe (b) Lamina externa
(c) Lamina Interna (d) Epiphysis

888. What is the name given to the base of the furcula?
(a) Hypocledium (b) Synsarcosis
(c) Wish bone (d) None of the above

889. 'Dew claw' is formed by the combination of which two digits?
(a) 3rd & 4th (b) 1st & 5th
(c) 2nd & 5th (d) 2nd & 5th

890. Scapular index in case of dog is:
(a) 1 : 1 (b) 1 : 0.7
(c) 1 : 0.6 (d) 1 : 0.5

891. Condyles of femur articulate with tibia with the help of:
(a) Collateral ligament
(b) Cruciate ligament
(c) Menescii
(d) Gamellus muscle

892. Os sufferaginus is the name given to:
(a) 2nd phalynx of forelimb

(b) 1st phalynx of hindlimb
(c) 2nd phalynx of hindlimb
(d) 1st phalynx of forelimb

893. Presence of Interior ischiatic crest is the characteristics of.
(a) Ox (b) Fowl
(c) Horse (d) Dog

894. Trochanteric fossa gives attachment to which of the following muscles?
(a) Gamellus muscle
(b) Illiacus muscle
(c) Trochanteric Muscle
(d) Psoas major muscle

895. What is string halt?
(a) Upward fixation of patella
(b) Sideways fixation of knee cap
(c) Downward fixation of patella
(d) Upward fixation of claride

896. Tuber coxae of ox consist of how many tuberosities?
(a) 3 (b) 4
(c) 2 (d) 1

897. Crista unguicularis is the name given to the
(a) Bony ridge on 3rd phalynx
(b) Bony ridge on Ist phalynx
(c) Crest on 3rd phalynx
(d) Crest on 2nd phalynx

898. What is synsarcosis?
(a) Attachment of muscles to lateral wall of thorax
(b) Attachment of bones to ligament
(c) None of above
(d) Both of above

899. Trochanter tertius present in which animal?
(a) Horse (b) Ox
(c) Fowl (d) Dog

900. Tuber coxae is quadratic in which case?
(a) Horse (b) Dog
(c) Fowl (d) Ox

901. Acromian process is rudimentary in the scapula of
(a) Ox (b) Horse
(c) Dog (d) Pig

902. Schindylesis is which type of joint?
(a) Synovial (b) Cartilagenous
(c) Fibrous joint (d) Fibrous

903. Which one of the following is muscle of lateral aspect of thigh?
(a) Tensor fascia lata (b) Pronator teres
(c) Teres major (d) None

904. Fold of mucous membrane between the lower lip and gum is known as:
(a) Planum
(b) Papila salivalis
(c) Frenum labii inferioris
(d) None

905. Canine tooth are absent in:
(a) Dog (b) Pig
(c) Rabbit (d) None

906. Margoplicatus is characteristic of the stomach of:
(a) Ox (b) Pig
(c) Dog (d) Horse

907. Correct order of various layers of meninges in brain from inner to outer surface:
(a) Piamater, Duramater, Arachanoid
(b) Duramater, Piamater, Arachanoid
(c) Arachanoid, Piamater, Duramater
(d) Piamater, Arachanoid, Duramater

908. Preganglionic fibres are shorter than post-ganglionic fibres in:
(a) Sympathetic neurons
(b) Parasympathetic neurons
(c) Both
(d) None

909. Retina of eye is conventionally arranged in how many layers:
(a) 7 (b) 11
(c) 10 (d) 14

910. Osteological term "Hamulus" refers to
(a) A pulley like grooved articular surface
(b) An elongated elevation
(c) Curved horn like process
(d) A large protection

911. Fovea capitis is present in which of the following bones:
(a) Tibia (b) Femur
(c) Radius (d) Metacarpal

912. Biggest sinus in case of horse is:

(a) Ethmoid (b) Frontal
(c) Maxillary (d) Sphenopalatine

913. Biggest sinus in case of cattle is:
(a) Frontal (b) Maxillary
(c) Ethmoid (d) Sphenopalatine

914. Greater trochanter is present in femur of which of the following species:
(a) Equine (b) Ovine
(c) Bovine (d) Canine

915. Which of the following nerve is desensitized in case of surgical removal of horn?
(a) Infra orbital (b) Maxillary
(c) Cornual (d) Mandibular

916. The fibrous tunic of eye comprises of
(a) Sclera alone (b) Cornea & choroid
(c) Sclera & cornea (d) Choroid alone

917. Bursa running between tendon of biceps brachii muscle & the intertubercular groove of humerus is called as:
(a) Interosseus cubital bursa
(b) Bicipital bursa
(c) Bursa anserina
(d) Fleischmann's bursa

918. The fold of peritoneum which is attached to stomach is:
(a) Mesentery (b) Broad ligament
(c) Omentum (d) Mesorectum

919. Muscle of hind limb is:
(a) Brachialis (b) Biceps brachii
(c) Anconeus (d) Biceps femores

920. Third/Tertiary trachanter is present in femur of:
(a) Ox (b) Dog
(c) Horse (d) Pig

921. The proximal end of fibular tarsal is known as:
(a) Calcaneous (b) Sustentaculum tali
(c) Tuber calcis (d) Talus

922. Number of bones in the carpus of dog is:
(a) 7 (b) 5
(c) 6 (d) 4

923. Intermediate carpal in ox is:
(a) Cunciform (b) Scaphoid
(c) Semilunar (d) Unciform

924. The distal projected end of ulna is known as:-
(a) Olecranon process
(b) Styloid process
(c) Semilunar notch
(d) Anconeus process

925. Curved horn like process is known as:
(a) Hamulus (b) Incisura
(c) Spine (d) Crest

926. Hard milker condition involves:
(a) Lactiferous duct (b) Lactiferous duct
(c) Papillary duct (d) None of the above

927. Teeth used as defencive weapons in boar are:
(a) Incisor (b) Canines
(c) Molar (d) Dolf teeth

928. Which one is absent in pigs:
(a) Pharyngeal tonsils (b) Lingual tonsils
(c) Palatine tonsils (d) All of the above

929. Which one is not a natural orifice is wall of abdomen:
(a) Deep inguinal ring
(b) Epiploic foramen
(c) Umbilicus
(d) Pelvic inlet

930. Which hepatic ligament is absent in pigs:
(a) Pt triangular ligament
(b) Caudate ligament
(c) Coronary ligament
(d) Falciform ligament

931. Nerve supply in the teeth of upper dental arcade in ruminants:
(a) Infra orbital (b) Lingual
(c) Supra orbital (d) Alveolar

932. What is trochlea?
(a) Pully like articulae surface
(b) Small articulae surface
(c) Depression on bony surface
(d) Large projection

933. How many number of bones are in fere limb of ox?
(a) 88 (b) 80
(c) 40 (d) 48

934. Give vertebrae formula of pig?
(a) $C_7 T_{13} L_6 S_5 Cy_{15-25}$
(b) $C_7 T_{18} L_6 S_5 Cy_{15-22}$
(c) $C_7 T_{14-15} L_{6-7} S_4 Cy_{18-24}$
(d) $C_7 T_{15} L_7 S_3 Cy_{18-25}$

935. Which muscle is not of fore limb?
(a) Gracialis (b) Trapezius
(c) Deep pectoral (d) Teresominor

936. What is the Dental formula of horse?
(a) $I_{0+0/3-3}$, $C_{0-0/1-1}$, $P_{3-3/3-3}$, $M_{3-3/3-3}$
(b) $I_{3-3/3-3}$, $C_{1-1/1-1}$, $P_{4-4/4-4}$, $M_{3-3/3-3}$
(c) $I_{3-3/3-3}$, $C_{1-1/1-1}$, $P_{4-4/4-4}$, $M_{2-2/3-3}$
(d) $I_{3-3/3-3}$, $C_{1-1/1-1}$, $P_{3-3/3-3}$, $M_{3-3/3-3}$

937. In which species of animal 37 pairs of spinal nerve are present?
(a) Pig (b) Horse
(c) Dog (d) Ox

938. Which of the following is IX cranial nerve?
(a) Facial nerve
(b) Glossopharyngeal nerve
(c) Trigeminal nerve
(d) None of these

939. Which muscle is absent in Ox:
(a) Tenson facialata
(b) Superficial gluteus muscle
(c) Biceps femoris
(d) Biceps brachi

940. Extensive and flat muscle covering most of the lateral aspect of hip and high is:
(a) Tensor facialates
(b) Superficial glutes muscle
(c) Biceps femoris
(d) Biceps brachi

941. Mental foramen is situated in which bone:
(a) Frontal bone (b) Molar bone
(c) Mandible (d) None of the above

942. Which is/are not a synovial joint:
(a) Amphiarthoidal (b) Synarthoidal
(c) Diarthioidal (d) Both a and b

943. Foramen ovale in present in bone:
(a) Presphenoid (b) Basisphenoid
(c) Ptery goid (d) Post sphenoid

944. Which is seen in the heart?
(a) Os penis (b) Os cordis
(c) Os heartis (d) None of the above

945. Blood supply to diaphram is through:
(a) Intercostal artery (b) Thoracic asota
(c) Left unival artery (d) Phrenic artery

946. Margo plicatus is found in stomach of:
(a) Dog (b) Horse
(c) Ox (d) Rabbit

947. Supra trochlear foramen is present in humerous of-
(a) Ox (b) Dog
(c) Horse (d) Fowl

948. Angular process is present in the mandible of-
(a) Dog (b) Horse
(c) Ox (d) Fowl

949. Quadrat bone is present in the skull of-
(a) Horse (b) Dog
(c) Fowl (d) Ox

950. Accessory ligament is present in the hip joint of which animal:
(a) Ox (b) Horse
(c) Pig (d) Dog

951. Tentosium cerebelli is a fold of duramater present between:
(a) The cerebral hemispheres
(b) The cerebellum & cerebral hemispheres
(c) The cerebellums spinal cord
(d) None of the above

952. Trochlear nerve supplies to:
(a) Ventral & medial rectus muscles
(b) Retractor oculi & dorsal rectus muscle
(c) Lateral rectus & dorsal oblique muscles
(d) None of the above

953. What percentage of calcium phosphate is in the bone composition?
(a) 86% (b) 5.8%
(c) 3% (d) 5.2%

954. Number of bones in fowl skull?
(a) 34 (b) 30
(c) 32 (d) 40

955. Term facet is:
(a) A depression
(b) Elongated depression
(c) A small articular surface
(d) A notch like depression

956. Total number of bones in ox?
(a) 208 (b) 200
(c) 291 (d) 274

957. How many surfaces are present in scapula?
(a) 2 (b) 3

(c) 4 (d) 5

958. The surface away from the axis called:
(a) Caudal (b) Planter
(c) Axial (d) Abaxial

959. The ratio between the inorganic mineral salt and organic matter are in the bone is:
(a) 1:1 (b) 1:2
(c) 1:3 (d) 1:4

960. A small projection adjacent to a condyle
(a) Epicondyle (b) Forsa
(c) Forea (d) Ineixure

961. The lateral surface of scapula of cattle is divided into unequal parts in the ratio of:
(a) 1:1 (b) 1:2
(c) 1:3 (d) 1:4

962. Which cranial bone is single?
(a) Sphenoid (b) Temporal
(c) Interperietal (d) Frontal

963 Left and right palatoglossal arches formed:
(a) Tonsilar sinuses (b) Aditus pharyngic
(c) Palatoglossal arch (d) Posterior pillur

964. The muscle providing stabilizing centripetal force on a joint.
(a) Spurt muscle (b) Shunt muscle
(c) Red muscle (d) Creviate muscle

965. Which muscle is related to posterior-medial aspect of hind-limb?
(a) Gastro cnemius (b) Extender brevis
(c) Peroneus longus (d) Tibialis articus

966. Islets of lengerhens are the endocrine part of:
(a) Liver (b) Pancrease
(c) Intestine (d) Testis

967. Which is not the part of female genital organs?
(a) Cervics (b) Seminal vesicles
(c) Vagina (d) Vulva

968. Any plane which is at right angle to the sagittal plane is:
(a) Transverse plane (b) Coronal plane
(c) Frontal plane (d) Paramedian plane

969. Os-penis is:-
(a) Short bone (b) Flat bone
(c) Viseral bone (d) Sesamoid bone

970. Fovea dentis articulates with:-
(a) Mandible (b) Olecranon process
(c) Coronoid process (d) Odontoid process

971. Peroneus torsus is an example of:
(a) Spiral muscle (b) Parallel muscle
(c) Pennate muscle (d) Cruciat muscle

972. The greater sac & lesser sac of peritoneal cavity communicate with each other through:
(a) Epiploic foramen (b) Foramen megnum
(c) Alar foramen (d) Foramen of monero

973. Sinus which acts as baroreceptor:
(a) Cranial venous sinuses
(b) Sphenoid sinus
(c) Ethmoid sinus
(d) Carotid sinus

974. A thin layer of grey matter placed on the outer surface of external capsule is:
(a) Putamen (b) Claustrum
(c) Globus pellidus (d) Lamina splendens

975. Which cartilage actually forms the shape of the ear?
(a) Scutiform cartilage
(b) Annular cartilage
(c) Condral cartilage
(d) Alar cartilage

976. Hypophysis cerebri (Pituitary gland) develops from:
(a) Stenson's duct (b) Rothke's pouch
(c) Utricle (d) Wharton's duct

977. Esophagus is supplied by:
(a) Common carotid (b) Oesophageal artery
(c) Reticular artery (d) All of these

978. The interior of which organ is honey comb in appearance:
(a) Rumen (b) Reticulum
(c) Omasum (d) Abomasum

979. In case of fowl, at about the middle portion of Jejunum a short closed remnant of yolk sac is present, known as-
(a) Adreson's diverticulum
(b) Haydin's diverticulum
(c) Meckel's diverticulum
(d) Brian's diverticulum

980. The duct of parotid gland is known as:
(a) Stensons' duct (b) Watson's duct
(c) David's duct (d) Bond's duct

981. The spleen tissue containing splenic sinusoids & splenic cords infiltrated by circulating blood is known as-
(a) White pulp (b) Red pulp
(c) Both A & B (d) Non of these

982. In case of ox, which cartilage of larynx is largest?
(a) Cricoid (b) Arytenoid
(c) Thyroid (d) Epiglottis

983. Point of hip is animal is formed by:
(a) Lateral angle of ilium
(b) Medial angle of ilium
(c) External angle of ischium
(d) Internal angle of ischium

984. Deltoid tuberosity is found in:
(a) Humerus (b) Femur
(c) Radius ulna (d) Tibia

985. Largest bone of face is:
(a) Hyoid (b) Frontal
(c) Mandible (d) Nasal

986. Opening of pancreas occurs in
(a) Duodenum (b) Jejunum
(c) Ileum (d) Large intestine

987. Number of True ribs in canine
(a) 9 (b) 10
(c) 11 (d) 12

988. Acetabulum cavity is formed by
(a) Ileum (b) Ischium
(c) Pubis (d) All

989. Capacity of stomach of Dog
(a) 2 liter (b) 3 liter
(c) 2.5 liter (d) 4 liter

990. Length of small intestine in Dog
(a) 2 meter (b) 3 meter
(c) 4 meter (d) 5 meter

991. Primary loop is the brachial plexus is formed between which nerves
(a) Median, scapulae
(b) Medial, musculo-cutaneous
(c) Median ulnar
(d) None of the above

992. The central & fourth tarsal bones are fused to form lag bone in:
(a) Ox (b) Horse
(c) Dog (d) Fowl

993. Bronchial artery is a branch of
(a) Common carotid artery
(b) Thoracic artery
(c) Axillary artery
(d) Branchial artery

994. Utero-ovarian artery is a branch of-
(a) Abdominal arota
(b) Cordiac artery
(c) Internal iliac artery
(d) External artery

995. The ribs of the fowl can be distinguished because of-
(a) Absence of costal cartilage
(b) Presence of unicinate process
(c) Seven pairs
(d) All of the above

996. Characteristic feature of skull of fowl are-
(a) Single ocipical candyle
(b) Very large tympanic cavity
(c) Presence of quarter base
(d) All of the above

997. Ovulation fossa is present in:-
(a) Ox (b) Horse
(c) Bitch (d) Fowl

998. Tibia is as long as fibula in:-
(a) Camel (b) Horse
(c) Dog (d) Fowl

999. Organ which related to equilibrium of body is:-
(a) Ear (b) Nose
(c) Nose (d) Trachea

1000. Syrinx is present in:-
(a) Bird (b) Goat
(c) Sheep (d) Camel

1001. Name the largest foramen of the body
(a) Acetabulum
(b) Foramen ovale
(c) Obturator foramen
(d) Foramen orbito rotundum

1002. Fibular tarsal is known as:-
(a) Calcaneous (b) Talus
(c) Malleolus (d) Tarsometatarsus

1003. Cranial bone which is not paired:-
(a) Parietal (b) Occipital
(c) Frontal (d) Temporal

1004. Facial bone which is not paired:-
(a) Molar (b) Nasal
(c) Vomar (d) Maxilla

1005. Name the largest turbinate:-
(a) Dorsal (b) Middle
(c) Ventral (d) Ethmoturbinate

1006. Leathery eggs are found in-
(a) Amphibian (b) Reptiles
(c) Mammals (d) Birds

1007. Gall bladder is absent in the liver of which animal-
(a) Ox (b) Dog
(c) Horse (d) Pig

1008. Larynx is not the sound producing organ in-
(a) Fowl (b) Horse
(c) Ox (d) Dog

1009. Amnion is formed at about which day of fertlization.
(a) Same (b) Next
(c) 18th (d) 32nd

1010. Which one is an incomplete cleavage of cells-
(a) Parthenogenesis (b) Superfoetation
(c) Polyspermy (d) Super facendation

Match the following

A.

Q.	Tissue type	Related Function
1.	Epithelial tissue	A. Circulation
2.	Musculer tissue	B. conduction
3.	Nervous tissue	C. Contraction
4.	Blood	D. Protection

B.

Q.	Epithelium Tissue		Location
1.	Squamous	A.	Digestive tract
2.	Cuboidal	B.	Blood vessel
3.	Endothelium	C.	Thyroid gland
4.	Columnar	D.	Kidney

C

Q.	Branch of science		Area studied
1.	Arthrology	A.	Muscles
2.	Myology	B.	Joints
3.	Splanchnology	C.	Sense organs
4.	Aesthesiology	D.	Viscera

D.

Q	Branch of science		Area studied
1.	Nuclear remnants of RBC	A.	Howell Jolly body
2.	Lead Poisoning	B.	Plumbism
3.	Production site of blood coagulating proteins	C.	Plasma cell
4.	Precursor of β lymphocyte	D.	Liver

E.

1.	Babesiosis in cattle	A	Minor cross match
2.	Test using donor's plasma and recipient's cells	B	Intravascular hemolysis
3.	Marginal bodies	C	Milk
4.	Poor source of iron	D	Major cross match
5.	Test using recipients plasma and donor cells	E	Anaplasma

F.

1.	Free nuclei from metarubriocytes	A	Curschmann's spirals
2.	Mucous casts formed in small bronchioles	B	Hematogenous
3.	Basophilic nuclear debris in macrophage	C	Tringible bodies
4.	Elongate double pyramidal structure formed by coalescence of eosinophillic granules	D	Chariot – legden crystals

G.

1.	Scutiform cartilage	A.	Anvil shaped
2.	Aduitory ossicles	B.	Hammer shaped
3.	Malleus bone	C.	Middle ear
4.	Incus	D.	Ear muscles

H.

1. Cerebral aqueduct	A. Cerebral peduncles
2. Crura cerebri	B. Aqueduct of sylvius
3. Corpora quadrigemina	C. Telencephalon
4. Olfactory bulbs	D. Quadrigeminal bodies

I.

1. Vater Pacinian corpuscles	A. Metencephalon
2. Proprioception	B. Sickle shaped fold
3. Falx cerebri	C. Subcutaneous connective tissue
4. Pons	D. Muscle sense

Match the following:

Answers

A
1 D
2 C
3 B
4 A

B
1 D
2 C
3 B
4 A

C
1 B
2 A
3 D
4 C

D
1 A
2 B
3 D
4 C

E
1 B
2 A
3 E
4 C
5 D

F.
1 B
2 A
3 C
4 D

G
1 D
2 C
3 B
4 A

H
1 B
2 A
3 D
4 C

I.
1 C
2 D
3 B
4 A

Write T for True and F for false statements:

1. Fourth ventricle is located between cerebellum above and pons and medulla below.
2. Hydrocephalus means water in heart.
3. Dura mater is loose fibrous covering of CNS.
4. Coverings of brains and spinal cord are called springes.
5. Habencular nuclei is found in epithalamus.
6. Tuber cinereum attaches pituitary gland to brain.
7. Basal nuclei represent gray matter of corpus striatum.
8. Sweating is parasympathetic activity of sweat gland.
9. Peristalsis is a sympathetic activity.
10. Vasodilation of blood vessel is a sympathetic action.
11. Parasympathetic drugs are used as laxatives or cathartics.
12. Chorda tympani is responsible for taste sensation.
13. Chorda tympani is a branch of facial nerve.
14. Base of tongue is sensitive to bitter taste.
15. Lateral side of tongue is sensitive to sour and salt.
16. Tip of tongue is sensitive to bitter taste only.
17. Macula lutea is central area of retina in man.
18. Central area of retina contains only cones.
19. Lateral rectus and medial rectus muscles rotate the eyeball around a horizontal axis.
20. Dorsal and ventral rectus muscles rotate eyeball around a vertical axis.
21. Nictitating membrane is a cartilage.
22. Articular cartilage is a hyaline cartilage.
23. Diaphysis is a cylindrical shaft of long bone.

Answers

1.	(a)	2.	(b)	3.	(d)
4.	(a)	5.	(c)	6.	(a)
7.	(b)	8.	(d)	9.	(a)
10.	(c)	11.	(b)	12.	(b)
13.	(b)	14.	(a)	15.	(d)
16.	(a)	17.	(c)	18.	(a)
19.	(b)	20.	(b)	21.	(a)
22.	(c)	23.	(a)	24.	(b)
25.	(a)	26.	(c)	27.	(a)
28.	(c)	29.	(d)	30.	(a)
31.	(b)	32.	(d)	33.	(c)

34.	(d)	35.	(a)	36.	(a)
37.	(c)	38.	(c)	39.	(a)
40.	(b)	41.	(c)	42.	(d)
43.	(c)	44.	(d)	45.	(c)
46.	(b)	47.	(b)	48.	(d)
49.	(d)	50.	(b)	51.	(b)
52.	(a)	53.	(b)	54.	(b)
55.	(d)	56.	(d)	57.	(a)
58.	(a)	59.	(b)	60.	(d)
61.	(b)	62.	(b)	63.	(c)
64.	(a)	65.	(b)	66.	(b)
67.	(c)	68.	(a)	69.	(b)
70.	(b)	71.	(c)	72.	(a)
73.	(c)	74	(d)	75	(a)
76	(b)	77	(a)	78	(b)
79	(c)	80	(a)	81	(c)
82	(b)	83	(a)	84	(b)
85	(c)	86	(d)	87	(a)
88	(b)	89	(c)	90	(a)
91	(b)	92	(c)	93	(d)
94	(a)	95	(b)	96	(d)
97	(a)	98	(a)	99	(b)
100	(c)	101	(a)	102	(b)
103	(a)	104	(b)	105	(a)
106	(c)	107	(b)	108	(d)
109	(c)	110	(b)	111	(d)
112	(a)	113	(c)	114	(a).
115	(b)	116	(b)	117	(c)
118	(c)	119	(b)	120	(c)
121	(c)	122	(d)	123	(c)
124	(c)	125	(b)	126	(c)
127	(c)	128	(d)	129	(c)
130	(c)	131	(c)	132	(c)
133	(d)	134	(d)	135	(d)
136	(c)	137	(a)	138	(b)
139	(b)	140	(b)	141	(a)
142	(a)	143	(a)	144	(d)
145	(c)	146	(b)	147	(a)
148	(b)	149	(c)	150	(a)
151	(a)	152	(a)	153	(a)
154	(b)	155	(b)	156	(a)
157	(c)	158	(c)	159	(c)
160	(c)	161	(b)	162	(a)
163	(c)	164	(d)	165	(d)
166	(a)	167	(b)	168	(a)
169	(c)	170	(c)	171	(b)
172	(c)	173	(c)	174	(b)

175	(a)	176	(a)	177	(d)
178	(b)	179	(a)	180	(d)
181	(a)	182	(b)	183.	(c)
184	(d)	185	(d)	186	(b)
187	(a)	188	(b)	189	(b)
190	(a)	191	(c)	192	(c)
193	(d)	194	(c)	195	(d)
196.	(a)	197	(a)	198	(b)
199	(a)	200	(a)	201	(a)
202	(a)	203	(c)	204	(c)
205	(d)	206	(d)	207	(b)
208	(c)	209	(a)	210	(d)
211	(a)	212	(a)	213	(d)
214	(a)	215	(b)	216	(b)
217	(a)	218	(a)	219	(c)
220	(c)	221	(a)	222	(a)
223	(d)	224	(a)	225	(b)
226	(c)	227	(b)	228	(d)
229	(c)	230	(a)	231	(a)
232	(a)	233	(b)	234	(b)
235	(c)	236	(b)	237	(b)
238	(a)	239	(b)	240	(a)
241	(d)	242	(b)	243	(b)
244	(d)	245	(b)	246	(d)
247	(c)	248	(d)	249	(c)
250	(d)	251	(d)	252	(c)
253	(b)	254	(b)	255	(a)
256	(d)	257	(a)	258	(d)
259	(c)	260	(a)	261	(b)
262	(a)	263	(d)	264	(a)
265	(b)	266	(c)	267	(b)
268	(c)	269	(d)	270	(c)
271	(b)	272	(a)	273	(c)
274	(b)	275	(a)	276	(b)
277	(c)	278	(a)	279	(c)
280	(a)	281	(b)	282	(c)
283	(b)	284	(b)	285	(a)
286	(c)	287	(a)	288	(c)
289	(a)	290	(b)	291	(a)
292	(b)	293	(c)	294	(b)
295	(b)	296	(a)	297	(b)
298	(d)	299	(d)	300	(c)
301	(a)	302	(a)	303	(d)
304	(b)	305	(b)	306	(a)
307	(b)	308	(b)	309	(c)
310	(a)	311	(b)	312	(c)
313	(d)	314	(d)	315	(c)

316	(a)	317	(a)	318	(c)	459	(b)	460	(c)	461	(b)
319	(b)	320	(b)	321	(d)	462	(b)	463	(c)	465	(a)
322	(b)	323	(b)	324.	(b)	466	(d)	467	(a)	468	(d)
325	(a)	326	(a)	327	(a)	469	(c)	470	(a)	471	(b)
328	(a)	329	(c)	330	(a)	472	(c)	473	(b)	474	(a)
331	(c)	332	(d)	333	(c)	475	(a)	476	(a)	477	(b)
334	(b)	335	(b)	336	(c)	478	(c)	479	(d)	480.	(a)
337	(c)	338	(a)	339	(c)	481	(a)	482	(b)	483	(a)
340	(b)	341	(b)	342	(b)	484	(d)	485	(a)	486	(a)
343	(b)	344	(c)	345	(c)	487	(b)	488	(b)	489	(a)
346	(a)	347	(d)	348	(b)	490	(a)	491	(b)	492	(a)
349	(a)	350	(d)	351	(a)	493	(c)	494	(b)	495	(a)
352	(a)	353	(a)	354	(a)	496	(b)	497	(a)	498	(b)
355	(c)	356	(c)	357	(d)	499	(a)	500	(a)	501	(d)
358	(a)	359	(c)	360	(c)	502	(a)	503	(b)	504	(a)
361	(d)	362	(c)	363	(a)	505.	(a)	506.	(d)	507.	(a)
364	(b)	365	(d)	366	(d)	508.	(b)	509.	(a)	510.	(a)
367	(b)	368	(a)	370	(b)	511.	(a)	512.	(b)	513.	(d)
371	(a)	372	(b)	373	(a)	514.	(d)	515.	(a)	516.	(a)
374	(b)	375	(a)	376	(a)	517.	(c)	518.	(b)	519.	(d)
377	(b)	378	(a)	379	(a)	520.	(b)	521.	(a)	522.	(d)
380	(b)	381	(a)	382	(b)	523.	(a)	524.	(c)	525.	(b)
384	(b)	385	(b)	386	(a)	526.	(d)	527.	(a)	528.	(b)
387	(c)	388	(b)	389	(d)	529.	(a)	530.	(b)	531.	(a)
390	(d)	391	(b)	392	(c)	532.	(b)	533.	(a)	534.	(d)
393	(d)	394	(c)	395	(b)	535.	(a)	536.	(a)	537.	(c)
396	(a)	397	(a)	398	(b)	538.	(b)	539.	(d)	540.	(a)
399	(a)	400	(a)	401	(b)	541.	(a)	542.	(c)	543.	(b)
402	(c)	403	(c)	404	(a)	544.	(b)	545.	(a)	546.	(c)
405	(a)	406	(b)	407	(c)	547.	(b)	548.	(c)	549.	(b)
408	(d)	409	(c)	410	(a)	550.	(a)	551.	(c)	552.	(a)
411	(b)	412	(c)	413	(d)	553.	(a)	554.	(b)	555.	(c)
414	(b)	415	(a)	416	(a)	556.	(c)	557.	(a)	558.	(d)
417	(d)	418.	(a)	419	(b)	559.	(d)	560.	(a)	561.	(c)
420	(b)	421	(a)	422	(c)	562.	(d)	563.	(d)	564.	(a)
423	(c)	424	(a)	425	(b)	565.	(b)	566.	(a)	567.	(a)
426	(a)	427	(c)	428	(b)	568	(d)	569.	(d)	570	(c)
429	(d)	430	(d)	431	(a)	571.	(d)	572.	(a)	573.	(d)
432	(d)	433	(d)	434	(a)	574.	(b)	575.	(a)	576.	(b)
435	(a)	436	(a)	437	(b)	577.	(a)	578.	(b)	579.	(d)
438	(b)	439	(b)	440	(b)	580.	(d)	581.	(c)	582.	(d)
441	(a)	442	(a)	443	(b)	583.	(b)	584.	(b)	585.	(d)
444	(a)	445	(c)	446.	(d)	586.	(b)	587.	(b)	588.	(b)
447	(c)	448	(a)	449	(a)	589.	(a)	590.	(c)	591.	(c)
450	(b)	451	(a)	452	(d)	592.	(b)	593.	(b)	594.	(a)
453.	(d)	454	(a)	455	(c)	595.	(b)	596.	(b)	597.	(a)
456	(b)	457	(d)	458	(a)	598.	(a)	599.	(a)	600.	(c)

601.	(c)	602.	(c)	603.	(a)
604.	(b)	605.	(c)	606.	(d)
607.	(b)	608.	(b)	609.	(b)
610.	(d)	611.	(d)	612.	(a)
613.	(c)	614.	(d)	615.	(a)
616.	(b)	617.	(c)	618.	(a)
619.	(b)	620.	(a)	621.	(b)
622.	(a)	623.	(d)	624.	(d)
625.	(d)	626.	(c)	627.	(c)
628.	(d)	629.	(d)	630.	(d)
631.	(d)	632.	(a)	633.	(b)
634.	(c)	635.	(a)	636.	(a)
637.	(b)	638.	(d)	639.	(b)
640.	(a)	641.	(c)	642.	(b)
643.	(a)	644.	(b)	645.	(a)
646.	(b)	647.	(c)	648.	(a)
649.	(b)	650.	(a)	651	(a)
652.	(b)	653.	(a)	654.	(b)
655.	(a)	656.	(c)	657.	(c)
658.	(d)	659.	(c)	660.	(a)
661.	(a)	662.	(b)	663.	(a)
664.	(b)	665.	(a)	666.	(a)
667.	(d)	668	(b)	669.	(b)
670.	(c)	671.	(c)	672.	(d)
673.	(a)	674.	(d)	675.	(c)
676.	(a)	677.	(a)	678.	(a)
679.	(d)	680.	(a)	681.	(b)
682.	(d)	683.	(d)	684.	(d)
685.	(b)	686.	(c)	687.	(b)
689.	(a)	690.	(c)	691.	(c)
692.	(b)	693.	(c)	694.	(b)
695.	(a)	696.	(a)	697.	(b)
698.	(a)	699.	(d)	700.	(b)
701.	(d)	702.	(d)	703.	(c)
704.	(c)	705.	(a)	706.	(d)
707.	(c)	708.	(a)	709.	(a)
710.	(a)	711.	(a)	712.	(a)
713.	(a)	714.	(a)	715.	(b)
716.	(a)	717.	(a)	718.	(a)
719.	(a)	720.	(d)	721.	(a)
722.	(a)	723.	(c)	724.	(d)
725.	(c)	726.	(d)	727.	(a)
728.	(b)	729.	(c)	730.	(b)
731.	(c)	732.	(a)	733.	(a)
734.	(d)	735.	(a)	736.	(a)
737.	(c)	738.	(a)	739.	(b)
740.	(a)	741.	(d)	742.	(b)

743.	(a)	744.	(a)	745.	(c)
746.	(c)	747.	(d)	748.	(b)
749.	(c)	750.	(b)	751.	(c)
752.	(b)	753.	(c)	754.	(a)
755.	(a)	756.	(c)	757.	(c)
758.	(d)	759.	(c)	760.	(a)
761.	(b)	762.	(c)	763.	(b)
764.	(b)	765.	(d)	766.	(d)
767.	(d)	768.	(d)	769.	(d)
770.	(c)	771.	(b)	772.	(d)
773.	(a)	776.	(c)	777.	(a)
778.	(c)	779.	(a)	780.	(d)
781.	(d)	782.	(a)	783.	(d)
784.	(d)	785.	(d)	786.	(a)
787.	(a)	788.	(b)	789.	(d)
790.	(a)	791.	(c)	792.	(b)
793.	(d)	794.	(c)	795.	(a)
796.	(c)	797.	(b)	798.	(c)
799.	(b)	800.	(c)	801.	(c)
802.	(b)	803.	(b)	804.	(c)
805.	(b)	806.	(a)	807.	(d)
808.	(c)	809.	(c)	810.	(c)
811.	(a)	812.	(c)	813.	(b)
814.	(c)	815.	(a)	816.	(c)
817.	(b)	818.	(c)	819.	(c)
820.	(a)	821.	(a)	822.	(b)
823.	(a)	824.	(c)	825.	(c)
826.	(b)	827.	(d)	828.	(a)
829.	(a)	830.	(c)	831.	(b)
832.	(b)	833.	(b)	834.	(b)
835.	(a)	836.	(c)	837.	(b)
838.	(b)	839.	(a)	840.	(c)
841.	(b)	842.	(c)	843.	(c)
844.	(a)	845.	(a)	846.	(c)
847.	(c)	848.	(d)	849.	(a)
850.	(b)	851.	(c)	852.	(c)
853.	(b)	854.	(b)	855.	(a)
856.	(a)	857.	(c)	858.	(d)
859.	(c)	860.	(a)	861.	(b)
862.	(b)	863.	(b)	864.	(b)
865.	(b)	866.	(b)	867.	(b)
868.	(b)	869.	(b)	870.	(a)
871.	(d)	872.	(d)	873.	(d)
874.	(d)	875.	(a)	876.	(b)
877.	(d)	878.	(b)	879.	(d)
880.	(a)	881.	(a)	882.	(a)

883. (a) 884. (c) 885. (c)
886. (b) 887. (a) 888. (a)
889. (d) 890. (a) 891. (c)
892. (d) 893. (c) 894. (a)
895. (a) 896. (a) 897. (a)
898. (a) 899. (a) 900. (a)
901. (d) 902. (c) 903. (a)
904. (c) 905. (c) 906. (d)
907. (d) 908. (a) 909. (c)
910 (c) 911. (b) 912. (c)
913. (a) 914. (a) 915. (c)
916. (c) 917. (b) 918. (c)
919. (d) 920. (c) 921. (c)
922. (a) 923. (c) 924. (b)
925. (a) 926. (c) 927. (b)
928. (c) 929. (a) 930. (b)
931. (a) 932. (a) 933. (d)
934. (c) 935. (a) 936. (d)
937. (d) 938. (b) 939. (b)
940. (c) 941. (c) 942. (d)
943. (d) 944. (b) 945. (d)
946. (b) 947. (b) 948. (a)
949. (c) 950. (b) 951. (b)
952. (b) 953. (a) 954. (d)
955. (c) 956. (a) 957. (a)
958. (d) 959. (b) 960. (a)
961. (c) 962. (a) 963. (b)
964. (b) 965. (a) 966. (b)
967. (b) 968. (b) 969. (c)

970. (d) 971. (c) 972. (a)
973. (d) 974. (b) 975. (c)
976. (b) 977. (d) 978. (b)
979. (c) 980. (a) 981. (b)
982. (c) 983. (a) 984. (a)
985. (c) 986. (a) 987. (a)
988. (d) 989. (c) 990. (c)
991. (b) 992. (a) 993. (a)
994. (a) 995. (d) 996. (d)
997. (b) 998. (c) 999. (a)
1000. (a) 1001. (c) 1002. (a)
1003. (b) 1004. (c) 1005. (a)
1006. (b) 1007. (c) 1008. (a)
1009. (c)
1010. (d)

Q. No.	**Ans**	**Q. No.**	**Ans**	**Q. No.**	**Ans**
1.	T	9.	F	17.	F
2.	F	10.	F	18.	T
3.	F	11.	T	19.	F
4.	F	12.	T	20.	F
5.	T	13.	T	21.	T
6.	T	14.	T	22.	T
7.	T	15.	T	23.	T
8.	F	16.	F		

5 Veterinary Parasitology

Salient Points

1. Trypanosoma, Leishmania are hemoflagellates of zoomastigophora class.
2. *Trypanosoma evansi* is the first pathogenic trypanosome discovered in India by Veterinarian Dr. G. Evans.
3. Trypanosoma is chiefly monomorphic, with slender leaf like body. Transmission occurs mechanically by blood sucking flies.
4. *Trypanosoma theileri* causes "**turning sickness**", anthrax like disease.
5. Trypanosoma is extra cellular while Leishmania is intracellular parasite.
6. Leishmania is cyclically transmitted by blood sucking sand flies *(Phlebotomus)*.
7. Trichomonads reproduce asexually by binary fission. Cysts are typically absent.
8. Trichomona causes abortion in first quarter of pregnancy.
9. *Histomonas meleagrides* is atypical trichomonad, found in caeca and liver of turkey and causes black head disease.
10. Histomonas is transmitted by embryonated egg of *Heterakis gallinarum* nematode.
11. Coccidia are intracellular parasites, reproduce by schizogony or endodygony. Infective stage is sporulated oocysts.
12. Overcrowding and insanitary conditions are two predisposing factors for coccidiosis.
13. *Eimeria brunette* causes rectal coccidiosis.
14. *Fasciola hepatica* is commonly found in hilly area.
15. *Ascaridia galli* is most common nematode of poultry.
16. *Ascaridia galli* also transmits through egg.
17. Anaplasmosis is not a contagious disease.
18. Calves are much more resistant to anaplasmosis that older cattle.
19. Schistosomiasis is also known as ***Bilharzia***.
20. East coast fever is caused by ***Theileria parva***.

Questions

1. Protozoa was seen for the first time by-
   (a) Leeuwenhock (b) John listor
   (c) Pasteur d Ronald Ross
2. Discovery of transmission of Human Malaria was done by -
   (a) Leeuwenhock (b) Pasteur
   (c) Johan listor (d) Ronald Ross
3. Kalaazar is caused by-
   (a) *Leishmania donovani*
   (b) *Trypanosoma evansi*
   (c) *Babesia bigemina*
   (d) *Theileria parva*
4. Protozoa is-
   (a) *Unicellular prokaryotic*
   (b) *Unicellular eukaryotic*
   (c) *Multicellular prokaryotic*
   (d) *Multicellular eukaryotic*
5. Which of the Phylum is not included under PROTOZOA?
   (a) Apicomplexa (b) Celophora

(c) Myxospora (d) None

6. Apical complex help protozoa for-
(a) Growth
(b) Host cell penetration
(c) Host cell lyses
(d) All

7. Which of the following protozoa form spores during multiplication?
(a) Apicomplexa (b) Celiophora
(c) Myxospora (d) All

8. Vesicular nucleus is found in which type of protozoa?
(a) Flagellates (b) Ciliates
(c) Both (d) None

9. Compact nucleus is found in which type of protozoa?
(a) Flagellates (b) Ciliates
(c) Both (d) None

10. Which nucleus in protozoa performs vegetative function?
(a) Macronucleus (b) Micronucleus
(c) Both (d) None

11. Which nucleus in protozoa performs reproductive function?
(a) Macronucleus (b) Micronucleus
(c) Both (d) None

12. Arrangement of microtubules in axoneme of flagella is-
(a) 11+2 (b) 9+2
(c) 7+2 (d) 13+2

13. Point in cytoplasm of protozoan from which axoneme originates is called
(a) Kinetosome (b) Blepheroplast
(c) Basal granule (d) All

14. How many flagella originate from a Kinetosome in protozoa?
(a) Many (b) 2 - 3
(c) 1 (d) 10 - 12

15. Which of the following help in gliding movement of protozoa?
(a) Cilia (b) Flagella
(c) Pseudopodia (d) Microtubules

16. Trypanosomes undergo which type of nutrition-
(a) Holophytic (b) Holozoic
(c) Saprozoic (d) Any

17. Free living protozoa undergo which type of nutrition-
(a) Holophytic (b) Holozoic
(c) Saprozoic (d) Any

18. Cytosome & Cytopyge is possessed by which type of protozoa?
(a) Holophytic (b) Holozoic
(c) Saprozoic (d) None

19. Flagellate protozoa undergo which type of binary fission?
(a) Longitudinal (b) Transverse
(c) Any (d) None

20. Ciliated protozoa undergo which type of binary fission?
(a) Longitudinal (b) Transverse
(c) Any (d) None

21. Which one is the sexual method of protozoan reproduction?
(a) Schizogony (b) Merogony
(c) Both (d) Syngamy

22. Which one is the asexual method of protozoan reproduction?
(a) Schizogony (b) Merogony
(c) Both (d) Syngamy

23. When the 2 gametes fusing together for the production of zygote are of same size, it is known as-
(a) Isogamy (b) Syngamy
(c) Anisogamy (d) Neogamy

24. When the 2 gametes fusing together to form a zygote are of different sizes it is known as-
(a) Isogamy (b) Syngamy
(c) Anisogamy (d) Neogamy

25. Cells in protozoa which give rise to gametes are known as-
(a) Gamonts (b) Gametocytes
(c) Both (d) None

26. Which of the following is the resting stage of a protozoan?
(a) Cyst (b) Sporozoite
(c) Trophozoite (d) Ookinete

27. Which of the following protozoan undergoes direct life cycle?
(a) Eimeria (b) Trypanosoma

(c) Babesia (d) Plasmodium

28. Which of the following protozoan undergoes indirect life cycle?
(a) Eimeria (b) Giardia
(c) Coccidia (d) Trypanosoma

29. Which of the following Trypanosoma, mode of transmission is coitus?
(a) *T. evansi* (b) *T. vivax*
(c) *T. equiperdum* (d) *T. equinum*

30. In which of the following transuterine transmission occurs?
(a) Babesia (b) Amoeba
(c) Toxoplasma (d) Zoomastigophora

31. Trypanosoma comes under which order of zoomastigophora?
(a) Trichomonadida (b) Diplomonadida
(c) Kinetoplastida (d) All

32. In which form of protozoa flagella is absent?
(a) Amastigote (b) Promastigote
(c) Trypomastigote (d) None

33. Which Trypanosoma is an amastigote?
(a) *T. vivax* (b) *T. evansi*
(c) *T. equinum* (d) T. cruzi

34. Which form of Trypanosoma is not found in vertebrates?
(a) Amastigote (b) Promastigote
(c) Trypomastigote (d) Epimastigote

35. Trypomastigote is the only form in the life cycle of
(a) *T. vivax* (b) *T.* evansi
(c) *T. equinum* (d) *T. cruzi*

36. Trypanosoma under salivarian is also known as-
(a) Anterior station group
(b) Posterior station group
(c) Both
(d) None

37. Trypanosoma under stercoraria is also known -
(a) Anterior station group
(b) Posterior station group
(c) Both
(d) None

38. Cyclical development with non contaminative mode of transmission is seen in Trypanosomes under-
(a) Salevaria (b) Stercoraria
(c) Both (d) None

39. Cyclical development with contaminative mode of transmission is seen in trypanosoma under-
(a) Salevaria (b) Stercoraria
(c) Both (d) None

40. Which of the following trypanosomes are transmitted by glossina?
(a) *T. vivax* (b) *T. evansi*
(c) *T. brucei* (d) All

41. Sleeping sickness in man is caused by which trypanosoma-
(a) *T. vivax* (b) *T. congolense*
(c) *T. gambiense* (d) *T. evansi*

42. Which of the following trypansome is not included under salivarea?
(a) *T. vivax* (b) *T. brucei*
(c) *T. cruzi* (d) *T. evansi*

43. Which Trypanosoma is not included under stercoraria?
(a) *T. cruzi* (b) *T. thelere*
(c) *T. lewesi* (d) *T. brucei*

44. *T. curzi* is transmitted by-
(a) Glossina (b) Tabanus
(c) Kissing bugs (d) Oribated mites

45. Surra is caused by which *trypanosoma-*
(a) *T. evansi* (b) *T. vivax*
(c) *T. cruzi* (d) All

46. Which of the following flies are interrupted feeders?
(a) Tabanied bylessina
(b) Stomoxys
(c) Both
(d) None

47. Tibersa is trypansoma infection specifically in-
(a) Cattle (b) Horse
(c) Sheep (d) Camel

48. Which of the following tests is meant for diagnosis of surra?
(a) Formal gel test
(b) Stilbamidinae test
(c) Mercuric Chloride test
(d) All

49. Which of the following drugs can be used for the

treatment of Trypanosomiasis?
(a) Diminazine aceturate
(b) Homidium bromide
(c) Quinapyramine prosalt
(d) All

50. Chagas disease in man is caused by-
(a) *T. evansi* (b) *T. equinum*
(c) *T. cruzi* (d) *T. brucei*

51. Which of the following forms is not seen in case of Leishmania?
(a) Amastigote (b) Promastigote
(c) Epomastigote (d) None

52. Leishmania is transmitted by-
(a) Nasal bot (b) Bot fly
(c) Warble fly (d) Sand fly

53. Chinese kala azar is caused by which leishmania-
(a) *L. donovani* (b) *L. infantium*
(c) *L. chagasi* (d) None

54. American kala azar is caused by which Leishmania-
(a) *L. donovani* (b) *L. infantium*
(c) *L. chagasi* (d) *L. tropica*

55. Cutaneous kala azar is caused by which Leishmania-
(a) *L. donovani* (b) *L. infantium*
(c) *L. chagasi* (d) *L. tropica*

56. Which of the following is caused by *Leishmania tropica?*
(a) Cutaneous (b) Delhi boil
(c) Aleppobutton (d) All

57. Which of the following is synonym for mucocutaneous leishmaniasis-?
(a) Utah (b) Espundia
(c) Delhi boil (d) (a and b)

58. What is the arrangement of flagella in case of Tritrichomonas?
(a) 3+1 (b) 4+1
(c) 5+1 (d) 6+1

59. Black head of Turkey is caused by-
(a) Histomonas
(b) Trichomonas
(c) Tritrichomonas
(d) Heterakis gallinarum

60. Sporogony occurs outside the host in case of -
(a) Eimeridae (b) Sarco cystidae
(c) Cryptosporidae (d) All

61. How many sporocysts are present in an oocyst of Eimeria?
(a) 2 (b) 4
(c) 8 (d) 16

62. How many sporocysts are present in an oocyst of Isospora?
(a) 2 (b) 4
(c) 8 (d) 16

63. How many sporozoites are present in an oocyst of Eimeria?
(a) 2 (b) 4
(c) 8 (d) 16

64. How many sporozoites are present in an oocyst of Wenylenlla?
(a) 2 (b) 4
(c) 8 (d) 16

65. How many sporozoites are present in an oocyst of Cryptosporidium?
(a) 2 (b) 4
(c) 8 (d) 16

66. Which of the following Eimeria is found in abomasum of sheep and goat?
(a) *E. ahsata* (b) *E. gilruthi*
(c) *E. granulosa* (d) *E. truncata*

67. Caecal coccidiosis is caused by-
(a) *E. nicatrix* (b) *E. tenella*
(c) *E. brunette* (d) None

68. Rectal cocccidiosis is caused by-
(a) *E. nicatrix* (b) *E. tenella*
(c) *E. brunette* (d) None

69. Which of the following causes Intestinal coccidiosis of rabbit?
(a) *E. magna* (b) *E. media*
(c) Both (d) None

70. Which of the following causes Hepatic coccidiosis of rabbit?
(a) *E. magna* (b) *E. stedae*
(c) *E. media* (d) None

71. Which of the following causes Coccidiosis in pig-?
(a) *E. deblieck* (b) *E. spinosa*
(c) *Isosopra suis* (d) All

72. Which of the following Coccidia is present in Kidney tubules of equines?

(a) *E. lcukarti* (b) *E. solepidum*
(c) *Klossiella equi* (d) All

73. Which Coccidia is present in kidney tubules of duck and geese?
(a) *E. anatis* (b) *E. anseris*
(c) *E. trunata* (d) *E. battakhi*

74. *Hepatozoan canis* is transmitted by-
(a) Brown dog tick (b) Red dog tick
(c) Sand fly (d) None

75. Plasmodium is transmitted in birds by which mosquito-
(a) Anophelies mosquito
(b) Culicine mosquito
(c) Both
(d) None

76. Plasmodium is transmitted in mammals by-
(a) Anophelies (b) Culex
(c) Both (d) None

77. Toxoplasma was discovered for the first time from a-
(a) Bird (b) Pig
(c) Rodent (d) Bat

78. Cat acts as which host for Toxoplasma-
(a) Definitive (b) Intermediate
(c) Both (d) None

79. Man acts as which host for Toxoplasma-
(a) Definitive (b) Intermediate
(c) Both (d) None

80. Tissue cyst of Toxoplasma is formed of-
(a) Bradyzoites (b) Tachyzoites
(c) Sporozoites (d) All

81. Which of the following is a rapidly dividing form of Toxoplasma?
(a) Bradyzoite (b) Tachyzoite
(c) Sporozoite (d) None

82. Which form of Toxoplasma infects definitive host?
(a) Bradyzoite (b) Tachyzoite
(c) Sporozoite (d) Sporocyst

83. Torch Test in man is done for the diagnosis of
(a) Coccidia (b) Trypanosoma
(c) Toxoplasma (d) Leishmania

84. Sebin-feldman dye test is used for the diagnosis of-
(a) Cocudia (b) Trypanosoma
(c) Toxoplasma (d) Leishmania

85. Which of the following are not included under flat worms?
(a) Nematodes (b) Cestodes
(c) Trematodes (d) Cotylodes

86. Which of the following are considered non-parasitic?
(a) Flat worms (b) Round worms
(c) Pin worms (d) Eddy worms

87. Non parasitic group of Platyhelmenthes come under-
(a) Trematoda (b) Cestoda
(c) Turbillaria (d) Cotyloda

88. Which of the following are termed as Pseudotapeworms?
(a) Tremiatoda (b) Eucestoda
(c) Cotyloda (d) Turbilleria

89. Which of the following are parasites of fish?
(a) Trematoda (b) Eucestoda
(c) Cotyloda (d) Turbilleria

90. Which of the following trematodes is not a hermaphrodite?
(a) Fasciola (b) Amphisotomes
(c) Gigantocotyle (d) Schistosomes

91. Which of the following orders is known as True trematodes?
(a) Monogenea (b) Aspidobothria
(c) Digenea (d) All

92. Maximum no. of intermediate hosts in the life cycle of a termatode can be-
(a) 1 (b) 2
(c) 3 (d) All

93. In which of the following termatodes, embryonated eggs are passed in the faeces of definitive host-
(a) Amphistome (b) Liver fluke
(c) Schistosoma (d) All

94. Which of the following stages is absent in case of Schistosomes-
(a) Corcaria (b) Miracidia
(c) Sporocyst (d) Redia

95. Tail of cercaria of Amphistosomes is-
(a) Oveidal (b) Flask likes
(c) Trunk like (d) Bifurcated

96. Tail of cercaria of Schistosomes is-
    (a) Oveidal (b) Flask likes
    (c) Trunk like (d) Bifurcated
97. I Intermediate host in case of Echinostome is-
    (a) Snail (b) Fish
    (c) Crab (d) All
98. II Intermediate host in case of Paragoniomus is-
    (a) Snail (b) Fish
    (c) Crab (d) All
99. III Intermediate host in case of Paragonimus is-
    (a) Snail (b) Fish
    (c) Crab (d) All
100. Which of the following can never act as intermediate host of termatode?
    (a) Snail (b) Fish
    (c) Crab (d) Ant
101. Which of the following is commonly known as Lancet fluke?
    (a) Dicrocoelium (b) Schistosome
    (c) Gigantocotyle (d) Paramphistomum
102. Which of fluke is present in bile duct of sheep & goat-?
    (a) Dicrocoelium (b) Schistosome
    (c) Gigantocotyle (d) Paramphistomum
103. Cercariae of which one is known as Cercaria vitrina-
    (a) Dicrocoelium (b) Schistosome
    (c) Gigantocotyle (d) Paramphistomum
104. Fluke present in pancreatic duct of sheep & goat-
    (a) Dicrocoelium (b) Gigantocotyle
    (c) Clonorchis (d) Eurytrerma
105. II intermediate host of *Eurytrema pancreaticum* is-
    (a) Fish (b) Crab
    (c) Grasshopper (d) Snail
106. II intermediate host of *Heterophyes heterophyes* is-
    (a) Fish (b) Crab
    (c) Grasshopper (d) Snail
107. Which one is commonly known as cat liver fluke?
    (a) *Fasciola hepatica*
    (b) *Opisthorchis tenuicollis*
    (c) *Clonorchis clonorchis*
    (d) *Eurytrema pancreaticum*
108. Prosthogonimus is a bird fluke present in-
    (a) Bursa fabricius (b) Oviduct
    (c) Posterior (d) All
109. Which one acts as IIintermediate host of Prosthogonimus?
    (a) Sand fly (b) Warble fly
    (c) Black fly (d) Dragon fly
110. Naids refer to nymphal stage of-
    (a) Sand fly (b) Warble fly
    (c) Black fly (d) Dragon fly
111. Bottle jaw condition occurs as a result of which infection-
    (a) Fasciola (b) Fasciolopsis
    (c) Both (d) None
112. Which of the following is commonly known as Lung fluke?
    (a) Paragonimus westermani
    (b) *Ogmocotyle indicia*
    (c) Echinostoma revoutum
    (d) None
113. Which of the following infection cause pulmonary distomosis?
    (a) Paragonimus (b) Ogmocotyle
    (c) Both (d) None
114. Which of the following parasites is not found in rumen or reticulum of cattle & buffalo?
    (a) *Paramphistomum cervi*
    (b) *Cotylophoran*
    (c) *Gigantocotyle*
    (d) None
115. Which parasite is found in bile duct of buffaloes?
    (a) *Paramphistomum cervi*
    (b) *Cotylophoran*
    (c) *Gigantocotyle*
    (d) None
116. Which of the following species of snail can act as intermediate host?
    (a) Guraulus (b) Indoplanorbis
    (c) Bulinus (d) All
117. Which of the following infections causes fluke diarrheoa?
    (a) *Paramphistomosis*
    (b) *Fasciolosis*
    (c) *Paragonimosis*
    (d) All
118. Which of the flukes is found only in non rumi-

nants?
(a) Gigantocotyle (b) Ogmocotyle
(c) Gastodiscus (d) Cotylophoron

119. Which parasite is found in colon of horse?
(a) Gastrodiscus (b) Gigantocotyle
(c) Gastroiscoidus (d) None

120. Which parasite is found in colon of horse & equines?
(a) Gastrodiscoidis (b) Pseudodiscus
(c) Gastrodiscus (d) Gigantocotyle

121. Which fluke is found in mesentric vein?
(a) Amphistome (b) Schistosome
(c) Gastrodiscus (d) Pseudodiscus

122. Which snail acts as intermediate host for schistosomes-?
(a) Gyrausleis (b) Bulinus
(c) Indoplanorbis (d) Lymena

123. Which stage is absent in life cycle of schistosomes-
(a) Cercariae (b) Redia
(c) Miracidia (d) Sporocyst

124. Which species of schistosomes is found in mesentric vein of pigs, dogs & rodents?
(a) *S. nasale* (b) *S. indicum*
(c) *S. incognitum* (d) *S. bovis*

125. Which species of Schistosomes in not found in India?
(a) *S. bovis* (b) *S. mansoni*
(c) *S. japonicum* (d) All

126. Which schistosome is found in mesentric vein of man?
(a) *S. japonicum* (b) *S. hematobium*
(c) *S. indicum* (d) All

127. Snoring disease is caused by which schistosome-
(a) *S. boris* (b) *S. nasale*
(c) *S. indicum* (d) *S. mansoni*

128. Which syndrome is caused by schistosomes?
(a) Acute intestinal
(b) Chronic Hepatic syndrome
(c) Both
(d) None

129. Cercarial dermatitis is caused due to-
(a) Hypoderma (b) Schistosome
(c) Mange (d) Tick infestation

130. Synonym for cercarial dermatitis-
(a) Swimmer's itch (b) Dhobi itch
(c) Rice paddy itch (d) All

131. Tapeworms of equids & ruminants are studied under which order of Eucestoda-
(a) Anoplocephalidea (b) Davaineidea
(c) Dilepididea (d) Hymenolepidea

132. Tapeworm of which order are found in poultry-
(a) *Dilepididea* (b) *Davaineidea*
(c) *Thysanosomidae* (d) *Hymenolepidea*

133. Which one is the tapeworm of ruminant?
(a) Thysanosoma (b) Avitellina
(c) Thysaniezia (d) All

134. Which tapeworm is found in bile duct of ruminants?
(a) Stilesia (b) Thysanosoma
(c) Avitellina (d) Thysaniezia

135. Which one is the commonest tapeworm of domestic fowl?
(a) Davainea (b) Raillietina
(c) Cotugnia (d) None

136. Which one is the tape worm of dog, cat & man?
(a) Choanotaenea (b) Dipylidium
(c) Davainea (d) None

137. Which tapeworm is found in both mammals & poultry?
(a) Davainea (b) Dipylidium
(c) Choanotaenea (d) Hymenolepis

138. Adult stage of which parasite is found in man-
(a) Taenia (b) Echinococcus
(c) Both (d) None

139. Metacestode stage of which parasite is found in man-
(a) Taenia (b) Echinococcus
(c) Both (d) None

140. Which tapeworm is particularly found in carnivores?
(a) Diphyllobothrium
(b) Spirometra
(c) Taenia
(d) Ecinococcus

141. Suckers are absent in-
(a) Eucestoda (b) Cotyloda
(c) Both (d) None

142. Gravid preglottids are found in-

(a) Eucestoda (b) Cotyloda
(c) Both (d) None

143. Only 1 set of reproductive organs can be found in the proglottid of-
(a) Eucestoda (b) Cotyloda
(c) Both (d) None

144. Uterine opening is absent in-
(a) Eucestoda (b) Cotyloda
(c) Both (d) None

145. Egg with Hexacanth embryo is characteristic of-
(a) Eucestoda (b) Cotyloda
(c) Both (d) None

146. Coracidium, a ciliated hexacanth embryo is a characteristic of-
(a) Eucestoda (b) Cotyloda
(c) Both (d) None

147. Which one is the innermost membrane of an egg of eucestoda?
(a) Capsule
(b) Embryophore
(c) Onchospheral membrane
(d) Coracidium

148. How many intermediate hosts are required in life cycle of Eucestodes-?
(a) 1 (b) 2
(c) 3 (d) Many

149. Eggs are non embryonated in case of-
(a) Eucestoda (b) Cotyloda
(c) Both (d) None

150. Eggs are embryonated in case of-
(a) Eucestoda (b) Cotyloda
(c) Both (d) None

151. *Rhipicephalus evertsi* is commonly known as-
(a) Blue tick (b) Brown ear tick
(c) Red leg tick (d) Bont tick

152. Which carcal stage is found in Anaplocephalidae?
(a) Cenurus (b) Cysticercoid
(c) Hydatid cyst (d) None

153. Which one is known as fringed tapeworm of sheep?
(a) *Stilesia hepatica*
(b) *Avilellina centripunclata*
(c) *Thysanosome actinoides*
(d) *None*

154. Genital pore is marginal in which Moneizia-
(a) *M. expansa* (b) *M. benedeni*
(c) Both (d) None

155. Intermediate host for Moneizia is-
(a) Snail (b) Fish
(c) Crab (d) Oribated mites

156. Which of the following acts as IH for Dipylidum?
(a) Dog louse (b) Dog flea
(c) Human flea (d) All

157. Which one is known as Dwarf Tapeworm?
(a) Dipylidium (b) Moneizia
(c) Hymenolepis (d) All

158. Which Hymenolepis is found in Turkey?
(a) *H. nana* (b) *H. diminuta*
(c) *H. carica* (d) None

159. Intermediate host for Hymenolepis nana-
(a) Floor beettle (b) Rat flea
(c) dung beettle (d) All

160. Intermediate host for Hymenolepis diminuta-
(a) Floor beettle (b) Rat flea
(c) dung beettle (d) All

161. IH for *Hymenolepis carioca-*
(a) Floor beettle (b) Rat flea
(c) Dung beettle (d) All

162. Life cycle of Hymenolepis is-
(a) Direct
(b) Indirect
(c) Both
(d) May be direct or indirect

163. Which one is the smallest tapeworm of poultry?
(a) Davainea (b) Rallietina
(c) Cotugnia (d) None

164. Davainea in poultry is found in-
(a) Crop (b) Liver
(c) Duodenum (d) Caecum

165. Intermediate host for davainea is-
(a) Snail (b) Fish
(c) Crab (d) Oribated mites

166. Intermediate host for Ralleitina is-
(a) Snail (b) Fish
(c) Crab (d) Ant

167. Which one is known as Beef tapeworm?
(a) *Taenia saginata* (b) *T. solium*
(c) *T. ovis* (d) *T. multiceps*

168. Which one is known as Pork tapeworm?
(a) *Taenia saginata* (b) *T. solium*
(c) *T. ovis* (d) *T. multiceps*

169. Dog acts as definitive host for which Taenia-
(a) *T. multiceps* (b) *T. hydatigena*
(c) *T. ovis* (d) All

170. Dog is which kind of host for *Taenia ovis*-
(a) Definitive (b) Intermediate
(c) Both (d) None

171. Man acts as which host for *Taenia solium*-
(a) Definitive (b) Intermediate
(c) Both (d) None

172. Intermediate host for *Taenia saginata* is-
(a) Cattle (b) Man
(c) Pig (d) Sheep

173. Intermediate host for *Taenia solium* is-
(a) Cattle (b) Man
(c) Pig (d) Sheep

174. Definitive host for *Taenia saginata* is-
(a) Cattle (b) Man
(c) Pig (d) Sheep

175. Intermediate host for *Taenia multiceps* is-
(a) Cattle (b) Dog
(c) Pig (d) All

176. Intermediate host for *Taenia hydatigina* is-
(a) Sheep (b) Goat
(c) Pig (d) All

177. Intermediate host for T. solium is-
(a) Wild boars (b) lab animals
(c) Both (d) All

178. Larval stage of *Taenia saginata* is-
(a) *Cysticercus bovis*
(b) *Cysticercus cellulose*
(c) *Cysticercus tenuicollis*
(d) *All*

179. Larval stage of *Taenia solium* is-
(a) Cysticercus bovis
(b) Cysticercus cellulose
(c) Cysticercus tenuicollis
(d) All

180. Cerebral cystecercosis is caused due to -
(a) *Taenia solium* (b) *T. saginata*
(c) *T. multiceps* (d) *T.hydatigena*

181. Larval stage of *Taenia multiceps* is-
(a) Cystecercus (b) Cysticercoid
(c) Coenurus (d) Hydated cyst

182. Site of prediliction of larva of *T. sagenata* is-
(a) Muscles
(b) Muscles, brain & heart
(c) Brain
(d) Peritoneum

183. Site of prediliction of larva of *T. solium* is-
(a) Muscles
(b) Muscles brain & heart
(c) Brain
(d) Peritoneum

184. Site of prediliction of larvae of *T. multiceps*-
(a) Muscles
(b) Muscles brain & heart
(c) Brain
(d) Peritoneum

185. Site of prediliction of larvae of *T. hyatigena*-
(a) Muscles
(b) Muscles brain & heart
(c) Brain
(d) Peritoneum

186. Site of prediliction of larvae of *T. ovis*-
(a) Muscles
(b) Muscles brain & heart
(c) Brain
(d) Peritoneum

187. Larva of T. ovis is Cysticercus-
(a) *C. bouis* (b) *C. cellulose*
(c) *C. ovis* (d) *C. tenuicollis*

188. Larval stage of T. hydatigina is which cysticercus-
(a) *C. bouis* (b) *C. cellulose*
(c) *C. ovis* (d) *C. tenuicollis*

189. GID is caused by which species of Taenia-
(a) *T. soluim* (b) *T. saginata*
(c) *T. hydatigena* (d) *T. multiceps*

190. Definitive host for *Taenia pessiformis* is-
(a) Dog (b) Man
(c) Pig (d) Cattle

191. Intermediate host for *Taenia pessiformis* is-
(a) Dog (b) Cat
(c) Man (d) Rabbit

192. Site for prediliction for larvae of *Taenia pessiformis* is-
(a) Brain (b) Heart
(c) Lever (d) Peritoneum

193. Site of prediliction for larvae of *Taenia serialis* is-
(a) Brain (b) Peritoneum
(c) Muscles (d) Connective tissue

194. *T. teniaformis* is a tapeworm of-
(a) Dog (b) Cat
(c) Man (d) Pig

195. Intermediate host for *T. taeniaformis* is
(a) Dog (b) Cat
(c) Rodents (d) Pig

196. Larval stage of *T. taeniaformis* is-
(a) *C. cellulose* (b) *C. formis*
(c) *C. fasceolaris* (d) None

197. Site of prediliction of larvae of *T. taeniaformis*-
(a) Brain (b) Heart
(c) Muscles (d) Liver

198. *T. tarandi* is tapeworm of-
(a) Dog (b) Cat
(c) Man (d) Pig

199. Intermediate host for *T. tarandi* is-
(a) Dog (b) Rabbit
(c) Reindeer (d) Cattle

200. Site of prediliction of larvae of *Taenia taradies*
(a) Liver (b) Brain
(c) Heart (d) Muscles

201. After how many days of Trypanosoma infection parasitemia may be observed-
(a) Same day (b) After 1-3 weeks
(c) After 2 months (d) After 1 week

202. Jugular pulse during Trypanosomosis can be observed at which stage of infection-
(a) Initial (b) Middle
(c) Terminal (d) All stages

203. Drug of choice for trypanosomosis in pigs is-
(a) Berenil (b) Trypacide
(c) Oxytetracycline (d) All

204. Drug of choice for Trypanosomosis in cattle is-
(a) Berenil (b) Trypacide
(c) Oxytetracycline (d) All

205. Diaminazine accurate is toxic in-
(a) Dog (b) Cattle
(c) Horse (d) Camel

206. Hepatozoon canis can be demonstrated in-
(a) Monocytes (b) Lymphocyte
(c) Neutrophill (d) All

207. Ehrlichia in dog can be demonstrated in-
(a) Monocytes (b) Lymphocytes
(c) Neutrophill (d) All

208. Ehrlichia in sheep & cat can be demonstrated in-
(a) Monocytes (b) Lymphocytes
(c) Neutrophill (d) All

209. Koch's blue bodies can be demonstrated in-
(a) Monocytes (b) Lymphocytes
(c) Neutrophill (d) All

210. Drug of choice in case of Anaplasmosis-
(a) Berenil (b) Trypacide
(c) Oxytetracycline (d) None

211. Trypanosomes can be demonstrated in which type of blood smear-
(a) Wet smear (b) Thin smear
(c) Thick smear (d) All

212. Nematode *Dracunculus medinensis* is
(a) Smallest (b) Largest
(c) Commonest (d) None

213. Metacestode stage of Echinococcus is-
(a) Coenurus (b) Cysticercus
(c) Hydatid cyst (d) All

214. Which segment of Echinococcus is gravid?
(a) First (b) Penultimate
(c) Terminal (d) All

215. Which one acts as first intermediate host in the life cycle of *Diphyllobothrium latum*?
(a) Mollusc (b) Crustaceans
(c) Both a & b (d) Fish

216. Which one acts as second intermediate host in the life cycle of *Diphyllobothrium latum*?
(a) Molluse (b) Crustaceans
(c) Both a & b (d) Fish

217. Which one acts as second intermediate host in the life cycle of *Spirometra Mansoni*?
(a) Fish (b) Reptiles
(c) Birds (d) All

218. Sparganosis is caused due to-
(a) Echinococcus
(b) Trypanosomes

(c) Diphyllobothrium
(d) Spirometra

219. Which type of migration is observed during development of *Toxocara vitulrum*?
(a) Somatic (b) Trachial
(c) Both (d) None

220. Visceral larvae migrans in dogs occurs due to-
(a) Echinococcus (b) *Taenia multiceps*
(c) Toxocara (d) None

221. Which larvae of Oxycuris equi is pathogenic & feeds on intestinal mucosa-
(a) L_1 (b) L_2
(c) L_3 (d) L_4

222. Members of family oxyuridae are commonly known as-
(a) Whip worms (b) Hook worms
(c) Pin worms (d) Red worms

223 Pin worms is a common name of members of which family-
(a) Oxyuridae (b) Rhabditidae
(c) Heterakidae (d) Stephanuridae

224. Oxyuris equi is found in-
(a) Esophagus (b) Stomach
(c) Caecum (d) Kidney

225. Rat tailed appearance of horse occurs due to-
(a) *Trypanosoma equiperdum*
(b) *Oxyuris equi*
(c) *Setaria equina*
(d) *Strongylus* vulgaris

226. *Heterakis gallinarum* is commonly known as-
(a) Pinworm of Poultry
(b) Hook worm of poultry
(c) Caecal worm of poultry
(d) Faecal worm of poultry

227. *Heterakis gallinarum* acts as carrier for a protozoan parasite called-
(a) *Histomonas meleagridis*
(b) *Cryptosporiduim baileyi*
(c) Haemoproteus
(d) Leucocytozoon

228. *Histomonas meleagridis* leads to which disease in turkey-
(a) Black head of turkey
(b) Infectious enterohepatitis
(c) Both
(d) None

229. Which one is the true ascarid worm of poultry?
(a) *Heterakis gallinarum*
(b) *Ascaredia galli*
(c) *Amoeba taenia*
(d) *Ascaridia columbae*

230. Largest Nematode found in poultry is-
(a) *Heterakis gallinarum*
(b) *Ascaredia galli*
(c) *Amoeba taenia*
(d) *Ascaridia columbae*

231. Paratenic host in case of *Ascridia galli* infections-
(a) Fish (b) Molluse
(c) Earthworm (d) Ant

232. Rhabitiform esophagus is present in-
(a) Ascaridia (b) Oxyliris
(c) Strogyloides (d) Fasciola

233. In case of strogyloides-
(a) Only females are pathogenic
(b). Only male are pathogenic
(c) Both are pathogenic
(d) Both are non pathogenic

234. Which type of esophagus is found in free living members of family Rhabditidae?
(a) Rhabditiform (b) Filariform
(c) Both (d) None

235. Which type of esophaus is found in parasitic members of family Rhabditidae?
(a) Rhabditiform (b) Filariform
(c) Both (d) None

236. Enteritis in all hosts is caused by which species of Rhabditis-
(a) *R. axei* (b) *R. bovis*
(c) *R. gingivalis* (d) *R. strongylides*

237. Parasitic otitis in cattle is caused by which species of Rhabditis-
(a) *R. axei* (b) *R. bovis*
(c) *R. gingivalis* (d) *R. strongylides*

238. Gum granuloma in horses is caused by which species of Rhabditis-
(a) *R. axei* (b) *R. bovis*
(c) *R. gingivalis* (d) *R. strongylides*

239. Which species of Rhabdites hides in skin of dog

& cat-
(a) R. axei (b) R. bovis
(c) R. gingivalis (d) *R. strongylides*

240. *Strongyloides papillosus* infects-
(a) Ruminants (b) Pigs
(c) Horse (d) Humans

241. *Strongyloides ransomi* infects-
(a) Ruminants (b) Pigs
(c) Horse (d) Humans

242. *Strongyloides westermani* infects-
(a) Ruminants (b) Pigs
(c) Horse (d) Humans

243. *Strongyloides stercoralis* infects-
(a) Ruminants (b) Pigs
(c) Horse (d) Humans

244. Which species of strongyloides is associated with tumor in cats?
(a) *S. stercoralis* (b) *S. westermani*
(c) *S. tumifaciense* (d) *S. cati*

245. Strongyloides are transmitted by which mode-
(a) Skin (b) Colestral
(c) Parenatral (d) All

246. Which larva of strongyloides is infective for definitive host?
(a) L_1 (b) L_2
(c) L_3 (d) L_4

247. Largest nematode found in colon of ruminants is-
(a) *Chabertia ovina* (b) *Trychostrongylus*
(c) *Trichuris ovis* (d) *Oesophagostmum*

248. *Stephanurus dentatus* is commonly called as-
(a) Faecal worm of pig
(b) Kidney worm of pigs
(c) Liver worm of pig
(d) Muscle worm of pigs

249. *Syngamus tracheai* is a-
(a) Nematode (b) Cestode
(c) Trematode (d) Cotylod

250. Who proved that *Trichodects canis* is the developmental host for *Dipylidium caninum*?
(a) Metnikoff (b) Carlos Fenlay
(c) Theobald Smith (d) None

251. Theory that mosquito transmits yellow fever pathogen was given by-
(a) Metnikoff (b) Carlos Fenlay
(c) Carlos Chagas (d) Ronald Ross

252. *Boophillus annulatus* transmits Babesiosis. This fact was discovered by-
(a) Theobald Smith (b) F.L. Kelbourne
(c) Both (d) None

253. Who found the zygote of Malaria parasite in mosquito?
(a) Theobald Smith (b) Carlos Fenlay
(c) Ronald Ross (d) None

254. Who proved those human malaria parasites are transmitted by Anopheles mosquito?
(a) Ronald Ross (b) Theobald smith
(c) Carlos Fenlay (d) Grassy & associates

255. Who proved that Dengue is transmitted by *Ades aegypti*?
(a) H. Grahm (b) Machie
(c) Brue (d) Thobald

256. Who proved that Relapsing fever organism is transmitted by human body louse?
(a) H. Grahm (b) Machie
(c) Brue (d) Thobald

257. Who proved that Cone nose bug is vector of *Trypanosome cruzi*-
(a) Carlos Fenlay (b) Carlos Chagas
(c) Machie (d) Brue

258. Which of the following acts as vector of *Trypansoma cruzi*?
(a) Bed bug (b) Tabanid fly
(c) Glossina (d) Cone nose bug

259. Who proved that *Trypanosoma congolense* is transmitted by Tse-Tse fly?
(a) Machie (b) Theanid fly
(c) Brue (d) Carlos chagas

260. Who demonstrated the development of *Wuchereia broncroftii* in the body of *Culex pipens*?
(a) Metnikoff (b) Patrie Manson
(c) Brue (d) Machie

261. Who proved transmission of surra pathogen occurs by Tabanus?
(a) Mitzmain (b) Machie
(c) Metnikoff (d) None

262. Onchosphere has how many sets of hooks
(a) 3 (b) 4
(c) 6 (d) 1

263. Winged insects are classified under-
(a) Pterygota (b) Apterygota
(c) Diplopoda (d) Chilopoda

264. Grasshopper are classified under-
(a) Orthoptera (b) Plecoptera
(c) Psocoptera (d) Odonata

265. Stone flies are classified under-
(a) Orthoptera (b) Plecoptera
(c) Psocoptera (d) Odonata

266. Dragon flies are classified under-
(a) Orthoptera (b) Plecoptera
(c) Psocoptera (d) Odonata

267. Book lice are classified under-
(a) Orthoptera (b) Plecoptera
(c) Psocoptera (d) Odonata

268. Bugs are classified under-
(a) Hemeptera (b) Coleoptera
(c) Hymenoptera (d) None

269. Beetles are classified under-
(a) Hemeptera (b) Coleoptera
(c) Hymenoptera (d) None

270. Hymenoptera includes includes-
(a) Bees (b) Wasps
(c) Ants (d) All

271. Lepidoptera includes-
(a) Beettles (b) Bugs
(c) Butterflies (d) Ant

272. Fleas are classifieds under-
(a) Henuptera (b) Coleoptera
(c) Siphonoptera (d) None

273. All true flies are classified under-
(a) Diptera (b) Siphonoptera
(c) Sipheeneulata (d) None

274. Biting lices are classified under-
(a) Siphunculata (b) Mallophage
(c) Psocoptera (d) None

275. Sucking lice are classified under-
(a) Siphunculata (b) Mallophage
(c) Psocoptera (d) None

276. Termites are classified under-
(a) Isoptera (b) Hemptera
(c) Coleoptera (d) Psocoptera

277. Spiders are classified under-
(a) Arancidia (b) Acrina
(c) Arachnida (d) None

278. Eyes of insects when meet on mid line are known as-
(a) Holoptic (b) Dichoptic
(c) Both (d) None

279. Eyes of insects when lie wide apart, are known as-
(a) Holoptic (b) Dichoptic
(c) Both (d) None

280. Biting & Chewing type of mouth parts are found in-
(a) Beetle (b) Biting lice
(c) Cockroach (d) All

281. Piercing & sucking type of mouth parts are-
(a) Mosquito (b) Flea
(c) Ticks (d) All

282. Lapping & Sponging type of mouth parts are found in-
(a) Musca (b) Mosquito
(c) Flea (d) Cockroach

283. Cutting & sponging type of mouth parts are found in-
(a) Musca (b) Tabanus
(c) Mosquito (d) Ticks

284. Which of the following flies are larviparous?
(a) Musca (b) Sarcophaga
(c) Glossina (d) All

285. Which of the following flies are oviparous?
(a) Musca (b) Sarcophaga
(c) Glossena (d) All

286. Which of the following flies are pupiparous?
(a) Musca (b) Sarcophaga
(c) Glossina (d) All

287. Oestrus ovis is-
(a) Oviparous (b) Larvipaeous
(c) Pupiparous (d) None

288. Flies & fleas undergo which type of life cycle-
(a) Holometabolus (b) Hemimetabolus
(c) Both (d) None

289. Members of Endopterygota undergo which type of life cycle-
(a) Holometabolus (b) Hemimetabolus
(c) Both (d) None

290. Egg, Nymph, Adult is a which type of life cycle-
(a) Holometabolus (b) Hemimetabolus
(c) Both (d) None

291. Polypod larva is found in which of the following-
(a) Caterpillar (b) Beetle
(c) Musca (d) Tabanus

292. Oligopod larva is found in which of the following-
(a) Caterpillar (b) Beetle
(c) Musca (d) Tabanus

293. Apodous larvae is found in which of the following-
(a) Musca (b) Stomoxys
(c) Tabanus (d) All

294. Which type of larvae is known as maggots?
(a) Polypod (b) Oligopod
(c) Apodous (d) All

295. How many total pair of legs is present on polypod larvae of an insect?
(a) 3 (b) 5
(c) 8 (d) 10

296. How many total pair of legs is present on an oligopod larva of an insect?
(a) 3 (b) 5
(c) 8 (d) 10

297. Exarate pupa is present in case of -
(a) Beetles (b) Mosquito
(c) Butterfly (d) All

298. Obtectate pupa is present in case of-
(a) Beetles (b) Mosquito
(c) Butterfly (d) All

299. Coarctate pupa is present is in case of-
(a) Musca (b) Stongoxs
(c) Glossina (d) All

300. Which type of pupa is present in case of horsefly?
(a) Exarate (b) Obtectate
(c) Coarctate (d) None

301. Which Helminth is found in the Abomasum of cattle?
(a) *Mecistocirrus digitaus*
(b) *Cooperia punctata*
(c) *Trichuris globulosa*
(d) *Toxocara vitulorun*

302. Which helminth is found in the liver and pancreas of cattle?
(a) *Dictyocaulus viviparus*
(b) *Cotylophoron spp.*
(c) *Fasciola gigantica*
(d) *Ostertagia ostertagi*

303. Which helminth is found in the blood vessels of cattle?
(a) *Paracooperia nodulosa*
(b) *Elaeophora poeli*
(c) *Nematoderus battus*
(d) *Cooperia pectinala*

304. Which helmith is found in the lungs of cattle?
(a) *Haemonchus similis*
(b) *Fasciola hepatica*
(c) *Fasciloa gigantica*
(d) *Mammomonogamus nasicola*

305. Which helminth is found in the brain of cattle?
(a) *Coenurus cerebalis*
(b) *Ixodes ricinus*
(c) *Thelazia spp.*
(d) *Schistosoma nasalis*

306. Which helminth is found in the eye of cattle?
(a) *Cysticercus bovis* (b) *Stephanofilaria spp.*
(c) *Theleazia spp.* (d) *Schistosoma nasalis*

307. Which helminth is not found in the abomasum of cattle?
(a) *Haemonchs controtus*
(b) *Cysticercus tenuicollis*
(c) *Ostertagia ostertagi*
(d) *Haemaochus similis*

308. Which helminth is not found in the liver and pancreas of cattle?
(a) *Trichuris globulosa* (b) *Dicocoelium hospis*
(c) *Fasciola hepatica* (d) *Fasciola gigantica*

309. Which helminth is not found in the lungs of cattle?
(a) *Dictyocaulus viviparus*
(b) *Moniezia expansa*
(c) *Mammomonogamus laryngeus*
(d) *Mammomonogamus nasicola*

310. Which helminth is not found in the blood vessels of cattle?
(a) *Onchocerca armillata*
(b) *Elaeophora poeli*
(c) *Schistosoma bovis*
(d) *Coenurus cerebralis*

311. Which helminth is found in the abomasum of sheep and goats?
(a) *Avitellina centripunctata*
(b) *Chabertia ovina*
(c) *Parabronema spp.*
(d) *Cotylophoraon spp.*

312. Which helminth is found in the brain of sheep and goats?
(a) *Coenurus cerbralis* (b) *Cysticercus ovis*
(c) Butterfly (d) All

313. Which helminth is found in the brain of sheep and goats?
(a) *Schistosoma spp.*
(b) *Stilesia hepatica*
(c) *Cooperia surnabada*
(d) *Parabronema spp.*

314. Which helminth is found in the lungs of sheep and goats?
(a) *Gaigeria pachyscelis*
(b) *Moniezua expansa*
(c) *Gongylonema pulchrusm*
(d) *Spiculocausus spp.*

315 Which helminth is found in the blood vessels of sheep and goats?
(a) *Haemonchus contortus*
(b) *Trichuris ovis*
(c) *Elaeophora schneideri*
(d) *Coenurus cerebralis*

316. Which helminth is not found in the abomasum of sheep and goats?
(a) *Thysanosoma actinioides*
(b) *Haemonchus contortus*
(c) *Ostertagia trifurcata*
(d) *Parabronema spp.*

317. Which helminth is not found in the liver of sheep and goats?
(a) *Dicrocelium hospes*
(b) *Muellerius capillaris*
(c) *Thysanosoma actinoides*
(d) *Dicrocoelium dendriticum*

318. Which helminth is not found in the lungs of sheep and goats?
(a) *Fascioloides magna*
(b) *Neostrogyluys spp.*
(c) *Disctyocaulus filaria*
(d) None

319. Which helminth is found in the oesophagus and forestomachs of cattle?
(a) Ostertaig ostertagi
(b) *Bunoslomum phlebotomum*
(c) *Cotylophoron spp.*
(d) *Cooperia oncophora*

320. Which helminth is not found in the oesophagus and forestomachs of cattle?
(a) *Ceylonocotyle spp.*
(b) *Haemonchus digitatus*
(c) *Paramphistomum spp.*
(d) *Gongylonema verrucosum*

321. Which helminth is found in the small intestine of cattle?
(a) *Onchocerca armillata*
(b) *Oxyuris spp.*
(c) *Thelazia spp.*
(d) *Avitellina centripunctata*

322. Which helminth is not found in the small intestine of cattle?
(a) *Bunastomum phlebotomum*
(b) *Schistosoma bovis*
(c) *Nematodirus battus*
(d) *Toxocara vitulorum*

323. Which helminth is found in the large intestine of cattle?
(a) *Nematodirus helvetianus*
(b) *Stilesia globipunctata*
(c) *Trichuris discolor*
(d) *Fascioloides magna*

324. Which helminth is found in the muscle, skin and connective tissue of cattle?
(a) *Homlogaster spp.*
(b) *Oesophagostomum radiatum*
(c) *Trichuris globulosa*
(d) *Eurytrema pancreaticum*

325. Which helminth is not found in muscle, skin and connective tissue of cattle?
(a) *Nematodirus helvetianus*
(b) *Onchocerca spp.*
(c) *Homologaster spp.*
(d) *Schistosoma bovis*

326. Infective stage of tapeworm is
(a) Metacestode (b) Oocyst

(c) Nymph (d) Eucestode

327. Which helminth is found in the oesophagus and forestomachs of sheep and goat?
(a) *Cotylophoron spp.*
(b) *Cysticercus tenuicollis*
(c) *Muellerius capillaris*
(d) *Schistosoma spp.*

328. Which helminth is not found in the Oesophagus and forestomachs of sheep and goats?
(a) *Cotylophoron spp.*
(b) *Schistosoma spp.*
(c) *Gongylonema pulchrum*
(d) *Paramphistomum spp.*

329. Which helminths are found in the small Intestine of sheep and goats?
(a) *Fascioloides magna* (b) *Dictyocaulus filaris*
(c) *Cysticercus ovis* (d) *Cooperia curticei*

330. Which helminth is not found in the small intestine of sheep and goats?
(a) *Thysanosoma actinioides*
(b) *Avitellina spp.*
(c) *Trichostrongylus vitrinus*
(d) *Cooperia curticei*

331. Which helminths are found in the large Intestine of sheep and goats?
(a) *Spiculocaulus spp.*
(b) *Chabertia ovina*
(c) *Ostertaia trifurcata*
(d) *Dicroceliym hospes*

332. Which helminths are not found in the large intestine of sheep and goats?
(a) *Skrjabinema ovis*
(b) *Oesphagostomum venulosum*
(c) *Cystocaulus spp.*
(d) *Chabertia ovina*

333. Which helminths are found in the Oesophagus and stomach of Pigs?
(a) *Schistosoma spp.*
(b) *Simmondsia paradoxa*
(c) *Systicerus cellulose*
(d) *Stephanurus dentatus*

334. Which helminths are found in the small intestine of pigs?
(a) *Fasciolopsis buski* (b) *Metastrongylus salmi*
(c) *Ollulanus tricuspis* (d) *Ascarops strongylina*

335. Which helminths are found in the large intestine of pigs?
(a) *Fasciola hepatica*
(b) *Trichinella spiralis*
(c) *Hyostrongylus rubidus*
(d) *Trichuris suis*

336. Which helminths are found in the lungs of pigs?
(a) Strongloides ransomi
(b) Ascaris suum
(c) Metastongylus salmi
(d) Ascarops strongylina

337. Which helminth is found in the liver of pigs?
(a) *Fasciola hepatica* (b) *Ascaris suum*
(c) *Fasciolopsis buski* (d) *Trichinella spiralis*

338. Which helminth is found in the blood vessels of pigs?
(a) *Oesophagostomum dentatum*
(b) *Schistosoma spp.*
(c) *Gongylonema pulchrum*
(d) *Strongyloides ransomi*

339. Which helminth is found in the muscle, skin and connective tissue of pigs?
(a) *Hysotrongylus rubidus*
(b) *Gnathostoma hispidum*
(c) *Cysticercus cellulose*
(d) *Trichurus suis*

340. Which helminth is found in the Kidneys of pigs?
(a) *Oesophagtrongylus apri*
(b) *Simmondisia paradoxa*
(c) *Gnathostoma doloresi*
(d) *Stephanurus dentatus*

341. Which helminth is not found in the Oesophagus and stomach of pigs-
(a) *Gnathostoma doloresi*
(b) *Stephanurus dentatus*
(c) *Trichuris suis*
(d) *Fasciolopsis buski*

342. Which helminth is not found in the small intestine of Pigs?
(a) *Trichuris suis* (b) *Fasciolopsis buski*
(c) *Trichinella spiralis* (d) *Ascaris suum*

343. Which helminth is not found in the large intestine of pigs?
(a) *Oesophagostomum brevicaudum*
(b) *Trichuris suis*

(c) *Schistosoma spp.*
(d) *Oesophagostomum granatensis*

344. Which helminth is not found in the lungs of pigs?
(a) *Metastongylus pudendotectus*
(b) *Metastrongylus salmi*
(c) *Metastrongylus apri*
(d) *Physocephalus senalatus*

345. Which helminth is found in the stomach of horses and donkeys?
(a) *Dictyocaulus arnfieldi*
(b) *Draschia megastoma*
(c) *Thelazia lacrymalis*
(d) *Parascaris equorum*

346. Which helminth is found in the small intestine of horses and donkeys?
(a) *Anoplocephala magna*
(b) *Oxyuris equi*
(c) *Elaeophora bohmi*
(d) *Cylicocyclus spp.*

347. Which helminth is found in the lungs of horses?
(a) *Anoplocephala perfoliata*
(b) *Habronema muscae*
(c) *Gastrodiscus spp.*
(d) *Onchocerca reticulata*

348. Which helminth is found in the lungs of horses?
(a) *Triodontophorus serratus*
(b) *Dictyocaulus arnfieldi*
(c) Cyathostomum spp.
(d) *Habronema inicrostoma*

349. Which helminth is found in the liver of horses?
(a) *Setaria equina*
(b) *Gastrodiscus spp.*
(c) *Metastrongylus apri*
(d) *Physocephalus senalatus*

350. Which helminth is found in the blood vessels of horses?
(a) *Elaeophora bohmi* (b) *Draschia megastoma*
(c) *Parascaris equorum* (d) *Strongyloides westeri*

351. Which helminth is found in the muscle, skin and connective tissue of horses?
(a) *Thelazia lacrymalis*
(b) *Parafilaris multipapillosa*
(c) *Parascaris equorum*
(d) *Elaeophora bohmi*

352. Which helminth is found in the brain of horses?
(a) *Halicephalobus deletrix*
(b) *Cylicocyclus spp.*
(c) *Gastrodiscus spp.*
(d) *Strongylus edentatus*

353. Which helminth is found in the two eye of horses?
(a) *Stongylus vulgaris*
(b) *Triodontophorus minor*
(c) *Theliazia lacrymalis*
(d) *Cyathostomum spp.*

354. Which helminth is not found in the stomach of horses?
(a) *Onchocerca reticulata*
(b) *Draschia megastoma*
(c) *Habronema muscae*
(d) *Trichostrongylus axei*

355. Which helminth is not found in the small intestine of horses?
(a) *Anoplocephala magna*
(b) *Oxyuris equi*
(c) *Parascaris equorum*
(d) *Stongyloides westri*

356. Which helminth is not found in the large intestine of horses?
(a) *Setaria equina*
(b) *Gastrodiscus spp.*
(c) *Metastrongylus apri*
(d) *Physocephalus senalatus*

357. Which helminth is not found in the muscle, skin and connective tissue of horses?
(a) *Onchocerca reticulata*
(b) *Parafilaria multipapillosa*
(c) *Triodontophorus tenuicollis*
(d) *Setaria equina*

358. Which helminth is found in the oesophagus of dogs and cats?
(a) *Ollulanus tricupis*
(b) *Spirocerca lupi*
(c) *Alaria spp.*
(d) *Trichuris vulpis*

359. Which helminth is found in the stomach of dogs and cats?
(a) *Spirurarity pliurites*
(b) *Spirometra spp.*
(c) *Metahelazia spp.*
(d) *Metorchis spp.*

360. Which helminth is found in the small intestine of dogs and cats?
(a) *Ollulanus ricurpis* (b) *Opisthorochis spp.*
(c) *Dirofilaria imitis* (d) *Taenia ovis*

361. Which helminth is found in the large intestine of dogs and cats?
(a) *Taenia serialis* (b) *Trichuris serrata*
(c) *Filaroides milksi* (d) *Trichinella spiralis*

362. Which helminth is found the lungs of dogs and cats?
(a) *Toxocara cati* (b) *Spirometra spp.*
(c) *Filaroides milksi* (d) *Trichinella spiralis*

363. Which helminth is found in the liver of dogs and cats?
(a) *Crenosoma vulpis* (b) *Capillaria hepatica*
(c) *Nanophyetus spp.* (d) *Filarodies hirthi*

364. Which helminth is found in the blood vessels of dogs and cats?
(a) *Toxoscaris leonia* (b) *Gurltia spp.*
(c) *Dirofilaria repens* (d) *Capillaira plice*

365. Which helminth is found in the eye of dogs and cats?
(a) *Rhabditis spp.*
(b) *Physaloptera spp.*
(c) *Trichuris serrata*
(d) *Platynosomum fastosum*

366. Which helminth is found in the eye of dogs and cats?
(a) *Echinococcus granulosus*
(b) *Ancylostoma caninum*
(c) *Thelazia californiensis*
(d) *Dirofilaria repens*

367. Which helminth is found in the urinary tract of dogs and cats?
(a) *Dipyliduim caninum*
(b) Taenia krabbei
(c) Spirocerca lupi
(d) *Dioctopyma renale*

368. Which helminth is not found in the stomach of dogs and cats?
(a) *Gnathostoma spinigerum*
(b) *Toxocara cati*
(c) *Physaloptera spp.*
(d) *Spirura ritypleurites*

369. Which helminth is not found in the small intestine of dogs and cats?
(a) *Metathelazia spp.*
(b) *Ancylostoma brazilinese*
(c) *Metastrongylus apri*
(d) *Physocephalus senalatus*

370. Which helminth is not found in the lungs of dogs and cats?
(a) *Filaroides herthi* (b) *Capillaria aerophila*
(c) *Paragaonimus spp.* (d) *Dirofilaria immitis*

371. Which helminth is not found in the liver of dogs and cats?
(a) *Capillarea hepatica* (b) *Capillaria plica*
(c) *Opistorchis spp.* (d) *Metorchis spp.*

372. Which helminth is not found the in the blood vessels of dogs and cats?
(a) *Dirofilaria immitis*
(b) *Schistosoma incognitum*
(c) *Anafilarioides spp.*
(d) *Gurltia spp.*

373. Which helminth is not found in the muscle, skin and connective tissue of dog and cats?
(a) *Trichinella spiralis*
(b) *Dirofilaria repens*
(c) *Dipetalonema reconditum*
(d) *Rhabditis spp.*

374. Which helminth is found in the oesophagus of domestic birds?
(a) *Heterakis gallinarum*
(b) *Capillaria controta*
(c) *Cheilospirura spp.*
(d) *Streptocara spp.*

375. Which helminth is found in the Proventriculus of domestic birds?
(a) *Echinuria spp.* (b) *Syngamus trachea*
(c) *Ascaridia galli* (d) *Histiocephalus spp.*

376. Which helminth is found in the Gizzard of domestic birds?
(a) *Dispharynm spp.*
(b) *Capillaria obsignata*
(c) *Amidostomum anseris*
(d) *Filicolis spp.*

377. Which helminth is found in the small intestine of domestic birds?
(a) *Cherlospirura spp.* (b) *Capillaria caudinflata*
(c) *Tetrameres spp.* (d) *Strongyloides ovium*

378. Which helminth is found in the large intestine of domestic birds?
(a) *Filicollis spp.* (b) *Hartertia spp.*
(c) *Heteraksi isolonche* (d) *Polymorphus spp.*

379. Which helminth is found in the lungs of domestic birds?
(a) *Syngamus trachea*
(b) *Histiocephalus spp.*
(c) *Davainea proglottina*
(d) *Amidostomum anseris*

380. Which helminth is not found in the Oesophagus of domestic birds?
(a) *Capllaria controta*
(b) *Ornithostrongylus quadriradiatus*
(c) *Gongylonema ingluvicola*
(d) *Tetrameres spp.*

381. Which helminth is not found in the Proventriculus of domestic birds?
(a) *Dispharynz spp.*
(b) *Trichostrongylus tenuis*
(c) *Echinuria spp.*
(d) *Tetrameres spp.*

382. Which helminth is not found in the Gizzard of domestic birds?
(a) *Amidostomum anseris*
(b) *Histocephalus spp.*
(c) *Syngamus trachea*
(d) *Streptocara spp.*

383. Which helminth is not found in the small intestine of domestic birds?
(a) *Gongylonema ingluvicola*
(b) *Ascaridia galli*
(c) *Polymorphus spp.*
(d) *Strongyloides ovium*

384. Which helminth is not found in the large intestine of domestic birds?
(a) *Heterakis gallinarum*
(b) *Heterakis isolonche*
(c) *Tricholstongylus tenuis*
(d) *Davainea proglottina*

385. In domestic birds, *Amoebotaenia spheoides* is found in the
(a) Large Intestine (b) Small Intestine
(c) Lungs (d) Gizzard

386. In domestic birds, *Ornithostrongylus quadriradiatus* is found in the
(a) Oesophagus (b) Proventriculus
(c) Gizzard (d) Lungs

387. In dogs and cats, *Crenosoma vulpis* is found in the
(a) Stomach (b) Oesophagus
(c) Lungs (d) Liver

388. In dogs and cats, *Diphyllobothrum latum* is found in the
(a) Blood vessels (b) Liver
(c) Large intestine (d) Small intestine

389. In dogs and cats, *Thelazia californiensis* is found in the
(a) Eye (b) Muscles
(c) Urinary tract (d) Stomach

390. In dogs and cats, *Schistosoma incognitum* is found in the
(a) Liver (b) Blood vessels
(c) Muscles (d) Eye

391. In horses, *Probstmayria vivipara* is found in the
(a) Stomach (b) Small intestine
(c) Large intestine (d) Lungs

392. In horses, *Halicephalobus deletrix* is found in the
(a) Lungs (b) Liver
(c) Muscles (d) Brain

393. In horses, Fasciola hepatica is found in the
(a) Lungs (b) Liver
(c) Muscles (d) Brain

394. In pigs, Stephanurus dentatus is found in the
(a) Blood vessels (b) Liver
(c) Kidneys (d) Skin

395. In pigs, *Metastrongylus pudendotectus* is found in the
(a) Lungs (b) Liver
(c) Blood vessels (d) Kidney

396. In sheep and Goats, *Coenurus cerebralis* is found in the
(a) Abomasum (b) Brain
(c) Lungs (d) Liver.

397. In sheep and Goats, *Marshallagia marshalli* is found in the
(a) Oesophagus (b) Blood vessels
(c) Abomasum (d) Lungs

398. In sheep and Goats, *Nenatidurys filicollis* is found in the
(a) Lungs (b) Liver

(c) Small intestine (d) Large intestine

399. In cattle, *Dicrocoelium dedriticum* is found in the
(a) Large intestine (b) Liver and pancreas
(c) Lungs (d) Abomasum

400. In cattle, *Nematodirus helvetianus* is found in the
(a) Small intestine (b) Large intestine
(c) Liver (d) Lungs

401. In which type of pupa legs and wings of insect developing inside can be externally seen & are free from body of pupa-
(a) Exarate (b) Obtectate
(c) Coarctate (d) All

402. In which type of pupa wings and legs attached to the body with the help of moulting fluid and are visible externally-
(a) Exarate (b) Obtectate
(c) Coarctate (d) All

403. In which type of pupa, pupa is enclosed in the cast skin of last larval stage known as puparium-
(a) Exarate (b) Obtectate
(c) Coarctate (d) All

404. Biting lices found on elephant are grouped under-
(a) Amblycera (b) Ischnocera
(c) Rincofthrina (d) None

405. Mammalian biting lices are grouped under-
(a) Amblycera (b) Ischnocera
(c) Rincofthrina (d) None

406. In which type of louse legs terminate into paired claw-
(a) Poultry (b) Mammalian
(c) Both (d) None

407. In which type of louse legs terminate into single claw-
(a) Poultry (b) Mammalian
(c) Both (d) None

408. Which of the following is commonly known as shaft louse of poultry?
(a) *Menopon gallinae*
(b) *Menacanthus strameneus*
(c) *Gonadis gigas*
(d) *Goniocites gallinae*

409. Which one is commonly known as Body louse of poultry?
(a) *Menopon gallinae*
(b) *Menacanthus strameneus*
(c) *Gonadis gigas*
(d) *Goniocites gallinae*

410. Which one is commonly known as large body louse of poultry?
(a) *Menopon gallinae*
(b) *Menacanthus strameneus*
(c) *Gonadis gigas*
(d) *Goniocites gallinae*

411. Which of the following is known as Fluff louse of poultry?
(a) *Menopon gallinae*
(b) *Menacanthus strameneus*
(c) *Gonadis gigas*
(d) *Goniocites gallinae*

412. Which one is known as Wing louse of poultry?
(a) *Lipeurus caponis*
(b) *Lipeurus heterographus*
(c) Both
(d) None

413. Which one is known as Head louse of poultry?
(a) *Lipeurus caponis*
(b) *Lipeurus heterographus*
(c) Both
(d) None

414. Which one is commonly known as Short nose cattle louse?
(a) *Hematopinus eurysternus*
(b) *Linognathus vituli*
(c) *Linognathus ovillus*
(d) *Linognathus pedalis*

415. Which one is commonly known as Long nose cattle louse?
(a) *Hematopinus eurysternus*
(b) *Linognathus vituli*
(c) *Linognathus ovillus*
(d) *Linognathus pedalis*

416. Which one is commonly known as body louse of sheep?
(a) *Hematopinus eurysternus*
(b) *Linognathus vituli*
(c) *Linognathus ovillus*
(d) *Linognathus pedalis*

417. Which one is commonly known as foot louse of sheep?

(a) *Hematopinus eurysternus*
(b) *Linognathus vituli*
(c) *Linognathus ovillus*
(d) *Linognathus pedalis*

418. Which one is commonly known as Body louse of Man?
(a) *Pediculus humanus caporis*
(b) *Pediculus humanus capitis*
(c) *Pthyrus pubis*
(d) All

419. Which one is commonly known as head louse of Man?
(a) *Pediculus humanis caporis*
(b) *Pediculus humanus capitis*
(c) *Pthyrus pubis*
(d) All

420. Which one is commonly known as Human pubic louse?
(a) *Pediculus humanis caporis*
(b) *Pediculus humanus capitis*
(c) *Pthyrus pubis*
(d) All

421. Which one is commonly known as crab louse?
(a) *Pediculus humanis caporis*
(b) *Pediculus humanus capitis*
(c) *Pthyrus pubis*
(d) All

422. Nits develop into adults in about-
(a) 3 days (b) 10-15 days
(c) 14-21 days (d) 3 Months

423. Canine filariasis is caused by-
(a) Dirofilaria
(b) *Dipetalonema reconditum*
(c) *Borrelia prowazaki*
(d) *Borrelia recurrentis*

424. Epidemis typhus is caused by-
(a) Dirofilaria
(b) *Dipetalonema reconditum*
(c) *Borrelia prowazaki*
(d) *Borrelia recurrentis*

425. Epidemic relapsing fever is caused by-
(a) *Dirofilaria*
(b) *Dipetalonema reconditum*
(c) *Borrelia prowazaki*
(d) *Borrelia recurrentis*

426. Louse borne typhus is caused by-
(a) Dirofilaria
(b) *Dipetalonema reconditum*
(c) *Borrelia prowazaki*
(d) *Borrelia recurrentis*

427. Trench fever is caused by-
(a) *Borelia prowazaki*
(b) *Borelia recurrentis*
(c) *Rochelimia quintana*
(d) None

428. Louse born typhus is transmitted by-
(a) *Trichodectis canis* (b) *Legnonathus vituli*
(c) *Pediculus humans* (d) *Heterodoxus sphiniger*

429. Dipylidium caminum is transmitted by-
(a) *Trichodectis canis*
(b) *Legnonathus vituli*
(c) *Rochelimia quintana*
(d) *Heterodoxus sphiniger*

430. Canine filariasis is transmitted by-
(a) *Trichodectis canis*
(b) *Legnonathus vituli*
(c) *Rochelimia quintana*
(d) *Heterodoxus sphiniger*

431. Epidemis relapsing fever is transmitted by-
(a) *Trichodectis canis*
(b) *Legnonathus vituli*
(c) *Rochelimia quintana*
(d) *Heterodoxus sphiniger*

432. Trench fever is transmitted by-
(a) *Trichodectis canis*
(b) *Legnonathus vituli*
(c) *Rochelimia quintana*
(d) *Heterodoxus sphiniger*

433. How many segments are present in antennae of Nematocera?
(a) 3 (b) >5
(c) >8 (d) >10

434. Witted appearance is present in antennae of -
(a) Nematocera (b) Brachycera
(c) Cyclorapha (d) All

435. How many segments are present in antennae of brachycera?
(a) 3 (b) 5
(c) 8 (d) 10

436. How many segments are present in antennae of cyclorapha?
(a) 3 (b) 5
(c) 8 (d) 10

437. Last segment of antennae has got annulations in case of-
(a) Nematocera (b) Brachycera
(c) Cyclorapha (d) All

438. Last segment of antennae is club shaped in case of-
(a) Nematocera (b) Brachycera
(c) Cyclorapha (d) All

439. How many pairs of legs are present in mosquito?
(a) 3 (b) 6
(c) 2 (d) 10

440. Mosquito undergoes which type of life cycle?
(a) Holometa bolus (b) Hemimetabolus
(c) Both (d) None

441. Which type of larvae is found in case of Anopheles?
(a) Apodous (b) Polypodous
(c) Oligopodus (d) All

442. Respiratory siphon is present in-
(a) Anopheles (b) Culex
(c) Both (d) None

443. Respiratory siphon is absent in-
(a) Anopheles (b) Culex
(c) Both (d) None

444. Probosis & abdomen are in straight sloped line in-
(a) Anopheles (b) Culex
(c) Both (d) None

445. Which mosquito protect their head downwards for resting surface-
(a) Anopheles (b) Culex
(c) Both (d) None

446. Hemelytra refers to which pair of wings of Hemiptera-
(a) Anterior (b) Posterior
(c) Both (d) None

447. Which pair of wings of Hemiptera is membranous?
(a) Anterior (b) Posterior
(c) Both (d) None

448. Which of the following bugs attacks man & animals?
(a) *Cimex lectularius* (b) *Cimex hemipterus*
(c) Both (d) None

449. Which of the following bugs attack poultry?
(a) *Cimex lectularius* (b) *Cimex hemipterus*
(c) Both (d) None

450. Reduvid bugs are also known as-
(a) Kissing bugs (b) Assasing bugs
(c) Cone nose bugs (d) All

451. Chagas disease in human beings is transmitted by-
(a) Kissing bugs (b) Assasing bugs
(c) Cone nose bugs (d) All

452. Which one is commonly known as Dog flea?
(a) Trichodectes canis
(b) Ctenocephalidis canis
(c) Xenopsylla cheopis
(d) All

453. Which one is commonly called Oriental rat flea?
(a) *Trichodectes canis* (b) *Ctenocephalidis canis*
(c) *Xenopsylla cheopis* (d) All

454. Which one is commonly called Black rat flea?
(a) *Trichodectes canis* (b) *Ctenocephalidis canis*
(c) *Xenopsylla cheopis* (d) All

455. Which one is commonly called as Human flea?
(a) *Trichodectes canis* (b) *Ctenocephalidis canis*
(c) *Xenopsylla cheopis* (d) *Pulex irritans*

456. Which one is commonly called as Jigger flea?
(a) *Tunga penetrans*
(b) *Ceratophullus gallenae*
(c) *Ceratophyllus columbae*
(d) *Echinophaga gallinacca*

457. Which one is commonly called as Chigoa flea?
(a) *Tunga penetrans*
(b) *Ceratophullus gallenae*
(c) *Ceratophyllus columbae*
(d) *Echidnophaga gallinacia*

458. Which one is commonly called as common flea of chicken?
(a) *Tunga penetrans*
(b) *Ceratophullus gallenae*
(c) *Ceratophyllus columbae*
(d) *Echidnophaga gallinacia*

459. Which one is commonly called as Stick tight flea of poultry?

(a) *Tunga penetrans*
(b) *Ceratophullus gallenae*
(c) *Ceratophyllus columbae*
(d) *Echidnophaga gallinacia*

460. Sensilluim is present in which segment of abdomen of flea-
(a) 3rd (b) 1st
(c) 9th (d) 10th

461. Which comb is present on head of flea?
(a) Genal comb (b) Pronotal comb
(c) Both (d) None

462. Which comb is present on 1st thoracic segment of flea?
(a) Pronotal (b) Genal
(c) Both (d) None

463. Anal struts are present on which segment of abdomen of flea-
(a) 3rd (b) 5th
(c) 9th (d) 10th

464. Which larvae of fleas build puparium around it?
(a) L_1 (b) L_2
(c) L_3 (d) L_4

465. Flea infestation is associated with miliary dermatitis & alopecia in-
(a) Cat (b) Dog
(c) Pig (d) Cattle

466. Oriental rat flea transmits-
(a) *Yersinia pestes* (b) Tularaemia
(c) Boobanic plague (d) All

467. Antennae in female mosquito is-
(a) Plumose (b) Pilose
(c) Both (d) None

468. Antennae in male mosquito is-
(a) Plumose (b) Pilose
(c) Both (d) None

469. When as insect bites all components of probosis are inserted into the host tissue except -
(a) Labium (b) Labrum
(c) Mandibles (d) Maxillae

470. Mosquitos breed in-
(a) Water (b) Air
(c) Cracks & crevices (d) Underground

471. Eggs are layed singly in case of-
(a) Anopheles (b) Aedes
(c) Both (d) None

472. Egg are laid in patches forming egg rafts in-
(a) Anopheles (b) Aedes
(c) Both (d) None

473. How many larval instars are present in life cycle of mosquito?
(a) 1 (b) 2
(c) 3 (d) 4

474. Eggs of Anopheles mosquito are-
(a) Ovoid (b) Spherical
(c) Irregular (d) Boat shaped

475. Anopheles female acts as which host for human malaria-
(a) Definitive (b) Intermediate
(c) Both (d) None

476. Which mosquito acts as DH of Bird Malaria?
(a) Culex (b) Aedes
(c) Theobaldia (d) All

477. Which mosquito acts as IH of *Wuchereria bancofti?*
(a) Anopheles (b) Thebaldia
(c) Mansonia (d) All

478. Which mosquito acts as IH of *Brugia malayi?*
(a) Mansonia (b) Anopheles
(c) Both (d) None

479. Which mosquito acts as IH of Dirofilaria immitis?
(a) Anopheles (b) Culex
(c) Mansonia (d) All

480. Culex transmits-
(a) Eastern equine encephalitis
(b) Western equine encephalitis
(c) Japanese encephalites
(d) All

481. Aedes aegypti transmits-
(a) Yellow fever (b) Dengue fever
(c) Both (d) None

482. Eggs of biting midges are-
(a) Ovoid (b) Boat shaped
(c) Banana shaped (d) Irregular

483. Probosis of biting midges by-
(a) Piercing type (b) Sucking type
(c) Biting type (d) Sponging type

484. Anal gills are present in larvae of-
(a) Biting midges (b) Lice
(c) Flea (d) Culex

485. Biting midge infection in horses causes-
(a) Summers itch (b) Queen's land itch
(c) Sweet itch (d) All

486. Sweet itch in horse is caused due to infection of -
(a) Biting mideges (b) Lice
(c) Flea (d) Bugs

487. *Onchocerca cervicalis* transmits-
(a) *Culicoides nubeculosus*
(b) *Culicoides perstanse*
(c) Both
(d) None

488. *Onhocerea egypsoni* transmits-
(a) *Culicoides nubeculosus*
(b) *Culicoides perstanse*
(c) Both
(d) None

489. Which of the following is known as Black flies?
(a) Simuluim (b) Culicoides
(c) Siphunculata (d) All

490. Simulium is also known as-
(a) Black flies (b) Buffalo gnats
(c) Both (d) None

491. *Simulium indicum* is also known as-
(a) Black fly (b) Potu fly
(c) Green fly (d) All

492. Eggs of simulium are laid-
(a) On stones
(b) On plants
(c) Just below slow moving water
(d) All

493. Simulium transmits-
(a) Leucocytozoon in turkey
(b) Hemoproteus in ducks
(c) Onchocerea gaturosa
(d) All

494. Phlebotomus are also known as-
(a) Black fly (b) Sand fly
(c) Potu flies (d) All

495. Phlebotomus transmits-
(a) Trypansomosis (b) Leishmaniosis
(c) Babesiosis (d) Theleriosis

496. Tropical leishmaniosis is transmitted by-
(a) *Phlebotomus papatasi*
(b) *Phlebotomus sergenti*
(c) *Phlebotomus major*
(d) All

497. Kala-azar is transmitted by
(a) *Phlebotomus major*
(b) *Phlebotomus papatasi*
(c) Phlebotomus sergenti
(d) *Phlebotomus argentypes*

498. Flies under *Tabandae* family are known as -
(a) Tabanid fly (b) Breeze fly
(c) Horse fly (d) All

499. Which of the following tabanid flies are host of veterinary importance -
(a) Tabanus (b) Chrysops
(c) Hematopota (d) Pangonia

500. Labella is terminal expansion of-
(a) Labium (b) Labrum
(c) Mandible (d) Maxilla

501. Male tabanid flies do not suck blood because they do not have-
(a) Labium (b) Labrum
(c) Mandible (d) Maxilla

502. Type of eyes of male tabanid flies are
(a) Holoptic (b) Dichoptic
(c) Both (d) None

503. Type of eyes of female tabanid flies are
(a) Holoptic (b) Dichoptic
(c) Both (d) None

504. Wings sprinkled with brown spots are typical morphological character of-
(a) Tabanus (b) Stomoxys
(c) Hematopota (d) Chrysops

505. Dark band across the wings is present in case of -
(a) Tabanus (b) Stomoxys
(c) Hematopota (d) Chrysops

506. Annulations are present in which segment of antennae of Tabanes -
(a) 1st (b) 2nd
(c) 3rd (d) 4th

507. How many annulations are present in 3rd segment of antennae of Tabanus -
(a) 1 (b) 2
(c) 3 (d) 4

508. Function of Graber's organ in the larvae of Tabanus is -

(a) To acquire nutrition
(b) Supporting organ
(c) Adhesive
(d) Sensory organ

509. Tabanus transmits which of the following diseases-
(a) Human African trypanosomosis
(b) Nagana
(c) Malde
(d) All

510. *Pasteurella tularensis* is transmitted by -
(a) *Chrysops discalis* (b) Hematopota
(c) *Chrysops dimidiata* (d) All

511. Loa-Loa is transmitted by -
(a) *Chrysops discalis* (b) Hematopota
(c) *Chrysops dimidiata* (d) All

512. Human filariosis is transmitted by -
(a) *Chrysops discalis* (b) Hematopota
(c) *Chrysops dimidiata* (d) All

513. *Trypanosoma theileri* is transmitted by -
(a) *Chrysops discalis* (b) Hematopota
(c) *Chrysops dimidiata* (d) All

514. Which of the following is commonly known as Horse bot fly -
(a) Hematopota (b) Gastrophillus
(c) Phlebotomus (d) Simuluim

515. Which species of Gastrophillus is commonly known as Horse stomach bot fly -
(a) *G. intestinalis* (b) *G. nasalis*
(c) *G. hemorrhoidalis* (d) *G. pecorum*

516. Which gastrophillus is commonly known as Horse nose bot fly -
(a) *G. intestinalis* (b) *G. nasalis*
(c) *G. hemorrhoidalis* (d) *G. pecorum*

517. Which Gastrophillus is commonly known as Horse throat bot fly -
(a) *G. intestinalis* (b) *G. nasalis*
(c) *G. hemorrhoidalis* (d) *G. pecorum*

518. The colour of larva of *Gastrophillus intestinalis* is
(a) Red (b) Green
(c) Yellow (d) Blue

519. The colour of larva of *Gastrophillus nasalis* is
(a) Red (b) Green
(c) Yellow (d) Blue

520. Larvae of *Gastrophillus intestinalis* is found at -
(a) Cardiac region
(b) Liver
(c) Pylorus & duodenum
(d) Caecum & colon

521. Larvae of gastrophillus nasalis is found in at.
(a) Cardiac region
(b) Liver
(c) Pylorus & duodenum
(d) Caecum & colon

522. Dose rate of Crabon di sulphide for the treatment of Gastrophillus infection in horses is -
(a) 2-5 ml/kg body weight
(b) 20 ml/kg body weight
(c) 10-15 ml/kg body weight
(d) 1-2 ml/kg body weight

523. Which species of Musca is commonly known as face fly -
(a) *M. domestica* (b) *M. conducens*
(c) *M. autumanlis* (d) All

524. Which species of Musca is known as House fly.
(a) *M. domestica* (b) *M. conducens*
(c) *M. autumanlis* (d) All

525. 4 distinct dark brown longitudinal stripes is a morphological characteristic of -
(a) Musca (b) Gastrophillus
(c) Simullum (d) None

526. Musca transmits -
(a) Typhoid
(b) Cholera
(c) Poliomyelitis virus
(d) All

527. Which of the following flies are known as Biting house flies
(a) Musca (b) Stomoxys
(c) Tabanus (d) Chrysops

528. *Stomoxys calcitans* is commonly known as -
(a) Face fly (b) House fly
(c) Stable fly (d) Biting house fly

529. Glossina is commonly known as -
(a) Tse-Tse fly (b) Tse fly
(c) Biting flies (d) All

530. Hatchet is present in the wings of -
(a) Tabanus (b) Musca
(c) Glossina (d) Stomoxys

531. Which one is the characteristic of wing of Glossina -
(a) Cleaver cell (b) Hatchet
(c) Both (d) None

532. Which flies are commonly known as Horn flies -
(a) Tabanid (b) Hematobia
(c) Glossina (d) None

533. Which species of *Hematobia* is commonly known as Buffalo fly -
(a) *H. irritans* (b) *H. exiqua*
(c) Both (d) None

534. Hematobia transmits -
(a) Trypanosomes (b) Tersinea
(c) Pasteurella (d) Stephanofilaria

535. Myiasis is caused by the larvae of -
(a) Calliphoridae (b) Sarcophagidae
(c) Oestridae (d) All

536. Larvae of which of the following parasite is facultative parasite -
(a) Lucilia (b) Calliphora
(c) Both (d) Oestrus ovis

537. Larvae of which of the following is an oblogatory parasite -
(a) Lucilia (b) Calliphora
(c) Both (d) Oestrus ovis

538. Cutaneous myiasis is caused by -
(a) Lucilia (b) Oestrus
(c) Hypoderma (d) All

539. Nasal myiasis is caused by -
(a) Lucilia (b) Oestrus
(c) Hypoderma (d) All

540. Somatic myiasis is caused by -
(a) Lucilia (b) Oestrus
(c) Hypoderma (d) All

541. Which one is known as green bottle fly -
(a) Lucilla (b) Phormia
(c) Chysomia (d) None

542. Which one is known as Black bottle fly -
(a) Lucilla (b) Phormia
(c) Chysomia (d) None

543. Which one is known as Blue bottle fly -
(a) Lucilla (b) Phormia
(c) Chysomia (d) None

544. Which flies are commonly known as bottle flies.
(a) Callephoridae (b) Sarcophagidae
(c) Oestridae (d) All

545. Blow strike is caused by the larvae of -
(a) Callephoridae (b) Sarcophagidae
(c) Oestridae (d) All

546. Myiasis of which of the following parts is known as Pizzle-rot -
(a) Tail (b) Body
(c) Poll (d) Penile sheath

547. Skrew-worm Myiasis is caused by larvae of -
(a) Chrysomia baziani
(b) Cochloiomyia hominivorax
(c) Cochliomyia macillaria
(d) All

548. Which one is commonly known as Tomb fly -
(a) *Chrysomia baziani*
(b) *Cordylobia anthropophaga*
(c) *Cochleomyia macillaria*
(d) All

549. Which species of Hypoderma infects deer -
(a) *H. bovis* (b) *H. lineatum*
(c) *H. diana* (d) All

550. *Hypoderma bovis* lays eggs -
(a) Singly, below the hocks
(b) In rows, below the hocks
(c) Singly, above the hocks
(d) In rows, above the hocks

551. *Hypodrma lineatum* lays eggs -
(a) Singly, below the hocks
(b) In rows, below the hocks
(c) Singly, above the hocks
(d) Iin rows, above the hocks

552. Which flies are commonly known as Warble flies-
(a) Oestrus (b) Hypoderma
(c) Phormia (d) Chrysomia

553. Which flies are commonly known as Nasal bots -
(a) Oestrus (b) Hypoderma
(c) Phormia (d) Chrysomia

554. False gid is caused by the larvae of -
(a) Oestrus (b) Hypoderma
(c) Phormia (d) Chrysomia

555. Which flies are commonly known as Louse flies -
(a) Hippoboscidae (b) Callephoridae
(c) Sarcophagidae (d) All

556. *Malophagus Ovinus* is commonly known as -
(a) Sheepked (b) Wingless fly
(c) Both (d) None

557. *Pseudolynchia canariensis* is commonly known as -
(a) Pigeon fly (b) Bot fly
(c) Chicken fly (d) None

558. *Hemoproteus columbae* can be transmitted by -
(a) Melophagus (b) Pseudolynchia
(c) Hypoderma (d) All

559. *Lipoptena cervi* infects -
(a) Cattle (b) Sheep
(c) Pig (d) Deer

560. Which of the following flies after locating host, looses wings -
(a) Hippobosca (b) Pseudolynchia
(c) Lipoptena (d) All

561. Gastrophillus lays eggs on -
(a) Hair (b) Around mouth
(c) Hump (d) Any where

562. Oestrus ovis lays eggs on -
(a) Hair (b) Around mouth
(c) Hsump (d) Any where

563. Hypoderma lays eggs on -
(a) Hair (b) Around mouth
(c) Hump (d) Any where

564. How many hosts are involved in life cycle of sheep ked -
(a) 1 (b) 2
(c) 3 (d) 4

565. Which of the following is associated with abortions -
(a) Anaplasmosis (b) Theileriosis
(c) Babesiosis (d) All

566. CoccidiosIs is not considered clinical up to which number of oocyst per gm of faeces -
(a) 5000 (b) 1000
(c) 10000 (d) 1 lac

567. Intermediate host for Neosporosis is -
(a) Bovines (b) Dog
(c) Deer (d) Pig

568. Definitive host for Neosporosis is -
(a) Bovines (b) Dog
(c) Deer (d) Pig

569. Which species of Sarcocyst infects cattle -
(a) *S. cruzi* (b) *S. hominis*
(c) *S. tenella* (d) Both a and b

570. Infection of Sarcocyst in intermediate host occurs due to ingestion of -
(a) Sporulated oocyst
(b) Meant of another intermediate host
(c) Both
(d) None

571. Cyst present in the muscles of intermediate host infected with sarcocystosis consists of -
(a) Merozoites (b) Tachyzoites
(c) Bradyzoites (d) Trophozoites

572. Intraepithelial lymphocyte infiltration in jejunum & villous atrophy is characteristic of which infection -
(a) Coccidiosis (b) Giardiosis
(c) Besnoitiosis (d) All

573. White crust formation in bunches in intestinal lumen is characteristic of which infection -
(a) Coccidiosis (b) Giardiosis
(c) Besnoitiosis (d) All

574. During coccidiosis, endothelium of intestine is invaded by -
(a) Merozoites (b) Brady zoites
(c) Trophozoites (d) None

575. Which of the following can be demonstrated in intestinal mucosa, in giardiasis -
(a) Merozoites (b) Brady zoites
(c) Trophozoites (d) None

576. Udder & perianal area of cattle becomes characteristically yellow in case of -
(a) Anaplasmosis (b) Theileriosis
(c) Babesiosis (d) Trypanosomosis

577. Deep orange liver & pulpy spleen is characteristic of which infection -
(a) Anaplasmosis (b) Theileriosis
(c) Babesiosis (d) Trypanosomosis

578. Punched ulcers on abomasum are characteristic of which infection -
(a) Anaplasmosis (b) Theileriosis
(c) Babesiosis (d) Trypanosomosis

579. Koch's blue bodies can be demonstrated in lymphocytes in case of -
(a) Anaplasmosis (b) Theileriosis

(c) Babesiosis (d) Trypanosomosis

580. Haemoglobinuria is characteristic of which infection -
(a) Anaplasmosis (b) Theileriosis
(c) Babesiosis (d) Trypanosomosis

581. Corneal opacity & subcutaneous edema are associated with -
(a) Anaplasmosis (b) Theileriosis
(c) Babesiosis (d) Trypanosomosis

582. During Babesiosis, haemoglobinuria is not observed in -
(a) Cattle (b) Sheep
(c) Pig (d) Horse

583. Babesiosis is associated with -
(a) Haemoglobinuria
(b) Haemolytic anaemia
(c) Thrombocytopaenia
(d) All

584. Trypanosomiosis is associated with -
(a) Corneal opacity
(b) Decreased blood glucose
(c) Subcuteneous edema
(d) All

585. Mal-de Cadres is caused by which trypanosome -
(a) *T. equinium* (b) *T. cruzi*
(c) *T. vivax* (d) *T. brucei*

586. Mal-de chagas is caused by which trypanosome -
(a) *T. equinium* (b) *T. cruzi*
(c) *T. vivax* (d) *T. brucei*

587. Mal-de cadres is a disease of -
(a) Equines (b) Cattle
(c) Human (d) Dog

588. Which of the following acts as reservoir of Mal-de cadres?
(a) Equines (b) Cattle
(c) Human (d) Dog

589. Malde chagas is a disease of -
(a) Human (b) Equine
(c) Deer (d) Dog

590. Which of the following acts as reservoir of Malde chagas?
(a) Human (b) Equine
(c) Deer (d) Dog

591. Toxoplasmosis is associated with-
(a) Encephalitis (b) Pneumonia
(c) Still birth (d) All

592. Cat acts as which host in case of Toxoplasmosis -
(a) Intermediate (b) Definitive
(c) Both (d) None

593. Toxoplasma infection in definitive host occurs by-
(a) Ingestion of cyst with bradyzoites
(b) Ingestion of faeces with sporulated oocyst
(c) Coitus
(d) Transuterine

594. Toxoplasma infection in Intermediate host occurs by -
(a) Ingestion of cyst with bradyzoites
(b) Ingestion of faces with sporulated oocyst
(c) Coitus
(d) Transuterine

595. Multiple proliferative & necrotic granulomas on necropsy is characteristic of -
(a) Coccidioses (b) Giardiosis
(c) Toxoplasmosis (d) Sarcocystosis

596. Toxoplasma cyst present in muscles of intermediate host is consists of -
(a) Merozoites (b) Trophozoites
(c) Tachyzoites (d) Bradyzoites

597. S_{48} strain vaccine of Toxoplasma consists of -
(a) Merozoites (b) Trophozoites
(c) Tachyzoites (d) Bradyzoites

598. Infective dose of oocyst in case of Cryptosporidiasis -
(a) 10^2 oocyst / gm of faeces
(b) 10^{10} ocyst/gm of faeces
(c) 10^5 - 10^7 oocyst/gm of faeces
(d) 10^{20} ocyst/gm of faeces

599. Mal-de chagas is transmitted by -
(a) Stomoxys (b) Tabanus
(c) Both (d) Reduvid insects

600. Malde cadres is transmitted by -
(a) Stomoxys (b) Tabanies
(c) Both (d) Reduvid insects

601. Only arthropod having indirect life cycle is
(a) Wood lice (b) Tongue worm
(c) Insecta (d) None

602. in cestodes, one egg gives how many cysticercoid
(a) One (b) Two

(c) Three (d) Four

603. Apolysis is seen in
(a) Roundworm (b) Tapeworm
(c) Fasciola (d) None

604. Infective stage of tapeworm is
(a) Metacestode (b) Oocyst
(c) Nymph (d) Eucestode

605. Correct sequence of stages in life cycle of mite is
(a) Egg-larva-nymph – adult
(b) Llarva-egg-adult
(c) Egg-nymph – adult
(d) Egg-nymph-larva-adult

606. Correct sequence of Life cycle of lice is
(a) Egg- nymph – larva-adult
(b) Egg-nymph -adult
(c) Nymph-larva – adult
(d) None

607. Acarology is the study of
(a) Mites (b) Ticks
(c) Both a and b (d) Snakes

608. Ascaris competes with host for
(a) Carbohydrate (b) protein
(c) Fat (d) Vitamin

609. . Pimply gut is peculiar to infection of
(a) Oesophagostomum
(b) Schistosoma
(c) Theileria
(d) Coccidia

610. Which one may cause abortion most likely?
(a) Sarcocystis (b) Milk fever
(c) Fasciola (d) Round worms

611. Which one arachnid is endoparasite?
(a) Red mite (b) Soft tick
(c) Air sac mite. (d) None

612. Mange mite belongs to
(a) Sarcoptiformes (b) Tombidiformes
(c) Ixodidae (d) Mesostigmata

613. Ciliates in rumen represent
(a) Innocuous parasitism
(b) Phoresis
(c) Predation
(d) Mutualism

614. Which one is monoxenous parasite?
(a) Haemophilus (b) Fasciola
(c) Trichinella (d) Theileria

615. Mice is paratinic host of
(a) Ascaridia (b) Toxocara canis
(c) Fasciola (d) Dicrocoelium

616. Strongyloides belongs to
(a) Ovoparous group
(b) Ovoviviparous group
(c) Larvaeparous group
(d) None

617. Which one is called as Pallisade Worm?
(a) Ascaridia (b) Strongylus
(c) Chabertia (d) None

618. Moniezia sp. is a
(a) Coccidia (b) Tapeworm
(c) Roundworm (d) None

619. Redwater fever is caused by
(a) Moniezia b Babesia
(c) Theileria (d) Anaplasma

620. Father of parasitology is
(a) F. Redi (b) Pasteur
(c) Rudolphi (d) Lamarck

621. Bacteria and amoebic cyst on legs of housefly and beetles represents which type of symbiosis-
(a) Mutation (b) Phoresis
(c) Predation (d) None

622. Choose the parasite with direct life cycle
(a) Heterakis (b) Chabertia
(c) Ascaridia (d) All of the above

623. Which species of Amblyoma cause 'Hard water' disease of cattle, sheep & goat -
(a) *Amblyoma habreum*
(b) *A. americana*
(c) *A. variegatum*
(d) All

624. Which species of Amblyoma is known as Bont tick?
(a) *Amblyoma habreum*
(b) *A. americana*
(c) *A. variegatum*
(d) All

625. Which species of Amblyoma is known as variegated tick?
(a) *Amblyoma habreum*
(b) *A. americana*

(c) *A. variegatum*
(d) All

626. Which species of Amblyoma is known as Tropical bont tick?
(a) *Amblyoma habreum*
(b) *A. americana*
(c) *A. variegatum*
(d) All

627. Which species of Amblyoma is known as Lone star tick?
(a) *Amblyoma habreum*
(b) *A. americana*
(c) *A. variegatum*
(d) All

628. Tick infestation in cattle may lead to -
(a) Tick worry (b) Tick paralysis
(c) Tick toxicosis (d) All

629. Sweating sickness in animals is caused due to infestation of -
(a) Ticks (b) Mites
(c) Lice (d) Fleas

630. Sweating sickness is cattle is mostly due to infestation of-
(a) Hyaloma spp
(b) Dermacenter spp
(c) Rhephicephalus spp
(d) Hemophysalis spp

631. Biological control of ticks can be done by the use of -
(a) Ants (b) Rodents
(c) Birds (d) All

632. Larvae of mites are known as -
(a) Harvest mites (b) Shigger mites
(c) Both (d) None

633. Which species of Trombicula is known as Harvest mite of Europe -
(a) *T. autumnalis* (b) *T. akanushi*
(c) *T. delhiences* (d) *T. sarcina*

634. Black soil itch of sheep is caused by which species of Trombicula.
(a) *T. autumnalis* (b) *T. akanushi*
(c) *T. delhicnces* (d) *T. sarcina*

635. Which of the mite is known as follicular mites -
(a) Trombicula (b) Demodex
(c) both (d) None

636. Which type of Demodicosis is known as Red mange -
(a) Squamous (b) Pustular
(c) Both (d) None

637. *Sarcoptes scabeii* causes -
(a) Mange in animals (b) Scabies in man
(c) Both (d) None

638. In male sarcoptes caruncles are present on which pair of legs -
(a) 1, 2, 4 (b) 1, 2
(c) 4 (d) All

639. In female sarcoptes caruncles are present on which pair of legs -
(a) 1, 2, 4 (b) 1, 2
(c) 4 (d) All

640. Dec planning itch in birds occurs due to -
(a) *Cnemidocoptes gallinae*
(b) *Cnemidocoptes mutans*
(c) Both
(d) None

641. Scaly leg in fowl occurs due to -
(a) *Chemidocoptes gallinae*
(b) *Cnemidocoptes mutans*
(c) Both
(d) None

642. Foot mange or itchy leg in horses is caused by.
(a) Chorioptes (b) Psoroptes
(c) Sarcoptes (d) Otodectes

643. Ear mange in carnivores is caused by -
(a) Chorioptes (b) Psoroptes
(c) Sarcoptes (d) Otodectes

644. Which one is known as Air sac mite -
(a) Cytodites (b) Otodectes
(c) Nematoderes (d) Psoroptes

645. *Linguatula serrata* is also known as -
(a) Whipworm (b) Gum worm
(c) Tongue worm (d) Gut worm

646. Anaplasma is transmitted by -
(a) Ixoded ticks (b) Tabanus
(c) Stomoxys (d) All

647. Hemoglobenuria is never seen in case of -
(a) Babeseoses (b) Theilereosis
(c) Anaplasmosis (d) All

648. Antibiotic of Choice in case of Anaplasmosis -
(a) Oxytetracyclene (b) Cefotaxim
(c) Gentamycine (d) Sulfadimedine

649. Hepatozoon canis is found in which cell -
(a) Neutrophill (b) Eosinophill
(c) Macrophage (d) Monocyte

650. Ehrlichia canis is found in which cell -
(a) Neutrophill (b) Eosinophill
(c) Macrophage (d) Monocyte

651. Which infection is known as tropical canine pancytopaenia -
(a) Babeseosis (b) Anaplasmosis
(c) Trypanosomosis (d) Ehrlichiosis

652. Which stage of toxoplasma is infective for IH -
(a) Tachyzoites (b) Bradyzoites
(c) Tissue cyst (d) All

653. In case of Sarcocystosis, which stage is infective for intermediate host -
(a) Sarcocyst (b) Sporozoite
(c) Tachyzoites (d) All

654. In case of Sarcocystosis which stage is infective for definitive host -
(a) Sarcocyst (b) Sporozoite
(c) Tachyzoites (d) All

655. Which Eimeria present biggest oocyte -
(a) *E. buckidnonensis* (b) *E. bores*
(c) *E. leukarti* (d) *E. parva*

656. Which Eimeria presents biggest oocyte in cattle & buffalo -
(a) *E. buckidnonensis* (b) *E. bores*
(c) *E. leukarti* (d) *E. parva*

657. Strongyloides causes -
(a) Foot rot in sheep
(b) parasitic gastroenterites in pigs
(c) Respiratory distress
(d) All

658. Which one is commonly known as whip worm -
(a) Ascaris (b) Oxyuris
(c) Trichuris (d) Moneizia

659. Rat tailed appearance in horses occur due to -
(a) Ascaris (b) Oxyuris
(c) Trichuris (d) Moneizia

660. During Trichuriasis mortality occurs only in -
(a) Sheep (b) Goat
(c) Horse (d) Pig

661. Infective stage for host in case of Trichuriasis is -
(a) L_1 (b) L_2
(c) L_3 (d) L_4

662. Which of the following is known as Barber's pole disease -
(a) Trichurliasis (b) Hemonchosis
(c) Strongyloidosis (d) Moneizia infection

663. Which mineral deficiency makes animals less susceptible for Hemonchosis-
(a) Cu (b) Co
(c) Mn (d) Mg

664. Infective larvae in case of hemonchosis is -
(a) L_1 (b) L_2
(c) L_3 (d) L_4

665. L_4 of Hemonchos undergoes histotropism in -
(a) Rumen (b) Liver
(c) Kidney (d) Abomasum

666. L_4 of Hemonchos takes how much blood/day -
(a) 0.05 ml (b) 0.5 ml
(c) 0.2 ml (d) 02 ml

667. What changes can be seen in case of animal suffering with Hemonchosis -
(a) Increase in abomasal pH
(b) Increase in pepsinogen level
(c) Malabsorption
(d) All

668. Nodule formation at the junction of jejeinum & duodenum occur due to infection of -
(a) Stilesia (b) Oesophagostomum
(c) Amoebotaenia (d) Ancylostoma

669. Nodular tapeworm disease of fowl is caused by -
(a) Raillietina (b) Daveinea
(c) Echinobothridia (d) None

670. Canine heart worm disease is caused by -
(a) *Ancy lostoma* (b) *Hepatozoon canis*
(c) *Amoeba taenia* (d) *Dirofilaria immitis*

671. Adult *Dirofilaria immitis* is found in -
(a) Myocardium (b) Atrium
(c) Pulmonary trunk (d) Ventricle

672. Which one acts as intermediate host for *Dirofilaria immitis* -
(a) Ant (b) Beetle
(c) Mosquito (d) Musca

673. *Dirofilaria immitis* is present in which side of heart-
(a) Right (b) Left
(c) Both (d) Any

674. Venacaval syndrome due to *Dirofilaria immitis* refers to -
(a) Hemolysis (b) Haemoglobinuria
(c) Bilirubenemia (d) All

675. Which drug should be given when microfilarae are present in blood.
(a) Diaminazine aceturate
(b) Thiasitarsamide
(c) Oxytetracycline
(d) All

676. Cooked rice grain like segments in faeces indicate which infection -
(a) Avitellina (b) Moneizia
(c) Stilesia (d) All

677. An Ancylostoma can suck how much blood/day.
(a) 0.1 ml (b) 0.01 ml
(c) 0.2 ml (d) 1 ml

678. Ancylostoma infection occurs in dogs of which age -
(a) < 1yr (b) < 2 yr
(c) 6 month (d) 3 month

679. Which of the following is known as globose mite -
(a) Psoroptes (b) Sarcorptes
(c) Chorioptes (d) Cnemidocoptes

680. Which one is known as Red mite of poultry -
(a) *Dermanyssces gallinae*
(b) *Cnemidocoptes gallinae*
(c) Choreoptes
(d) Sarcoptes

681. What % of benzylbenzoate is used for the treatment of mites -
(a) 1% (b) 2%
(c) 5% (d) 10%

682. Which one is known as soft tick of poultry?
(a) *Dermanyssus gallinae*
(b) *Cnemidocqptes gallinae*
(c) *Argas persicus*
(d) All

683. Which stage of *Hepatozoon canis* is found in neutrophill?
(a) Schizont (b) Gamont
(c) Sporozoite (d) Any

684. Nucleus of gamont of *Hepatozoon canis* stains -
(a) Pink (b) Violet
(c) Icy blue (d) Yellow

685. Cytoplasm of gamont of *Hepatozoon canis* stains -
(a) Pink (b) Violet
(c) Icy blue (d) Yellow

686. *Pulex irretants* is a flea which infects.
(a) Man (b) Horse
(c) Pig (d) Cattle

687. Which stage of Hepatozoon occurs in dog -
(a) Syngamy (b) Schizogony
(c) Sporogony (d) All

688. Infection of *Hepatozoon canis* in dog occurs by -
(a) Accidental ingestion
(b) Transovarian
(c) Coitus
(d) Skin penetration

689. Which of the following is a Reduvid bug -
(a) Rhodinus (b) Triatoma
(c) Penstrongylus (d) All

690. Which Trypanosoma is an intracellular parasite?
(a) *T. evansi* (b) *T. brucei*
(c) *T. cruzi* (d) *T. vivax*

691. In macrophages which form of trypanosoma is found -
(a) Epimastigote (b) Promastigote
(c) Amastigote (d) Trypomastigote

692. In reduvid bug which form of Trypanosomes are found -
(a) Epimastigote (b) Promastigote
(c) Amastigote (d) Trypomastigote

693. Flea jumps with the help of -
(a) First pair of legs (b) Third pair of legs
(c) Wings (d) Halters

694. First & second spine of genal comb is of equal size in -
(a) *Ctenocephalidis canis*
(b) *Ctenocephalides felis*
(c) *Xenopsiella cheopis*
(d) All

695. 1st spine is ½ in length of 2nd spine of genal comb in -

(a) *Ctenocephalidis canis*
(b) *Ctenocephalides felis*
(c) *Xenopsiella cheopis*
(d) All

696. Genal combs are absent in -
(a) *Ctenocephalidis canis*
(b) *Ctenocephalides felis*
(c) *Ceratophylus gallinae*
(d) All

697. *Strongyle spp.* in horses is found in -
(a) Intestine (b) Mesenteric artery
(c) Lymph node (d) Muscles

698. Strongyloses in horses is also known as -
(a) Red worm infection
(b) Hook worm infection
(c) Black worm infection
(d) Whip worm infection

699. Verminous arteritis in horses is caused by -
(a) Strongyle worms
(b) Oxyures equi
(c) Trypanosoma equiperdum
(d) None

700. Infective larvae for horses in case of strongylosis.
(a) L_1 (b) L_2
(c) L_3 (d) All

701. Larvae of which species of Strongyle spends 3months of it's life cycle in hepatorenal ligament-
(a) *S. edentatus* (b) *S. equinus*
(c) *S. vulgaris* (d) All

702. Infective larva in case of Ascarias is -
(a) L_1 (b) L_2
(c) L_3 (d) L_4

703. Thin sow syndrome occurs due to infection of -
(a) *Hyostrongylus rubidus*
(b) *Ascarops strongylena*
(c) *Ascarops dentata*
(d) All

704. Which of the following parasites leads to Rhabditis in cattle?
(a) *Pelodera strongyloides*
(b) *Strongylus vulgaris*
(c) *Strongylus edentatus*
(d) *Hyostrongylus rubidus*

705. Hemonchus contortus in ruminants is known as -
(a) Stomach worm (b) Wire worm
(c) both (d) None

706. What % of $K_2Cr_2O_4$ is used for sporulation of coccidian oocyst?
(a) 1% (b) 2.5%
(c) 5% (d) 2%

707. Critical test is used for the studies of -
(a) *Dictyocaulus viviparous*
(b) *Fasciola hepatica*
(c) Both
(d) None

708. What % of alcohol is used for preservation of fleas?
(a) 10% (b) 50%
(c) 70% (d) 100%

709. Oocyst of *Cryptosporidium parvum* can be destroyed by -
(a) 10% formalin (b) 5% NH_4OH
(c) 5% NaOH (d) All

710. Vaccination of *Toxoplasma gondii* is done using which strain -
(a) S_{40} (b) S_{19}
(c) S_{48} (d) T_{48}

711. Cryptosporidiasis is most prevalent in which age group of animals -
(a) Adults (b) 5-30 days
(c) 6 months (d) All ages

712. Oocyst wall formation in case of coccidia occurs in -
(a) Intestine (b) Environment
(c) Both (d) Any where

713. Oocyst wall formation in case of Cryptosporidiasis occurs in -
(a) Intestine (b) Environment
(c) Both (d) Any where

714. Count of oocyst per gm. of faeces considered clinical in case of Cryptosporidiasis is -
(a) 10^2 (b) 10^3-10^4
(c) 10^5-10^7 (d) 10^{10}-10^{12}

715. Loose and frequent faces are characteristic of which infection.
(a) Ascariasis (b) Coccidiasis
(c) Giadiasis (d) Cryptosporidiasis

716. Mucus with soft dropping is characteristic of which infection.

(a) Ascariasis (b) Cocidiosis
(c) Giardiasis (d) Cryptosporidiasis

717. Cysts of giardia consist of -
(a) Trophozoites (b) Merozoites
(c) Bradyzoites (d) All

718. Which of the following is known as Lancet fluke-
(a) Fasciola (b) Fascioloides
(c) Dicrocoelium (d) Gigantocotyle

719. Surra in Asia & Africa is caused by
(a) *Trypanosoma evansi*
(b) *Trypanosoma vivax*
(c) Both
(d) None

720. Surra in Latin America is caused by -
(a) *T. evansi* (b) *T. vivax*
(c) Both (d) None

721. Stilbamedine test is used for the diagnosis of -
(a) Trypanosomosis (b) Babesiosis
(c) Anaplasmosis (d) Theileriosis

722. Sabin-feld men dye test is used for the diagnosis of -
(a) Trypanosomosis (b) Toxoplasmosis
(c) Babesiosis (d) Coccidiosis

723. Genal & pronotal combs are absent in -
(a) Xenopsiella cheopis
(b) Ceratophyllus
(c) Ctenocephalidis canis
(d) Ctenocephalidis felis

724. Genal combs are absent but pronotal combs are present in -
(a) *Xenopsiella cheopis*
(b) Ceratophyllus
(c) *Ctenocephaldis canis*
(d) *Ctenocephalidis felis*

725. Which of the following is not an intracellular parasite?
(a) Leishmania (b) *Trypanosoma cruzi*
(c) Babesia (d) None

726. How many segments are present in Abdomen of lice?
(a) 7 (b) 8
(c) 9 (d) 10

727. How many segments are present in abdomen of flea?
(a) 7 (b) 8
(c) 9 (d) 10

728. Saliva of flea acts as -
(a) Antigen (b) Hapten
(c) Antibody (d) Epitope

729. Fleabite allergy occurs when saliva of flea binds with -
(a) RBC (b) WBC
(c) Skin collagen (d) Actin & myosin

730. Minimum time required by coccidian oocyst to sporulate in $K_2Cr_2O_4$ is -
(a) 1 week (b) 2 week
(c) 20 days (d) 1 month

731. Parasite which lodges accidentally in a site others than it's natural site of predilection is called -
(a) Accidental parasite
(b) Abberant parasite
(c) Both
(d) None

732. Parasite which lodges accidentally in a host other than it's natural host is called-
(a) Accidental parasite
(b) Abberant parasite
(c) Both
(d) None

733. How many nucleuses are present in cyst of *Entamoeba coli*?
(a) 4 (b) 8
(c) 10 (d) 12

734. How many nucleuses are present in cyst of *Entamoeba histolytica*?
(a) 4 (b) 8
(c) 10 (d) 12

735. Which one is commonly known as fringed tapeworm -
(a) *Thysanosoma actiniodes*
(b) Thysaneizia
(c) Avitellina
(d) Stilezia

736. Which of the following can be used as fixatives for the mount of Nematodes -
(a) Corrosive acetic solution
(b) Bouins picroformal solution
(c) Formal acetic acid
(d) All

737. Which of the following are difficult to stain & mount in DPX or canadabalsam-
(a) Nematodes (b) Cestodes
(c) Trematodes (d) All

738. *Opisthorchic tenuicollis* is commonly known as -
(a) Cat liver fluke
(b) Dog liver fluke
(c) Poultry liver fluke
(d) Cattle liver fluke

739. Which one is known as Giant liver fluke -
(a) *Fasciola gigantica* (b) *Fasciola hepatica*
(c) *Fasciola jacksoni* (d) *Fasciolopsis buski*

740. Which one is known as Giant intestinal fluke -
(a) *F. gigantica* (b) *F. jacksoni*
(c) *F. hepatica* (d) *Fasciolopsis buski*

741. Ingestion of calthrops & water chestnut may lead to which infection in man -
(a) *F. gigantica* (b) *F. Jacksoni*
(c) *F. hepatica* (d) *Fasciolopsis buski*

742. Which of the following act as I & II intermediate host of Echinochasmus respectively -
(a) Snail, fish (b) Ant, snail
(c) Fish, snail (d) Ant, fish

743. Which of the following is commonly known as oriental lung fluke?
(a) Echunostoma (b) Echinochasmus
(c) Notocotylus (d) Paragonimus

744. Which of the following act as I & II intermediate host of Paragonimus respectively-
(a) Snail, crab (b) Crab, fish
(c) Snail, fish (d) Crab, ant

745. Which of the following is known as 'Rumen fluke'?
(a) *Paramphistomum cervi*
(b) *Cotylophoron cotylophoron*
(c) *Gastrothylax crumenifer*
(d) All

746. Which one is known as 'Biliary amphistome'?
(a) *Gastrothylax crumenifer*
(b) *Gigantocotyl explanatum*
(c) Gastrodiscus
(d) None

747. Which Fluke is found in colon of elephants?
(a) *Gastrodiscus aegyptiacus*
(b) *Gastrodiscus secundus*
(c) *Fischoederius elongatus*
(d) *Oliveria indica*

748. Which species of Schistosoma uses Lymnaea species of snail as intermediate host?
(a) *S. Spindale* (b) *S. nasale*
(c) *S. indicum* (d) *S. incognitum*

749. Which species of Schistosoma is not found in mesenteric & portal veins?
(a) *S. spindale* (b) *S. nasale*
(c) *S. indicum* (d) None

750. Male of which species of Schistosoma has atuberculate tegument -
(a) *S. spindale* (b) *S. nasale*
(c) *S. indicum* (d) None

751. In which species of Schistosoma ovary is post-equitorial.
(a) *S. spindale* (b) *S. nasale*
(c) *S. indicum* (d) *S. incognitum*

752. Boomerang shaped eggs are laid by which species of Schistosoma -
(a) *S. spindale* (b) *S. nasale*
(c) *S. indicum* (d) *S. incognitum*

753. Napolean hat shaped eggs are laid by which species of Schistosoma -
(a) *S. spindale* (b) *S. nasale*
(c) *S. indicium* (d) *S. incognitum*

754. Cercariae of blood flukes have bravicaudum tail in which case -
(a) Avian (b) Mammalian
(c) both (d) None

755. Cercariae of blood flukes have longicaudum tail in which case.
(a) Avian (b) Mammalian
(c) both (d) None

756. Cercareae of blood flukes have ocellate nervous system in which case -
(a) Avian (b) Mammalian
(c) Both (d) None

757. Cercariae of blood flukes have non-ocellate nervous system in which case -
(a) Avian (b) Mammalian
(c) both (d) None

758. Which of the following is smallest tapeworm of

equines?
(a) *Paranoplocephala mammillana*
(b) *Anoplocephala perfoliata*
(c) both
(d) None

759. Which one is known as Dwarf tapeworm of horses?
(a) *Paranoplocephala mammillana*
(b) *Anoplocephala perfoliata*
(c) both
(d) None

760. Lappet below each sucker is present in which one-
(a) *Anoplocephala perfoliata*
(b) *Paranoplocephala mammillana*
(c) *Anoplocephala manga*
(d) All

761. Slit like suckers are found in which of the following -
(a) *Anoplocephala perfoliata*
(b) *Paranoplocephala mammillan*
(c) *Anoplocephala magna*
(d) All

762. Which of the following has single genitalia in each segment?
(a) Moneizia (b) Thysanosoma
(c) Stilesia (d) Avitellina

763. Which of the following has double genitalia in each segment?
(a) Moneizia (b) Thysanosoma
(c) Both a and b (d) None

764. How many paruterine organs are present per gravid segment in Stilesia -
(a) 1 (b) 2
(c) 5 (d) Many

765. Which of the following is zoonotic?
(a) Echinococcus (b) Hymenolepis
(c) Taenia (d) All

766. Echinococcus uses which one as organs of attachment.
(a) Suckers (b) Bothria
(c) both (d) None

767. Diphyllobothrium uses which one as organs of attachment.
(a) Suckers (b) Bothria
(c) both (d) None

768. Which segment of Echinococcus is mature & contains genital organs?
(a) 1st (b) Penultimate
(c) Ultimate (d) All

769. Ovary of Echinococcus is - shaped -
(a) Spherical (b) Kidney
(c) Boomerang (d) Spindle

770. Which ascarid worm is found in large intestine of definitive host?
(a) Ascaris (b) Heterakes
(c) Toxocara (d) Ascaridea

771. Oesophagus of which of the following canine ascarid worm lacks posterior bulb-
(a) *Toxocara canis* (b) Toxocara cati
(c) *Toxocara leonina* (d) All

772. Egg shell of which Toxocara is smooth -
(a) *T. canis* (b) *T. cati*
(c) *T. leonina* (d) All

773. Lips are divided into anterior & posterior parts in which of the following-
(a) *Ascaris suum* (b) *Parascaris equorum*
(c) *Toxocara vitulorum* (d) All

774. Male of which of the following lacks bursa -
(a) Strongyloides (b) Strongylus
(c) Chabertia (d) Oesophagostomum

775. Which of the following are voracious blood sucker?
(a) Strongy loides (b) Strongylus
(c) Chabertia (d) Oesophagostomum

776. Which of the following produce nodules in large intestine of their host?
(a) Storngyloides (b) Strongylus
(c) Chabertia (d) Oesophagostomum

777. Which of the following are mucosal plug feeders?
(a) Strongylus (b) Chabertia
(c) Oesophagostomum (d) None

778. 2 rows of corona radiata are present in -
(a) Strongylus (b) Oesophagostomum
(c) Chabertia (d) All

779. Which species of strongyle worms are characterized by absence of teeth -
(a) *S. vulgaris* (b) *S. edentatus*
(c) *S. equinus* (d) All

780. Which species of strongyle is characterized by

the presence of 3 chitinous teeth in buccal capsule-
(a) *S. vulgaris* (b) *S. edentatus*
(c) *S. equinus* (d) All

781. Which species of strongyle is characterized by the presence of 2 ear-shaped teeth in buccal capsule?
(a) *S. vulgaris* (b) *S. edentatus*
(c) *S. equinus* (d) All

782. Which of the following is known as Kidney worm of pigs?
(a) Stephanurus (b) Syngamus
(c) Agristomum (d) Ancylostoma

783. Which one is known as gape worm?
(a) Stephanurus (b) Syngamus
(c) Ancylostoma (d) Bunostomum

784. Which one causes cutaneous larva migrans in man?
(a) Ancylostoma (b) Agriostomum
(c) Stephanurus (d) Syngamus

785. *Syngamus trachea* is found in permanent copulation & give appearance of which letter -
(a) L (b) Y
(c) M (d) A

786. *Hemonchus contortus* is also know as -
(a) Stomach worm (b) Wire worm
(c) Bancrupt worm (d) All

787. Which one is known as Black scour worm -
(a) *Ostertagia ostertagi*
(b) *Trichostrongylus colubriformis*
(c) *Cooperia curticel*
(d) *Paracooperia*

788. Which of the following is also known as geohelminth?
(a) Dictyocaulus (b) Protostrongylus
(c) Mullerius (d) None

789. Which of the following can be grouped under biohelminth?
(a) Proto strongylus (b) Muellerius
(c) Metastrongylus (d) All

790. Which one can be found in aorta of carnivores?
(a) Habronema (b) Thelazia
(c) Spirocerca (d) Gongylonema

791. Which one can be found in conjunctional sac or lacrymal duct of mammals & birds?
(a) Habronema (b) Oxiuris
(c) Spirocerca (d) Gongylonema

792. Which one is found in conjunctival sac or lacrymal duct of mammals & birds?
(a) Habronema (b) Thelazia
(c) Spirocerca (d) Gongylonema

793. Which one is found in rumen of ruminants & crop of fowl?
(a) Habronema (b) Thelazia
(c) Spirocerca (d) Gongylonema

794. Which one is known as Eye worm?
(a) Habronema (b) Thelazia
(c) Spirocerca (d) Gongylonema

795. *Gongylonema pulchrum* is also known as -
(a) Gullet worm
(b) Zigzag worm
(c) Tailor stitch worms
(d) All

796. Larvae of Habronema causes -
(a) Summer sores (b) Granular dermatitis
(c) Bursati (d) All

797. Bursati is caused by the larva of -
(a) Habronema (b) Thelazia
(c) Spirocerca (d) All

798. Which of the following causes Hump-sore?
(a) Dirofilaria (b) Stephanofilaria
(c) Stephanurus (d) Setaria

799. Which parasite leads to the formation of nodules or worm nest in the skin?
(a) Onchocerca (b) Setaria
(c) Stephanofilaria (d) None

800. In sheep & goat Setaria causes-
(a) Cerebrospinal nematodiasis
(b) Kumri
(c) Lumber paralysis
(d) All

801. Which of the following is known as Guinea – worm?
(a) Dracunculus (b) Trichinella
(c) Trichuris (d) Dioctophyma

802. Which of the following is known as whip worm?
(a) Dracunculus (b) Trichinella
(c) Trichuris (d) Dioctophyma

803. Which of the following is known as kidney worm?

(a) Dracunculus (b) Trichinella
(c) Trichuris (d) Dioctophyma

804. Macracanthorhynchus is commonly known as -
(a) Kidney worm
(b) Thorny headed worm
(c) Guinea worm
(d) Whipworm

805. Where does the adult female of Drancunculus reside -
(a) Subcut connective tissue
(b) Muscles
(c) Intestine
(d) Caecal mucosa

806. Paralysis of respiratory muscles may be associated with which parasitic infection-
(a) Dracunculus (b) Trichinella
(c) Trichuris (d) All

807. Dephtheritic inflammation of caecal mucosa is associated with -
(a) Dracunculus (b) Trichinella
(c) Trichuris (d) None

808. Granuloma formation at the site of attachment in intestine is associated with -
(a) Dracunculus
(b) Macracathorhynchus
(c) Trichuris
(d) All

809. How many intermediate host are required in Life Cycle of members of order spirurida.
(a) 1 (b) 2
(c) 3 (d) 4

810. Which of the following is a member of Trichostrongylidae?
(a) Ostertagia (b) Mullereus
(c) Oxyuris (d) Gongylonema

811. Which of the following is a member of Protostrongyliae?
(a) Ostertagia (b) Mullereus
(c) Oxyuris (d) Gongylonema

812. Which of the following is not an ascarid worm?
(a) Hetuabis (b) Oxyuris
(c) Ostertagia (d) None

813. Which of the following is not a member of Ancylostomatidae?
(a) Ancylostoma (b) Agreistomun
(c) Bunostomum (d) All

814. Outermost covering of body is called Tegument in -
(a) Trematode (b) Cestode
(c) Nematode (d) Both a & b

815. Outermost covering of body is called cuticle in -
(a) Trematode (b) Cestode
(c) Nematode (d) All

816. Internal organs remain embedded in parenchyma in -
(a) Trematode (b) Cestode
(c) Both (d) Nematode

817. Internal organs bath in perienteric fluid in -
(a) Trematodes (b) Cestodes
(c) both (d) Nematodes

818. Anus is absent in cases of -
(a) Nematodes (b) Trematodes
(c) both (d) None

819. Whole digestive system is absent in -
(a) Trematodes (b) Nematodes
(c) Cestodes (d) All

820. Members of which of the following are hermaphrodites -
(a) Trematodes (b) Cestodes
(c) Nematodes (d) Both a & b

821. Which of the following are monoecious -
(a) Trematodes (b) Cestodes
(c) Both (d) Nematodes

822. Which of the following are known as pseudo tape worms?
(a) Eucestoda (b) Cotyloda
(c) Cestoda (d) Trematoda

823. Life cycle of which of the following tape worm is direct -
(a) *Ascaridia galli* (b) *Taenia solium*
(c) *Hymenolepis nana* (d) All

824. Cuticle is modified to form circular thickenings in case of -
(a) Gongylonema (b) Hemonchus
(c) ancylostoma (d) None

825. Buccal cavity posses three pairs of teeth in -
(a) Ancylostoma (b) Bunostomum
(c) Hemonchus (d) All

826. Cutting plates are present in buccal cavity in -
(a) Bunostomum (b) Ancylostoma
(c) Hemonchus (d) All

827. Lasscets are present in buccal cavity in -
(a) Bunostomum (b) Ancylostoma
(c) Hemonchus (d) All

828. Nematodes may be
(a) Oviparous (b) Ovoviviparous
(c) Larviparous (d) All

829. What is the side of predilection of Leishmania -
(a) Macrophages
(b) Liver & Caeca
(c) Reproductive tract
(d) Erythrocytes

830. *Theileria spp* can be found in -
(a) Lymphocytes (b) Lymphoblasts
(c) Erythrocytes (d) All

831. Babesia can be found in -
(a) Lymphocytes (b) Lymphoblasts
(c) Erthrocytes (d) All

832. Which of the following can be found intracellularly in liver & caeca?
(a) Leishmania
(b) *Tritrichomonas foetus*
(c) *Histomonas meleagridis*
(d) *Entamoeba histolytica*

833. Which of the following insects are wingless?
(a) Lice (b) Sheep ked
(c) Fleas (d) All

834. Which of the following undergo complete metamorphosis?
(a) Mosquitoes (b) Fleas
(c) Housefly (d) All

835. Which one undergoes incomplete metamorphosis?
(a) Mosquitoes (b) Fleas
(c) Housefly (d) Lice

836. How many pairs of legs are presents in an adult insect?
(a) 3 (b) 4
(c) 5 (d) 6

837. How many pairs of legs are present in larvae of an insect?
(a) 3 (b) 4
(c) 5 (d) 6

838. Which solution can be used to preserve ticks in their natural colours?
(a) Chloroform in 10% formalin
(b) Formalin in 10% chloroforms
(c) 30% acetic acid
(d) 20% formalin

839. Mites can be stored in which solution -
(a) 70% alcohol (b) 5% glycerol
(c) Both (d) None

840. To digest the tissue debris, skin scrappings are boiled in which solution -
(a) 10% KOH (b) 15% KOH
(c) 20% KOH (d) 100% KOH

841. Which one acts as II intermediate host in the life cycle of *Dicrocoelium dendriticum*?
(a) Ants (b) Grasshopper
(c) Crab (d) Fish

842. Indoplanorbis (snail) acts as intermediate host in Life Cycle of -
(a) *Fasiola gigantica*
(b) Amphistomes
(c) *Dicrocoelium dendriticum*
(d) All

843. Bulinus species of snail acts as intermediate host in case of -
(a) Amphistomes (b) Dicrocoeliem
(c) Echinostoma (d) Echinochasmus

844. Naids of Dragon fly act as II intermediate host in case of -
(a) Echinostoma (b) Dicrocoelium
(c) Prosthogonimus (d) All

845. Which one acts as II intermediate host in case of *Eurytrema pancreaticum*?
(a) Grass hoppers (b) Fish
(c) Ant (d) Crabs

846. Bithynia species of snail acts as intermediate host for -
(a) Opisthorchis (b) Echinochasmus
(c) both (d) Notocotylus

847. Lymnaea species of snail acts as intermediate host for
(a) Schistosomes
(b) Echinostoma revolutum

(c) Fasciola gigantica
(d) All

848. Snail may act as both I & II intermediate host in case of -
(a) *Echinostoma revolutum*
(b) Echinochasmus
(c) Prosthogonimus
(d) Notocolylus

849. There is no II intermediate host in case of -
(a) Schistosomes (b) Notocotylus
(c) Fasciolopsis (d) All

850. Which species of snail acts as intermediate host for *Eurytrema pancreaticum*?
(a) Brady baena (b) Bithynia
(c) Lymnaea (d) Bulinus

851. Which of the following require 2 IH for completing their life cycle?
(a) Cestodes (b) Cotylodes
(c) Both (d) None

852. Which of the following have cysticercoid as their metacestode stage?
(a) Anoplocephalidea (b) Davaineidea
(c) Dilepididea (d) All

853. Which of the following doesn't have cysticercus as its metacestode stage?
(a) *T. solium* (b) *T. saginata*
(c) *T. ovis* (d) *T. multiceps*

854. Which metacestode shows single evaginated scolex withdrawn into a vesicle with no cavity?
(a) Cysticercoid (b) Cysticercus
(c) Coenurus (d) Hydatid cyst

855. Which metacestode stage shows single scolex invaginated into a fluid containing bladder & vesicle?
(a) Cysticercoid (b) Cysticercus
(c) Coenurus (d) Hydatid cyst

856. Which metacestode is a large fluid containing bladder with many invaginated scolices arranged in clusters?
(a) Cysticercoid (b) Cysticercus
(c) Coenurus (d) Hydatid cyst

857. Which metacestode is a large fluid containing bladder with many daughter cysts which contain brood capsules with many invaginated scolices?
(a) Cysticercoid (b) Cysticercus
(c) Coenurus (d) Hydatid cyst

858. Which metacestode is a single non-invaginated scolex, attached to a fluid containing bladder by a long segmented strobila?
(a) Strobilocercus (b) Procercoid
(c) Plerocercoid (d) All

859. Which metacestode is a solid bodied metacestode with hooks in cercomer region?
(a) Strobilocercus (b) Procercoid
(c) Plerocercoid (d) All

860. Which metacestode is elongate, solid bodied metacestode with bothria in the scolex?
(a) Strobilocercus (b) Procercoid
(c) Pleurocercoid (d) None

861. *Taenia taeniaeformis* shows which metacestode -
(a) Strobilocercus (b) Procercoid
(c) Pleurocercoid (d) None

862. Catarrhal enteritis in ruminants may be associated with -
(a) Coccidiosis
(b) Gastro-intestinal nematodes
(c) Both
(d) None

863. Nodules in intestine of ruminants may be due to -
(a) Oesophagostomum
(b) Spirocerca
(c) Mullerius
(d) Hemonchus

864. Nodules in esophagus of dog may be associated with -
(a) Paracooperia (b) *Spirocerea lupi*
(c) Mullerius (d) None

865. Nodules in intestine of poultry may be due to -
(a) Paracooperia (b) Coccidea
(c) *Ascaridia galli* (d) Raillietina

866. *Oxyuris spp.* is also called as
(a) Pin worm (b) Caecal worm
(c) Hookworm (d) None of above

867. Nodules in lungs of sheep & goat may be due to -
(a) Hermonchus (b) Mullerius
(c) Coccidia (d) None

868. Ulcers in abomasum of sheep & goat may be due to -

(a) Hemonchus (b) Mullerius
(c) Coccidia (d) None

869. Circumscribed necrotic areas on liver on poultry indicate which infection -
(a) Hemonchus (b) Coccidia
(c) Histomonas (d) Thelazia

870. Which parasitic infection may lead to dermatitis?
(a) Fasciolosis (b) Histomonas
(c) Stephanofilaria (d) Stephanurus

871. Typhlitis in poultry can be associated with -
(a) Coccidia (b) Histomonas
(c) Both (d) None

872. Which of the following can be used for preservation of helminthes?
(a) 70% alcohol (b) 5-10% formalin
(c) Both (d) None

873. Which type of blood smear is used to see intercellular parasites?
(a) Wet smear
(b) Microhematocrit test
(c) Thin smear
(d) All

874. Which type of blood smear is mostly used to see intracellular parasites?
(a) Wet smear
(b) Microhematocrit test
(c) Thin smear
(d) All

875. For preparing thin blood smear, the spreader slide should be at which angle -
(a) 10° (b) 20-30°
(c) 30°-40° (d) 90°

876. For how much time the dry smear should be fixed in absolute methanol before staining -
(a) 1 minute (b) 30 sec-1 minute
(c) 1 seconds (d) Indefinite

877. What dilution of Giemsa stain should be used?
(a) 1 : 10 (b) 1 : 20
(c) 1 : 25 (d) 1 : 30

878. What should be the pH of distilled water used for diluting giemsa stain to stain mammalian blood -
(a) 6.5-6.7 (b) 7-7.2
(c) 1 (d) 5-6

879. What should be the pH of distilled water used for diluting giemsa stain to stain avian blood -
(a) 6.5-6.7 (b) 7-7.2
(c) 5.5-6.5 (d) 2-4

880. Which of the following stains does not require fixation with alcohol before staining?
(a) Leishman (b) Wright's
(c) Both (d) Giemsa

881. Which of the following is not Romanowsky stain?
(a) Leishman (b) Wright's
(c) Both (d) Giemsa

882. Which type of blood smear is preferred when there is low parasitemia?
(a) Thin smear (b) Thick smear
(c) Wet smear (d) None

883. Which of the following is not a qualitative method of faecal sample examination?
(a) Direct smear
(b) Concentration method
(c) Mac master's egg counting slide
(d) None

884. Which of the following solutions can be used for floation of helminth eggs?
(a) Saturated NaCl solution
(b) 33% $Znso_4$ solution
(c) Sheather's sugar solution
(d) All

885. 33% $ZnSO_4$ solution cannot float eggs of which helminths-
(a) Nematodes (b) Trematodes
(c) Cestodes (d) All

886. Which of the following solution can float fluke egg?
(a) Saturated NaCl solution
(b) Saturated $ZnSO_4$
(c) 33% $ZnSO_4$ solution
(d) Sheather's sugar solution

887. What is the quantity of floatation method used in concentration method?
(a) 5 ml (b) 10 ml
(c) 12 ml (d) 15 ml

888. What is the volume of the chamber under one of the squares in McMaster egg counting slide?
(a) 0.1 ml (b) 0.12 ml
(c) 0.15 ml (d) 0.2 ml

889. 0.15 ml faecal suspension represents how many grams of faeces-
(a) 1 gm (b) 1/100 gm
(c) 1/1000 gm (d) 0.0001 gm

890. What is the common multiple factor for Normal pelleted faeces of sheep?
(a) 1x egg/gm of faeces
(b) 1-1.5 x egg/gm of faeces
(c) 2 x egg /gm of faeces
(d) 4 x egg /gm of faeces

891. What is the common multiple factor for soft formed faeces of sheep?
(a) 1x egg/gm of faeces
(b) 1-1.5 x egg/gm of faeces
(c) 2 x egg /gm of faeces
(d) 4 x egg /gm of faeces

892. What is the common multiple factor for soft formed faeces of sheep?
(a) 1x egg/gm of faeces
(b) 1-1.5 x egg/gm of faeces
(c) 2 x egg /gm of faeces
(d) 4 x egg / gm of faeces

893. What is the common multiple factors used for diarrhoeic faeces of sheep?
(a) 1x egg/gm of faeces
(b) 1-1.5 x egg/gm of faeces
(c) 2 x egg /gm of faeces
(d) 4 x egg /gm of faeces

894. Baermann technique is used for separation of which larvae-
(a) Nematode (b) Trematode
(c) Cestode (d) Cotylod

895. What is the specific gravity of saturated NaCl solution?
(a) 1.20 (b) 1.30
(c) 1.25 (d) 0.89

896. Which of the following is not used in the preparation of lactophenol?
(a) Lactic acid (b) Crabolic acid
(c) Glycerine (d) Phenol

897. Solution used for destaining of overstained helminth parasite does not contain-
(a) 70% ethyl alcohol (b) Concentrated HCL
(c) Phenol (d) None

898. Which one acts as II IH for Echinochasmus perfoliatus?
(a) Fish (b) Crab
(c) Ant (d) Grasshopper

899. Stagnicola species of snail acts as I IH for-
(a) Echinostoma revolution
(b) Echinochasmus perfoliatus
(c) Prosthogonimus
(d) Opisthorchis

900. Trichinella can be found in-
(a) Tongue
(b) Intercostal muscles
(c) Diapharagmatic muscles
(d) All

901. Tandem testes are found in which of the following-
(a) *Dicrocoelium dendriticum*
(b) *Heterophyes heterophyes*
(c) *Eurytrema paneraticum*
(d) *Prosthogonimus ovatus*

902. Second intermediate host in case of *Heterophyes heterophyes* is-
(a) Fish (b) Crab
(c) Grasshopper (d) Ant

903. Carcinoma of liver & pancreas can be associated with-
(a) Prosthogonimus (b) Heterophyes
(c) Eurytrema (d) Dicrocoelium

904. Egg production is hampered due to which of the following parasite-
(a) Dicrocoelium (b) Eurytrema
(c) Heterophyes (d) Prosthogonimus

905. Which of the following does not posses horizontal tests?
(a) Prosthogonimus (b) Heterophyes
(c) Eurytrema (d) Dicrocoelium

906. Fasciolopsis buski has which type of testes-
(a) Verticle (b) Horizontal
(c) Tandem (d) Irregular

907. Second intermediate host in case of Echinochasmus is-
(a) Snail (b) Crab
(c) Fresh water fish (d) All

908. Second intermediate host in case of Paragonimus

is-
(a) Snail (b) Crab
(c) Fish (d) Ant

909. Which of the following is a monostome?
(a) Notocotylus (b) Paragonimus
(c) Echinochasmus (d) All

910. Ventral Sucker is larger & present in anterior one third of body in case of -
(a) Echinostoma (b) Echinochasmus
(c) Both (d) None

911. Cysts are Hazel nut shaped in case of-
(a) Echinostoma (b) Echinochasmus
(c) Paragonimus (d) Notocotylus

912. Cyst of paragonimus westermanni is found in -
(a) Lungs (b) Kidney
(c) Crop (d) Gizzard

913. Watery diarrhoea & edema in animals is associated with-
(a) Fasciolosis (b) Fasciolopsis
(c) Amphistomes (d) All

914. Testes are diagonal in case of-
(a) *Cotylophoron cotylophoron*
(b) *Gigantocotyle explanatum*
(c) *Gastrothylax crumenifer*
(d) *Fischoederices elongatus*

915. Genital pore is present infront of intestinal bifurcation in-
(a) *Gastodiscus aegyptiacus*
(b) *Gastrodiscus secundus*
(c) Both
(d) None

916. Genital pore is present below the intestinal bifurcation in case of-
(a) *Gastrodiscus aegyptiacus*
(b) *Gastrodiscus secundus*
(c) Both
(d) None

917. What is the function of palps in mosquito?
(a) Act as sensory organ
(b) Act as biting jaws
(c) Act as upper lip
(d) Act as lower lip

918. What is the function of labium in mosquito?
(a) Act as sensory organ
(b) Act as biting jaws
(c) Act as upper lip
(d) Act as lower lip

919. What is the function of labrum in mosquito?
(a) Act as sensory organ
(b) Act as biting jaws
(c) Act as lower lip
(d) Act as upper lip

920. What is the function of mandibles in mosquito?
(a) Act as sensory organ
(b) Act as biting jaws
(c) Act as upper lip
(d) Act as lower lip

921. What is the function of maxilla in mosquito?
(a) Act as sensory organ
(b) Act as biting jaws
(c) Act as upper lip
(d) Act as lower lip

922. How many segments are generally present in the antennae of a mosquito?
(a) 1-12 (b) 2-3
(c) 1 (d) 14-15

923. Epipharynx is fused with which of the following in mosquito-
(a) Labrum (b) Labium
(c) Mandibles (d) Maxilla

924. Eggs of which of the following is boat shaped-
(a) Anopheles (b) Culex
(c) Aedes (d) All

925. Eggs are laid in masses called egg rafts by-
(a) Anopheles (b) Culex
(c) Aedes (d) All

926. Palps are as long as probocis but not clubbed in case of -
(a) Male Anopheles (b) Female Anopheles
(c) Female Culex (d) All

927. Pulps are as long as probocis & are clubbed in-
(a) Male Anopheles (b) Female Anopheles
(c) Male Culex (d) Female culex

928. Palps are very short in length than probocis in -
(a) Male Anopheles (b) Female Anopheles
(c) Male Culex (d) Female culex

929. Larva of which mosquito bears palmate hairs -
(a) Anopheles (b) Culex
(c) Aedes (d) All

930. Respiratory siphon is _ in which of the following-
(a) Anopheles (b) Culex
(c) Aedes (d) All

931. Breathing trumpets are present in which developmental stage of mosquito-
(a) Larva (b) Pupa
(c) Adult (d) All

932. Which of the following can not be preserved in formalin?
(a) Lice (b) Flea
(c) Tick (d) Mite

933. Which of the following can be preserved in lactophenol?
(a) Lice (b) Flea
(c) Both (d) None

934. Parasitemia is detectable after how much time in case of Trypanosomosis-
(a) 1-3 Week (b) 3-6 Week
(c) 6-9 Week (d) 9-12 Week

935. Chawere in case of Trypanosomosis is-
(a) Inflammatory swelling
(b) Bite mark
(c) Exudative deposition
(d) None

936. Study of ticks & mites comes under-
(a) Entomology (b) Acarology
(c) Protozoology (d) Helminthology

937. Study of mosquito comes under-
(a) Entomology (b) Acarology
(c) Protozoology (d) Helminthology

938. Under which of the following the microscopic parasite present in blood are studied-
(a) Entomology (b) Acarology
(c) Protozoology (d) Helminthology

939. Study of nematodes comes under-
(a) Entomology (b) Acarology
(c) Protozoology (d) Helminthology

940. Which of the following is known as common Indian centripede?
(a) *Scolopendra gigantica*
(b) *Blatella germanica*
(c) *Supella supelectilium*
(d) *Periplanta americana*

941. *Blatella germanica* is commonly known as-
(a) German cockroach
(b) Oriental cockroach
(c) American cockroach
(d) Black beetle

942. *Blatella germanica* is commonly known as -
(a) Croton bug (b) German cockroach
(c) Both (d) None

943. *Supella supelectilium* is commonly known as-
(a) Brown banded cockroach
(b) Tropical cockroach
(c) Both
(d) None

944. *Blatta orentalis* is commonly known as-
(a) Oriental Cockroach
(b) Croton bug
(c) German cockroach
(d) Both b & C

945. *Periplanta american* is commonly known as-
(a) Croton bug
(b) German cockroach
(c) American cockroach
(d) All

946. *Menacanthus stramineus* is commonly known as-
(a) Chicken body louse
(b) Head Louse of poultry
(c) Wing louse of poultry
(d) Fluff louse

947. Tetramisole is effective against
(a) Lungworm (b) Bunostomum
(c) Oestertagia (d) All of above

948. Coumpaphos is used to control
(a) Grub (b) Ascaris
(c) Oestertagia (d) None

949. *Goniocotes gallinae* is commonly known as-
(a) Chicken body louse
(b) Head Louse of poultry
(c) Wing louse of poultry
(d) Fluff louse

950. Identify hardtack from following
(a) Ixodid (b) Argas
(c) Metophagus (d) None of above

951. Which of the following is a duck louse?
(a) *Columbicola columbae*
(b) *Anaticola crossicornis*

(c) *Gonocotes gallinae*
(d) *Goniocotes gigas*

952. Horn fly is
(a) *Haemotobis irritans*
(b) *Stomoxys calcitrans*
(c) *Habronema*
(d) *Cooperia*

953. *Pulex irritans* is commonly known as-
(a) Human crab louse (b) Human flea
(c) Rat flea (d) None

954. *Xenopsiella cheopis* is commonly known as-
(a) Rat flea (b) Human flea
(c) Dog flea (d) Cat flea

955. Which species of Phlebotomus is known as owl midges?
(a) *P. papatasi* (b) *P. sergento*
(c) *P. major* (d) All

956. *Tabanus striatus* is also known as-
(a) Horse fly (b) Breeze fly
(c) Gad fly (d) All

957. *Musca autumalis* is commonly known as-
(a) Face fly (b) Stable fly
(c) Horn fly (d) Buffalo fly

958. *Stomoxys calcitrans* is commonly known as-
(a) Face fly (b) Stable fly
(c) Horn fly (d) Buffalo fly

959. *Hematobia irritans* is commonly known as-
(a) Face fly (b) Stable fly
(c) Horn fly (d) Buffalo fly

960. *Hematobia exigua* is commonly known as-
(a) Face fly (b) Stable fly
(c) Horn fly (d) Buffalo fly

961. *Cephalopira titillator* is commonly known as-
(a) Camel nasal fly (b) Ox nasal fly
(c) Buffalo fly (d) All

962. *Hypeoderma lineatum* is commonly known as-
(a) Ox warble fly
(b) Heel fly
(c) Northern cattle grub
(d) All

963. Which of the following is blue bottle fly?
(a) *Calliphora erythrocephala*
(b) *Lucilia cuprina*
(c) *Lucillia sericata*
(d) Both b & c

964. Which of the following is known as green bottle fly?
(a) *Calliphora erythrociphala*
(b) *Lucilia cuprina*
(c) *Lucillia sericata*
(d) Both b & c

965. *Chrysomia bezziana* is commonly known as-
(a) Screw worm fly
(b) Flesh fly
(c) Old world flesh fly
(d) Forest fly

966. *Sarcophaga dux* is commonly known as-
(a) Screw worm fly
(b) Flesh fly
(c) Old world flesh fly
(d) Forest fly

967. *Wohlfahrtia magnifica* is commonly known as-
(a) Screw worm fly
(b) Flesh fly
(c) Old world flesh fly
(d) Forest fly

968. *Hippobosca maculata* is commonly known as-
(a) Screw worm fly
(b) Flesh fly
(c) Old world flesh fly
(d) Forest fly

969. Which of the following is called pigeon fly?
(a) *Pseudolynchia canariensis*
(b) *Lipoptina cuprina*
(c) Both
(d) None

970. Which of the following is called goat fly?
(a) *Pseudolynchia canariensis*
(b) *Lipoptina cuprina*
(c) Both
(d) None

971. *Otobius magnini* is commonly known as-
(a) Spinose ear tick
(b) Castor been tick
(c) North American cattle tick
(d) Tropical cattle tick

972. *Ixodes ricinus* is commonly known as-
(a) Spinose ear tick
(b) Castor been tick

(c) North American cattle tick
(d) Tropical cattle tick

973. *Boophillus annulatus* is commonly known as-
(a) Spinose ear tick
(b) Caster been tick
(c) North American cattle tick
(d) Tropical cattle tick

974. *Boophillus microplus* is commonly known as-
(a) Spinose ear tick
(b) Caster been tick
(c) North American cattle tick
(d) Tropical cattle tick

975. *Argas persicus* is commonly known as
(a) Castor been tick (b) Fowl tick
(c) Pigeon tick (d) Camel tick

976. *Boophillus decoloratus* is commonly known as-
(a) Blue tick (b) Red leg tick
(c) Yellow dog tick (d) Brown ear tick

977. *Rhipicephalus appendiculatus* is commonly-
(a) Blue tick (b) Brown ear tick
(c) Red leg tick (d) Yellow dog tick

978. *Rhipicephalus sanguineus* is commonly known as-
(a) Blue tick (b) Brown ear tick
(c) Brown dog tick (d) Red leg tick

979. *Haemaphysalis leachi* is commonly known as-
(a) Yellow dog tick (b) Brown dog tick
(c) Brown ear tick (d) All

980. *Dermacentor andersoni* is commonly known as-
(a) Rocky mountain wood tick
(b) American dog tick
(c) Bont tick
(d) Varigated tick

981. Life cycle is completed within 7 days involving egg laying after first blood meal which result six legged larval upon hatching followed by blood sucking nymphs which became adults. Identify the parasitic with such life cycle.
(a) Demodex (b) Dermanyssus
(c) Argas (d) Ear tick

982. Earthworm is intermediate host for
(a) Capillaria (b) Strongylus
(c) Fasciola (d) Argas

983. *Chabertia ovina* affects which part of digestive system:
(a) Colon (b) Crop
(c) Rumen (d) None

984. Which species of Amblyomma is known as cone star tick?
(a) *A. americanum* (b) *A. maculatum*
(c) Both (d) None

985. Which species of Amblyomma is known as gulf coast tick?
(a) *A. americanum* (b) *A. maculatum*
(c) Both (d) None

986. *Cytodites nudus* is commonly known as -
(a) Airsac mites (b) Grain itch mite
(c) Harvest mite (d) Red mite of poultry

987. Which of the following is chigger mite?
(a) *Thrombicola autumnalis* (b) *Thrombicola akamush*
(c) Both (d) None

988. *Thrombicola akamush* is commonly known as-
(a) Air sac mite (b) Harvest mite
(c) Grain itch mite (d) Red mite of poultry

989. *Pediculoides ventricosus* is commonly known as-
(a) Grain itch mite
(b) Subcut mite of fowl
(c) Red mite of poultry
(d) Soft tick of poultry

990. *Laminosioptes cysticola* is commonly known as-
(a) Grain itch mite
(b) Subcut mite of fowl
(c) Red mite of poultry
(d) Soft tick of poultry

991. *Dermanyssees gallinae* is commonly known as-
(a) Grain itch mite
(b) Subcut mite of fowl
(c) Red mite of poultry
(d) Soft tick of poultry

992. *Argas persicus* commonly known as-
(a) Grain itch mite
(b) Subcut mite of fowl
(c) Red mite of poultry
(d) Soft tick of poultry

993. *Cotugnia diagonophora* is known as-
(a) Double pored tapeworm of poultry
(b) Smallest tape worm of poultry

(c) Both
(d) None

994. Which species of tapeworm is known as Zipper tapeworm?
(a) Taenia (b) Cotugnia
(c) Spirometra (d) None

995. *Enterobius vermicularis* is commonly known as-
(a) Pin worm (b) Seat worm
(c) Both (d) None

996. *Opisthorchis tenuicollis* is commonly known as-
(a) Dog liver fluke (b) Cat liver fluke
(c) Ox liver fluke (d) None

997. Which of the following is Liver fluke of Elephant?
(a) F. hepatica (b) F. gigantica
(c) F. jacksoni (d) All

998. Type of Parasitism when entire life is parasitic is called
(a) Obligatory (b) Facultative
(c) Erratic (d) Temporary

999. Which antibiotic may be indicated for Ascaris sp.
(a) Phenothiazine (b) Tetracycline
(c) Hygromycin B (d) Cephalosporin

Write true or false for the following statement

1. No development occurs in transport host.
2. Trematodes are oviparous.
3. *Trichinella sp.* is autoheteroxenous parasite.
4. Snail is intermediate host of Fasciola.
5. Armed oral sucker is peculiar characteristic to family Echinostomatidae.
6. Metcercaria is infective stage of digenetic trema tode.
7. Ventral sucker is also known as acetabulum.
8. Egg of digenetic trematodes is operculated except of blood flukes.
9. Redia stage is found in life cycle of Schistosoma.
10. Cotugnia and Moniezia are double pored tapeworms.
11. Bothria is present in Eucestodes.
12. Pleurocercoid is infective stage of Cotyloda.

Answers

1	2	3	4	5	6	7
T	T	T	T	T	T	T
8	9	10	11	12		
T	F	T	F	T		

A. Match the following:

	Common name		Genus
1.	Soft tick	A.	*Damalina*
2.	Seep tick	B	Argas
3.	Biting tick	C	Metophagus
4.	Roost mite	D	*Dermanyssus gallinae*

Answers

1. B 2. C 3. A 4. D

B. Match the following

1.	Sucking louse	A.	*Boophilus annulatum*
2.	Texas fever tick	B.	*Hematopinus suis*
3.	Spinose ear tick	C.	*Otobius magnimi*
4.	Heel fly	D.	*Hypodorma lineatum*

Answer

1 – B, 2 – A, 3 – C, 4 – D

Answer

1.	(a)	2.	(d)	3.	(a)
4.	(b)	5.	(d)	6.	(b)
7.	(c)	8.	(a)	9.	(b)
10.	(a)	11.	(b)	12.	(b)
13.	(d)	14.	(c)	15.	(d)
16.	(c)	17.	(a)	18.	(b)
19.	(a)	20.	(b)	21.	(d)
22.	(c)	23.	(a)	24.	(c)
25.	(c)	26.	(a)	27.	(a)
28.	(d)	29.	(c)	30.	(c)
31.	(c)	32.	(a)	33.	(d)
34.	(b)	35.	(b)	36.	(a)
37.	(b)	38.	(a)	39.	(b)
40.	(d)	41.	(c)	42.	(c)
43.	(d)	44.	(c)	45.	(a)
46.	(a)	47.	(d)	48.	(d)
49.	(d)	50.	(c)	51.	(c)
52.	(d)	53.	(b)	54.	(c)
55.	(d)	56.	(d)	57.	(d)

58.	(a)	59.	(a)	60.	(a)
61.	(b)	62.	(a)	63.	(c)
64.	(d)	65.	(b)	66.	(b)
67.	(b)	68.	(c)	69.	(c)
70.	(b)	71.	(d)	72.	(c)
73.	(c)	74.	(a)	75.	(b)
76.	(a)	77.	(c)	78.	(c)
79.	(b)	80.	(a)	81.	(b)
82.	(a)	83.	(c)	84.	(c)
85.	(a)	86.	(d)	87.	(c)
88.	(c)	89.	(c)	90.	(d)
91.	(c)	92.	(b)	93.	(c)
94.	(d)	95.	(c)	96.	(d)
97.	(a)	98.	(b)	99.	(c)
100.	(d)	101.	(a)	102.	(a)
103.	(a)	104.	(d)	105.	(c)
106.	(a)	107.	(b)	108.	(d)
109.	(d)	110.	(d)	111.	(a)
112.	(a)	113.	(a)	114.	(c)
115.	(c)	116.	(d)	117.	(c)
118.	(b)	119.	(c)	120.	(b)
121.	(b)	122.	(c)	123.	(b)
124.	(c)	125.	(d)	126.	(b)
127.	(b)	128.	(c)	129.	(b)
130.	(d)	131.	(a)	132.	(b)
133.	(d)	134.	(a)	135.	(a)
136.	(b)	137.	(d)	138.	(a)
139.	(b)	140.	(b)	141.	(b)
142.	(a)	143.	(b)	144.	(a)
145.	(c)	146.	(b)	147.	(c)
148.	(a)	149.	(b)	150.	(a)
151	(c)	152.	(b)	153.	(c)
154.	(a)	155.	(d)	156.	(d)
157.	(c)	158.	(a)	159.	(a)
160.	(b)	161.	(c)	162.	(d)
163.	(a)	164.	(c)	165.	(a)
166.	(d)	167.	(a)	168.	(b)
169.	(d)	170.	(a)	171.	(c)
172.	(a)	173.	(c)	174.	(b)
175.	(a)	176.	(d)	177.	(c)
178.	(a)	179.	(b)	180.	(a)
181.	(c)	182.	(a)	183.	(b)
184.	(c)	185.	(d)	186.	(a)
187.	(c)	188.	(d)	189.	(d)
190.	(a)	191.	(d)	192.	(d)
193.	(d)	194.	(b)	195.	(c)

196.	(c)	197.	(d)	198.	(a)
199.	(c)	200.	(d)	201.	(b)
202.	(c)	203.	(b)	204.	(a)
205.	(d)	206.	(c)	207.	(a)
208.	(c)	209.	(b)	210.	(c)
211.	(d)	212.	(b)	213.	(c)
214.	(c)	215.	(c)	216.	(d)
217.	(d)	218.	(d)	219.	(a)
220.	(c)	221.	(d)	222.	(c)
223	(a)	224.	(c)	225.	(b)
226.	(c)	227.	(a)	228.	(c)
229.	(b)	230.	(b)	231.	(c)
232.	(c)	233.	(a)	234.	(a)
235.	(b)	236.	(a)	237.	(b)
238.	(c)	239.	(d)	240.	(a)
241.	(b)	242.	(c)	243.	(d)
244.	(c)	245.	(d)	246.	(c)
247.	(a)	248.	(b)	249.	(a)
250.	(a)	251.	(b)	252.	(c)
253.	(c)	254.	(d)	255.	(a)
256.	(b)	257.	(b)	258.	(d)
259.	(c)	260.	(b)	261.	(a).
262.	(a)	263.	(a)	264.	(a)
265.	(b)	266.	(d)	267.	(c)
268.	(a)	269.	(b)	270.	(d)
271.	(c)	272.	(c)	273.	(a)
274.	(b)	275.	(a)	276.	(a)
277.	(a)	278.	(a)	279.	(b)
280.	(d)	281.	(d)	282.	(a)
283.	(b)	284.	(b)	285.	(a)
286.	(c)	287.	(b)	288.	(a)
289.	(a)	290.	(b)	291.	(a)
292.	(b)	293.	(d)	294.	(c)
295.	(c)	296.	(c)	297.	(a)
298.	(b)	299.	(d)	300.	(b)
301.	(a)	302.	(c)	303.	(b)
304.	(d)	305.	(a)	306.	(c)
307.	(b)	308.	(a)	309.	(b)
310.	(d)	311.	(c)	312.	(a)
313.	(a)	314.	(d)	315	(c)
316.	(a)	317.	(b)	318.	(a)
319.	(c)	320.	(b)	321.	(d)
322.	(b)	323.	(c)	324.	(d)
325.	(b)	326.	(a)	327.	(a)
328.	(b)	329.	(d)	330.	(a)
331.	(b)	332.	(c)	333.	(b)

334.	(a)	335.	(d)	336.	(c)
337.	(a)	338.	(b)	339.	(c)
340.	(d)	341.	(b)	342.	(a)
343.	(c)	344.	(d)	345.	(b)
346.	(a)	347.	(c)	348.	(b)
349.	(b)	350.	(a)	351.	(b)
352.	(a)	353.	(c)	354.	(a)
355.	(b)	356.	(d)	357.	(c)
358.	(b)	359.	(a)	360.	(d)
361.	(b)	362.	(c)	363.	(b)
364.	(b)	365.	(a)	366.	(c)
367.	(d)	368.	(b)	369.	(a)
370.	(d)	371.	(b)	372.	(c)
373.	(a)	374.	(b)	375.	(a)
376.	(c)	377.	(b)	378.	(c)
379.	(a)	380.	(d)	381.	(b)
382.	(c)	383.	(a)	384.	(d)
385.	(b)	386.	(a)	387.	(c)
388.	(d)	389.	(a)	390.	(b)
391.	(c)	392.	(d)	393.	(b)
394.	(c)	395.	(a)	396.	(b)
397.	(c)	398.	(c)	399.	(b)
400.	(a)	401.	(a)	402.	(b)
403.	(c)	404.	(c)	405.	(b)
406.	(a)	407.	(b)	408.	(a)
409.	(b)	410.	(c)	411.	(d)
412.	(a)	413.	(b)	414.	(a)
415.	(b)	416.	(c)	417.	(d)
418.	(a)	419.	(b)	420.	(c)
421.	(c)	422.	(c)	423.	(b)
424.	(c)	425.	(d)	426.	(c)
427.	(c)	428.	(c)	429.	(a)
430.	(d)	431.	(c)	432.	(c)
433.	(c)	434.	(a)	435.	(a)
436.	(a)	437.	(b)	438.	(c)
439.	(a)	440.	(a)	441.	(a)
442.	(b)	443.	(a)	444.	(a)
445.	(b)	446.	(a)	447.	(b)
448.	(a)	449.	(b)	450.	(d)
451.	(d)	452.	(b)	453.	(c)
454.	(c)	455.	(d)	456.	(a)
457.	(a)	458.	(b)	459.	(d)
460.	(c)	461.	(a)	462.	(a)
463.	(d)	464.	(c)	465.	(a)
466.	(d)	467.	(b)	468.	(a)
469.	(a)	470.	(a)	471.	(c)
472.	(d)	473.	(d)	474.	(d)

475.	(a)	476.	(d)	477.	(c)
478.	(c)	479.	(d)	480.	(d)
481.	(c)	482.	(c)	483.	(a)
484.	(a)	485.	(d)	486.	(a)
487.	(a)	488.	(b)	489.	(a)
490.	(c)	491.	(b)	492.	(d)
493.	(d)	494.	(b)	495.	(b)
496.	(d)	497.	(d)	498.	(d)
499.	(d)	500.	(a)	501.	(c)
502.	(a)	503.	(b)	504.	(c)
505.	(d)	506.	(c)	507.	(d)
508.	(d)	509.	(d)	510.	(a)
511.	(b)	512.	(b)	513.	(c)
514.	(b)	515.	(a)	516.	(c)
517.	(b)	518.	(a)	519.	(c)
520.	(a)	521.	(c)	522.	(a)
523.	(c)	524.	(a)	525.	(a)
526.	(d)	527.	(b)	528.	(c)
529.	(d)	530.	(c)	531.	(c)
532.	(b)	533.	(b)	534.	(d)
535.	(d)	536.	(c)	537.	(d)
538.	(a)	539.	(b)	540.	(c)
541.	(a)	542.	(b)	543.	(c)
544.	(a)	545.	(d)	546.	(d)
547.	(d)	548.	(c)	549.	(c)
550.	(c)	551.	(b)	552.	(b)
553.	(a)	554.	(a)	555.	(a)
556.	(c)	557.	(a)	558.	(b)
559.	(d)	560.	(c)	561.	(a)
562.	(b)	563.	(c)	564.	(a)
565.	(a)	566.	(a)	567.	(a)
568.	(b)	569.	(d)	570.	(a)
571.	(c)	572.	(b)	573.	(a)
574.	(a)	575.	(c)	576.	(a)
577.	(a)	578.	(b)	579.	(b)
580.	(c)	581.	(d)	582.	(d)
583.	(d)	584.	(d)	585.	(a)
586.	(b)	587.	(a)	588.	(b)
589.	(a)	590.	(d)	591.	(d)
592.	(c)	593.	(a)	594.	(b)
595.	(c)	596.	(c)	597.	(c)
598.	(c)	599.	(d)	600.	(c)
601.	(b)	602.	(a)	603.	(b)
604.	(a)	605.	(a)	606.	(b)
607.	(c)	608.	(a)	609.	(a)
610.	(a)	611.	(c)	612.	(a)
613.	(a)	614.	(a)	615.	(b)

616.	(b)	617.	(b)	618.	(b)	757.	(b)	758.	(a)	759.	(a)
619.	(b)	620.	(c)	621.	(b)	760.	(a)	761.	(b)	762.	(c)
622.	(d)	623.	(a)	624.	(a)	763.	(c)	764.	(b)	765.	(d)
625.	(c)	626.	(c)	627.	(b)	766.	(a)	767.	(b)	768.	(b)
628.	(d)	629.	(a)	630.	(a)	769.	(b)	770.	(b)	771.	(c)
631.	(d)	632.	(c)	633.	(d)	772.	(c)	773.	(b)	774.	(a)
634.	(d)	635.	(b)	636.	(b)	775.	(b)	776.	(d)	777.	(b)
637.	(c)	638.	(a)	639.	(b)	778.	(c)	779.	(b)	780.	(c)
640.	(a)	641.	(b)	642.	(a)	781.	(a)	782.	(a)	783.	(b)
643.	(d)	644.	(a)	645.	(c)	784.	(a)	785.	(b)	786.	(d)
646.	(d)	647.	(c)	648.	(a)	787.	(b)	788.	(a)	789.	(d)
649.	(a)	650.	(d)	651.	(d)	790.	(c)	791.	(a)	792.	(b)
652.	(d)	653.	(b)	654.	(a)	793.	(d)	794.	(b)	795.	(d)
655.	(b)	656.	(a)	657.	(d)	796.	(d)	797.	(a)	798.	(b)
658.	(c)	659.	(b)	660.	(d)	799.	(a)	800.	(d)	801.	(a)
661.	(a)	662.	(b)	663.	(b)	802.	(c)	803.	(d)	804.	(b)
664.	(c)	665.	(d)	666.	(a)	805.	(a)	806.	(b)	807.	(c)
667.	(d)	668.	(a)	669.	(c)	808.	(b)	809.	(a)	810.	(a)
670.	(d)	671.	(c)	672.	(c)	811.	(b)	812.	(c)	813.	(c)
673.	(a)	674.	(d)	675.	(b)	814.	(d)	815.	(c)	816.	(b)
676.	(b)	677.	(a)	678.	(a)	817.	(d)	818.	(b)	819.	(c)
679.	(d)	680.	(a)	681.	(d)	820.	(d)	821.	(c)	822.	(b)
682.	(c)	683.	(b)	684.	(a)	823.	(c)	824.	(a)	825.	(a)
685.	(c)	686.	(a)	687.	(b)	826.	(a)	827.	(c)	828.	(d)
688.	(a)	689.	(b)	690.	(c)	829.	(a)	830.	(d)	831.	(c)
691.	(c)	692.	(a)	693.	(b)	832.	(c)	833.	(d)	834.	(d)
694.	(b)	695.	(a)	696.	(c)	835.	(d)	836.	(a)	837.	(b)
697.	(b)	698.	(a)	699.	(a)	838.	(a)	839.	(c)	840.	(a)
700.	(c)	701.	(a)	702.	(b)	841.	(a)	842.	(b)	843.	(d)
703.	(d)	704.	(a)	705.	(c)	844.	(c)	845.	(a)	846.	(a)
706.	(b)	707.	(c)	708.	(c)	847.	(d)	848.	(a)	849.	(d)
709.	(d)	710.	(c)	711.	(b)	850.	(a)	851.	(b)	852.	(d)
712.	(b)	713.	(a)	714.	(c)	853.	(d)	854.	(a)	855.	(b)
715.	(c)	716.	(d)	717.	(a)	856.	(c)	857.	(d)	858.	(a)
718.	(c)	719.	(a)	720.	(b)	859.	(b)	860.	(c)	861.	(c)
721.	(a)	722.	(b)	723.	(a)	862.	(c)	863.	(a)	864.	(b)
724.	(b)	725.	(d)	726.	(c)	865.	(d)	866.	(a)	867.	(b)
727.	(d)	728.	(b)	729.	(c)	868.	(a)	869.	(c)	870.	(c)
730.	(a)	731.	(b)	732.	(a)	871.	(c)	872.	(c)	873.	(a)
733.	(b)	734.	(a)	735.	(a)	874.	(c)	875.	(c)	876.	(b)
736.	(d)	737.	(a)	738.	(a)	877.	(b)	878.	(b)	879.	(a)
739.	(a)	740.	(d)	741.	(d)	880.	(c)	881.	(d)	882.	(b)
742.	(a)	743.	(d)	744.	(a)	883.	(c)	884.	(d)	885.	(b)
745.	(d)	746.	(b)	747.	(b)	886.	(b)	887.	(c)	888.	(b)
748.	(d)	749.	(b)	750.	(a)	889.	(b)	890.	(a)	891.	(b)
751.	(c)	752.	(b)	753.	(a)	892.	(c)	893.	(d)	894.	(a)
754.	(a)	755.	(b)	756.	(a)	895.	(a)	896.	(d)	897.	(c)

898.	(a)	899.	(a)	900.	(d)	949.	(d)	950.	(a)	951.	(b)
901.	(a)	902.	(a)	903.	(a)	952.	(a)	953.	(b)	954.	(a)
904.	(d)	905.	(d)	906.	(c)	955.	(d)	956.	(d)	957.	(a)
907.	(c)	908.	(b)	909.	(a)	958.	(b)	959.	(c)	960.	(d)
910.	(c)	911.	(c)	912.	(a)	961.	(a)	962.	(d)	963.	(a)
913.	(c)	914.	(a)	915.	(a)	964.	(d)	965.	(a)	966.	(b)
916.	(b)	917.	(a)	918.	(d)	967.	(c)	968.	(d)	969.	(a)
919.	(d)	920.	(b)	921.	(b)	970.	(b)	971.	(a)	972.	(b)
922.	(d)	923.	(a)	924.	(a)	973.	(c)	974.	(d)	975.	(b)
925.	(b)	926.	(b)	927.	(a)	976.	(a)	977.	(b)	978.	(c)
928.	(d)	929.	(a)	930.	(a)	979.	(a)	980.	(a)	981.	(b).
931.	(b)	932.	(b)	933.	(c)	982.	(a)	983.	(a)	984.	(a)
934.	(a)	935.	(a)	936.	(b)	985.	(b)	986.	(a)	987.	(c)
937.	(a)	938.	(c)	939.	(d)	988.	(b)	989.	(a)	990.	(b)
940.	(a)	941.	(a)	942.	(c)	991.	(c)	992.	(d)	993.	(a)
943.	(c)	944.	(a)	945.	(c)	994.	(c)	995.	(c)	996.	(b)
946.	(a)	947.	(d).	948.	(a)	997.	(c)	998.	(a)	999.	(c)

6 Veterinary Pharmacology

Salient Points

- Father of toxicology is M. J. B. Orfla
- O. W. Holmes coined term Anaesthesia.
- Neurotransmitter was discovered by Otto.
- Posology is the study of dosage.
- Asafetida is a gum resin.
- Camphor is an essential oil.
- Polar ionized water and soluble drugs are excreted through kidney.
- Receptor is a complement of tissue to which a drug interacts to produce its effect.
- Piperidine nucleus is responsible for activity of morphine.
- Affinity is a character of drug to combine with a particular type of receptor.
- Naloxone is antagonist of morphine.
- Agonist must possess intensive activity and affinity.
- Antagonist lacks intrinsic activity.
- Phenoxy benzamine produces irreversible antagonism.
- Potency of a drug depends on affinity and efficacy of drug.
- Salbutamol is B adrenergic agonist.
- Atropine is antagonist of organo-phosphorus compound.
- Lead poisoning can be antidoted by $CaNa_2EDTA$.
- Dimercaprol Arsenic, Mercury poisoning.
- Drug passes across membranes mainly by passive diffusion.
- In ruminants, most of drugs are absorbed in rumen.
- Catalepsy refers to waxy rigidity of muscles so that animal remains in position of placement.
- Anesthesia is characterized by loss of consciousness, loss of sensation and state of amnesia.
- Dissociative anesthesia is characterized by catalepsy and amnesia
- Aspirin is a non narcotic analgesic.
- Neurolepsia is also known as Ataraxia.
- Anaesthetic triad consists of muscular relaxant and anaesthetics.
- Atropine blocks muscarinic receptor only not block nicotinic receptor.
- Adrenergic receptors are two types: alpha and beta.
- Propranolol is competitive and non selective blocking both beta-1 and beta-2 receptors.
- Quinidine, class-1 antiarrythmics, is effective in supraventricular and ventricular arrythmias.
- Nitroglycerine relaxes vascular smooth muscle.
- Hydralazine is arterial vasodilator.
- Positive inotrops increase the strength of cardiac muscle contraction by increasing the quantity of intracellular calcium available for binding by muscle protein.
- Dopamine is an endogenous catecholamine precursor with sensitive beta-1 activity. It also stimulates the release of nor-epinephrine.
- Astringents act locally by precipitating proteins.

They do not penetrate tissues.

- Epoetin alfa is the synthetic form of human glycoprotein and indicated in anaemia with chronic renal failure in dogs and cats.
- Folic acid is needed for DNA and RNA synthesis.

Questions

1. Sweat glands in horses receive which type of autonomic fibres
(a) Adrenergic fibers (b) Cholinergic fibres
(c) Both of the above (d) None of the above
2. Post ganglionic autonomic fibres innervate
(a) Heat (b) Smooth muscles
(c) Both 'a' and 'b' (d) Hair follicles
3. Adrenergic against are also called as
(a) Sympathomimetic agents
(b) Parasympathomimetic agents
(c) Sympatholytic agents
(d) None
4. Adrenaline increases blood pressure due to
(a) Alfa effect
(b) Beta 2 effect
(c) Alfa and Beta both
(d) None
5. Adrenaline is readily deaminated by
(a) MAO (b) COMT
(c) Protease (d) None
6. MAO is
(a) Monoamine oxidase
(b) Methylated ammonium oxide
(c) Morphine anhydrous oxide
(d) None
7. Nor adrenaline exerts same effects of Adrenaline except
(a) Relaxation of smooth muscles
(b) Glycogenolysis
(c) Respiratory secretions
(d) All of the above
8. Clonidine is a
(a) Centrally acting antihypertensive agents
(b) Locally acting antihypertensive agents
(c) Beta – Adrenergic agonist
(d) None
9. Dobutamine stimulates heart without
(a) Lowering blood pressure
(b) Increasing blood pressure
(c) Producing diseases
(d) None
10. Which one of following sympatholytic agent
(a) Phenoxybenzamine
(b) Amphetamine
(c) Adrenaline
(d) None
11. Ketanserin is a
(a) 5 – HT antagonist
(b) 5 – HT agonist
(c) Beta 2 – antagonist
(d) None
12. Ephedrine is
(a) Alkaloid
(b) Beta – adrenergic agonist
(c) Bronchodilator
(d) All of the above
13. Cholinesterase inhibitors are used for the treatment of
(a) Glaucoma (b) Paralytic ileus
(c) Rumen atony (d) All of the above
14. Diacetyl monoxime is a cholinesterase
(a) Reactivator (b) Inhibitor
(c) Both (d) None
15. Belladonna alkaloids are
(a) Antimuscarinic drugs
(b) Cholinesterase Inhibitors
(c) Cholinergic agonist
(d) None
16. Half life of Atropine is man is
(a) 4 hours (b) 1 hours
(c) 10 hours (d) 15 hours
17. Atropine produces
(a) Complete cycloplegia
(b) Incomplete cycloplegia
(c) Mydriasis
(d) Only A & C
18. Tubocurorine or obtained
(a) Strychnos plant (b) Atropa belladonna
(c) Hyoscimus plant (d) None
19. Atropine in used for treatment of
(a) Spasmodic colic

(b) Organophosphate poisoning
(c) Carbamate poisoning
(d) All of the above

20. Antagonist of Benzodiazepines is
(a) Flumazenil (b) Yohimbine
(c) Xylazine (d) None

21. Xylazine is an
(a) Alfa$_2$ against (b) Alfa$_1$ against
(c) Alfa$_2$ against (d) None

22. Xylazine is an
(a) Emesis in cat (b) Alpha-$_1$ agonist
(c) Alfa$_2$ antagonist (d) None

23. Acepromazine prevents
(a) Arrhythmia by adrenaline
(b) Bradycardia
(c) Vagal stimulation
(d) None

24. Neuroleptanalgesia is produced by
(a) Droperidiol + opiates
(b) Azaperone + opiate
(c) Diazepam + Droperidol
(d) None

25. Phenobarbital Na causes
(a) Sedation (b) Hypnotism
(c) Anticonvulsation (d) All of the above

26. Morphine in obtained from
(a) Papaver somniferum
(b) Atropa belladonna
(c) Scindapsus sp.
(d) None

27. Morphine has affinity for
(a) μ receptor (b) Alfa receptor
(c) Beta receptor (d) None

28. Morphine is not used in
(a) Strychnine poisoning
(b) Tetanus
(c) Epilepsy
(d) All of the above

29. Specific antagonist of etorphine is
(a) Morphine
(b) Diprenorphrine HCl
(c) Acepromazine
(d) None

30. Ketamine causes
(a) Salivation (b) Analgesia
(c) Anesthesia (d) All

31. CNS depressant effect of Chloral hydrate or due to
(a) Trichloroethanol (b) Methanol
(c) Tetraethylalcohol (d) None

32. Procaine is metabolized by
(a) Hepatic cholinesterase
(b) Kidney enzymes
(c) Both
(d) None

33. Which of the following is a common local anesthetic?
(a) Lidocaine (b) Bupivacaine
(c) Cocaine (d) None

34. Histamine is
(a) A biogenic amine
(b) Alcoholic compound
(c) Enzyme
(d) None

35. Histamine is
(a) A biogenic amine
(b) Alcoholic compound
(c) Enzyme
(d) None

36. Triple response is produced by intradermal injection of
(a) Histamine (b) Lidocaine
(c) Ethyl chloride (d) None

37. Frostbite pain in skin is produced by spray of?
(a) Ethyl chloride (b) Halothane
(c) Tetracaine (d) None

38. Cimetidine is
(a) H_2 antagonist (b) H_1 antagonist
(c) Alfa agonist (d) All of the above

39. Which of the following is an ergot derivative?
(a) Membrane lipids (b) Membrane protein
(c) Methysergide (d) None

40. Eicosanoids are derived from
(a) Membrane lipids (b) Membrane protein
(c) Cytoplasm (d) None

41. Glucocorticoids induce synthesis of
(a) Eicosanoids (b) Lipocortin
(c) Histamine (d) None

42. Prostaglandins are
(a) Hypotensive in general
(b) Hypotensive in general
(c) Analgesic
(d) None

43. $PGF_{2\,alpha}$ is a hormone which causes
(a) Glycolysis (b) Luteolysis
(c) Thrombolyser (d) All of the above

44. $PGF_{2\,alfa}$ is used for
(a) Synchronisation of estrous
(b) Induction of parturition
(c) Luteolysis
(d) All of the above

45. Aspirin relieve pain inflammation by
(a) Inhibiting cyclooxygenase
(b) Inhibiting leukotrienes
(c) Both
(d) All of the above

46. Gastric Prostaglandins inhibit
(a) Secretion of acid (b) Mucus secretion
(c) Both (d) None

47. Cats are especially susceptible to NSAIDs toxicity because
(a) Lack of glucuronyl transferase
(b) Lack of MAO
(c) Both
(d) None

48. Salicylates increase
(a) O_2 consumption (b) CO_2 consumption
(c) Both (d) None

49. Fenamates are
(a) PG_s antagonists (b) PGs agonist
(c) 5 – HT antagonist (d) None

50. Meclofenamic acid antagonizes effect of
(a) Bradykinin (b) Histamine
(c) Kallikrein (d) None

51. Overdosing of Phenylbutazone produces
(a) Mucosal petechiae
(b) Mouth ulcers
(c) Colic
(d) All of the above

52. Which of the following is not a NSAID?
(a) Aspirin
(b) Naproxen
(c) Meclofenamic acid
(d) Cimetidine

53. Which of the following may be used even in case of peptic ulcers
(a) Acetaminophen
(b) Aspirin
(c) Acetylsalicylic acid
(d) Naproxen

54. GnRH is used for
(a) Induction of orulatory estrus
(b) To treat cystic ovaries
(c) Both
(d) None

55. Somatostatin is produced in
(a) Hypothalamus (b) D cells of pancreas
(c) GI mucosa (d) All of the above

56. Adrenocorticosteroids have negative feed back control over
(a) Corticotropin release hormone
(b) Thyrotropin release hormone
(c) Prostaglandins
(d) None

57. Luteinizing hormone causes
(a) Maturation of follicles
(b) Production of estrogen
(c) Release of progesterone
(d) All of the above

58. Ovarian cysts may be treated by
(a) FSH (b) LH
(c) CRH (d) None

59. PMSG in produced by
(a) Hypothalamus (b) Endometrium
(c) Pituitary Gland (d) None

60. Human chorionic gonadotropin is produced by
(a) Human placenta
(b) Human ovary
(c) Human hypothalamus
(d) None

61. hCG is a
(a) Glycoprotein (b) Glycolipid
(c) Protein (d) None

62. hCG causes
(a) Ovulation (b) Luteinization
(c) Both (d) None

63. Ergot alkaloids inhibit release of
(a) ACTH (b) Prolactin
(c) GnRH (d) None

64. Oxytocin and vasopressin are
(a) Nanopeptides (b) Decapeptides
(c) Octapeptides (d) None

65. Hypertonicity of plasma promotes release of
(a) Oxytocin (b) Vasopressin
(c) Both (d) None

66. ADH deficiency produces
(a) Diabetes mellitus (b) Diabetes insipidus
(c) Abortion (d) None

67. Oxytocin is stored in
(a) Hypothalamus (b) Posterior pituitary
(c) Anterior pituitary (d) None

68. Uterine inertia may be treated by
(a) Oxytocin (b) Vasopressin
(c) Prostaglandin (d) Histamine

69. Testosterone causes feed back inhibition of release of
(a) Hypothalamic GnRH
(b) ACTH
(c) ADH
(d) None

70. Reduced form of Testosterone is
(a) Dihydrotestosterone
(b) Dinitrotestosterone
(c) Dialkyl testosterone
(d) None

71. Testosterone is used to treat
(a) Mammary carcinoma
(b) Male infertility
(c) Aloepecia in castrated dog
(d) All of the above

72. Toxic effects of testosterone are
(a) Edema
(b) Jaundice
(c) Disturbed estrous cycle
(d) All of above

73. Competitive antagonist of androgens is
(a) Zeranol (b) Estrogen
(c) Cyproterone (d) None

74. Estradiol is oxidized to
(a) Estrone (b) Estriol
(c) Both (d) None

75. Estrogens are
(a) Luteolytic in cow (b) Luteotropic in sow
(c) Epitheliotropic (d) All of the above

76. Misalliance in dogs can be nullified by use of
(a) Estrogen (b) Testosterone
(c) Histamine (d) None

77. Nonsteroidal estrogen is
(a) Diethylstilbestrol (b) Clomiphene
(c) Flutamide (d) None

78. Clomiphene is competitive antagonist of
(a) Estrogen (b) Testosterone
(c) Histamine (d) None

79. Progesterone suppresses
(a) Uterine milk secretion
(b) Ovulation
(c) Both
(d) None

80. Progestins on prolong use may produce
(a) Cystic hyperplasia of uterine
(b) Mammary carcinomas
(c) Abortion
(d) None

81. Competitive antagonist of progesterone is
(a) Mifepistfrone (b) Proligestone
(c) Clomiphene (d) None

82. Glucocorticoids promote
(a) Gluconeogenesis (b) Lipolysis
(c) Growth (d) All of above

83. Corticosteroids are synthesized mainly in
(a) Adrenal cortex (b) Pituitary gland
(c) Hypothalamus (d) All of above

84. Glucocorticoids are used in
(a) Addison's disease (b) Bovine ketosis
(c) Hay fever (d) All of above

85. What is best for Glucocorticoid Administration?
(a) Smallest dose for long period
(b) Large dose for long period
(c) Small dose for long period
(d) None

86. Glucocorticoids should not be used in
(a) Late pregnancy (b) Corneal ulcers
(c) Diabetes mellitus (d) All of above

87. Which drug competes for thyroxine binding sites?

(a) Aspirin (b) Flucinolone
(c) Progestin (d) None

88. $T_3 + T_4$ act by binding to
(a) Nuclear chromatin
(b) Mitochondria
(c) Cell wall
(d) None

89. $T_3 + T_4$ are
(a) Thyroxine and Triiodothyronine
(b) Thyronin and Triidothyronin
(c) Thyroglobins
(d) None

90. T_4 is reduced to T_3 by
(a) 5 – deiodinase (b) 5 – HT
(c) Oxidase (d) None

91. $T_3 + T_4$ are used for
(a) Cretinism (b) Hairless calf
(c) Myxedems (d) All of above

92. Early signs of thyroid toxicity is/are
(a) Arrhythmia (b) Osteoporosis
(c) Restlessness (d) All of above

93. Hormone secreted in response to hypocalcemia is
(a) Calcitonin
(b) Parathyroid hormone
(c) Glucagon
(d) None

94. Calcitonin produces
(a) Hypocalcemia
(b) Hypercalcemia
(c) Hypophosphatmia
(d) Both A and C

95. Hypoparathyroidism in dog is treated by
(a) Calcium borogluconate
(b) Dexamethasone
(c) Lugol's solution
(d) None

96. Distal tubular reabsorption of Ca^{++} is enhanced by
(a) Calcitonin
(b) Parathyroid hormone
(c) Glucagon
(d) None

97. Somatostatin inhibits
(a) Glucagon secretion
(b) Insulin secretion
(c) Both
(d) None

98. Glucagon and insulin is produced in pancreas by
(a) Alfa cells and beta islets respectively
(b) Beta islets and alpha cells respectively
(c) Delta cells and beta islets respectively
(d) None

99. Growth promoting effects of insulation is based on its
(a) IGF – 1 agonist action
(b) IGF agonist action
(c) IGF – 1 antagonist action
(d) None of above

100. Calcitriol is synthesized in
(a) Renal mitochondria
(b) hypothalamus
(c) Liver
(d) None

101. FSH release is inhibited by
(a) Gastrin (b) Calcitriol
(c) Inhibin (d) None

102. Which of the following is most applicable for the variation in the drug?
(a) Species of animal
(b) The intended effect of the drug.
(c) The individual susceptibility to the drug.
(d) All of the above.

103. Abnormalities of the genetic materials (genes, chromosomes) caused by the drugs is called.
(a) Mutogeneris (b) Oncogeneris
(c) Tiratogeneris (d) All of the above

104. Solution that contains bacteristics agents:
(a) Cannot be tested far sterility.
(b) Must be diluted beyond the bacteristastic level for sterility tests.
(c) Do not require a sterility test.
(d) None of the above

105. The heptic injury induced by the carbon tetrachloride is mediated its metabolites.
(a) Trichoromehyl from radical CCl3
(b) Trichloromethyl proxy free radical (Cl_3COO)
(c) Trichlaromethyl free radical as well as Cl_3COO.

(d) None of the above

106. A chemical compound becomes a useful drug
(a) If it is passes therapeutic activity
(b) If it is free of toxicity.
(c) If it is superior to any of the existing medicoments.
(d) All of the above

107. The following statement regarding passage of drugs across cell membrane is correct;
(a) Ionized drug is not diffusible.
(b) Acidic environment of stomach favours absorption of alkaline drugs
(c) Polar drugs readily cross all membrane.
(d) All of the above

108. Active transport across the cell membrane is
(a) Carrier mediated
(b) Energy dependent
(c) Along concentration gradient
(d) Both a & b

109. Which one of the following statements about drug absorption from gastro intestal tract is correct?
(a) Stomach is the major site of drug absorption.
(b) Stomach is the site of drug absorption
(c) Sublingual drug administration gives quick onset
(d) All of the above

110. Following is not true regarding oral administration
(a) All soluble drugs are absorbed from gastro intestinal tract.
(b) Benzyl pencillin is absorbed from stomach.
(c) Both a & b.
(d) None of the above

111. Drug administration by inhalation is
(a) Is only possible for gases & volatile liquids.
(b) Is far systemic as local effects
(c) Leads to cough & bronchpneumonia
(d) Will have bronchiolar effect only if the particle size is 40 mm or less.

112. The following is true regarding plasma protein binding
(a) Acidic drug are bound to the albumen fraction.
(b) Basic drugs are not bound to the proteins.
(c) Highly plasma protein bound drugs have short plasma t1/2.
(d) Plamsa protein binding of drugs sites is non specific.

113. High plasma protein binding of drug results in
(a) Increased efficiency
(b) Increases distribution
(c) Increased rate of metabolism
(d) Increased plasma t1/2

114. The following drugs easily cross the blood brain barriers
(a) Mathyl dopa & isoniazid
(b) Methyl dopa & dopamins.
(c) Isoniazid & streptomycin
(d) Quarternary Ammonium compounds

115. If drug is subject to the hepatic tissue, first pars effect
(a) It may be effective orally if given in high dosages.
(b) A chemical analogue resistant to hepatic metabolism may be done given orally.
(c) Response to the oral drug is more in presence of hepatic dysfunction.
(d) All of the above

116. Which of the following is classified as an Anti viral agent?
(a) Vidarabini (b) Gentomincin
(c) Ribaflinpin (d) Novobiocin

117. Which of the following drug undergoes marked hydrolysis in gastrointestinal tract?
(a) Asprin (b) Hydrocartisone
(c) Penicillin G (d) Chlortetracyclin

118. If a central nervous system drug is extensiovally ionized at the pH of blood, it will
(a) Penetrate the blood brain barrier slowly.
(b) Penetrate the blood brain barrier rapidly.
(c) Not penetrate the blood brain barrier
(d) Be eliminated slowly

119. An advantage of cyclocillin over ampicillin is
(a) It has a broader spectrum
(b) It may be given orally
(c) It produces a lower incidence of diarrhoea
(d) It is more stable

120. Tetracyclinis tend to farm complexes with
(a) Calcium ions

(b) Mercury ions
(c) Iron ions & Alluminium ions
(d) All of the above

121. Most drugs are
(a) Strong electrolytes
(b) Wheak electralytes
(c) Non electralytes
(d) Highly ionic

122. Hyaluronidase has property to
(a) Prevent oxidation of drugs.
(b) Increase absorption of injected drugs
(c) Produce sustained action
(d) Increase detoxification

123. Ranitidine is used primarily to treat
(a) Ulcer
(b) Diarrhoea
(c) Staphylococcal infections
(d) Colic

124. Which of the following compounds of undecylinic acid is most commonly used in therapy?
(a) Zn (b) Mg
(c) Mn (d) Ag

125 A vitamin that stains the urine is
(a) Vitamin D (b) Thiomine
(c) Riboflavin (d) Niacin

126. Diuretics tend to increase salt toxicity due to
(a) Sodium depletion
(b) Potassium deplition
(c) Direct drug introduction
(d) Increased absorption

127. Which of the following is an oral antifungal agent?
(a) Sopronol (b) Disenix
(c) Undecylinic acid (d) Grisiofulvin

128. Mitrofurantain is most active when the pH of urinary tract is
(a) Neutral (b) 0ver 9.5
(c) Between 6 to 7 (d) 5.5 or less

129. Alaes are used to treat which of the following
(a) Burns (b) Cartritis
(c) Carcinomas (d) Vertigo

130. Which of the following can cause discolouration of teeth?
(a) Chloromycetin (b) Penicillin
(c) Achromycin (d) Kanomycin

131. Which of the following can increase the serum level of penicllins significantly?
(a) Solicylates (b) Probenecid
(c) Kaolin (d) Antacids

132. Which of the following can increase the serum level of pencillins significantly?
(a) Salicylats (b) Probenecid
(c) Kaolin (d) Antacids

133. Which of the following diuretics is quite effective seen in presence of electrolytic imbalance?
(a) Ethacrynic acid (b) NH4Cl
(c) Chlorothiazide (d) Acetazolamids

134. Methotrikats should never be used concurrently with
(a) Aspirin (b) Penicillin
(c) Epinephrine (d) Tetracycline

135. Which of the following drugs is commonly used to treat schistosomiasis?
(a) Methylene blue
(b) Praziqunatel biltricide
(c) Chloroquine
(d) Oxyetrocycline

136. Salicyclic acid is used primarily as which of the following
(a) Analgesic
(b) Antipyretic
(c) Cough suppressant
(d) Kerotolytic agent

137. Which of the following is expectorant agent?
(a) Glyceryl guiachalate (b) Codine
(c) Wild cherry syrup (d) Glycerine

138. Which one of the following statements regarding drug ionization is correct?
(a) pka & pH are identical
(b) pka = Log ka
(c) Most of drugs are weak electrolytes
(d) Both b & c

139 Econozole nitrate (spectozole) is most effective against
(a) Fungal infections (b) Viruses
(c) Rictettsia (d) Tape worm

140. Hetocillin is converted by the body to
(a) Ampicillin (b) Penicilline G
(c) Penicillin V (d) Carbamicillin

141. Which anthelmintic is effective against multiple infestations?
(a) Talnaftals (b) Griseofulvin
(c) Flucytosine (d) Thiobendazole

142. Ampicillin may give a false positive diagnostic test for
(a) Uric acid (b) Glucose
(c) Cholesteral (d) Billrubin

143. Which of the following antibiotics has exceptionally good antifungal action?
(a) Bactracin (b) Spectinomyein
(c) Condicidin (d) Polymyxin

144. Which of the following is very similar to the cephalosporin?
(a) Doxycycline (b) Minocycline
(c) Carbenicillin (d) Moxalactam

145. Clindomycin interacts with
(a) Lactose (b) Kaolin
(c) Most luxatiues (d) Marcotic analgerics

146. Moxan (Moxalactam) is most closely related to which classes of Anti infectives
(a) Aminoglycoside (b) Sulfonamide
(c) Cephalosporine (d) Oleandomycine

147. Spectinomycin is used primarily as an alternative to
(a) Penicillin G (b) Bacitracin
(c) Kanamycin (d) Streptomycin

148. Which of the following is the most effective in treating rickettiatal infections?
(a) Pencillins (b) Tetracyclines
(c) Sulfonamides (d) Cephalosporin

149. The treatment of choice for leprosy is
(a) Penicillin therapy
(b) Broad spectrum antibiotic therapy
(c) Susfone therapy
(d) Chloromycetin therapy

150. The route of administration of bacitracin is
(a) Intra venous (b) Intra muscular
(c) Topical (d) Oral

151. Which of the following is not produced by moulds?
(a) Penicllin (b) Terromycin
(c) Streptomycin (d) Bacitracin

152. Which of the following is used exclusively for urinary tract infections?
(a) Pyrimethomin (b) Metronidazole
(c) Ticarcillin (d) Nalidixic acid

153. Which one is very effective in treating amaebiasis?
(a) Emetine HCl (b) Miconazole
(c) Trimethoprim (d) Cephalosporidine

154. Vancomycin should be well diluted to minimize
(a) Thrombophlebitis (b) Residual effect
(c) Ear damage (d) Chance of over dosing

155. Metronidozole is used mainly to treat
(a) Syphilis
(b) Trichomonas
(c) Resistant staphylococcus
(d) Pneumonia

156. In young ones tetracylcine often cause
(a) Agranulocytosis
(b) Discolouration of teeth
(c) Conjuctivitis
(d) Muscular ulceration

157. Which of the following has longest serum half life?
(a) Doxycyclin (b) Dixechlocycline
(c) Tetracycline (d) Oxytetracycline

158. Nitrofurantoin is used mainly to treat
(a) Respiratory tract infection
(b) Urinary tract infections
(c) Gastrointestinal tract infection
(d) Rickettesial infection

159. The route of administration of bacitracin is
(a) Intravenous (b) Intramuscular
(c) Topical (d) Oral

160. Which of the following should be used for severe fatal fungal infection?
(a) Nystatin (b) Grisiofulvin
(c) Amphotericin B (d) Condidicin

161. Histoplasmosis is best treated with
(a) Penicillin G (b) Amphotericin B
(c) Ampicllin (d) Tetracycline

162. Acyclovir is classified as which of the following
(a) Antiviral (b) Anthelmintic
(c) Antirickettsial (d) Penicillin

163. Which one is used to treat serious pseudomonas infection

(a) Ampicllin (b) Oxocillin
(c) Cloxacillin (d) Carbenicillin

164. Which is best to treat ring worm of the body?
(a) Boric acid (b) Tolnafate
(c) Iodofarm (d) Gentamicin

165. Vancomucins is effective primarily against
(a) Gram positive Bacilli
(b) Gram negative Bacilli
(c) Gram positive cocci
(d) Gram negative cocci

166. A bacteriostatic agent has which of the following property
(a) It kills bacteria on contact
(b) It dihydrates the bacteria
(c) It inhibits multiplication of bacteria
(d) It induces spore formation

167. Nystatin is used mainly to treat
(a) Blastomycosis (b) Coccidiomycosis
(c) Histoplasmosis (d) Candida infection

168. Penicillins can be obtained commercially from
(a) Yeast (b) Mold
(c) Fungi (d) Bacteria

169. Niclosamide is most effective against
(a) Tape worms (b) Pin worms
(c) Whip worms (d) Hook worms

170. Vancomycin is used to tract
(a) Urinary tract infections
(b) Skin infection
(c) Serious infection resistant to other drugs
(d) Burns

171. An advantage of Amoxicillin over ampicillin is that it
(a) Is more rapidly absorbed
(b) Less toxic
(c) Has a brooder spectrum
(d) Has a longer duration of action

172. A drug based in treating 2nd as 3rd degree burns is
(a) Mafinide (b) Sulfoxazole
(c) Mitrofurantoin (d) Polymyxin

173. A broad spectrum antibiotic that is effective against resistant staphylococcus infection is
(a) Vibromycin (b) Hinocylcine
(c) Dimeclocycline (d) Tetracycline

174. Which of the following antifungals also has amaebicidal properties?
(a) Nystatin (b) Flucytosine
(c) Miconazole (d) Metronidazole

175. Which of following is not metobalized by liver?
(a) Phenobarbital (b) Barbital
(c) Pentobarbital (d) Secobarbital

176. Vancomycin is
(a) Preferably administered intravenous
(b) Well observed orally
(c) Single chemical entity
(d) Isolated from a strain of bacillus

177. Pyridoxine is
(a) Vitamin B_6 (b) Vitamin A
(c) Vitamin B_1 (d) Vitamin B_2

178. Which of the following drug is used to treat fungal infestations of eye?
(a) Mafcillin (b) Nectomycin
(c) Amikacin (d) Idoxurine

179. Mutilmycin is classified as which of the following
(a) Penicillin (b) Aminoglycoside
(c) Tetracycline (d) Antifungal

180. Which of the following is a typical ingradient of Antacid preparations
(a) MgO (b) MgCO3
(c) CaCO3 (d) All of three

181 Betadine contains
(a) Benzocaine
(b) Betemethionine
(c) Povidine iodine complex
(d) Gention violet

182. Sulpha drug that is widely used to treat opthalmic infections
(a) Sulfapyridale (b) Sulfasinazole
(c) Sulfadiazine (d) Sulfacetamide

183. An agent commonly combined with local anesthetics is
(a) Epinephrine (b) Ephedrine
(c) Isoproterenol (d) None of these

184. Antidote for DDT poisoning is
(a) Adrenalin (b) Atropine
(c) Barbiturate (d) Amphitamine

185. One specific side effect of tridione administration is

(a) Gingival hyperplasia
(b) Glare phenomenon
(c) Rispiratary depression
(d) Cerebral depression

186. Colchicine is used mainly to treat
(a) Gout (b) Arthritis
(c) Diabetes (d) All

187. Tirbutaline has preference far stimatulation of which of the following receptors
(a) Alpha (b) b_1
(c) b (d) Dopominegic

188. Streptomycin can cause
(a) IV cranial nerve damage
(b) VIII cranial nerve damage
(c) X cranial nerve damage
(d) VI cranial nerve damage

189. Methanol may cause
(a) Blindness (b) Deafness
(c) Tetany (d) Gastritis

190. Which of the following agent is used for carcinoma of the liver?
(a) Vinblastine (b) Floxuridine
(c) Vincristine (d) Cytarabine

191. One of the epinephrine actions on the heart is
(a) Acceleration due to depression of vagus
(b) Increase in refractory period
(c) Depression of SA node
(d) Increase in concentration of the enzyme phosphorylase

192. Sulfonamides combine as
(a) Acetyl derivative (b) Amino derivative
(c) Sulfate derivative (d) Glycine conjugate

193. An Antifungas that release acetic acid only in the presence of the fungus is
(a) Enzactin (b) Viaform
(c) Gresiafalvin (d) Mycostatin

194 Which of the following is fastest acting anticoagulant?
(a) Warfarin (b) Heparin
(c) Ovabain (d) Vitamin K

195. Which of the following is a gamitocidal against malaria?
(a) Primaquine (b) Quinine
(c) Atabrine (d) Acalin

196. Clotrimazole is effective in treating
(a) Abortion (b) Diarrhaea
(c) Both a & b (d) Moniliasis

197. A specific narcotic antagonist is
(a) Mepiridine (b) Nalorphine
(c) Meprobamate (d) None of three

198. A very common side effect of marphine is
(a) Allergic response (b) Constipation
(c) Liver damage (d) Visceral pain

199. The most effective drug for prophylaxis against meningitis is
(a) Piniclin G (b) Penicillin V
(c) Erythromycin (d) Sulfisoxazole

200. Cimentadine is used to treat which of the following
(a) Hypertension
(b) Ulcers
(c) Edema
(d) Congestive heart failure

201. A class of plant alkaloids that are widely used to treat migraine are
(a) Ergot alkaloid
(b) Vinca alkaloid
(c) Stramonium alkaloid
(d) Balladona alkaloid

202. Viderakine is effective against which of the following
(a) Syphilis (b) Typhoid
(c) Herpes simplex (d) None of three

203. Which of the following is classified as an antiviral agent?
(a) Vidarakine (b) Gentamicin
(c) Rifampin (d) Novobiocin

204. Most useful antibiotic to treat serous infection caused by *Pseudomonas aeruginosa* strains is
(a) Rifampin (b) Novabiocin
(c) Kanomycin (d) Gentamicin

205. Which of the following groups depresses the activity of grisiofulvin?
(a) Barbiturates (b) Topical antifungals
(c) Dibenzazepines (d) Anticoagulants

206. The therapeutic uses of thyroid hormons includes which of the following
(a) Myxaedema (b) Cretinism

(c) Simple goitre (d) All the above

207. Which of the following drug is clinically effective in reflux oesophagitis?
(a) Metaclopramide (b) Domperidone
(c) Ranitidine (d) All of the above

208. Drug used in respiratory depression is
(a) Amphetamine (b) Dorapram
(c) Methylphenidate (d) Naetrexone

209. Which of the following imparts a pale blue fluorescence to urine?
(a) Trimeterene (b) Ribaflovin
(c) Nitrofurantoin (d) All of the above

210. An effect which is result of two chemicals acting together while simple sum of their effects when acting independently is
(a) Antagonistic effect
(b) Synergistic effect
(c) Additive effect
(d) Anti synergistic effect

211. Which drug does not produce its action by enzyme inhibition?
(a) Pencillins (b) Caffine
(c) Isoproperenol (d) Asprin

212. A example of competitive drug antagonist is
(a) Acetylcholine & atropine
(b) Epinephrine & Nistatine
(c) Histamine & acetylcholine
(d) Acetyl choline & neostigmine

213. Neostigmin is preferred to physostigmin in the treatment of myasthenia gravis because
(a) It is peripherally acting
(b) It has less chollinergic side effects
(c) It has prolonged action
(d) None of the above

214. Which one of the following drug stimulates dopamine receptors in the periphery?
(a) Adrenaline (b) I-Dopa
(c) Dobutamine (d) None of three

215. Term selective toxicity was given by
(a) Unlenheath (b) Paul Ehrlich
(c) Loeffler (d) Eisenberg

216. Drug receptor therapy was given by
(a) Paul Ehrlich (b) Domagic
(c) A. Flaming (d) Florey & Chain

217. First anti bacterial agent used in modern history was
(a) Penicillins (b) Sulfonamides
(c) Tetracyclines (d) Aminoglycosides

218. Sulfonamides inhibits the enzymes
(a) Dihydrofolate reductase
(b) DNA gyrase
(c) Topoisomerase IV
(d) Dihydropteroate synthetase

219. Resistance develops against sulfonamides by
(a) Mutation & conjugation
(b) Transduction
(c) Transformation
(d) None

220. Crystalurea occur due to toxicity of
(a) Penicllins (b) Tetracyclines
(c) Sulfonamides (d) Aminoglycosides

221. Photosensatization occurs due to toxicity of sulfonamides is
(a) Primary (b) Secondary
(c) Both (d) None

222. Trimethoprim blocks the enyzmes for this action
(a) Dihydrofolate reductase
(b) Topoisomerase IV
(c) Acotinase
(d) Dihydrofolate synthetase

223. Quinolons inhibit the enzyme for this effect
(a) DNA glyrase (b) Topoisomerase IV
(c) Actinase (d) Both a & b

224. Ciprofloxacin is a
(a) First generation quinolon
(b) Second generation quinolon
(c) Third generation quinalon
(d) None

225. Furazolidone act by
(a) Blocking oxidative dicarboxylation
(b) Blocking of cell wall synthesis
(c) Blocking protein synthesis
(d) None

226. First pinicillin which was obtained was
(a) Penicllin-V (b) Penicllin A
(c) Penicllin-G (d) Methyla penicllin

227. Natural penicillins are stable at a pH
(a) Between 3.5-5.0 (b) Between 9.5-10.5

(c) Between 6.0-7.0 (d) Between 1.5-3.5

228. 1 mg of penicllin-G sodium is equavalent to
(a) 1667 units (b) 1595 units
(c) 1676 units (d) 1955 units

229. 1 mg of pencillin-G potassium is equvalant to
(a) 1667 units (b) 1595 units
(c) 1559 units (d) 1676 units

230. Penicllins are mainly effective against
(a) Gram +ve
(b) Gram-ve
(c) Both gram +ve & -ve
(d) Acid fast organism

231. Carbenicilin is mainly effective against
(a) *Psudomanas sp.*
(b) *Staphylococcus sp.*
(c) *Eimeria sp.*
(d) *Salmonella sp.*

232. Clovulonic acid inhibit the B lactamare enzyme
(a) Reversibly (b) Irreversibly
(c) Chemically (d) None

233. Cephalosporine consist of
(a) Dihydrothiazine ring
(b) B-lactum ring
(c) Thiazolindine ring
(d) Both a & b

234. Cepalosporins are sensitive to
(a) Penicillinare (b) Cephalosporinase
(c) Both a & b (d) None

235. All tetracycline antibiotics
(a) Have same chemical structure but are stereotypic isomere
(b) Are isolated from steriptococcus rinosus
(c) Produce same side effects
(d) Are distroyed by alkali hydroxides?

236. Tetracyclines were discovered by
(a) Duggar (b) Allxander Flaming
(c) Poul Ehrilich (d) Damagle

237. Tetracyclines are
(a) Bacteriostatic (b) Bactericidal
(c) Fungistatic (d) None

238. Tetracyclins inhibits protein synthesis by binding at
(a) 50 S subunits (b) 40 S subunits
(c) 30 S subunits (d) 60 S subunits

239. The volume of distribution for tetracyclines is:
(a) Equal to body water
(b) Larger than body water
(c) Smaller than body water
(d) Very less distribution

240. Transport of aminoglycosides across the cytoplasmic membrane is
(a) An O_2 dependent active process
(b) An O_2 dependent passive process
(c) An CO_2 dependent passive process
(d) A CO_2 dependent active process

241. Aminoglycosides are
(a) Ionized at all physiological pH.
(b) Unionized at all physiological pH
(c) Ionized at acidic pH
(d) Ionized at basic pH

242. Curare like effect is due to toxicity of
(a) Penicillins (b) Tetra cyclines
(c) Quinolons (d) Aminoglycosides

243. Ototoxicity & nephrotoxicity found in long term use of
(a) Gentamicin (b) Tirromycin
(c) Erythromycin (d) Linomycin

244. Erythromycin is drug of choice for
(a) *E-coli* (b) *Leptospira sp.*
(c) PPLO (d) *Salmonilla sp.*

245. Macrosides inhibit protein synthesis by biding
(a) 30 S subunits (b) 60 S subunits
(c) 40 S subunits (d) 5 S subunits

246. Half life of erythromycin is
(a) 6-8 hrs (b) 1-2 hrs.
(c) 12-16 hrs. (d) 24-28 hrs.

247. Grey body syndromsccur due to toxicity of
(a) Macrolides (b) Aminoglycosides
(c) Chloramphenical (d) Polymixins

248. Drug of choice far salmonellosis is
(a) Chloramphenicol (b) Polymixin-E
(c) Penicllin-G (d) Erythromycin

249. Polymixin is:
(a) Palypeptide & basic in nature
(b) Nitrobenzin
(c) Polypeptid & acidic in nature
(d) Lactons

250. Rifampacin act through

(a) Inhibition of protein synthesis
(b) Inhibition of cell walls synthesis
(c) Inhibition of DNA dependent RNA polymase
(d) Inhibition of DNA synthesis

251. Antineoplastic antibiotic is
(a) Rifampicin (b) Bleomycin
(c) Methenamine (d) Tiamulin

252. Antiparasitic antibiotic is
(a) Bleomycin (b) Erythromycin
(c) Kanamycin (d) Hygromycin

253. Antifungal action of grisiofulin is by
(a) Inhibition of cell wall synthesis
(b) Increasing permiability of cell
(c) Inhibition of fungal mitosis
(d) Inhibition of protein synthesis

254. Chloramphenicol is obtained from
(a) *Streptomyces linolinsis*
(b) *Streptomyces unezuele*
(c) *Streptomyces fradiae*
(d) Both a & b

255. Father of chemotherapy was
(a) Paul Ehrlich (b) Unlen Teeth
(c) Laiffles (d) Eisenbery

256. Who discovered methyline blue?
(a) Paul Ehrlich (b) Domagk
(c) A-flaming (d) Ramnovsky

257. Chemotherapeutic properties of sulfonamides was discovered by
(a) Paul Ehrlich (b) Domagk
(c) A flaming (d) Ramnovsky

258. Which of the organism is frequently responsible for super infection?
(a) Salnomella (b) *E. coli*
(c) Leptospira (d) Klebulla

259. Choose the antimicrobial which acts by interfiring with DNA function in the bacteria
(a) Chloramphenicol (b) Ciprofloxacin
(c) Streptomycin (d) Vancomycin

260. Which antibiotic is primarily bacteriostiatic but becomes bacteriacidal at higher concentrations
(a) Erythromycin (b) Tetracycline
(c) Chloramphinicol (d) Ampicillin

261. Select the antibiotic that has a high therapeutic index
(a) Streptomycin (b) Doxycycline
(c) Cephalixin (d) Vancomycin

262. The following organism is notorious for developing antimicrobial resistance rapidly
(a) *Streptococcus pyogenes*
(b) *Meningococcus sp.*
(c) *Treponima pallidum*
(d) *Escherichia coli*

263. The most important mechanism of concurrent acquisition of multi drug resistance among bacteria is
(a) Mutation (b) Conjugation
(c) Transduction (d) Transformation

264. Drug destroying type of bacterial resistance is important far the following antibiotics except
(a) Cephalosporins (b) Tetracyclines
(c) Chloramphinicol (d) Aminoglycosides

265. Acquisition of inducible energy dependent efflux protein by bacteria serves to
(a) Secrete exotoxins
(b) Enhance virulence
(c) Lyse host tissue
(d) Confer antibiotic resistance

266. Super infections are more common with
(a) Use of narrow spectrum antibiotics
(b) Short courses of antibiotics
(c) Use of antibiotics that are completely absorbed from the small intestine
(d) Use of antibiotics combinations covering both gram +ve & gram -ve bacteria

267. The following organism are frequently responsible for super infections except
(a) *Psudomanas aeroginasa*
(b) *Salmonella typhi*
(c) *Clostridium diffucle*
(d) *Condida albicans*

268. Which antimicrobial should be avoid in patients of liver disease
(a) Tetracyclines (b) Cotrimoxozole
(c) Cephaexin (d) Ethambutal

269. Bacteriostateic drugs are unlikely to effect cure of bacterial infection in the following category of patients except

(a) Diabetic patients
(b) Patients with allergic disorders
(c) Patients on corticosteroid therapy
(d) Subactute bacterial endocarditis patients

270. Surgical antibiotic prophylaxis for clean electric surgery standard just before operation should be continued for
(a) One day (b) Two days
(c) Five days (d) Seven days

271. Indicate the sulfonomide whose sodium salts yields a nearly neutral solution which is suitable for topical use in the eye
(a) Sulfadiazine (b) Sulfacitamide
(c) Sulfadosine (d) Sulfamoxole

272. A higher incidence of adverse effect to cotrimoxozole occurs when this drug is used far
(a) Typhoid fever
(b) Whooping cough
(c) Pneumocystic carinii pneumonia in AIDS patients
(d) All

273. The following quinolans antimicrobial agent is not useful in systemic infections
(a) Lomefloxacin (b) Oflaxacin
(c) Nalidixic acid (d) Pifloxacin

274. Indicate the enzymes inhibited by fluroroquinolanes
(a) Tapoiscmerase II (b) Topoisomerase IV
(c) Both a & c (d) DND gyrase

275. Select the antimicrobial drug which is used orally only for urinary tract bacterial infection
(a) Nalidixic acid (b) Azithromycin
(c) Bacampicillin (d) All

276. Nalidixic acid is primarily active against
(a) Cocci
(b) Bacilli
(c) Gram positive bacteria
(d) Gram negative bacteria

277. Adverse effects of sulpha are referable primarily to the following except
(a) Gartro intestinal tract
(b) Kidney
(c) Skin
(d) None

278. A single oral dose of the following drug can cure most cases of uncomplicated ganorrhaea
(a) Ciprofloxocin (b) Cotrimaxozole
(c) Doxycycline (d) All

279. Which fluoroquinalone has enhanced activity against gram positive bacteria & anaerobes?
(a) Pifloxocin (b) Ciprofloxacin
(c) Sparfloxacin (d) Marfloxacin

280. Ciprofloxacin is not active against
(a) *H. influenzae* (b) *Leptospira Sp.*
(c) *E. coli* (d) *Bacteroides frogilis*

281. Currently the drug of choice for imperic treatment of typhoid fever is
(a) Chloramphenical (b) Lincomycin
(c) Ciproflaxacin (d) Ampicillin

282. The following drug may cure typhoid fever but does not prevent development of carrier state
(a) Ciprofloxacin (b) Tetracyclin
(c) Chloramphenicol (d) Lincomycin

283. Intradermal test for penicillin sensitivity test should be performed by injecting the following quantity of sodium binzyl penicillin
(a) 10 U (b) 100 U
(c) 1000 U (d) 50000 U

284. Through penicillin kills the causative organism, it has adjuvant value to
(a) Diphtheric
(b) Subacute bacterial endocarditis
(c) Syphilis
(d) Anthrax

285. Which of the following is not semisynthetic penicillin?
(a) Procaine penicillin
(b) Ampicillin
(c) Cloxocillin
(d) Carbinicillin

286. Cloxocillin is indicated in infections caused by the following organisms
(a) Staphylococci (b) Streptococci
(c) Conococci (d) All the above

287. The most frequent side effect of oral ampicillin is
(a) Nausea & vomiting
(b) Loose motions
(c) Constipation
(d) Urticaria

288. Amoxicillin is inferior to ampicillin for treatment of the following infection
(a) Typhoid
(b) *Shigella enteritis*
(c) Subacute bacterial endocarditis
(d) Gonorrhaea

289. Select the semi synthetic penicillin which is not acid resistant
(a) Phenoxymethyl penicillin
(b) Ampicillin
(c) Carbenicllin
(d) Cloxacillin

290. Clavulanic acid is combined with amoxicillin because
(a) It kills bacterial that are not killed by amoxicillin.
(b) It inhibits beta lactamares that distroy amoxicillin.
(c) It counteracts the adverse effects of amoxicillin.
(d) All of the above

291. Bactericidal action of aminoglycoside antibiotics is due to
(a) Inhibition of bacterial protein synthesis.
(b) Alternation of bacterial membrane permeability.
(c) Damage to bacterial cell wall
(d) Inhibition of bacterial oxidative metabolism.

292. Streptomycin sulfate is not absorbed orally because it is
(a) Degraded by gastro intestinal enzymes
(b) Destroyed by gastric acid.
(c) Highly ionized at a wide range of pH values.
(d) Insolable in water.

293. Clarithromycin is used for the following
(a) Multi drug resistant *M. tuberculosis* infection.
(b) *M. ovium* complex infection in AIDS patient.
(c) *M. tuberculosis* infection in a patient who develops Jaundice due to first line antitubercular drugs.
(d) Both a & c are correct.

294. In the short course regimin far treatment of tuberculosis, pyrozinamide & ethombutol are used for
(a) Initial one month (b) Initial two month
(c) Last two month (d) Throughout the course

295. Conciclovir is preferred over acyclovin in the following condition
(a) Herpes simplex keratitis
(b) Herpes zoster
(c) Chicken pox
(d) Cytomegalovirus retinitis in AIDS patients

296. Currently monotherapy with zidovudine is recommended for
(a) Asymptomatic HIV positive subjects with CD_4 cell count more than 200/ml.
(b) Asmptomatic HIV positive subjects with CD4 cell count less than 200 /ml
(c) HIV positive subjects with opportunistic infection
(d) None of the above

297. Though the following drug reduces HIV titre, it is used only to treat associated cytomegalovirus infections in AIDS patients
(a) Didanosine (b) Foscarnet
(c) Acyclovir (d) Saquinovir

298. The following Anti HIV drug should not be combined with zidovedine because of mutual organism
(a) Stavudine (b) Lamivudine
(c) Musirapine (d) Didanosine

299. Select the drug that is active against both HIV & Hepatitis B virus
(a) Lamivudine (b) Indinavir
(c) Didanasine (d) Etavirinz

300. Antiretroviral treatment affords the following benefits in HIV infection
(a) Increases CD4 lucocyte count.
(b) Reduces the incidence of opportunistic infection in AIDS patients
(c) Increase survival time in AIDS patients
(d) All of the above

301. Autonomous nervous system is
(a) Voluntry (b) Involuntry
(c) Both a & b (d) None

302. Which of the following is the characteristic feature of sympathetic nurvous system?
(a) Thoracolumber origin
(b) Pre ganglionic nerve fibres are shorter than post ganglionic
(c) Dynamic in nature
(d) All of above

303. Para sympathetic nurvous system is characterized by
(a) Origin at cranosaccral region
(b) Preganglionic nerve fibre is longer than ganglionic
(c) Dynamic in nature
(d) All of above

304. Sympathetic nurvous system is related to
(a) Conservation of energy
(b) Spending of energy
(c) Not related to a & b
(d) Both a & b

305. Which of the following system is related to para sympathetic nurvous system
(a) Conservation of energy
(b) Spending of energy
(c) Not of above
(d) Both a & b

306. Which of the following compound inhibits axonal condition by preserving "increase in permiability for Na^+ ions".
(a) Tetradotoxin (b) Batrachotoxin
(c) Adrenalined (d) Nor Adernal

307. Which of the following compound inhibits axonal conduction by increasing the permiability for Na+ ions?
(a) Batrochotoxin (b) Irbadotoxin
(c) Digitoxin (d) All of the above

308. Distance between pre & post Junctional segment is
(a) 500 A° (b) 50 A°
(c) 5000 A° (d) 50×10^{-3}A°

309. Receptors are macro molecular substances that are present on
(a) All surfaces (b) Cell cytoplasm
(c) Both a & b (d) Nuclear only

310. Which of the following is a parasympathetic activity?
(a) Increase Heart Rate
(b) Dialatation of pupil
(c) Bronchial dialatation
(d) Increases intestinal motility

311. Order of a- receptor adrenergi activity of cholamines is
(a) Epinephrine > Nor epinephrine < Isopnenaline
(b) Isopnenaline > Nor epinephrine > Epinephrine
(c) Epinephrine> Isopnenaline > Nor epinephrine
(d) None

312. Correct order of b receptor adrenergic activity of catecholamine
(a) Epinephrine > Nor epiprephrine < Isopnenaline
(b) Isopnenaline > Nor epiprephrine > Epinephrine
(c) Epinephrine> Isopnenaline > Nor epinephrine
(d) None

313. All a1 adnenergic receptors are
(a) Excitatory in nature
(b) Some are Excitatory some are depressant
(c) Inhibitory in nature
(d) All of above

314. Synonyms for Isoprenaline are
(a) Isoproterenol
(b) Isopropyl norepinephrine
(c) Isophopyl adrenol
(d) All of above

315. Epinephrine is
(a) Vasoconstructor (b) Bronchiodialators
(c) Cause mydriasis (d) All of above

316. Drug of choice for heart black is
(a) Adrenaline (b) Noradrenaline
(c) Isoproperenol (d) Acetylcholine

317. Which of the following drug shows the phinomina of Tachyphylaxis?
(a) Acetyl choline (b) Ephrine
(c) Carbachol (d) Moshgmine

318. Which of the following is/are b_2 bronchiodialators?
(a) Isoxpuprine (b) Clenbutamol

(c) Salbutamol (d) All

319. Which of the following is non competitive/ preversible a_1 blocker?
(a) Phenoxy benzamine
(b) Tolazaline
(c) Phentolamine
(d) All

320. Which of the following is a competitive a_1 blocker?
(a) Phenoxy Binzamine
(b) Tolazoline
(c) Phentolamine
(d) All

321. Which of the following is best & commonly used b-Blocker Agent?
(a) Properonolol (b) Practolol
(c) Prozosin (d) All

322. Which of the following is an a1 Blocking Agent?
(a) Labetolol (b) Propranolo
(c) Pracholol (d) Prazosin

323. Cholenergic receptors one classified into
(a) Nicotonic (b) Muscarinic
(c) Adrenergic (d) Both a & b

324. Which of the following muscarininc receptors (M) are present in heart?
(a) M_1 type (b) M_2 type
(c) M_3 type (d) M_4 type

325. To inhibit parasympathetic action which of the following compound inhibit 1 block transport of choline in to chalenergic fibre?
(a) Hemicholinium (b) Botulinum toxin
(c) Acetyl choline (d) None

326. To inhibit parasympathetic action which compound block release of Acetyle chlorine by cholenergic fibre?
(a) Hemicholinium (b) Botulinum toxin
(c) Acetyl choline (d) None

327. Major parasympathetic action of Acetyl choline is
(a) Decrease in heart rate
(b) Increases tone & motility of gastro intestinal motility
(c) Increase salutation
(d) All of above

328. Effect of acetyl choline on skeletal muscle is/are
(a) Muscle farciculation
(b) Asynchronus contration
(c) De polarizing paralysis
(d) All

329. Dose of carbachol for the treatment of colic & intestinal impaction in horse
(a) 1-2 mg subcutaneous
(b) 2-3 mg intramuscular
(c) 0.5 mg intramuscular
(d) 10 mg Intraperitoneal

330. Which of the following is/are cholinominiatic alkaloides?
(a) Pilocarpine & arecholine
(b) Muscorine
(c) Nicotine
(d) All

331. Which of the following is/are reversible cholinestrase inhibitors?
(a) Physostigmine (b) Niostigmine
(c) Edrophonium (d) All

332. Which of the following is/are irreversible cholinestrase inhibitors?
(a) Organophophorus compound
(b) PAM
(c) Both
(d) None

333. Antidote for organophosphorus compound toxicity is
(a) PAM
(b) Atropine
(c) Tetra ethyl pyrophosphate
(d) None

334. PAM is contra-indicated in which of the following toxicity
(a) Organo phosphrus toxicity
(b) Carbonate poisoning
(c) Organo chlorine toxicity
(d) Urea poisoning

335. Which of the following are natural parasympatholytic alkaloides?
(a) Atropine (b) Scopolamine
(c) Both (d) None

336. Synthetic anti cholinergic agent is

(a) Glycopyrolate & oxyphenonium
(b) Methontheline
(c) Prienzopine & Telenzepine
(d) All

337. Large dose of nicotine shows
(a) Initial stimulation followed by depression
(b) Only stimulation
(c) Only depression
(d) Initial depression followed by stimulation

338. Examples of Autocoids are
(a) Histamine (b) Serotonin
(c) Prostaglandine (d) All

339. "Triple Response" is related to which compound
(a) Histamine (b) Serotonin
(c) Prostaglandin (d) Kinins

340. H_1 Histominic blockers are
(a) Promethazine
(b) Chlor phineramine maleate
(c) Diamin hydromine
(d) All

341. H_2 Histominic blockers are
(a) Cimetidine (b) Ranitidine
(c) Burimamide (d) All

342. Angiotensin is spolypeptide Autocoid has following functions
(a) Vaso constrictor
(b) Na+ ion constriction
(c) Water absorption
(d) All

343. Inhibitors of Angiotensin converting enzyme are
(a) Captopril (b) Enalpril
(c) Teprotide (d) All

344. Which of the following prostaglandin is potent leuteolytic agent?
(a) Ph E (b) PG F_2á
(c) PGAs (d) PGI

345. Dose rate of PGF2á as a luteolytic agent in cow is
(a) 25-30mg/kg Bwt
(b) 25-30 mg total dose
(c) 10-15 mg total dose
(d) 50 I.U.

346. Hunger centre is located in
(a) Medulla (b) Pons
(c) Hypothalamus (d) Spinal cord

347. Which of the following drug promote gastric emptying?
(a) Hydrazine sulphate
(b) Metoclopromide
(c) BZP
(d) None

348. Centre for emesis control is
(a) Medulla (b) Pons
(c) Hypothalamus (d) Cerebelum

349. Which of the following is example of reflex emetics?
(a) $CuSO_4$ (b) $ZnSO_4$
(c) NaCl (d) All

350. Which of the following is/are anti emetic substance?
(a) Anti histamincs (b) Antichoinergic
(c) Prokinetics (d) All

351. Any inert bland substance which prevent the contact of gestric mucosa from toxic substance are termed as
(a) Adsorbends (b) Demulants
(c) Astringent (d) None

352. Management of peptic ulcer include
(a) Neutrilization of gastric acid
(b) Reduction of gastric acid secretion
(c) Healing of ulcer
(d) All

353. Which of the following is a systemic antacid?
(a) Sodium bicarbonate
(b) Sodium citrate
(c) Both
(d) None

354. Example of non systemic antacid is
(a) MgOH, $MgCO_3$ (b) $Al_2(OH)_3$
(c) $CaCO_3$ (d) All

355. Safest drug used for the treatment of gastroduodenal ulcer
(a) Sucralfate (b) Sodium citrate
(c) $CaCO_3$ (d) Megaldrate

356. Examples of prokinetic drug are
(a) Cholinergics (b) Metoclopromide
(c) Dompetridone (d) Cisapride

357. The substance that leads to semi solid and fluid faeces respectively called as

(a) Laxative & purgative
(b) Purgative & laxative
(c) Diarrhoeic substance
(d) Prokinetics

358. Which is an example of bulk purgative?
(a) Bran (b) Plantago seed
(c) Methyl cellulose (d) All

359. Examples of irritant/stimutant purgatives are
(a) Diphenylmethane derivative
(b) Emodine purgative
(c) Both
(d) None

360. Mechanism of Achon for irritant purgative is
(a) Increase intestinal motility
(b) Inhibits Na-K ATPase
(c) Hypokalemia
(d) All

361. One, the best drug used in acute heart failure is
(a) Epinephrine (b) Nor epinephrine
(c) Isophaline (d) All

362. Which of the following are reflex cardiac stimulants used in field practice
(a) Ammonia (b) CH_3COOH
(c) Alcohol (d) All

363. Substance that improves funchonal capacity of any organ up to it's optimum functional level are termed as
(a) Stimulant (b) Inducers
(c) Tonics (d) Expectorants

364. One of the best drugs used in treatment of congestive heart failure
(a) Digitoxin (b) Isoprimaline
(c) Adkenaline (d) Nor adtinaline

365. Mechanism of action of digitalis alkaloids is
(a) Inhibition of Na, K and ATPase enzyme
(b) Direct action on heart
(c) Activation of Na, K and ATPase enzyme.
(d) Decrease Ca^{+2} influxes in heart

366. Arrhythemia is characterized by abnormality in
(a) Heart rate only
(b) Conduction of impulse only
(c)
(d) Site of impulse generation only

367. Which of the following is a direct acting vasodilator?
(a) Amyl nitrate (b) Nitroglycerine
(c) Both (d) None

368. Which of the following is/are example(s) of Ca+2 channel blocks?
(a) Nifedipine (b) Minodipine
(c) Dilitiazam (d) All

369. Circulatory form of iron in blood is
(a) Transferrin (b) Ferritin
(c) Apoterritin (d) All

370. Soluble form of Iron is
(a) Transferrin (b) Ferritin
(c) Apoferritin (d) All

371. Blaud is pills contains following ingredients
(a) FeSO4 (b) K2CO3
(c) FeSO5 + K2SO3 (d) FeSO4+Na2CO3

372. Which of the following are examples of topical anti coagulant?
(a) Thromboplastin (b) Thrombin
(c) Fibrin (d) All

373. Which of the following topical anti coagulant is used to dust surgical glooves?
(a) Calcium alginate (b) Gelatin spong
(c) Thrombin (d) Oxidizid cellulose

374. Which of the following is an example of astringent coagulant?
(a) Shong solution of $FeCl_3$
(b) Alum
(c) 2% Tonnic acid & Tincture benzoin
(d) All

375. Example of parentral coagulants
(a) Melonic acid & oxalic acid
(b) Alum
(c) Tannic acid
(d) All

376. Strongest acid in body which act as natural anti coagulant property
(a) Heparin (b) HCl
(c) H_2SO_4 (d) Acetic acid

377. Examples of plasma expenders are
(a) Dextran (b) Acacia solution
(c) Strerile gelatin (d) All

378. Metabolic acidosis in animals is mainly due to
(a) Increase intake of carbohydrate

(b) Fault in fat metabolism
(c) Fault in protein mtabolism
(d) All

379. Mechanism of action of cardiovascular diuretics
(a) Increase renal blood flow & glomerular filteration
(b) Decrease in tubular reabsoption
(c) Inhibits release of ADH
(d) All

380. Example of loop diurstics
(a) Frusemide (b) Ethacynic acid
(c) Bumetenide (d) All

381. Which of the following hormone control urine volume?
(a) Adrinalene (b) ADH
(c) Oxytocin (d) Corticosteroides

382. Examples of osmotic diuretics
(a) Sugar (b) Salt
(c) Both (d) None

383. Substances which are used to relieve of suppress coughing
(a) Emulscene (b) Expectorants
(c) Both (d) None

384. Example of narcotic Emulscene
(a) Codine (b) Morphine hydrate
(c) Codoxime (d) All

385. Example of non narcotic antitissue agents
(a) Butarphanon (b) Aminophyline
(c) Ephedrine (d) All

386. Agents which liquify & increase pulmonary secretions & expel them out are known as
(a) Expectorants (b) Inhaller
(c) Anodyne (d) Analgesics

387. Example of gassous expectorants is
(a) CO_2 (b) O_2
(c) SO_2 (d) All

388. Agents which soften soothes, lubircate & protect skin against irritation are called
(a) Emollients (b) Demulscent
(c) Anodyne (d) Adsorbents

389. Examples of counter irritants is/are
(a) Ammonia liniment
(b) Ointment of red iodide of mercury
(c) Canthradine
(d) All

390. Which of the following is capable to present itching & irritation?
(a) White lotion (b) Callamine lotion
(c) Ammonia (d) All

391. Glucocorticoides has following action
(a) Immuno suppressive
(b) Anti inflammatory, antiallergic
(c) Catabolism of protein & fat
(d) All

392. Dose rate of corticosteroids drug fall in the range of
(a) 0.0001 mg to 5 mg/ kg bwt
(b) 0.0001-5 mg total dose
(c) 0.001 mg to 0.5gm/kg bwt
(d) None

393. Use of cortcosteroides is contra-indicated in
(a) Pregnancy
(b) Along with vaccination
(c) In infectious diseases
(d) All

394. Secretion of K+ in the distal tubule and collecting ducts of kidney depends on
(a) Intracellular K+ content
(b) Unabsorbed Na+ load presented to the distal segment
(c) Aldosterone level
(d) All of the above

395. Select the diuretic which is orally active, effective in acidic as well as alkaline pH, causes diuresis even in renal failure and has additional carbonic antihydrate inhibitory action
(a) Mannital (b) Bonzithiazide
(c) Indapamide (d) Furosemide

396. Furosemide acts by inhibiting the following at the end tubular cell
(a) Na^+,K^+,Cl^- and ca+ ion transport
(b) Na^+ and Cl^- transport
(c) $Na^{+ and} H^+$ transport
(d) $Na^+ K^+$ and ATPase transport

397. The following diuretic abolishes the corticomedullary osmotic gradient in the kidney
(a) Acetozolamide
(b) Furosemide
(c) Hydrochlothiazide

(d) Spirondactome

398. Parenteral furosemide is an alternative diuretic to mannitol in the following condition.
(a) Pulmarny edema (b) Cirrhotic edema
(c) Cerebral edema (d) Cardiac edema

399. The Na+-Cl- symporter in the early distal convaluted tubule of the kidney is inhibited by
(a) Thiazides (b) Metolazone
(c) Xipamide (d) All of the above

400. The primary site of action of thiazide diuretics is
(a) Proximal tubule
(b) Ascending limb of loop of heart
(c) Cortical diluting segment
(d) Collecting of ducts

401. Long-term thiazide therapy can cause hyperglycoma by
(a) Reducing insulin release
(b) Increasing corticosteroid secretion
(c) Increasing symphetic activity
(d) Decreasing corticosteroid secretion

402. In addition to contemporary potassium loss, following consequence of thiazide/furosemide therapy may also occur
(a) Hyper viremia
(b) Rise in pharma LDL-cholesterol
(c) Magnesium loss
(d) Both 'A' & 'C' are correct

403. At equintrinsic doses which diuretic causes the maximum K+ loss?
(a) Furosemide
(b) Hydrochlorothiazide
(c) Acetazatamide
(d) Amiloride

404. Which of the following has a 'self limiting diuretic' action?
(a) Indaparide (b) Spironolactrine
(c) Xipamide (d) Acetazatamide

405. The following is not itself on efficacious diuretic, and is used only as an adjuvant/corrective to other diver tics.
(a) Actazolamide (b) Metolazone
(c) Spironolactone (d) Indaparide

406. Spironolactone can be usefully combined with the following diuretics except
(a) Furosemide
(b) Amiloride
(c) Hydrochlorothiazide
(d) Chlorthalidone

407. The correct therapeutic induction of acetazolamide is
(a) Congestive heart failure
(b) Renal insufficiency
(c) Cerrhosis of liver
(d) Glaucoma

408. Amiloride inhibits K^+ excretion is the distal tubules & collecting ducts by blocking
(a) Electrogenic K^+ channels
(b) Electrogenic Na^+ channels
(c) Non electrogenic Na^+ & Cl^- symporter
(d) H^+, K^+ and APTase

409. Which of the following is a 'K' retaining diuretics
(a) Triamterene (b) Trimethoprim
(c) Tizanidine (d) Trimetazidine

410. Use of 'K' sparing diuretics in patients receiving the following drug needs close monitoring
(a) Furosemide
(b) Hydrochlorothiazide
(c) Cuptoril
(d) Verapamil

411. Which of the following peptide is a selective vasopressin viz receptor against
(a) Arginine vasopressin
(b) Desmopressin
(c) Lypressin
(d) Terlipressin

412. The following tissue is most sensitive to vasopressin
(a) Renal collecting ducts
(b) Intestinal smooth muscle
(c) Vascular smooth muscle
(d) Uterus

413. Indications of desmopressin includes the following except
(a) Neurogenic diabetes insipidus
(b) Nephrozonic diabetes insipidus
(c) Bedwetting in children
(d) Bleeding due to haemophilia

414. Choose the antimicrobial which acts by interfering with DNA function in the bacteria

(a) Chloramphenicol (b) Ciprofloxacin
(c) Streptamycin (d) Vancomycin

415. Which antibiotic is primarily bacteriostetic but becomes becteriocidal at high dose
(a) Erythromycin (b) Tetracycline
(c) Chloramphenicol (d) Ampicillin

416. Select the antiobiotics that has high theraputic index
(a) Streptomycin (b) Doxycycline
(c) Cepthalexin (d) Vancomycin

417. The following organism is notorious for developing anti microbial resistance rapidly
(a) *Streptococcous pyogenies*
(b) *Meningococcus sp.*
(c) *Treponema pellidum*
(d) *Escherichia coli*

418. The most important mechanism of concurrent acquistion of matching resistance among bacteria is
(a) Mutation (b) Conjugation
(c) Trasnduction (d) Transformation

419. Drug destroyor of bacteria is important for the following antibiotics except
(a) Cephalosporins (b) Tetracyclins
(c) Chloramphenicol (d) Aminoglycosides

420. The concentration of Nitrofurazone solution as used opthalamically
(a) 2% (b) 20%
(c) 0.02% (d) 1%

421. Select the antibioitic whose dose must be reduced in patients with renal insufficiency.
(a) Ampicillin (b) Chloramphenicol
(c) Tobramycin (d) Erythromycin

422. Which antimicrobial should be avoided in patients of liver disease?
(a) Tetracycline (b) Cotrimoxazole
(c) Cephalexin (d) Ethambutol

423. Choose the condition which is mostly tracted with a combination of antimicrobials
(a) Lobar pneumonia (b) Typhoid
(c) Peritonitis (d) Syphilis

424. The therapeutic use of nesigmine bromide is: -
(a) Neuromuscular blocker
(b) Treatment of curare poisoning
(c) Muscle relaxant
(d) All of these

425. The following quinolone antimicrobial agent is not useful in systemic infection
(a) Lamefloxacin (b) Oflaxacin
(c) Nalidixic acid (d) Refloxacin

426. Indicate the enzyme (s) inhibited by fluroquinolones
(a) Both 'a' & 'c' (b) Topoisomerase II
(c) Topoisomerase IV (d) DNA gyrase

127. The drug that can be used to treated osteoporosis are
(a) Raloxifene (b) Alendronate
(c) Pamidranate (d) Both 'a' & 'b'

128. Adverse effects of ciprofloxacin are referable primarily to the following except
(a) Gastrointestinal tract
(b) Kidney
(c) Skin
(d) Nervous system

429. A single oral dose of the following drug can be used in most cases of uncomplicated gonorrhea
(a) Ciprofloxacin (b) Cotrimaxazole
(c) Spectinomycin (d) Doxycycline

430. Ciprofloxacin is not active against
(a) *H. influenza*
(b) *E. coli*
(c) *Enterobactor spp.*
(d) *Bacteroides fragiles*

431. The beta lactam antibiotics include the following
(a) Cephalosporins (b) Monobactans
(c) Carbapenems (d) All of the above

432. Which of the following is not semisynthetic penicllin?
(a) Procaine penicillin
(b) Ampicllin
(c) Cloxacillin
(d) Carbenicilla

433. The most frequent side effect of oral amipicillin is
(a) Naursea & vomiting
(b) Loose motions
(c) Constipation
(d) Urtiaria

434. Amoxillin in inferior to ampicillin for the treatment of the following infection

(a) Typhoid
(b) Shigella enteritis
(c) Subacute bacterial endocordities
(d) Gonorrhoea

435. Select the semisynthetic panicillin which is not acid resistant
(a) Phenoxymethyl penicillin
(b) Ampicillins
(c) Carbenicillin
(d) Cloxacillin

436. Select 4th generation cephelosporin among the following
(a) Cefpirome (b) Ceftizoxime
(c) Ceftazidine (d) Cefuroxime

437. Select the most potent tetracycline antibiotic
(a) Demeclocycline (b) Oxytetracycline
(c) Ceftazidine (d) Cefuroxime

438. The following tetracycline has the potential to cause vesticular toxicity
(a) Minocycline (b) Demectocycline
(c) Minocycline (d) Doxycycline

439. The following anticancer drug has high emetoganic potential
(a) Vincristine (b) Chlorambacil
(c) 6-nercaphopurine (d) Cisplatin

440. Which of the following neoplastic disease is almost curable by chemotherapy?
(a) Branchogenic carcinoma
(b) Cholicarcinoma
(c) Malignant melanoma
(d) Colorectal carcinoma

441. The most important target of action of chlorambucil is
(a) Myocordial tissue (b) Lymphoid tissue
(c) Neural tissue (d) Skin

442. The following antineoplastic drug is a mitotic inhibitor and causes metaphase arrest
(a) Bushlfan (b) Vincristine
(c) Cytarabine (d) Procarbazine

443. Select the cell cycle non specific antipneoplastic drug
(a) Vincristine (b) Bleomycin
(c) Methotrexate (d) 5-Fluoronracil

444. The characteristic toxicity of dexorubictin is
(a) Kidney damage (b) Liver damage
(c) Cordiomyopathy (d) Pulmonary fibrosis

445. Patients treated with the following anticancer drug are likely to develop a disuffiron like reaction on taking alcohol.
(a) Decarbazine (b) Procarbozine
(c) Melphelon (d) Hydroxyurea

446. Which of the following is a selective H1 receptor against?
(a) 4-methyl histamine
(b) Impromidine
(c) 2-thiazolymethylamine
(d) Chlorpheniramine

447. The drug that can directly release histamine from most cells without involving antigen-antibody reaction is
(a) Aspirin (b) Procaine
(c) Morphine (d) Sulfadizine

448. High anticholinergic property is present in the following antihistaminic
(a) Diphenhydromine
(b) Astemizole
(c) Cetrizine
(d) Terfenadine

449. The conventional H_1 antihistamics posses the following additional properties except
(a) Local anaesthetic (b) Vasopresin
(c) Antiarrhythmic (d) Catecholamine

450. Selective H1 antihistaminic which is used topically in the nose for allergic rhities
(a) Laroladine (b) Cetrizine
(c) Fexofenadine (d) Azelastine

451. The following 5-HT receptor is not a G protein coupled receptor
(a) 5-HT1 (b) 5-HT2
(c) 5-HT3 (d) 5-HT4

452. The site of action of d-tubocurarine is
(a) Spinal neurone (b) Motor nerve ending
(c) Muscle end-plate (d) Sodium channels in the muscle fibre

453. Succinylcholine produces spastic paralysis in
(a) Rabbit (b) Frogs
(c) Birds (d) All of the above

454. The fall in blood-pressure caused by

detubocurarine is due to
(a) Reduced venous return
(b) Ganglian blockade
(c) Histamine release
(d) All of the above

455. The following antibiotic accentuates the nuromuscular blockade produced by procuranium
(a) Spephomycin (b) Erythromycin
(c) Penicillin (d) Chloramphenicol

456. Which of the following is a centrally acting skeletal muscle relaxant?
(a) Carisoprodal (b) Dantrolene sodium
(c) Quinine (d) Decanethorium

457. The following is a skeletal muscle relaxant that acts as a central á1 adrenegic against
(a) Carisoprodal (b) Dantrolene sodium
(c) Quinine (d) Decanethorium

458. Diazepam is used on a muscle relaxant for
(a) Deep intro-abdominal operation
(b) Tracheal intubation
(c) Tetanus
(d) Diagnosis of myasthenia gravis

459. Which sensation is blocked first by concentration of a local anaesthetic?
(a) Pain (b) Temperature
(c) Touch (d) Deep pressure

460. The following local anaesthtic raised BP instead of tending to cause a fall
(a) Cocaine (b) Dibucaine
(c) Lignocaine (d) Procaine

461. Toxicity of local anaesthetics involves the following organs except
(a) Heart
(b) Brain
(c) Kidney
(d) Skin & subcutoneas tissue

462. The local anaesthetic with the largest duration of action is
(a) Procaine (b) Chlornoprocaine
(c) Lignocaine (d) Dibutaine

463. Which of the following is a poor surface anaesthetic?
(a) Procaine (b) Lignocaine
(c) Tetracaine (d) Bonoxinetic

464. The local anaesthetic having high cordiotoxic & arrhythmogenic potential is
(a) Lignocaine (b) Procaine
(c) Bupivacine (d) Ropivacaine

465. None surgical operation should be performed during in following stage of anaesthesia
(a) Stage I (b) Stage II
(c) Stage III, Phase I (d) Stage III, Phase III

466. Select the inhelational anaesthetic that is metabolized in the body to a significant extent
(a) Sevoflurane (b) Isoflurene
(c) Ether (d) Halothane

467. The anasthetic that can be used by the open drop method
(a) Ether (b) Desflurane
(c) Halothane (d) Isothane

468. The minimal absorber concentration (MAC) of helothane is
(a) 75% (b) 25%
(c) 7.5% (d) 0.75%

469. The following general anaesthetic has poor muscle relexant action
(a) Ether (b) Nitrous oxide
(c) Helothane (d) Isoflurane

470. The daily dose of elemental iron for maximal haemopoietic response in an anaemic adult is
(a) 30 mg (b) 100 mg
(c) 200 mg (d) 500 mg

471. 'Fe' sarbitol-citric acid differs from iron dextron in that
(a) It can not be injected I.V.
(b) It is not excreted in urine.
(c) It is not bound to transferrin in plasma
(d) It produces fewer side effects

472. The daily dietary requirement of vit B_{12} by an adult is
(a) 1-3 mg (b) 50-100 mg
(c) 0.1-0.5 mg (d) 1-3 mg

473. The following factor is required for the absorption of dietary vit. B_{12}.
(a) Gastric acid
(b) Gestric intrinsic factor
(c) Both a & b
(d) None

474. Blood level of which clotting factor declines most rapidly after the initiation by warfarin therapy
(a) Factor VIII (b) Factor IX
(c) Factor X (d) Prothrombin

475. The following drug reduces the effect of oral anticoagulants
(a) Broad spectrum antibiotic
(b) Cimetidine
(c) Aspirin
(d) Oral contraceptive

476. Select the fibrinolytic drug that is antigenic
(a) Streptophase (b) Urokinase
(c) Alteplase (d) Both 'a' & 'b'

477. For healing duodenal ulcer, the duration of the blocker thearpy is
(a) 4 weeks (b) 6 weeks
(c) 8 weeks. (d) 12 weeks

478. Gynaecomastia can occur as a side effect of
(a) Broncocriptive (b) Cimetidine
(c) Foamotidine (d) Levodopa

479. The first choice drug for non steroidal anti-inflammatory drug associated gastric ulcer is
(a) Omeprozole (b) Misoprostol
(c) Panictidine (d) Sucraffate

480. Any drug is select on, the basis of
(a) Safety (b) Potency
(c) Efficacy (d) All of the above

481. The following is a competitive antagonist of GABA but a non competitive antganist of diazepam
(a) Picrotoxin (b) Muscimal
(c) Flumazenil (d) Bicuculline

482. The elderly patients are relatively intolerant to
(a) Digoxin (b) Silbutamol
(c) Propronalol (d) Nife dipine

483. Tricyclic antidepressants abolish the antihypertensive action of the following drug
(a) Enalapril (b) Clonidine
(c) Atenolol (d) Diltriazem

484. Imipramine produces the following actions except
(a) Euphoria
(b) Dryness of mouth
(c) Tachycardia
(d) Lowering of seizure threshold

485. The percentage of elemental iron in hydrated ferrous sulfate is
(a) 5% (b) 10%
(c) 20% (d) 33%

486. The thyroid inhibitor which produces the fastest response is
(a) Lugol's iodine (b) Radioactive iodine
(c) Propylthioracil (d) Lithium carbonate

487. Dextromethorphan is an
(a) Analgesic (b) Antitussive
(c) Expectorant (d) Anti histaminic

871. Nitrofurantion is used mainly to treat: -
(a) Gastro intestinal tract infection
(b) Urinary tract infections
(c) Rickettesial infection
(d) Myocarditis

872. The drug that may be used for treating rickettsial infections is: -
(a) Penicillin (b) Tetracycline
(c) Closental (d) Cephalosporin

490. The following expectorent acts both directly on the airway as well as reflexly
(a) Potassium iodine (b) Gualyshenestin
(c) Terph hydrite (d) Bromhexine

491. Codeine is used clinically as
(a) Analgeic (b) Antitussive
(c) Antidirrhoeal (d) All of the above

492. Which of the following is used topically as a cardiovascular agent?
(a) Propranolol (b) Procainamide
(c) Nitroglycerine (d) Lidocaine

493. The following antiasthma drug not a bronchodilater
(a) Iproatropium bromide
(b) Theophylline
(c) Formotent
(d) Sodium cromoglycate

494. Select the fastest acting inhaled bronchodilater
(a) Ipratropium bromide
(b) Formoterol
(c) Selbutemol
(d) Selmatenol

495. The following vascular net is constricted by caffine

(a) Coronery (b) Cutaneous
(c) Cranial (d) Mesentric

496. Intranasal spray of budesonide is indicated in
(a) Common cold
(b) Acute sinusitis
(c) Perinial vesicular rhinitis
(d) Epistaxic

497. The vitamins that is regarded to be a hormone is
(a) Vit D (b) Vit C
(c) Vit B_{12} (d) Vit A

498. The drug of choice of hypoparathyridism is
(a) Parathormone (b) Calcium lactate
(c) Vit D (d) Pamichromite

499. Biphosphonates are beneficial in the following condition except
(a) Paget's disease
(b) Senite osteoporosis
(c) Rickets
(d) Osteolytic bony metastesis

500. Suramin drug is present in
(A) Germanin (B) Berenil
(C) Samorin (D) Ganaseg

501. Cymelarsan is effective against
(A) *Trypanosoma evansi*
(B) *T. vivax*
(C) *T. simiae*
(D) *T. brucei*

502. Which one is used in prophylaxis of trypanosomiasis?
(A) Cymelarsan (B) Suramin
(C) Quinapyramine (D) Diaminazine

503. The hepatic injury induced by carbon tetrachloride is mediated:
(a) Trichloromethylperoxy free radical (Cl_3COO)
(b) Trichloromethyl free radical
(c) Trichloromethyl free radical (CCl_3)
(d) None of the above

504. The most sensitive method for the analysis of toxicants is:-
(a) Column chromatography
(b) Gas-liquid chromatography
(c) UV spectrophotography
(d) None of the above

505. Strychnine acts by: -
(a) Producing postsynaptic inhibition in the spinal cord
(b) Stimulating the motor cortex
(c) Stimulacing somatic nerve endings.
(d) None of the above

506. The severity of organophosphorus insecticides toxicity signs are best correlated with extent of inhibition of:
(a) Brain acetylcholinesterase
(b) Plasma cholinesterase
(c) Both
(d) None of the above

507. The suitable anticoagulant for toxicological analysis is: -
(a) EDTA (b) Potassium oxalate
(c) Heparin (d) None of the above

508. The drug of choice for eviction of toxin from the intestine is: -
(a) Magnesium sulphate
(b) 1,8-dihydroxyanthraquinone
(c) Carbachol
(d) None of the above

509. The basic toxicant present in biological sample is efficiently extracted by adding:
(a) Acid (b) Alkali
(c) Alcohal (d) None of these

510. The poisoning of cyanogenetic glycosides in cattle can be diagnosed by:
(a) Smell of garlic like odor
(b) Smell of phenol like odor
(c) Smell of bitter almond like odor
(d) None of the above

511. The toxic effects of malathion is due to: -
(a) Malaoxon (b) Malathion
(c) Both (d) None of these

512. The toxic signs of nitrite appear on levels of blood methaemoglobin more than:
(a) 5 % (b) 10 %
(c) 20 % (d) None of these

513. Interaction of silver nitrate and sodium chloride produces: -
(a) Strychnine tannate
(b) Calcium floride
(c) Silver chloride

(d) Cyanomethaemoglobin

514. Interaction of fluoride and calcium lactate produces: -
(a) Silver chloride
(b) Strychnine tannate
(c) Calcium floride
(d) Cyanomethemoglobin

515. Interaction of Strychnine and tannic acid produce:
(a) Silver chloride
(b) Calcium floride
(c) Strychnine tannate
(d) Cyanomethaemoglobin

516. Interaction of cyanide and methaemoglobin produces -
(a) Silver chloride
(d) Cyanomethaemoglobin
(c) Strychnine tannte
(b) Calcium floride

517. Leucomethylene in nitrite poisoning act by: -
(a) Converting methaemoglobin
(b) Adsorption
(c) Chelation
(d) None of above

518. In lead poisoning, calcium sodium acts by: -
(a) Converting methaemoglobin
(b) Chelation
(c) Adsorption
(d) None of above

519. In copper poisoning, penicillamine act by: -
(a) Converts methaemoglobin
(b) Chelation
(c) Adsorption
(d) None of above

520. In DDT poisoning, activated charcol acts by: -
(a) Adsorption
(b) Chelation
(c) Converts methaemoglobin
(d) None of above

521. How British antilewisite acts in arsenic poisoning: -
(a) Converts methaemoglobin
(b) Chelation
(c) Adsorption
(d) None of above

522. How fluoroacetate acts in acetate poisoning: -
(a) Converts methaemoglobin
(b) Chelation
(c) Adsorption
(d) Competitive substitution

523. How drugs enter and distributed across cell boundaries: -
(a) Filtration (b) Diffusion
(c) Active transport (d) All of these

524. Log dose-response curves of agonist, given with or without antagonist may be parallel: -
(a) When the drug antagonism is physiological
(b) When the drug antagonism is non- competitive
(c) When the drug antagonism is competitive
(d) None of the above

525. The appropriate statements for active transport of drugs is/are: -
(a) It utilize carrier substances
(b) It require energy expenditure
(c) It is transport against a concentration gradient.
(d) All of the above

526. Ionisable groups, when tend to lose an H + then it is called: -
(a) An acid (b) A base
(c) A free radical (d) None of these

527. Which of the following statement is incorrect for rapid excretion of drugs:
(a) High glomerular filtration rate
(b) Drug should be ionized
(c) Drug should have high protein binding capacity
(d) Drug should be unionized

528. In the drug resistance the phage involved is: -
(a) Transformation (b) Transduction
(c) Mutation (d) None

529. The first pharmacopeia was compiled by: -
(a) Englishman (b) German
(c) Egyptian (d) Indian

530. The first laboratory for the study of pharmacology was established by: -
(a) Ruaolph Buclcim (b) Friedrieh Serturner
(c) John J. Abel (d) Oswald Selsiedeberg

531. Most of a does of aspirin is absorbed from the

small intestine because: -
(a) The surface area is large
(b) The pH is alkaline
(c) The pH is acidic
(d) None of the above

532. The most appropriate statement for distribution of the drug from blood is:
(a) The extent or protein bindings
(h) Pka of the drug
(c) Differences in blood flow
(d) All of the above.

533. Solutions that contain bacteriostatic agents: -
(a) May not be tested for sterility
(b) Must be diluted beyond the bacteriostatic level for sterility tests
(c) Do not require a sterility test.
(d) All of the above

534. The bond strength of the hydrogen bond is: -
(a) 2-5 K cal/mole
(b) 10-20 K calories/mole
(c) 50 to 150 K cal/mole
(d) Less than one K cal/mole

535. The drug which is free in the blood: -
(a) May be pharmacologically active but non-diffusible
(b) May not be available for metabolism as they are non-diffusible
(c) Both
(d) None of the above

536. Ebers papyrus was written about: -
(a) 1550 B.(C) (b) 3000 B.(C)
(c) 5000 B.(C) (d) 7000 B.C.

537. Which of the following is most applicable for the variation in the dosage of a drug: -
(a) Species of animal
(b) The intended effect of the drug
(c) The individual susceptibility to the drug
(d) All of the above

538. Abnormalities of genetic material caused by the drugs is known as: -
(a) Teraogenesis (b) Oncogenesis
(c) Mutagenesis (d) All of the above.

539. Double-reciprocal plot is applied widely for the analysis of: -
(a) Competitive antagonism
(b) Non-competitive antagonism
(c) Both of the above
(d) None of the above

540. A chemical compound converts in useful drug when: -
(a) If it possess therapeutic activity
(b) If it is free of toxicity
(c) Both of the above
(d) None of the above

541. Under steady state conditions, if plasma concentration of a drug is 30 mg/100 ml after a dose of 5 mg/kg, the plasma concentration of the drug will be: -
(a) 50 mg/100 ml
(b) 30 mg/100 ml
(c) More than 35 mg/ ml
(d) None of the above

542. After thalidomide disaster which of the following animal tests is mandatory for a new drugs: -
(a) Administration of the drugs in either sex before mating
(b) Administration of the drug through-out pregnancy
(c) Observation of the animal from birth to maturity
(d) All of the above

543. Elimination of a drug 'X' obeys first order kinetics. 'X' is bound to plasma proteins by 95% and its half-life is 6 hours. In presence of another drug 'Y' which competes with drug 'X' for the same binding sites, X is bound to the extent of 90%. Half-life of X will be approximately.
(a) 1 hours (b) 3 hours
(c) 6 hours (d) 4 hours

544. The following statement regarding passage of drugs across cell membrane is correct: -
(a) Acidic environment of stomach favours absorption of alkaline drugs
(b) Polar drugs readily cross all membrane
(c) Ionized drug is not diffusible
(d) All of the above

545. Administration of sodabicarbonate with sulphonamides will: -
(a) Increase the excretion of sulphonamides from renal tubule

(b) Decrease the excretion of sulphonamides from renal tubule
(c) Increase the absorption of sulphonamides
(d) Decrease the absorption of sulphonamides

546. Active transport across the cell members is: -
(a) Carrier mediated (b) Energy dependent
(c) Both a and b (d) None of above

547. The time taken to achieve a steady condition of pharmacokinetics is directly proportional to: -
(a) Plasma clearance rate
(b) Plasma drug concentration
(c) Half-life a
(d) Both b and c

548. Correct statement regarding drug ionization: -
(a) pka - Log Ka
(b) Most of drugs are weak electrolytes
(c) pka and pH are identical
(d) Both a and b

549. The equation which correctly shows the relationship between the drug dose D(ug), the interval between successive doses T (h), the mean steady-state plasma drug concentration with pss (ug/ml) and the clearance CI (l/h) is : -
(a) D/T with pss x CI
(b) T/D = with pss x CI
(c) DT = with pss x CI
(d) D/T = pss/CI

550. Correct statement about drug absorption from gastro-intestinal tract is:-
(a) Stomach is the major site of drug absorption
(b) Colon is incapable of absorption of drugs
(c) Sublingual drug administration gives quick onset of action
(d) All of the above

551. If a drug has a half life of 5 hours, on administering @ 5 mg/kg will have the following half-life at a dose of 10 mg/kg, if other factors remaining constant: -
(a) 2 hrs (b) 3 hrs
(c) 5 hrs (d) 6 hrs

552. Sublingual administration can be adopted for the following drug: -
(a) Glycery trinitrate (b) Methyl testosterone
(c) Both of the above (d) None of the above

553. Ethanol is eliminated mainly by: -
(a) Acetylation in the liver
(b) Excretion in the expired air
(c) Excretion in the liver
(d) Oxidation in the liver

554. Following statement is true regarding rectal administration of drugs: -
(a) It is a convenient mode of the administration in presence of vomiting
(b) Rectal administration of drugs may produce systemic effects
(c) This bypasses chemical reactions at upper part of intestine
(d) All of the above

555. Under stationary conditions, plasma concentration of a drug at any given time can be obtained by the formula: -
(a) Area under the concentration versus time curve divided by volume of distribution
(b) Area under the concentration versus time curve divided by the dose of the drug in mg/kg
(c) Volume of distribution divided by interval between doses
(d) Area under the concentration versus time curve divided by interval between doses

556. Following is true regarding oral administration: -
(a) All soluble drugs are absorbed from Gastro intestinal tract
(b) Benzyl penicillin is absorbed from stomach
(c) Both a and b
(d) None of these

557. The equation which correctly describes the relationship between the plasma concentration half-time T1/2 (min), the distribution volume V (ml) and clearance Cl (ml/min) of a drug is: -
(a) T = 0.7 (1/V) x CI
(b) T 1/2 = 0.7 V x CI
(c) T 1/2 = 0.7 CI/V
(d) T 1/2 = 0.7 V/CI

558. Drug administration by inhalation is: -
(a) Is only possible for gases and volatile liquids
(b) Is for systemic or local effects
(c) Leads to cough and bronchospasm

(d) Both a and b are correct

559. The concurrent administration of phenobarbitone increases the dosage of warfarin requires for effective anticoagulant therapy because: -
(a) It induces liver microsomal oxidase
(b) It forms an inactive complex with warfarin
(c) It displaces warfarin from albumin binding
(d) It diminishes the renal tubular reabsorption of warfarin

560. The bioavailability by oral rout is a ratio between:
(a) The oral does and I. V. does
(b) Maximum plasma concentration by oral rout and the Maximum plasma concentration I.V dose.
(c) T maximum by oral rout & T maximum I.V rout.
(d) None of the above

561. Digoxin has a longer plasma concentration half-time than gentamicin because:-
(a) Digoxin has a much greater effective volume of distribution
(b) The renal clearance of digoxin is smaller
(c) Dixoxin is metabolized less rapidly
(d) None of the above

562. The following is true regarding plasma protein binding: -
(a) Highly plasma protein bound drugs have short plasma T1/2
(b) Basic drugs are not bound to the proteins
(c) Acidic drugs are bound with the albumen fraction
(d) Plasma protein binding sites are non-specific

563. All of the following factors except one will improve the bioavailability: -
(a) Hydrous crystalline form
(b) Amorphus form
(c) Highly water soluble form
(d) Smaller particle size

564. High plasma-protein binding of drugs results in: -
(a) Increased plasma T ½
(b) Decreased efficiency
(c) Decreased distribution
(d) Increased rate of metabolism

565. Bioavailability of a drug depends on: -
(a) Size of drug particle
(c) Crystal hydration
(d) Crystal form
(b) All of the above

566. The following drugs easily cross blood brain barrier: -
(a) Methyl dopa and dopamine
(b) Isoniazid and streptomycin
(c) Mathyl dopa and isoniazid
(d) All of the above

567. Which one of the following neurotransmitters is amine: -
(a) Noradrenaline (b) Phenylethylamine
(c) Both (d) None of the above

568. The purpose of biotransformation is: -
(a) To convert drugs into water soluble compounds
(b) To inactivate drugs
(c) To break down complex chemicals into simple compounds
(d) All of the above

569. Which of the following may show tachyphylaxis:
(a) Ephedrine (b) Noradrenaline
(c) Both (d) None of these

570. Phase I metabolism reaction includes: -
(a) Acetylation
(b) Methylation and sulphation
(c) Oxidation and reduction
(d) All of the above

571. Which one of the following blocks histamine, muscarinic and 5-TH receptors: -
(a) Cyproheptadine (b) Promethazine
(c) Methysergide (d) None of the above

572. First pass effect include which of the following: -
(a) Hepatic metabolism
(b) Metabolism by intestinal wall enzymes
(c) Metabolism by intestinal flora
(d) All of the above

573. Which of the following blocks histamine 2 receptors: -
(a) Mepyramine (b) Metiamide
(c) Both of these (d) None of these

574. Which of the following expected pharmacological actions contribute to the antihypertensive action of propranolol: -

(a) Down regulation of aortic and carotid receptors
(b) Vasodilatation
(c) Both of these
(d) None of the above.

575. If a drug is subject to 'Hepatic first pass effect: -
(a) It may be effective orally
(b) A chemical analogue may be resistant to hepatic metabolism
(c) Both of these
(d) None of the above

576. Which one of the following is a selective adrenergic alpha 2 blocking agent:-
(a) Yohimbine (b) Clonidine
(c) Both of these (d) None of these

577. Enzyme induction: -
(a) Is seen with most of drugs
(b) Relates to all metabolizing enzymes
(c) Both of these (d) None of these

578. Which one is a selective postsynaptic á and b receptor blocking agent:-
(a) Phentolamine (b) Yohimbine
(c) Prazocine (d) None of these

579. Inhibition of hepatic cytochrome p-450 activity may be achieved by: -
(a) Cietidine (b) Spironolactone
(c) Ethylestradiol (d) All of the above

580. Which one blocks both adrenergic á and b receptors: -
(a) Atenolol (b) Labetolol
(c) Pindolol (d) None of these

581. True statement in severe hepatic disease is:-
(a) Oxidative reaction is unaffected
(b) Conjugation reactions on the unaffected
(c) Lonizable drugs can be prescribed normally
(d) All of the above

582. Which one of the following is selective adrenergic â2 receptor antagonist:-
(a) Butoxamine (b) Practalol
(c) Timolol (d) None of these

583. Enterohepatic circulation:-
(a) Is decreased by drugs which sterilize the gut
(b) Does not affected plasma 1/2 of drugs
(c) Takes place with drugs which are excreted in the free from bile
(d) All of the above

584. Which one of the following is a selective adrenergic â2 receptor agonist:-
(a) Atenolol (b) Salbutamol
(c) Adrenaline (d) All of the these

585. True statement for the 'first order' of kinetics of drugs clearance is:-
(a) The plasma concentration- time curve is linear
(b) A fixed amount of drug is eliminated in a unit time
(c) Plasma concentration is reduced to 25% after 2t 1/2
(d) Urinary excretion is the primary mode of clearance

586. Which one of the following adrenergic â blockers has a marked membrane stabilizing action: -
(a) Propranolol (b) Metoprolol
(c) Acebutolol (d) All of these

587. Which of the following statement is true regarding Zero order' kinetics:-
(a) The rate of elimination is independent of plasma concentration
(b) This is also called' saturation kinetics'
(c) In this case the metabolizing enzyme is saturated
(d) All of the above

588. Which one of the following is a selective adrenergic â receptor antagonist:-
(a) Acebutolol (b) Atenolol
(c) Metoprolol (d) None of these

589. In repeated administration of fixed amount of a drug, a steady state level is achieved, then:-
(a) Does- response relationship will be linear
(b) Long does - response curve is sigmoid
(c) ED_0 is the minimum does at which there is no effect
(d) All of these

590. The adrenergic â-receptor thought to be an enzyme is: -
(a) Adenyl cyclase (b) Phophokinase
(c) Phosphdiesterase (d) None of these

591. The characteristics of competitive antagonism is/are:-
(a) It binds to the agonist reversibly
(b) It is surmountable
(c) The antagonism has affinity for the receptor but weak intrinsic activity
(d) Both a and b

592. Which one of the following stimulates dopamine receptors: -
(a) Adrenaline (c) Dobutamine
(b) I - dopa (d) All of these

593. Which one is true for spare receptors:-
(a) They determine the efficiency of receptor-effectors interaction
(b) If present in large number, increase sensitivity of the tissue to the drug
(c) Both a and b (d) None of these

594. Which one of the following drugs stimulates dopamine receptors in CNS:-
(a) Amantadine (b) Deprenyl
(c) Tyramine (d) None of these

595. The true statement regarding lingand gated plasma membrane channels is/are:-
(a) They are present on the cell surface
(b) They regulate the flow of ions through membrane channels
(c) Several amino acid neurotransmitters act by this mechanism
(d) All of the above

596. Atropine is contraindicated in which of the following: -
(a) Partial heart block
(b) Bronchial asthma
(c) Urinary retention
(d) All of the above

597. True statement regarding 'pharmacologic potency' and 'maximal efficacy:-
(a) Clinical effectiveness of drugs depends on its maximal efficacy
(b) Efficacy refers to the maximal response that can be achieved in high does
(c) Potency refers to concentration of drug required to produce a specified effect
(d) All of the above

598. Neostigmine is preferred over physostigmine for the treatment of myasthenia gravis because: -
(a) It is longer acting
(b) It has fewer side effects
(c) It is peripherally acting
(d) None of the above

599. One of the antiviral agent among following is: -
(a) Gentamicin (b) Novobicin
(c) Ribfampin (d) Vidarabine

600. Atropine is contraindicated in glaucoma as:
(a) It increases intraocular circulation
(b) It decreases the drainage of intraocular fluids
(c) It increases the secretion of intraocular fluids
(d) None of the above

601. Atropine can completely block the actions of: -
(a) Carbachol (b) Acetylcholine
(c) Arecholine (d) All of these

602. Idiosyncratic drug response is: -
(a) Usually caused by the genetic differences
(b) Regulated by the immunologic mechanisms
(c) A form of hypersensitive reaction
(d) Both a and b

603. Pirenzepine is: -
(a) An antagonist for muscarinic M_1 receptor
(b) An antagonist for muscarinic M_2 receptors
(c) An antagonist for both M1 and M2 receptors
(d) All of the above

604. Which of the following statement is true: -
(a) Tolerance develops to all the actions of a drug
(b) Acute type of tolerance is known as tachyphytaxis
(c) Species variation may be responsible for tolerance
(d) Both b and c

605. The specific affinity label for muscarinic cholinoceptors is: -
(a) Benzolycholine mustard
(b) Decamethonium
(c) â haloalkylamines
(d) a - bungarotoxin

606. The organs interacted by both sympathetic and

parasympathetic nerves are: -
(a) Spleen, sweet gland and radial muscle of iris
(b) Smooth muscles of gut, bronchus, urinary bladder
(c) Arterioles and veins
(d) Cerebral blood vessels

607. Delayed neurotoxicity may be observed in hen following exposure to: -
(a) Leptophos (b) Carbaryl
(c) Malathion (d) All of above

608. Pentazocine is said to be a partial antagonist of morphine because: -
(a) It partly blocks the m receptor but has intrinsic motion at the k receptor
(b) It has affinity for the m receptor but partly blocks k receptor
(c) It has intrinsic activity at the m receptor but also blocks k receptor
(d) None of the above

609. Denervation supersensitivity occurs in: -
(a) In the skeletal muscles after denervation
(b) In the blood vessels after sympathetectomy
(c) Due to regulation of receptors
(d) All of the above

610. Acetylcholinesterase is: -
(a) Hydrolyses acetylcholine only
(b) Is identical with plasma cholinesterase
(c) May show genetic variation
(d) Is present in all cholinergic neurons

611. The presynaptic nerve terminals of ANS have the following characteristics except: -
(a) They are not sensitive to the transmitters released by the neuron
(b) The presynaptic inhibition may be homotropic as well as heterotropic
(c) They release more than one transmitter in response to nerve impulses
(d) They synthesize, store and release transmitters in response to nerve impulses

612. A receptor antagonist has which of the following:
(a) Only intrinsic activity
(b) Both affinity and intrinsic activity
(c) Only affinity for the receptor
(d) None of the above

613. The noradrenaline release from the post ganglionic sympathetic nerve may be:-
(a) Facilitated by angiotensim II
(b) Inhibited by noradernaline via a_2 receptors
(c) Inhibited by enkephaline via d receptors
(d) All of the above

614. DDT decreaes: -
(a) Firing threshold
(b) Neuronal excitability
(c) Both
(d) None of the above

615. Selenium produces toxicity by: -
(a) Replacing sulfur incertain tissues
(b) Inhibiting sulfurdryl enzymes
(c) Both a and b
(d) None of the above

616. Acetylcholine: -
(a) Release adernaline
(b) Is released from sympathetic nerve
(c) Both a and b
(d) None of the above

617. Amphetamine: -
(a) Is central nervous system stimulant
(b) Acts directly on adrenergic receptors
(c) l-form is biologically more active
(d) Is commonly used in obesity

618. Cocaine: -
(a) Is widely used as local anesthetic
(b) Is a direct sympathomimetic drug
(c) Is an alkaloid from erythroxyloncoca
(d) Produces passive mydriasis

619. Bradykinin: -
(a) Causes pain & itching locally
(b) Releases catecholamine from adrenal medulla
(c) Causes vasodilatation
(d) All of the above

620. Ouabain is: -
(a) Obtained from digitalis purpurea leaf
(b) Rapidly absorbed from intestine
(c) Highly bound to plasma protein
(d) None of the above

621. Amiodarone is: -
(a) A safe drug with minimum side effects
(b) A pure Na channel blocker

(c) Having extremely short half life
(d) A powerful inhibitor of abnormal automaticity

622. Lignocaine is: -
(a) Very useful in suppressing arrhythmias
(b) Least cardiotoxic
(c) Both a and b
(d) None of the above

623. Prazosin is: -
(a) A good dewormer
(b) Used in moderate hypertension and congestive heart failure
(c) Both a and b
(d) None of the above

624. Azathioprine is used primarily as: -
(a) Immunosuppressive
(b) Cardiotonic
(c) Transquilizer
(d) Antihypertensive

625. Oral hypoglycemic agents increase the metabolism of: -
(a) Digitoxin (b) Propanolol
(c) Lidocaine (d) Morphine

626. A source of anticarcinogenic drugs is: -
(a) Belladona (c) Vincarosla
(b) Nux vomica (d) Digitalis

627. Which of the following is not correct about Chloramphenicol: -
(a) It is devoid of toxicity and is well tolerated
(b) May have a febrile period follows the administration
(c) It is well absorbed by the oral routs and diffuses well into tissues
(d) None of the above

628. Most drugs are: -
(a) Strong electrolytes
(b) Weak electrolytes
(c) Non electrolytes
(d) Highly ionic

629. A vitamin stains the urine is: -
(a) Vitamin A (b) Thiamine
(c) Niacin (d) Riboflavin

630. Radioactive decay follows a: -
(a) I order rate (d) II order rate
(c) III order rate (b) Zero order rates

631. An antidote for heparin over dosage is: -
(a) Dicumerol (b) Atropine
(c) Ca salt (d) Protamine suphate

632. AlCl3 is used mainly as: -
(a) Antiemetic (b) Urinary acidifier
(c) Luxative (d) Antiperspirant

633. Prostaglandin E is used in the form of: -
(a) Capsules (b) Tablets
(c) Solution (d) Vaginal suppositories

634. Chlorambucil acts as: -
(a) Antimetabolite (b) Antibiotic
(c) Alkylating agent (d) Mitotic inhibitor

635. A disadvantage of chloralhydrate is: -
(a) Disagreeable odour
(b) Lack of absorption
(c) Rapid elimination
(d) Allergic reaction

636. Calcium EDTA chelates lead from: -
(a) Blood (b) Bones
(d) Erythrocytes (d) None of the above

637. The action of acetylcholine released from nerve terminals is limited by: -
(a) Acetylcholinesterase
(b) Cholineacetylase
(c) Both a and b
(d) Pseudocholinesterase

638. Death in animals occurs immediately when the carbon monoxide content of air is: -
(a) > 0.1 % (b) > 0.5 %
(c) > 3 % (d) None of these

639. Physostigmine is: -
(a) Drug of choice of myesthenia gravis
(b) Potentiates the action of carbachol
(c) Is a quaternary ammonium ion
(d) Competitor with acetylcholine for true cholinesterase

640. According to patons scheme agonist receptor complex leads to picking up of: -
(a) Extracellular potassium
(b) Extracellular potassium
(c) Membrane bond Ca++
(d) None of the above

641. True statement for amphetamine is: -
(a) Dextro isomer has potent peripheral action
(b) Levo isomer has potent central actions
(c) Levo isomer has potent peripheral actions
(d) Both levo and dextro isomers have potent central actions

642. Which drug not produces its action by enzyme inhibition: -
(a) Isoproterenol (b) Penicillins
(c) Caffeine (d) Aspirin

643. Cholinergic drugs may be used in: -
(a) Alzheimer's disease
(b) Myasthenia gravis
(c) Acute angle - closure glaucoma
(d) All of the above

644. Cholinergic drugs are contraindicated in: -
(a) Bronchial asthma (b) Hyperthyroidism
(c) Peptic ulcer (d) All of the above

645. Which one of the following is the most neuro-toxic: -
(a) Carbon tetrachloride
(b) Benzene
(c) Cadmium
(d) Carbon disulphide

646. Pyridoxine is: -
(a) Vitamin A (b) Vitamin B_1
(c) Vitamin B_2 (d) Vitamin B_6

647. The indirect effect of Acetyl choline is: -
(a) Decrease in heart rate
(b) Increase in vagal tone
(c) Miosis
(d) Tachycardia

648. Toxicity of pyrithrins is: -
(a) Least (b) Acute
(c) Subacute (d) Chronic
(e) Aminophylline

649. Theophylline: -
(a) Inhibitis phosphiesterase
(b) Prevents degradation of intracellular cAMP
(c) Causes relaxation of all vascular smooth muscles except cerebral vessels
(d) All of the above

650. Cimetidine can prolong the duration of action of:
(a) Propranolol (b) Phenytion
(c) Diazepam (d) All of the above

651. The adverse effects of testosterone include: -
(a) Gynaecomastia
(b) Aggressive behaviour
(c) Increased in libido
(d) Masculiniziation in females

652. An antiviral agent is: -
(a) Novobiocin (b) Gentamicin
(c) Rifampin (d) Vidarabine

653. An antidote for curare poisoning: -
(a) Atropine (b) Hexamethonium
(c) Neostigmine (d) None of these

654. Contraindicated drug in the presence of active tuberculosis is: -
(a) Streptomycin (b) PABA
(c) Hydrocortisone (d) None of these

655. Epinephrine's action is: -
(a) Depression of vagus
(b) Depression of SA node
(c) Increase in refractory period of heart
(d) Increase in concentration of the enzyme phosphrylase A

656. First toxic symptoms of the digitalis poisoning is:
(a) Flushing of skin
(b) Gastro intestinal irritation
(c) Undue depression of heart rate
(d) Cerebral excitement

657. Colchicine is used mainly to treat: -
(a) Carcinomas (b) Arthritis
(c) Diabetes (d) Gout
(e) Antifungal

658. Antacid may be: -
(a) MgO (b) $MgCO_3$
(c) $CaCO_3$ (d) All of these

659. An advantage of amoxicillin over ampicillin is: -
(a) Broader spectrum
(b) Less toxic
(c) Rapid absorption
(d) Longer duration of action

660. Suitable combination of Gentamicin to treat serious pseudomonas infection is:-
(a) Carbenicillin (b) Ampicillin
(c) Cloxacillin (d) Oxacillin

661. Which of the following is produced by moulds: -
(a) Bacitracin (b) Penicillin
(c) Streptomycin (d) Both b and c

662. Clindomycin interacts with: -
(a) Lactose
(b) Most laxatives
(c) Narcotic analgesics
(d) Kaolin

663. Salicylic acid is used as: -
(a) Keratolytic agent
(b) Antipyretic
(c) Cough suppressant
(d) Analgesic

664. Suitable drug to offset the effects of caumarin derivatives is: -
(a) Calcium (b) Adrenalin
(c) Vitamin K (d) All of them

665. Absorption of vitamin A from the gastro intestinal tract depends on: -
(a) pH of the intestine
(b) Acid base balance
(c) The presence of bile in the intestine
(d) None of thee

666. Discoloration of teeth occurs by: -
(a) Achromycin (b) Penicillin
(c) Chloromycetin (d) Kanamycin

667. Hemin is derived from:-
(a) Vitamin B_{12} (b) Liver
(c) RBC (d) Ferric compounds

668. Pale blue fluorescence to urine may be obtained following administration of: -
(a) Nitrofurantion (b) Riboflavin
(c) Triamterene (d) All of the above

669. Iron preparations may stain the urine:-
(a) Yellow (b) Brown
(c) Purple (d) Black

670. The true statements regarding neuroleptanalgesia is: -
(a) It can be induced by a combination of fentany & droperidol
(b) It can be induced by a combination of morphine& droperidol
(c) It has minimal respiratory depression
(d) All of the above

671. Hypotensive action of guanethidine is due to: -
(a) Depletion of nordrenaline from neurons
(b) Direct vasodilation
(c) a - adrenergic blockade
(d) Prevention of release of noradrenaline

672. The route of drug administration is governed by:
(a) Physical and chemical character of the drug
(b) The intensity of the action desired
(c) The completeness of absorption of the drug
(d) All of the above

673. Therapeutic uses of digoxin include: -
(a) Low output failure of heart
(b) Atrial fibrillation
(c) Prophylactically prior to cardiacsurgery
(d) All of the above

674. The correct mechanisms of actions of potassium sparing diuretic is: -
(a) Mechanism of action of amiloside is similar to that of triamterene
(b) Prevent depletion of intracellular K^+
(c) Triamterene directly inhibits Na transport in the collecting tubules
(d) All of the above

675. PGE_{2a} is responsible for: -
(a) Bronchoconstriction
(b) Uterine contraction
(c) Vasoconstriction
(d) All of the above

676. Side effects of H1 receptor antagonists may be: -
(a) Loss of vision
(b) Contact dermatitis on local application
(c) Dryness of mouth
(d) All of the above

677. H_1 receptor antagonists are indicated in: -
(a) Angioneurotic oedema
(b) Motion sickness
(c) Insect bite
(d) All of the above

678. H_2 receptor antagonists are indicated in:-
(a) Duodenal ulcer
(b) Reflux oesophagitis
(c) Acute ulcerative colitis
(d) All of the above

679. Following dugs are selective H_2 receptor antidote:-
(a) Ranitidine (b) Fomitidien

(c) Cimetidine (d) All of the above

680. Which of the following are histamine releasers: -
(a) Morphine & polymixin
(b) d-tybopcurarine
(c) Succinylcholine
(d) All of the above

681. Lignocaine: -
(a) Produces convulsions in large doses
(b) Is used in atrial fibrillation
(c) Has surface anesthetic action
(d) Antagonizes the effects of sulphonamide

682. Local anaesthetics: -
(a) Have sympathomimetic actions
(b) Affect only myelunated fibers
(c) Block calcium channels
(d) Prevent generation and propagation of impulses

683. Solutions that contain bacteriostatic agents: -
(a) Do not require a sterility test
(b) Can not be tested for sterility
(c) Must be diluted beyond the bacteriostatic level for sterility tests
(d) None of the above

684. The drugs which blocks an autonomic ganglion by persistent depolarization is:
(a) Nicotine in large does
(b) TMA
(c) DMPP
(c) TEA

685. The drugs that can be used as nasal contestant and vasopressor is: -
(a) Clonidine (b) Exhedrine
(c) Prometazoline (d) Noradrenaline

686. Hyoscine differs from atropine in which of the following: -
(a) It has greater ability to cross blood brain barrier
(b) It is more effective in motion sickness
(c) It is more effective in glandular secretions
(d) All of the above

687. Correct statements for belladonna is: -
(a) *Datura stramonium* contains hyoscine
(b) Racemic isomers are more potent than l-isomers
(c) Belladonna in Italian means 'Beautiful Lady'
(d) None of the above

688. Belladonna alkaloids are: -
(a) Esters of the tropic acid
(b) Water soluble
(c) Able to block all cholinergic receptors
(d) All of these

689. Nicotinic receptors of acetylcholine are present at: -
(a) Suprarenal medulla
(b) Autonomic ganglia
(c) Skeletal muscle
(d) None of the above

690. Gluathione involved in the detoxification of various electrophilic compounds is:
(a) Glutamylcysteinylvaline e
(b) Glutamylcysteinylaglycine
(c) Glutamylcysteinylalanin
(d) None of the above.

691. Muscarinic actions of acetyl choline include: -
(a) Tachycardia
(b) Release of adrenaline from adrenal medulla
(c). Colic pain in abdomen and excessive salivation
(d) All of these

692. Photosensitization in *Lantana camara* poisoning is due to: -
(a) A mixture of several photodynamic substances
(b) Phyloerythrin
(c) Chlorophyll
(d) None of the above

693. Neostigmine is: -
(a) Acts only by inhibiting acetylcholinesterase
(b) Not completely blocked by atropine
(c) A tertary amine
(d) None of the above

694. Carbamates act by interacting at: -
(a) Anionic site of AchE
(b) Esteratic site of AchE
(c) Both a and b
(d) None of the above

695. Butyrylcholinesterase is: -

(a) Present in plasma and liver
(b) Different from pseudocholinesterase
(c) Reversibly inhibited by DFP
(d) Hydrolyses procaine but not succinylcholine

696. Glucuronide formation is mediated by: -
(a) Microsomal enzymes
(b) Non-microsomal enzymes
(c) Both a and b
(d) None of the above

697. Incorrect statement about cholinergic agents is: -
(a) Echothiophate is used in glaucoma
(b) Pilocarpine is used as a miotic
(c) Carbachol has a very short duration of action
(d) Amanita muscarina is a poisonous mushroom

698. True statement in relation to dextio isomer of 3 hydroxy N-methyl morphinan is: -
(a) It is an antitussive and lacks analgesic activity
(b) It is both antitussive and analgesic
(c) Only levo isomer is potent antitussive agent
(d) Levo isomer lacks both analgesic and antitussive property

699. In myasthenia gravis: -
(a) Quinine is contraindicated
(b) Atropine prevents the adverse action of neostigmine
(c) Edrophenuim exaggerates myasthenic crisis
(d) Both a and b

700. Which of the group of drugs are isosters: -
(a) Carbachol, Methacholine, Hemicholinium
(b) Norepinephrine, Isopreterenol, Epinephrine
(c) Amphetmine, Ephedrine, Isoproterenol
(d) Isoprenaline, Salbutamol, Cabuterol

701. Neostigmine potentiates the parasympathomimetic effects of: -
(a) Methacholine (b) Muscarine
(c) Pilocarpine (d) Carbachol

702. Parasympathomimetics can be used for the treatment of: -
(a) Atony of bladder following surgery and glaucoma
(b) Bronchial pneumonia
(c) Parkinsonism
(d) Gastritis

703. Isosteres are: -
(a) Chemicals of homologues series
(b) Optical isomers
(c) Chemicals acting on same receptors
(d) Atoms, groups of atoms or molecules with general resemblances but different electronic properties

704. Atropine decreases the following secretions: -
(a) Sweat secretions
(b) Lachrymal secretions
(c) Salivary secretions
(d) All of the above

705. Atropine is: -
(a) Obtained from *Hyoscyamus niger*
(b) A tertiary amine blocks M and M_2 receptors
(c) Same as l-hyoscyamine
(d) None of above

706. True statement regarding geomectrical isomerism is: -
(a) Trans isomers of tripolidine and thioxanthines are more active
(b) Cis isomer of tripolidine and thioxanthines are more active
(c) Both a and b
(d) None of the above.

707. Mushroom poisoning is: -
(a) Occurs due to Amanita muscaria
(b) Occur by Aphalloides
(c) Treated symptomatically
(d) All of the above

708. Adrenergic neurotransmitters and B-haloalkylamines in low concentrations interact with receptor: -
(a) In irreversible manner
(b) B-haloalkylamine anactivate receptors
(c) In competitive manner
(d) None of the above

709. Anticholinergic drugs may be used as preanaesthetic agent as they: -

(a) Depress salivary secretion
(b) Depress bronchial secretion
(c) Prevent laryngospasm
(d) All of the above

710. For irreversible antagonism which of the statement is true: -
(a) There is strong bond between drug and receptor
(b) The antagonism is non-surmountable
(c) In presence of antagonist maximal response is reduced
(d) All of the above

711. An example of competitive drug antagonism is: -
(a) Epinephrine and histamine
(b) Histamine and acetyl choline
(c) Acetylcholine and Neostigmine
(d) Acetyl choline and atropine

712. The neuronal uptake of nor-adrenaline has following characteristic: -
(a) Sympathetectomy increases this process
(b) It has equal affinity for all catecholamines
(c) It is Na+ dependent and is blocked selectively by cocaine and imipramine
(d) Guanithidine is a substrate for uptake

713. BAL and penicillin produce therapeutically useful action by: -
(a) Conversion into metabolically active drug
(b) Chelation
(c) Oxidation
(d) Receptor mediated action

714. The extraneuronal uptake of nor-adrenaline has following characteristics: -
(a) Reserpine acts on both uptake 1 and uptake 2 mechanism
(b) It is present in non neuronal tissues like heart, blood vessels and intestine
(c) It is inhibited uptake 1 inhibitors
(d) It has equal affinity for all catecholamines

715. The drug-receptor interaction involve: -
(a) Hydrophobic bonds
(b) Elctrostatic bonds
(c) Covalent bond
(d) All of the above bonds

716. Monoamine oxidase: -
(a) Inactivates exogenous amine like tyramine
(b) Causes oxidative deamination of biogenic amines
(c) Is a mitochondrial enzyme
(d) All of the above

717. The putative anesthetic/hypnotic action of barbiturates: -
(a) Due to their GABA-mimetic action
(b) Due to metabolic conversion into active metabolite
(c) Due to their physicochemical action
(d) All of the above

718. The drug acting by non receptor mediated action is: -
(a) Strychnine (b) Neostigmin
(c) Carbachol (d) Halothane

719. COMT is a: -
(a) Cytoplasmic enzyme in liver and kidney
(b) It converter of nor adrenaline and adrenaline into nor metanephrine and metanephrine
(c) It converts of diaminated products of catecholamine into VMA
(d) All of the above

720. d - tubocurarine is: -
(a) Completely metabolized in liver
(b) Obtained from *Chondodendron tementosum*
(c) Rapidly absorbed orally
(d) A glycoside

721. Protamine antagonizes the action of heparin by: -
(a) Receptor mediated action
(b) Making the basic groups
(c) Making the acidic group
(d) Physiochemical actions

722. Following drugs produce hypotension as they are a_2 agonist: -
(a) Guanethidine
(b) Hexamethonium
(c) a -methyl dopa & clonidine
(d) Reserpine

723. For sensitization test, the animals preferably used are: -
(a) Guinea pigs (b) Rabbits
(c) Dogs (d) Rats

724. The main excretory products of catecholamine in the urine may be: -

(a) HVA
(b) VMA
(c) Normetanephrine and metanephrine
(d) All of the above

725. Gallamine: -
(a) Releases histamine
(b) Produces tachycardia
(c) Produces hypotension due to the ganglion blockade
(d) Safe drug for cardiac renal diseases

726. Charecteristics of curve obtained between log does and the proportion of animals dead, drawn on a graph is: -
(a) Sigmoid (b) Normal Curve
(c) Linear (d) Hyperbola

727. Propranolol produces following effects on CVS: -
(a) Reduces myocardial oxygen demand
(b) Negative chronotropic and intropic effects on heart
(c) Products central sympathoplegia resulting in hypocardial
(d) All of the above

728. Covalent linkage of the absorbed chemicals with products of the phase I reactions formed such as glutathione is an example of: -
(a) Phase I reaction (b) Phase II reaction
(c) Phase III reaction (d) Elimination reaction

729. Fluoride inhibits conversion of glyceric acid to pyruvic acid by inhibiting:-
(a) Transminase (b) Adenylase
(c) Enolase (d) Phosphatase

730. Te tendency of an organism towards maintenance of physiological and psychological stability is: -
(a) Homeostasis (b) Haemodialysis
(c) Hemolysis (d) Apoptosis

731. Ames Salmonella test on *Salmonella typhimurium* and dominant lethal test on rodents generally is preferred for: -
(a) Teratogenic potential of a chemical
(b) Carcinogenic potential of a chemical
(c) Mutagenic potential of a chemical
(d) All of the above

732. Conversion of normal cell to tumor cell without any mutation is called: -
(a) Teratogenesis
(b) Mutation
(c) Carcinogenesis
(d) Epigenetic transformation

733. During meningitis the transport of drug into CSF is: -
(a) Unaffected (b) Increased
(c) Decreased (d) None of the above

734. Expectorants:
(a) Increase bronchial secretions
(b) Reduce its viscosity of bronchial secretions
(c) Facilitating removal of bronchial secretions
(d) All of the above

735. Oxytocin: -
(a) Stimulates both the frequency and force of myometrial contraction
(b) Acts best on pregnant uterus
(c) Causes marked contraction of umbilical arteries & veins
(d) All of the above

736. Synthetic glucocorticoids are used in: -
(a) Ulcerative colitis
(b) Osteoarthritis
(c) Rheumatoid arthritis
(d) All of the above

737. The B_1 agonist drugs that can be used and for heart block and refractory congestive heart failure is: -
(a) Amphetamine (b) Dobutamine
(c) Isoprenaline (d) None of these

738. The true statement following use of local anaesthetics is: -
(a) Somatomotor nerve fibers are affected last
(b) Autonomic fibers are affected first
(c) Loss of motor power loss of sensation
(d) Both a & b

739. The oral administration of pentachlophenol interrupts enterohepatic circulation by using: -
(a) Magnesium oxide (b) Cholestyramine
(c) Polythiol resin (d) None of the above

740. The osmotic diuretics: -
(a) Reduce intracranial pressure
(b) Remain unabsorbed form the nephrone
(c) Reduce intraocular pressure
(d) All of the above

741. Bretylium: -
(a) Used in emergency treatment of ventricular fibrillation
(b) Raises the threshold of ventricular fibrillation
(c) Reverses the shortening of action potential duration
(d) All of the above

742. Angiotenein converting enzyme (ACE) inhibitions: -
(a) Blocks angiotensin II receptors
(b) Prevents conversion of angiotensin to agiotensin II
(c) Prevents conversion of angiotensinogen to andiotensin 1
(d) Directly inhibit the release of aidoterone

743. Enflurane has the following advantages as a general anesthetic agent: -
(a) Induces marked muscle relaxation
(b) Induces bronchodilatation, so safer in asthmatic patients
(c) Has minimal adverse cardivascular effects
(d) All of the above

744. Which of the following types of tissues frequently store drugs: -
(a) Muscle tissue (b) Protein tissue
(c) Fatty tissue (d) Both b & c

745. Strong iodine solution contains K1 for the purpose of: -
(a) Increasing potency
(b) Reducing agent
(c) Preservation
(d) None of these

746. Which of the following compounds of undecylenic acid is most commonly used in therapy: -
(a) Ag (b) Mg
(c) Mn (d) Zn

747. Glucogon may be used as a diagnostic agent in radio graphic examination of the:
(a) Liver (b) Brian
(c) Bones (d) Gastro intestinal tract

748. The non-aquos vehicle used in the injections is: -
(a) Alcohol
(b) Vegetable oils
(c) Glycerol
(d) Wax or liquid petroleum

749. The concerntration of nitrofurazone solution used ophthalamically is: -
(a) 1 % (b) 2 %
(c) 0.02 % (d) 20 %

750. Moxan (Moxalactan) is most closely related to: -
(a) Oleandomycins (b) Sulfenamides
(c) Cephalosporims (d) Aminoglycosides

751. One of the following drugs is not a competitive receptor antagonist of autonomic ganglia: -
(a) Suxamethonium (b) Hexamethonium
(c) Pentolinium (d) Mecamylamine

752. Parameters studied for reproductive toxicity of a chemical are: -
(a) Fertility index (b) Gestation index
(c) Viability index (d) All of the above

753. Sub acute exposure of a chemical is defined as: -
(a) Exposure of a chemical for less than 24 hours
(b) Repeated exposure to a chemical for one month or less
(c) Repeated exposure of a chemical for 1 to 3 moths
(d) None of the above

754. An antagonist drug should have: -
(a) Affinity
(b) Affinity as well as intrinsic activity
(c) Affinity with no intrinsic activity
(d) Intrinsic activity

755. Mucolytic agents do not include: -
(a) Acetyl cysteine
(b) K1 (potassium iodide)
(c) Atropine sulphate
(d) Bromhexine

756. Mecamylamine is: -
(a) Quaternary ammonium compound (b) Effectively orally
(c) Both b and c
(d) None of these

757. The electrophils formed during reactive intermediate metabolites in the body can react with: -
(a) Glutathione
(b) Glutathione disulfide
(c) Glutathione disulfide as well as glutathione

(d) None of the above

758. Blockade of ganglionic transmission by hexamethonium is likely to: -
(a) Have no effect on vision
(b) Increase salivary secretions
(c) Cause urgency in micturtion
(d) Reduce B.P. and the intestinal contractions

759. Digitalis toxicity may cause: -
(a) Ventricular tachycardia
(b) Heart block
(c) Sinus bradycardia
(d) All of the above

760. The following is not good choice for the control of hypertensive crisis: -
(a) Propranolol
(b) Sodium nitroprusside
(c) Ansolysen
(d) Hydralazine

761. The first evidence that a drug is being stored in tissue may be: -
(a) Decrease of metabolites in urine
(b) Large apparent volume of the distribution
(c) Decrease of drug in urine
(d) Small apparent volume of the distribution

762. Route of administration for drugs which distribute poorly is: -
(a) Subcutaneous (b) Intracerebral
(c) Intra muscular (d) Intra venous

763. Diuretics such as furosemide facilitate elimination of toxicants by: -
(a) Altering their passive reabsorption
(b) Accelerating their active transport
(c) Both a and b
(d) None of the above

764. Opium is obtained by: -
(a) Extraction from leaves of a plant
(b) Chemical synthesis
(c) Slitting capsules of a plant
(d) Grinding a plant

765. Which of the following may be side effect of cimetidine: -
(a) Rash (b) Constipation
(c) Dizziness (d) Both a and c

766. Ampicillin may give a fake positive diagnostic test for: -
(a) Bilirubin (b) Glucose
(c) Cholesterol (d) Uric acid

767. Which of the following is used exclusively for urinary tract infections: -
(a) Nalidixic acid (b) Ticarcillin
(c) Metronidazole (d) Pyrimethamine

768. The longest serum half life is of: -
(a) Doxycyline (b) Oxytetracycline
(c) Tetracycline (d) Demechlocyline

769. A drug used in treating 2nd or 3rd degree burns is: -
(a) Mafenide (b) Polymyxin
(c) Sulfisoxazole (d) Nitrofurantion

770. When tolmetin is used it may produce a false positive test for: -
(a) Haemoglobinemia
(b) Uric acid
(c) Glucose
(d) Protenuria

771. The drug having both antidepressant and antihypertensive property: -
(a) Paragyline (b) Doxepin
(c) Amitrptyline (d) Imipramine

772. Morphine stimulates: -
(a) Non propulsive contraction of small intestine
(b) Propulsive peristalsis waves in colon
(c) Biliary & pancreatic secretions
(d) All of the above

773. Strychnine acts by: -
(a) Depressing inhibitory centers in spinal cord
(b) Inhibiting cholinesterase
(c) Stimulating acetylcholine production
(d) None of the above

774. Strychnine may cause: -
(a) Cardiac failure
(b) Exhaustion of respiratory center
(c) Fatigue of spinal reflexes
(d) Fatigue of respiratory muscles

775. Streptomycin can cause: -
(a) VII cranial nerve damage
(b) VIII cranial nerve damage
(c) IX cranial nerve damage
(d) X cranial damage

776. Insulin need may be increase by: -
(a) Prednisolone (b) Isoniazid
(c) Penicillin (d) Glyceryl guaicolate

777. Mydriasis and rise in systolic B.P. occurs due to S/C injection of:-
(a) Atropine and adrenaline
(b) Cocaine
(c) Hexamethonium
(d) Salbutamol

778. The barriers which protect the nervous system from certain neurotoxins are: -
(a) Blood brain barrier
(b) Blood nerve barrier
(c) Both a and b
(d) None of the above

779. Antidote of arsenic poison: -
(a) Nicotine (b) Dimercaprol
(c) Obdioxime (d) Rotenone

780. Vitamin D may be used in: -
(a) Hypoparathyroidism
(b) Oesteomalacia
(c) Rickets
(d) All of the above

781. Which one is used for the analysis of toxicants and their metabolites in biological samples: -
(a) UV spectrophotometry
(b) Column chromatography
(c) Gas-liquid chromatogrphy
(d) None of the above

782. The local anaesthetic which can not absorb so used as dusting powder: -
(a) Bupivacaine (b) Procaine
(c) Benzocaine (d) Lignocaine

783. Compounds which undergo phase I and phase II reaction is: -
(a) Lipophilic (b) Lipophobic
(c) Both a and b (d) None of these

784. Regarding nicotinic the correct statements may be: -
(a) Decreases tone of skeletal muscles and tendon reflexes
(b) Stimulates central nervous system
(c) Stimulates nicotine receptors in the small does and depress in the large doses
(d) All of the above

785. Tetraethyl lead damages the skin on contact and when absorbed it causes damage to central nervous system, it is: -
(a) Local effect (b) Systemic effect
(c) Both a and b (d) None of the above

786. Action of d-tubocurrarine is amplified by: -
(a) Aminoglycoside antibiotics
(b) Inhalant anesthetics like isoflurane
(c) Coexisting upper motor neuron disease
(d) All of the above

787. The three routes of exposure are:-
(a) Lungs, Skin, Kidney
(b) Skin, Lungs, Gut
(c) Skin, Lungs, Liver
(d) None of the above

788. Suxamethonium is:-
(a) An ester of choline with 2 molecules of succinic acid
(b) Rapidly metabolized by pseudocholinesterase
(c) Both a and b
(d) None of the above

789. An effect of two chemicals acting together independently is:-
(a) Antagonistic effect
(b) Synergistic effect
(c) Anti-synergistic effect
(d) Additive effect

790. Sodium channel is not inactivated by:-
(a) Batrachotoxin (b) Verapamil
(c) Tetrodoxin (d) Lidocame

791. Halothane as a general anesthetic agent is:-
(a) Non-inflammable
(b) Having property of post operative recovery more rapid than ether
(c) Non irritant to tracheobronchial mucosa
(d) All of the above

792. The hepatic injury induced by carbon tetrachloride is mediated by: -
(a) Trichloromethyl free radical
(b) Trichloromethylperxy free radical
(c) Both a and b
(d) None of the above

793. A common side effect of ephedrine is: -
(a) Ulcers (b) Nervousness

(c) Drowsiness (d) Rashes

794. Most useful antibiotic to treat *Pseudomonas aeruginosa* infection is: -
(a) Kanamycin (b) Rifampin
(c) Novobiocin (d) Gentamicin

795. Inflammation caused by a substance on skin and mucus membranes following immediate contact is called: -
(a) Oxidizing (b) Explosive
(c) Corrosive (d) Irritant

796. Duration of local anesthetic procaine can be prolonged by: -
(a) Combining with zinc
(b) Combining with PABA
(c) Combining with adrenaline
(d) Combining with probenecid

797. Lethal synthesis is the result of: -
(a) Bioactivation (b) Detoxification
(d) Biomagnification (c) Biotoxification

798. In one compartment model, the urinary excretion rate of drug is obtained by: -
(a) Urinary excretion rate = elimination rate constant (Ke) x apparent volume of distribution
(b) Urinary excretion rate = renal clearance x plasma drug concentration
(c) Urinary excretion rate = renal clearance/ plasma concentration of drug
(d) None of the above

799. Absorption of a chemical usually decreases in the following order: -
(a) G.I. Tract, Lungs, Skin
(b) G.I. Tract, Skin, Lungs
(c) Skin, Lungs, G.I. Tract
(d) Lungs, G.I. Tract, Skin

800. Histamine causes: -
(a) Fall in blood pressure
(b) Increased in capillary permeability
(c) Bronchospasm
(d) All of the above

801. Histamine release is characterized by: -
(a) Anaphylactic shock
(b) Bronchospasm
(c) Skin rash
(d) All of the above

802. Histamine H1 receptor stimulation causes: -
(a) Increased vascular permeability
(b) Increased mucus secretion
(c) Both a and b
(d) Increased secretion of HCL

803. Histamine H2 receptor stimulation causes: -
(a) Vascular dilation
(b) Increase in cyclic AMP in cells
(c) Increase in gastric acid secretion
(d) All of the above

804. Toxaphene can persist in body fat for: -
(a) 1 months (b) 2 months
(c) 3 months (d) 4 months

805. The following is correct regarding disopyramide:-
(a) It is used for ventiricular arrythmia
(b) It has membrane stabilizing activity
(c) Its cardiac antimuscarinic effects are more marked than of quinidine
(d) All of these

806. Thipentone as an anesthetic agent has the following disadvantages: -
(a) Local extravasations can occur
(b) Laryngeal spasm may occur during induction
(c) Anesthesia is of very short duration
(d) All of the above

807. The unpredictability of entericcoated tablets is due to: -
(a) Effect of pH
(b) State of health of patient
(c) Failure to release drug
(d) Premature release of drug

808. Pinocytosis requires: -
(a) No energy (b) Energy
(c) A carrier system (d) A carrier as well as energy

809. Biological half life of drug is more if drug has: -
(a) Higher protein binding
(b) Less protein binding
(c) Higher rate of excretion
(d) Higher rate of biotransformation

810. Hypersensitivity reactions caused by toxicants are mediated by: -
(a) Macrophages
(b) Sensitized T-lymphocytes

(c) Both a and b
(d) None of the above

811. Phorate gives protection in how many weeks after use: -
(a) 10 (b) 20
(c) 30 (d) 40

812. Therapy of ketoacidosis includes: -
(a) Continuous administration of regular crystalline insulin
(b) Correction of the acidosis by the bicarbonate infusion
(c) Both a and b
(d) None of the above

813. Growth hormone may: -
(a) Exerts a diabetogenic effect
(b) Increases intestinal calcium absorption
(c) Induce positive nitrogen absorption
(d) All of the above

814. Plant alkaloids used to treat migraine has: -
(a) Ergot alkaloid
(b) Belladona alkaloid
(c) Stramonium alkaloid
(d) Vinca alkaloid

815. A tranquillizer which may cause hypertensive is:-
(a) Meprobamate (b) Sparine
(c) Reserpine (d) None of these

816. An overdose of d-tubocurarine may cause: -
(a) Paralysis of ANS
(b) Paralysis of respiratory muscles
(c) Interference with oxidative enzymes
(d) All of these

817. Which of the following may cause asthma: -
(a) Viral infections (b) Bacterial infections
(c) Both a and b (d) None of the above

818. Antidote for DDT poisoning is: -
(a) Atropine (b) Amphetamine
(c) Adrenalin (d) Barbiturate

819. Drug may be used to treat fungal infections of eye: -
(a) Amikacin (d) Idoxurine
(c) Nafcillin (b) Natamycin

820. Acyclovir is an: -
(a) Antifungal (b) Anthelmintic
(c) Antirickettesial (d) Antiviral

821. Which of the following antibiotics is an antifungal also: -
(a) Bacitracin (b) Candicidin
(c) Spectinomycin (d) Polymyxin

822. Oral hypoglycemic is useful in: -
(a) Weak diabetes
(b) Labile diabetes
(c) Juvenile diabetes
(d) Uncomplicated diabetes

823. Which of the following is a loop diuretic: -
(a) Furosemide (b) Spironolactone
(c) Triamterene (d) All of these

824. Ranitidine is used primarily to treat: -
(a) Ulcers
(b) Colic
(c) Diarrhoea
(d) Staphylococcal infections

825. Oral administration of Lidocaine is prohibited because: -
(a) It is inflective by this route
(b) Unstable
(c) It is toxic
(d) It is acidic

826. The advantages of cyclopropane as a general anesthetic is: -
(a) Good muscle relaxation
(b) Rapid recovery
(c) Smooth induction
(d) All of the above

827. The binding of toxicants in circulation is usually made by: -
(a) á -l acid glycoprotein
(b) Plasma globulins
(c) Plasma albumin
(d) None of the above

828. Therapeutic uses of prostaglandins include: -
(a) Termination of pregnancy in 2nd trimester
(b) Reduction of gastric acid secretion
(c) Induction of labor at full term
(d) All of the above

829. Ranitidine: -
(a) Reduces volume of gastric juice
(b) Reduces nocturnal secretion of acid
(c) Increases pH of gastric juice

(d) All of the above

830. Ranitidine is preferred over Cimetidine because it: -
(a) Is much less & convenient to patient
(b) Does not increase prolactin level
(c) Does not inhibit hepatic microsomal enzyme
(d) All of the above

831. H_1 blockers are not effective in: -
(a) Bronchial asthma (b) Motion sickness
(c) Hay fever (d) Urticaria

832. Blood levels following should be monitored during use of diuretic: -
(a) Ca^+ (b) K
(c) Cl (d) Na and glucose

833. Treatment of congestive heart failure without digitalis include: -
(a) Amrinene (b) Dobutamine
(c) Orazosine (d) All of these

834. The neurotransmitters responsible for CTZ activity may be: -
(a) 5-hydroxytryptamine
(b) Acetylcholine
(c) Dopamine
(d) All of the above

835. The resistant species to DNOL poisoning is: -
(a) Cattle (b) Cat
(c) Dog (d) Horse

836. The advantageous effects of digitalis in congestive heart failure are due to:-
(a) Dilates the coronary vessels
(b) Increases myocardial contractility
(c) Increases myocardial excitability
(d) Delays AV conduction

837. The anesthetics used by inhalation: -
(a) Ether (b) Halothane
(c) Enflurane (d) All of the above

838. The factors not altering the rate of absorption is: -
(a) Viscosifty
(b) Chemical stability
(c) Reversible complication
(d) Biological half life

839. Weakly basic drugs are eliminated best from: -
(a) Neutral urine
(b) Acidic urine
(c) Alkaline urine
(d) Lack of biotransformation

840. Which of the following drugs is commonly used to the treat schistosomisis: -
(a) Ivermectin (b) Praziquantel
(c) Closental (d) Oxytetacycline

841. Dimethylsulphoxide is no longer used clinically because it causes: -
(a) Agranulocytosis (b) Carcinomas
(c) Skin damage (d) Eye damage

842. The drug preferred in fatal infection: -
(a) Candidicin (b) Griseofulvin
(c) Amphotericin B (d) Nystatin

843. Penicillin is obtained from: -
(a) Fungi (b) Mold
(c) Yeast (d) Bacteria

844. Antifungal that has antiprotozoal properties: -
(a) Miconazole (b) Flucytosine
(c) Nystatin (d) Metronidazole

845. Which statement is correct about the solubility of alkaloids: -
(a) Insoluble in water insoluble in non polar solvent
(b) Sparingly soluble in water, soluble in non polar solvent
(c) Sparingly soluble in water, insoluble in dilute acid
(d) Sparingly soluble in water, soluble in dilute acid

846. An agent normally used combined with local anesthetic is: -
(a) Epinephrine (b) Isoproterenol
(c) Ephedrine (d) Amphetamine

847. The action of quinidine differing from the digitalis: -
(a) It has increasing irritability abality to cardiac muscle
(b) It has reducing ability for conductivity
(c) It has decreasing irritability ability to cardiac muscle
(d) None of the above

848. Single oral lethal does of DNOL in pigs (mg/kg) ranges between: -

(a) 5-10 (b) 10-50
(c) 50-100 (d) 100-150

849. Metronidazole is used mainly to treat: -
(a) Bronchitis (b) Trichomonas
(c) Syphilis (d) Pneumonia

850. Angiotensin II: -
(a) Receptor can be blocked by saralasin
(b) Stimulate adrenal medulla to release catecholamines
(c) Stimulate release of aldosterone
(d) All of the above

851. Which of the following fluorescence to urine: -
(a) Nitrofurantion (b) Riboflavin
(c) Triamterene (d) All of the above

852. The following statements pertaining to natural mineralocorticosteroid is true: -
(a) Aldosterone is most potent sodium retaining
(b) 11-desoxycorticosterone is most potent sodium retaining
(c) Cortisone has weaker corticoid activity compared to glucocorticoid
(d) All of these

853. Which of the following transmitter inhibits prolactin release: -
(a) GABA (b) Noradrenaline
(c) Dopamine (d) Acetylcholine

854. Following autacoids are mediators of inflammatory reactions: -
(a) Bradykinin
(b) Prostaglandin
(c) 5-Hydroxytryptamine
(d) All of the above

855. An advantage of cyclacillin over ampicillin is: -
(a) It may be given orally
(b) It is more stable
(c) It produces a lower incidence of diarrhoea
(d) It has a broader spectrum

856. Rotenone is obtained from: -
(a) Chryosathemum (b) Oleander
(c) Lanchocorpus (d) Stramonium

857. Cardiac glycosides have following actions: -
(a) Positive ionotropic action
(b) Increases myocardial excitability
(c) Both a and b
(d) none of these

858. If a central nervous system drug is extensively ionized in blood it will: -
(a) Not penetrate the blood brain barrier
(b) Penetrate the blood brain barrier rapidly
(c) Penetrate the blood brain barrier slowly
(d) Be eliminated slowly

859. Methotrexate should never be used concurrently with: -
(a) Aspirin (b) Epinephrine
(c) Penicillin (d) Tetracycline

860. Probenecid should not be used in the treatment of gout in conjunction with salicylates because: -
(a) Therapeutic actions are antagonistic
(b) Probenecid is not effective in gout
(c) Toxicity of probenecid is increased by acidic salicylates
(d) None of the above

861. PGE_2 causes: -
(a) Aggregation of platelets
(b) Contraction of bronchial muscles
(c) Constriction of blood vessels
(d) Decrease gastric acid secretion and mediation for thermoregulation

862. Barium intoxication can be prevented by administration of: -
(a) Aluminium (b) Calcium
(c) Zine (d) Sodium

863. In organophosphorus insecticides poisoning, animal show inhibition of: -
(a) Brian acetylcholinesterase
(b) Brain neurotoxicesterase
(c) Plasma cholinesterase
(d) None of the above

864. Acute bronchchial asthma occurs in all, except: -
(a) Ephephrine (b) Aminophylline
(c) Ephedrine (d) Bradykinin

865. Strychnine acts by: -
(a) Stimulating somatic nerve endings
(b) Producing postsynaptic inhibition in the spinal cord
(c) Stimulating the motor cortex
(d) None of the above

866. HCG is used for: -
(a) Cryptorchism (b) Female infertility
(c) Male infertility (d) All of the above

867. Widely used drugs to treat mild hypertension is: -
(a) Diuretics (b) Sympathetic blockers
(c) MAO inhibitors (d) Ganglionec blockers

868. Which one is not representing action of quinidine on the myocarduim: -
(a) Slow conduction
(b) Increases force of contraction of the muscle
(c) Increases the refractory period
(d) Blocks vagal effects on heart

869. Clotriamazole is effective in treating: -
(a) Abortion (b) Diarrhoea
(c) Moniliasis (d) Both a & b

870. The action of digitalis is improved by: -
(a) Na (b) Mg
(c) Cl (d) Ca

871. Betadine contains: -
(a) Gentian violet
(b) Betamethionine
(c) Povidine - iodine complex
(d) Benzocaine

872. Deferoxamine is used to treat intoxication due to:-
(a) Cadmium (b) Arsenic
(c) Iron (d) None of these

873. Aloes are used to treat: -
(a) Burns (b) Carcinomas
(c) Gastritis (d) Vertigo

874. Cardiac effects of digitalis are due to: -
(a) Inhibition of Na K ATP ase
(b) Increased availability of intracellular Ca
(c) Both a and b
(d) Facilitation of entry of Ca^2 by voltage operated channels

875. Fluoide inhibits synthesis of: -
(a) Angiotensin
(b) Phosphatase
(c) Norepineinephrine
(d) Citric acid

876. Therapeutic agents used in the respiratory suppression are: -
(a) Naltrexone (b) Doxapran
(c) Methylphenidate (d) Amphetamine

877. Cough is: -
(a) A protective reflex for expulsion things from air passages
(b) Formed due to pharyngitis often responds to a demulcent
(c) Formed in respons to a steam and benzoin inhibition
(d) All of the above

878. Action of insulin is opposes by glucagon through:-
(a) Inhibition of the release of insulin
(b) Stimulation of glycogenolysis
(c) Induction of neoglycogensis
(d) All of the above

879. Hypothamic peptide hormones indirectly control the synthesis and release of: -
(a) Thyroxine (b) Oestrogen
(c) Glucocorticoids (d) All of the above

880. Hypokalemia, as a side effect of diuretic may be reduced by useing: -
(a) Citrus fruits (b) Mixed electrolytes
(c) Potassium salt (d) Salt

881. The site of action of thiazide diuretics is: -
(a) Loop of henle
(b) Proximal tubule
(c) Both a & b
(d) Tubule just beyond the loop of henle

882. Prednisolone is classified as a: -
(a) Anti histaminic
(b) Analgesic
(c) Anti inflammatory
(d) Antifungal

883. An antifungal that releases acetic acid in the presence of fungus is: -
(a) Vitamin K (b) Griseofulvin
(c) Vioform (d) Enzactin

884. Epinephrine HCI has little effect on: -
(a) Pupil (b) Conjunctiva
(c) Nasal mucosa (d) Unbroken skin

885. Which of the following I contraindicated in myasthenia gravis: -

(a) Atropine (b) Digitalis
(c) Prostigmine (d) Curare

886. The brain-stem centers affected most strongly by barbiturates are the: -
(a) Cardio inhibitory centers
(b) Vasomotor center
(c) Respiratory center
(d) None of these

887. Which sulpha drug is widely used to treat ophthalmic infections: -
(a) Sulfadiazine (b) Sulfisoxazine
(c) Sulfapyridole (d) Sulfacetamide

888. Nystatin is used to treat: -
(a) Histoplasmosis (b) Caccidiomycosis
(c) Blastomycosis (d) Candida infection

889. Which of the following antibiotic is similar to the cephalosporins: -
(a) Carbenicillin (b) Doxycycline
(c) Ninocycline (d) Moxalactam

890. Propranolol is used with extreme caution in patient suffering from:
(a) Hypertension (b) Cardiac arrythmias
(c) Diabetes (d) Depunion

891. An oral antifungal agent is: -
(a) Desenex (b) Undecylenic acid
(c) Sopronol (d) Griseofulvin

892. Under does of which one may cause marked hydrolysis in gastro-intestinal tract:-
(a) Chlortetracyline (b) Hydrocortisone
(c) Penicillin G (d) Aspirin

893. The advantages use of thiopentone sodium as a general anesthetic agent is: -
(a) Rapid hypnosis and anesthesia
(b) Induction is without excitement
(c) It is used as preanesthetic prior to inhalation anesthetic
(d) All of the above

894. Class IB drugs have following properties: -
(a) Do not suppress the AV nodal conduction
(b) Do not have negative inotropic activity
(c) Have mainly central nervous system toxicities
(d) All of the above

895. Arsenic increases blood circulation in pig's by: -
(a) Vasocostriction (b) Paralysis
(c) Irritation (d) None of these

896. Which one is clinically effective in reflux oesphagitis: -
(a) Ranitidine (b) Domperidone
(c) Metoclopramide (d) All of the above

897. Testosterone secretion is: -
(a) Increased by follicle stimulating hormone
(b) Increased by growth hormone
(c) Increased by luteinizing hormone
(d) All of the above

898. Titanium dioxide is used in which of the following preparations:-
(a) Burn treatment
(b) Sunscreen
(c) Topical anaesthetic
(d) Cough

899. The therapeutic uses of the thyroid hormones includes: -
(a) Goitre (b) Myxoedema
(c) Cretinism (d) All of the above

900. Aminophlline is used most frequently in: -
(a) Diabetes insipidus
(b) Lowering cerebral pressure
(c) Nephritic oedema
(d) Asthma

901. A narcotic antagonist is: -
(a) Meprobamate (b) Nalorphine
(c) Meperidine (d) None of these

902. The disadvantage in the use of meperidine is: -
(a) High B.P. (b) Low B.P.
(c) Addiction (d) All of these

903. Glucagon is used as a anticholinergics in the radiology of: -
(a) Spleen
(b) Heart
(c) Liver
(d) Gastro intestinal tract

904. EDTA is and antidote for which of the following:-
(a) Lead (b) Sodium chloride
(c) Aspirin (d) Zinc

905. Which of following is not significantly absorbed orally: -

(a) Ephedrine (b) Cromolyn
(c) Osoproterenol (d) Theophylline

906. Which of the following drugs is used to treat both constipation and diarrhoea:
(a) Polycarbophil (b) Metamucil
(c) Parepectolin (d) Phenophthalein

907. The hypnotic does of a barbiturate acts mainly on: -
(a) Cerebral cortex (b) Brain stem
(c) Thalmus (d) Entire Central nervous system

908. Overuse of digitatis may result in: -
(a) Tolerance (b) Addiction
(c) Habituation (d) Cumulative poisoning

909. One specific side effect of tridione administration is: -
(a) Respiratory suppression
(b) Glare phenomenon
(c) Gingival hyperplasia
(d) Cerebral depression

910. Barrier cream is quite useful in preventing: -
(a) Drug allergies (b) Psoriasis
(c) Dry skin (d) Poison sumae

911. The dosage of anticonvulsant is adjusted: -
(a) Every 2 weeks (b) Every 2 months
(c) Every 2 years (d) When attacks occur frequently

912. Sulfonamides are executed free and combined as the: -
(a) Acetyl derivative (b) Glycine conjugates
(c) Sulfate derivative (d) Amino derivative

913. Enzymatic oxidation of trapped iodides is blocked in the thyroid gland by:-
(a) Penicillin (b) Thiouracils
(c) Iodides (d) Thyroxin

914. Netilmycin is classified as: -
(a) Penicillin (b) Aminoglycoside
(c) Tetracycline (d) None of these

915. In young ones, tetracycline causes: -
(a) Conjunctivitis
(b) Discoloration of teeth
(c) Agranulocytosis
(d) Muscular weakness

916. Aminocaproic acid is used to treat: -
(a) Protein loss (b) Haemorrhage
(c) Hypertension (d) Warts

917. A rich source of vitamin A is which of the following: -
(a) Milk (b) Meat
(c) Honey (d) Fish liver oils

918. g - globulin fraction is separated from serum by: -
(a) Filtration (b) Centrifugation
(c) Chromatography (d) Dialysis

919. Premedication before general anesthesia should comprise: -
(a) Analgesic (b) Sedative
(c) Anti muscarinic (d) All of the above

920. Following treatment of congestive heart failure with digoxin there is increase in: -
(a) Venous pressure (b) Body weight
(c) Size of heart (d) Stroke volume

921. Alpha methyl dopa: -
(a) Acts by he synthesis of a false transmitter
(b) Has a t 1/2 of 2 hours
(c) Has a high bioavalability
(d) Has no central action

922. Procainamide: -
(a) Shortens cardiac refractory period
(b) Has more antimuscarinic action than quinidine
(c) Is more useful in supraventricular arrythmias
(d) Is a sodium channel blocker

923. Following should be done for the treatment of digitalis toxicity: -
(a) Administration of lidocaine
(b) Withdrawal of K depleting diuretics
(c) Withdrawal or reduction of the does
(d) All of the above

924. Tetracyclines tend to from complexes with: -
(a) Hg ions (b) Iron ions
(c) Calcium ions (d) All of the above

925. A drug that reverses plasma - pretein binding is often referred as: -
(a) Displacer (b) Prptein hyrolysate
(c) Carrier substance (d) Enzyme

926. Hetacillin is converted in the body to: -

(a) Carbenicillin (b) Penicillin V
(c) Penicillin G (d) Ampicillin

927. The route of administration of bacitracin is: -
(a) Oral (b) Intra muscular
(c) Topical (d) Intra venous

928. Vancomycin is used to treat: -
(a) Skin infection
(b) Urinary tract infections
(c) Burns
(d) Serious infection resistant to other drugs

929. Which one is not metabolized in liver: -
(a) Secobarbital (b) Barbital
(c) Pentobarbital (d) Phenobarbital

930. Treatment of digitalis intoxication may be done by: -
(a) Give K salts
(b) Stop the administration of drug
(c) Administer diuretics
(d) Administer quinidine

931. Continued use of dicumarol may lead to cumulative poisoning of: -
(a) Cytarabine (b) Vitamin K
(c) Heparin (d) Thrombin

932. Non reactive carcinogens are converted to carcinogens *in vivo* by: -
(a) Arylesterases
(b) N-acetyl transferases
(c) Cytochrome p-450 dependent monooxygenases of endoplasmic reticulum
(d) None of the above

933. Which one not enhances the potential effects of digitalis on the heart: -
(a) Alkatosis
(b) High serum calcium
(c) Myocardial anoxia
(d) Increased renal clearance

934. The difference in competitive and non-competitive inhibition is: -
(a) Degree of agonism
(b) Extent of receptor site blocking
(c) Whether inhibition occurs
(d) Extent of enzyme inhibition

935. Which of the following groups depresses the activity of griseofulvin: -
(a) Anticoagulents (b) Barbiturates
(c) Dibenzazepines (d) Topical antifungals

936. The hormones that oppose the action of insulin include: -
(a) Adrenalin
(b) Glucagon & growth hormone
(c) Hydrocortisone
(d) All of the above

937. Which of the following may be stimulant purgatives: -
(a) Bisacodyl (b) Phenophthalein
(c) Senna (d) All of the above

938. Correct statement about the calcium channel blockers is: -
(a) Dilate arterioles and veins equally
(b) Dilate arterioles more than veins
(c) Are used in treatment of hypercalcemia
(d) Co-administation with b -blockers may aggravate AV block and cardiac failure

939. Particle size reduction will not enhance the absorption of: -
(a) Weak acids
(b) Weak bases
(c) Hydrophillic compounds
(d) Hydrophillic compounds

940. Surface active agents enhance absorption by: -
(a) Reduction of interfacial tension
(b) Effects of dissolution rate of drugs
(c) Effects on biological membrane
(d) All of the above

941. Effective diuretics in presence of electrolyte imbalance is: -
(a) NH_4CI (b) Chlorothiazide
(c) Acetazolamide (d) Ethacrynic acid

942. The most prevalent adverse reaction of selenium sulfide is: -
(a) Discoloration of hair
(b) Loss of hair
(c) Dryness of scalp
(d) Irritation of skin

943. Spectinomycin is used as an alternative to: -
(a) Penicillin G (b) Kanamycin
(c) Bacitracin (d) Streptomycin

944. Vacomycin should be well diluted to minimize: -
(a) Chance of over dosing
(b) Thrombophlebitis

(c) Residual effect
(d) Ear damage

945. Niclosamide is effective against: -
(a) Tape worms (b) Hook worms
(c) Whip worms (d) Pin worms

946. Which of the following symptoms is present in digitalis intoxication: -
(a) AV block
(b) Ventricular tachycardia
(c) Vomiting
(d) All of these

947. Which of the following may not be toxic effect of the local anesthetics: -
(a) Central nervous system depression
(b) Tachycardia
(c) Local ischemia
(d) None of these

948. The most effective drug for prophylaxis of meningitis is: -
(a) Erythromycin (b) Penicillin V
(c) Penicillin G (d) Sulfisoxazole

949. Antihistamines have little effect on which actions of histamine: -
(a) Gastric secretion (b) Whal & flare
(c) Hypotension (d) Bronchospasm

950. Which of the following is bulk-forming purgative:-
(a) Isabgula husk (b) Carboxymethyl cellulose
(c) Whole bran (d) All of the above

951. Drug produces its action on receptor if it has got:-
(a) High affinity
(b) High intrinsic activity
(c) Both a and b
(d) All of the above

952. In case of complete heart block & cardiac arrest use of the following is helpful:-
(a) Molar lactate solution intravenously
(b) Mechanical electronic pacemaker
(c) Catecholamines such as isoprenaline and adrenaline
(d) All of the above

953. Long term use of thiazide diuretics in hypertension may cause: -
(a) Hypuraemia (b) Hypoglycaemia
(c) Hypocalcaemia (d) Hypokalaemia

954. Most major operations are done in stage II, which is identified by: -
(a) Loss of corneal reflex
(b) Pupils normal size
(c) Cessation of eyeball movements
(d) All of the above

955. Ether has the following advantages as an anesthetic agent: -
(a) It induces good muscle relaxation
(b) Cardiac arrhythmias are uncommon
(c) Has a wide margin of safety
(d) All of the above

956. Antimuscarinic agents like atropine or hyoscine are used as preanesthetic to:
(a) Prevent reflex bradycardia
(b) Prevent bronchospasm
(c) Reduce bronchial and salivary secretions
(d) All of the above

957. What may happen if the distribution of drugs is slower than the processes ofbiotransformation: -
(a) Potentiation
(b) Low blood levels of drug
(d) High blood levels of drug
(d) Failure to attain diffusion equilibrium

958. Hyaluronidase has been used as an adjunct to: -
(a) Prevent oxidation of drugs
(b) Increase detoxication
(c) Produces sustained action
(b) Increase absorption of injected drugs

959. Which one is not a major pathway of biotransformation: -
(a) Deamination (b) Oxidation
(c) Conjugation (d) Reduction

960. Protein that is involved in plasma-protein binding:-
(a) Fibrin & plasmin
(b) Albumin & Globulin
(c) Globulin & plasmin
(d) Plasminogea & fibrin

961. Diuretics enhance salt toxicity by: -
(a) Potassium depletion
(b) Direct drug interaction
(c) Increased absorption

(d) Sodium depletion

962. Nitrofurantion is most active when the pH of the urinary tract is: -
(a) 5.5 or less (b) Over 9.5
(c) Between 6 to 7 (d) Neutral

963. Which of the following may increase the serum levels of penicillin: -
(a) Antacids (b) Probenecid
(c) Kaolin (d) Salicylates

964. Plasma levels of vitamin A may be significantly affected by: -
(a) Aspirin
(b) Oral contraceptives
(c) Vitamin D

965. Which of the following may be used as plasma expanders: -
(a) Dextrans (b) Na salts
(c) Strach (d) Ca salts

966. For ophthalmic use, boric acid solution should be diluted with: -
(a) An equal volume of sterile distilled water
(b) An equal volume of isotonic saline solution
(c) An equal volume of distilled water
(d) An equal volume of alcohol

967. Which of the following is not an expectorant agent:-
(a) Codeine (b) Wild chery syrup
(c) Glycerine (d) All of above

968. Econazole nitrate is most effective against: -
(a) Bacteria (b) Rickettsia
(c) Tape worm (d) Fungal infestations

969. Which anathematic is effective against multiple infestations: -
(a) Tolnaftale (b) Griseofulvin
(c) Flucytosine (d) None of these

970. The microsomal mixed function oxidase enzymes are specific for: -
(a) Functional groups as well as for substrates
(b) Substrates but not for functional groups
(c) Functional groups but not for substrates
(d) None of the above.

971. The treatment of choice for leprosy is: -
(a) Sulfone therapy
(b) Broad spectrum antibiotic therapy
(c) Penicillin therapy
(d) Chloromycetin therapy

972. Which is very effective in treating amoebiasis: -
(a) Cephalosporidine (b) Miconazole
(c) Trimethoprim (d) Emetine HCL

973. Histoplasmosis is best treated with: -
(a) Tetracycline (b) Amphotericin B
(c) Ampicilin (d) Penicillin G

974. Vancomycin is effective primarily against: -
(a) Gram negative bacilli
(b) Gram positive bacilli
(c) Gram positive cocci
(d) Gram negative cocci

975. A bacteriostatic agent has which of the following effects: -
(a) It induces spore formation
(b) It kills bacteria on contact
(c) It dehydrates the bacteria
(d) It inhibits multiplication of bacteria

976. A broad spectrum antibiotic effective even against resistant Staph. infection is: -
(a) Vibramycin (b) Hinocycline
(c) Demecloycline (d) Tetracycline

977. Vitamin K is associated with: -
(a) Pellagra
(b) Bones
(c) Haemoglobin concentration
(d) Blood clotting

978. Which of the following is found in vitamin B_{12}: -
(a) Co (b) Ni
(c) Mg (d) Fe

979. Which of the following is not a natural alkaloid: -
(a) Scopolamine (b) Apomorphine
(c) Papaverine (d) Lobeline

980. Which of the following ions plays a significant role in preventing convulsions: -
(a) Na (b) Li
(c) Mg (d) K

981. The emetic action of morphine in due to: -
(a) Stimulation of medullary vomiting center
(b) Stimulation of cerebral cortex
(c) Irritation of Gastro intestinal tract
(d) Stimulation of emetic CTZ

982. A drug administered by inhalation as a prophylactic for asthma is: -
(a) Epinephrine (b) Isoproterenol
(c) Ephedrine (d) Disoduim cromolyn

983. N-acetyl cysteine is classified as: -
(a) Protein hydrolysate
(b) Antitussive
(c) Mucolytic agent
(d) Analgesic

984. A drug which creates increased contraction of the sphincter iridis on local application is: -
(a) A parasympathomimetic drug
(b) A sympatholytic drug
(c) A ympathomimetic drug
(d) A parasympatholytic drug

985. Terbutaline has preference for stimulation of which receptors: -
(a) á (b) b_1
(c) b_2 (d) Dopaminergic

986. The toxicity of methanol is due to is conversion in: -
(a) Acetaldehyde
(b) Methane
(c) Carbonic acid
(d) Formic acid and formaldehyde

987. Alternate day steroid therapy is most useful in treating: -
(a) Asthma (b) Insulin shock
(c) Ulcers (d) Carcinoma of lung

988. The antispasmodic action of papaverince on smooth muscle is exerted via stimulation of: -
(a) Parasympathetic ganglia in intestinal wall
(b) Sympathetic ganglia in intestinal wall
(c) Directly on muscle cell
(d) All of these

989. Which of the following is the fastest acting anticoagulant: -
(a) Vitamin K (b) Heparin
(c) Ouabain (d) Warfarin

990. Which of the following is a gametocidal agent in malaria: -
(a) Primaquine (b) Atabrine
(c) Quinine (d) Acalen

991. Excessive use of the tolbutamide will lead to: -
(a) Glycosuria
(b) Prolonged hypoglycemia
(c) Acidosis
(d) Diarrhoea

992. The drug of choice for the treatment of hypertensive crisis is: -
(a) Diazoxide (b) Propranolol
(c) Clonidine (d) Reserpine

993. A very common side effect of morphine is: -
(a) Visceral pain (b) Constipation
(c) Liver damage (d) Allergic response

994. Ergotoxine alkaloids predominantly block which receptors: -
(a) Alpha - 2 adrenergic
(b) Alpha - 1 adrenergic
(c) Beta adrenergic
(d) All of the above.

995. Spironolactone acts by antagonizing: -
(a) Glucagon (b) Histamine
(c) Aldosterone (d) Insulin

996. Magnessium ion is necessary in: -
(a) Stimulating enzyme system
(b) Nerve conduction
(c) Musclar contraction
(d) All of the above

997. Vitamin A and D ointment is useful in treating: -
(a) Avitaminosis
(b) Puncture wounds
(c) Rickets
(d) Minor burn and Skin irritation

998. Which of the following is a serotonin antagonist:-
(a) Tolbutamide (b) Glutehimide
(c) Methysergide (d) Caffeine

999. Thiazide diuretics may produce an increase in blood levels of uric acid and: -
(a) Urea (b) BUN
(c) K (d) Glucose

1000. Ethacrynic acid is used primarily as: -
(a) Antiemetic (b) Sedative
(c) Luxative (d) Diuretic

1001. Which of the following is used to relieve gastro intestinal muscle spasm:-
(a) Edrophonium (b) Dicyclomine

(c) Bethanechol (d) Guanethidine

1002. Which is an antidote for malathion poisoning: -
(a) Edrophonium (b) Nalorphine
(c) Pralidoxime (d) Vitamin K

1003. Cyelosporine is used for: -
(a) Allergies (b) Steroid deficiency
(c) Lead poisoning (d) Transplant rejection

1004. Vidarakine is effective against: -
(a) Typhoid (b) Syphilis
(c) Herpes simplex (d) None of these

1005. Function of thyroid peroxidase includes: -
(a) Iodination of tyrosine to mono & di-iodotyrosine
(b) Conversion of iodide to its active form iodine
(c) Coupling of two di-iodotyrosine moeities to from T4
(d) All of the above

1006. Metabolic actions of estrogens include: -
(a) Increased High density lipid cholesterol
(b) Increased Low density lipid cholesterol
(c) Weak anabolic activity
(d) All of the above

1007. The secretion of insulin by the beta-cells of the islets of langerhans is stimulated by: -
(a) Cholecystokinin
(b) Glucose given orally
(c) Gastrine and secretin
(d) All of the above

1008. Stimulation of which gastric mucosal receptors may increase gastric acid secretion:
(a) Adrenergic b receptors
(b) Cholinergic M_1 & M_2 receptors
(c) Cholinergic M_1 & histaminergic H_2 receptors
(d) Histaminergic H_1 & H_2 receptors

1009. Which of the following are osmotic laxative: -
(a) Sorbitol
(b) Milk of magnesia
(c) Sodium phosphate
(d) All of the above.

1010. Parathion gets converted into paraoxon by oxidative reaction through: -
(a) Reduction
(b) No change in activity
(c) Inactivation
(d) Toxicity

1011. Pituitary gland found in: -
(a) Vertebrate kingdom
(b) Highly mammal
(c) Avertebrate
(d) Both a and b

1012. Ketamine has the following disadvantages when used as an anesthesia agent: -
(a) It is contraindicated in epilepsy
(b) It is not suitable for neurosurgery
(c) It produce dissociative anesthesia
(d) All of the above

1013. Which of the following interacts with vasopressin:-
(a) Dicumarol (b) Chlorpropamide
(c) Chloramphenicol (d) All of these

1014. An antiemetic containing carbohydrate derivatives is: -
(a) Emetcol (b) Magnesium sulfate
(c) Vesprin (d) None of these

1015. Which is best for treatment of ring worm: -
(a) Tolnaftale (b) Gentamicin
(c) Iodoform (d) Boric acid

1016. Most diarrhoea remedies contain: -
(a) Kaolin (b) Benzocaine
(c) Citrates (d) Aluminium oxide

1017. An advantage of ephidrine sulfate over epiephrine is: -
(a) Non toxic (b) More patients
(c) Effective orally (d) All of these

1018. Which one is signs of barbiturate poisoning: -
(a) Diuresis
(b) Hypertension
(c) Alkalosis
(d) Decreases respiratory volume

1019. The correct statements pertaining to estrogens: -
(a) Decrease follicle stimulating hormone secretion
(b) Have biphasic effect on luteinizing hormone secretion
(c) Both a & b
(d) None of them

Answers

1.	(a)	2.	(c)	3.	(a)
4.	(a)	5.	(a)	6.	(a)
7.	(d)	8.	(a)	9.	(b)
10.	(a)	11.	(a)	12.	(d)
13.	(d)	14.	(a)	15.	(a)
16.	(a)	17.	(d)	18.	(a)
19.	(d)	20.	(a)	21.	(a)
22.	(c)	23.	(a)	24.	(a)
25.	(d)	26.	(a)	27.	(a)
28.	(d)	29.	(b)	30.	(d)
31.	(a)	32.	(a)	33.	(a)
34.	(a)	35.	(a)	36.	(a)
37.	(a)	38.	(a)	39.	(c)
40.	(a)	41.	(b)	42.	(a)
43.	(b)	44.	(d)	45.	(a)
46.	(a)	47.	(a)	48.	(c)
49.	(a)	50.	(a)	51.	(d)
52.	(d)	53.	(a)	54.	(c)
55.	(d)	56.	(a)	57.	(d)
58.	(b)	59.	(b)	60.	(a)
61.	(a)	62.	(c)	63.	(b)
64.	(a)	65.	(c)	66.	(b)
67.	(b)	68.	(a)	69.	(a)
70.	(a)	71.	(d)	72.	(d)
73.	(c)	74.	(c)	75.	(d)
76.	(a)	77.	(a)	78.	(a)
79.	(b)	80.	(a)	81.	(a)
82.	(d)	83.	(a)	84.	(d)
85.	(a)	86.	(d)	87.	(a)
88.	(a)	89.	(a)	90.	(a)
91.	(d)	92.	(d)	93.	(b)
94.	(d)	95.	(a)	96.	(b)
97.	(c)	98.	(a)	99.	(a)
100.	(a)	101.	(c)	102.	(d)
103.	(a)	104.	(a)	105.	(c)
106.	(d)	107.	(a)	108.	(d)
109.	(c)	110.	(a)	111.	(a)
112.	(a)	113.	(d)	114.	(a)
115.	(d)	116.	(a)	117.	(c)
118.	(c)	119.	(c)	120.	(d)
121.	(b)	122.	(b)	123.	(a)
124.	(a)	125.	(c)	126.	(a)
127.	(d)	128.	(d)	129.	(a)
130.	(c)	131.	(b)	132.	(b)
133.	(a)	134.	(a)	135.	(b)
136.	(b)	137.	(b)	138.	(d)
139.	(a)	140.	(a)	141.	(d)
142.	(a)	143.	(c)	144.	(d)
145.	(b)	146.	(c)	147.	(a)
148.	(b)	149.	(c)	150.	(c)
151.	(d)	152.	(d)	153.	(b)
154.	(a)	155.	(b)	156.	(b)
157.	(a)	158.	(b)	159.	(c)
160.	(c)	161.	(b)	162.	(a)
163.	(d)	164.	(b)	165.	(c)
166.	(c)	167.	(d)	168.	(b)
169.	(a)	170.	(c)	171.	(a)
172.	(a)	173.	(b)	174.	(d)
175.	(b)	176.	(a)	177.	(a)
178.	(b)	179.	(b)	180.	(d)
181.	(c)	182.	(d)	183.	(a)
184.	(c)	185.	(b)	186.	(a)
187.	(c)	188.	(b)	189.	(a)
190.	(b)	191.	(c)	192.	(a)
193.	(c)	194.	(b)	195.	(a)
196.	(d)	197.	(b)	198.	(b)
199.	(d)	200.	(b)	201.	(d)
202.	(c)	203.	(a)	204.	(d)
205.	(c)	206.	(d)	207.	(d)
208.	(d)	209.	(a)	210.	(c)
211.	(c)	212.	(a)	213.	(a)
214.	(c)	215.	(b)	216.	(a)
217.	(b)	218.	(d)	219.	(c)
220.	(c)	221.	(c)	222.	(a)
223.	(d)	224.	(b)	225.	(a)
226.	(c)	227.	(c)	228.	(a)
229.	(b)	230.	(a)	231.	(a)
232.	(b)	233.	(c)	234.	(b)
235.	(d)	236.	(a)	237.	(a)
238.	(c)	239.	(b)	240.	(a)
241.	(c)	242.	(d)	243.	(a)
244.	(c)	245.	(d)	246.	(b)
247.	(c)	248.	(a)	249.	(a)
250.	(c)	251.	(b)	252.	(d)
253.	(d)	254.	(b)	255.	(a)
256.	(d)	257.	(b)	258.	(a)
259.	(b)	260.	(a)	261.	(c)
262.	(d)	263.	(b)	264.	(b)
265.	(d)	266.	(d)	267.	(b)
268.	(a)	269.	(b)	270.	(a)
271.	(b)	272.	(c)	273.	(c)
274.	(d)	275.	(a)	276.	(d)

277. (c) 278. (a) 279. (c)
280. (d) 281. (a) 282. (c)
283. (a) 284. (b) 285. (a)
286. (d) 287. (b) 288. (b)
289. (c) 290. (b) 291. (b)
292. (c) 293. (b) 294. (b)
295. (d) 296. (d) 297. (b)
298. (a) 299. (a) 300. (d)
301. (b) 302. (d) 303. (d)
304. (b) 305. (a) 306. (a)
307. (a) 308. (a) 309. (c)
310. (d) 311. (a) 312. (a)
313. (b) 314. (d) 315. (d)
316. (c) 317. (b) 318. (d)
319. (a) 320. (c) 321. (a)
322. (a) 323. (d) 324. (b)
325. (a) 326. (b) 327. (d)
328. (d) 329. (a) 330. (d)
331. (d) 332. (a) 333. (a)
334. (b) 335. (c) 336. (d)
337. (a) 338. (b) 339. (a)
340. (d) 341. (d) 342. (d)
343. (d) 344. (b) 345. (b)
346. (c) 347. (b) 348. (a)
349. (d) 350. (d) 351. (b)
352. (d) 353. (d) 354. (d)
355. (a) 356. (c) 357. (a)
358. (c) 359. (d) 360. (d)
361. (a) 362. (d) 363. (d)
364. (a) 365. (a) 366. (d)
367. (c) 368. (d) 369. (a)
370. (b) 371. (c) 372. (d)
373. (a) 374. (b) 375. (d)
376. (a) 377. (d) 378. (d)
379. (d) 380. (b) 381. (c)
382. (a) 383. (c) 384. (d)
385. (d) 386. (a) 387. (a)
388. (a) 389. (d) 390. (d)
391. (d) 392. (a) 393. (d)
394. (d) 395. (a) 396. (b)
397. (b) 398. (c) 399. (d)
400. (c) 401. (a) 402. (c)
403. (c) 404. (d) 405. (c)
406. (b) 407. (d) 408. (b)
409. (a) 410. (c) 411. (b)
412. (a) 413. (b) 414. (b)
415. (a) 416. (c) 417. (d)

418. (b) 419. (b) 420. (c)
421. (c) 422. (a) 423. (c)
424. (b) 425. (c) 426. (d)
427. (d) 428. (c) 429. (a)
430. (d) 431. (d) 432. (a)
433. (b) 434. (b) 435. (c)
436. (a) 437. (a) 438. (d)
439. (b) 440. (b) 441. (b)
442. (d) 443. (c) 444. (b)
445. (c) 446. (c) 447. (d)
448. (b) 449. (d) 450. (c)
451. (c) 452. (c) 453. (d)
454. (a) 455. (a) 456. (a)
457. (c) 458. (a) 459. (a)
460. (c) 461. (d) 462. (a)
463. (c) 464. (b) 465. (d)
466. (d) 467. (a) 468. (b)
469. (c) 470. (a) 471. (a)
472. (c) 473. (a) 474. (d)
475. (a) 476. (a) 477. (b)
478. (a) 479. (d) 480. (d)
481. (a) 482. (b) 483. (a)
484. (d) 485. (c) 486. (d)
487. (a) 488. (d) 489. (c)
490. (d) 491. (c) 492. (c)
493. (c) 494. (a) 495. (c)
496. (c) 497. (a) 498. (a)
499. (c) 500. (b) 501. (b)
502. (a) 503. (a) 504. (c)
505. (a) 506. (b) 507. (c)
508. (a) 509. (c) 510. (c)
511. (c) 512. (c) 513. (d)
514. (a) 515. (b) 516. (b)
517. (a) 518. (b) 519. (d)
520. (b) 521. (c) 522. (d)
523. (a) 524. (d) 525. (b)
526. (b) 527. (a) 528. (a)
529. (d) 530. (b) 531. (a)
532. (d) 533. (a) 534. (d)
535. (c) 536. (c) 537. (c)
538. (b) 539. (d) 540. (b)
541. (c) 542. (a) 543. (c)
544. (d) 545. (d) 546. (a)
547. (c) 548. (c) 549. (c)
550. (d) 551. (d) 552. (d)
553. (d) 554. (d) 555. (d)
556. (a) 557. (d) 558. (a)

559.	(c)	560.	(a)	561.	(a)
562.	(b)	563.	(c)	564.	(a)
565.	(a)	566.	(c)	567.	(c)
568.	(a)	569.	(d)	570.	(b)
571.	(a)	572.	(c)	573.	(a)
574.	(c)	575.	(c)	576.	(d)
577.	(b)	578.	(c)	579.	(a)
580.	(a)	581.	(b)	582.	(c)
583.	(a)	584.	(d)	585.	(b)
586.	(b)	587.	(a)	588.	(b)
589.	(c)	590.	(c)	591.	(a)
592.	(d)	593.	(c)	594.	(d)
595.	(c)	596.	(d)	597.	(b)
598.	(a)	599.	(d)	600.	(a)
601.	(d)	602.	(a)	603.	(b)
604.	(a)	605.	(b)	606.	(d)
607.	(d)	608.	(a)	609.	(c)
610.	(d)	611.	(a)	612.	(c)
613.	(c)	614.	(a)	615.	(c)
616.	(d)	617.	(d)	618.	(d)
619.	(c)	620.	(d)	621.	(a)
622.	(a)	623.	(c)	624.	(a)
625.	(b)	626.	(d)	627.	(b)
628.	(d)	629.	(d)	630.	(d)
631.	(c)	632.	(a)	633.	(a)
634.	(a)	635.	(c)	636.	(c)
637.	(a)	638.	(c)	639.	(a)
640.	(d)	641.	(d)	642.	(d)
643.	(d)	644.	(d)	645.	(a)
646.	(d)	647.	(d)	648.	(d)
649.	(d)	650.	(d)	651.	(c)
652.	(c)	653.	(d)	654.	(b)
655.	(d)	656.	(d)	657.	(c)
658.	(a)	659.	(a)	660.	(d)
661.	(a)	662.	(c)	663.	(a)
664.	(a)	665.	(c)	666.	(c)
667.	(d)	668.	(a)	669.	(d)
670.	(d)	671.	(d)	672.	(d)
673.	(d)	674.	(d)	675.	(d)
676.	(d)	677.	(d)	678.	(d)
679.	(c)	680.	(d)	681.	(c)
682.	(a)	683.	(b)	684.	(d)
685.	(c)	686.	(a)	687.	(c)
688.	(b)	689.	(c)	690.	(b)
691.	(b)	692.	(c)	693.	(a)
694.	(a)	695.	(c)	696.	(a)
697.	(d)	698.	(d)	699.	(a)

700.	(a)	701.	(d)	702.	(d)
703.	(b)	704.	(b)	705.	(d)
706.	(c)	707.	(d)	708.	(c)
709.	(d)	710.	(c)	711.	(b)
712.	(b)	713.	(d)	714.	(d)
715.	(a)	716.	(d)	717.	(d)
718.	(b)	719.	(b)	720.	(c)
721.	(a)	722.	(d)	723.	(b)
724.	(a)	725.	(d)	726.	(b)
727.	(c)	728.	(a)	729.	(c)
730.	(d)	731.	(b)	732.	(d)
733.	(d)	734.	(d)	735.	(d)
736.	(d)	737.	(b)	738.	(d)
739.	(d)	740.	(b)	741.	(d)
742.	(d)	743.	(d)	744.	(d)
745.	(d)	746.	(b)	747.	(c)
748.	(c)	749.	(a)	750.	(d)
751.	(b)	752.	(d)	753.	(c)
754.	(c)	755.	(c)	756.	(a)
757.	(d)	758.	(d)	759.	(a)
760.	(b)	761.	(d)	762.	(a)
763.	(c)	764.	(d)	765.	(b)
766.	(a)	767.	(a)	768.	(a)
769.	(d)	770.	(a)	771.	(a)
772.	(a)	773.	(b)	774.	(b)
775.	(a)	776.	(a)	777.	(c)
778.	(b)	779.	(d)	780.	(c)
781.	(c)	782.	(a)	783.	(d)
784.	(c)	785.	(d)	786.	(b)
787.	(c)	788.	(d)	789.	(b)
790.	(d)	791.	(c)	792.	(b)
793.	(d)	794.	(d)	795.	(c)
796.	(c)	797.	(b)	798.	(d)
799.	(d)	800.	(d)	801.	(c)
802.	(d)	803.	(a)	804.	(d)
805.	(d)	806.	(c)	807.	(b)
808.	(a)	809.	(c)	810.	(a)
811.	(c)	812.	(d)	813.	(a)
814.	(c)	815.	(b)	816.	(b)
817.	(c)	818.	(d)	819.	(b)
820.	(c)	821.	(b)	822.	(d)
823.	(a)	824.	(a)	825.	(a)
826.	(d)	827.	(c)	828.	(d)
829.	(d)	830.	(d)	831.	(a)
832.	(d)	833.	(d)	834.	(d)
835.	(a)	836.	(b)	837.	(d)
838.	(d)	839.	(b)	840.	(b)

841.	(d)	842.	(c)	843.	(a)
844.	(d)	845.	(b)	846.	(a)
847.	(c)	848.	(c)	849.	(b)
850.	(d)	851.	(c)	852.	(a)
853.	(c)	854.	(d)	855.	(c)
856.	(a)	857.	(c)	858.	(c)
859.	(a)	860.	(a)	861.	(d)
862.	(d)	863.	(a)	864.	(d)
865.	(b)	866.	(d)	867.	(a)
868.	(b)	869.	(c)	870.	(d)
871.	(c)	872.	(c)	873.	(a)
874.	(c)	875.	(d)	876.	(b)
877.	(d)	878.	(d)	879.	(d)
880.	(a)	881.	(d)	882.	(c)
883.	(d)	884.	(d)	885.	(d)
886.	(c)	887.	(d)	888.	(d)
889.	(d)	890.	(c)	891.	(d)
892.	(c)	893.	(d)	894.	(d)
895.	(b)	896.	(d)	897.	(d)
898.	(b)	899.	(d)	900.	(d)
901.	(b)	902.	(c)	903.	(d)
904.	(a)	905.	(b)	906.	(a)
907.	(a)	908.	(d)	909.	(b)
910.	(d)	911.	(d)	912.	(a)
913.	(b)	914.	(b)	915.	(b)
916.	(b)	917.	(d)	918.	(d)
919.	(d)	920.	(d)	921.	(a)
922.	(d)	923.	(d)	924.	(d)
925.	(b)	926.	(a)	927.	(c)
928.	(d)	929.	(b)	930.	(a)

931.	(b)	932.	(c)	933.	(d)
934.	(d)	935.	(b)	936.	(d)
937.	(d)	938.	(c)	939.	(d)
940.	(d)	941.	(d)	942.	(d)
943.	(a)	944.	(b)	945.	(a)
946.	(d)	947.	(d)	948.	(d)
949.	(a)	950.	(d)	951.	(c)
952.	(d)	953.	(d)	954.	(d)
955.	(d)	956.	(d)	957.	(d)
958.	(b)	959.	(b)	960.	(b)
961.	(d)	962.	(a)	963.	(b)
964.	(b)	965.	(a)	966.	(a)
967.	(d)	968.	(d)	969.	(d)
970.	(c)	971.	(a)	972.	(c)
973.	(b)	974.	(c)	975.	(d)
976.	(b)	977.	(d)	978.	(a)
979.	(b)	980.	(c)	981.	(d)
982.	(d)	983.	(c)	984.	(a)
985.	(c)	986.	(d)	987.	(c)
988.	(b)	989.	(b)	990.	(a)
991.	(b)	992.	(a)	993.	(b)
994.	(b)	995.	(c)	996.	(d)
997.	(d)	998.	(c)	999.	(d)
1000.	(d)	1001.	(b)	1002.	(c)
1003.	(d)	1004.	(c)	1005.	(d)
1006.	(d)	1007.	(d)	1008.	(c)
1009.	(d)	1010.	(d)	1011.	(d)
1012.	(d)	1013.	(b)	1014.	(a)
1015.	(a)	1016.	(a)	1017.	(c)
1018.	(d)	1019.	(c)		

7 Microbiology & Immunology

Salient Points:

1. Chronic respiratory disease is a Mycoplasmal disease of poultry.
2. **IgA** = found in high concentration in external secretions colostrum, tear, saliva, intestinal and bronchial secretions. it is a part of Ist line of defense (DL-1)
3. Milk contains greater quantity of Ig A than Ig G.
4. Ig E is homocytotropic. Responsible for allergic reaction and syndromes of Asthma and Hay fever involved in protection against metazoan parasites – intestinal worm.
5. Antigen – binding sites are known as Paratopes.
6. Allotypes: are epitopes that differ among individuals of same species. Genetically different antigenic determinants on proteins of individuals of same species.
7. Antisera produced to heat denatured or chemically denatured Ig may react only to denatured Ig; not with native Ig.
8. Idiotype: a set of unique antigenic determinants (Idiotopes) on V region of homologous/ monoclonal antibodies.
9. Idiotope = an epitope on V region of antibody.
10. ANTIGEN is molecular species capable of inducing immune response and of being recognized by antibody.
11. Interleukin is produced by T-cells.
12. Mature antibody producing cells are calls plasma cells.
13. Neonatal bursectomy in birds causes reduced Ig level.
14. Detection of surface Ig best demonstrates that the lymphocytes in leukemic animals are B-cells.
15. Neonatal thymectomy does not cause increased susceptibility to disease.
16. Vit. E enhances B-cell proliferation enhances lymphocytes response to mitogen enhances macrophage phagocytosis of *Streptococcus pneumoniae*.
17. Tuberculosis is caused by *Mycobacterium tuberculosis*.
18. Rat flea is involved in transmission of plague.
19. Leeuvenhoek was first to report cell under microscope.
20. Acid fast stain was discovered by **Ehrlich**.
21. Edward Jenner for the first time vaccinated against small pox using **cow pox** vesicle.
22. Joseph Lister developed the **Aseptic** techniques. (Father of aseptic surgery)
23. **Pasteur** coined the term vaccine.
24. **Metchnikoff** discovered defensive mechanism of phagocytosis.
25. **J. Bordet** discovered complement and complement fixation test.
26. R. Koch is known as the father of **bacteriology**.
27. **Lister** is known as the father of antiseptic surgery.
28. Rous isolated virus causing **Sarcoma** in fowls.
29. **Resolving power** of microscope is the shortest distance by which two particles are separated to

give distinct images.

30. India ink is a **negative** stain.
31. Lacto phenol cotton blue stain is used to study **fungi**.
32. Rickettsias can be stained using **Giemsa** stain.
33. Fontana stain is used to study **spirochaetes**.
34. The highest percentage of **lipids** is found in Mycobacterium.
35. Dipicolinic acid is found in **spore**.
36. Protoplasts are prepared from Gram **positive** bacteria.
37. Pilli are common in Gram **negative** bacilli.
38. Lophotrichous bacteria have cluster of flagella at **one** pole.
39. Extracytoplasmic DNA in bacteria is known as **plasmid**.
40. Structure in bacteria equivalent to mitochondria is **mesosome**.
41. Site of eukaryotic cell respiration is **mitochondria**.
42. Protein moiety of an enzyme is called **apoenzyme**.
43. ATP releases **7.3** K cal energy per mol.
44. Uracil is a nitrogenous base of **RNA**.
45. Chain terminating codons are also known as **Non – Sense** codons.
46. AUG and GUG are chain **initiating** codons.
47. Same amino acid may be coded by **more than one** codon.
48. Single codon codes for single **amino acid**.
49. Bacterial conjugation was first observed in **E. coli**.
50. Antibiotic resistance in bacteria is transmitted by **R** plasmids.
51. In bacteria sex factor is determined by **F** factor.
52. Penicillin was discovered by **Flemming**.
53. Actinomycin D inhibits the synthesis of **RNA**.
54. Mytomicin C inhibits synthesis of **DNA**.
55. The term antibiotic was first used by **Waksman**.
56. Fungi cell wall consists of **chitin**.
57. Capsules can be stained by **India** ink.
58. **Cuboidal** form of cocci is known as sarcinae
59. Staphylococcus aureus produces golden **yellow** colony.
60. Hot – cold lysis is produced by á haemolysin.
61. Selective medium for staphylococci is **Mannitol salt** agar.
62. O_2 **labile** form of á – heterolysis is caused by streptolysin O.
63. á – haemolysin produces no haemolysis.
64. Hotis test is used for *Streptococcus agalactiae*.
65. Scarlet fever is detected by **Dick** test.
66. Dick toxin is **erythrogenic**.
67. Streptococcus equi causes **strangles** in horses.
68. **Mc. Fadyean's** reaction is produced by *Bacillus anthracis* capsule.
69. **String of Pearls** on nutrient agar colonies is produced by *Bacillus anthracis*.
70. Black quarter in cattle is caused by *Clostridium chauvoei*.
71. Shape of spores of *Clostridium tetani* is **drum stick**.
72. *Clostridium welchii* type b causes **lamb dysentery**.
73. Lamsiekte in cattle is caused by *Cl. botulinum* type **D**.
74. **Limberneck**, in chickens is caused by *Cl. botulinum* type C
75. *Cl tetani* digests and turns meat colour into **black**.
76. Serological types of *Cl. tetani* can be distinguished by **H** antigens.
77. Nagler's reaction with Cl. Perfringens on egg yolk agar is caused by **lecithinase**.
78. *Cl. septicum* causes **braxy** in sheep.
79. **Anton's** eye test is done for *Listeria monocytogenes*.
80. **Diamond skin** disease in swine disease is caused by *Erysipelothrix rhusiopathiae.*
81. Schick test determines susceptibility to **diphtheria**.
82. **Pseudotuberculosis** in sheep is caused by *Erysipelothrix rhusiopathiae*.
83. Ray fungus belongs to **Actinomyces** genus.
84. Wooden tongue is caused by **Actinobacillus** ligniresi.
85. *Nocardia* causes bovine **farcy**.

86. *Corynebacterium* is now known as **Rhodococcus**.
87. Leprosy bacillus is also known as **Hansen's** bacillus.
88. Serpentine cards are produced by **Mycobacterium**.
89. **Johne's disease** is caused by *M. paratuberculosis*.
90. Lowenstein – Jensen medium is used to grow pathogenic **Mycobacteria**.
91. Timothy hay bacillus is ***Mycobacterium phlei***.
92. Iron is essential for growth of **Mycobacteria**.
93. Lactose fermenting bacteria are collectively known as **coliform**.
94. **Capsular** antigens of *E. coli* are known as K antigens.
95. Bismuth sulphate agar is used for *Salmonella typhi*.
96. Klebsiella pneumoniae is also known as **fried lander's** bacillus.
97. ***E. coli*** causes white scour in calves.
98. Fowl typhoid is caused by *Salmonella* ***gallinarum***.
99. **Vi** antigen is found an Salmonella surface.
100. Transduction was discovered by **Zinder** and **Lederberg** in Salmonella typhi bacteria.
101. Conjugation was discovered in **E. coli**.
102. Transformation was first found in Pneumococci by **Griffith**.
103. Bacillary dysentery is known as **shigellosis**.
104. **Shiga** toxin is produced by *Shigella dysenteriae*.
105. *Actinomyces bovis* causes **Lumpy jaw**.
106. Wooden Tongue is caused by *Actinobacillus* ***lignieresii***.
107. *Haemophilus aegyptius* is also known as **Koch weeks** bacillus.
108. Bang's disease is caused by *Brucella* ***abortus***.
109. *Brucella abortus* requires 5-10 % CO_2 for growth.
110. *Brucella abortus* produces **Strauss** test.
111. Brucella causes abortion in **third** trimester.
112. *Brucella abortus* has special affinity for **erythritol** present in uterus.
113. Kennel cough is caused by ***Bordetella bronchiseptica***.
114. Nature of Bordetella toxin is **dermonecrotising**.
115. Sweetish aromatic odour on ordinary media is produced by ***Pseudomonas aeruginosa***.
116. Whitemore's bacillus is nick name of ***Pseudomonas pseudomallei***.
117. *Pseudomonas mallei* cause **glanders** in equines.
118. Mallein is a filtrate of **bacterial** extract.
119. Vibrio cholerae is facultative **anaerobes**.
120. El tor is a biotype of ***Vibrio cholerae***.
121. Thiol medium is used for isolation of ***Campylobacter fetus***.
122. **Fried eggs** like colonies with nipple are produced by Mycoplasma on solid media.
123. Chronic respiratory disease in poultry is caused by ***Mycoplasma***.
124. ***Mycoplasma*** is also known as Eaton agents.
125. Shape of spirochetes is **helical**.
126. Borrelia causes **lyme** disease in man.
127. **Weil's** disease is caused by *Leptospira interrogans* serotype icterohaemorrhagica.
128. Weil – Felix reaction is used for diagnosis of **endemic typhus**.
129. Brooder's pneumonia is caused by ***Aspergillus flavus***.
130. Aflatoxin is produced by ***Aspergillus flavus***.
131. *Trichophyton schoenleinii* causes **favus**.
132. Colonies of *A. fumigatus* are **green** is colour.
133. *Histoplasma capsulatum* is found inside **macrophages**.
134. Tinea pedis is caused by ***Trichophyton mentagrophytes***.

Questions:

1. Acid fast stain was first discovered by
   (a) Christian Gram (b) Ehrlich
   (c) Ziehl-Neelsen (d) Koch
2. The concept of chemotherapy originated from;
   (a) Pasture (b) Waksman
   (c) Fleming (d) Ehrlich
3. Waksman is associated with:
   (a) Erythromycin (b) Streptomycin
   (c) Bacitracin (d) None of the above

4. The *Staphylococcus* infection partial hemolysis of the basis of-
(a) Coagulase test (b) Dick test
(c) CAMP test (d) None of the above

5. Important toxin related to the food poising in *Staphylococcus ssp.* is-
(a) Lethal toxin (b) Dermeto toxin
(c) Enterotoxin (d) None of the above

6. Most commonly used Media for Streptococcus is-
(a) MSA (b) McConkey agar
(c) Edward mediam (d) None of above

7. Which is responsible for strangle in horse-
(a) *S. equi* (b) *S. faecalis*
(c) *S. bovis* (d) None of the above

8. Hemolytic streptococci is-
(a) Classified by Lancefield
(b) Basis in nature of CHO sub.
(c) Decided group from A to U
(d) All are corrected

9. Dick test is performed in-
(a) Staphylococcus (b) Erysipelothrix
(c) Streptococcus (d) Corynebacteria

10. Circling disease caused by
(a) *L. monocytogenes* (b) Erysipelothrix
(c) Leptospira (d) Anthrax.

11. In which animal *Erysipelothrix*, produces diamond shaped bodies-
(a) Rat (b) Sheep & Goat
(c) Pig (d) None of the above

12. Brucellosis is also called as
(a) Undulant fever (b) Malta fever
(c) Both (d) None

13. Which of the following combination is dissimilar?
(a) *B. melitensis,* in sheep & goat
(b) *B. ovis*-in Sheep.
(c) *B. neotomae*- man
(d) None of the above

14. Which test is capable to detect the incomplete antibody?
(a) ELISA (b) Coomb's test
(c) CFT (d) All are correct.

15. Fowl cholera now named pasteurella in the honour
(a) Bruce (b) Pasteur
(c) Bang (d) None

16. Which of the following colony is most pathogenic?
(a) Blue colony (b) Intermediate
(c) Fluorescent (d) None

17. Braxy in sheep caused by which of the following-
(a) *Cl. hemalyticum* (b) *Cl. septcium*
(c) *Cl. novyi* (d) None

18. Potent neurotoxin which interfere with release of GABA
(a) Tetanospasmin (b) á-toxin
(c) â-toxin (d) None

19. Pulpy kidney disease is caused by
(a) *Cl. perfringens* type A
(b) *Cl. perfringens* type B
(c) *Cl. perfringens* type D
(d) None

20. Whooping cough is caused by which of the following
(a) *Bordetella pertussis*
(b) *Clostridium sp.*
(c) *Erysipelothrix sp.*
(d) None

21. Filamentous bacterium, first isolated by Nocard is which of the following.
(a) Aeromonas (b) Bordetella
(c) Nocardia (d) Corynebacterium

22. Fish *pathogen which is motile & unable to grow at 37 is*
(a) Aeromonoas hydrophilla
(b) *A. salmonicida*
(c) Both
(d) None

23. Which test is performed for *Corynebacterium*
(a) Elek's test (b) Dick test
(c) Coomb's test (d) All of these

24. The bacteriophage along with gene toxin inject in the bacteria
(a) Nocordia (b) Pseudomonas
(c) Corynebacterium (d) All

25. The somatic cell antigen which is
(a) 'O' antigen (b) 'K' antigen
(c) 'H' antigen (d) All of these

26. Which one of following is not correct?

(a) 'O' antigen - somatic antigen
(b) 'K' antigen - capsulor antigen
(c) 'H' antigen - somotic antigen
(d) None

27. The prominent capsule is the most disinct feature of which bacteria
(a) *Klebsiella sp.* (b) *E. coli*
(c) *Salmonella sp.* (d) None

28. Swelling reaction is performed in
(a) *E. coli* (b) Enterobactor
(c) Klebsiella (d) All

29. In *E. coli*, which of the test is prefored?
(a) Eijkman test (b) Coomb's test
(c) Both (d) None

30. Toxin which are product by *E. coli*
(a) Enterotoxin (b) Verotoxin
(c) Both (d) None

31. IMVIC pattern found in *E. coli* is
(a) + – + – (b) – – + +
(c) + + – – (d) + – – +

32. The character which is not found in Enterobacteriaceae
(a) Gram-ve
(b) Grow on Mc conkey agar
(c) Produce enterotaxaemia
(d) None of the above

33. Medium which is differentiate LF & MLF
(a) Mc conkey agar (b) Blood agar
(c) MSA agar (d) All

34. Medium of choice for *E. coli is*
(a) EMB (b) Nutrient agar
(c) Nutrient broth (d) All

35. Kauffman white scheme is present in-
(a) Shigella (b) Salmonella
(c) Proteus (d) None

36. Red water disease is caused by
(a) Erysipelothrix (b) Yersinia
(c) Leptospira (d) None

37. Which of the following organism is responsible for the infectious coryza
(a) *Haemophilus gallinarum*
(b) *H. parogallinarum*
(c) *Haemophillus canis*
(d) Both a & b

38. Gram-ve small rod with rounded end, I[st] time identified by Pfeiffer's is-
(a) Haemophillus (b) Mycobacterium
(c) Leptospira (d) All

39. The organism which can grow on cell free medium
(a) Mycoplasma (b) Chlamydia
(c) Virus (d) All

40. Peptidoglycan may be present in cell wall of
(a) Mycoplasma
(b) Bacteria
(c) Rickettsia & Chlamydia
(d) Both B & C

41. Organisms which are not filterable through 450 mm spore size filter is
(a) Bacteria
(b) My coplasma & Virus
(c) Rickettsia
(d) Both b & c

42. In 1963 Petergell & Robert comb classify the Hypersensitivity
(a) 4 type (b) 3 type
(c) 5 type (d) 2 type

43. *Yersimia pestes* which produce plague is spread by
(a) Dog flea (b) Rat
(c) Ely (d) None

44. Which is causative organism of 'Johnes' disease
(a) *M. bovis* (b) *M. paratuberulosis*
(c) *M. tuberculosis* (d) All

45. Medium which is used for culturing Mycobacterium
(a) Lowenstein Jensen medium
(b) Dorset medium
(c) Ogawa medium
(d) All are correct

46. Gram-ve anerobes are
(a) Fusobacterium (b) Bacteroides
(c) Both (d) None

47. Calf diphtheria is produced by-
(a) *F. necrophorum* (b) *E. coli*
(c) *Mycobacterium sp.* (d) All

48. Foot rot in sheep produced by
(a) Spherophorus necrophorum
(b) Bacteroides

(c) Both
(d) None

49. The medium used for culturing *Leptospira* is
(a) Blood agar
(b) BGA
(c) Korthop & fletcher
(d) None

50. Which organism is sensitive to digitoxin
(a) Mycoplasma (b) Acholephasma
(c) Both (d) None

51. The organism which is responsible for the wool sorter disease in human is
(a) Campylobactor (b) *Bacillus anthracis*
(c) Vibrio (d) All

52. The following species of *Bacillus* helpful for stoppage of spilling oil taps-
(a) *B. lickeniformis* (b) *B. Polymyxa*
(c) *B. subtilis* (d) *B. anthracis*

53. The colony of *Bacillus* given the appearance of
(a) Medusa head (b) Fried egg
(c) Bladed (d) All of these

54. Extra cellular toxins produced by *Bacillus* is
(a) Edema factor (b) Protection factor
(c) Lethal factor (d) All

55. For diagnosis for Anthrax following test is preformed
(a) Dick test (b) Shick test
(c) Ascoli's test (d) Dye test

56. The father of Microbiology is
(a) Antony van Laeuwenhock
(b) Levis pasture
(c) Robert Koch
(d) Jenner

57. The father of Bacteriology is
(a) Antony van laeuwanhock
(b) Louis Pasteur
(c) Robert Koch
(d) Jenner

58. Who discovered the tubercle bacilli?
(a) Pasture
(b) Robert Koch
(c) Antonym van Laeuwanhock
(d) None

59. Beta-lectamase enzyme is produce by
(a) P. aeruginosa (b) Bacillus anthracis
(c) S. typhimurium (d) All

60. Bacteria which requires cholesterol for its growth is
(a) Mycoplasma (b) Leptospira
(c) Spirochaeta (d) None

61. Unstained living bacteria can preferably be best resolved by
(a) Dark background illumination
(b) Light Microscope
(c) Electron microscope
(d) None of the above

62. In general, important spp. of chlamydia are
(a) 4 (b) 3
(c) 5 (d) 6

63. The size of elementary body of Chlamydia is
(a) 50-100 nm (b) 100-150 nm
(c) 200-300 nm (d) 300-400 nm

64. Chalamydia lose infectivity with in hours at
(a) 15-17°C (b) 20-22°C
(c) 30-32°C (d) 35-37°C

65. Virulence of Bacteria depends upon
(a) Host defence mechanism
(b) Number of Bacterise preent
(c) Tissue affinity
(d) All

66. The Ultra violet microscopy is developed by
(a) Antony von Leewenhock
(b) Barnard
(c) Robert hook
(d) Noll and Ruska

67. Cell wall of Bacteria act as major part of
(a) Endotoxin (b) Exotoxin
(c) Both (d) None

68. Certain enteric bacteria possess fibre & these belong to the genus
(a) Klebsilla (b) Escheresia
(c) Enterococi (d) None

69. The revision of code of conduct of nomenclature of bacteria came into being in
(a) 1900 (b) 1960
(c) 1976 (d) 1980

70. The heat resistance of spore bearing bacteria is due to

(a) Dipicolinic acid (b) Mucopeptides
(c) Hereditary (d) None

71. The only indispensable layer present in mycoplasma group of bacteria is
(a) Cell wall (b) Cell membrane
(c) Both a & b (d) None

72. In bacteria, two subunits of DNA which form ribosomes are.
(a) 40S & 50S (b) 355 & 355
(c) 505 & 205 (d) 205 & 505

73. Lipid A moiety of LPS pathogenic bacteria is
(a) Toxic (b) Non toxic
(c) Induce resistance (d) All

74. Immune response is
(a) Antigen specific (b) Species specific
(c) Hereditary (d) None

75. The dry weight of bacteria varies between.
(a) 40-60 % (b) 5-15 %
(c) 10-40 % (d) None

76. Which part of the bacteria cell possess phage receptors
(a) Cell wall (b) Capsule
(c) Cell membrane (d) Spore

77. Medium which is suitable for the growth of specific organisms is termed as
(a) Selective media (b) Minimal media
(c) Complex media (d) None of the above

78. *Staphylococci* are relatively
(a) Heat tolerant (b) Salt tolerant
(c) Resistant to dye (d) Both a & b

79. Selective medium for staphylococci-
(a) Blood agar (b) Mannital salt agar
(c) Nutrient agar (d) None

80. Select one of the following enzymes which activates plasminogen system-
(a) Coagulase (b) Staphylokinase
(c) Lipase (d) Hyluronidase

81. Food poising due to *Staph. aureus* is caused by one of the following toxin-
(a) Haemolysin (b) Leucocidin
(c) Entero toxin (d) Lethal toxin

82. In carreiers *Staphlococcus* are found in the following sites except
(a) Skin (b) Nose
(c) Throat (d) Tears

83. *Staphylococcus* is quite susceptible to
(a) Methelin green (b) Crystal violet
(c) Acid fast srain (d) None

84. Hotis test is specific for
(a) Str. agalactiae (b) Str. dyslactiae
(c) Str. *ubris* (d) None

85. *Str. agalactiae* produce CAMP test in presence of
(a) Staphylococcus á- haemolysis
(b) Staphylococcus â- haemolysis
(c) Staphylococcus ã - haemolysis
(d) Staphylococcus ä-haemolysis

86. Lancefield classification of Streptococci is based on
(a) M & T antigen (b) MTR antigen
(c) C antigen (d) Montigen

87. Dick test is done to detect susceptibility for
(a) Sore throat (b) Diarrhoea
(c) Tetanus (d) Scarlet fever

88. Common sub acute endocarditis can be caused by
(a) Staphylococcus
(b) Pneumococcus
(c) á-haemolytic Strep.
(d) None

89. *Str. pneumoniae* can be differentiated from á-haemolytic *Strep.* by
(a) Growth characteristic
(b) Morphology
(c) Bile solubility
(d) None

90. The pneumococcal antigen are resistants to phagocytosis & used in specific serotyping is-
(a) Capsular polysacharide
(b) Leumcodin
(c) Nucleoprotein
(d) None

91. The most common infection due to â-haemolytic Streptococcai are following except-
(a) Streptococcal sore throat
(b) Mastitis in cattle & buffalo
(c) Strangles in horses
(d) Acute & sub acute endocarditis

92. Dick toxin is

(a) Streptolysin (b) Streptolysin 'O'
(c) Erythrogenic (d) None

93. Which of the following antigens of streptococcus is related to its virulence?
(a) M (b) T
(c) R (d) None of the above

94. Vegetative form of *Bacillus* sp. have-
(a) O Antigens (b) H antigens
(c) Both a & b (d) None

95. *Bracillus anthracis* spore are formed
(a) Outside the body in presence of O_2
(b) Abundantly formed in preence of CO_2
(c) Both a & b
(d) None

96. Spores of all the following bacteria are formed inside the body except-
(a) *Cl. chauvoi* (b) *Cl. tetani*
(c) *B. anthracis* (d) *cl. welchi*

97. The string of pearls on nutrient agar colonies is produced by
(a) *Proteus* (b) *B. anthracis*
(c) *Pneumococci* (d) *Salmonalla*

98. Cutaneous anthrax is also known as-
(a) Pulmonary anthrax
(b) Malignant anthrax
(c) Visceral anthrax
(d) None

99. Canned food is responsible for food poisoning denote
(a) *Staphy.* enterotoxin
(b) *Cl. welchi toxin*
(c) Salmonella toxin
(d) *Cl. botulinum* toxin

100. The following clostridias produces pink colour on Robertson cooked meat medium except.
(a) *Cl. septicum* (b) *Cl. oedematiens*
(c) *Cl. tetani* (d) *Cl. wechi*

101. Which of the following clostridia digest the meat & terns it black & produce foul odour-
(a) Cl. tetani (b) Cl. chauvoei
(c) *Cl. speticum* (d) *Cl. welchi*

102. The most powerful neuro toxin among following clostridia is that of-
(a) Cl. welchii
(b) Cl tetani
(c) *Cl.* botulinum
(d) Cl. oedematiens

103. Serological types of *Cl. tatani* can be distinguished by-
(a) 'O' Antigens (b) H Antigens
(c) Exotoxins (d) All above

104. Clostridia are
(a) Atrichous (b) Amphitrichous
(c) Lophotrichous (d) Peritrichous

105. The following clostridia are motile except-
(a) *Cl. septicum* (b) *Cl. welchii*
(c) *Cl. botulinum* (d) *Cl. tetani*

106. The following clostridia are non-capsulated except-
(a) *Cl. welchi* (b) *Cl. Chauvoei*
(c) *Cl. oedoematiens* (d) *Cl. septicum*

107. Among following micro-organisms, most powerful toxin is produced by
(a) *Staph. aureus* (b) *Cl. diptheriae*
(c) *Cl. botulinum* (d) *Cl. welchii*

108. Magleris reaction with *Cl. perfringens* on egg yolk agar is due
(a) Haemolysin (b) Lecithinase
(c) Hyaluronidase (d) Leucocidin

109. *Mycobacterium leprae* can be cultivated in following except-
(a) Artificial media (b) Foot pad of mice
(c) Both (d) None

110. The growth of *M. tuberculosis* on solid medium appears-
(a) Moist (b) Glistening
(c) Dry & granular (d) Smooth

111. The shortest generation time observed for tubercle bacillus inrich media is about-
(a) 30 minutes (b) 1 hours
(c) 8 hours (d) 12 hours

112. Yellowish-orange pigment is produced by
(a) *M. bovis* (b) *M. avium*
(c) *M. tuberculosis* (d) In all species

113. A good growth of pathogenic sp. of Mylobacterium is seen in
(a) 24 hour (b) 1 week
(c) 4 to 6 week (d) 3 month

114. The following give acid fast staiing except.
(a) Mycobacterium (b) Nocardia
(c) Bacterial spore (d) Leptospira

115. The mycolic acid is present in the cell wall of the following bacteria except-
(a) Nocardia (b) Corynebacteria
(c) Mycobacteria (d) Eryseplothrix

116. B.C.G. is prepared from-
(a) *M. tuberculosis* (b) *M. bovis*
(c) *M. avium* (d) None of above

117. In Coliform bacilli the generation time is about-
(a) 10 minutes (b) 20 minutes
(c) 45 minutes (d) 1 hours

118. On Wilson & Blair's medium the growth of *E. coli* is due to
(a) Brillent green (b) Bismuth sulphite
(c) Sod. Sulphate (d) All

119. In tetrathionate broth which of the following bacteria grow
(a) *Escherisia coli*
(b) Slamanella & Proteus.
(c) Salmonella & Shigella
(d) Proteus & Shigella

120. Black coloured colonies of salmonella are produced on
(a) Mackonkey agar
(b) DCA
(c) Wilson & Blair's medium
(d) BGA

121. Salmonella differs from Shigella in following properties except-
(a) Motility (b) H_2S production
(c) MR & VP test (d) H Antigen

122. Which one is not a coliform bacteria -
(a) *E. coli* (b) *Kelebsiell*
(c) Both a & b (d) None

123. Escherichia differ from Klebsiella in the following accept-
(a) Motility
(b) IMVC test
(c) Both a & b
(d) Lactose fermentation

124. Name the Salmonella serotype, generally responsible for food poisoning-
(a) *Sal. typhimurim* (b) Sal. paratyphoid
(c) *Sal. pullorum* (d) All

125. The main virulence factor of Shigellae is-
(a) Exotoxin (b) Endotoxin
(c) Neurotoxin (d) None

126. The following media is used for *H. influenza* cultivation except-
(a) Chocalate agar (b) Levinthals medium
(c) Fildes medium (d) Blood agar

127. The species causing conjunctivitis in Man is-
(a) *H influenza* (b) *H. aegyptius*
(c) *H. haemalyticas* (d) *H. ducrgi*

128. Toxin production in *Cl. tetani* in animal host is dependent upon factor like-
(a) Anaerobic condition
(b) Concurrent infections
(c) Aerobic condition
(d) Inclement weather

129. Retained placenta & decomposed foetus in case of abortion of cattle is usually due to bacteria belonging to the genus-
(a) *Listeria* (b) *Leptospira*
(c) *Brucella* (d) *Campylobactor*

130. Brown rat is considered reservior of-
(a) *Leptospira* (b) *M. laprae*
(c) *Brucella* (d) None

131. Leptospira organism can preferably be isolated from infected animals-
(a) Faeces (b) Nasal discharge
(c) Urine (d) All of the above

132. In suspected case of Leptospirosis in sheep, the organisms can be isolated from-
(a) Faeces (b) Brain
(c) Blood (d) Nasal discharge

133. Toxoids are used as immunogens in-
(a) Tuberculosis (b) Glanders
(c) Tetanus (d) None

134. Hyper immune serum is of high therapeutic value in-
(a) Subacute infection
(b) Acute
(c) Chronic
(d) None

135. Soil borne infection is attributed to those patho-

genic bacteria which bear-
(a) Capsule (b) Spore
(c) Fimbrae (d) Flagella

136. The undulant fever in man is caused by-
(a) *B. abortus* (b) *B. suis*
(c) *B. metitenis* (d) All of above

137. *M. paratuberculosis* may be examine in laboratory with the help of
(a) Sputum (b) Faeces
(c) Blood (d) None of the above

138. Staining of acid fast organism is done by-
(a) Alberts method
(b) Zeihl Neelsen Method
(c) Hiss method
(d) Gram's stained method

139. Mcfaydean reaction is used to diagnose Anthrax being-
(a) Capsule (b) Elagella
(c) Spore (d) All

140. Leptospira can best survive for days in
(a) Lake water (b) Sewage
(c) Alkaline water (d) Clean cowdung

141. Presumptive diagnosis of *Str. agalactiae* is done by
(a) CAMP test (b) BAIF Mastitis test
(c) Gram staining (d) None

142. The appearance of red colour colony of *Salmonella* on BGA plate is due to
(a) Pigment of Bacteria
(b) Peptone hydrolysis
(c) Metabolites of Bacteria
(d) None of the above

143. The V_1 antigen found in-
(a) *Salmonella typhi*
(b) *Salmonella galinarum*
(c) *E. coli*
(d) *Streptococci*

144. Leptospira, in infected animal usually localize at-
(a) Kidney (b) Spleen
(c) Joints (d) Bone marrow

145. The positive complement fixation antibody titter in glanders is-
(a) 1:16 (b) 1:32
(c) 1:64 (d) < 1:64

146. The different type of *Cl. welchii* can be identified by test like-
(a) CPT
(b) PPT
(c) Neutralization test
(d) Coagulating test

147. Enterotoxaemia in sheep (struck) is caused by-
(a) *Cl. welchii A* (b) *Cl. welchii type C*
(c) type B (d) *Salmonella enteritidis*

148. Oedema disease in pig is caused by
(a) *B. anthracis* (b) *Cl. novyi*
(c) *E. coli* (d) None

149. High natural resistant to T.B. in contained in animal like-
(a) Horse (b) Cross breed cattle
(c) Pig (d) Sheep & goat

150. The name of salmonella is in the memory of-
(a) Salmon & Smith (b) Eberth
(c) Cauffmonn (d) None

151. *Brucella abortus* has biotypes numbering
(a) 9 (b) 3
(c) 4 (d) None

152. Erythrital is present in-
(a) Testicular tissue (b) Udder
(c) Ovaries (d) Placenta

153. Capsules in *P. multocida* can best be demonstrated in
(a) Blood agar (b) Nutrient agar
(c) Both a & b (d) None

154. *P. multocida* stains isolated from cattle are pathogenic for
(a) Ducks & chickens (b) Mice & rabbit
(c) Both a & b (d) None

155. In case of outbreak of pasteurellosis, the foremost contral measures to be adopted as-
(a) Chemotherapy
(b) Vaccination
(c) Passive immunization
(d) None

156. Black quarter is caused by
(a) *Cl. chauvoei* (b) *Cl. septicum*
(c) *Cl. tetani* (d) None

157. Alpha toxin is produced in large amounts by *Cl. perfringens*
(a) Type A (b) type B

(c) type C (d) Type D

158. Theta toxin production by *Cl. perfringens* is enhanced by the addition of-
(a) Sucrose (b) Maltose
(c) Lactose (d) Glucose

159. The optimum pH for he growth of *Clostridia* is
(a) 7.0 to 7.4 (b) 6.8 to 7.0
(c) 6.0 to 9.0 (d) None of the above

160. The thermophilic *Clostridia* grow at
(a) 50 to 60°C (b) 37°C
(c) 37-45°C (d) Below 30°C

161. Acyclovir is a drug of choice for
(a) Calicivirus infection
(b) Poxvirus infection
(c) Rhabdovirus infection
(d) Herpesvirus infection

162. Interactions of viruses occurs by
(a) Carbohydrates (b) Protein
(c) Lipids (d) Nucleic acid

163. Infectious bovine rhinotracheitis virus belongs to family-
(a) Herpesviridae (b) Poxiviridae
(c) Togaviridae (d) None

164. The nucleic acid of Rinderpest virus is-
(a) ds. DNA (b) ss DNA
(c) ds RNA (d) ss RNA

165. The nucleic acid of Avian erterovirus causing avion encephlolomyelitis is-
(a) ss DNA (b) ds DHA
(c) dS RNA (d) ss RNA

166. ICH virus belongs to family-
(a) Hepatomaviridae (b) Herpesviridae
(c) Adenoviridae (d) Picornaviridae

167. Plague assay was introduced into animal virology by
(a) Dulbecco (b) Rous
(c) Prof. Bong (d) None

168. Rabies virus agglutination-
(a) Chicken RBC (b) Human RBC
(c) Gooese RBC (d) Rat RBC

169. Equine infectious anaemia virus belongs to family
(a) Retro viridae (b) Vegaviridae
(c) Elaviviridae (d) None

170. Idio type present in-
(a) Viral envelope
(b) Viral nuleic acid
(c) Variable region of Antibodies
(d) Constant region of Antibodies

171. Ether can inactivate
(a) Enveloped virus
(b) Non enveloped virus
(c) Both a & b
(d) None

172. In poultry M.D. virus induced tumor of
(a) Sarcoma (b) Lipoma
(c) Osteoporosis (d) All

173. The genomic nuclei acid of T-even phase is-
(a) DNA (b) RNA
(c) a RNA (d) All above

174. Borna diseases virus of equire belong to-
(a) Goroviridae (b) Picornaviridae
(c) Filaviviridae (d) Bornaviridae

175. The causative agent of scrapie in sheep is
(a) Virioid (b) Virusoid
(c) Prion (d) All above

176. The genome of African swine fever is-
(a) ds DNA (b) ss DNA
(c) ds RNA (d) ss RNA

177. Birnaviridae members are-
(a) Enveloped (b) Non enveloped
(c) Both a & b (d) None

178. Antigenic variation in virus was first identified in-
(a) Tobacco Mosaic virus
(b) Rabies virus
(c) FMD virus
(d) Rous sarcoma virus

179. Independent heredity transcription & translation in viruses is associated with the-
(a) dS DNA (b) ss DNA
(c) ds RNA (d) ss RNA

180. Ring shaped long coposomeres arranged in hexagonal pattern showing 32 visible holes in
(a) Bunya virus (b) Rota virus
(c) Calcivirus (d) Corona virus

181. Viral nucleic acid extracted from heat inactivated virus preparation is-
(a) Antigenic (b) Infectious

(c) Non infectious (d) None

182. Viral protein capsid is transcriptional product of-
(a) Immediate early gene
(b) Delayed early gene
(c) Delayed gene
(d) Post transcriptional process of mRNA

183. ss DNA virus is
(a) Hepatitis B virus (b) Bunya virus
(c) Parvo virus (d) None

184. ds RNA segment genome is the characteristic feature of-
(a) Paramyxovirus (b) Orthomyxo virus
(c) Retro virus (d) Reo virus

185. Which one of the virus is different amongst following on the basis of structure-
(a) Adenovirus (b) Picornavirus
(c) Papova virus (d) Corona virus

186. Viruses having heterogenic effect belonged to the family-
(a) Reoviridae (b) Herpesviridae
(c) Adenoviridae (d) Caluviridae

187. Defective interfeare virus particle, interfere in replication of
(a) Heterologous virus
(b) Homologous virus
(c) Related virus
(d) None

188. Which of the following RNA virus polymers is mach pron
(a) Polio virus (b) FMDV
(c) Influenza virus (d) Rabies virus

189. The following is a plasmid vector of *E. coli*-
(a) PSE 101 (b) RSF 1010
(c) RWW 0 (d) None

190. Equine herpes virus-1 causes-
(a) Respiratory neurological disease & abortion in mares
(b) Hepatic disease in equines
(c) Both a & b
(d) None of the above

191. RNA of vasculor examthema virus of swine-
(a) Infectious (b) Non infectious
(c) Both (d) None

192. Rinderpest can occur in camels & in epidemiology of rinderpest
(a) Camels are important
(b) Camels do not play important role
(c) Role of camel is not known
(d) None of the above

193. Wild animals are not important for spread of-
(a) Rinderpest (b) PPR
(c) Both (d) None

194. Most susceptible species for African horse sickness is-
(a) Horse (b) Mules
(c) Donkeys (d) Deer

195. Bovine viral diarrhoea virus can be detected in cell culture by
(a) FAT (b) Viral interference
(c) Both (d) CPE

196. New castle disease virus can transmit which of the following to man & cow
(a) Conjuctivitis (b) Diarrhoea
(c) Fatality (d) All of the above

197. Which cell culture is most sensitive for isolation of FMD virus-
(a) Primary calf kidney
(b) PK-15
(c) BHK-21
(d) Calf thyroid

198. Most enveloped viruses are released by-
(a) Cell lysis (b) Budding
(c) Endocytosis (d) None

199. Virus does not possess the following property-
(a) They lack enzyme necessary for protein & H.A. Synthesis
(b) They multiply by complex mechanism.
(c) They multiply by binary fission.
(d) They are unaffected by antibacterial Antibiotics.

200. Electron microscope was introduced by
(a) Antony van leeuwenhock
(b) Elford
(c) Ruska
(d) L. Pasteur.

201. Who for the firt time observed that FMD was caused by a filterable agent
(a) Beijerinck (b) Loeffler & Frosch

(c) Walter Reed (d) Edward Jenner

202. The term vaccine was coined by
(a) Robert Koch (b) Zinke
(c) J. Bordet (d) L. pasteur

203. Who first produced tobacco mosaic disease by filterable agent.
(a) Stanley (b) Iwanowski
(c) Henle (d) Twort

204. Who first crystallized tobacco mosaci virus (TMV)
(a) Berkefield (b) Lindenmann
(c) Stanley (d) Kitosato

205. The symmetric protein shell of the viruses which incloses viral nucleic acid is known as-
(a) Envelope (b) Capsid
(c) Copsomere (d) Nucleocapsid

206. Outside host cell, the virus nucleic acid without coat is
(a) Infective (b) Inert
(c) Virulent (d) Non virulent

207. Which one of following is incorrect about viruses
(a) Unicellular organism
(b) Contain both DNA & RNA
(c) Haploid in nature
(d) Multiply by binary fission

208. The viruses are
(a) Susceptible to antibiotics
(b) Susceptible to interferons
(c) Grow in artificial media
(d) Can be seen under light micros

209. Clear area due to virus multiplication on agar overlay cell culture is known as-
(a) Pock (b) Plague
(c) Focal CPE (d) None

210. Ultrasonic waves release the virus from infected cell by
(a) Sailing the cell membrane
(b) Shrinking the cell
(c) Disrupting cell
(d) None

211. The production of progeny virus that carries traits not found in either-
(a) Interference (b) Complementation
(c) Recombination (d) All

212. The following viruses induce tumour formation except
(a) Retroviruses (b) Herpesviruses
(c) Iridoviridae (d) Parvoviruses

213. Name virus families which are induce malignant tumour in domestic animals except one-
(a) Retroviridae (b) Parvoviridae
(c). Papovarvidae (d) Herpesviridae

214. Papilloma virus produces carcinoma
(a) Naturally (b) Experimentally
(c) Both a & b (d) None

215. Papilloma virus produces tumour
(a) Naturally
(b) Experimentally in rodents
(c) Naturally & experimentally in infants
(d) None

216. Adenoviruses produce tumour
(a) Naturally
(b) Experimentally in rodent
(c) Naturally & experimentally in infants
(d) All of the above

217. Following viral infections occurs via skin except
(a) Pox disease
(b) Herpesviruses
(c) Tumour due to papilloma viruses
(d) Blue tongue disease

218. The incubation period of infectious canine hepatitis is
(a) < 1 weeks (b) 2.3 weeks
(c) 4 weeks (d) 5-6 weeks

219. ICH in day produces
(a) Pink eye (b) Blue eye
(c) Pearly eye (d) None

220. ICH virus is execrated from body through
(a) Nasal discharge (b) Urine
(c) Faeces (d) All of he above

221. Which of the following laboratory animal is most suitable for typing of FMD virus
(a) Guinea pig (b) Hamester
(c) Rat (d) Unweaned mice

222. Typing of Apthous virus is done by
(a) ELISA
(b) Virus neutralization test
(c) CDT

(d) All of above

223. The most of effective chemical disinfectant to kill FMD virus is
(a) 2 % farmaline
(b) 70 % alcohol
(c) 2 % Sodium hypochloride
(d) 2 % Na_2CO_3

224. An animal become infected by more than one type of Apthavirus due to
(a) Poor immunity (b) Antigen diversity
(c) Antigenic drift (d) All

225. Haemagglutinin are
(a) Polysaicharides (b) Proteins
(c) Glycoprotein (d) Lypoprotein

226. Haemagglutination test is given by
(a) Live viruses (b) Killed viruses
(c) A & b both (d) None

227. Freund's complete adjuvant contains a potent non specific immunostimulant obtained from
(a) *M. leprae* (b) *C. parium*
(c) *M. phlei* (d) *E. coli*

228. Incubation period of rabies in dogs in most cases is
(a) 1-2 weeks (b) 2-10 weeks
(c) 3-6 months (d) 6-12 months

229. Rabid dog in dumb form
(a) Always bites (b) Often bites
(c) Seldom bites (d) Never bites

230. Among following laboratory animals which animal is most preferred for isolation of street rabies virus.
(a) Rabbits (b) Guinea pig
(c) Suckling mice (d) White rate

231. Sylvatic type of rabies is transmitted by
(a) Dogs (b) Domestic animals
(c) Wild animals (d) Vampire bats

232. From rabid animals viruses secreted in the following specimens excepts.
(a) Milk (b) Saliva
(c) Blood (d) Tears

233. In rabies endemic area if a street dog has bitten a person the dog must be quarantined for
(a) At least 3 day (b) At least 5 day
(c) At least 10 days (d) At least 14 days

234. Original source of Flury strain of rabies virus was-
(a) Chicken (b) Dog
(c) Human (d) Rabbit

235. From the following rabies vaccines; Select one which is free form post vaccinal reactions-
(a) Samples vaccine
(b) Duck embry vaccine
(c) Mouse brain vaccine
(d) Human diploid cell culture vaccine

236. What is the incubation period of the New castle disease
(a) 2-3 days (b) 5-6 days
(c) 1-3 days (d) 2-3 months

237. What is the incubation period by equine influenza virus
(a) 2 month (b) 4 month
(c) 1-3 day (d) 1-3 weeks.

238. What is the incubation period of the PPR
(a) 2-3 days (b) 4-9 days
(c) 1-3 days (d) 1 Month

239. What is the incubation period of Canine distemper
(a) 5-8 day (b) 2-4 day
(c) 10 day (d) 14 day

240. What is the incubation period of the Foot & Mouth disease
(a) 2-5 days (b) 2-10 days
(c) 2-14 days (d) 2-28 days

241. What is the incubation period of the Rabies in Man.
(a) 21 days to 2-3 Month (b) 10 days
(c) 14 days (d) 1 Years

242. What is the incubation period the Blue tongue disease
(a) 6-7 days (b) 2-3 days
(c) 1 Month (d) 2 Months

243. What is the incubation period of the Rabies in dog
(a) 1-2 weeks (b) 3-10 weeks
(c) 14 weeks (d) 28 weeks

244. What is the incubation period of Swine fever
(a) 1-2 weeks (b) 3-10 weeks
(c) 14 weeks (d) 28 weeks

245. Which one is method of cultivation of virus
(a) Cell culture (b) Serological test

(c) Agglutination test (d) Milk ringtest

246. For Pox virus cell line are
(a) Hela cell line (b) Liver cell
(c) MD BK (d) All

247. Transformed cell do not die & are capable of multiplication for indefinite period known as
(a) Cell line (b) Secondary cell line
(c) Cell culture (d) All of the above

248. Prolonged storage of virus can be achieved by
(a) Lyophilisation (b) Freeze drying
(c) Frozen at 70°C (d) None

249. Which virus is associated with development by syncytia in cell culture
(a) Aphtha virus (b) Hog cholera virus
(c) Rinderpest virus (d) Buffalo pox virus

250. The Blue tongue virus is transmitted through
(a) Semen only
(b) Arthropod bite only
(c) Congenital mode only
(d) All of the above type

251. Virus capable of infecting & destroying primary Lymphoid organ-
(a) Canine distemper virus
(b) African swine fever virus
(c) Infectious bursal disease virus
(d) BVD virus

252. Adenoviruses are so because of presence of-
(a) Sand particle (b) Ribosomes
(c) Lipid droplets (d) All of the above

253. Multiplication of virus in Cytoplasm occurs in
(a) Papava viridae (b) Adeno viridae
(c) Herpes viridae (d) Irido viridae

254. Embryonated eggs are used for virus cultivation over tissue culture because of
(a) Easily available & cheap also
(b) Manipulation with less effort
(c) They are devoid of natural defence system
(d) All of the above

255. Allantoic membrane is used for the cultivation of
(a) Toga virus (b) Myxo virus
(c) Pox virus (d) Influenza & mumps

256. Ig class with highest concentration in bovine milk is
(A) Ig G_1 (B) Ig G_2
(C) Ig A (D) Ig M

257. Ig with highest concentration on body surface of pigs is
(A) IgM (B) Ig A
(C) Ig G_1 (D) IgG_2

258. Cholesterol antibodies can not be absorbed by neonate calf after
(A) 24 hours of age (B) 48 hours of age
(C) 7 days of age (D) 36 hours of age

259. Term Immunization was coined by
(A) J. Lister (B) L. Pasteur
(C) E. Jenner (D) None

260. First vaccine against fowl cholera was developed by
(A) L. Pasteur (B) E. Jenner
(C) Leuwenhock (D) None

261. Site of class I histocompatibility antigens is
(A) b - cells (B) Macrophages
(C) All nucleated cells (D) T cells only

262. Which marker is especially present on helper T - cells
(A) CD -2 (B) CD -4
(C) CD -3 (D) None

263. Site of T- lymphocytes in lymphodes is
(A) Paracortical zone (B) Cortex
(C) Medulla (D) None

264. Calcium dipicolinic acid is found in which state of bacterial cell -
(a) Vegetative state
(b) Spore state
(c) Reproduction state
(d) Dividing state

265. Maximum growth rate of a bacterium is dependent upon -
(a) Genetic make up (b) Environment
(c) Nutrition (d) None of the above

266. Lag phase in the bacterial growth refers to -
(a) Adaptation to the old environment
(b) Adaptation to new environment
(c) Dormancy
(d) None of the above

267. Cell wall is present in
(A) Bacteria (B) Rickettsia

(C) Fungi (D) All of the above

268. Which of the following is eukaryotic cell?
(A) Bacteria (B) Rickettsia
(C) Fungi (D) All of the above

269. Comma shaped bacteria
(A) Spirilla (B) Spirochaeta
(C) Vibrio (D) None

270. *E. coli* is a
(A) Cocci (B) Bacilli
(C) Coccobacillus (D) None

271. Several vertical divisions of coccus results
(A) Staphylococci (B) Streptococci
(C) Tetrad (D) None

272. Membrane bound organelles are absent in
(A) Bacteria (B) Virus
(C) Virions (D) All of above

273. Babes Ernst granules are
(A) Polymetaphosphate
(B) Reserve
(C) Both
(D) None

274. Fluid mosaic model is a model for
(A) Cell wall (B) Cytoplasm
(C) Cell structure (D) None

275. Teichoic acid is present in
(A) Gram poitive bacteria
(B) Gram negative bacteria
(C) Both
(D) None

276. Gram negative bacteria contain
(A) Teichoic acid (B) Lipopolysaccharide
(C) Both (D) None

277. Structural backbone of bacteria is
(A) Carbon (B) Phosphorous
(C) Sodium (D) None

278. Growth rate of bacteria is zero in
(A) Lag phase (B) Log phase
(C) Stationary phase (D) None

279. Catalase test is positive for
(A) Staphylococcus (B) Streptococcus
(C) Both (D) None

280. Acid fast staining was developed by
(A) Ehrlich (B) Waksman
(C) Hesse (D) None

281. Concept of Attenuation was given by
(A) Pasteur (B) Jenner
(C) Schutz (D) None

282. Vaccines against Fowl cholera, Rabies, Anthrax were first developed by
(A) Pasteur (B) Jenner
(C) Schutz (D) None

283. Who isolated fowl sarcoma virus
(A) Rous (B) Rickets
(C) R. Koch (D) None

284. Clonal selection theory was proposed by
(A) Jerne (B) Burnet
(C) Haeckel (D) None

285. Five kingdom classification was proposed by
(A) Jerne (B) Whittacker
(C) Burnet (D) None

286. Bacteria belongs to
(A) Protista (B) Monera
(C) Planta (D) None

287. Peptidoglycan is found in cell wall of
(A) Bacteria (B) Fungi
(C) Mycoplasma (D) None

288. Suitable media for fungi is
(A) BGA (B) SDA
(C) L J media (D) None

289. Agar solidifies at
(A) 45^0 C (B) 50^0 C
(C) 25^0 C (D) None

290. Nucleoside consists of
(A) N_2 Base (B) Pentose sugar
(C) Both (D) None

291. Nucleotide is made up of
(A) Nucleoside (B) Phosphate
(C) Both (D) None

292. TCA cycle results
(A) 38 ATP (B) 20 ATP
(C) 8 ATP (D) None

293. Blood agar contain blood
(A) 1 % (B) 5-10 %
(C) 20 % (D) None

294. Which one is called as soluble RNA?
(A) rRNA (B) tRNA

(C) mRNA (D) None

295. Which one involves bacteriophage?
(A) Conjugation (B) Transduction
(C) Transformation (D) None

296. Selective medium for staphylococcus is
(A) Mannitol salt agar (B) Urea medium
(C) BOA (D) None

297. Nature of staphylococcal toxin is
(A) Dermonecrotoxin (B) Hemolysin
(C) Enterotoxin (D) All

298. Streptococcal mastitis can be diagnosed by
(A) Dick test (B) CAMP test
(C) Ascoli test (D) All

299. Blood does not clot in which disease –
(A) Haemophilia (B) Anthrax
(C) Both (D) None

300. Ascoli test is a
(A) Thermoercipitation test
(B) Agglutination test
(C) Diffusion test
(D) None

301. Anthrax is also known as
(A) Splenic fever
(B) Wool sorters disease
(C) Charbon
(D) All

302. *B. anthracis* produces medusa head like colony on which of the following media
(A) Nutrient Agar (B) Blood Agar
(C) Lactose Agar (D) None

303. On nutrient Agar, *B. anthracis* produces which type of colony
(A) Strings of pearls (B) Medusa head
(C) Dewdrop like (D) None

304. Sterne vaccine is used against
(A) Anthrax (B) Scarlet fever
(C) Malta fever (D) All

305. Common sequelae of Brucellosis is
(A) Retention of placenta
(B) Metritis
(C) Abortion
(D) All

306. To diagnose Brucellosis, which test is used –
(A) Card test
(B) ABR test
(C) Blood Agglutination test
(D) All

307. Brucella is
(A) Intracellular organism
(B) Extracellular organism
(C) Acellular organism
(D) None

308. Stock yard disease is
(A) H. S. (B) FMD
(C) Brucellosis (D) None

309. H. S. is also known as
(A) Cornstalk disease (B) Transit fever
(C) Barbone (D) All

310. *Pasteurella multocida* causes H. S. It is
(A) Aerobic (B) Anaerobic
(C) Capsular (D) Both A & B

311. Franscisella requires following for growth –
(A) Cystine (B) Cytosine
(C) Methionine (D) None

312. Tularemia is caused by
(A) Pasteurella (B) Brucella
(C) Franscisella (D) None

313. Struck is caused by *Clostridium perfringens* type
(A) Type C (B) Type A
(C) Type D (D) Type B

314. *Cl. septicum* causes
(A) Braxy (B) Gas gangrene
(C) Both A & B (D) None

315. Clostridium is
(A) Gram positive bacteria
(B) Anaerobic bacteria
(C) Endospore forming bacteria
(D) All

316. Earliest sign in horse affected with *Cl. tetani*
(A) Bloat
(B) Prolapse of 3rd eyelid
(C) Both
(D) None

317. Spore of *Cl. tetani* has shape of
(A) Drumstick (B) Boomerang
(C) Oval (D) None

318. *Cl. botulinum* type D causes
(A) Lamziekte

(B) Shaker foal syndrome
(C) Limberneck
(D) All

319. Multiplication of *Cl. nouveii* B is favored by
(A) Fasciola infection (B) Brucella infection
(C) Viral infection (D) None

320. Red water disease is caused by *Cl. nouveii* type
(A) A (B) D
(C) C (D) B

321. Symptomatic anthrax is caused by
(A) Bacillus (B) Clostridium
(C) Brucella (D) None

322. Cord factor of Mycobacteria cell wall is
(A) Lipid (B) Protein
(C) Carbohydrate (D) None

323. Mycolic acid of mycobacterium is
(A) Glycolipid (B) Protein
(C) Carbohydrate (D) None

324. Mineral associated with severity of Johnes' disease
(A) Cu (B) Fe
(C) Mn (D) None

325. Koch's adenitis is caused by
(A) Mycobacteria (B) Brucella
(C) Clostridium (D) None

326. Vallee's vaccine is used to prevent
(A) Paratuberculosis (B) Tuberculosis
(C) Brucellosis (D) None

327. Infectious jaundice is caused by
(A) Leptospira (B) Brucella
(C) Virus (D) None

328. Canine typhus is also known as
(A) Weil's disease
(B) Stuttgart disease
(C) Infectious jaundice
(D) All of above

329. Cold mastitis is caused by
(A) Streptococccus (B) Staphylococcus
(C) *E. coli* (D) Leptospira

330. Enteric form of Salmonella is seen generally in
(A) Adult (B) Young
(C) Neonates (D) All

331. Bacillary white diarrhea in chicks is also known as
(A) Pullorum disease (B) Keel disease
(C) Fowl typhoid (D) None

332. Turkey egg appearance is seen in Salmonella infection in
(A) Liver (B) Kidney
(C) Intestine (D) None

333. Surface antigen of *E. coli* causing diarrhea in calves is
(A) K_{88} (B) K_{99}
(C) K_{12} (D) None

334. IMViC pattern for *E. coli* is
(A) ++ - - B - - ++
(C) - + - + (D) None

335. Salmonella has which of the following IMViC pattern
(A) - + - + (B) ++ - -
(C) - - ++ (D) None

336. Which one is H_2S and urease positive –
(A) Proteus (B) *E. coli*
(C) Salmonella (D) Shigella

337. Swarming phenomenon is shown by
(A) Proteus (B) Salmonella
(C) E coli (D) Shigella

338. Bismuth sulfate is most suitable for isolation of
(A) Streptococci (B) Salmonella
(C) Mycobacteria (D) None

339. Lumpy jaw is caused by
(A) Actinomyces (B) Actinobacillus
(C) Mycobacteria (D) None

340. Actinobacillus causes
(A) Lumpy jaw (B) Wooden tongue
(C) Charbone (D) Barbone

341. Summer mastitis is caused by
(A) Leptospira (B) Actinomyces
(C) Actinobacillus (D) None

342. Glanders is caused by
(A) Actinobacillus (B) Actinomyces
(C) Brucella (D) None

343. Mallein test is used for
(A) Strangle (B) Tuberculosis
(C) Paratuberculosis (D) Glanders

344. *Streptococcus equi* causes
(A) Strangle (B) Glander
(C) Mastitis (D) None

345. Drug of choice for Pseudomonas is
(A) Polymixin (B) Erythromycin
(C) Iodine (D) None

346. Iodide is used preferably in
(A) Salmonellosis (B) Actinomycosis
(C) AIDS (D) PPLO infection

347. Farcy is also known as
(A) Glanders (B) Strangle
(C) Distemper (D) None

348. Generally bacteria fail to survive on skin because of
(A) Presence of lactic acid in sweat
(B) Absence of lactic acid in sweat
(C) Low pH (D) Only 1 & 3

349. Azurophilic granules of neutrophils contains
(A) Myeloperoxidase (B) Lactoferin
(C) Lysozyme (D) None

350. Horse shoe nucleus is found in
(A) Macrophase (B) Neutrophil
(C) Bacteria (D) Fungi

351. Macrophage present in liver is known as
(A) Kuffer cell (B) Mesengial cell
(C) Microglia (D) None

352. Site of lymphoid differentiation in bird is
(A) Bursa (B) Thymus
(C) Spleen (D) None

353. Antibody is
(A) Glycoprotein (B) Glycolipid
(C) Lipoprotein (D) None

354. Highest concentration in serum is found for Ig
(A) G (B) A
(C) M (D) D

355. Pilli are found in which of the following -
(a) Gram positive bacteria
(b) Gram negative bacteria
(c) Both of the above
(d) Fungi

356. Ig having maximum sedimentation coefficient is
(A) A (B) M
(C) G (D) E

357. Which Ig is found in external secretions?
(A) Ig A (B) Ig G
(C) Ig M (D) Ig E

358. Which Ig is known as lupus erythematous factor
(A) Ig A (B) Ig F
(C) Ig M (D) Ig E

359. Which Ig is very active during anaphylaxis?
(A) Ig G (B) Ig M
(C) Ig E (D) Ig D

360. Which Ig is very active during anaphylaxis
(a) Cause delayed hypersensitivity
(b) Destroy abnormal cells
(c) Combat virus infections
(d) Combat intracellular bacteria

361. The primary immune response is characterized by
(a) Induction by one dose of antigen
(b) Along lag period
(c) Low levels of antibody produced
(d) All of the above

362. Vaccination using cowpox (vaccinia) was first described by
(a) Louis Pasteur
(b) Lady Mary Montagu
(c) Emile von Behring
(d) Edward Jenner

363. Antibodies are
(a) Foreign substances that stimulate an immune response
(b) A form of vaccine
(c) Serum proteins that protect the body
(d) A type of cells that protects the body

364. A secondary immune response
(a) Occurs after several months
(b) Has a very short lag period
(c) Is medicated by cells
(d) Only occurs against toxoid

365. Rejection of a foreign skin graft is an example of
(a) Destruction of virus-infected cells
(b) Tolerance
(c) Antibody-medicated immunity
(d) A cell-medicated immune response

366. Graft rejection occurs because
(a) Transplantation is bad for the body
(b) Grafts resemble foreign organisms
(c) The body destroys foreign cells
(d) Grafts act as infectious agents

367. Tolerance is a

(a) Failure to make any antibodies
(b) Defect in the cell-medicated immune system
(c) Method of inducing autoimmunity
(d) Method of preventing autoimmunity

368. Antibodies are necessary to
(a) Help destroy invading bacteria
(b) Destroy foreign grafts
(c) Help develop tolerance
(d) Cause autoimmunity

369. The first successful vaccine was against
(a) Cowpox (b) Smallpox
(c) Fowl cholera (d) Anthrax

370. The outer coat of budding viruses is the
(a) Nucleoprotein
(b) Capsid
(c) Envelope
(d) Cell surface antigens

371. Which of the following are obligate intracellular organisms?
(a) Bacteria (b) Viruses
(c) Protozoa (d) Helminthes

372. A pathogenic organism is one that
(a) Does not cause disease
(b) Grows within cells
(c) Stimulates an immune response
(d) Cause disease

373. An exotoxin is a
(a) Toxin that works outside the body
(b) Protein toxin with specific activity
(c) Bacterial lipo-polysaccharide
(d) Viral subunit

374. A virus particle is a
(a) Capsid (b) Nucleocapsid
(c) Capsomere (d) Viroid

375. A retrovirus is a virus that
(a) Uses DNA as its nuclear material
(b) Uses a reverse transcriptase
(c) Causes immunosuppression
(d) Has a cell surface envelope

376. Protozoa are parasites that
(a) Use RNA as their nuclear material
(b) Are exclusively found in blood
(c) Are eukaryotic organisms
(d) Are gram-negative organisms

377. Immunosuppression causes increased susceptibility to
(a) Protozoan disease (b) Viral disease
(c) Bacterial disease (d) All of the above

378. Proteoglycans are major cell wall components in
(a) Gram-positive bacteria
(b) Protozoa
(c) Helminthes
(d) Gram-negative bacteria

379. Transcription occurs when
(a) The amino acid sequence in a protein is converted to a corresponding nucleotide sequence in RNA
(b) The nucleotide sequence in mRNA is converted to a corresponding sequence in DNA
(c) The nucleotide sequence in mRNA is converted to a corresponding amino acid sequence in protein
(d) The nucleotide sequence in DNA is converted to a corresponding sequence in mRNA

380. Translation occurs when
(a) The amino acid sequence in a protein is converted to a corresponding nucleotide sequence in RNA
(b) The nucleotide sequence in mRNA is converted to a corresponding sequence in DNA
(c) The nucleotide sequence in mRNA is converted to a corresponding amino acid sequence in prodein
(d) The nucleotide sequence in DNA is converted to a corresponding amino acid sequence in protein

381. Introns are segments of DNA that
(a) Are expressed as genes
(b) Regulate mRNA production
(c) Code for long sequences of amino acids
(d) Are inserted between expressed genes

382. Disulfied bonds can be formed
(a) Between chains as well as within a single chain
(b) Between glycine and serine residues

(c) Between two different peptide chains only
(d) Between peptides and nucleic acids

383. The primary structure of a protein refers to its
(a) Molecular weight
(b) Carbohydrate side chains
(c) Polymerization between subunits
(d) Amino acid sequence

384. A well-defined structural region within a protein is called
(a) Aregion (b) A domain
(c) The N-terminus (d) A variable region

385. When many protein molecules make use of the same basic structural unit, this is called a (n)
(a) Super family (b) Gene complex
(c) Oligo-peptide (d) Polypeptide

386. Protein molecules that differ in a few amino acid residues are called
(a) Polymers (b) Isoforms
(c) Glycoforms (d) Isotypes

387. Which one of the following is not immunogenic?
(a) Keyhole limpet hemocyanin
(b) Bovine serum albumuin
(c) Bacterial lipopolysaccharide
(d) Glucose

388. Locomotory organ of spirochaeta bacteria are -
(a) Flegella (b) Pilli
(c) Axial filaments (d) Prendopodia

389. Cross-relations may be due to
(a) Nonspecific antinbodies
(b) Dissimilar epitomes on antigens
(c) Similar epitopes on antigens
(d) Chemical reactions with antigens

390. An epitope determinant is about the size of
(a) 1 amino acid residue
(b) 5 amino acid residure
(c) 20 amino acid residure
(d) 50 amino acid residure

391. Which one of the following properties of a molecule does not influence its antigenicity?
(a) Conformation (b) Complexity
(c) Color (d) Sability

392. In penicillin allergy, the penicillin acts as a (n)
(a) Antibody (b) Carrier
(c) Hapten (d) Antigen

393. A hapten is a (n)
(a) Carbohydrate side chain
(b) Amino acid side chain
(c) Small molecule attached to a protein
(d) Large protein attached to a small molecule

394. The ability of an antibody that binds blood group antigens to also react with some *Escherichia coli* bacteria is an example of
(a) Cross-reactivity
(b) Autoimmunity
(c) Passive immunity
(d) Transfusion reaction

395. Which of the following is most likely to induce a strong immune response?
(a) Glycoprotein (b) Phospholipid
(c) Glycolipid (d) Simple carbohydrate

396. An autoantigen is a (n)
(a) Antigen from bacteria
(b) Self-antigen
(c) Artificial antigen
(d) Carbohydrate antigen

397. Plastics are not good antigens because they are
(a) Degraded too fast
(b) Synthetic
(c) Toxic
(d) Degraded too slowly

398. The predominant typed of leukocytes in the blood is the
(a) Monocyte (b) Eosinophils
(c) Basophile (d) Neutrophils

399. The movement of neutrophils under the influence of external chemical gradients is called
(a) Endocytosis (b) Chemotaxis
c.- Phagocytosis (d) Chemolysis

400. Which of the following is a potent chemotactic factor for neutrophils?
(a) Creative protein (b) Interleukin-8
(c) Arachidonic acid (d) Complement

401. What is an opsonin?
(a) A chemotactic factor
(b) A type of granulocytes
(c) Achemokin
(d) A substance that enhances phagocytosis

402. The key cell surface molecule that initiates the respiratory burst is
(a) Hypohalide
(b) Myeloperoxidase
(c) Superoxide dismutase
(d) NADPH-oxidase

403. A receptor that binds immunoglobulin (antibody) to a cell surface is called a (n)
(a) Fc receptor
(b) Complement receptor
(c) Integrin
(d) CD molecule

404. One function of eosinophil major basic protein is to
(a) Destroy invading bacteria
(b) Destroy helminth parasites
(c) Cause acute inflammation
(d) Cause asthma

405. Integrins are
(a) Opsonins
(b) Chemotactic factors
(c) Cell surface adhesive proteins
(d) Complement components

406. Macrophages produce
a- IL-2 and IL-3 b- IL-2 and IL-1
c- IL4 and IL-1 d- IL-12 and IL-1

407. Bacteria are cleared from the bloodstream mainly by
a- Lung capillaries
b- Spleen and liver macrophages
c- Circulating neutrophils
d- Marinating neutrophils

408. Particles given intravenously are mainly trapped in the
a- Lung b- Thymus
c- Lymph nodes d- Spleen

409. The constituent cells of the mononuclear-phagocytic system are
a- Eosinophils b- Basophiles
c- Neutrophils d- Lymphocytes

410. The form of macrophage lining the sinuses of the liver is the
a- Histiocyte b- Kupffer cell
c- Monocyte d- Astrocyte

411. Macrophages can be activated by
a- Neutrophils b- Antibodies
c- Complement d- All of the above

412. Activated macrophages can kill intracellular organisms
a- Nitric oxide b- Antibodies
c- Proteases d- Interferons

413. The key protein produced by macrophages on exposure to microorganisms and other stimuli is
a- Complement b- Integrins
c- Interleukin-1 d- Interleukin-2

414. Septic shock is mediated by which macrophage-derived product?
a- Tumor necrosis factor-a
b- Nitric oxide
c- Singlet oxygen
d- Interleukin-12

415- FcyRI is receptors for
a- Interleukins b- Antibodies
c- Complement d- TNF

416- The receptor glyoproteins that bind foreign antigen belong to the
a- Immunoglobulin super family
b- Selectin super family
c- Integrin super family
d- Receptor super family
e- Cytokin super family

417- The b2 family of integrins contains which of the following proteins?
a- CD29 and CD18 b- CD16 and CD32
c- CD11 and CD18 d- CD11 and CD42
e- CD16 and CD18

418- The major tyrosine kinase associated with lymphocyte receptors is called
a- fos b- lck
c- ras d- erb

419- The uptake of fluid by cells is through a process called
a- Pleocytosis b- Exocytosis
c- pinocytosis d- endocytosis

420- Exogenous processing mainly occurs within
a- T lymphocytes b- Neutrophils
c- Plasma cells d- Macrophages

421- Class I MHC molecules are found on

a- B cells and macrophages
b- Erythrocytes, B cells and T cells
c- T cells only
d- All nucleated cells

422- An individual's HLA haplotype is
a- Achromosome segment
b- One allele at each MHC class I locus
c- One allele at each MHC class II locus
d The individual's complete set of MHC alleles

423- b2-Microglobulin is an integral part of
a- Immunoglobulin M
b- MHC class II molecules
c- MHC class I molecules
d- T-cell antigen receptor

424- Exogenous antigen processing mainly occurs within
a- T lymphocytes b- Neutrophils
c- Plasma cells d- Macrophages

425- Class II MHC molecules contain
a- One g and d chain
b- One a chin and one b chain
c- Two light and two heavy chins
d- One y chain

426- b2-Microglobulin is an integral part of
a- Immunoglobulin M
b- MHC class II molecules
c- MHC class I molecules
d- T-cell antigen receptor

427- Neonatal bursectomy in birds causes
a- Sharp reduction in circulating lymphocytes
b- Cancer in chicks
c- Impaired rejection of skin grafts
d- Reduction in serum immunoglobulin levels

428- Lymph nodes perform the following functions except
a- Trapping antigen on dendritic cell processes
b- Pumping returning lymph
c- Exposing trapped material to macrophages
d- Exposing trapped material to lymphocytes
e- Filtering lymph

429- B lymphocytes in the spleen are largely found in
a- The marginal zone
b- The red pulp
c- The periarteriolar lymphoid sheath
d- The follicular areas

430- The thymus is
a- A primary lymphoid organ
b- A secondary lymphoid organ
c- A reticuloendothelial organ
d- A lymphoreticular organ

431- In which area of the lymph node are T cells mainly found?
a- Subcapsular b- Sinusoids
c- Primary follicles d- Paracortex

432- Where in the lymph node are memory cells for antibody production generated?
a- Sub capsular b- Sinusoids
c- Primary follicles d- Germinal center

433. Acid fast staining was discovered by -
(a) Zeihl and Neelson
(b) Erhlich
(c) Both of the above
(d) None of them

434- Germinal centers of lymphoid tissues largely contains
a- Macrophages b- Neutrophils
c- T cells d- Plasma cells

435- One the basis of morphology, T and B cells can be distinguished by
a- Size differences
b- Microvilous projections on cells surfaces
c- Secretory granules
d- Cytoplasmic structures

436- One characteristic cell surface molecule largely restricted to human thymocytes is
a- Cd4 b- Cd8
c- TCR d- Thy-1

437- The flow cytometer is an instrument that
a- speartes blood cells
b- Detects different leukocyte populations
c- Measures T-cell responses
d- Measures antibody

438- CD8 is a receptor for
a- Antigen
b- MHC class II molecules
c- Antibody

d- MHC class I molecules

439- In addition to T cells and B cells, there is a third distinct type of lymphocyte called

a- MHC cells b- IgG cells
c- Langerhans cells d- NK cells

440- The CD4 molecule is

a- A heterodimer
b- A receptor for MHC class II molecules
c- Part of the BCR
d- A complement receptor

441- The major cytokines secreted by Th 1 cells are

a- IL-1 and IL-6 b- IL-4 and IL-5
c- IL2 and IFN-g d- IL-10 and IL-12

442- The helper cell population that promotes IgE production is composed of

a- Th 1 cells b- Th2 cells
c- Th0 cells d- Tdh cells

443- Helper T cells recognize antigen-presenting cells as antigen

a- Wlone
b- With MHC class I product
c- With MHC class II product
d- With both class I and class II products
e- With complement

444- The term "MHC restriction" refers to the

a- Inheritance of MHC antigen
b- Need for antigen to be recognized in association with MHC molecules
c- Need for MHC genes to control complement activity
d- Problems associated with allograft rejection
e- Need for MHC molecules in order to reject grafts

445- To induce an immune response, antigen-presenting cells must also secrete

a- IL-6 b- IL-2
c- TNF-a d- IL-1

446- Interferon-g enhances

a- ADCC
b- NK-cell activity
c- Macrophage activity
d- T-cell-mediated cytotoxicity

447- Three major cytokines secreted by macrophages are

a- IL-1, IL-2 and IL-3
b- IL-2, IFN-g and IL-12
c- IL-1, and IL-12 and TNF-a
d- IL-1, IL-12 and TNF-a

448- Interleukin-2 is produced by

a- B cells b- Th 1 cells
c- Macrophages d- Neutrophils

449- Septic shock is the toxic manifestation of the release of large amounts of

a- Interleukin-2
b- Interferon-g
c- Transforming growth factor-b
d- Tumor necrosis factor-a

450- The key cytokines produced by Th 1 cells are

a- IL-4 and IL-10 b- IL-1 and TNF-a
c- IL-2 and TNF-g d- IL-2 and TNF-a

451- A major role of IL-4 is to promote the

a- Cell-mediated immune responses
b- IgE responses
c- Macrophage activation
d- IgG responses

452- How many constant domains does the heavy chain of IgE contain?

a- Two b- Three
c- Four d- Five

453- Which class of immunoglobulin activates complement upon binding with antigen?

a- IgM b- IgA
c- IgD d- IgE
e- All of the above

454- Serum IgM molecules usually have

a- 10 light chains
b- 10 heavy chains
c- Apentameric structure
d- A J chain

455- The major forces linking antigen to antibody are

a- Hydrogen bonds b- Coloumbic bonds
c- Covalent links d- Hydrophobic bonds

456- Immunoglobulin binding to receptors on effecter cells (e.g., phagocytes, mast cells) is due to which portion of the immunoglobulin molecule?

a- Fab b- Fc
c- Fd d- Light chain

457- The hinge region of an immuboglobulin is flexible

be cause it contains a large amount of which amino acid?

a- Serine b- Cysteine
c- Threonine d- Proline

458- The complementarity-determining regions of immunoglobulins
a- Activate complement
b- Bind to cells
c- Mediate opsonization
d- Bind to antigen

459- A hybridoma is a cell formed by fusion of a
a- Plasma cell with a plasma cell of another species
b- T cell with a myeloma cell
c- Macrophage with myeloma cell
d- Plasma cell with a myeloma cell

460. Negative staining is useful for the demonstration of -
(a) Spirochaetes (b) Bacterial capsules
(c) Both of the above (d) None of the above

461- Which T-cells-derived cytokin triggers the class switch from IgM to IgE production?
a- Il-2 b- IFN-g
c- TGF-b d- IL-5

462- What is the major activity occurring within germinal centers?
a- Antibody production
b- Antigen trapping
c- Somatic mutation
d- Antigen presentation

463- The B-cell antigen receptor typically consists of
a- CD3 and receptor immunoglobulin
b- z chain and receptor immunoglobulin
c- Ig-a/b and CD3
d- Ig-a/b and receptor immunoglobulin

464- A common feature of T-independent antigens is that they are
a- Globular proteins
b- Simple repeating polymers
c- Very large molecules
d- Carbohydrate

465- Which genes code for an immunoglobulin light chain?
a- One V gene, one C_L gene
b- One V gene, one J gene, one C_L gene
c- One light-chain gene
d- One V gene, one J gene, one C_H gene

466- One characteristic that distinguishes the construction of immunoglobulin heavy chains from that of light chains is
a- Somatic mutation
b- The use of V gene segments
c- Looping out of gene segments
d- The use of a D gene segment

467- The k and l gene families code for
a- Immunoglobulin heavy chains
b- Immunoglobulin light chains
c- TCR heavy chains
d- Immunoglobulin constant regions

468- The immunoglobulin class switch results from
a- Deletion of D gene segments
b- Somatic mutation
c- Deletion of unwanted C gene segments
d- Deletion of unwanted J gene segments

469- The only two immunoglobulin classes that can be expressed simultaneously on a B-cell surface are
a- IgM and Igg b- IgA and IgG
c- IgG and IgD d- IgM and IgD

470. Which of the following is not a differential staining -
(a) Gram's staining
(b) Methylene blue staining
(c) Acid fast staining
(d) All of the above

471- Which complement component produces an anaphylatoxin?
a- C1 b- C2
c- C3 d- Properdin

472- Complement used for serological tests is usually derived from
a- Horses b- Guinea pigs
c- Sheep d- Rabbits

473- Which complement component has chemotactic properties?
a- C1a b- C2a
c- C4a d- C5a

474- Normally interaction of antigen occurs with
a- At least two IgG molecules
b- Five IgG molecules

c- An Iga molecule
d- A single IgG molecule

475- The ligand for the small protein avidin is
a- Immunoglobulin b- Biotin
c- Fluorescein d- Ferritin

476- Immune complex precipitates are formed in
a- Antigen excess
b- Antibody excess
c- The zone of equivalence of antigen and antibody
d- The presence of concentrated acid

477. Flegella in salmonella typhii have the pattern of -
(a) Lophotrichous (b) Peritrichous
(c) Monotrichous (d) Amphitrichous

478- *M. tuberculosis* infection is diagnosed by a (n)
a- Intradermal skin test
b- Complement fixation
c- Indirect fluorescent antibody test
d- Passive hemagglutination test

479- A typical delayed hypersensitivity reaction reaches maximum size in
a- seconds b- Minutes
c- 6 to 10 hours d- 24 to 48 hours

480- The process of physiologically mediated cell death is called
a- Necrosis b- Lysis
c- Hemolysis d- Apoptosis

481- At least one of the functions of CD8 on the surface of lymphocytes interacting with another cell is to
a- bind antigen
b- Bind to MHC class I molecules
c- Bind to MHC class II molecules
d- Bind to Fc receptors

482- Transplanted cells are mainly destroyed by
a- B cells b- Macrophages
c- Neutrophils d- T cells

483- Corticosteroids mainly suppress allograft rejection by suppressing
a- macrophage function
b- T-cell function
c- Neutrophil function
d- Antibody synthesis

484- One mechanism by which tumors evade immunological destruction is
a- Secretion of anticomplementary factors
b- Release of lymphotoxins
c- Production of immunosuppressive molecules
d- Destruction of neutrophils

485- NK cells develop from which cell lineage?
a- T cell b- B cell
c- Myeloid d- Erythroid

486- Tolerance is most readily induced in
a- Older animals
b- Female animals
c- Immunologically stimulated animals
d- Young animals

487- When a T cell is made tolerant by receiving insufficient or inappropriate stimulation, this is called
a- Negative selection
b- Clonal energy
c- Clonal selection
d- Positive selection

488- Clonal abortion is a mechanism of inducing tolerance in
a- T cells b- B cells
c- NK cells d- TIL cells
e- V regions

489- T-independent antigens only induce antibodies of which class?
a- IgG b- IgA
c- IgM d- IgE

490. Type of staining during which the cell is killed -
(a) Vital staining
(b) Intra vital staining
(c) Supra vital staining
(d) None of the above

491- Secretory IgA contains
a- Four light chains b- Four heavy chains
c- One J chain d- All of the above

492- Lactoferrin found in milk inhibits bacterial growth by
a- Binding calcium
b- Binding iron
c- Acting as an opsonin
d- Stimulating IgA formation
e- Acting as a chemotactic agent

493- The major disadvantage of passive immunization is that it
a- Is ineffective
b- Is expensive
c- Is liable to cause serum sickness
d- Induces short-lived immunity

494- The major disadvantage of active immunization is that it
a- Cause prolonged immunity
b- Induces rapid onset of immunity
c- Induces slow onset of immunity
d- Cause serum sickness

495- One of the most potent adjuvant known is called
a- Alum
b- Saponin
c- Freund's complete adjuvant
d- Liposomes

496- One reason why vaccines fail to work in very young infants is the presence of
a- Maternal antibodies
b- Glycoproteins
c- Endotoxin
d- Adjuvant

497- One problem associated with the use of modified live vaccines is
a- Toxicity b- Fevers
c- Muscle pain d- Residual virulence

498- Major changes in the antigenic structure of influenza viruses are called
a- Antigenic variation
b- Signal transduction
c- Antigenic shift
d- Attenuation

499- Among the most potent bactericidal factors produced by activated macrophages is
a- Nitric oxide b- Lysozyme
c- Transferring d- Complement
e- Hemolysis

500- The main lesion that occurs in combined immunodeficiency is loss of
a- T and NK cells
b- B and T cells
c- Neutrophils and macrophages
d- Helper and cytotoxic T cells

501- The failure of the thymus and parathyroid to develop is called
a- Reticular dysgenesis
b- Combined immunodeficiency
c- Secondary immunodeficiency
d- DiGeorge anomaly

502- Which strain of mice fails to develop a thymus?
a- New Zealand white
b- Lpr
c- Deige
d- Nude

503- The causal agent of AIDS is
a- EBV b- IDV
c- HTLY II d- HIV

504- Which of the following species can contract a lentivirus infection that cause an immunodeficiency similar to that seen in AIDS?
a- Dog b- Cat
c- Horse d- Rabbit

505. Bacterial flegella is made up of which of the following -
(a) Pillin protein (b) Flagellin protein
(c) Gelatin protein (d) Core protein

506- The key cells involved in mediating delayed hypersensitivity are
a- Neutrophils b- Immune complexes
c- T cells d- Mast cells

507. "Quelling reaction" is the capsule of bacteria result of -
(a) Absorption of water by capsule
(b) Antigen antibody reaction
(c) Both of the above
(d) None of the above

508- Interleukin-I causes a fever as a result of acting of the
a- Spleen b- Thymus
c- Adrenals d- Hypothalamus

509- The metabolism of the long-chain unsaturated fatty acid arachidonic acid through the actions of lipoxygenases generates
a- Prostaglandins b- Thromboxanes
c- Prostaglandins d- Leukotrienes

510- Mast-cell granules contain
a- Immunoglobulin b- Complement

c- Epinephrine d- Histamine

511- Allergial contact dermatitis is diagnosed by
a- Complement fixation test
b- Provocation test
c- Patch test
d- Intradermal skin test

512- Hemolytic disease of newborn infants can be prevented by
a- Allergy shots
b- Exchange transfusion
c- Administration of allergen
d- Administration of anti-Rh antibodies

513. Sharply defined viscid material around the cell surface of bacteria is called as -
(a) Slime layer (b) Capsule
(c) Both of above (d) None of them

514. Capsule of bacteria generally made up of -
(a) Polypeptide (b) Polysaccharide
(c) Lipids (d) Mixture of the protein and the carbohydrates

515. Capsule of *Bacillus anthracis* bacteria is made up of -
(a) Polypeptides (b) Polysaccharides
(c) Complex lipids (d) Peptidoglycan

516. Capsule can be easily demonstrated by which of the following -
(a) Methylene blue (b) Giemsa stain
(c) Acid fast stain (d) India ink

517. The gene coding for prion protion is normally
(a) Absent (b) Present
(c) Not known (d) None

518. Only diagnostic tool to confirm BSE is -
(a) Histopathology (b) ELISA
(c) PCR (d) None

519. Abortion due to trichomonas foetus is followed by
(a) Sterility (b) Pyometra
(c) Both (d) None

520. Encephalitis may be seen in
(a) Toxoplasmosis (b) Ascariasis
(c) Coccidiosis (d) None

521. Bacterial cell have which ribosomes
(a) 70 s (b) 60 s
(c) 80 s (d) 40 s

522. Vesicular convoluted or multilaminated structures in bacterial cell formed as invagination of plasma membrane into cytoplasm are called -
(a) Vacuoles
(b) Chondroids
(c) Endoplasmic reticulum
(d) Chromosomes

523. Mesosomes in bacterial cells are analogous to which of the following organelles of cukey tic cell-
(a) Endoplasmic reticulum
(b) Ribosomes
(c) Plastids
(d) Mitochondria

524. Volutin granules are characteristically, present in cytoplasm of which of the following-
(a) *Corynebacterium diphtheriae*
(b) *Clostridium species*
(c) *Bacillus species*
(d) All gram positive bacteria

525. Deoxyribonucleioprotein found in which of the following -
(a) Prokaryotic cells (b) Eukaryotic cells
(c) Both of the above (d) None of them

526. Extra nuclear circular self replicating DNA of the bacteria is called as -
(a) Chromosome (b) Episome
(c) Ribosome (d) Centrosome

527. Papilloma virus has which oncogene?
(a) Src (b) Raf
(c) Myc (d) All of above

528. Acid Fastness of mycobacteria specres is due to -
(a) High molecular weight of cell wall content
(b) Mycolic acid
(c) Both are combined responsible
(d) None of the above

529. Bacteria which remain red colored after Zn staining are -
(a) Acid Fast bacteria
(b) Partial acid fast bacteria
(c) Non acid fast bacteria
(d) Gram variable bacteria

530. The bacteria of pathogenic importance commonly measures -

(a) Length 1-6 μm and diameter 0.2-1.5μm
(b) Length 1-6 mm and diameter 0.2-1.5mm
(c) Length 10-50 μm and diameter 1-20μm
(d) Length 10-50 nm and diameter 1-20 nm

531. Which of the following are the uniform rod shape bacteria -
(a) *Coryne bacteria* (b) *Bacillus anthracis*
(c) *Mycobacterium* (d) *Strepococci*

532. Which is club shaped Bacillus bacteria -
(a) *Bacillus anthracis* (b) *Corynebacteria*
(c) *Mycobacteria* (d) None of them

533. Cause of late abortions in cattle is
(a) BHV-1 (b) Rotavirus
(c) Corona virus (d) Piconavirus

534. Which of the following is the bacterial cell cytoplasmic property -
(a) Endoplasmic reticulum present
(b) Mitochondria present
(c) Cytoplasmic streaming present
(d) None of the above

535. Cause of hypersensitivity pneumonitis is
(a) Allergens (b) Parasites
(c) Moldy hay (d) All of above

536. A foreign material capable of inducing the production of antibodies in animal is called -
(a) Agglutinin (b) Antigen
(c) Antipyretic (d) Antidote

537. Which one is not an adjuvant
(a) Oil (b) Wax
(c) Alum (d) Glucose

538. IgD is found abundantly in
(a) Cow (b) Rat
(c) Sheep (d) Horse

539. IgE is fond in very low concentration in serum which has the property to bind with receptors present on
(a) Neutrophils (b) Eosinophils
(c) T-lymphocytes (d) Mast cells

540. IgD in not found in serum due to lysis by
(a) Bacteria (b) Proteaes
(c) Endonucleases (d) Peroxidases

541. Processing of antigen by macrophasges is comparatively less efficient due to lysis of antigen by
(a) Proteases (b) Peroxidases
(c) Endonucleases (d) Lipases

542. There is a latent period in antibody production on exposure to any antigen which is
(a) 6 days (b) 20 days
(c) 25 days (d) 4 weeks

543. The peak antibody titres are seen at
(a) 2 days (b) 20 days
(c) 25 days (d) 4 weeks

544. The exogenous antigen are processed in dendritic cells/macrophages and along with which of the following molecule it is presented to Th cells
(a) MHC class Ia (b) MHC class II
(c) MHC class III (d) MHC class Ib

545. T-cytotoxic cells recognize which one specifically to destroys them
(a) Bacteria
(b) Virus
(c) Ag containing cells
(d) Fungi

546. Anaphylaxis is also called which type of hypersensitivity
(a) Type I (b) Type II
(c) Type III (d) Type IV

547. Secretary type of antibody is
(a) IgA (b) IgD
(c) IgM (d) IgE

548. Sensitized T- cells mediate
(a) Type I hypersetity
(b) Type hypersensitity
(c) Both
(d) DTH reactions

549. Cimbined immunodeficiency syndrome occurs as a result of absence of
(a) Stem cells (b) B - cells
(c) T -cells (d) Macrophages

550. Autoimmunity developes in body when immue mechnisms are directed toward whgich antigens.
(a) Self (b) Foreign
(c) Protein (d) Bacterial

551. In respriatory mucosa secretions this antibody is mainly found.
(a) IgG (b) IgM
(c) IgA (d) IgE

552. Corticosteroids bind with receptors present on

which cells leading to decrease in antibody production.
(a) T-helper (b) Macrophages
(c) B-cells (d) T-suppressor

553. Primery staining for the Gram's staining method of bacteria is -
(a) Gram's Iodine (b) Safronin
(c) Crystal violet (d) None of them

554. Safronin used in Gram's staining act as which of the following -
(a) Primary staining (b) Counter staining
(c) Mordant (d) Decolorizer

555. The bacteria which remain purple (violet) color by Gram's staining is called as -
(a) Gram Negative (b) Gram positive
(c) Both of above (d) None of them

556. Which are acid fast bacteria -
(a) Gram Positive
(b) Gram Negative
(c) Both of the above
(d) Gram variable bacteria

557. The resolution power of Electron Microscope is -
(a) 1Å (b) 1 nm
(c) 1μ (d) 10 Å

558. Reduction in T cell found in
(a) Equire herpes virus
(b) Equine pesti virus
(c) Both
(d) None

559. Petechial haemorrhages are of what size
(a) 1 mm (b) 2 mm
(c) 5 mm (d) 10 mm

560. Programmed cell death in living body is called
(a) Apoptosis (b) Necrosis
(c) Autolysis (d) None of the above

561. Immunopathology/immodeficiency disorder of animals falls under the branch of.
(a) Cytopathology
(b) Humoral pathology
(c) Microscopic pathology
(d) Immnopathology

562. Erythrocytes having minute dark spots are called
(a) Heinz bodies
(b) Theleira
(c) Basophilic stippling
(d) None

563. Macrocytic normochromic anemia is -
(a) Large size RBC
(b) Decreased Hb
(c) Small size RBC
(d) Large size RBC and normal Hb

564. Depletion of lymphoid tissue from follicles of bursa
(a) Neutropenia
(b) R.P.
(c) Hypogammaglobulimia
(d) Salmonellosis

565. Decrease in the number of all components of leucocytes is known as
(a) Leucopenia (b) Panleucopenia
(c) Leucocytosis (d) Leukemia

566. Eosinophilia occur in which type of infection
(a) Bacterial (b) Prion
(c) Viral (d) Parasitic

567. C_3 component of complement is found in which type of glomerulonephritis (MPGN)
(a) Type I (b) Type II
(c) Type III (d) Type IV

568. Inflammation of hair follicle or sebaceous gland called as
(a) Acne (b) Folliculitis
(c) Fissure (d) Bleb

569. A break in the continuity of the epidermis exposing dermis is called as -
(a) Erosion (b) Ulcer
(c) Fissure (d) Vesicle

570. Hyperkeratosis is the thicking of
(a) Prickle cell layer (b) Stratum lucidum
(c) Stratum corneum (d) Dermis

571. Superficial loss of epithelium on skin or mucons membrane is called
(a) Erosion (b) Abrasion
(c) Ulcer (d) Fissure

572. Papule is hyperplasia of
(a) Stratum corneum (b) Stratum lucidum
(c) Stratum spinosum (d) Dermis

573. Retention of nucleus in keratin layer of skin is called

(a) Hyperkeratosis (b) Parakeratosis
(c) Urticaria (d) Acanthosis

574. Which animal is not resistant to fline panluopnia virus infaction?
(a) Dog (b) Cattle
(c) Cat (d) Pig

575. Natural immunity do not include
(a) Tears (b) NK cells
(c) Cytoginus (d) Sersitized T cells

576. A foreign material capable of including the producteir of antibodeiy in animal in called -
(a) Agglotinin (b) Antigen
(c) Antipycetic (d) Antidate

577. Anitbodes are chemically
(a) Lipopolysaccharide
(b) Lipid
(c) Gycoprotein
(d) Protein

578. Which one not an adjuvant
(a) Oil (b) Wax
(c) Alum (d) Glucose

579. Serum cantain mainly antibody -
(a) IgG (b) IgM
(c) IgA (d) IgD

580. The interference microscopy is used for -
(a) Study of cell organelles
(b) Quantitative measurement of the chemical constituents of cell organelles
(c) Both of the above
(d) None of the above

581. IgE is found in very low cencertration in serum which has the property to bind with receptor present in
(a) Neulrophils (b) Eosinophils
(c) T-lumphocyte (d) Mast Cell

582. IgD is not found in serum due to lysis by
(a) Bacteria (b) Proteases
(c) Endoneucleases (d) Peroxidases

583. Processing of antigen by macrophages is comparetively less efficeent due to lysis of antigen by -
(a) Protases (b) Peroxidases
(c) Endonucleoses (d) Lipase

584. There in latent priod in antibody production on exposure to any antigen this is
(a) 2 day (b) 20 day
(c) 25 day (d) 4 Weeks

585. The exogenous antigen are presented by dendritic cell/marophages along with
(a) MHC Class I (b) MHC Class II
(c) MHC Class III (d) MHC Class Ib

586. T-cytotoxic cells recognize specifically to destroys
(a) Bacteria
(b) Virus
(c) Antigen cantaining cells
(d) Fungi

587. Anaphylaxis is also called which type of hypersenitivity
(a) Type I (b) Type II
(c) Type III (d) Type IV

588. Equine infection anemia virus may causes which type of hypersensitivity
(a) Type I (b) Type II
(c) Type III (d) Type IV

589. Reagin type of anitbody is
(a) IgA (b) IgD
(c) IgM (d) IgE

590. DTH Reuter is mediated by
(a) IgA (b) IgD
(c) IgM (d) Sensitized T-cells

591. Combined immunodyiciency syndrome occur as a result of absence of
(a) Setem (b) B cells
(c) T cells (d) Macrophage

592. Autoimmunity develops in body when immune mechanism is directed towards which type of antigens.
(a) Self (b) Non Self
(c) Protein (d) Bacterial

593. In Repiratory mucosa secretion the antibody manly found is
(a) Igh (b) IgM
(c) IgA (d) IgE

594. Canine distemper virus activates which type of cells
(a) T-helper (b) T- suppressor cells
(c) Maerophages (d) B-cells

595. Surgery may enhance the activity of - cells and

therefore moclulate the immune response
(a) T - helper cells (b) T- cytotoxic cells
(c) T - supressor (d) Macrophages

596. Pesticides are common contaminats of environment and may cause
(a) Immunosuppression
(b) Autoimmunity
(c) Hyper sensitivity
(d) All of the above

597. Lead, mrcury and codmium may lead to
(a) Immunopotentiation
(b) Immurnosuppretion
(c) Activation of macrophages
(d) Reduction of complement

598. Aspirin decreases.
(a) Antibody production
(b) Phagacytosis
(c) Both of the above
(d) None of the above

599. Bovine viral diorrhrea virus reduces.
(a) T – suppressor cells
(b) IL- I
(c) IL - 2
(d) Interoferons

600. Equine hrpes virus (EHV – I) cause reduction in
(a) B - cells (b) T - cells
(c) Macrophage (d) NK cells

601. In liquifactive nerosis, which cells are present?
(a) Monocytes (b) Lymphocytes
(c) Eosinophils (d) Neutrophils

602. Programmed cell death is called
(a) Apoptosis (b) Necrosis
(c) Autolysis (d) None of the above

603. Turbidostat provides a means of maintaining culture in:-
(a) Exponential phase
(b) Lag phase
(c) Stationary phase
(d) None of the above

604. Medium which is suitable for the growth of a specific organism is termed as:-
(a) Selective media (b) Minimal media
(d) Complete media (d) None of the above

605. A total count of bacteria refers to:-
(a) Number of living and dead cells
(b) Dead only
(c) Living only
(d) None of the above

606. Antibody producing cells are:-
(a) Macrophages (b) Eosinophils
(c) Plasma cells (d) T and B cells

607. The resolving power of a microscope is at best:-
(a) 0.2 micron (b) 0.05 micron
(c) 0.1 micron (d) None of the above

608. Which of the following drug was first synthesized and used by Paul Ehrlich in treatment of syphilis:-
(a) Penicillin (b) Amoxycillin
(c) Arsphenamide (d) None of the above

609 Dark field microscope is used for examination of-
(a) Cocci bacteria (b) Bacillus bacteria
(c) Spirochaetes (d) Viruses

610. The penicillin destroying enzyme betalactamase is produced is by:-
(a) *Pseudomonas aeruginosa*
(b) *Bacillus anthracis*
(c) *Salmonella typhimurium*
(d) None of the above

611. Which of the following antibiotics is acid resistant and can be given orally:-
(a) Penicillin V (b) Carbencillin
(c) Clocacillin (d) None of the above

612. In contrast with eukaryotes non growing prokaryotes have simple genetic system and are:-
(a) Haploid
(b) Diploid
(c) Possess more than 2 chromosomes
(d) None of the above

613. The bacteriophage lytic cycle differs from animal or plant virus replication cycle by:-
(a) That only nucleic acid penetrates into the bacteria cell
(b) Pinocytosis
(d) Unknown
(d) None of the above

614. All pathogenic bacteria require one of the following for synthesis and growth:-
(a) Reduced organic molecules
(b) Proteins and lipids

(c) Inorganic molecules
(d) None of the above

615. Microaerophilic bacteria are:-
(a) Strict aerobes
(b) Partial aerobes
(c) Facultative aerobes
(d) None of the above

616. Rupture of cell wall at some point followed by extruding of protoplasm from there is called:-
(a) Plasmoptysis (b) Plasmolysis
(c) Sheroplasts (d) None of the above

617. The number of flagella per cell in a motile bacterium may be:-
(a) 1-20 (b) 20-50
(c) More than 50 (d) None above

618. Sporulation in a culture medium first occurs:-
(a) At the end of log phase
(b) During stationary phase
(c) Beginning of decline phase
(d) None of the above

619. The habitual presence of an animal disease in a certain geographic area is called:-
(a) Enzootic (b) Axenic
(c) Outbreak (d) Epizootic

620. Endotoxins are major part of:-
(a) Cell wall (b) Cell membrane
(c) Cytoplasm (d) None of the above

621. Bacteria lacking cholesterol in cytoplasmic membrane are:-
(a) Mycoplasma (b) Chlamydia
(c) Corynebacterium (d) None of the above

622. Bacteriophage lytic cycle differs from animals and plant viruses by:-
(a) Penetration of nucleic acid into bacterial cells
(b) Pinocytosis
(c) Unknown
(d) None of the above

623. The wide variety of antibiotics is produced by pure cultures of soil organisms as:-
(a) Actinomycetes (b) Arthrobacter
(c) Bacillus (d) Micrococcus

624. In which type of the flowing water the number of bacteria could possibly be highest:-
(a) Hail (b) Snow
(c) Rain (d) None of the above

625. Which of the following type of water destroy the sewage bacteria:-
(a) Snow water (b) Lake water
(c) Hail water (d) Sea water

626. Growth media which inhibit the growth of some bacteria but help the growth of specific organisms are termed as:-
(a) Complete media (b) Enrichment media
(c) Selective media (d) None of the above

627. The most common mode of transmission of typhoid bacilli in man is through the agency of :-
(a) Shell fish
(b) Swimming pools
(c) Milk obtained from infected cow
(d) None of the above

628. The milk obtained from poisonous plants eaten by the cow may cause:-
(a) Milk sickness (b) Diarrhoea
(c) Dermatitis (d) Food poisoning

629. The transfer of resistance to some antibiotics is seen particularly in:-
(a) Enteric organism
(b) Staphylococci
(c) Pseudomonas
(d) Any pathogenic bacteria

630. Transfer of genetic material from one bacterium to another through the agency of bacteriophage is called:-
(a) Transduction (b) Transformation
(c) Mutation (d) None of the above

631. Pathogenic organisms which have high salt tolerance belong to the genus:-
(a) Staphylococci (b) Streptococci
(c) Escherichia (d) Pseudomonas

632. For isolation of staphylococci from air and dehydrated food it is best to isolate them on:-
(a) Nutrient agar or blood agar
(b) Selective media
(c) Nutrient broth
(d) All of the above

633. Which of the following is responsible for liquefaction of purulent exudates:-

(a) Hyaluronidase (b) Streptodernase
(c) Streptokinase (d) None of the above

634. Toxin production in *Clostridium tetani* in animal host is dependent:-
(a) Anaerobic condition
(b) Aerobic condition
(c) Concurrent parasitic infection
(d) Inclement weather

635. Retained placenta and decomposed foetus in seen in:-
(a) Listeria (b) Leptospira
(c) Brucella (d) Campylobacter

636. Brown rats are considered reservoir of:-
(a) Leptospira
(b) *Mycobacterium laprae*
(c) Brucella
(d) Campylobacter

637. Leptospira organisms can preferably be isolated from:-
(a) Faeces (b) Nasal discharge
(c) Urine (d) None of the above

638. In suspected case of listeriosis in sheep preferably the organisms can be isolated from:-
(a) Faeces (b) Brain
(d) Blood (c) Nasal discharge

639. Soil borne infections are attributed to those pathogenic bacteria which bear:-
(a) Capsule (b) Spore
(c) Fimbrae (d) Flagella

640. *Mycobacterium paratuberculosis* infection is diagnosed by the examination of:-
(a) Sputum (b) Faeces
(c) Blood (d) None of the above

641. Staining of acid fast organism is done by:-
(a) Albert's method
(b) Ziehl Neelsen method
(c) Hiss method
(d) Gram's method

642. Mcfaydean reactions is used to diagnose anthrax bacilli bearing:-
(a) Capsule (b) Flagella
(c) Spore (d) Cut ends of bacilli

643. Leptospira can best survive for days in:-
(a) Lake water (b) Sewage
(c) Alkaline water (d) Clean water

644. Presumptive diagnosis of *Str. agalactiae* is done by:-
(a) CAMP test (b) BAIF Mastitis test
(c) Gram staining (d) None of the above

645. The appearance of red colour colonies of salmonella on Brilliant Green Agar Medium is due to:-
(a) Pigment production
(b) Peptone hydrolsis
(c) Metabolites of the bacteria
(d) None of the above

646. The flagella antigens of salmonella which cannot be shared by other members are designated by:-
(a) a,b,c (b) 1,2,3
(c) i,ii,iii (d) A,B,C

647. Lancefield classification is based on group specific carbohydrate antigen using precipitation test and belongs to the genus:-
(a) Cestridium (b) Staphylocci
(c) Salmonella (d) Streptococci

648. Leptaspira in infected animals/ carriers usually localizes in:-
(a) Kidney (b) Spleen
(c) Joints (d) Bone marrow

649. The positive complement fixation antibody titer in glanders is:-
(a) 1: 16 (b) 1: 32
(c) 1: 64 (d) More than 1: 64

650. *Clostridum chauvoei* and *Clostridium septicum* infection is best be identified by:-
(a) FAT
(b) Size and shape of spore
(c) Culture method
(d) None of the above

651. The different types of *Cl. welchii* can be identified by carries out test like -
(a) CPT
(b) Precipitation test
(c) Neutralization test
(d) Conglutination test

652. Cartex 1967. classified *Past. Multocida* into types A-E based on-
(a) Capsule antigens
(b) Cell wall antigens

(c) Fimbrae antigens
(d) Whole cell extract antigens

653. O.H.K fimbrial common antigens (CA) are represent at antigens of bacteria belonging to the genus -
(a) Campylobacter (b) Salmonella
(c) Escherichia (d) None of the above

654 High natural resistance to tuberculosis is encountered in animals like -
(a) Horses (b) Cross bred cattle
(c) Pigs (d) Sheeps & goats
(e) Dog and Cats

655. The major four lethal toxins which help in differentiating type of <u>*Cl. welchii*</u> are-
(a) Lambda, Mu, Nu and Delta toxin
(b) Alpha, Beta, Episolonand lota
(c) Alpha, Beta, Lambda, Gamma toxin
(d) None of the above

656. Metachromatic granules are characteristics of the genus -
(a) Corynebacterium (b) Pseudomonas
(c) Escherichia (d) Mycobacterium

657. *Cl. botulinum* produces its toxins -
(a) In living tissue
(b) In food stuffs outside the living host
(c) In blood of the animal
(d) None of the above

658. The name Salmonella is in the memory of -
(a) Salmon and Smith (b) Eberth
(c) Cauffmann (d) None of the above

659. Streptococci which can stand a temperature of 45^{0}C belongs to-
(a) Viridans (b) Lactic
(c) Pyogenic (d) None above

660. Capsule in *Past. multocida* can best be demonstrated from culture of:-
(a) Selective medium
(b) Nutrient agar medium
(c) Blood origin
(d) None of the above

661. In case of outbreak of HS in cattle, the control measure should begin with-
(a) Chemotherapy
(b) Vaccination
(c) Passive immunization
(d) None of the above

662. The various species of Brucella in culture media are differentiated by employing -
(a) Dyes
(b) Antibiotics
(c) Monospecific antisera
(d) None of the above

663. The test in brucellosis that helps to differentiate vaccination and infection animals is -
(a) SAT (b) ELISA
(c) IHA (d) CFT

664. Erythritol is present in -
(a) Testicular tissue (b) Udder
(c) Ovaries (d) None of the above

665. The antigen processing cells are -
(a) Neutrophil (b) Macrophages
(c) Epithelial cells (d) T-cells

666. Immune response is -
(a) Antigen specific
(b) Species specific
(c) Hereditary process
(d) None of the above

667. Immunoglobulin class produced in primary immune response is -
(a) Ig G (b) Ig M
(c) Ig n A (d) Ig E

668. A nonprotein molecule that can bind with specific antobody combining sites but can not by itself initiate an immune response is called -
(a) Complement (b) Hapten
(c) Adjuvant (d) Both a and c

669. Antibody producing cells are -
(a) Macrophages (b) Eosinophils
(c) Plasma cells (d) T and B cells

670. After the alteration or suppression of normal flora, the infection that develops is called as -
(a) Super infection
(b) Secondary invader
(c) Altered microflora
(d) None of the above

671. Drugs specifically binding to the large 50S ribosomal subunit inhibiting thereby protein synthesis are -

(a) Erythromycin (b) Cycloserine
(c) Corbencillin (d) None of the above

672. Brucella in culture media are differentiated may have a high rate of storage of polymers like -
(a) Glycogen
(b) Phosphates
(c) Inorganic compounds
(d) Both a and b

673. All count of bacteria refers to -
(a) Number of cells living or not
(b) Dead only
(c) Living only
(d) None of the above

674. The penicillin destroying enzyme betalactamase is produced by -
(a) *Bacillus anthracis*
(b) *Pseudomonas aeruginosa*
(c) *Salmonella typhimurium*
(d) None of the above

675. Which of the following antibiotics is acid resistant and can be given orally-
(a) Penicillin (b) Corboncillin
(c) Cloxacillin (d) None of the above

676. Bacitracin is derived from a strain of -
(a) *Bacillus megatherium*
(b) *Bacillus cereus*
(c) *Bacillus subtilis*
(d) None of the above

677. Simultaneous action of bactericidal and bacteriostatic by drug a drug combination is -
(a) Antagonistic (b) Synergistic
(c) Toxic (d) None of the above

678. In contrast with eukaryotes non growing prokaryotes have simple genetic system and are-
(a) Haploid
(b) Diploid
(c) Possess more than 2 chromosomes
(d) None of the above

679. Microaerophilic bacteria are -
(a) Facultative aerobes
(b) Partial aerobes
(c) Strict aerobes
(d) None of the above

680. The number of flagella per cell in a motile bacterium may be -
(a) 1-20 (b) 20-50
(c) More than 50 (d) None of the above

681. Certain enteric bacilli posses fimbriae and they belong to the genus -
(a) Klebsiella (b) Escherichia
(c) Pseudosomonas (d) None of the above

682. Sporulation in a culture medium first occurs -
(a) At the end of log phase
(b) During stationary phase
(c) Begining of decline phase
(d) None of the above

683. The habitual presence of an animal disease in a certain geographic area is called-
(a) Enzootic (b) Axanic
(c) Outbreak (d) Epizootic

6 84. Gamma rays are used commercially to sterilize -
(a) Powders
(b) Fats and oils
(c) Disposable syringes, needles, plastic equipments
(d) None of the above

685. In purification of water, the ultraviolet rays penetrate only upto -
(a) 1.5 meters
(b) 15 meters
(c) More than 15 meters
(d) None of the above

686. The most common mode of transmission of typhoid bacilli in man is through the agency of -
(a) Milk obtained from infected cow
(b) Swimming pools
(c) Shell fish
(d) None of the above

687. Number per cell of common fimbriae present in Enterobacteriaccea is?
(a) 1-5 (b) 10-25
(c) 50-100 (d) 10,000 or more

688. Examination of wet films or hanging drop indicates -
(a) Shape of bacteria
(b) Shape and size of bacteria
(c) Shape, size and arrangement of bacteria
(d) Shape, size arrangement and motility of bacteria

689. Living cells can be viewed by -
 (a) Light microscope
 (b) Dark field microscope
 (c) Phase contrast microscope
 (d) Electron microscope

Answers

1. (b) 2. (d) 3. (b) 4.
(c) 5. (c) 6. (c) 7. (a)
8. (d) 9. (c) 10. (a) 11. (c)
12. (c) 13. (c) 14. (b) 15. (b)
16. (c) 17. (b) 18. (a) 19. (c)
20. (a) 21. (c) 22. (b) 23. (a)
24. (c) 25. (a) 26. (c) 27. (a)
28. (c) 29. (a) 30. (c) 31. (c)
32. (c) 33. (a) 34. (a) 35. (b)
36. (c) 37. (d) 38. (a) 39. (a)
40. (d) 41. (a) 42. (a) 43. (b)
44. (b) 45. (d) 46. (c) 47. (a)
48. (a) 49. (c) 50. (a) 51. (b)
52. (c) 53. (a) 54. (d) 55. (c)
56. (a) 57. (c) 58. (b) 59. (a)
60. (a) 61. (a) 62. (b) 63. (c)
64. (d) 65. (a) 66. (b) 67. (b)
68. (a) 69. (c) 70. (a) 71. (b)
72. (a) 73. (a) 74. (a) 75. (a)
76. (a) 77. (a) 78. (b) 79. (b)
80. (b) 81. (c) 82. (c) 83. (b)
84. (a) 85. (b) 86. (c) 87. (d)
88. (b) 89. (c) 90. (a) 91. (d)
92. (c) 93. (a) 94. (c) 95. (a)
96. (c) 97. (b) 98. (b) 99. (b)
100. (c) 101. (a) 102. (c) 103. (b)
104. (b) 105. (b) 106. (a) 107. (c)
108. (b) 109. (a) 110. (c) 111. (d)
112. (c) 113. (c) 114. (d) 115. (d)
116. (b) 117. (b) 118. (d) 119. (c)
120. (c) 121. (c) 122. (c) 123. (d)
124. (d) 125. (b) 126. (d) 127. (b)
128. (a) 129. (c) 130. (a) 131. (c)
132. (b) 133. (c) 134. (b) 135. (b)
136. (a) 137. (d) 138. (b) 139. (a)
140. (c) 141. (a) 142. (c) 143. (a)
144. (a) 145. (b) 146. (c) 147. (b)
148. (b) 149. (a) 150. (a) 151. (a)
152. (d) 153. (d) 154. (a) 155. (b)
156. (a) 157. (a) 158. (d) 159. (a)

160. (a) 161. (d) 162. (d)
163. (a) 164. (d) 165. (d)
166. (c) 167. (a) 168. (c)
169. (a) 170. (c) 171. (a)
172. (b) 173. (a) 174. (d)
175. (c) 176. (c) 177. (c)
178. (c) 179. (d) 180. (b)
181. (b) 182. (d) 183. (c)
184. (d) 185. (d) 186. (c)
187. (b) 188. (c) 189. (a)
190. (a) 191. (a) 192. (a)
193. (b) 194. (a) 195. (c)
196. (a) 197. (d) 198. (b)
199. (c) 200. (c) 201. (b)
202. (d) 203. (b) 204. (c)
205. (b) 206. (b) 207. (b)
208. (b) 209. (d) 210. (a)
211. (b) 212. (c) 213. (b)
214. (c) 215. (b) 216. (b)
217. (c) 218. (a) 219. (b)
220. (d) 221. (d) 222. (d)
223. (d) 224. (d) 225. (c)
226. (c) 227 (b) 228. (b)
229. (c) 230. (c) 231. (c)
232. (d) 233. (c) 234. (c)
235. (d) 236. (b) 237. (c)
238. (b) 239. (a) 240. (a)
241. (a) 242. (a) 243. (b)
244. (b) 245. (a) 246. (b)
247. (c) 248. (b) 249. (b)
250. (d) 251. (c) 252. (b)
253. (d) 254. (d) 255. (c)
256. (a) 257. (b) 258. (c)
259. (c) 260. (a) 261. (c)
262. (b) 263. (a) 264 (d)
265. (a) 266. (b) 267. (d)
268. (c) 269. (c) 270. (c)
271. (b) 272. (d) 273. (c)
274. (a) 275. (a) 276. (b)
277. (a) 278. (a) 279. (a)
280. (a) 281. (a) 282. (a)
283. (a) 284. (b) 285. (b)
286. (b) 287. (a) 288. (b)
289. (a) 290. (a) 291. (c)
292. (a) 293. (b) 294. (a)
295. (b) 296. (a) 297. (c)
298. (b) 299. (c) 300. (a)

301. (d) 302. (a) 303. (b)
304. (a) 305. (d) 306. (d)
307. (a) 308. (a) 309. (d)
310. (d) 311. (b) 312. (c)
313. (a) 314. (a) 315. (d)
316. (b) 317. (a) 318. (a)
319. (a) 320. (c) 321. (b)
322. (a) 323. (a) 324. (a)
325. (a) 326. (a) 327. (a)
328. (d) 329. (c) 330. (b)
331. (a) 332. (b) 333. (b)
334. (a) 335. (a) 336. (a)
337. (a) 338. (b) 339. (a)
340. (b) 341. (b) 342. (d)
343. (d) 344. (a) 345. (a)
346. (b) 347. (a) 348. (d)
349. (d) 350. (a) 351. (a)
352. (a) 353. (a) 354. (a)
355. (b) 356. (a) 357. (a)
358. (a) 359. (c) 360. (b)
361. (d) 362. (d) 363. (c)
364. (b) 365. (d) 366. (b)
367. (a) 368. (a) 369. (c)
370. (c) 371. (b) 372. (d)
373. (b) 374. (b) 375. (b)
376. (c) 377. (d) 378. (a)
379. (d) 380. (c) 381. (d)
382. (a) 383. (c) 384. (b)
385. (d) 386. (d) 387. (d)
388. (a) 389. (c) 390. (b)
391. (c) 392. (c) 393. (c)
394. (a) 395. (a) 396. (b)
397. (b) 398. (d) 399. (b)
400. (b) 401. (d) 402. (d)
403. (a) 404. (b) 405. (c)
406. (d) 407. (b) 408. (d)
409. (d) 410. (b) 411. (d)
412. (a) 413. (c) 414. (a)
415. (b) 416. (a) 417. (c)
418. (c) 419. (c) 420. (d)
421. (d) 422. (d) 423. (c)
424. (d) 425. (b) 426. (c)
427. (d) 428. (b) 429. (d)
430. (a) 431. (d) 432. (d)
433 (a) 434. (d) 435. (a)
436. (d) 437. (b) 438. (d)
439. (d) 440. (b) 441. (c)

442. (b) 443. (c) 444. (b)
445. (d) 446. (d) 447. (c)
448. (b) 449. (d) 450. (b)
451. (b) 452. (b) 453. (a)
454. (c) 455. (a) 456. (b)
457. (d) 458. (d) 459. (d)
460 (c) 461. (d) 462. (c)
463. (d) 464. (b) 465. (d)
466. (d) 467. (b) 468. (b)
469. (d) 470 (b) 471. (c)
472. (d) 473. (d) 474. (d)
475. (b) 476. (c) 447. (b)
478. (a) 479. (d) 480. (d)
481. (b) 482. (d) 483. (b)
484. (c) 485. (c) 486. (a)
487. (b) 488. (b) 489. (c)
490 (c) 491. (d) 492. (b)
493. (d) 494. (c) 495. (c)
496. (a) 497. (d) 498. (c)
499. (a) 500. (b) 501. (d)
502. (d) 503. (d) 504. (b)
505 (b) 506. (c) 507 (c)
508. (d) 509. (d) 510. (d)
511. (d) 512. (d) 513. (b)
514. (b) 515. (a) 516. (d)
517. (c) 518. (a) 519. (c)
520. (a) 521. (d) 522. (b)
523. (d) 524. (a) 525. (b)
526. (b) 527. (d) 528. (c)
529. (a) 530. (a) 531. (a)
532. (b) 533. (a) 534. (d)
535. (d) 536. (b) 537. (d)
538. (b) 539. (b) 540. (b)
541. (b) 542. (b) 543. (d)
544. (b) 545. (c) 546. (a)
547. (a) 548. (d) 549. (c)
550. (a) 551. (c) 552. (c)
553. (a) 554. (b) 555. (a)
556. (a) 557. (a) 558. (c)
559. (a) 560. (a) 561. (d)
562. (a) 563. (d) 564. (c)
565. (b) 566. (d) 567. (c)
568. (a) 569. (b) 570. (c)
571. (b) 572. (c) 573. (b)
574. (c) 575. (d) 576. (b)
577. (c) 578. (d) 579. (a)
580. (c) 581. (b) 582. (b)

583. (a) 584. (b) 585. (b)
586. (c) 587. (a) 588. (d)
589. (d) 590. (d) 591. (c)
592. (a) 593. (c) 594. (b)
595. (c) 596. (d) 597. (b)
598. (c) 599. (b) 600. (b)
601. (d) 602. (a) 603. (a)
604. (a) 605. (a) 606. (c)
607. (a) 608. (c) 609. (c)
610. (a) 611. (a) 612. (a)
613. (b) 614. (a) 615. (a)
616. (a) 617. (a) 618. (a)
619. (a) 620. (a) 621. (a)
622. (a) 623. (a) 624. (a)
625. (d) 626. (c) 627. (a)
628. (a) 629. (a) 630. (a)
631. (a) 632. (a) 633. (b)
634. (a) 635. (a) 636. (a)

637. (c) 638. (b) 639. (b)
640. (b) 641. (b) 642. (a)
643. (c) 644. (a) 645. (b)
646. (a) 647. (d) 648. (a)
649. (b) 650. (a) 651. (c)
652. (a) 653. (c) 654. (a)
655. (b) 656. (a) 657. (b)
658. (a) 659. (a) 660. (c)
661. (b) 662. (a) 663. (d)
664. (a) 665. (b) 666. (a)
667. (b) 668. (b) 669. (c)
670. (a) 671. (a) 672. (a)
673. (a) 674. (b) 675. (a)
676. (b) 677. (a) 678. (a)
679. (c) 680. (a) 681. (b)
682. (a) 683. (a) 684. (c)
685. (a) 686. (c) 687. (c)
688. (d) 689. (c)

8 Veterinary Pathology

Salient Points

- Hypertrophy is not seen in CNS.
- Metaplasia is transformation of one cell type to other type.
- Necrobiosis is programmed cell death.
- Pyknosis is condensation of nuclear material in nucleus.
- Karyorrhexis is fragmentation of nucleus.
- Caseative necrosis is characterized by loss of both architectural and cellular details.
- Coagulative necrosis is a condition when cellular details are lost and architectural details are maintained.
- Symptom is defined as subjective evidence and thing felt by patient. ex- Pain, It cannot be recorded.
- Lesion is functional or morphological abnormality in tissue.
- Aflatoxins are produced by *Aspergillus flavus*. Aflatoxins affect liver, bile duct and kidney.
- Inflammation is characterized by 5 cardinal signs like 1. redness: 2.swelling: 3. pain: 4.heat: 5.loss of function .
- C_{567}, C_{3a5a}, Kellikrein, Lymphokines are chemo attractants for Monocytes.
- Secretion of C_{567}, C_{3a5a}, I L-1, LT-B_4, LPS by tissue attracts Neutrophils.
- T cells appear late in inflammation.
- Plasma cells are absent in blood and possess cartwheel nucleus.
- Kuffer's cells are found in liver.
- Septal cells are present in lungs.
- EPITHELOID CELLS possess eccentric nucleus and involved in tuberculosis lesion.
- Langhan's type giant cells have nuclei arrange in Horse Shoe shaped.
  Ex. Tuberculosis.
- Serous exudate is clear fluid secreted from oedema. It shows first stage of inflammation.
- Cellulitis / Phlegmon is acute purulent exudates in subcutaneous tissue.
- Boil or furuncle is abscess on skin surface.
- Ulcer is oozing abscess with loss of basement membrane.
- Pus beneath epidermis is known as pustule.
- Opsonization is first stage of phagocytosis.
- SADDLE Thrombi is arterial thrombi.
- Emboli are sequelae of thrombi.
- Emboli are mostly seen in arteries.
- Fat emboli are formed by entering fat in circulation accidentally.
- Infarction refers to local area of necrosis due to ischemia.

Important Terms

- **Hyalinization:** Change from normal to variable degrees of smooth eosinophilic appearance of tissue. Eosinophilia indicates presence of protein. Thickening of basement membrane.
- **Corpora amylacea**: Circular laminated concre-

tions found in glandular tissue or free in secretions.

- **Calciphylaxis**: Widespread deposition of calcium in tissue treated with calcium sensitizer.
- **Necrobiosis**: Entire process of degeneration and death of cells.
- **Pyknosis**: Condensation of nuclear chromatin into a dark, round, homogeneous mass smaller than in a normal nucleus.
- **Coagulation necrosis**: Type of necrosis with recognizable gross and microscopic architectures of tissue.
- **Caseative necrosis**: Loss of tissue architecture along with necrosis.
- **Liquefactive necrosis:** Semisolid or fluid mass, undergoing self digestion. Ex. Abscess
- **Erosion**: Shallow area of necrosis of epidermis that heals without scarring.
- **Ulcer**: Excavation of surface produced by necrosis and sloughing of necrotic debris, involving tissue below surface layer.
- **Gangrene**: Combination of necrosis and putrefaction, involving saprophytic bacteria.
- **Steatitis**: Inflammation of fat.
- **Infarction**: Process of making infarct due to ischemia resulting necrosis.
- **Shock**: Generalized failure of peripheral circulation.
- **Diapedesis**: Flow out of blood cells through intact vessel wall.
- **Purpura**: Animal with extensive petechial and ecchymotic haemorrhages on serous and mucous surfaces.
- **Hemorrhagic diathesis**: Diseases that result in marked bleeding tendencies.
- **Cellulitis**: Acute purulent exudates in subcutaneous tissues.
- **Agenesis**: Tissue or organ did not develop and is absent.
- **Aplasia**: Organ is present but reduced in size from normal.
- **Hypoplasia**: Incomplete growth. It is an anomaly.
- **Atrophy**: Decrease in amount of tissue after full normal growth.
- **Dysplasia**: Abnormally developed tissue.
- **Retroplasia**: Decreased growth activity through injury or aging.
- **Anaplasia**: Cells and tissue that are poorly differentiated.
- **Metaplasia:** Transformation of fully differentiated normal adult tissue in a related type of adult tissue.
- **Teratology**: Study of anomalies.
- **Hamar tomas:** Improper mixtures of tissue and grossly resembles tumors ex. Moles in humans.

Questions

1. Cardinal sign of inflammation is:
   (a) Itching (b) Loss of hairs
   (c) Swelling (d) None
2. Which cells are feature of avian inflammation
   (a) Epithelial (b) Lymphoid
   (c) Heterophil (d) Giant
3. Avian inflammation caused by PHA or con A is characterized by infiltration of
   (a) Heterophil (b) Monocytes
   (c) Basophils (d) All above
4. Avian inflammation is characterized by increased permeability in
   (a) Venules (b) Arterioles
   (c) Both (d) None
5. In Avian inflammation which cells are seen in abundance in comparison to mammals?
   (a) Eosinophils (b) Basophils
   (c) Neutrophils (d) None
6. Mn deficiency is characterized by
   (a) Perosis (b) Chondrodystrophy
   (c) Osteodystrophy (d) All of above
7. Selenium deficiency may cause absence of what in embryo
   (a) Beak (b) Eye
   (c) Limb (d) All of above
8. Hypovitaminosis B1 in birds is responsible for atrophy of
   (a) Testes (b) Ovary
   (c) Both (d) None

9. Pica in Birds may occur due to deficiency of
(a) Calcium (b) Vitamin B
(c) Phosphorus (d) None

10. Perosis occurs in birds due to deficiency of
(a) Choline (b) Biotin
(c) Zinc (d) All of above

11. Curled toe paralysis in chicks occurs due to deficiency of
(a) Vitamin A (b) Vitamin B_1
(c) Vitamin C (d) None

12. Star gazing condition in chicks is caused by deficiency of
(a) Vitamin A (b) Vitamin B1
(c) Vitamin C (d) None

13. Excess of Fluorine in water of birds may cause
(a) Retarded growth (b) Deformity in bones
(c) Both (d) None

14. Crazy chick disease is caused by deficiency of
(a) Vitamin A (b) Vitamin B
(c) Vitamin C (d) Vitamin E

15. Nutritional roup occurs in poultry due to deficiency of
(a) Vitamin A (b) Vitamin B
(c) Vitamin C (d) Vitamin E

16. Hydro pericardium syndrome is caused by
(a) Adeno virus (b) Herpes virus
(c) Calci virus (d) Entero virus

17. Egg drop syndrome is characterized by
(a) Decrease in egg production
(b) Increase in egg production
(c) Stopped egg production
(d) None

18. Chicken anaemia agent is a
(a) DNA virus (b) RNA virus
(c) Both (d) None

19. Inclusion body hepatitis is caused by
(a) Hepdna virus (b) Reo virus
(c) Adenovirus (d) None

20. Avian pock lesion include
(a) Papule (b) Vesicle
(c) Both (d) None

21. Epidemic tremor disease is caused by
(a) Entero virus (b) Herpes virus
(c) Reo virus (d) Alpha virus

22. Viral nephritis is also known as
(a) Baby chick nephropathy
(b) Grower nephropathy
(c) Both
(d) None

23. Avian stunting syndrome is caused by
(a) Reo virus (b) Birna virus
(c) Herpes virus (d) Orbi virus

24. Avian stunting syndrome is characterized by
(a) Low wt. gain
(b) Pasty vent
(c) Atrophy of pancreas
(d) All of the above

25. In Tenosynovitis, rupture of which muscle occur
(a) Gastrocnemius (b) Messator
(c) Both (d) None

26. Tenosynovitis is caused by
(a) Adenovirus (b) Reo virus
(c) Rotavirus (d) Herpes virus

27. The inclusion in infectious laryngo tracheitis is
(a) Intra cytoplasmic (b) Intra nuclear
(c) Both (d) None

28. In infectious laryngo-tracheitis, there is plugging of respiratory passage by cheesy material at the junction of
(a) Larynx - trachea (b) Trachea- bronchi
(c) Bronchi-lung (d) All of above

29. Infectious laryngo tracheitis (ILT) is caused by
(a) Corona virus (b) Paramyxo virus
(c) Reovirus (d) Herpes virus

30. Infectious bronchitis is characterized by
(a) Thin watery yolk (b) Misshapen eggs
(c) Both (d) None

31. In infectious bronchitis, there is plugging of respiratory passage by cheesy material at the junction of
(a) Larynx-trachea (b) Trachea-bronchi
(c) Bronchi-lung (d) All of above

32. In IBD, bursa shows
(a) Oedema (b) Haemorrhage
(c) Atrophy (d) All of above

33. IBD is caused by
(a) Reovirus (b) Picorna virus
(c) Birna virus (d) Lenti virus

34. IBD is also known as
(a) Gamboro (b) New castle
(c) Ranikhet (d) None

35. Avian leucosis complex includes
(a) Lymphoid leucosis
(b) Osteoporosis
(c) Myeloblastosis
(d) All

36. Avian leucosis is also known as
(a) Big spleen (b) Big liver
(c) Big head (d) None

37. Which one is mostly observed in Marek's disease?
(a) Malignant melanoma
(b) Malignant adenoma
(c) Malignant lymphoma
(d) None

38. MATSA is produced in Marek's disease as
(a) Tumour specific antigen
(b) Tumour specific antibody
(c) Type specific antigen
(d) Type specific antibody

39. Marek's disease is caused by
(a) Herpes virus (b) Togavirus
(c) Poxvirus (d) Lentivirus

40. Avian influenza is characterized by oedema of
(a) Head (b) Face
(c) Leg (d) Chest

41. Avian influenza is caused by
(a) Myxovirus (b) Orthomyxovirus
(c) Paramyxovirus (d) None

42. Avian influenza is also known as
(a) Fowl cholera (b) Fowl plague
(c) Both (d) None

43. Which one is most characteristic lesion seen in Ranikhet disease.
(a) Ulcer at cecal tonsils
(b) Pneumonia
(c) Diarrhoea
(d) None

44. Ranikhet disease is also known as
(a) Ornithosis
(b) Degnala disease
(c) New castle disease
(d) None

45. Highly virulent Ranikhet disease virus is
(a) Lentogenic (b) Mesogenic
(c) Velogenic (d) None

46. Salmonellosis in poultry is characterized by which colour of liver
(a) Silver (b) Gold
(c) Bronze (d) None

47. Coli septicaemia is characterized by ________ in birds
(a) Fibrinous pericarditis
(b) Fibrinous hepatitis
(c) Both
(d) None

48. Hjarre's disease is caused by
(a) *E. coli*
(b) *Salmonella sp.*
(c) Mycobacterium sp.
(d) None

49. Which one is associated in chronic respiratory disease with mycoplasma
(a) *E.coli* (b) Salmonella
(c) Pasteurella (d) None

50. In Omphalitis the yolk becomes
(a) Thin (b) Watery
(c) Coagulated (d) All of above

51. Infectious coryza is characterized by
(a) Swollen head (b) Swollen leg
(c) Both (d) None

52. Fowl cholera is caused by
(a) Vibrio cholarea (b) Pasteurella
(c) E.coli (d) Salmonella sp.

53. Necrotic enteritis due to clostridia occurs after
(a) Necrotic hepatitis (b) Hydro pericardium
(c) Catarrhal enteritis (d) All of above

54. Campylobacter hepatitis is characterized by
(a) Neurotic hepatitis (b) Hydro pericardium
(c) Catarrhal enteritis (d) All of above

55. In birds, *Stephylococcus aureus* causes
(a) Gangrenous dermatitis
(b) Puslutar dermatitis
(c) Vesicular dermatitis
(d) None

56. Acariasis is
(a) Bacteria (b) Virus

(c) Chlamydia (d) Mite

57. Fowl cholera is characterized by
(a) Red coloured comb
(b) Yellow coloured comb
(c) Blue coloured comb
(d) Pale coloured comb

58. Pink colour in Mc conkey agar & white on BGA are seen due to
(a) Salmonella (b) *E. coli*
(c) Both (d) None

59. Coli garnuloma is characterized by presence of what in intestines
(a) Nodules (b) Ulcers
(c) Erosions (d) None

60. Salmonellosis is characterized by
(a) Necrosis on liver (b) Omphelitis
(c) Marbling (d) All of above

61. Ornithosis is a disease of
(a) Parrots (b) Pigeons
(c) Poultry (d) All of above

62. Chlamydiosis in birds is also known as
(a) Ornithosis (b) Psittacosis
(c) Both (d) None

63. Ornithosis is characterized by
(a) Serofibrinous pericarditis
(b) Air sacculitis
(c) Enteritis
(d) All of above

64. In Ornithiosis, which colour diarrhoea occurs?
(a) Brown (b) Red
(c) Greenish (d) Black

65. Ornithosis is caused by
(a) *Chylamydia psittacii*
(b) *Chlamydia trachomatis*
(c) Both
(d) None

66. Chronic respiratory disease is caused by
(a) *Mycoplasma gallisepticum*
(b) *E. coli*
(c) Both
(d) None

67. Infectious synovitis in birds is caused by
(a) *E. coli* (b) *Mycoplasma synoviae*
(c) Both (d) None

68. In Avian infectious synovitis joints are filled with
(a) Cheesy material (b) Serous exudates
(c) Suppurative mass (d) All of above

69. Chronic respiratory disease occurs in flocks maintained under
(a) Poor management
(b) Good management
(c) Fair management
(d) Excellent management

70. Infectious synovitis is complicated by
(a) *E. coli*
(b) *Pasteurella gallinarum*
(c) Both
(d) None

71. Fowl spirochaetosis is caused by
(a) *Reptospira sp* (b) *Spirochaeta sp.*
(c) *Borrelia sp.* (d) None

72. Which type of diarrhoea occurs in spirochaetosis in birds?
(a) Reddish (b) Yellowish
(c) Greenish (d) Blackish

73. The spirochaetosis is also known as
(a) Mite (b) Tick paralysis
(c) Lice (d) Fly

74. Fowl spirochaetosis is also known as
(a) Tick fever (b) Tick paralysis
(c) Both (d) None

75. Which type of haemorrhage is seen in proventriculus in spirochaetosis?
(a) Patechial (b) Ecchymotic
(c) Linear (d) All

76. Aspergillosis in chick is caused by
(a) *Aspergillus fumigatus*
(b) *Aspergillus niger*
(c) *Aspergillus flavus*
(d) All of above

77. Brooders pneumonia is also known as
(a) Aspergillosis (b) Candidiosis
(c) Favus (d) Thrush

78. Favus is caused by
(a) *Trichophyton maginini*
(b) *Trichophyton verucosum*
(c) Both
(d) None

79. Candidiosis is characterized by
(a) Turkish towel like crop
(b) Turkish towel like oesophagus
(c) Both
(d) None

80. Histoplasmosis is caused by
(a) *Histoplasma capsulatum*
(b) *Histomonas meleagridis*
(c) Both
(d) None

81. Aflatoxicosis is characterized by
(a) Hepatitis
(b) Immunosuppression
(c) Cancer
(d) All of above

82. In Aflatoxicosis there is
(a) Nephrosis (b) Visceral gout
(c) Pale bone marrow (d) All of above

83. Which aflatoxin causes disease?
(a) B_1 (b) A_1
(c) C_1 (d) All

84. Candidiosis is also known as
(a) Favus
(b) Thrush
(c) White comb disease
(d) None

85. Candidiosis is caused by
(a) *Candida albicans* (b) *Monilia albicans*
(c) Both (d) None

86. Cannibalism in poultry is what type of habit
(a) Bad (b) Good
(c) Fair (d) None

87. Cannibalism is aggravated by
(a) Overcrowding (b) Prolapse of cloaca
(c) Wounds (d) All of above

88. Pica stroke is characterized by
(a) Calcium (b) Phosphorus
(c) Magnesium (d) None

89. Heat stroke is characterized by
(a) Open beak (b) Paralysis
(c) Both (d) None

90. Gout may occur due to excess of
(a) Protein (b) Fat
(c) Minerals (d) Vitamin B_1

91. Theileriosis in wild animals is characterized by what coloured faeces
(a) Red (b) Clay
(c) Both (d) None

92. Babesiosis in leopard is characterized by
(a) Icterus
(b) Haemoglobinuria
(c) Pulmonary oedema
(d) All of above

93. *Anaplasma marginale* causes anaplasmosis in leopard that is characterized by
(a) Lymphocytosis (b) Leucocytosis
(c) Basophilia (d) None

94. Common disease of pheasant's include
(a) Coli septicaemia (b) Leucosis
(c) Marek's disease (d) None

95. Trypamosomiasis in wild animals is characterized by haemorrhages in __
(a) Liver (b) Kidneys
(c) Lungs (d) All

96. Tyzzer's disease in mouse is caused by ______
(a) *Bacillus piliformis* (b) *Bacillus subtilis*
(c) Both (d) None

97. Diarrhoea in infant mouse is caused by
(a) Clostridia (b) Coccidia
(c) Rotavirus (d) None

98. Reovirus infection in mice cause
(a) Jaundice (b) Pneumonia
(c) Nephritis (d) None

99. Wet tail disease of hamster is caused by
(a) *E. coli* (b) *Salmonella*
(c) Rotavirus (d) None

100. In Rats, hepatitis is caused by
(a) *E. coli* (b) *Salmonella*
(c) Rotavirus (d) None

101. Coagulative necrosis of the myocardium in calves is seen in
(a) Rinderpest
(b) Necrophorous infection
(c) Both a & b
(d) Mycoplasmal infection

102. Which of the inflammatory cells is not present in circulation?
(a) Neutrophil (b) Basophil

(c) Monocyte (d) Plasma cells

103. Localised dilatation of an artery, vein or a cardiac chamber is called as
(a) Arteritis (b) Aneurysm
(c) Arteriosclerosis (d) Ball thrombi

104. Vitamin A deficiency produces which of the following
(a) Hyperlasia (b) Metaplasia
(c) Dysplasia (d) Anaplasia

105. Osteoporosis is seen in which of the following
(a) Hyperplasia (b) Metaplasia
(c) Dysplasia (d) Anaplasia

106. Horn cancer is malignant tumor of which cells
(a) Squamous (b) Columnar
(c) Cuboidal (d) Transitional

107. Babes noduls in rabies is formed due to collection of
(a) Astrocytes (b) Oligodendroglia
(c) Microglia (d) Ependymal cells

108. Curled toe paralysis in the chicks is due to deficiency of
(a) Vit B_1 (b) Vit. B_2
(c) Vit. A (d) Vit. E

109. Type of necrosis in abscess is
(a) Fat necrosis
(b) Liquifactive necrosis
(c) Coagulative necrosis
(d) Caseous necrosis

110. Dystrophic calcification occurs due to
(a) Hypercalcaemia
(b) Excess of Vitamin D
(c) Necrosis of the cells
(d) Hyperglycaemia

111. Caisson disease is caused by
(a) Low atmospheric pressure
(b) High atmospheric pressure
(c) Narrowing of blood vessels
(d) None of the above

112. Sago-spleen is caused by the deposition of
(a) Amyloid (b) Lipid
(c) Glycogen (d) Mucopolysaccharides

113. The first line of cellular defence is
(a) Neutrophils (b) Monocytes
(c) Lymphocytes (d) Macrophage

114. In granulomatous inflammation the predominant cells are
(a) Neutrophils (b) Lymphocytes
(c) Macrophage (d) Eosinophils

115. White muscle disease of calf is caused by deficiency of
(a) Vitamin A (b) Vitamin C
(c) Vitamin E (d) Vitamin D

116. Caseative necrosis is seen in which of the following
(a) Tuberculosis nodule
(b) Caseous lymphadenitis
(c) Fungal granuloma
(d) All of the above

117. Mucoid degeneration occur in which
(a) GIT mucosa (b) Respiratory mucosa
(c) Both a & b (d) None of the above

118. Glycogen infiltration occurs due to disturbance in which metabolism
(a) Protein (b) Mineral
(c) Fat (d) Carbohydrate

119. Failure of which occurs in the cloudy swelling of cells
(a) Protein synthesis (b) Energy mechanism
(c) Fat synthesis (d) None

120. Neutral fat in tissue sections is stained by
(a) Osmic stain (b) M & E
(c) Both a & b (d) None above

121. Ingestion of foreign material by a cell is known as
(a) Phagocytosis (b) Pinocytosis
(c) Exocytosis (d) None of above

122. Most infarct tissues undergo Coagulative necrosis except in
(a) Kidney (b) Brain
(c) Liver (d) Lungs

123. Removal of dead neurons by microglia or oligodendroglia cells is known as
(a) Neuronophagia (b) Satellitosis
(c) Shrinkage (d) Chromatolysis

124. Granulocytes are formed in
(a) Lymph nodes (b) bone marrow
(c) Spleen (d) Liver

125. Which is nucleated cell in erythrocytic series?

(a) Rubricyte (b) Metarubricyte
(c) Reticulocyte (d) Normoblast

126. Mycloid: erythroid ratio is increased in
(a) Erythrocytic hypoplasia
(b) Erythrocytic hyperplasia
(c) Leukopenia
(d) Leukocytosis

127. The cellular reaction in transplant rejection comprises
(a) T cells
(b) B cells
(c) B & T cells
(d) T cells & macrophages

128. Surface marker on killer T cells is which of the following
(a) CD_2 (b) CD_3
(c) CD_3 & CD_8 (d) CD_5

129. Basophillic erythrocytic cytoplasm is typically seen in
(a) Hypochromasia (b) Polychromasia
(c) Hyperchromasia (d) Digochromasia

130. An elliptical erythrocyte is called
(a) Spherocyte (b) Leptocyte
(c) Ovalocyte (d) Myelocyte

131. Which is related with increased erythrocytic count?
(a) Reticulocytosis (b) Erythrocytosis
(c) Poikilocytosis (d) Anisocytosis

132. Young erythrocyte that takes up the stain new methylene blue is called
(a) Macrocyte (b) Reticulocyte
(c) Normocyte (d) None above

133. Variation in size of erythrocytes is called
(a) Microcytosis (b) Poikilocytosis
(c) Anisosytosis (d) None

134. Which cytokines are produced by activated T-cells?
(a) Interleukin-2 (b) IL-3
(c) IL-4 (d) All of above

135. Cytokines induces which of the following
(a) Autocrine effect (b) Paracrine
(c) Endocrine (d) All above

136. Which of the following is Amyloidosis
(a) Immune disorder
(b) Autoimmune disorder
(c) Immunodeficiency disorder
(d) None

137. The antigen substances should have molecular weight
(a) 5000 kd (b) 7000 kd
(c) 6000 kd (d) 8000 kd or high

138. Complete lack of cellular development is known as
(a) Hypoplasia (b) Aplasia
(c) Hyperplasia (d) Agenesis

139. Which type of T-cells is more numerous?
(a) Killer cells (b) Helper T cells
(c) Suppressor T cells (d) Cytotoxic cells

140. Anticoagulant is
(a) Sodium hydroxide
(b) Sodium citrate
(c) Sodium tartrate
(d) None

141. Generally T cells are considered to be of
(a) One type (b) Three types
(c) Two types (d) Four types

142. Which is not an immediate hypersensitive reaction (involved)
(a) IgM (b) IgA
(c) IgG & IgM (d) IgE

143. The cytotoxic T-cells are especially lethal to
(a) Cancer cells
(b) Heat transplant cells
(c) Virus infected cells
(d) All above

144. Albuminous degeneration is the synonym of
(a) Hydrophic degeneration
(b) Hyaline degeneration
(c) Mucinous degeneration
(d) None

145. Neutropenia occurs in which of the following
(a) Typhoid fever (b) Paratyphoid fever
(c) Aplastic anemia (d) All

146. Which antibody constitutes the major share in normal individuals?
(a) IgM (b) IgA
(c) IgG (d) IgE

147. The cytotoxic substances are released by T-cells

are
(a) Lysosomal enzymes
(b) Isoenzymes
(c) Hormones
(d) Inorganic substances

148. Presence of lipids in visible forms in blood called
(a) Lipemia (b) Rouleux
(c) Polychromasia (d) Leukaemia

149. N.K. cells are also known as
(a) Small lymphocytes
(b) Large Lymphocytes
(c) Large agranular lymphocytes
(d) Large granular lymphocytes

150. Tissue collected from a living individual is known as
(a) Autopsy (b) Biopsy
(c) Necropsy (d) None

151. Liquifactive necrosis is seen in which of the following
(a) Myocardium (b) Brain
(c) Lung (d) Kidney

152. Lymphocytic thyroiditis occurs spontaneously in
(a) Dogs (b) Rats
(c) Chicken (d) All above

153. CD_{19} & CD_{20} surface markers are associated with
(a) B lymphocytes (b) T lymphocytes
(c) Both (d) None

154. Prior recognition by B lymphocytes antigen is processed by
(a) Eosinophils (b) Macrophages
(c) Microphages (d) Basophils

155. Anasarca is the result of
(a) Protein deficiency (b) Fat deficiency
(c) CHO deficiency (d) None

156. Most of the cardinal signs of inflammation were described by
(a) Metchrikoff (b) Galen
(c) Cohnheim (d) Celsus

157. Valvular insufficiency will result into
(a) Chronic general passive hyperemia
(b) General edema
(c) Regurgitation of blood into preceding chamber
(d) All above

158. The healing of an open wound is occur by
(a) Regeneration
(b) Primary union
(c) Granulation tissue
(d) All

159. The fluid cytoplasm outside the membrane of the endoplasmic reticulum is called
(a) Exoplasm (b) Hyloplasm
(c) Karyoplasm (d) Endoplasm

160. Corpora amylacea are example of
(a) Amyloidosis
(b) Epithelial hyaline
(c) Connective hyaline
(d) None

161. Morbid changes are
(a) Alteration found in tissue at necropsy
(b) Alteration found in tissue at biopsy
(c) Alteration found in tissue at symptom
(d) None

162. P.M. examination in human medicine is known as
(a) Necropsy (b) Autopsy
(c) Biopsy (d) All above

163. P.M. examination of veterinary medicine is known as
(a) Necropsy (b) Autopsy
(c) Biopsy (d) All

164. Father of medicine
(a) Hippocrates (b) Aristotle
(c) Claudius Galen (d) Celsus

165. Antemortem first conducted by
(a) Hippocratis (b) Aristotle
(c) Claudius Galen (d) Celsus

166. Four elements are
(a) Air, blood, Fire, Water
(b) Air, Water, Fire, Earth
(c) Blood, Phlegm, Yellow bile, Black bile
(d) Blood, Water, Fire, Phlegm

167. How many elements & humors Hippocrates used
(a) 2 elements & 2 humours
(b) 4 elements & 2 humours
(c) 4 elements & 4 humours
(d) 2 elements and 4 humours

168. Four humours are which of the following

(a) Air, blood, fire, water
(b) Air, water, fire, earth
(c) Blood, phlegm, yellow bile, black bile
(d) Blood, phlegm, water, fire

169. Liver is the source of which type of humour
(a) Blood (b) Phlegm
(c) Yellow bile (d) Black bile

170. Heart is the source of which humour
(a) Blood (b) Phlegm
(c) Yellow bile (d) Black bile

171. Brain is the source of which type of humour
(a) Blood (b) Phlegm
(c) Yellow bile (d) None

172. Spleen is the source of which of the following humour
(a) Blood (b) Phlegm
(c) Yellow bile (d) Black bile

173. Beginner of modern pathology
(a) G.B. Morgagni (b) Renatius Vegetive
(c) Bichat (d) Virchow

174. Father of cellular pathology
(a) Morgagni (b) Vegetius
(c) Bichat (d) Virchow

175. First experimental pathologist
(a) John hunter (b) Louis pasture
(c) Robert Koch (d) Carl

176. Originator of modern experimental pathology
(a) Cohnheim (b) Negri
(c) Thedoald Smith (d) Knoll & Ruska

177. Father of pathology
(a) Edward Tenner (b) Antonio Benevieni
(c) Metchnikoff (d) Virchow

178. Ist lesion in cell injury is which of the following
(a) Gross lesion
(b) Ultra structural lesion
(c) Biochemical lesion
(d) Light microscopic lesion

179. Which free radicle is most reactive in cell damage?
(a) Superoxide (b) Hydrogen peroxide
(c) Hydroxy radical (d) Singlet oxygen

180. Cell injury which is caused by mildest irritants
(a) Cloudy swelling
(b) Hydropic swelling
(c) Mucinous digeneration
(d) Autolytic changes

181. Ground glass appearance of cytoplasm and par boiled appearance of organ occur in
(a) Hydropic swelling
(b) Cloudy swelling
(c) Mucinous degeneration
(d) Autolytic changes

182. Water/Vacuolar/Ballooning degeneration is synonym for
(a) Cloudy swelling
(b) Hydropic swelling
(c) Mucinous degeneration
(d) Autolytic changes

183. Changes which are retrogressive but the nucleus is preserved
(a) Degeneration (b) Necrosis
(c) Gangrene (d) All of above

184. Cell swelling is which type of change
(a) Irreversible (b) Reversible
(c) Both (d) None of above

185. Cloudy swelling occur in
(a) Fresh tissue
(b) Well fixed tissue
(c) Old & nonfixed tissue
(d) All of the above
(e) Both a & b

186. Autolytic changes occur in
(a) Fresh tissue
(b) well fixed tissue
(c) Old & non fixed tissue
(d) All of above

187. Granules of cloudy swelling is dissolved in
(a) Lipid solvent (b) Benzene
(c) Acetic acid (d) All of above

188. In which condition hydropic swelling occur
(a) Degeneration (b) During necrosis
(c) During regeneration (d) All of above

189. Mucoid degeneration occur in which of the following
(a) Neoplasm (b) Malnutrition
(c) Myxedema (d) All of above

190. Amyloid infiltration or waxy degeneration occur

in
(a) Between the cells
(b) With in the cells
(c) Between & within the cells
(d) None

191. Iodine gives which color to amyloid
(a) Red
(b) Rose red with surrounding tissue blue
(c) Mahogany brown
(d) Black or blue

192. Disturbance in carbohydrate metabolism causes
(a) Fibrinoid
(b) Gout
(c) Hyaline
(d) Glycogen infiltration

193. Example of connective tissue hyaline is
(a) Arteriosclerosis (b) Corpora amylaceae
(c) Scar tissue (d) Both a & c

194. Antigen-antibody reaction (Hyperglobulinaemia) is the cause of
(a) Amyloidosis
(b) Fibrinoid degeneration
(c) Cloudy swelling
(d) both a & b

195. Epithelial hyaline is which of the following
(a) Arteriosclerosis (b) Corpora amylaceae
(c) Hyperkeratosis (d) both b & c

196. In hyaline degeneration which bodies are present in hepatitis?
(a) Russel's body (b) Council man's body
(c) Mallory body (d) Negri body

197. Inflammation is the cause of which hyperemia
(a) Active (b) Passive
(c) Congestion (d) None

198. The cause of fatty infiltration is
(a) Choline deficiency in liver
(b) Disturbance in fat metabolism
(c) Both a & b
(d) Disturbance in carbohydrate metabolism

199. Thrush breast heart/tabby cat heart occur in
(a) Glycogen infiltration
(b) Fatty infiltration
(c) Amyloid infiltration
(d) both a & b

200. Glycogen infiltration mainly occur in
(a) Liver & Kidney (b) Spleen & intestine
(c) Liver & Spleen (d) Liver and intestine

201. Anaplasia is characteristic of
(a) Benign tumor (b) Malignant tumor
(c) Both of the above (d) None of the above

202. Tumor arising out of an embryonic defect and consist of tissue developing from all germinal layers is known as
(a) Epithelial benign tumor
(b) Epithelial malignant tumor
(c) CT benign tumor
(d) Teratoma

203. Tumor of smooth muscle is known as -
(a) Leiomyoma (b) Rhabdomyoma
(c) Sarcoma (d) Haemoangioma

204. Tumor of striated muscle is
(a) Leiomyoma (b) Sarcoma
(c) Rhabdomyoma (d) Haemangioma

205. Metastasis does not occurs in-
(a) Mycloma
(b) Adenocarcinoma
(c) Basal cell carcinoma
(d) Squamons cell carcinoma

206. Dermoid cyst is an example of-
(a) Epithelial benign tumor
(b) Teratoma
(c) Epithelial malignant tumor
(d) Squamous cell carcinoma

207. Seminoma is an example of
(a) Tumor of testes
(b) Tumor of thyroid
(c) Tumor of prostate
(d) Tumor of parathyroid

208. Melanoma arises from-
(a) DOPA negative cells
(b) DOPA positive cell
(c) DOPA cell
(d) All of the above

209. Venereal tumor are found most commonly in-
(a) Cow (b) Dog
(c) Bitch (d) Ewe

210. Venereal granuloma is a tumor of-
(a) Younger dog (b) Older dog

(c) Pup (d) Bitch

211. Papilloma is a tumor of
(a) Epithelial tissue (b) Connective tissue
(c) Both of the above (d) None of the above

212. Papilloma shows
(a) Finger like projections
(b) Polypoid growths
(c) Cauliflower like growth
(d) None of the above

213. Squamous cell carcinoma shows-
(a) Islands/Pearls
(b) Finger like projections
(c) Cauliflower like growth
(d) All of these

214. Squamous cell carcinoma is a
(a) Benign tumor
(b) Malignant tumor
(c) None of the above
(d) All of the above

215. Transformation of cartilage to bone is a example of
(a) Metaplasia (b) Hypoplasia
(c) Hyperplasia (d) Aplasia

216. When cause is removed, metaplastic epithelium
(a) Remain as such
(b) Revert to its original cell type
(c) Changes of metaplastic epithelium minimized
(d) Any of the above

217. Rodent/Jacob's ulcer or hair matrix carcinoma is
(a) Squamous cell carcinoma
(b) Adeno carcinoma
(c) Basal cell carcinoma
(d) Myeloma

218. In which metastasis does not occur-
(a) Squamous cell carcinoma
(b) Adeno carcinoma
(c) Basal cell carcinoma
(d) Mycloma

219. Adenoma is tumor of
(a) Glandular epithelium
(b) Connective tissue
(c) Both of the above
(d) None of the above

220. Myoxoma is tumor of
(a) Glandular tissue
(b) Embryonic fibrous connective tissue
(c) Connective tissue
(d) None of the above

221. Tumor arising from cartilage cells is
(a) Liposarcoma (b) Chondroma
(c) Osteoma (d) Papilloma

222. Haemongioma is
(a) Benign tumor of endothelial cells
(b) Malignant tumor of endothelial cells
(c) Tumor of epithelial tissues
(d) Tumor of glandular epithelium

223. Lymphocytoma/Reticulum cell sarcoma/Hodkin's disease is symptoms of
(a) Lymphosarcoma (b) Osteosarcoma
(c) Liposarcoma (d) Adenocarcinoma

224. Tumor of old dogs is
(a) Osteosarcoma (b) Lipoma
(c) Mastosarcoma (d) Histiosarcoma

225. Tumor of young dog is
(a) Mastosarcoma (b) Seminoma
(c) Histiosarcoma (d) Osteosarcoma

226. Venereal granuloma/Canine condyloma is synonym of
(a) Histiosarcoma (b) Mastosarcoma
(c) Osteosarcoma (d) Adenocarcinoma

227. Mesothelioma is
(a) Tumor of epithelial tissues
(b) Tumor of connective tissues
(c) Tumor of mesothelial lining of serous cavities
(d) Tumor of meanings of brain

228. Footh and mouth disease is caused by
(a) *Orthopox cameli* (b) Apthovirus
(c) Picorna virus (d) Both b & c

229. In Parvo virus disease, pan leucopenia is caused by
(a) Parvo virus (b) Morbilli virus
(c) Herpes virus (d) Ritro virus

230. Louping ill is caused by
(a) Orbi virus (b) Pesti virus
(c) Flavi virus (d) Lenti virus

231. Tigroid heart appearance is seen in
(a) PPR (b) Vesicular stomatitis

(c) FMD (d) Vesicular exanthema

232. Hepatitis blue eye is found in
(a) Canine distemper
(b) Infectious canine hepatitis
(c) Parvo virus disease
(d) Rabies

233. Hard pad disease/ canine influenza is synonym for
(a) Infectious canine hepatitis
(b) Rabies
(c) Parvo virus disease
(d) Canine distemper

234. Vesicles formed in FMD is an example of
(a) Cell swelling
(b) Fatty infiltration
(c) Hydropic degeneration
(d) None of the above

235. Corrugations in intestinal mucosa are seen in
(a) Tuberculosis (b) Johne's disease
(c) Actinobacillosis (d) None

236. Tetanus is caused by
(a) *Clostridium tetani*
(b) *Clostridium novyi*
(c) *Clostridium septicum*
(d) *Clostridium perfringens*

237. False BQ is caused by
(a) *Clostridium chauvoei*
(b) *Clostridium septicum*
(c) *Clostridium novyi*
(d) *Clostridium botulinum*

238. Enterotoxaemia is caused by
(a) *Clostridium tetani*
(b) *Clostridium perfringens* type D
(c) *Clostridium novyi*
(d) *Clostridium chauvoei*

239. Struck is caused by
(a) *Clostridium perfringens* type B
(b) *Clostridium perfringens* type C
(c) *Clostridium perfringens* type D
(d) Mixed *Clostridium* infection

240. Necrotic haemorrhagic enteritis is caused by
(a) *Clostridium perfringens* type B
(b) *Clostridium perfringens* type E
(c) *Clostridium perfringens* type C
(d) Mixed *Clostridium* infection

241. Enterotoxaemia is known as
(a) Pulpy kidney disease
(b) Over eating disease
(c) Both
(d) None

242. Actinobacillosis is caused by-
(a) *Actinobacillus mallei*
(b) *Actinomyces bovis*
(c) Actinobacillus lignieresii
(d) *Streptococus equi*

243. Actinomycosis is caused by
(a) *Actinobacillus bovis*
(b) *Actinomyces bovis*
(c) *Actinomycosis hirci*
(d) *Actinocabacillosis lignieresii*

244. Actinobacillosis is also known as
(a) Wooden tongue (b) Lumpy Jaw
(c) Both (d) None

245. Causative organism of T.B. is
(a) *Mycobacterium tuberculosis*
(b) *Mycobacterium paratuberculosis*
(c) Both
(d) None

246. *Mycobacterium tuberculosis* is
(a) Gram positive
(b) Gram negative
(c) Acid fast organism
(d) None

247. Johne's disease/Paratuberculosis is caused by
(a) Mycoplasma
(b) *Mycobacterium tuberculosis*
(c) *Mycobacterium paratuberculosis*
(d) None

248. Causative organism of B2/Black leg is
(a) *Clostridium botulinum*
(b) *Clostridium septicum*
(c) *Clostridium chauvoei*
(d) *Clostridium novyi*

249. Bovine bacillary haemoglobinuria/infectious icterohaemoglobinuria is caused by
(a) *Clostridium botulium*
(b) *Clostridium septicum*
(c) *Clostridium hemolyticum*
(d) *Clostridium novyi*

250. Malignant oedema/Gas gangrene is caused by-
(a) *Clostridium hemolyticum*
(b) *Clostridium chauvoei*
(c) *Clostridium novyi*
(d) *Clostridium septicum*

251. Braxy is also known as
(a) Black quarter (b) Black leg
(c) Bradsot (d) Bacillary haemoglobinuria

252. Symptomatic Anthrax is
(a) Bradsot
(b) Bacillary haemoglobinuria
(c) Pulpy kidney disease
(d) Black quarter

253. Actinobacillosis is caused by
(a) Gram positive organism
(b) Gram negative organism
(c) Acid fast organism
(d) None

254. Limber neck condition is observed in
(a) Barxy (b) Tetanus
(c) Rabies (d) Botulism

255. Causative agent of strangles is
(a) *Staphylococcus aureus*
(b) *Streptococcus equi*
(c) *Burkholdirie mallei*
(d) *Actinomyces bovis*

256. Strangles is also known as
(a) Adenitis Equorum
(b) Braxy
(c) Splenic fever
(d) None

257. Wool sorter disease/splenic fever is
(a) Strangle
(b) Anthrax
(c) Haemorrhagic septicemia
(d) T.B.

258. Tarry colored blood is observed in
(a) Strangle
(b) Haemorrhagic septicemia
(c) Anthrax
(d) T.B.

259. Purpura haemorrhagica is a complication of
(a) Anthrax
(b) T.B.
(c) Strangle
(d) Haemorrhagic septicemia

260. Spleenomegaly occurs
(a) Strangle (b) Anthrax
(c) HS (d) T.B.

261. Pearl's disease is
(a) Strangle (b) Anthrax
(c) HS (d) T.B.

262. Type of colony of *B. anthracis* is
(a) Medusa head colony type
(b) Linear
(c) Polyp type
(d) All of above

263. Ascoli's thermoprecipitation test is for
(a) Strangle (b) N.S.
(c) Anthrax (d) Botulism

264. Mc Fadyean reaction is used for-
(a) Anthrax (b) H. S.
(c) T.B. (d) Tetanus

265. Farcy is
(a) Acute form of Glanders
(b) Chronic form of Glanders
(c) Both
(d) None

266. Haemorrhagic septicemia is also known as
(a) Septicemic Pasteurellosis
(b) Barbone
(c) Both
(d) None

267. Causative agent of Haemorrhagic septicemia is
(a) *Pasteurella hemolytica*
(b) *Pasteurella multocida*
(c) *Pseudomonas mallei*
(d) *Actinobacillus lignirasi*

268. Weil's disease is another synonym for-
(a) Listeriosis (b) Leptospirosis
(c) Pasteurellosis (d) None

269. Chief source of organism in Leptospirosis is
(a) Drinking water
(b) Feed
(c) Contaminated pasture
(d) Urine

270. Lock jaw condition & prolapse of third eyelid

occurs in
(a) Tetanus (b) Botulism
(c) Rabies (d) B.Q

271. Focal gangrene, emphysematous swelling and crepitating is a symptom of which disease
(a) Tetanus (b) B.Q
(c) Botulism (d) Braxy

272. Toxins of *Clostridium tetani* is
(a) Neurotoxin (b) Haemolysin
(c) Fibrinolysin (d) All

273. Abortion caused by *Campylobacter foetus* occurs in
(a) 7-9 months of gestation
(b) 2-3 months of gestation
(c) 4-7 months of gestation
(d) All of the above

274. Pyometra is a feature of
(a) Leptospirosis (b) Vibriosis
(c) Listeriosis (d) Trichomoniasis

275. The causal virus of which disease have type O, A, C, SAT 1, 2, 3 subtype-
(a) PPR (b) FMD
(c) Rinderpest (d) None

276. Arthropod transmitted viral disease is
(a) Ephemeral fever (b) Blue tongue
(c) Both a & b (d) None

277. Epizootic lymphangitis is caused by
(a) *Aspergillus flavus*
(b) *Histioplasma farciminosum*
(c) Both
(d) None

278. Brooder's pneumonia is caused by-
(a) *Aspergillus flavus*
(b) *Histoplasma cepsulatum*
(c) Trichophyton
(d) None

279. Lumpy Jaw/Suppurative granulomatous osteomyelitis is synonym for
(a) *Actinobacillus lignieresii*
(b) *Actinomyces bovis*
(c) *Mycobacterium bovis*
(d) *Corynebacterium pyogenes*

280. FMD occurs in
(a) Cloven footed animals
(b) Odd footed animals
(c) Both
(d) None

281. FMD like disease is
(a) Vesicular exanthema
(b) FMD
(c) Vesicular stomatitis
(d) Contagious ecthyma

282. Abortion due to *Brucella* occurs in-
(a) First trimester of pregnancy
(b) 5-6 months of pregnancy
(c) Last trimester of pregnancy
(d) Any of the above

283. In males *Brucella* causes
(a) Abortion
(b) Epididymitis
(c) Hygroma & Abscess
(d) None

284. Saddle curve temperature is characteristic symptom of -
(a) Rabies
(b) Canine distemper
(c) Listeriosis
(d) Infections canine hepatitis

285. Rubarth disease is
(a) Canine distemper
(b) Rabies
(c) Infections canine hepatitis
(d) Parvo disease

286. Choria is after effect of which disease
(a) Rabies (b) Canine distemper
(c) ICH (d) Parvo virus disease

287. Scrapie is a
(a) Febrile disease
(b) Oedema disease
(c) Non febrile disease
(d) None of the above

288. Scrapie is also known as
(a) Mad cow disease
(b) Kuru
(c) Ovine spongiform encephalopathy
(d) None of the above

289. Mad cow disease is
(a) Scrapie
(b) Bovine spongiform encephalopathy

(c) Ovine spongiform encephalopathy
(d) None

290. Blind staggers or Equine encephalomyelitis is caused by
(a) Morbillis virus
(b) Herpes virus
(c) Group A abrovirus
(d) None

291. Which strain of Equine encephalomyelitis virus is most pathogenic?
(a) Western strain (b) Eastern strain
(c) Venezuelan strain (d) None

292. Three day sickness/ bovine epizootic fever is synonym for
(a) FMD
(b) Rinderpest
(c) Vesicular stomatitis
(d) Ephemeral fever

293. Lungs showing granulomatous lesions with caseation but without calcification in
(a) Tuberculosis (b) Fasciolosis
(c) Histoplasmosis (d) Aspergillosis

294. Guttural pouch empyema occurs in
(a) Botulism (b) Dourine
(c) Glanders (d) Strangle

295. Disease transmitted by coitus is
(a) Nagana (b) Surra
(c) Sleeping sickness (d) Dourine

296. Synonyms of Leptospirosis is
(a) Weil's disease
(b) Rice field worker's disease
(c) Stutgart's disease
(d) All of the above

297. Silver staining technique/ Dark field microscopy is used for
(a) *Brucella* (b) *Leptospira*
(c) *Pseudomonas* (d) *Bacillus*

298. MAT is used in diagnosis of-
(a) Brucellosis (b) Actinomycosis
(c) Trichomoniasis (d) Leptospirosis

299. Anaplasia is a characteristic feature of
(a) Benign tumor (b) Malignant tumor
(c) Both (d) None

300. Grading of tumor refers to-
(a) Extent of spread of tumor
(b) Degree of differentiation
(c) Degree of malignancy
(d) None

301. Sago-spleen is caused by the deposition of-
(a) Amyloid (b) lipid
(c) Glycogen (d) Mucopolysaccharides

302. The protein contents are least in
(a) Serous exudates (b) Fibrinous exudates
(c) Mucous exudates (d) Transudate

303. Infarcts have
(a) Coagulative necrosis
(b) Caseous necrosis
(c) Liquefactive necrosis
(d) Fat necrosis

304. Caseous necrosis found in
(a) TB
(b) Oesophagostomasis
(c) Caseous lymphadenitis
(d) All of the above

305. In the skin vessicles formation occuss as a result of
(a) Cloudy sewelling
(b) Hydropic degeneration
(c) Glycogen storage
(d) Fatty changes

306. In viral diarrhoea and rhinitis there is-
(a) Mucinous degeneration
(b) Mucus degeneration
(c) Mucoid degeneration
(d) Both a & b

307. Renal casts, arteriosclerosis, scar tissue are examples of
(a) Epithelial hyalinisation
(b) Connective tissue hyalinisation
(c) Kertohyalinisation
(d) Mucoid degeneration

308. Which of the following is example of Ag-Ab reaction (hyperglobulineria)
(a) Amylodosis
(b) Fibrinoid degeneration
(c) Collagen disease
(d) All of the above

309. Red infarct occurs in

(a) Liver/ Lungs (b) Kidney
(c) Heart (d) Spleen

310. Which cells never undergo hyperplasia?
(a) Cardiac muscle (b) Smooth muscle
(c) Brain cells (d) Hepatocytes

311. Staining of fat by which dye gives black colour
(a) Sudan III (b) Sudan IV
(c) Osmic acid (d) PAS

312. Hepatosis dietetica occurs due to deficiency of -
(a) Vit. E (b) Vit A
(c) Vit K (d) Vit. B complex

313. In catarrhal inflammation mucus is stained blue by-
(a) Haematoxylin (b) Eosin
(c) Acetic acid (d) Methylene blue

314. Stenosis of left AV valve is example of-
(a) Adaptive hypertrophy
(b) Compensatory hypertrophy
(c) Pseudo hypertrophy
(d) Physiological hypertrophy

315. Transformation of less specialised cells into hyperspecialised cells is called-
(a) Anaplasia (b) Dysplasia
(c) Metaplasia (d) Hyperplasia

316. The first four cardinal signs of inflammation are given by-
(a) Galen (b) Celsus
(c) Bichat (d) Morgagni

317. Chemical mediator of inflammation from plasma is-
(a) Histamine (b) Serotonin
(c) Bradykinin (d) Prostaglandins

318. Basophils contributes to-
(a) Exudates formation
(b) release of histamine & S-HT
(c) Both
(d) None

319. Special feature of viral infection and chronic inflammatory condition
(a) Neutrophils (b) Eosinophils
(c) Monocytes (d) Lymphocytes

320. The following cells are characteristic feature of pus and cannot proliferate-
(a) Neutrophils (b) Eosinophils
(c) Basophils (d) Lymphocytes

321. The cells which does not exist in blood but tissues-
(a) Macrophages (b) plasma cells
(c) Both (d) None

322. Heart failure cells are macrophages laden with-
(a) Fat (b) Hemosiderin
(c) Amyloid (d) None

323. Type of giant cell found in T.B.
(a) Tumour giant cell
(b) Foreign body giant cell
(c) Langhan's type giant cell
(d) Both b and c

324. In membranous inflammation chief constituents are-
(a) Fibrin
(b) Mucus
(c) Inflammatory cells & necrotic denuded epithelial cells
(d) All

325. Collection of pus within body cavity-
(a) Abscess (b) Empyema
(c) Sinus (d) Fistula

326. Carrel Trephone Theory is given for
(a) Inflammation (b) Healing & repair
(c) Hyperemia (d) None

327. Amino acid essential for formation of granulation tissue-
(a) Arginine (b) Lysine
(c) Tryptophan (d) Methionine

328. Vitamin essential for healing-
(a) Vit C (b) Vit D
(c) Thiamine (d) All

329. Select the option in terms of regeneration power-
(a) Nerve cell < Tendon < muscle < fibroblast
(b) Bone < nerve cell < Tendon < muscle
(c) Both
(d) None

330. Condition found in intussusceptions & strangulations
(a) Acute local passive hyperemia
(b) Acute general passive hyperemia
(c) Chronic local passive hyperemia
(d) Chronic general passive hyperemia

331. Organs affected from infarction-
(a) Heart (b) Brain
(c) Kidney (d) All

332. Terminology for blood in the sputum-
(a) Epistaxis (b) Hemoptysis
(c) Hematemesis (d) Both b and c

333. Brain haemorrhage and loss of consciousness is called-
(a) Metrorrhagia (b) Encephaloplasia
(c) Apoplexy (d) Enterorrhagia

334. Phlebolith is presence of stone in-
(a) Artery (b) Capillary
(c) Vein (d) Aorta

335. PM clot is composed of-
(a) Plate lets (b) Fibrin
(c) Both (d) None

336. Emboli generally lodges in-
(a) Artery (b) Capillary
(c) Vein (d) Both a & b

337. Caisson's disease occurs due to -
(a) High atmospheric pressure
(b) Low atmospheric pressure
(c) High relative humidity & temp.
(d) Low RM & temperature

338. Metaplasia of esophageal glandular duct in poultry is-
(a) Nutritional roup (b) Thrush
(c) Epulis (d) None

339. Sequelae to edema may be-
(a) Exudate formation(b) Fibrosis
(c) Both (d) None

340. In congenital icthyosis the skin of calves resembles with the skin of
(a) Toad (b) Fish
(c) Tortoise (d) Zebra

341. Acanthosis is of skin epithelium
(a) Hypoplasia (b) Hyperplasia
(c) Aplasia (d) Anaplasia

342. Idiosyncrasy is-
(a) Individual susceptibility of a disease
(b) Individual resistance to disease
(c) Susceptibility to disease in a group of people
(d) Any of the above

343. First change in the blood vessel during inflammation-
(a) Momentary constriction
(b) Vasodilatation
(c) Increased endothelial permeability
(d) Any of the above

344. Pseudomulin found only in-
(a) Dentigerous cyst
(b) Cyst of coenurus cerebralis
(c) Ovarian cyst
(d) All of the above

345. Mucoid degeneration occurs in-
(a) Neoplasm (Myxoma)
(b) Malnutrition
(c) Myxedema
(d) All

346. Collagen diseases are example of which degeneration-
(a) Fibrinoid
(b) Gout
(c) Hyaline
(d) Glycogen infiltration

347. Mucin takes which colour with H & E-
(a) Purple red (b) Blue
(c) Pink (d) All of these

348. Pseudomucin takes which colour with H & E-
(a) Blue (b) Pink
(c) Red (d) Black

349. Cause of spongiform encephalopathy is
(a) Virus (b) Viroids
(c) Prions (d) Deficiency of B_{12}

350. Which ingredient remove fat, during processing-
(a) Xylene (b) Xylol
(c) Benzene (d) PVP

351. In passive hyperemia organs/body has which colour-
(a) Bluish red (cyanotic)
(b) Red (bright)
(c) Pink
(d) None

352. Hypostatic congestion which occurs at the time of death-
(a) PM congestion

(b) AM congestion
(c) Agonal congestion
(d) Postgonal congestion

353. Haemorrhage occurs by-
(a) Rhexis (b) Diapedesis
(c) Both a & b (d) None

354. Suffusions are haemorrhages when-
(a) Less than 1 mm diameter
(b) Over 1-2 cm in diameter
(c) Approx. 1 cm in diameter
(d) Diffuse, flat, irregular areas of bleeding

355. Which thrombi is attached to wall -
(a) Valvular (b) Mural
(c) Ball (d) All of above

356. Thrombi which are attached to entire circumference of vessel
(a) Lateral (b) Canalized
(c) Saddle (d) Occluding

357. Thrombosis in end arteries results in-
(a) Red or current jelly clots
(b) Oedema
(c) Yellow clots
(d) Infraction

358. Endothelial injury is the cause for-
(a) Thrombus (b) PM clot
(c) Both a & b (d) None

359. Which gas is mainly responsible for gas/air emboli?
(a) Hydrogen (b) Carbon
(c) Oxygen (d) Nitrogen

360. Colliquative necrosis occurs in which type of infarct-
(a) Infarct of kidney (b) Infarct of brain
(c) Infarct of spleen (d) Infarct of heart

361. Oedema in ventricle of brain is-
(a) Ascites (b) Anasarca
(c) Hydrocephalus (d) Hydro-pericardium

362. Oedematous fluid is-
(a) Non-inflammatory
(b) Low in protein
(c) Low in specific gravity than exudates
(d) All of above

363. The cause of parasitic, renal, nutritional and cachectic oedema is-
(a) Increased hydrostatic pressure
(b) Decreased osmotic pressure
(c) Lymphatic obstruction
(d) Sodium retention

364. In lung thrombi is formed by which of the following -
(a) Platelet
(b) Platelet & leucocyte
(c) Platelet, leucocyte & fibrin
(d) All of above

365. Which organ is among the first to show senile changes-
(a) Respiratory (b) Digestive
(c) Nervous (d) Reproductive

366. Hypertrophy and hyperplasia both develop concurrently in-
(a) CNS
(b) Prostate, uterus, goiter
(c) Cardiac & skeletal muscle
(d) All of above

367. Compensatory hypertrophy occurs in-
(a) Kidney (paired organ)
(b) Heart (unpaired organ)
(c) Intestine
(d) All

368. In metaplasia which is permanent alteration-
(a) Bone
(b) Stratified squamous epithelium
(c) Cartilage
(d) Both a & c

369. Which is the precancerous stage?
(a) Metaplasia (b) Hyperplasia
(c) Dysplasia (d) Hypertrophy

370. Which process induce necrosis-
(a) Enzymic digestion of cell
(b) Denaturation of proteins
(c) Both a & b
(d) None

371. Cracks on nuclear membrane is known as-
(a) Karyoschisis (b) Karyorhexis
(c) Karyolysis (d) Chrometolysis

372. Fragmentation of nucleus is known as -
(a) Karyoschisis (b) Karyorhexis
(c) Karyolysis (d) Chrometolysis

373. In which type, both architectural and cellular details are lost-
(a) Coagulative (b) Caseous
(c) Liquifactive (d) Both b & c

374. In extremities which type of gangrene occurs?
(a) Apoptosis
(b) Dry gangrene
(c) Moist gangrene
(d) Pathological calcification

375. Colour of gangrene is due to-
(a) Barium sulphate (b) Iron sulphide
(c) Silver chloride (d) All

376. Moist gangrene occurs in-
(a) Extremities (b) internal organ
(c) Both a & b (d) None

377. Clostridial organism produced which types of gangrene-
(a) Moist (b) Gas
(c) Dry (d) All

378. Klotz Theory is related to which type of calcification-
(a) Metastatic calcification
(b) Dystrophic calcification
(c) Both a & b
(d) None

379. With Von Kossa's silver nitrate stain calcified tissue takes which stain-
(a) Black (b) Blue
(c) Pink (d) Purple

380. Dystrophic calcification occurs in-
(a) TB, abscess and degenerating tumors
(b) Phlebolith
(c) Renal tubular epithelium
(d) All

381. Accumulation of lead is known as-
(a) Anthracosis (b) Silicosis
(c) Plumbism (d) Pneumoconiosis

382. All exogenous pigment cause fibrosis of lung known as-
(a) Anthracosis (b) Pneumoconiosis
(c) Plumbism (d) Silicosis

383. Rigor mortis starts at-
(a) 20-30 hrs after death
(b) 20-30 hrs before death
(c) 1-8 hrs after death
(d) 1-8 hrs before death

384. Most commonly displaced organ after death-
(a) Liver (b) Intestine
(c) Kidney (d) Lungs

385. Which is acidic in nature?
(a) Exudate (b) Transudate
(c) Oedematous fluid (d) All

386. If exudate is suppurative, it leads to-
(a) Fibrosis (b) Regeneration
(c) Both a & b (d) Abscess formation

387. Pus is-
(a) Alkaline (b) Acidic
(c) Neutral (d) None

388. Which of the following produce black pus?
(a) Staphylococcus
(b) Corynebacterium
(c) Disintegrating hoof material
(d) None

389. Which wound is healed by I intension
(a) Excessive loss of tissue
(b) Healing of open wound
(c) Healing of close wound
(d) Both a & b

390. In which healing, resulting tissue is called cicatrix or scar
(a) Healing by I intension
(b) Healing by II intension
(c) Both a & b
(d) None

391. When scar continue to grow mass of C.T. called as-
(a) Keloid (b) Scar
(c) Proud flesh (d) Both a & c

392. Cells which cannot undergo mitotic division in postnatal life is known as
(a) Permanent or non-dividing cells
(b) Labile or continuously dividing cells
(c) Stable or quiescent celles
(d) None of above

393. Epithelium, cells of splenic lymphoid and haemopoietic tissue are of which type of cells
(a) Permanent (b) labile
(c) Stable (d) None of above

394. Erythropoiesis and granulopoiesis in poultry is-
(a) Extravascular (b) Intravascular
(c) Both (d) Liver

395. Dystrophic calcification occurs due to -
(a) Hypercalcemia
(b) Excess of Vit D
(c) Necrosis of the cells
(d) Hyperglycemia

396. In gout, which salts are deposited in tissues-
(a) Magnesium & sodium carbonate
(b) Ca & Mg citrate
(c) Ca and Na urates
(d) Ca oxalate & silicate

397. Epitheloid cells have?
(a) More endoplasmic reticulum & phagocytic vacuoles
(b) More endoplasmic reticulum, golgi apparatus
(c) Less golgi & phagocytic vacuoles
(d) None

398. An abscess of hair follicle or sebaceous gland is known as-
(a) Carbuncle (b) Furuncle
(c) Pustule (d) None

399. Thrombi found in the auricles of heart is-
(a) Cardiac thrombi
(b) Vegetation type thrombi
(c) Ball thrombi
(d) Vegetation type vacuolar thrombi

400. Which is the senile pigment?
(a) Haemosiderin (b) Lipofuscin
(c) Bile pigments (d) Porphysin

401. Bronchiectasis is-
(a) Rupture of lumen of bronchi
(b) Dilatation of the lumen of bronchi
(c) Constriction of lumen of bronchi
(d) All of the above

402. Caisson's disease is caused by-
(a) Low atmospheric pressure
(b) High atmospheric pressure
(c) Narrowing of blood vessels
(d) None of the above

403. White muscle disease of calf is caused by-
(a) Vitamin A deficiency
(b) Vitamin C deficiency
(c) Vitamin E deficiency
(d) Vitamin D deficiency

404. In tuberculosis, giant cells are found which are known as-
(a) Lang Han's type
(b) Foreign body type giant cell
(c) Both a & b
(d) None of the above

405. Which one is the inflammation of hip join?
(a) Coxitis (b) Arthritis
(c) Gonitis (d) Spavin

406. Which occurs in systemic anaphylaxis in guinea pigs?
(a) Contraction of bronchial vein
(b) Contraction of pulmonary artery
(c) Contraction of hepatic vein
(d) Cutaneous edema & dyspnea

407. Dysgammaglobulinemia of chickens is a primary immunodeficiency disease associated with defect of-
(a) B cells (b) T cells
(c) T & B cells (d) None of the above

408. Hemorrhage from nasal cavity is-
(a) Epistaxis
(b) Hemoptysis
(c) Hemotemesis
(d) Petechial hemorrhage

409. Narrowing of bronchial lumen due to obstruction is called as-
(a) Bronchiectasis (b) Bronchostenosis
(c) Bronchitis (d) None of the above

410. In which condition there is necrosis & gangrene of muscles
(a) Myositis
(b) Muscular dystrophy
(c) Both a & b
(d) None of the above

411. In Avian pox, Borrel bodies are present in ______ body
(a) Lung cells (b) Skin cells
(c) Heart cells (d) None

412. Sinusitis in turkey is caused by
(a) *M. gallisepticum* (b) *H. paragalinarum*

(c) *Chlamydia psittaci* (d) *P. Multocida*

413. Bulging muscles of a race horse are example of
(a) Cellular injury
(b) Necrosis
(c) Cellular adaptation
(d) Gangrene

414. Which gas is mostly responsible for air emboli?
(a) Hydrogen (b) Carbon
(c) Oxygen (d) Nitrogen

415. When animal expose to normal pressure from higher pressure suddenly then it is known as-
(a) Caisson disease
(b) Decompression sickness
(c) Bends
(d) All of the above

416. Accumulation of silicon in lungs is known as -
(a) Anthracosis (b) Silicosis
(c) Plumbism (d) Pneumoconiosis

417. Accumulation of lead in lungs-
(a) Anthracosis (b) Silicosis
(c) Plumbism (d) Pneumoconiosis

418. Blue line is produced by-
(a) Anthracosis (b) Silicosis
(c) Plumbism (d) Pneumoconiosis

419. Removal of dead neurons through microglial cells is called as -
(a) Satellitosis
(b) Neuronophagia
(c) Perivascular cuffing
(d) None

420. Accumulation of carbon particle in lung-
(a) Anthracosis (b) Silicosis
(c) Plumbism (d) Pneumoconiosis

421. PM changes are rapid in-
(a) High environment temperature
(b) Large size of individual
(c) Thick external insulation
(d) All of the above

422. Nerve cells & skeletal & cardiac cells are of which type of cells
(a) Permanent/Non dividing cells
(b) Labile/continuously dividing cells
(c) Stable/quiescent cells
(d) None of above

423. Which is commonly involved as secondary site in hematogenous dissemination?
(a) Liver & lung (b) Lung & Heart
(c) Heart & Kidney (d) All of above

424. In lungworm disease fecal sample is preserved by-
(a) Refrigeration
(b) Addition of 10% formation in 1:4 ratios of faecal material
(c) Addition of 20% formaldehyde in 1:4 ratio of faecal sample
(d) Addition of 40% formalin in 1:4 ratio of faecal material

425. Larvae of lung worm are detected by-
(a) Direct examination of feces
(b) Sedimentation
(c) Floatation
(d) Concentration

426. Which parasite is not diagnosed by floatation technique of fecal examination?
(a) Lung worm larvae
(b) Some trematodes
(c) Both of above
(d) Nematode only

427. In atrophic rhinitis of swine, which bone undergoes rarefaction
(a) Turbinate
(b) Maxillary
(c) All facial bones
(d) only frontal part of turbinate

428. Which type of necrosis occur in bull nose-
(a) Liquifactive
(b) Colligative
(c) Caseous
(d) pancreatic fat degeneration

429. In roaring which type of degeneration occur in left cricoaryknoids in -
(a) Albumenous (b) Hyaline
(c) Hydropic (d) Fatty

430. Narrowing of bronchial lumen is called as-
(a) Bronchostenosis (b) Bronchiectasis
(c) Both (d) None

431. Dilatation of bronchus is called as
(a) Bronchostenosis (b) Bronchiectasis
(c) Both (d) None

432. Uniform dilatation of bronchi-
(a) Saccular Bronchiectasis
(b) Cylindrical Bronchiectasis
(c) Columnar Bronchiectasis
(d) All of the above

433. An out pouching of bronchial wall is known as -
(a) Saccular Bronchiectasis
(b) Cylindrical Bronchiectasis
(c) Columnar Bronchiectasis
(d) All

434. Atelectosis is-
(a) Increased air in lungs
(b) Collapse of alveoli
(c) Failure of alveoli to open & contain air
(d) Both a & b

435. Emphysema is
(a) Increased air in lungs
(b) Alveoli collapse
(c) Failure of alveoli to open & contain air
(d) Both a & b

436. Collapse of alveoli is always-
(a) Generalized (b) Focal
(c) Both (d) None

437. Broken wind or heaves is-
(a) Acute alveolar emphysema
(b) Acute interstitial emphysema
(c) Chronic alveolar emphysema
(d) Both a & c

438. Sequelae of heaves is-
(a) Hypertrophy & dilation of right ventricles
(b) Hypertrophy & dilation of left ventricles
(c) Both
(d) None

439. Microscopic lesion of congestion of lung is-
(a) Alveoli & bronchi contain a pink stained homogenous material
(b) Blood may be found in alveoli, bronchioles & bronchi
(c) Alveoli, capillaries & septa is filled with blood
(d) Alveoli contain red cells & heart failure cells

440. Which route of infection is most common for pneumonia?
(a) Hematogenous
(b) Bronchogenous
(c) Via penetrating wounds
(d) None

441. Microscopic lesion of infarction of lungs is-
(a) Alveoli & bronchi pink stained homogenous material
(b) Blood in alveoli, bronchioles & bronchi
(c) Alveoli, capillaries & septa filled with blood
(d) Alveoli with red cells & heart failure cells

442. Microscopic lesion of hemorrhage of lung is-
(a) Alveoli, bronchi to pink stained homogenous material
(b) Blood in alveoli, bronchioles & bronchi
(c) Alveoli capillaries & septa filled to blood
(d) Alveoli to red cells & heart failure cells

443. Pneumonia in whole lobes may be affected & characterized by a catarrhal exudates of alveolar -
(a) Lobar/cropous pneumonia
(b) Lobular/catarrhal/broncho pneumonia
(c) Both
(d) None

444. Most frequent pneumonia in animals-
(a) Lobar (b) Lobular
(c) Both (d) None

445. Pneumonia with catarrhal exudates of alveolar & only a lobule or part of lobule is affected -
(a) Lobar (b) Lobular
(c) Both (d) None

446. In which stage, lung is not consolidate & does not sink in water-
(a) Stage of congestion
(b) Stage of red hepatisation
(c) Stage of grey hepatisation
(d) None

447. At which stage, liquefaction & removal of exudates occur-
(a) Stage of congestion
(b) Stage of red hepatisation
(c) Stage of grey hepatisation
(d) None

448. Part of lung commonly affected in bronchopneumonia-
(a) Anterior & dorsal part
(b) Ant. & ventral part

(c) Posterior & dorsal part
(d) Posteriro & ventral part

449. Part of lung is greenish or black in pneumonia-
(a) Lobar (b) Broncho
(c) Aspiration (d) None

450. Pneumonia due to helminthes-
(a) Gangrenous
(b) Verminous
(c) Metastatic Suppurative
(d) All

451. Which of the following is interstitial pneumonia?
(a) Inflammation of lung
(b) Inflammation of alveolar septa
(c) Inflammation of alveoli
(d) Inflammation of lung parenchyma

452. Characteristics of interstitial pneumonia-
(a) Presence of hyaline membrane
(b) Foetalization or epithelialisation of lung
(c) Both of above
(d) Nodular lesion

453. Characteristic of mycotic pneumonia-
(a) Presence of hyaline membrane
(b) Foetalization or epithelialisation of lung
(c) Both
(d) Nodular lesion

454. In mycotic pneumonia, lesions is found in-
(a) Trachea (b) Bronchi
(c) Air sacs (d) All

455. In which disease, alveoli show adenomatosis & lesions are focal-
(a) Jag siekte (b) Meadi
(c) Pneumothorax (d) Pleuropneumonia

456. Pleura is involved in pneumonia, condition known as-
(a) Jagsiekte (b) Meadi
(c) Pneumothorax (d) Pleuropneumonia

457. In which disease, lymphadenitis occur & inclusions present & lung is not collapsed while thorax is opened-
(a) Hydrothorax (b) Pneumothorax
(c) Both a & b (d) None

458. Which disease cases atelectasis of lung-?
(a) Hydrothorax (b) Pneumothorax
(c) Both a & b (d) None

459. Curvature of spine to a ventral convexity is called as-
(a) Kyphosis (b) Lordosis
(c) Apodia (d) Scoliosis

460. Abnormal lateral curvature of spine is known as-
(a) Kyphosis (b) Lordosis
(c) Apodia (d) Scoliosis

461. Abnormal curvature & dorsal prominence of spine is known as -
(a) Kyphosis (b) Lordosis
(c) Apodia (d) Scoliosis

462. Absence of posterior limbs-
(a) Kyphosis (b) Lordosis
(c) Apodia (d) Scoliosis

463. Absence of anterior limbs is known as -
(a) Abrachia (b) Amelia
(c) Micromelia (d) Apodia

464. Absence of limbs-
(a) Abrachia (b) Amelia
(c) Micromelia (d) Apodia

465. Absence of some of toes-
(a) Adactylism (b) Perodactyly
(c) Brachydactylism (d) Syndactylism

466. Absence of all the toes-
(a) Adactylism (b) Perodactyly
(c) Brachydactylism (d) Syndactylism

467. Fusion of toes-
(a) Adactylism (b) Perodactyly
(c) Brachydactyly (d) Syndactylism

468. Abnormal shortening of toes-
(a) Adactylism (b) Perodactyly
(c) Brachydactyly (d) Syndactylism

469. Steatorrhoea
(a) Vit D is not observed in presence of fat
(b) Def of a & Vit D presence of fat
(c) Def of Ca, P, Vit D
(d) All

470. Osteodystrophia fibrosa in horses-
(a) Bran disease (b) Big head disease
(c) Millers disease (d) All of above

471. Inflammation of vertebrae-
(a) Ostitis (b) Periostitis
(c) Ostiomyelitis (d) Spondylitis

472. Inflammation of bone-

(a) Ostetis (b) Periostitis
(c) Osteomyelitis (d) Spondylitis

473. Exostosis of osteophyte has the structure of -
(a) Compact bone (b) Spongy bone
(c) Spongy bone but do not have Haversion system
(d) Compact bone with a haversion system

474. If Exostosis is found on I or II phalanx, then, it is known as-
(a) Ringbone (b) Splint
(c) Spavin (d) Joint gall

475. Exostosis at end of Mc or Mt -
(a) Ringbone (b) Splint
(c) Spavin (d) Joint gall

476. Exostosis at medial portion of distal tarsal bone-
(a) Ringbone (b) Splint
(c) Spavin (d) Joint gall

477. When serous fluid is in considerable amount in joint is known as-
(a) Ringbone (b) Splint
(c) Spavin (d) Joint gall

478. Degenerative changes due to disturbance in cell metabolism of proteins is known as-
(a) Hyaline degeneration
(b) Mucinous degeneration
(c) Mucoid degeneration
(d) All of the above

479. Leiomyosarcoma is a -
(a) Malignant tumour of striated muscle
(b) Malignant tumour of the smooth muscle
(c) Malignant tumour of fibrous muscle
(d) None of the above

480. The protein contents are least in
(a) Serous exudate (b) Fibrinous exudate
(c) Mucous exudate (d) Transudate

481. Serous bursitis of hock joint in horses-
(a) Bog spavin
(b) Ankylosing spondylosis
(c) Hypoma of carpal joint
(d) Both a & c

482. Capped elbow in horse involves-
(a) Carpal joint (b) Shoulder joint
(c) Hock joint (d) Stifle joint

483. Poll evil involves-
(a) Carpal joint (b) Shoulder joint
(c) Hock joint (d) Stifle joint

484. Dystrophic calcification occurs due to-
(a) Hypocalcaemia
(b) Excess of vitamin D
(c) Necrosis of the cells
(d) Hyperglycemia

485. Cause of myasthenia gravis is-
(a) Hyperplasia of thymus gland
(b) Hypoplasia of thymus
(c) Hypoplasia of thymus & pineal
(d) Hyperplasia of adrenal cortex

486. Respiratory burst of Myeloperoxidase pathway is most effective way of phagocytosis in-
(a) Macrophage (b) Neutrophils
(c) Eosinophils (d) Basophils

487. Infraction in lungs & liver is rare due to-
(a) Double blood supply
(b) Little collateral blood supply
(c) Both are parenchymatous organs
(d) None

488. Which of the pneumoconiosis is more harmful?
(a) Chalicosis (b) Silicosis
(c) Anthracosis (d) Siderosis

489. Porcine atrophic Rhinitis is caused by-
(a) *Brucella bronchiseptica*
(b) *Bordetella bronchiseptica*
(c) *Clostridium septicum*
(d) None

490. Which is corpora amylaceae-?
(a) Epithelial hyaline
(b) Connective tissue hyaline
(c) Amyloidal spleen
(d) Muscle hyaline

491. Which have a stimulating effect on mitosis in wound healing-
(a) Urea
(b) Number of NH_3 compounds
(c) Allantion
(d) All of the above

492. Most damage in a cell is infected by influx of-
(a) Ca-ion (b) K-ion
(c) Fe-ion (d) Ammonium ion

493. Ionization refers to production of ions leading to

displacement of
(a) Ion (b) Proton
(c) Cation (d) Electron

494. Immunodeficiency with dwarfism is related with defect in-
(a) B-cell (b) T-cell
(c) Both (d) None

495. Complete failure of an organ or tissue to develop-
(a) Aplasia (b) Anomaly
(c) Atrophy (d) Anaplasia

496. Example of ketone bodies-
(a) Acetone (b) â-HBA
(c) Acetoacetic acid (d) All

497. Nutritional encephalomalacia is a disease of-
(a) Mink (b) Baby chicks
(c) Calves (d) Puppies

498. Parasitic edema is caused by-
(a) *Oestrus ovis* (b) Blood fluke
(c) Spirocerca (d) Liver fluke

499. Which can cause genetic injury?
(a) Compound 48/80 (b) 5-Bromouracil
(c) 5-fluerouracil (d) 6-mercaptopurine

500. Pigment ceroid is related to which-
(a) Fat (b) Protein
(c) Vitamin (d) Carbohydrate

501. Bovine Enzootic haematuria is which type of diseases
(a) Acute (b) Subacute
(c) Chronic (d) All the above

502. Microconcentration is used for-
(a) Calculi in uninary tubules
(b) Calculi in bile ducts
(c) Calculi in pelvis of kidney
(d) Calculi in bladder

503. Kumri in horses is caused by-
(a) *Toxoplasma gondii*
(b) *Seteria digitata*
(c) *Coenurus cerebralis*
(d) *Hypoderma bovis* larvae

504. Lumbar paralysis in sheep and goat is caused by-
(a) *Toxoplasma gondii*
(b) *Seteria digitata*
(c) *Coenurus cerebralis*
(d) *Hypoderma bovis* larvae

505. Which parasite is found in fat of vertebral canal?
(a) *Toxoplasma gondii*
(b) *Seteria digitata*
(c) *Coenurus cerebralis*
(d) *Hypoderma bovis* larvae

506. Which parasite causes coagulative necrosis in brain?
(a) *Toxoplasma gondii*
(b) *Seteria digitata*
(c) *Coenurus cerebralis*
(d) *Hypoderma bovis* larvae

507. Local dilatation of artery is known as-
(a) Aneurysm (b) Ball thrombi
(c) Arteritis (d) None above

508. Goiter is-
(a) Non-inflammatory enlargement of thyroid
(b) Non-neoplastic enlargement of thyroid
(c) Both a and b
(d) Inflammatory enlargement of thyroid

509. Grave's disease is
(a) Parenchymatous goiter
(b) Colloidal goiter
(c) Nodular goiter
(d) Exophthalmic goiter

510. Out of which goiter is called hyperplastic goiter
(a) Parenchymatous goiter
(b) Colloidal goiter
(c) Adenomatous goiter
(d) Exophthalmic goiter

511. Cushing syndrome is result of which
(a) Hyper-junction of adrenal cortex
(b) Hypo-junction of adrenal cortex
(c) Hypo-junction of adrenal medulla
(d) Hyper-junction of adrenal medulla

512. Heart failure cells are found in which of the following-
(a) Lungs (b) Heart
(c) Kidney (d) Liver

513. The first line of cellular defense is-
(a) Neutrophils (b) Monocytes
(c) Lymphocytes (d) Macrophages

514. Cattle of plain areas when taken to hills above 7000 feet for rearing, develop
(a) Caison's disease

(b) Cori's disease
(c) Anaemia & dyspnoea
(d) Brisket disease and polycythemia

515. Gout is primary a disease of primates and poultry because
(a) Both over feed on protein diet
(b) Both suffer from vit A deficiency
(c) Both suffer from inherent urciase enzyme deficiency
(d) None of the above

516. Endotoxic shock is caused by which of the following
(a) Gram –ve organism
(b) Gram +ve organism
(c) Both of these
(d) None of the above

517. Intussusception of intestine leads to which
(a) Chronic venous congestion
(b) Local venous congestion
(c) Local venous congestion & gangrene
(d) Infarction

518. Haemoprotozoan disease usually results in
(a) Anaemia only
(b) Anaemia and hemolytic jaundice
(c) Icterus only
(d) None of the above

519. Fever is a -
(a) Local but useful response
(b) Systemic but harmful response
(c) Systemic but useful response
(d) Systemic but useful response within limits

520. Zenker's necrosis is a special kind of necrosis occurring in
(a) Smooth muscles (b) Skeletal muscles
(c) Both a & b (d) None of the above

521. The causative factor of Equine abortion is
(a) RNA virus (b) Herpes virus
(c) Mycoplasma (d) None of the above

522. Chief lesion of ICH are
(a) Perianal edema & haemorrhage
(b) Gliosis and intracytoplasmic inclusion in liver
(c) Focal necrosis and intra nuclear inclusion in liver
(d) Periportal cirrhosis and intracytoplasmic inclusions

523. Virus of FMD disease is classified under the particular group of family picornaviridae
(a) Entero virus (b) Calcivirus
(c) Aptho virus (d) None of the above

524. Generally, pathological lesions of hog cholera are-
(a) Oedema and haemorrhages
(b) Neural degeneration & gliosis
(c) Leucocytosis & haemorrhagic enteritis
(d) Leukemia and button ulcers in caecum and colon

525. In nervous system, CD virus has affinity for
(a) Myelinated portion of brain and spinal cord
(b) Piamater and arachinoid
(c) Neurons of grey matter of cerebrum
(d) Capillaries network of hippocampus

526. The Rinderpest virus has affinity for
(a) Myeloid tissue and skin
(b) Lymphatic
(c) R.E. cells and capillary endothelial cells
(d) None o the above

527. The particular parasite can act as intermediate host and reservoir for swine influenza
(a) *Dictyocaulus viviparous*
(b) *Dictyocaulus fillaria*
(c) *Mullerius* sp.
(d) *Metastrongylus apri*

528. Which is not caused by "slow virus?"
(a) Maedi
(b) FMD in goats
(c) Jaaggsiekte
(d) Equine infectious anaemia

529. Presence of organisms at which location helps in diagnosis of Heart water-
(a) Cardiac muscle cells
(b) Endothelial cells of blood capillaries
(c) Kuffer's cells of liver
(d) R.E. cells in red pulp of spleen

530. Necrosis of brain is called
(a) Encephalomalacia
(b) Polioencephalomalacia
(c) Myelomalacia
(d) None

531. Winter diarrhoea of cattle is caused by
(a) *Vibrio foetus* (b) *Vibrio jejuni*
(c) Rota virus (d) None of the above

532. In case of BQ blackish discolouration of muscle is due to-
(a) Formation of iron sulphide
(b) Hyper pigmentation with melanin
(c) Lack of tyrosine
(d) Deposits of lead sulphide

533. Lesions of listeriosis in sheep may remain confined to
(a) Fourth ventricle and spinal cord
(b) Hippocampus
(c) Pones and cerebellum
(d) Medulla oblangata and spinal cord

534. The species of oesophagostomum which affects sheep and goat is
(a) *O. radiatum* (b) *O. dentatum*
(c) *O. columbianum* (d) None of the above

535. Immunosuppression is quite evident in the following disease-
(a) Equine Influenza (b) FMD
(c) Hog cholera (d) Canine hepatitis

536. Corridor disease in buffalo is caused by
(a) *Leishmania donovani*
(b) *Theileria mutans*
(c) *Theileria lawrencei*
(d) *Trypanosoma evansi*

537. Organism responsible for 'Gas gangrene' is
(a) *Pneumococcus sp.*
(b) *Clostridium septicum*
(c) *Clostridium hemolyticum*
(d) *Streprococcus sp.*

538. In gout salt deposited in tissue are
(a) Calcium and sodium carbonates
(b) Calcium and magnesium carbonates
(c) Calcium oxalate and silicates
(d) Calcium and sodium urates

539. Black tongue is caused by
(a) Virus
(b) Niacin deficiency
(c) Pyridoxine deficiency
(d) Melenosis in tongue due to heavy louse infection

540. Scurvy is caused by
(a) Pyridoxine deficiency
(b) Vitamin A deficiency
(c) Vit. B_{12} deficiency
(d) Ascorbic acid deficiency

541. Nutritional encephalomalacia will be caused by
(a) Excessive feeding of cod liver oil
(b) Riboflavin deficiency
(c) Chlorinated naphthalene poisoning
(d) Salt poisoning

542. Nutritional encephalomalacia is a disease of
(a) Mink (b) Baby chicks
(c) Calves (d) Puppies

543. Classic paralysis is caused by which of the following
(a) Riboflavin deficiency
(b) Pantothenic acid deficiency
(c) Choline deficiency
(d) None of the above

544. Colour of urine in a horse suffering from Monday morning sickness is
(a) Black due to iron sulphids
(b) Yellow due to bile squamous
(c) Brown due to iron sulphide
(d) None of the above

545. Vitamin A deficiency causes hyperkeratinisation of epithelium, the process is referred as-
(a) Anaplasia (b) Hyperplasia
(c) Metaplasia (d) None of the above

546. Inflammation of oviduct is called-
(a) Proctitis (b) Salphingitis
(c) Typhlitis (d) Chelitis

547. Caisson's disease is caused by
(a) Low atmospheric pressure
(b) High atmospheric pressure
(c) Narrowing of blood vessels
(d) None of the above

548. Which parasite causes catarrhal gastritis?
(a) *Habronema sp.* (b) *Gastrophillus sp.*
(c) *Strongylus sp.* (d) None of the above

549. Hair balls are
(a) Phytobezoars (b) Trichobezoars
(c) Enterolith (d) Coli granuloma

550. Mulberry heart disease commonly occurs in

which animal

(a) Cattle (b) Dog
(c). Fowl (d) Pig

551. Heart worm (*Dirofilaris immitis*) is a parasite of
(a) Heart (b) Pericardium
(c) Myocardium (d) Endocardium

552. Heart worm is found in which chamber of heart of dog.
(a) Right ventricle (b) Left ventricle
(c) Right auricle (d) Left auricle

553. Which animal is most susceptible for *Sarocystis tenella* in its heart muscle?
(a) Cattle (b) Pig
(c) Sheep (d) All the above

554. In Perpura haemmorrhagica of horse, which type of the haemorrhages are seen commonly-
(a) Diffused haemorrhages
(b) Echymosis
(c) Both the above
(d) Petechial

555. Rheumatic fever is commonest cause of which type of pericarditis
(a) Fibrinous pericarditis
(b) Uric acid pericarditis
(c) Suppurative pericarditis
(d) Constrictive pericarditis

556. Suppuration is present in T.B.
(a) Yes
(b) No
(c) In immune amount
(d) Full of pus

557. In sweet clover poisoning which type of haemorrhages are şeen commonly-
(a) Diffused haemorrhage
(b) Ecchymosed
(c) Both the above
(d) Petechial haemorrhages

558. Which thrombi is common in cattle in B.Q.
(a) Valvular thrombi
(b) Mural thrombi
(c) Ball thrombi
(d) Vegetation type valvular thrombi

559. Bleeding from nose is known as
(a) Apoplexy (b) Epistaxis
(c) Hematesis (d) Hemoptysis

560. Blood in sputum is known as
(a) Apoplexy (b) Epistaxis
(c) Haematemesis (d) Haemoptysis

561. Blood in vomit is known as
(a) Apoplexy (b) Epistaxis
(c) Haematemesis (d) Haemoptysis

562. Brain haemorrhage is known as
(a) Apoplexy (b) Epistaxis
(c) Haematemesis (d) Haemoptysis

563. In ICH, inclusion body is found in hepatocyte at location of
(a) Cytoplasm (b) Nucleus
(c) Both the above (d) None of the above

564. In rabies lesions in brain nerve are
(a) Suppurative encephalitis
(b) Non-suppurative encephalitis
(c) Coagulative lesions
(d) Both a & b

565. Farcy is-
(a) Acute form of actinomycosis
(b) Cutaneous form of glanders
(c) Subacute form of CBPP
(d) Chronic form of CBPP

566. Summer mastitis is caused by
(a) *Staphycococus aureus*
(b) *Acranobacter pyogenes*
(c) *Streptococus uberis*
(d) *Candida albicans*

567. In pox, there is -
(a) Hyperkeratosis
(b) Acanthosis & parakeratosis
(c) Acanthosis & hyperkeratosis
(d) Acanthosis, parakeratosis & Hyperkeratosis

568. Diabetes insipidus is under the influence of hormone secreted by
(a) Posterior pituitary
(b) Anterior pituitary
(c) Pancreas
(d) All the above

569. Microscopically rabies is diagnosed by the presence of
(a) Inclusion body in the cytoplasm of neuron

(b) Inclusion body in the nucleus of neuron
(c) Inclusion body in the glial cells
(d) All the above

570. White muscle disease of calf is caused by deficiency of
(a) Vitamin A (b) Vitamin B_1
(c) Vitamin E (d) Vitamin D

571. The disease farcy is seen in
(a) Pig (b) Cattle
(c) Horse (d) Sheep

572. In obstructive jaundice blood contains more of
(a) Haemoglobin (b) Urobilin
(c) Bilirubin (d) None of the above

573. Turkey egg appearance of kidney is an important feature of which disease of swine
(a) Swine fever
(b) Glasser's disease
(c) African swine fever
(d) Both a & b

574. J.D. in bovine is caused by which of the following-
(a) *Mycobacterium bovis*
(b) *Mycobacterium tuberculosis*
(c) *Mycobacterium intercellulare*
(d) *Mycobacterium paratuberculosis*

575. Babes nodule in rabies is formed due to collection of
(a) Astrocytes (b) Oligodendroglia
(c) Microglia (d) Ependymal cells

576. Abortion in last trimester in cattle is caused by
(a) *Brucella* infection
(b) *Vibrio* infection
(c) *Trichomonas* infection
(d) All the above

577. Mixed granulomatous inflammation does not occur in
(a) Actinobacillosis (b) Actinomycosis
(c) Aspergillosis (d) Tuberculosis

578. Acute thileriosis in India is caused by
(a) *T. annulata* (b) *T. mutans*
(c) *T. parva* (d) All of the above

579. Cow pox can be an example of
(a) An inadequate inflammatory
(b) An excessive inflammatory reaction
(c) A moderate inflammatory reaction
(d) None of these

580. Langhan's cells are seen in
(a) Tuberculosis (b) Glanders
(c) Black Quarters (d) Salmonellosis

581. Heart failure cells are found in
(a) Heart (b) Lung
(c) Liver (d) Kidney

582. Button shaped ulcer in large intestine is pathognomic lesion in which of the following disease
(a) Theileriosis (b) Swine fever
(c) Rinderpest (d) Rabies

583. Zebra-markings in large intestine is pathogenic lesion of which disease
(a) Theileriosis (b) Swine fever
(c) Rinderpest (d) Rabies

584. Punched out ulcers in Abomasum is pathognomic lesion in which disease
(a) Theileriosis (b) Swine fever
(c) Rinderpest (d) Rabies

585. Negri bodies in cells of hippocampus and cerebellum is pathogenic lesion of which disease
(a) Theileriosis (b) Swine fever
(c) Rinderpest (d) Rabies

586. Bloat is
(a) Structural change (b) Functional change
(c) Both the above (d) None of the above

587. Negri bodies, the pathognomic lesion in case of rabies are found in which part of the brain
(a) Hippocampus (b) Pons
(c) Cerebellum (d) Both a & c

588. In hyaline degeneration, which bodies are present in hepatocytes
(a) Russel's body (b) Council man body
(c) Mallory body (d) Negri body

589. In hyaline penetration, which bodies are present in hepatocytes
(a) Ketosis
(b) Glycogen infiltration
(c) Jaundice
(d) Both a & b

590. Vegetative endocarditis may be one of the chief lesions found in
(a) Bovine traumatic gastritis

(b) Swine Erysipelas
(c) Equine viral arteritis
(d) Hog cholera

591. Primary photosensitization is not related with
(a) Liver disease
(b) Sweet clover poisoning
(c) Buckmhert
(d) St. John's woit

592. Babesiosis is also known as
(a) Piroplasmosis (b) Red water disease
(c) Tick fever (d) All the above

593. CD is characterized by
(a) Continuous temperature
(b) Intermittent temperature
(c) Diphasic temperature
(d) Relapsing temperature

594. Murine respiratory mycoplasmosis is characterized by inflammation of respiratory tract and
(a) Conjunctiva (b) Nose
(c) External Ear (d) Internal Ear

595. The type of jaundice in which the level of conjugated billirubin increases is
(a) Pre-hepatic (b) Hepatic
(c) Post-hepatic (d) None of the above

596. Rickets is the disease of
(a) Young calves (b) Adult calves
(c) Old cattle (d) All the above

597. Enzootic ataxia in lambs is caused due to the deficiency of
(a) Copper (b) Selenium
(c) Manganese (d) Iron

598. "White velvety deposit" with little damage to oral mucosa is characteristic of
(a) Bacterial stomatitis
(b) Mycotic dermatitis
(c) Both the above
(d) None of the above

599. Pharyngeal paralysis is a typical sign of the disease
(a) Rabies (b) Botulism
(c) Both the above (d) None of the above

600. Blood stained saliva occurs in
(a) FMD (b) BMC
(c) RP (d) Blue tongue

601. Substitution of one type of cells by another type is known as
(a) Hyperplasia (b) Anaplasia
(c) Metaplasia (d) Aplasia

602. Reversion of cells to amore embryonic type and less differentiated is called as
(a) Hyperplasia (b) Neoplasia
(c) Anaplasia (d) Metaplasia

603. Hyperchromania and pleomorphism is a characteristic feature of
(a) Metaplasia (b) Hyperplasia
(c) Anaplasia (d) None

604. Neoplasms whose cells are anaplastic, metastasize are classified as
(a) Benign (b) Malignant
(c) Both (d) None

605. Obstruction of lymphatic by tumor cells disturbs lymphatic flow to facilitate metastasis at unusual site is known as
(a) Skip metastasis
(b) Retrograde metastasis
(c) Both
(d) None

606. Meningeal tumor spreads through
(a) Blood (b) Lymph
(c) Skin (d) CSF

607. Abnormal enzyme ATPase on cell surface promoter leading to chachexia in tumor patient
(a) Proteolysis (b) Glycolysis
(c) Both (d) None

608. Gene responsible for suppression of cell proliferation is known as-
(a) Oncogene (b) Antioncogene
(c) Both (d) None

609. V-onc and C-onc are having
(a) Homology (b) Heterology
(c) Both (d) None

610. Oxygen metabolites of neutrophils respiratory burnt out as
(a) Tumor initiator (b) Tumor promoter
(c) Both (d) None

611. Tumor cells develop certain biochemical alterations on their surface that is known as
(a) Tumor antigens (b) Tumor antibodies
(c) Anaplasia (d) None

612. Tumor necrosis factor is responsible for
(a) Promotion (b) Initiation
(c) Regression (d) None

613. Tumor antigen is
(a) Fetal antigens (b) Alpha fetoproteins
(c) Both (d) None

614. A stage T_2, N_2 & M_2 of tumor is considered with
(a) Good prognosis
(b) Fair prognosis
(c) Guarded prognosis
(d) Poor prognosis

615. A cytokine secreted by tumor cells, responsible for cachexia is known as
(a) Interleukin
(b) Tumor necrosis factor
(c) Cachetin
(d) None

616. In neoplasia, hepatocytes become
(a) Hypertrophied (b) Atrophied
(c) Hyperplastic (d) Hypoplastic

617. Which one is a feature of neoplasm?
(a) Hypocalcemia (b) Hypercalcemia
(c) Preneoplastic (d) None

618. Liposarcoma is which type of tumor of adipose cells
(a) Benign (b) Malignant
(c) Preneoplastic (d) None

619. Tumor of flat bones is known as-
(a) Compad osteoma (b) Spongy osteoma
(c) Both (d) None

620. Leiomyoma is benign tumor of
(a) Cardiac muscles (b) Smooth muscles
(c) Skeletal muscles (d) All of above

621. Mesothelioma is a neoplasm of
(a) Epithelium (b) Endothelium
(c) Mesothelium (d) None

622. Lymphosarcoma is a malignant neoplasm of
(a) Circulating lymphocytes
(b) Tissue lymphocytes
(c) Both
(d) None

623. Leukemia is a malignant neoplasia of
(a) Circulating lymphocytes
(b) Tissue lymphocyte
(c) Both
(d) None

624. Squamous cell carcinoma of which organ is more common
(a) Eyes (b) Lip
(c) Hoof (d) Horn

625. Epithelial pearls is a feature of
(a) Papilloma (b) Adenocarcinoma
(c) Lymphosarcoma (d) None

626. Basal cell carcinoma is also known as
(a) Horn cancer
(b) Eye cancer
(c) Hair cell carcinoma
(d) None

627. Cholangiocellular is a tumor of bile duct caused by-
(a) Aflatoxins
(b) Liver fluke infection
(c) Both
(d) None

628. Adomantinoma is a tumor of
(a) Adipose cells (b) Enamel
(c) Eye (d) Gum

629. Myxoma is a tumor
(a) Adipose tissue (b) Fibrous tissue
(c) Cardiac cells (d) Skeletal cells

630. Process of metastasis includes
(a) Penetration (b) Seperation
(c) Dinemination (d) All of the above

631. Viral agent in milk causing mammary gland carcinoma of mice is
(a) Bittner (b) Gross
(c) Lucke (d) Shope

632. Which of the following are epithelial neoplasms
(a) Papilloma (b) Lipoma
(c) Osteoma (d) Myxoma

633. Which of the following is non-epithelial neoplasma
(a) Lymphoma (b) Melanoma
(c) Adenoma (d) Papilloma

634. Cause of FMD in animals is
(a) DNA virus (b) Rota virus
(c) Picorna virus (d) Corona virus

635. FMD is characterised by presence of

(a) Vesicular lesions (b) Erosive lesions
(c) Ulcerative lesions (d) None

636. Vesicular stomatitis is caused by
(a) Picorna virus (b) Calcivirus
(c) Vesiculo virus (d) None

637. Sore mouth is synonymously used
(a) FMD
(b) Vesicular stomatitis
(c) Vesicular exanthema
(d) All of above

638. RP virus belongs to which group of paramyxo viridae family
(a) Orbi (b) Perti virus
(c) Flavi virus (d) Morbilli virus

639. Infectious canine hepatitis is caused by
(a) Herpes virus (b) Rhabdo virus
(c) Adeno virus (d) Corona virus

640. Rabies is characterised by
(a) Encephalitis (b) Negri bodies
(c) Bubes nodules (d) All of the above

641. In CD, inclusion bodies are
(a) Intracytoplasmic (b) Intranuclear
(c) Both (d) None

642. Blue tongue is caused by
(a) Pesti virus (b) Intranuclear
(c) Both (d) None

643. Blue eye is synonymously with
(a) Rabies (b) ICH
(c) CD (d) All of the above

644. Parvoviral infection in dogs is characterised by
(a) Necrotic enteritis
(b) Myocardial necrosis
(c) Both
(d) None

645. Zebra marking seen in
(a) RP (b) PPR
(c) MCF (d) All of the above

646. Maedi-visna is caused by
(a) Orbi virus (b) Lenti virus
(c) Pesti virus (d) None

647. Pulmonary adenomatosis is characterised by-
(a) Neoplasia (b) Anaplasia
(c) Metaplasia (d) Dysplasia

648. Equine infectious anemia is caused by
(a) Lenti virus (b) Pesti virus
(c) Orbi virus (d) All of above

649. Button ulcers are present in large intestine in
(a) Swine fever (b) Hog cholera
(c) Both (d) None

650. Equine plague is
(a) Equine encephalomyelitis
(b) Equine viral arteritis
(c) African horse sickness
(d) None

651. Equine encephalomyelitis is also known as-
(a) Staggers (b) Borna disease
(c) Forage poisoning (d) All of the above

652. Pseudorabies is also known as
(a) Rabies (b) Mad itch
(c) Mad cow disease (d) None

653. Shaped of Ephemeral fever virus is
(a) Wheel like (b) Bullet like
(c) Pin like (d) None

654. PPR is caused by
(a) Morbillivirus (b) Pestivirus
(c) Rubivirus (d) None

655. Maedi-visna is characterised by
(a) Metaplasia
(b) Gliosis
(c) Intra-cytoplasmic inclusions
(d) All of the above

656. Diarrhoea is manifested in
(a) RP (b) MCF
(c) Mucosal disease (d) All of the above

657. African horse sickness is caused by
(a) Orbi virus (b) Pesti virus
(c) Rota virus (d) None

658. CD is characterised by
(a) Pustular dermatitis
(b) Bronchopneumonia
(c) Hard pad
(d) All of the above

659. Late abortion in cattle are caused by
(a) BHV-I (b) Rota virus
(c) Corona virus (d) Picoma virus

660. PPR is caused by
(a) Morbilli virus (b) Pesti virus
(c) Rubi virus (d) None

661. Camel pox characterised by
(a) Papule (b) Pustule
(c) Vesicles (d) All of the above

662. Rabies is caused by
(a) Lyssa virus (b) Vesiculo virus
(c) Rhabdo virus (d) None

663. Rotavirus infection in calves characterised by
(a) Maldegeneration (b) Malabsorption
(c) Shortening of villi (d) All of the above

664. Presence of tuberculosis in pleura and mesentery are known as
(a) Johne's disease (b) Epithelial pearls
(c) Pearl's disease (d) None

665. In tuberculosis _____ type of giant cells are formed
(a) Langhan's (b) Tuton
(c) Tumor (d) All of the above

666. John's disease is caused by
(a) *Mycobacterium tuberculosis*
(b) *Mycobacterium avium*
(c) *Mycobacterium pseudotuberculosis*
(d) *Mycobacterium paratuberculosis*

667. *Brucella abortus* produces
(a) Granulomatous lésions
(b) Suppurative lésions
(c) Fibrinous lésions
(d) All of above

668. HS is characterised by
(a) Edema on neck (b) Dyspnea
(c) Pneumonia (d) All of the above

669. Braxy is caused by
(a) *Clostridium perfringens*
(b) *Clostridium tetani*
(c) *Clostridium welchi*
(d) *Clostridium septicum*

670. Pulpy kidney disease in sheep caused by
(a) *Clostridium welchi*
(b) *Clostridium perfringens*
(c) *Clostridium tetani*
(d) None

671. Gas gangrene is caused by
(a) *Fusarium sp.*
(b) *Clostridium chauvoei*
(c) *Clostridium welchi*
(d) None

672. Abortion in which months of gestations may occur due to brucellosis
(a) 5-6 (b) 7-9
(c) 3-4 (d) None

673. Painful swelling in thigh muscles with crepitating sound on touch known as
(a) Anthrax (b) HS
(c) Tetanus (d) BQ

674. In camels, enterotoxemia is caused by clostridium perfringens type-
(a) Colibacillosis (b) Pasteurellosis
(c) Black Quarter (d) All of above

675. Marbling in lungs with extensive sero-fibrinous lesions is found in
(a) Colibacillosis (b) Pasteurellosis
(c) Black quarter (d) All of the above

676. Listeriosis is characterised by
(a) Lepto-meningitis (b) Pachy-meningitis
(c) Sero-meningitis (d) None

677. Novel ill is caused by
(a) *Salmonella* (b) *E. Coli*
(c) Pasteurellla (d) None

678. Diamond skin disease also known as-
(a) Swine fever (b) Erysipelas
(c) Pseudorabies (d) CD

679. Lock jaw is feature of
(a) Glanders (b) Anthrax
(c) Actinomycosis (d) Tetanus

680. Empyema is feature of
(a) Glanders (b) Strangles
(c) Babesiosis (d) None

681. In tetanus death occurs due to
(a) Asphyxia (b) Paralysis
(c) Dehydration (d) None

682. Swine erysipelas is characterised by
(a) Haemorrhagic endocarditis
(b) Suppurative endocarditis
(c) Vegetative endocarditis
(d) None

683. In TB giant cells are found which are known as
(a) Foreign body type giant cell
(b) Langhan's type
(c) Both a & b
(d) None of the above

684. Botrymycosis is caused by
(a) Staphylococci (b) Streptococci
(c) Blastomycosis (d) None

685. Actinomycosis is characterised by
(a) Wooden tongue (b) Lumpy jaw
(c) Lock jaw (d) None

686. *Pseudomonas mallei* causes ________in horses
(a) Lymphangitis (b) Lymphadenitis
(c) Farcy (d) All of above

687. Actinobacillosis is characterised by-
(a) Wooden tongue (b) Lumpy jaw
(c) Lock jaw (d) All of above

688. Absence of rigor mortis
(a) Colibacillosis (b) Pasteruellosis
(c) Anthrax (d) None

689. Bovine farcy is also known as
(a) Tuberculosis (b) Johne's disease
(c) Brucellosis (d) Nocardiosis

690. Campylobacteriosis is characterised by
(a) Early abortion
(b) Suppurative metritis
(c) Both
(d) None

691. Tary color blood coming out from natural openings is features of
(a) HS (b) Anthrax
(c) BQ (d) Leptospirosis

692. Necrobacillosis is characterised by
(a) Necrosis of liver (b) Foot rot
(c) Diphtheria (d) All of above

693. Chlamydiosis in cattle is caused by
(a) *Chalmydia psittaci* (b) *Chalmydia abortus*
(c) Both (d) None

694. In calves, chlamydia causes
(a) Poly arthiritis (b) Pneumonia
(c) Diphtheria (d) All

695. Chlamydial infection in sheep is characterised by
(a) Pruritis (b) Myositis
(c) Neuritis (d) Abortion

696. Anaplasmosis is characterised by
(a) Icterus (b) Pneumonia
(c) Enterits (d) All of the above

697. Diagnosis of Anaplasmosis can be done by
(a) Blood smear examination
(b) Serum examination
(c) Lung tissue examination
(d) All of the above

698. Anaplasmosis is caused by
(a) *Anaplasma marginale*
(b) *Anaplasma centrale*
(c) Both
(d) None

699. CBPP is caused by
(a) *Mycoplasma mycoide*
(b) Mycobacterium
(c) Both
(d) None

700. Mycoplasma causes
(a) Mastitis (b) Pneumonia
(c) Abortion (d) All of the above

701. Common round worm of poultry is
(a) *Syngamus trachea* (b) *Ascardia galli*
(c) Both (d) None

702. In poultry, this worm is present under the mucosa of crop and causes emaciation and retardation of growth
(a) *Syngiamus trachea*
(b) *Ascardidai galli*
(c) *Gangylonema ingluvicola*
(d) None

703. Trematods of poultry are
(a) *Prasthoganimus macrorchis*
(b) *Echinostoma revolutum*
(c) Both
(d) None

704. The poultry ticks include
(a) *Argas persicus*
(b) *Aegylianella pullorum*
(c) Both
(d) None

705. The poultry red mite is
(a) *Cylodites nudus* (b) *Dermanysus gallinae*
(c) Both (d) None

706. Caecal coccidiosis is caused by
(a) *Eimeria mivati* (b) *Eimeria necatrix*
(c) *Eimeria mitis* (d) *Eimeria tennella*

707. Coccidia cause which type of enteritis in birds?

(a) Catarrhal (b) Haemorrhagic
(c) Fibrinous (d) None

708. Histomoniasis is also known as
(a) Black head (b) Swollen head
(c) Cyanotic head (d) None

709. Yellow round nodules in oesophagus and crop of pigeons are seen in__________
(a) Histomoniasis (b) Trichomoniasis
(c) Both (d) None

710. Shaped of *Hexamita meleagridis* is
(a) Almond (b) Bean
(c) Pear (d) None

711. Cannibalism is a which type of habit of poultry
(a) Bad (b) Good
(c) Fair (d) None

712. Cannibalism is aggravated by
(a) Overcrowding (b) Prolapse of cloaca
(c) Wounds (d) All of the above

713. Egg eating by birds occurs due to presence of what in poultry house
(a) Broken eggs (b) Feed
(c) Water (d) None

714. Pica occurs as a result due to deficiency of
(a) Calcium (b) Phosphorous
(c) Presence of water (d) None

715. Heat stroke is characterized by
(a) Open beak (b) Paralysis
(c) Both (d) None

716. Toxic fat syndrome is also known as
(a) Chick oedema disease
(b) Water belly
(c) Both
(d) None

717. Gout may occur due to excess of
(a) Protein (b) Fat
(c) Minerals (d) Vitamin B_1

718. Blue comb disease is also known as
(a) Monocytosis (b) Lymphocytosis
(c) Both (d) None

719. Fatty liver and kidney syndrome is characterized by
(a) Pale liver (b) Hydropericardium
(c) Pale kidney (d) All of the above

720. Prolapse of cloaca is seen due to
(a) Aflatoxicosis (b) Ochratoxicosis
(c) Fusariotoxicosis (d) None

721. Metaplasia of esophageal glands in poultry occurs due to deficiency of-
(a) Vit. A (b) Vit D
(c) Vit C (d) All of the above

722. Brooder's pneumonia is also known as
(a) Aspergillosis (b) Candidiasis
(c) Favus (d) Thrush

723. Favus is caused by
(a) *Trichophyton magnini*
(b) *Trichophyton verucosum*
(c) Both
(d) None

724. Candidiasis is characterized by
(a) Turkish towel like crop
(b) Turkish towel like oesophagus
(c) Both
(d) None

725. Histoplasmosis is caused by
(a) *Histoplasma capuilatum*
(b) *Histomonas melecpredis*
(c) Both
(d) None

726. Aflatoxicosis is characterized by
(a) Hepatitis
(b) Immunosuppression
(c) Cancer
(d) All of the above

727. Ochratoxicoris is characterized by
(a) Nephrosis
(b) Visceral gout
(c) Pale brown marrow
(d) All of above

728. Inflammation of crop is known
(a) Ingluvitis (b) Chelitis
(c) Typhlitis (d) Salpingitis

729. Candidiasis is also known as
(a) Favus
(b) Thrush
(c) White comb disease
(d) None

730. Candidiasis is caused by
(a) *Candida albicans* (b) *Monilia albicans*

(c) Both (d) None

731. Inflammation of tongue is known as-
(a) Proctitis (b) Stomatitis
(c) Glossitis (d) Gingivitis

732. Colour of diarrhoea in spirochaetosis is
(a) Reddish (b) Yellowish
(c) Greenish (d) Blackish

733. The spirochaete of fowl are transmitted through
(a) Mite (b) Tick
(c) Lice (d) Fly

734. Fowl spirochaetosis is also known as
(a) Tick fever (b) Tick paralysis
(c) Both (d) None

735. Kind of hemorrhage in proventriculus due to spirachaetosis in birds is
(a) Petechial (b) Ecchymotic
(c) Linear (d) All of above

736. Chronic respiratory disease is caused by
(a) *E. coli*
(b) *Mycoplasma gallisepticum*
(c) Both
(d) None

737. Parturition of a dead foetus on its full development and gestation is called
(a) Abortion (b) Still birth
(c) Premature birth (d) Normal birth

738. Neuritis is found in
(a) Mucosal disease
(b) Infectious bursal disease
(c) Marek's disease
(d) I L T

739. Avian influenza is characterized by oedema of
(a) Head (b) Face
(c) Leg (d) Chest

740. Marek's disease is caused by
(a) Herpes virus (b) Toga virus
(c) Pox virus (d) Lenti virus

741. Cause of summer mastitis is
(a) Staphylococci
(b) *Actinomyces pyogenes*
(c) Streptococci
(d) *Candida spp.*

742. Which is mostly observed in Marek's disease?
(a) Malignant melanoma
(b) Malignant adenoma
(c) Malignant lymphoma
(d) None

743. Avian leucosis is also known as
(a) Big spleen disease (b) Big liver disease
(c) Big head disease (d) None

744. Avian leucosis complex includes
(a) Lymphoid leucosis
(b) Osteoporosis
(c) Myeloblastosis
(d) All of the above

745. Infectious bursal disease is also known as
(a) Gumboro (b) New Castle
(c) Ranikhet (d) None

746. Infectious bursal disease is caused by
(a) Reovirus (b) Picornavirus
(c) Birnavirus (d) Lentivirus

747. In infectious bursal disease, bursa shows
(a) Oedema (b) Hemorrhage
(c) Atrophy (d) All of above

748. In infectious bronchitis plugging of respiratory passage occurs at
(a) Larynx-trachea (b) Trachea-bronchi
(c) Bronchi-lump (d) All of above

749. *Staphylococcus aureus* causes
(a) Gangrenous dermatitis
(b) Pustular dermatitis
(c) Vesicular dermatitis
(d) None

750. In tuberculous birds, Granulomatous nodules are seen in
(a) Liver (b) Spleen
(c) Air sacs (d) All of above

751. In Fowl cholera colour of combs becomes
(a) Red (b) Yellow
(c) Blue (d) Pale

752. Inflammation of caecum is-
(a) Proctitis (b) Gonitis
(c) Chelitis (d) Typhlitis

753. Coligranuloma following one is present in intestines
(a) Nodules (b) Ulcers
(c) Erosions (d) None

754. Salmonellosis is characterized by

(a) Necrosis in liver (b) Marbling in spleen
(c) Oophoritis (d) All of above

755. Highly virulent Ranikhet disease virus is
(a) Lentogenic (b) Mesogenic
(c) Velogenic (d) None

756. Ranikhet disease is also known as
(a) Ornithosis
(b) Degnala disease
(c) New castle disease
(d) All of above

757. Which is moral characteristic lesion seen in Ranikhet disease?
(a) Ulcer at caecal (b) Pneumonia
(c) Diarrhoea (d) None

758. Avian influenza is also known as
(a) Fowl cholera (b) Fowl plague
(c) Both (d) None

759. Presence of follicular cyst in ovary may lead to
(a) Sterlity hump
(b) Nymphmonia
(c) Continuous oestrous
(d) All the above

760. Retention of nucleus in keratin layer of skin is known as
(a) Hyperkeratosis (b) Parakeratosis
(c) Urticaira (d) Keratosis

761. Cause of mastitis is mostly
(a) Trauma
(b) Haematogenous infection
(c) Poisonous
(d) Infection

762. Chronic respiratory disease occurs due to what kind of managemental practices?
(a) Poor (b) Good
(c) Fair (d) Excellent

763. Infectious synovitis is complicated by
(a) *E. coli*
(b) *Pasteurella gallinarum*
(c) Both
(d) None

764. Inflammation of lips is
(a) Chelitis (b) Glossitis
(c) Gingivitis (d) Stomatitis

765. Chlamydiasis in birds is also known as ______
(a) Ornithosis (b) Psittacosis
(c) Both (d) None

766. Inflammation of spermatic cord
(a) Scirrous cord (b) Spermatitis
(c) Arthritis (d) None above

767. Accumulation of oedema fluid
(a) Ascites (b) Anasarca
(c) Peritonitis (d) All of above

768. Dissolution of chromatin is known as-
(a) Chromatolysis (b) Anasarca
(c) Peritonitis (d) All of above

769. Sensitized T cells play role in which of the following-
(a) Generalized anaphylaxis
(b) Acute allergic reaction
(c) Delayed hypersensitivity
(d) Cytotoxic hypersensitivity

770. Surface marker on killer T cells is which of the following
(a) CD_2 (b) CD_3
(c) CD_3 & CD_8 (d) CD_5

771. Basophilic erythrocytic cytoplasm is typically seen in-
(a) Hypochromasia (b) Polychromasia
(c) Hyperchromasia (d) Oligochromasia

772. An elliptical erythrocyte is called-
(a) Spherocyte (b) Leptocyte
(c) Ovalocyte (d) Myelocyte

773. Young erythrocyte that takes up the vital stain with methylene blue is called-
(a) Macrocyte (b) Reticulocyte
(c) Normocyte (d) None of the above

774. Small spherical, cresentric nuclear remnant in young erythrocyte is called-
(a) E.R. bodies
(b) Heinz bodies
(c) Howell Jolly bodies
(d) None of the above

775. Cause of Phimosis is
(a) Balanitis (b) Seminal vesicle
(c) Balenophosthitis (d) Prepuce

776. Most appropriate term for the messenger molecules of the immune system is-
(a) Lyphokine (b) Monokine

(c) Cytokine (d) None of the above

777. Primary response that occur to the first exposure to a specific antigen is characterized by -
(a) Rapid appearance, more potency short duration
(b) Rapid appearance, weak potency short duration
(c) Delay in appearance, weak potency & short duration
(d) Delay in appearance, more potency & longer duration

778. Westergren method is used for the determination of -
(a) Haemoglobin (b) Blood glucose
(c) E.S.R (d) R.B.C. count

779. Thickness of a blood smear depends upon-
(a) Size of the drop
(b) Angle of the spreader
(c) Both of the above
(d) None of the above

780. The normal range of haemoglobin in cattle is-
(a) 10-16 gm/100 ml of blood
(b) 8-15 gm/100 ml of blood
(c) 4-10 gm/100 ml of blood
(d) 10-20 gm/100 ml of blood

781. The agranulocytes include-
(a) Lymphocyte (b) Monocyte
(c) Both above (d) Neutrophil

782. Non-nucleated cell of erythrocytes serices in known as-
(a) Rubricyte (b) Prorubricyte
(c) Rubriblast (d) Reticulocyte

783. More than the normal number of nuclear lobes in neutrophils is called
(a) Aged cell (b) Shift to right
(c) Both above (d) Shift to left

784. Blue-black granules in the cytoplasm of neutrophils are typically seen in
(a) Dohle body (b) Heinz body
(c) Howell jolly body (d) E.R. body

785. Cytokines include which of the following
(a) Autocrine effect (b) Paracrine effect
(c) Endocrine effect (d) All of the above

786. Lupus erythematosis is a complex autoimmune disease of-
(a) Human being (b) Dog
(c) Both above (d) Cattle

787. Funiculitis is the inflammation of
(a) Schirrhous cord (b) Seminal vesicle
(c) Glans penis (d) Prepuce

788. The cells which form the first line of defense against tumor cells & virus infected cells are-
(a) Macrophages (b) B cells
(c) NK cells (d) T- cells

789. Macrocytes are typically seen in which deficiency?
(a) Folic acid (b) B_{12}
(c) Both (d) None

790. Basophilic stippling occurs in response to
(a) Anaemia
(b) Leucopenia
(c) Leukaemia
(d) Intense erythrogenesis

791. Erythrocyte containing precipitated strands of RNA is called-
(a) Basophillia (b) Heinz body
(c) Hyperchromatic (d) E.R. body

792. Injection of antigen in multiple doses at intervals of several weeks/month is based on the phenomenon of -
(a) Primary response of the body
(b) Secondary response of the body
(c) Tertiary response of the body
(d) None of the body

793. Antigenic substance should have molecular weight-
(a) 5000 (b) 7000
(c) 6000 (d) 8000 or high

794. Cell surface marker associated with all T-cells in the circulating blood are-
(a) CD_2 (b) CD_3
(c) CD_2 & CD_3 (d) CD_4

795. What means complete lack of cellular development?
(a) Aplasia (b) Hypoplasia
(c) Hyperplasia (d) Agenesis

796. Arrangement of erythrocytes in a roll of coin is known as-
(a) Shift to left (b) Band cell

(c) Rouleux (d) Ovalocyte

797. Which type of T-cells are more neurons-
(a) Killer cells (b) Helper T cells
(c) Supressor T celles (d) Cytotoxic T celles

798. Prefix 'A' means which of the following
(a) Not equal (b) Excessive
(c) Without (d) All of the above

799. Anticoagulant is-
(a) Sodium hydroxide
(b) Sodium citrate
(c) Sodium tartrate
(d) None of the above

800. Necropsy means-
(a) Post-mortem examination of the animal
(b) Post mortem examination of humans
(c) All of the human
(d) None of the above

801. Which lesion is related to Duck viral hepatitis infection;
A. Enlarged liver with foci up to 1 cm. in diameter.
B. Mottled spleen
C. Swollen kidney
D. All of above

802. Colibacillosis in bind results;
A. Fibrinopurulent airsacculitis
B. Mottled spleen
C. Hemorrhage on thigh
D. None of above

803. Enlarged, friable, mottled liver and spleen along with general darkening of skin is found in;
A. Colibacillosis B. Erysipelas infection
C. Mareks disease D. All of above

804. Hyperemic abdominal vasculature with swollen liver having multiple necrotic foci, are characteristic of;
A. Fowl cholera B. Ascaridia galli
C. Zn deficiency D. None

805. Visceral lymphoid tumors, enlarged feather follicles, enlarge nerves, anaplastic lymphoblastosis are peculiar to;
A. Marek's disease
B. Fowl Cholera
C. New Castle disease
D. None

806. Proventicular hemorrhages, necrotic caecal tonsils, mucoid respiratory exudates with thickened and opaque air sacs are seen in;
A. Ranikhet disease B. Marek's disease
C. Fowl cholera D. Parasitic infection

807. Accumulation of bubbly sero-sanguinous fluid in the subcutis and cooked appearance of musculature in bird at necropsy indicates;
A. Gangrenous dermatitis
B. Necrotic dermatitis
C. None of the above
D. Both of above

808. Zebra stripping haemorrhage in intestine is characteristic of;
A. Rinder pest B. Brucellosis
C. FMD D. None

809. Conjunctivitis, stomatitis, abnormal bleeding, necrosis of lower lips are seen in;
A. Ascaridia galli infection
B. PPR
C. Brucellosis
D. None

810. Edematous swelling of head, neck, brisket and sub serous petechial haemorrhage, bloody pericardial fluid are seen in;
A. FMD
B. Brucellosis
C. Haemorrhagic Septicaemia
D. PPR

811. Blue tongue disease is caused by;
A. Orbivirus B. Flavi virus
C. Orthopvirus D. None

812. Yellow fat disease or seatitis of swine occurs primarily as a result of;
A. Fish diets B. Maize diets
C. Bone meal diets D. All of above

813. Steatilis usually arises as a result of deficiency of;
A. Vit. E B. Vit. C
C. Vit. A D. None

814. Usual colour of wet gangrene is;
A. Black B. White
C. Red D. None

815. Gradual cooling of body after death is called;
A. Rigor mortis B. Livor mortis
C. Algor mortis D. None

816. Gravitational settling of blood to down side of the animal is known as;
A. Algor mortis B. Livor mortis
C. Rigor mortis D. All of the above

817. Which of the following disease has recreational exposure as means of spread to man;
A. Avian influenza B. Brucellosis
C. Rabies D. None

818. Anthrax is a;
A. Bacterial disease
B. Viral Disease
C. Mycoplasma Disease
D. None of the above

819. Which on spreads by ticks;
A. Bartinella B. Anthrax
C. Clostridium D. All of the above

820. Which one is caused by ingestion of undercooked ground beef;
A. Coliform infection
B. Rabies
C. Plague
D. Rat bite fever.

821. Tularemia is caused by;
A. Vibrio B. Mycobacterium
C. Rickettsia D. Francisella

822. Choose the rickettsial disease;
A. Tetanus B. Tularemia
C. Q-fever D. Rat bite fever

823. Typhus is commonly seen in;
A. Rat B. Flying squirrel
C. Bandicoots D. Cattle

824 Which one spreads via ingestion of raw or partially cooked infected fresh water fish:
A. Malaria B. Clonorchis
C. Anthrax D. None of the above

825. Which one is contact zoonosis;
A. Actinomycosis B. Sarcocystosis
C. Malaria D. None of the above

826. Bite of infected Phlebotomus sandflies may spread;
A. Anthrax B. Clonorchis
C. Leishmania D. Echinostomiasis

827. Choose a fungal disease;
A. Typhus B. Nocardiosis
C. Plague D. Glanders

828. African sleeping sickness is spread by bite of infected;
A. Tsetse fly
B. Anopheles mosquito
C. Tick
D. Lice

829. Coenuriasis is caused by;
A. *Taenia multiceps* B. *Bartinella studeri*
C. Fasciola D. Diphyllobothrium

830. Which one is tapeworm of dog;
A. Diphylidium B. Hymenolepis
C. Taenia D. Capillaria

831. African hemorrhagic fever is caused by;
A. Marburg virus B. *Bacillus anthracis*
C. Arena virus D. Junin virus

832. Which one spreads via occupational exposure;
A. Contagious ecthyma
B. Pseudo cowpox
C. Glanders
D. All of these

833. Principal host of Fasciolosis is;
A. Swine B. Dog
C. Water buffalo D. Rat

834. Cattle are the principal host of;
A. Bartinella B. Borrelia
C. Anthrax D. Plague

835. Which one of the following is caused by tapeworm;
A. Bartinellosis B. Metagonimiasis
C. Billharziasis D. Paragonimiasis

836. Ingestion of raw pork may result;
A. Toxoplasmosis B. Trypanosomiasis
C. Babesiosis D. Fasciolosis

837. Feline infectious anemia is caused by
A. Haemobartonella B. Babesia
C. Thieleria D. Amoeba

838. Identify the disease whose incubation period is 1-4 week. Primary clinical signs are intermittent fever, high mortality and anemia in cattle. It is transmitted by tse – tse fly.
A. Milk fever B. Brucellosis
C. Trypanosomiasis D. Fasciolosis

839. *Trypanosoma evansi* causes

A. East coast fever B. Bilharzia
C. Surra D. Dourine

840. Which is not a feature of scrapie in sheep?
A. Incoordination
B. Nibbling reflex
C. Wool nibbling and rubbing on fixed object
D. Prevented by vaccination

841. Scrapie affects
A. Cellular immunity
B. Humoral immunity
C. Both
D. None

842. An ewe with lumpy wool examined and revealed diffuse thick mats and crusts, with areas of erythema. The most likely cause is
A. Lymphadenitis B. FMD
C. Dermatophytosis D. Fleece rot

843. Sheep ked infection is most common is
A. Fall B. Winter
C. Both of above D. Summer

844. Udder impetigo (nodules, pustules and scabs on udder) of a milking goat is most likely caused by
A. Staphylococcus sp.
B. E coli
C. Corynebacterium
D. None

845. Which one greatest disease threat to commercial broilers –
A. Turkeys
B. Imported psittacines
C. Guinea fowl
D. Quail

846. Which virus in not directly associated with respiratory disease –
A. Reovirus B. Adenovirus
C. Coronavirus D. Herpes virus

847. Ranikhet disease virus (NCD) belongs to
A. Paramyxoviridae B. Coronaviridae
C. Birnaviridae D. None

848. Which respiratory disease among following is not caused by a virus
A. Infectious Coryza
B. Laryngotracheitis
C. Fowl Pox
D. Infectious bronchitis

849. Infectious bronchitis viruses differ from one another primarily by
A. Infectivity B. Strains
C. Pathotype D. None

850. Major difference among NCD viruses is
A. Pathogenicity (pathotype)
B. Strains
C. Infectivity
D. Tracheal area

851. Braken fern causes
(a) Haemolytic anemia
(b) Pyurea
(c) Burns
(d) Anurea

852. Typical consolidated lung in turkey with sudden increase in mortality is characteristic of
A. E coli infection B. IBD
C. I B D. Pasteurellosis

853. Gross lesions typically produced by Reovirus involve
A. Musculoskeletal system
B. Alimentory system
C. Both A & B
D. Respiratory and circulatory system

854. Which one is center of humoral system in birds?
A. Cecal tonsils B. Bursa Fabricius
C. Spleen D. None

855. IBD in chicken cause dysfunction of
A. Humoral immunity
B. Cellular immunity
C. Brain
D. Both A & B

856. Duck viral enteritis is another name of
A. Duck plague
B. Bird flu
C. Duck virus hepatitis
D. Black head

857. As Bursa of fabricius to birds, likewise bone marrow to
A. Amoeba B. Mammals
C. Spider D. None

858. Which one is preferred culture medium for *Chlamydia psittaci*

A. McConkey Agar
B. Tryptose
C. Yolk sac inoculation
D. None

859. Infectious disease of peripheral nerve is
A. Pullorum disease B. Epidemic tremor
C. Rickets D. Star grazing

860. Fowl plague is another name of
A. Epidemic tremor B. Avian influenza
C. Fowl typhoid D. None

861. Anemia resulted when there is
A. Copper deficiency B. Iron deficiency
C. Lead poisoning D. *All of above*

862. Which of the following is not one of the cardinal signs of inflammation?
a- Heat b- Redness
c- Pain d- Pus

863. An eosinophilia is suggestive of
a- Parasitic disease
b- Cancer
c- Autoimmune disease
d- Bacterial disease

864. Leptospirosis is chracterized by -
(a) Heamorrhage (b) Nephritis
(c) Icterus (d) All of above

865. Leptospirosis in females causes -
(a) Vaginitis (b) Cervicitis
(c) Abortion (d) All above

866. Which one is a feature of leptospirosis?
(a) Haematuria (b) Myoglobinuira
(c) Haemoglobinuria (d) None

867. Scarpie is caused by
(a) Virus (b) Bacteria
(c) Fungus (d) Prion

868. Cause of chlamydiosis in cattle is
(a) *Chlamydia psittacii* (b) *Chlamydia abortus*
(c) Both (d) None

869. Leptospisosis is transmitted through direct contact with
(a) Faecs (b) Urine
(c) Sweat (d) None of above

870. Which colour of foci is observed in the visceral organs of leptospira?
(a) Whitish (b) Yellowish
(c) Greyish (d) Redtish

871. Demonstration of leptospira becomes easy with urine sample under
(a) Dark field illumination
(b) Ligth field illumination
(c) Electrone microscope
(d) Ordinary microscope

872. Bovine spongi form encephalopathy is disease of
(a) Cattle (b) Buffalo
(c) Goat (d) Sheep

873. Mad cow disease in caused by a
(a) Virus (b) Protozoa
(c) Bacteria (d) Prion

874. Corona virus is the cause of -
(a) Plague (b) PPR
(c) RP (d) None

875. Rinderpest virus belonges to which group of paramxoviridae family.
(a) Orbi virus (b) Flavi virus
(c) Pesti virus (d) Morbilli virus

876. Rabies is characterized by
(a) Encephalitis (b) Negribodies
(c) Hyper salivation (d) All of above

877. Cryptorchidism may led to
(a) Hypolasia of testicles
(b) Aspermatogenesis
(c) Neoplasia of testicles
(d) All of the above

878. Ventral deviation of penis is called
(a) Corkscrew penis (b) Phylocampus
(c) Rainbow penis (d) None

879. Hydrocele is accumulation of serous fluid in
(a) Oviduct (b) Testis
(c) Mammary (d) Tunica vaginalis

880. Diarrhoea is manifested in
(a) Rinderpest (b) MCF
(c) Mucosal disease (d) All of above

881. Parasitic emboli are formed in dogs due to
(a) *Strongylus spp* (b) *Dirofilaria immitis*
(c) *Coccidia spp* (d) *Sarcoptes canis*

882. Metrorrhagia is haemorrhage from
(a) Intestine (b) Stomach
(c) Oviduct (d) Uterus

883. Septic thrombus must have what in it

(a) Virus (b) Parasite
(c) Fungi (d) Bacteria

884. Cloudy swelling is characterized by hazy cytoplasm due to swollen
(a) Endoplasmic (b) Golgi bodies
(c) Mitochondira (d) Nucleus

885. The mucus containing cells in mucous membranes are called
(a) Epithelial cells (b) Pearl cells
(c) Colmnar cells (d) Goblet cells

886. Mucin stains become pink by
(a) MB stain
(b) H & E stain
(c) Hematoxylin stain
(d) Corbol fuction stain

887. Sago spleen is found
(a) Amyloid (b) Mucin
(c) Hyaline (d) Pseudomucin

888. Epithelial pearl is an example of
(a) Amyloid (b) Mucin
(c) Hyaline (d) Cell swelling

889. Amyloid occurs in body as a result of
(a) Immune complexes
(b) Antigen
(c) Antibody
(d) Starch

890. In liquifactive necrosis which cells are present?
(a) Monocytes (b) Lymphocytes
(c) Eosinophils (d) Nueutrophils

891. Chalky white deposits are occur in which type of necrosis
(a) Coagulative (b) Liquifactive
(c) Fat (d) Caseative

892. Gangrene in lungs is an example of which type of gangrene
(a) Dry (b) Moist
(c) Gas (d) All of the above

893. Example of dry gangrene is
(a) Dagnala disease (b) JD
(c) TB (d) None of the above

894. Digestion of cells/tissues by their own enzymes is known as
(a) Necrosis (b) Autolysis
(c) Gangrene (d) Putrefaction

895. Greenish discoloration of tissues after death is also called
(a) Pseudomelanosis (b) Melanosis
(c) Necrosis (d) Imbibitions of bile

896. Algor mortis is the
(a) Stiffening of body (b) Cooling
(c) Hardening (d) Softening

897. Rigor mortis remains in body for
(a) 12 - 15 hrs (b) 20 - 30 hrs
(c) 35 - 48 hrs (d) 5 - 10 hrs

898. Lyses of chromatin material is called
(a) Karyolysis (b) Karyorhexis
(c) Chromatolysis (d) Caseation

899. Dystrophic calcification occurs in animals due to
(a) Tuberculosis (b) Parasitic infection
(c) Necrosis (d) All of the above

900. Melanosis is the brown/black discoloration of tissue/organ as a result of excessive accumulation of melanin due to
(a) Hyperadrenalism
(b) Hyperthyroidism
(c) Hyperparathyroidism
(d) Hypermelanemia

901. Hemosiderin is which colour pigment
(a) Green (b) Red
(c) Golden Yellow (d) Blue

902. Urobilinogen is which form of bilirubin.
(a) Unconjugated
(b) Conjugated and reduced
(c) Conjugated
(d) Conjugated and oxidised

903. Hemolysis may lead to
(a) Prehepatic icterus (b) Posthepatic icterus
(c) Toxic icterus (d) None of the above

904. Indirect Van den Berh reaction is an indication of
(a) Obstructive icterus
(b) Hemolytic icterus
(c) Hepatic jaundice
(d) None of the above

905. Deposition of carbon particles in lungs is called
(a) Silicosis (b) Asbestoses
(c) Anthracosis (d) All of the above

906. Gout is the deposition of what in tissues
(a) Uric acid crystals (b) Oxalate crystals

(c) Hemosiderin (d) Urobilin

907. In poultry, known cause of gout is absence of
(a) Trypsin (b) Lymphnodes
(c) Amylase (d) Uricase

908. First veterinary school established in year
(a) 1762 (b) 1884
(c) 1889 (d) 1773

909. The originator of modern experimental pathology is.
(a) Robert Koch (b) J. Cohnheim
(c) John hunter (d) R. Virchow

910. First veterinarian of the world
(a) Shalihotra (b) Aritotle
(c) Hippocrates (d) Nakul

911. 5th cardinal sign of inflammation lass of function described by
(a) Claudius Galen (b) Cornelius celsus
(c) Renatus vegetius (d) Hippocrates

912. Father of modern pathology.
(a) R. Virchow (b) Muller
(c) Carl Roktan (d) E. Jaest

913. The process of phogocytosis by macrophages first described by
(a) B. Muller (b) E. Metchnicoff
(c) Bittener (d) Bichat

914. Study of tumor is called
(a) Oncology (b) Clinical pathology
(c) Cytopathology (d) Chemical pathology

915. Study of zoonotic disease fall under the branch of pathology.
(a) Nutritional (b) Comparative
(c) Experimental (d) Systemic

916. Humoral pathology is the study of alteration in
(a) Antibodies (b) Fibrin
(c) Urine (d) Feaces

917. General pathology does not include one of the following
(a) Faty change (b) Embolism
(c) Inflammation (d) Digestive system

918. Examination of dead animal is called -
(a) Necropsy (b) Autopsy
(c) Lethopsy (d) Micorscopy

919. Nutritional romp is
(a) Nutritional Pathology
(b) Chemical
(c) Humoral
(d) Postmortem

920. Examination tissue recovered from living animal is known as
(a) Necropsy (b) Biopsy
(c) Postmortem (d) Operation

921. Process of development of a disease process is called
(a) Pathogenesis (b) Pathogenicity
(c) Virulence (d) Disease

922. Estimation of probable severity of disease by a clinician is called
(a) Diagnosis (b) History
(c) Prognosis (d) Etiology

923. Proportion of affected animal out of total population in a particular disease out break is
(a) Mortality rate (b) Morbidity
(c) Case fatality rate (d) None of these

924. Pathological alteration in structure & function that can be detectable is
(a) Lesion (b) Pathogenesis
(c) Symptom (d) Sign

925. Hog Cholera seen in
(a) Pig (b) Dog
(c) Horse (d) Cow

926. *Coxiella burnetti* came under
(a) Mycoplasma (b) Bacteria
(c) Rickettsia (d) Chlamydia

927. Cause of ringworm is
(a) Fungus (b) Virus
(c) Parasite (d) Bacteria

928. Rachischisis is a cleft in
(a) Spinal column (b) Abdomen
(c) Agmathia (d) Lip

929. Harelip is due to fissure in lip and called as -
(a) Palatoschisis (b) Cranioschisis
(c) Cheilioschisis (d) All of the above

930. Fusion of eye in monsters and is called as -
(a) Renarrcuatus (b) Columbia
(c) Polymelia (d) Polydactylia

931. Increased number of limbs in monsters is called -
(a) Polythelia (b) Polymastia
(c) Polymelia (d) Polydactylia

932. Dextrocardia in transposition of heart in
(a) Right thorax (b) Left thorax
(c) Neck (d) Abdomen

933. Tumor origin form embryonic defect and composed of more than two tissues
(a) Dermatoma (b) Hematoma
(c) Papilloma (d) Teratoma

934. A monster having two separate brains with bodies separately arranged at an acute angle.
(a) Cephalothorcopagus
(b) Craniopagus
(c) Dicephalus
(d) Gsonioschisis

935. A monster united at thorax region and with complete development as twin is known as
(a) Procopothora copogus
(b) Dipygus
(c) Thoracopegus
(d) Cephalothoracophegus

936. A monester having thorax and lumber portion of vertibral column united in twin
(a) Rachipagus (b) Cyamiopogus
(c) Thoracopagus (d) Dipagus

937. Cause of cerebral hypoplasia in calves is
(a) Adnovirus
(b) Rotavirus
(c) Bovine viral diarrhoea
(d) Corona virus

938. Increase in size of cells leading to increased size of organ is called
(a) Atrophy (b) Hyperplasia
(c) Hypertrophy (d) Metaplasia

939. Fibrosis may lead to
(a) Atrophy (b) Hyperplasia
(c) Dysplasia (d) Hypertrophy

940. Transformation one type cell to another type
(a) Lypoplasia (b) Dyphasia
(c) Anaplasia (d) Metaplasia

941. Increae in number of cells which increase the size and weight of organ
(a) Hypertrophy (b) Anaplasia
(c) Metaplasia (d) Hyperplasia

942. Environmental pollution may lead to lymphoides as
(a) Atrophy (b) Aplasia
(c) Agenesis (d) Hypoplasia

943. Failure of an organ to develop to its full size is known
(a) Hyperplasia (b) Aplasia
(c) Neoplasia (d) Hypoplasia

944. Petechial haemorrhage are of -size
(a) 1 mm (b) 2 mm
(c) 5 mm (d) 10 mm

945. Parasitic emboli are formed in dogs due to
(a) *Strongylus spp* (b) *Dirofilaria immitis*
(c) *Coccidia spp* (d) *Scrcoptes canis*

946. Uremia is caused by the increased level of
(a) Urea (b) Uric acid
(c) Creatinine (d) All of the above

947. Aflatoxins are produced by
(a) *Aspergillus flavus*
(b) *Aspergillus paramitions*
(c) *Pennicillium puberlum*
(d) All of above

948. Increased permeability of capillaries accumulation in tunica vaginalis
(a) Hydorthorex (b) Hydrocephalus
(c) Hydrocele (d) Anasarca

949. Sludge blood is agglutination of erythrocytes in the vascular system of an animal caused by
(a) Fluctuation in blood flow
(b) Slow rate of blood flow
(c) Both a & b
(d) None

950. Deficiency of phosphorus may lead to hypophosphatemia and characterized by
(a) Pica (b) Rheimatism
(c) Hemoglobinuria (d) All

951. Stunted growth in chicks due to deficiency of
(a) Pyridoxine (b) Pantothenic acid
(c) Folate (d) Biotin

952. Retardation, fibroplasia, scurvey in pigs, haemorrhage, swelling, ulcers and delayed wound healing conditions are due to deficiency
(a) Vitamin C (b) Vitamin D
(c) Vitamin E (d) Vitamin B_1

953. Transmission of biological causes occurs through direct contact or indirect in a animal of fomites

called -
(a) Horizontal transmission
(b) Lateral transmission
(c) A & B
(d) None

954. Hardening and thickening of intimal layer of large arteries ad aorta cause of.
(a) Thrombosis (b) Aplasia
(c) Emboli (d) Arteriosclerosis

955. Which condition is manifested in poultry?
(a) Ranikhet disease
(b) Brisket disease
(c) Endocarditis
(d) Mulberry heart disease

956. Inflammation of vein is
(a) Phlebitis (b) Arteritis
(c) Synovitis (d) None

957. Bread and butter appearance of heart is due to deposition of
(a) Fibrin (b) Neutrophils
(c) Fibroblasts (d) Collagen

958. Aneurysm is dilation of an artery or cardiac chamber leading to formation of sac which is caused by
(a) Aflatoxin (b) Infections emboli
(c) Arterioscleriosis (d) All above

959. Which strain of FMD is most common in India?
(a) O & A (b) O & C
(c) A & Asia 1 (d) O & Asia 1

960. Urethra may become infected by which virus
(a) Picorna (b) Herpes
(c) Birna (d) Adeno

961. Enlargement of sealed off hair follicle or sebaceous gland is called
(a) Acne (b) Folliculitis
(c) Fissure (d) Bled

962. A break in the continuity of epidermis exposing dermis is called
(a) Erosion (b) Fissure
(c) Vesicle (d) Ulcer

963. Hyperkeratosis is the thickening of -
(a) Prickle cell layer (b) Stratum lucidum
(c) Stratum corneum (d) Dermis

964. Superficial loss of epithelium on skin or mucous membrane is called -
(a) Erosion (b) Abrasion
(c) Ulcer (d) Fissure

965. Vesicle formation occurs in skin as a result of
(a) Cloudy swelling
(b) Hydropic degeneration
(c) Glycogen storage
(d) Fatty change

966. Which amino acid form calculi in animal which causes obstruction in urethra?
(a) Argenine (b) Leucine
(c) Cystine (d) None

967. Cause of degnala disease by feeding of -
(a) Wheat bran (b) Rice straw
(c) Wheat straw (d) Paddy

968. Other name of vesicular dermatitis is
(a) Hydropic degeneration
(b) Hydropic deronatitis
(c) Erythema
(d) Hyporkeratosis

969. Folliculitis is inflammation of
(a) Gland (b) Hair follicle
(c) Both (d) None

970. Equine rhabdomyolysis is called morning disease
(a) Sunday (b) Monday
(c) Tuesday (d) Wednesday

971. Accumulation of which one is responsible for hardening of muscle in azoturia.
(a) Lactic acid (b) Myoglobin
(c) Heamoglobin (d) Glycogen

972. White muscle disease is caused by deficiency of
(a) Vit -A (b) Vit -B
(c) Vit - D (d) Vit -E

973. Rickets is caused by deficiency of vitamin -
(a) A (b) D
(c) C (d) E

974. Fibrous osteodystrophy is characterised by -
(a) Lock Jaw condition
(b) Marble bone condition
(c) Bottle jaw condition
(d) None

975. Inflammation of bone marrow and bone is -
(a) Spondylitis (b) Arthritis
(c) Osteomyelitis (d) None

976. Brucella spp. may cause

(a) Osteopetrosis
(b) Spondylitis
(c) Rickets
(d) Pulmonary osteoarthropathy

977. Rheumatoid arthritis is caused by
(a) Ag - Ab complex (b) *E. Coli*
(c) Reovirus (d) *Brucella spp.*

978. Osteopetrosis is also called disease
(a) Brittle bone (b) Marble bone
(c) Both a & b (d) None

979. Lymphangits is inflammation of
(a) Lymph node (b) Lymph gland
(c) Lymph vessels (d) Lymphocytes

980. Phlebitis is the inflammation of
(a) Artery (b) Vein
(c) Lymph vessel (d) Capillary

981. Arteritis is caused by
(a) Equine viral (b) E. Coli
(c) Rota virus (d) Salmonella

982. Atherosclerosis is
(a) Hardening of blood vessels
(b) Softening of blood vessels
(c) Aneyursm of blood vessels
(d) Thinning of blood vessels

983. Arteriolosclerosis affect arterioles in
(a) Kidney (b) Spleen
(c) Pancreas (d) All of above

984. Haemoglobinurea is characterized by
(a) Coffee colour urine
(b) Anaemia
(c) a & b
(d) None

985. Cause of endocarditic is
(a) Actinomyces pyogenase
(b) Erysepelas
(c) Fiborblast/staphylococci
(d) All of above

986. Cause of vegetative growth in heart is
(a) Streptococci (b) Staphylococci
(c) Clostridia (d) Erysipelas

987. Not a cause of acute heart failure
(a) Anoxia
(b) Shock
(c) Cardiac temponade
(d) Fever

988. Left side heart failure is characterized by -
(a) Heart failure (b) Pulse jugular vein
(c) Shock (d) Oedema

989. Pneumoconiasis is characterized by what type of lesion in lungs
(a) Serous (b) Fibrinous
(c) Haemorrhagic (d) Granulamatous

990. Cause of hypersensitivity pneumonitis is
(a) Allergens (b) Parasites
(c) Moldy hay (d) All the above

991. Atelectasis neonatorum is characteristic feature of -
(a) Premature birth (b) Aborted foetus
(c) Still birth (d) None

992. Langarhan's type giant cells are characteristic feature of what type of pneumonia
(a) Tuberculous (b) Verminous
(c) Broncho (d) Pulmonary

993. Verminous pneumonia is caused by
(a) Mycoplasma (b) Clamydia
(c) Dictyocalus sp (d) E. Coli

994. Infection through aerogenous route might causes what type of pneumonia
(a) Lobar (b) Lobular
(c) Hypersensitivity (d) Fibrinous

995. Which are not pathological lesions of pneumonia?
(a) Congestion
(b) Red hepatization
(c) Yellow hepatization
(d) Resolution

996. Presence of caseous plug in bronchi at the point of entrance in lungs is characteristic
(a) Infectious bronchitis
(b) Infectious laryngotracheitis
(c) Air sacculitis
(d) Pleuritis

997. Cause of canine tracheobronchitis is
(a) Adeno virus (b) Influenza virus
(c) Herpes virus (d) All

998. Cause of nasal polyps are
(a) Schistosoma nasalis
(b) Rhinosporidium sceberi

(c) E .Coli
(d) Mycoplasma mycoides

999. Turkish towel like lesion are seen in -
(a) Candidiasis (b) Histomoniasis
(c) Moniliasis (d) Coccidiosis

1000. Erosive stomatitis is seen in case of
(a) Rinder pest (b) Mucosal disease
(c) Hog cholera (d) FMD

1001. In cattle, pyelonephritis is caused by -
(a) E. Coli (b) Proteus
(c) Corynebacterium (d) Actionmcyces

1002. Scurvy is hypovitaminosis of
(a) A (b) B
(c) C (d) D

1003. Ureteritis is the inflammation of
(a) Uterus (b) Uterine gland
(c) Ureter (d) Uterine tube

A. Match the following:

1.	Tumors of melanoblasts	A.	Melanosis
2.	Presence of melanin in abnormal Lacation	B.	Macrophage
3.	Caroid	C.	Thrombus
4.	Blood clot within vessel	D.	Melanomas
5.	Coloboma	A.	Nervous system
6.	Myelitis	B.	Female genital system
7.	Goiter	C.	Eye
8.	Salpingitis	D.	Endocrine system
9.	Myeloma	A.	Lymphocytes
10.	Lymphoma	B.	Adrenal medulla
11.	Polyp	C.	Plasma cells
12.	Pheochromocytoma	D.	Glandular epithelium

Answers

1-D, 2-A, 3-B, 4-C, 5- C, 6- A, 7- D, 8- B, 9- C, 10- A, 11- D, 12- B

B. Match the following:

	Disease		Lesion
1.	Reoviral infection	A.	Pulmonary cream colored plaques
2.	Botulism	B.	Rhinotracheitis
3.	Turkey Coryza	C.	Limberneck
4.	Aspergillosis	D.	Tenosynovitis

Answers

1-D, 2-C, 3-B, 4-A

Write True or False for following statements;

1. Tissue should not be frozen before fixation.
2. Fixed tissues should be protected from freezing.
3. For chemical preservation, denatured alcohol should not be used.
4. Blood urea nitrogen and creatinine are most often used to assess renal function.
5. Creatinine is produced as a waste product of muscle metabolism.
6. Blood creatinine level is used to estimate glomerular filtration rate.
7. Howell – Jolly bodies are tiny ruminants of nuclear chromatins.
8. Heinz bodies are pieces of unoxidized hemoglobin.
9. Bilirubinuria is seen with liver disease or hemolysis
10. Picket fence posts like shaped calcium oxalate crystals are typically seen in urine in ethylene glycol toxicity.
11. Presence of ammonium urate crystals strongly suggests liver disease
12. Blood borne organisms in plasma or WBC are concentrated in the buffy coat.
13. Aegyptionella sp. appears as round signet ring or irregular oval bodies in RBC.
14. Solitary prominent basophilic inclusion bodies are seen in hepatocytic nuclei of inclusion body hepatitis cases.
15. Airsaccullitis is a classic lesion of Colibacillosis.
16. Hyaline droplets are foci of proliferation of endoplasmic reticulum and indicate excess function or toxicity.
17. There is strong association between presence of fibrinoid and acute immunologic ally based reactions.
18. Xanthomatosis results from massive accumulation of lipids in macrophages.
19. Amyloid is best known in animals as a primary cause of uremia
20. Acute anoxia usually causes coagulation necrosis

Answers

Q	1	2	3	4	5	6	7	8	9	10
	True	True	True	True	True	True	True	False	True	True
Q	11	12	13	14	15	16	17	18	19	20
	True	True	True	True	True	True	True	True	True	True

Answers

1.	(d)	2.	(c)	3.	(a)
4.	(a)	5.	(b)	6.	(d)
7.	(d)	8.	(c)	9.	(c)
10.	(d)	11.	(d)	12.	(b)
13.	(c)	14.	(d)	15.	(a)
16.	(a)	17.	(a)	18.	(d)
19.	(c)	20.	(a)	21.	(a)
22.	(a)	23.	(b)	24.	(a)
25.	(a)	26.	(b)	27.	(b)
28.	(a)	29.	(d)	30.	(c)
31.	(b)	32.	(a)	33.	(c)
34.	(a)	35.	(d)	36.	(b)
37.	(c)	38.	(a)	39.	(a)
40.	(b)	41.	(b)	42.	(b)
43.	(a)	44.	(c)	45.	(c)
46.	(c)	47.	(c)	48.	(a)
49.	(a)	50.	(d)	51.	(a)
52.	(b)	53.	(c)	54.	(d)
55.	(a)	56.	(d)	57.	(c)
58.	(b)	59.	(a)	60.	(d)
61.	(d)	62.	(c)	63.	(d)
64.	(c)	65.	(a)	66.	(c)
67.	(b)	68.	(a)	69.	(a)
70.	(b)	71.	(c)	72.	(c)
73.	(b)	74.	(c)	75.	(c)
76.	(d)	77.	(a)	78.	(a)
79.	(c)	80.	(a)	81.	(d)
82.	(d)	83.	(a)	84.	(b)
85.	(c)	86.	(a)	87.	(d)
88.	(b)	89.	(c)	90.	(a)
91.	(b)	92.	(d)	93.	(b)
94.	(a)	95.	(d)	96.	(a)
97.	(c)	98.	(a)	99.	(a)
100.	(b)	101.	(d)	102.	(d)
103.	(b)	104.	(b)	105.	(d)
106.	(a)	107.	(c)	108.	(b)
109.	(b)	110.	(c)	111.	(b)
112.	(a)	113.	(a)	114.	(b)
115.	(c)	116.	(d)	117.	(d)
118.	(d)	119.	(b)	120.	(a)
121.	(a)	122.	(b)	123.	(a)
124.	(b)	125.	(a)	126.	(d)
127.	(d)	128.	(c)	129.	(b)
130.	(c)	131.	(b)	132.	(b)
133.	(c)	134.	(d)	135.	(d)
136.	(a)	137.	(d)	138.	(b)
139.	(b)	140.	(b)	141.	(b)
142.	(c)	143.	(d)	144.	(d)
145.	(d)	146.	(c)	147.	(a)
148.	(a)	149.	(d)	150.	(b)
151.	(b)	152.	(d)	153.	(a)
154.	(b)	155.	(a)	156.	(d)
157.	(d)	158.	(c)	159.	(b)
160.	(b)	161.	(a)	162.	(b)
163.	(a)	164.	(a)	165.	(c)
166.	(b)	167.	(c)	168.	(c)
169.	(c)	170.	(a)	171.	(d)
172.	(d)	173.	(a)	174.	(d)
175.	(a)	176.	(a)	177.	(b)
178.	(c)	179.	(c)	180.	(a)
181.	(b)	182.	(b)	183.	(a)
184.	(b)	185	(e)	186.	(c)
187.	(c)	188.	(d)	189.	(d)
190.	(a)	191.	(c)	192.	(d)
193.	(d)	194.	(d)	195.	(d)
196.	(b)	197.	(a)	198.	(c)
199.	(b)	200.	(a)	201.	(b)
202.	(d)	203.	(a)	204.	(c)
205.	(c)	206.	(b)	207.	(a)
208.	(b)	209.	(b)	210.	(b)
211.	(a)	212.	(a)	213.	(a)
214.	(b)	215.	(a)	216.	(b)
217.	(c)	218.	(c)	219.	(a)
220.	(b)	221.	(b)	222.	(a)
223.	(a)	224.	(c)	225.	(c)
226.	(a)	227.	(c)	228.	(d)
229.	(a)	230.	(c)	231.	(c)
232.	(b)	233.	(d)	234.	(c)
235.	(b)	236.	(a)	237.	(b)
238.	(c)	239.	(b)	240.	(c)
241.	(c)	242.	(b)	243.	(b)
244.	(a)	245.	(a)	246.	(c)
247.	(c)	248.	(c)	249.	(c)
250.	(d)	251.	(c)	252.	(d)
253.	(b)	254.	(d)	255.	(b)
256.	(a)	257.	(b)	258.	(c)
259.	(c)	260.	(b)	261.	(d)
262.	(a)	263.	(c)	264.	(a)
265.	(b)	266.	(c)	267.	(b)
268.	(b)	269.	(d)	270.	(a)
271.	(b)	272.	(d)	273.	(c)
274.	(d)	275.	(b)	276.	(c)

277.	(b)	278.	(a)	279.	(b)
280.	(a)	281.	(c)	282.	(c)
283.	(c)	284.	(d)	285.	(c)
286.	(b)	287.	(c)	288.	(c)
289.	(b)	290.	(c)	291.	(c)
292.	(d)	293.	(b)	294.	(d)
295.	(d)	296.	(d)	297.	(b)
298.	(d)	299.	(b)	300.	(b)
301.	(a)	302.	(d)	303.	(a)
304.	(d)	305.	(b)	306.	(d)
307.	(b)	308.	(d)	309.	(a)
310.	(a)	311.	(c)	312.	(a)
313.	(a)	314.	(b)	315.	(c)
316.	(b)	317.	(c)	318.	(c)
319.	(d)	320.	(a)	321.	(c)
322.	(b)	323.	(c)	324.	(d)
325.	(b)	326.	(b)	327.	(d)
328.	(d)	329.	(a)	330.	(a)
331.	(d)	332.	(b)	333.	(c)
334.	(c)	335.	(b)	336.	(d)
337.	(a)	338.	(a)	339.	(a)
340.	(b)	341.	(b)	342.	(a)
343.	(a)	344.	(c)	345.	(d)
346.	(a)	347.	(b)	348.	(b)
349.	(c)	350.	(b)	351.	(a)
352.	(c)	353.	(c)	354.	(d)
355.	(b)	356.	(d)	357.	(d)
358.	(a)	359.	(d)	360.	(b)
361.	(c)	362.	(d)	363.	(b)
364.	(c)	365.	(d)	366.	(c)
367.	(a)	368.	(d)	369.	(c)
370.	(c)	371.	(a)	372.	(b)
373.	(d)	374.	(b)	375.	(b)
376.	(b)	377.	(b)	378.	(b)
379.	(a)	380.	(d)	381.	(c)
382.	(b)	383.	(c)	384.	(b)
385.	(a)	386.	(d)	387.	(a)
388.	(c)	389.	(c)	390.	(b)
391.	(c)	392.	(a)	393.	(b)
394.	(b)	395.	(c)	396.	(c)
397.	(c)	398.	(b)	399.	(c)
400.	(b)	401.	(b)	402.	(b)
403.	(c)	404.	(c)	405.	(a)
406.	(a)	407.	(a)	408.	(a)
409.	(b)	410.	(b)	411.	(b)
412.	(a)	413.	(c)	414.	(d)

415.	(d)	416.	(b)	417.	(c)
418.	(c)	419.	(b)	420.	(a)
421.	(d)	422.	(a)	423.	(b)
424.	(b)	425	(a)	426	(a)
427.	(a)	428.	(c)	429.	(b)
430.	(a)	431.	(b)	432.	(b)
433.	(a)	434.	(c)	435.	(a)
436.	(b)	437.	(c)	438.	(a)
439.	(d)	440.	(b)	441.	(c)
442.	(b)	443.	(a)	444.	(b)
445.	(b)	446.	(a)	447.	(d)
448.	(b)	449.	(c)	450.	(c)
451.	(b)	452.	(c)	453.	(d)
454.	(d)	455.	(a)	456.	(d)
457.	(b)	458.	(b)	459.	(b)
460.	(d)	461.	(a)	462.	(c)
463.	(a)	464.	(b)	465.	(b)
466.	(a)	467.	(d)	468.	(c)
469.	(a)	470.	(d)	471.	(d)
472.	(a)	473.	(d)	474.	(a)
475.	(b)	476.	(c)	477.	(d)
478.	(d)	479.	(b)	480.	(d)
481.	(a)	482.	(a)	483.	(b)
484.	(c)	485.	(a)	486.	(b)
487.	(a)	488.	(b)	489.	(b)
490.	(a)	491.	(d)	492.	(a)
493.	(d)	494.	(d)	495.	(a)
496.	(d)	497.	(b)	498.	(c)
499.	(b)	500.	(a)	501.	(c)
502.	(d)	503.	(b)	504.	(b)
505.	(d)	506.	(a)	507.	(a)
508.	(c)	509.	(d)	510.	(a)
511.	(a)	512.	(a)	513.	(a)
514.	(d)	515.	(c)	516.	(a)
517.	(c)	518.	(b)	519.	(d)
520.	(b)	521.	(b)	522.	(c)
523.	(c)	524.	(d)	525.	(a)
526.	(d)	527.	(d)	528.	(b)
529.	(b)	530.	(a)	531.	(b)
532.	(a)	533.	(d)	534.	(c)
535.	(c)	536.	(c)	537.	(b)
538.	(d)	539.	(b)	540.	(d)
541.	(a)	542.	(b)	543.	(d)
544.	(d)	545.	(b)	546.	(b)
547.	(b)	548.	(b)	549.	(b)
550.	(d)	551.	(c)	552.	(a)

553. (d) 554. (c) 555. (a)
556. (b) 557. (d) 558. (b)
559. (b) 560. (d) 561. (c)
562. (a) 563. (b) 564. (b)
565. (b) 566. (b) 567. (d)
568. (a) 569. (a) 570. (c)
571. (c) 572. (c) 573. (a)
574. (d) 575. (c) 576. (a)
577. (c) 578. (a) 579. (b)
580. (a) 581. (b) 582. (b)
583. (c) 584. (a) 585. (d)
586. (b) 587. (d) 588. (b)
589. (d) 590. (b) 591. (a)
592. (d) 593. (c) 594. (a)
595. (c) 596. (a) 597. (a)
598. (b) 599. (c) 600. (a)
601. (c) 602. (c) 603. (c)
604. (b) 605. (b) 606. (d)
607. (b) 608. (b) 609. (a)
610. (b) 611. (a) 612. (c)
613. (c) 614. (d) 615. (c)
616. (b) 617. (b) 618. (b)
619. (a) 620. (b) 621. (c)
622. (b) 623. (a) 624. (b)
625. (a) 626. (c) 627. (d)
628. (b) 629. (b) 630. (a)
631. (a) 632. (a) 633. (a)
634. (c) 635. (a) 636. (c)
637. (b) 638. (d) 639. (c)
640. (d) 641. (c) 642. (a)
643. (b) 644. (d) 645. (d)
646. (b) 647. (c) 648. (a)
649. (a) 650. (c) 651. (d)
652. (b) 653. (b) 654. (a)
655. (d) 656. (d) 657. (a)
658. (d) 659. (a) 660. (a)
661. (d) 662. (a) 663. (d)
664. (c) 665. (a) 666. (d)
667. (a) 668. (d) 669. (d)
670. (b) 671. (b) 672. (b)
673. (d) 674. (d) 675. (a)
676. (b) 677. (b) 678. (b)
679. (d) 680. (a) 681. (a)
682. (c) 683. (c) 684. (a)
685. (b) 686. (d) 687. (a)
688. (c) 689. (d) 690. (c)

691. (b) 692. (d) 693. (a)
694. (d) 695. (a) 696. (a)
697. (a) 698. (c) 699. (a)
700. (d) 701. (b) 702. (c)
703. (c) 704. (c) 705. (b)
706. (d) 707. (b) 708. (a)
709. (c) 710. (a) 711. (a)
712. (d) 713. (a) 714. (b)
715. (c) 716. (c) 717. (a)
718. (a) 719. (d) 720. (c)
721. (a) 722. (a) 723. (a)
724. (c) 725. (a) 726. (d)
727. (d) 728. (a) 729. (b)
730. (c) 731. (c) 732. (c)
733. (b) 734. (c) 735. (c)
736. (c) 737. (b) 738. (c)
739. (b) 740. (a) 741. (b)
742. (c) 743. (b) 744. (d)
745. (a) 746. (c) 747. (d)
748. (b) 749. (a) 750. (d)
751. (c) 752. (d) 753. (a)
754. (d) 755. (c) 756. (c)
757. (a) 758. (b) 759. (d)
760 (b) 761. (d) 762. (a)
763. (b) 764. (a) 765. (c)
766. (a) 767. (a) 768. (a)
769. (c) 770. (c) 771. (b)
772. (c) 773. (b) 774. (c)
775. (c) 776. (c) 777. (c)
778. (c) 779. (c) 780. (a)
781. (c) 782. (d) 783. (c)
784. (a) 785. (d) 786. (c)
787. (a) 788. (c) 789. (c)
790. (d) 791. (a) 792. (b)
793. (d) 794. (a) 795. (a)
796. (c) 797. (b) 798. (c)
799. (b) 800. (a) 801. (d)
802. (a) 803. (b) 804. (a)
805. (a) 806. (a) 807. (d)
808. (a) 809. (b) 810. (c)
811. (a) 812. (a) 813. (a)
814. (a) 815. (c) 816. (B)
817. (d) 818. (a) 819. (a)
820. (a) 821. (d) 822. (c)
823. (b) 824. (b) 825. (a)
826. (c) 827. (b) 828. (a)

829. (a) 830. (a) 831. (a)
832. (d) 833. (c) 834. (c)
835. (a) 836. (a) 837. (a)
838. (c) 839. (c) 840. (d)
841. (d) 842. (c) 843. (c)
844. (a) 845. (b) 846. (a)
847. (a) 848. (a) 849. (b)
850. (a) 851 (a) 852. (d)
853. (c) 854. (b) 855. (a)
856. (a) 857. (b) 858. (c)
859. (b) 860. (b) 861. (d)
862. (d) 863. (a) 864. (d)
865. (d) 866. (c) 867. (d)
868. (c) 869. (b) 870. (b)
871. (a) 872. (a) 873. (d)
874. (d) 875. (d) 876. (d)
877. (d) 878. (c) 879. (d)
880. (d) 881. (b) 882. (d)
883. (d) 884. (d) 885. (d)
886. (c) 887. (a) 888. (c)
889. (a) 890. (d) 891. (d)
892. (c) 893. (a) 894. (b)
895. (a) 896. (b) 897. (b)
898. (c) 899. (d) 900. (d)
901. (c) 902. (b) 903. (a)
904. (b) 905. (c) 906. (a)
907. (d) 908. (a) 909. (b)
910. (d) 911. (a) 912. (a)
913. (b) 914. (a) 915. (b)
916. (a) 917. (d) 918. (a)

919. (a) 920. (b) 921. (a)
922. (c) 923. (b) 924. (a)
925. (a) 926. (c) 927. (a)
928. (a) 929. (c) 930. (b)
931. (c) 932. (a) 933. (d)
934. (b) 935. (d) 936. (a)
937. (c) 938. (c) 939. (d)
940. (d) 941. (d) 942. (b)
943. (d) 944. (a) 945. (b)
946. (a) 947. (a) 948. (c)
949. (c) 950. (d) 951. (b)
952. (a) 953. (c) 954. (d)
955. (a) 956. (a) 957. (a)
958. (d) 959. (a) 960. (b)
961. (a) 962. (d) 963. (c)
964. (b) 965. (b) 966. (c)
967. (b) 968. (a) 969. (b)
970. (b) 971. (a) 972. (d)
973. (b) 974. (b) 975. (c)
976. (b) 977. (a) 978. (c)
979. (c) 980. (b) 981. (a)
982. (a) 983. (d) 984. (c)
985. (b) 986. (d) 987. (d)
988. (b) 989. (d) 990. (d)
991. (c) 992. (a) 993. (c)
994. (b) 995. (c) 996. (a)
997. (a) 998. (a) 999. (a)
1000. (d) 1001. (c) 1002. (c)
1003. (c)

9 Veterinary Public Health

Salient Features

1. Veterinary Public Health is an interdisciplinary branch dealing with study of animal diseases, important for human health.
2. Zoonoses are diseases transmissible from animal to human and vice – versa.
3. Rabies is a direct zoonoses.
4. Taeniasis belongs to cyclozoonoses group.
5. Japanese encephalitis is a metazoonotic disease.
6. Metazoonotic diseases require both vertebrate and invertebrate species for cycle maintenance.
7. Histomoniasis is an excellent example of saprozoonoses.
8. Brucellosis, Anthrax, Tuberculosis Leptospirosis are important occupational diseases.
9. Kysannur forest disease is a viral (RNA) disease spread by bite of tick Haemophysalis spinigera. Transovarian transmission is also seen.
10. Hydatidosis is a non – obligatory cyclozoonoses.
11. Rota viral infection is a direct anthropozoonoses, zooanthroponoses.
12. All India Institute of Hygiene and Public Health is situated at Calcutta.
13. Trichinellosis spreads by ingestion of undreprocessed contaminated pork.
14. Fascioliasis is an excellent example of type III saprozoonoses, as it propagates and develops in inanimate object.

Questions

1. In India the milk market Industry started in the year;
   (a) 1950 - 51 (b) 1945 - 46
   (c) 1952 - 53 (d) 1980
2. Pasteurization and bottling of milk on a large scale for organized distribution was started at;
   (a) Aarey (b) Pune
   (c) Allhabad (d) Lucknow
3. Daily per capita milk consumption in India during the year 1975 was;
   (a) 120 gm (b) 226 gm.
   (c) 114 gm. (d) 138 gm.
4. Milk production in India during 1951 - 52 was;
   (a) 17.5 million (b) 20.0 million
   (c) 10.5 million (d) 34.09 million
5. PFA (Prevention of Food Adulteration) Act was enacted in the year;
   (a) 1951 (b) 1955
   (c) 1985 (d) 1976
6. On an average buffalo milk contain — % milk fat;
   (a) 6 % (b) 3.5%
   (c) 9% (d) 8.5%
7. Factors affecting composition of milk;
   (a) Species
   (b) Breed
   (c) Interval of milking
   (d) All of above
8. Milk fat gives energy;
   (a) 4.1 c/gm (b) 3.1 c/gm
   (c) 9.3 c/gm (d) None of above

9. Milk Protein gives energy equal to;
(a) 4.1 c/gm (b) 3.1 c/gm
(c) 9.3 c/gm (d) All of above

10. On an average the energy value of cow milk is;
(a) 41 c/gm (b) 75 c/gm
(c) 100 c/gm (d) None of above

11. On an average buffalo milk furnishes;
(a) 41 c/100 gm (b) 75 c/ 100 gm
(c) 100 c/ 100 gm (d) None of above

12. Milk is an excellent source of;
(a) Calcium
(b) Iron
(c) Both a & b
(d) None of them (a & b)

13. Milk is an excellent source of;
(a) Calcium (b) Phosphorus
(c) Vit. D (d) All of above

14. Milk is deficient in;
(a) Iron (b) Copper
(c) Vit C (d) All of above

15. In the process of Pasteurization loss of thiamine is about;
(a) 20% (b) 10%
(c) 0% (d) 100%

16. Expected losses of ascorbic acid during pasteurization is;
(a) 20% (b) 10%
(c) 100% (d) Not affected

17. Expected losses of Thiamine and ascorbic acid during sterilization are respectively;
(a) 30 - 50% (b) 100%
(c) 75% (d) Not affected

18. pH of normal, fresh cow milk usually varies from;
(a) 6.4 - 6.6 (b) 9.0 - 95
(c) 5.2 - 5.5 (d) 6.9 - 7.2

19. Main protein of milk is;
(a) Casein (b) Albumin
(c) A- lactalbumin (d) B – lactogubulins

20. The T.A. (titrable acidity) of cow milk varies from;
(a) 0.13 -0.14 (b) 0.17 - 0.2
(c) 0.14 - 0.15 (d) 0.13 - 0.2

21. pH of fresh, normal buffalo milk varies from;
(a) 6.4 - 6.6 (b) 6.7 - 6.8
(c) 6.1 - 6.2 (d) 7.9 - 8.0

22. The pasteurized milk (at the plant, in its final container) should have a spc/ml (org) not exceeding;
(a) 20,000 (b) 30000
(c) 15000 (d) 50,000

23. Addition of water to milk results lactometer reading;
(a) Increase (b) decrease
(c) Not affected (d) None of above

24. Formulation of standard of pasteurization consideration as taken;
(a) Bacterial distention
(b) Cream line reduction
(c) Phosphates inactivation
(d) All of above

25. Test is used to detect inadequate pasteurization;
(a) Catalase test (b) Whiteside test
(c) Phosphatase test (d) Chloride test

26. In the bottle pasteurization sealed bottles are held at 63 - 65^{0}c for;
(a) 15 min (b) 15 sec
(c) 30 min (d) 30 sec.

27. Low Temperature Long Time (LTLT) pasteurization is of;
(a) Water jacket type (b) Water spray type
(c) Cell - vet type (d) All of above

28. High Temperature Short Time (HTST) pasteurization was first developed by A.P.V. Co in United Kingdom in;
(a) 1970 (b) 1972
(c) 1980 (d) 1982

29. In HTST milk is heated to;
(a) 72^{0}c for 15 min (b) 72^{0}c for 15 sec
(c) 72^{0}c for 30 min (d) 72^{0}c for 30 sec

30. Raising or lowering of the fat and /or Solid Not Fat% is termed as;
(a) Standardization (b) Homogenization
(c) Pasteurizations (d) Sterilization

31. Direct microscopic count per ml (DMC) of good quality milk should not exceed from;
(a) Less than 50,000
(b) Less that 500000
(c) 5, 00, 000 to 20,00,000

(d) 100 – 500

32. SPC (Standard Plate Count)/ ml of good quality milk vary between;
(a) 2,00,000 (b) 200 - 10,000
(c) 100 - 500 (d) None of above

33. Sanitary analysis of milk can be done by;
(a) MBRT (b) Resasuin test
(c) Both of above (d) None of above

34. If the time taken for reduction of Methylene blue is 5 hour or above then the quality of milk is suggested.
(a) Very good (b) Good
(c) Fair (d) Poor

35. Plate form test for determination of milk quality is;
(a) Determination of pH
(b) Determination of T.A.
(c) Clot on boiling test
(d) All of above

36. If the milk is taken from cow having mastitis the pH of milk becomes;
(a) Alkaline (b) Acidic
(c) Neutral (d) Highly Acidic

37. In mastitis milk contain;
(a) More chloride content
(b) Less chloride contend
(c) Not contain chloride contain
(d) Very less chloride written

38. Milk sample contains abnormally high % of chloride, the red colour change into;
(a) Yellow (b) Dark red
(c) Voilet (d) Bleak

39. Hotis test gives the most acurate information about mastitis infection caused by;
(a) Saphylococcus
(b) *Streptococcus agalactiae*
(c) Both of above
(d) None of above.

40. In hotis test, indicator is used
(a) Bromocresol blue (b) Bromocresol purple
(c) Neutal red s (d) Phenol

41. In white side test ________ is used;
(a) NaOH (b) KOH
(c) Cr_2O_7 (d) None of above

42. California mastitis test contains;
(a) Silver Nitrate (b) Alkyl aryl sulfonote
(c) Both of above (d) None of above

43. California Mastitis Test (CMT) distermines the number of —— present in milk;
(a) RBC (b) WBC
(c) Both of above (d) None of above

44. In synthetic milk, being adding content are;
(a) Refined oil (b) Detergent
(c) Urea (d) All of above

45. For examination of milk for presence of Brucalla organism test is used;
(a) MBRT (b) Catalogue above
(c) STAT (d) All of above

46. In Milk Ring Test Antigen is stained with;
(a) Gimsa (b) Crystal voilet
(c) Haematoxylin (d) None of above

47. Handling water requirement for each liter of milk is;
(a) 2 lit (b) 5 lit
(c) 3 lit (d) 1 lit

48. According to histological development which is the earliest method of pasteurization;
(a) Batch hoder (b) Continuous holding
(c) Flash process (d) HTST

49. In HTST temperature is;
(a) 71 - 72^{0}C (b) 70 - 75^{0}C
(c) 74 - 75^{0}C (d) None of above

50. Milk is excellent source of;
(a) Thiamine (b) Riboflavin
(c) Vit C (d) Vit E

51. T.A. of buffalo milk generally varies;
(a) 0.14 - 0.15% (b) 0.17 - 0.2%
(c) 0.13 - 0.14% (d) None of above

52 Real acidity of natural fresh milk is due to;
(a) Lactic acid (b) Ascorbic acid
(c) Both of above (d) None of above

53. Water present in the milk in form of;
(a) Colloidal phase
(b) Neutal phase
(c) Contineous phases
(d) None of above

54. Average freezing point depression of cow milk is;
(a) 0.457^{0}C (b) 0.547^{0}C

(c) 0.512°C (d) None of above

55. Souring of milk is due to;
(a) Lactose (b) Voletile fatty acid
(c) Both of above (d) None of above

56. For formation of dahi the organism used is;
(a) *Strepto coccus lactis*
(b) *Streptococcus agalactiae*
(c) *Stephylacoccus thermophilus*
(d) None of above

57. Red colour of milk is due to;
(a) *Serratia marcescens*
(b) *Pseudomonas synxantha*
(c) Coli form
(d) All of above

58. Factor affecting homogenization is;
(a) Temperature
(b) Pressure of homogenization
(c) Both of above
(d) None of above

59. Boiling point of milk is;
(a) Less than boiling point of water
(b) Slightly higher than H_2O
(c) Both of above
(d) None of above

60. Saponification number of milk;
(a) 120 - 130 (b) 223 - 230
(c) 110 - 120 (d) 121 – 129

61. In polenske no. 0.1N alkali salution is used to neutralize;
(a) Voletile fatty acid
(b) Non volatile fatty acid
(c) Both of above
(d) None of above

62. In R.M. value 0.1N alkali solution is used to Neutraize;
(a) Voletile fatty acid
(b) Non volatile fatty acid
(c) Both of above
(d) None of above

63. Spray dried milk was started by;
(a) Amvi (b) AMUL
(c) Coxhlet's (d) None

64. Rancid flavour of milk is due to;
(a) Butyric acid (b) Latic acid
(c) Vit C (d) All of above

65. Spray died milk was started
(a) 1952 (b) 1960
(c) 1955 (d) 1986

66. Efficieny of homogenization is judged;
(a) Feral Indix
(b) Fat rise
(c) BY appearance of product
(d) All of above

67. Phosphatage inactivated at temperature;
(a) 61.1° c for 30 min.
(b) 65.1° c for 30 min.
(c) both of above
(d) All of above

68. Creem line reduction at temperature;
(a) 62.2°C for 30 min (b) 65.1°C for 30 min
(c) 60.1°C for 30 min (d) None of above

69. In milk main sugar is;
(a) Glucose (b) Lactose
(c) Fructose (d) All of above

70. Souring results;
(a) Lowering of freezing point
(b) Raising of freezing point
(c) Not affect F P
(d) very rise F P

71. Colour of whey is;
(a) Yellow (b) Blue
(c) Greewizh yellow (d) None of above

72. Ca insensitive protein is;
(a) K - casein (b) a cosein
(c) b casein (d) All of above

73. Fat globule memberane is formed by;
(a) Calcium casinate (b) Lacithin
(c) Cephalin (d) Spingomyelin

74. Fat soluble pigment is;
(a) Carotene (b) Xanthene
(c) Riboflavin (d) Both of a and b

75. Water soluble pigment is;
(a) Carotene (b) Xanthene
(c) Riboflavin (d) None of above

76. On pasteurization temperature antibiotics are not inactivated;
(a) Chlortetracycline (b) Oxytetracycline
(c) Streptomycin (d) all of above

77. Phosphatage test positive giving antibiotics are;
(a) Penicillin (b) Oxyteracyclin
(c) Both of above (d) None of above

78. Mastitis origenated from;
(a) Greek word (b) Latin word
(c) Both of above (d) None of above

79. Greates production loss in matitis is due to;
(a) *Streptococcus agalactia*
(b) *Streptococcus aureus*
(c) Nocardia
(d) All of above

80. Which vitamin deficiency contributing factor in mastitis
(a) Vit. B- complex (b) Vit A.
(c) Vit. D (d) All of above

81. Which organism in mastitis has higher infection rate and resistant to treatment.
(a) *Streptococcus agalactia*
(b) *Straphylococcus aureus*
(c) Nocardia
(d) Salmonella

82. Pathogen of normal flora of teat skin;
(a) *Stephylococcus warmin*
(b) *Stephylococcus simulus*
(c) *Stephylococcus epidermis*
(d) All of above

83. Mastitis is;
(a) Contagious disease
(b) Metabolic disease
(c) Infectious disease
(d) All of above

84. Biological value of protein does not decrease in;
(a) HTST (b) STHT
(c) Both (d) None

85. Inativation of lysine in long storage is due to;
(a) Maillard's reaction
(b) Niglar reaction
(c) Souring
(d) None of above

86. Sterilization does not require;
(a) Referegerated storage
(b) Ambient temperature
(c) Both
(d) None

87. Natually present inhibitory substance in milk is;
(a) Bifidus factor (b) Lactoferin
(c) Lysozymes (d) All of above

88. Peticides in milk are considered as antibiotic residue.
(a) Fat soluble (b) Water soluble
(c) Both (d) None

89. In IVRI Public Health division was established in;
(a) 1971 (b) 1876
(c) 1955 (d) None of above

90. Minimum daily need of milk per capita according to ICMR is;
(a) 226 gm (b) 280 gm
(c) 250 gm (d) 180 gm

91. Hygeine control of dairy equipments is necessary;
(a) To produce safe milk
(b) To incresse keeping quality
(c) Bacteriological standard
(d) All of above

92. Flash process of pasteuirization at;
(a) 75°C - 80°C (b) 71 - 72°C
(c) 80 - 100°C (d) 160 - 180°C

93. On boiling vit B_{12} is losses;
(a) 10% (b) 20%
(c) 80% (d) 100%

94. Coli form organisms are killed at;
(a) At pasteurization temperature
(b) At below pasteurizations
(c) At sterilization temperature
(d) All of above

95. On boiling of milk vit. C losses upto;
(a) 30% (b) 50%
(c) 100% (d) Not affected

96. For determination of time for which milk is exposed in holding unit test is used;
(a) Salt conductivity test
(b) Phosphatase inactivation test
(c) MBRT
(d) Resazurin test

97. The White Side Test what is determines;
(a) Milk fat (b) Leucocytes
(c) Both of above (d) None of above

98. The CMT determines;

(a) Milk fat (b) Leucocytes
(c) Both (d) None

99. In CMT milk is determined for mastitis;
(a) Alkaline milk (b) Acidic for mastitis
(c) Both (d) None

100. Which test is used for mastitis diagnosis;
(a) Catalase test (b) Coagula tion test
(c) Milk ring test (d) None of above

101. The word Hygiene has been derived from the Greak word;
(a) Hygiea (b) Hygieniea
(c) HYgieounea (d) None of the above

102. The diseases and infections which are transmitted between vertebrate animal and man are studied under zoonoses;
(a) Artificially (b) Naturally
(c) Any of the above (d) Both of the above

103. The Kaira District Milk Producers Union came in to existence in the year;
(a) 19 Dec 1946 (b) 15 Aug 1947
(c) 2 Oct 1947 (d) 26 Jan 1950

104. First Chairman of Khaira District Milk Producers Union was;
(a) Triubhuvan Das Patel
(b) Vergieus konrian
(c) Mani Bhai Bhem Bhai Besai
(d) Charls

105. Operation Flood was started in the year;
(a) 1996 (b) 1968
(c) 1947 (d) 1970

106. Operation Flood completed in the year;
(a) 1997 (b) 2002
(c) 1996 (d) 1970

107. India is having —— position in milk production in world;
(a) First (b) Second
(c) Third (d) None of above

108. The temperature in HTST is;
(a) 71 - 72^{0}C for 15 sec.
(b) 63.5^{0}C for 1 sec
(c) 62.5^{0}C for 90 min
(d) None of the above

109. Spore farming Bacteria is;
(a) *Bacillus stenottermophilus*
(b) *B. kaustophlus*
(c) *B. themaigufacinens*
(d) All of the above

110. Mastitis word is derived from word maston meaning breast which is a;
(a) Greek word (b) Latin word
(c) English word (d) Intalian word

111. Milk Borne intoxication is caused by;
(a) *Bacullus cereus* (b) Protozoa
(c) *E. coli* (d) both a & b

112. Milk borne toxi – infection is one caused by;
(a) *Clostridium butulinum*
(b) *Bacillus cerus*
(c) Fetergen
(d) None of the above

113. An increase of 5^{0}F or 3^{0}C in the pasteurization temperature is recommended for killing the organism;
(a) FMD virus (b) T.B Bacteria
(c) a + b both (d) *Coxiella burnette*

114. Anthrx is also known as;
(a) Charbon (b) Malignant burnette
(c) Milzbrand (d) All of the above

115. Which form is not found in case of Anthrax;
(a) Cutaneous (b) Pulmonary
(c) Intestinal (d) Nervous form

116. Medusa head like colonies are useful in diagnosis of which disease;
(a) T.B (b) Viral encephalitis
(c) Splenic lever (d) None of the above

117. Which test is used to diagnose Anthrax;
(a) Ascolis ppt test (b) String of pearl
(c) Both of the above (d) None of the above

118. Post Mortum is not advisable in which of the following diseases;
(a) Milz brand (b) B.Q.
(c) H.S. (d) Rabies

119. Which vaccine is used in anthrax;
(a) Sterne vaccine
(b) Wright vaccine
(c) Alum treated vaccine
(d) All of the above

120. Brucellosis is also known as;
(a) Undulating fever (b) Malta fever

(c) Bang's disease (d) All of the above

121. The most virulent Brucella is;
(a) *B. abortus* (b) *B. melitansis*
(c) B. neonatae (d) B. seuis

122. Brucella is;
(a) Gram +ive bacilli
(b) Gram -ive bacilli
(c) Gram -ive coccobacilli
(d) None of the above

123. In Brucella milk borne zoonoses;
(a) Cream is more heavely
(b) Milk is more infected than cream
(c) Both are equally infected
(d) None of the above

124. Brucella organism is;
(a) Non motile (b) Non capsulated
(c) Non spore former (d) All of the above

125. Herd screening test is also called as;
(a) Milk ring test (b) RBPT
(c) CFT (d) None of the above

126. Oral vaccine for Brucella is prepared by;
(a) *B. suisi* (b) B. aburtus 45/20
(c) B. abortus S -19 (d) None of above

127. Shigatoxin are produced by;
(a) Bacteria (b) Virus
(c) Fungi (d) Ricktessia

128. Rice water stool is found in case of;
(a) Cholera (b) *E. coli*
(c) Botulism (d) Caudria

129. All clostridia are motile except;
(a) *Clostridum botulimum*
(b) *C. perfirgens*
(c) Both of the above
(d) None of the above

130. Lethal dose of *Clostridium botulinum* in man is;
(a) 1 mg (b) < 1 mg
(c) > 1 mg (d) 10 mg

131. Leptospirosis is also called as;
(a) Cane cutter disease
(b) Mud fever
(c) Eucel's disease
(d) All of the above

132. Silver staining is used to diagnose;
(a) Listeria organism
(b) Leptosipra organism
(c) Pasteurella organism
(d) All of the above

133. Shipping fever is other name of;
(a) H.S (b) B.Q
(c) Typhiod (d) T.B

134. Bipolar staining is used to diagnose;
(a) H.S
(b) B.Q.
(c) F.M.D.
(d) Tick borne encepnalitis

135. Silage is an important source for the disease;
(a) Diptheria (b) Listeriosis
(c) Leptospirosis (d) H.S

136. Tumbling motility is found in;
(a) Lepltospira (b) *Coxiella burnetti*
(c) Listeriosis (d) None of the above

137. Rat bite fever is caused by;
(a) *Streptobacillus moniliformis*
(b) *Listeria monocitogenies*
(c) *Corynebacterium deptheriae*
(d) None of the above

138. Aflatoxicosis is cased by;
(a) *Aspergillus flavus* (b) *A. parasiticus*
(c) Both of the above (d) None of the abve

139. Most virulent Aflatoxin is;
(a) B_1 (b) M_1
(c) G_1 (d) B_2

140. Kangawa Phenomenon is related with organism;
(a) Yersinia
(b) Streptococcus
(c) *Vibrio parhaemolyticus*
(d) None of the above

141. Yersiniosis is caused by;
(a) *Yersinia enterocolitica*
(b) *Y. pseudotuberculosis*
(c) Both of the above
(d) None of the above

142. There are about _____ proteins in milk causing allergy;
(a) 30 (b) 1000
(c) 500 (d) 10

143. Reduction of the number of spores to 1/10 of the concentration is called as;
(a) Reduction time

(b) Sterlization time
(c) Pasteurization time
(d) Decimal reduction

144. No. of decimal reduction that heat treatment is able to effect is called as;
(a) Reduction time (b) sternation time
(c) Sterlization effect (d) Decimal reduction

145. In sterlized milk which vitamin is competely lossed;
(a) Vit. C (b) Thiamine
(c) Vit. B_{12} (d) B_6

146. In sterlized milk which vitamin has no effect of sterlization;
(a) Vit. A (b) Riboflavin
(c) Nicotinic Acid (d) All of the aboves

147. Septic sore throat is caued by;
(a) Staphyllococcuas
(b) Streprococcal food forming
(c) *Vibrio parahaemolyticus*
(d) None of the above

148. In Buffalo milk myco toxin should not be more than;
(a) 0.5 PPm (b) 5PPm
(c) 0.0005 PPm (d) 100 PPm

149. In feed mycotoxin should not be more than;
(a) 0.5 PPm (b) 20 PPm
(c) 20 PPb (d) 150 PPb

150. For Rat Bite fever milk is which type of medium for growth and serival or *Streptobacillus monaliformis*
(a) Favourable
(b) Unfavonable
(c) Meither favourble or untanonable
(d) Any of the above

151. Listeria organism having the flagella which is;
(a) Monotrichus (b) Peritrichus
(c) Amchus (d) None

152. Diptheria organism;
(a) Multiply in milk at ambient temperature
(b) Does not multiply in milk
(c) Occuarinally multiply
(d) None of the above

153. Leptospira affects;
(a) Dogs (b) Cattle
(c) Swine (d) All the the above

154. Most common serotype of leptospira is;
(a) *L. grippotyphosa* (b) *L. canicola*
(c) *L. pomona* (d) *L. hardjoi*

155. Which type of soil is favorable for leptospira organism;
(a) Acidic soil
(b) Alkaline soil
(c) Neither alkali nor acidic
(d) Both a & b

156. In tuberculin srains which one directly derived from udder;
(a) Multiply wilh in milk
(b) Do not multiply
(c) Multiply after 10 days
(d) None of the aboves

157. Double intradermal test is uesd to differnate between diseases Tuberculosis &;
(a) Jhone's disease (b) Paratuberculosis
(c) Both of the above (d) None of the above

158. *E. coli* causes;
(a) Traveler diarrhoea
(b) Delhi belly
(c) Mountagenas revenge
(d) All of the above

159. In canned food by seeing by seeing bulged cane one can suspect;
(a) *Clostridium botulinum*
(b) *Coxiella burnetti*
(c) Both of the above
(d) None of the above

160. Salmonella is a;
(a) Gram -ve bacilli spore forming
(b) G -ve nonspore forming bacilli
(c) Gram -ve spore foring coccobacilli
(d) G -ve nonspore forming coccei

161. Abortion in Brucella occus in;
(a) First trimester
(b) Second trimester
(c) Third Trimester
(d) With in 15 days of gestation

162. Post mo rtem is not Advisable in disease;
(a) Anthrax (b) Brucellosi
(c) B.Q (d) Tuberculois

163. Stern vaccine is;
(a) Live attenuated spore vaccine
(b) Killed Vaccine
(c) Both of the above
(d) None of the above

164. Anthrax vaccine was developed by;
(a) Adverd Jener (b) Lister
(c) Louis pasteur (d) Antony von Leuwen hock

165. MC fadgean test is used in diagnosis of;
(a) Anthrax (b) T.B
(c) Brucella (d) B.Q

166. Vegitative form of anthrax is;
(a) Resistant to pasteurization
(b) Suceptible to pasteurization
(c) Partially resistant
(d) None of the aboves

167. In *B. anthrasis* spore are produced;
(a) Out side the body
(b) Inside the body
(c) Both outside & inside
(d) Depends on Environment conditions

168. *B. anthrasis* can survive in milk;
(a) Always
(b) Depends upon severty of infection
(c) Does not come in milk
(d) None of the aboves

169. *B. anthrasis* can survive in milk for;
(a) 10 years (b) 40-60 years
(c) 200 - 50 years (d) None of the above

170. *B. anthrasis* survive in bones of dead animal for;
(a) 200 ± 50 years (b) 1000 years
(c) 10 years (d) 40 - 60 years

171. B. anthrasis survives in soil;
(a) 40 - 60 years (b) 10 year
(c) 200 ± 50 year (d) 2 month

172. HTST Pasteurization can;
(a) Kills the *C. bournetti*
(b) May not kill *C. bournetti*
(c) Both are correct
(d) None is correct

173. In tick borne encephalitis human are infected by;
(a) Milk (b) Tick bite
(c) Both of the above (d) None of the aboves

174. Apthization is a Practice in farm done in the disease;
(a) H.S (b) B.Q
(c) T.B (d) FMD

175. Lactic acid producing bacteria;
(a) Inhibit the growth of pathogenic organism
(b) Favour growth of pathogenic organism
(c) Do not effect
(d) None of the above

176. From mastitis production losses in the world are;
(a) 300 million tons / annum
(b) 5000 million tons / annum
(c) 30 million tons / annum
(d) 1300 million tons / annum

177. Which one is not an enteric bacteria;
(a) Salmonella
(b) Sheigella
(c) *Staphylococcus aureus*
(d) *Mycobacterium bovis*

178. Psychophilic bacteria grow at;
(a) 5 - 7°C (b) 55 - 70°C
(c) 100 - 200°C (d) -193°C

179. Most common organism that causes ropy milk is;
(a) *Alcaligenes viscosus*
(b) *Micrococcus epidermidis*
(c) *B. subtalis*
(d) *B. Thermoliquetaciemis*

180. Pseudomonas syncyanea gives colous to milk;
(a) Red (b) Black
(c) Purple (d) Blue

181. *Serratia marcescens* gives which color to milk;
(a) Red (b) Blue
(c) Orange (d) Purple

182. Yellow pigment in milk is produced by bacteria;
(a) *Micrococcus flavus*
(b) *M. cuterus*
(c) Bothe of the above
(d) None of the aboves

183. Draw backs of pasteurization;
(a) Reduces cream (b) Loss of vitamins
(c) Change in flavour (d) All of the above

184. Source of contamination after pasteurization are;
(a) Transportation
(b) Whole seller

(c) Chilling for storage
(d) All of the above

185. For pasteurization which one is not right combination;
(a) 63 ^{0}C 30 min (b) 72 ^{0}C 15 sec
(c) 89 ^{0}C 1 sec (d) None of the above

186. Which one is not method of pasteurization;
(a) Batch holder (b) Contineous holding
(c) Flash process (d) None of the above

187. Strip cup is used in the examination of milk;
(a) Physical Examination
(b) Chemical Examination
(c) Biological Examination
(d) None of the above

188. Indian institute of Hygeine and Public Health was started in the year;
(a) 1964 (b) 1965
(c) 1970 (d) 1950

189. VPH came in existance in year
(a) 1940 (b) 1970
(c) 1990 (d) 1905

190. Serological test used for the detection of Brucella organism;
(a) ABR (b) RBPT
(c) CFTS (d) All of the above

191. 10% Co_2 tension is requiredl for the Brucella
(a) *B. abortus* (b) *B. suis*
(c) *B. melitansis* (d) None of the above

192. In ziehl - neelsens test method methylene blue is;
(a) First stain (b) Secondary stain
(c) Tertiary stain (d) None of the above

193. Methods used for detecting *tubercle bacilli* in milk are;
(a) Microscopic method
(b) Culture method
(c) Animal inoculation test
(d) All of the above

194. Salmonella is considered as emerging zoonosion because;
(a) It has large No of serovars
(b) Adoptability robilety to vauable conditionis high
(c) Wide host range
(d) All of the above

195. Salmonella serovars found only in animals are;
(a) *S. abortus* (b) *S. gallinarum*
(c) Both of the above (d) None of the above

196. In acid fast staining chemical used is;
(a) Corbol fuschin (b) 3% Alcohol
(c) Methylen blue (d) All of the above

197. 4% NaOH is used in the;
(a) White side test (b) Rannet test
(c) CMT (d) Chloride test

198. Hotis test is used for detection of;
(a) *Streptococcus aureus*
(b) *Streptococuus aglactiae*
(c) *Staphylococus aureus*
(d) None of the above

199. Animal can be said suffering from mastitis when chloride contents in milk are;
(a) > 0.14% (b) = 0.14%
(c) < 0.14% (d) None fo the aboves

200. In case of animal previously expored to mastitis what changes are being effeted again mastitis;
(a) Double
(b) zero as it makes animal resistant for disease
(c) Half
(d) None of te above

201. Which one is coli form organism;
(a) Proteus vulgarius (b) Yersinia
(c) *E. coli* (d) All of the aboves

202. In MBRT
(a) Methylene Blue converted into leucomethylene blue
(b) Leucomethyline blue converted into methylen blue
(c) Rad colour is formed
(d) None of the above

203. Catalage test used to diagnose matitis measures;
(a) Co_2 (b) O_2
(c) H_2S (d) None of above

204. DMC and SPC tests used for sanitary analysis of milk are;
(a) Direct methods
(b) Indirect method
(c) Semi dirrect method
(d) None of above

205. Sanitary examination of milk can be done by;

(a) Hotis test (b) Chloride test
(c) Nitrate test (d) Alcohol test

206. Micorscopic factor for ditermination of sanitary examination of milk is;
(a) 5,00,000 (b) 50,00,000
(c) 500 (d) None of above

207. The first Foodborne disease virus reported was;
(a) FMD virus (b) Hepatitis
(c) Poliomylitis (d) Rabies

208. All zoonotic viruses are essentially;
(a) Food borne (b) Not food borne
(c) Poliomylitis (d) None of the above

209. The oncogenic Food borne virus are;
(a) Bovine leukosis virus
(b) Feline leukosis virus
(c) Avian leukosis virus
(d) Caprine leukosis virus

210. The most important widerspread zoonotic Food borne disease is;
(a) FMD virus (b) Coxackie B_5 virus
(c) Hepatitis (d) Poliomylitis

211. For maximum inactivation of virus in meat foods;
(a) Boiling is only alternative
(b) Irradiation is the Panacea
(c) Freezing at - 80 ^{0}C
(d) Pasteurization in ideal

212. A good presevative is a substance with any of the following properties;
(a) Destroy offernsive odours
(b) Destroys bacteria completely
(c) Prevents deterioration of food
(d) Destroys Pathagens and their toxins

213. World wide spread of a disease through food is known as;
(a) Spordic (b) Epedemic
(c) Pandemics (d) Endemic

214. Hazard Analysis Critical Control Point include;
(a) Risk analysis of food
(b) Determination of cirtical control point
(c) Assessment of abouse of finshed product
(d) All of the above

215. Vehicle of Poliomylitis food borne infection is;
(a) Milk (b) Air
(c) Water (d) None of the above

216. Hepatitis A is;
(a) Water borne disease
(b) Food borne disease
(c) Both a and b
(d) None of the above

217. Introduction of virus to food stuff after the event of harvest or slaughter is;
(a) Primary contamination
(b) Secondary contamination
(c) Both a and b
(d) Above

218. Inactivation of more deeply situated viruses in food is possible by;
(a) Ultraviolet irradiation
(b) Ionization irradiation
(c) Both a and b
(d) None

219. Inactivation of virus with in substance of a number of food is inhanced by;
(a) Acidity (b) Alkalinity
(c) Neutrality (d) None of the above

220. Food products of infected animal origin are most likely to be contaminated with in the;
(a) Deep tissue (b) surface
(c) Both a and b (d) Non of above

221. The yield of total by products from the meat animal is;
(a) 50% of live wt. (b) < 50% of live wt
(c) 20% of live wt. (d) 30% of live wt

222. Spoilage of canned food can be judged by observing;
(a) Leakage
(b) Bloating of the tins
(c) Change in colour of the product
(d) None

223. Nitrosamines can destroy the cell of;
(a) Kidney (b) Liver
(c) Both a and b (d) None of the above

224. A large number of organophosporus compounds have been developed as pesticides;
(a) Coumaphos (b) Malathion
(c) Diazinon (d) All of above

225. Which of the following disease has recreational exposure as means of spread to man;

(a) Avian influenza (b) Brucellosis
(c) Rabies (d) None

226. Cummulative poison which accumulates in animal body is;
(a) Arsenic (b) Lead
(c) Mercury (d) All of the above

227. Radiation is not an Ideal method for the inactivation of food borne viruses because;
(a) Viruses are not iactiveted
(b) Organoleptic changes are produced
(c) Both a and b
(d) None of the above

228. Vriuses in food may be inactivated by;
(a) Physical methods
(b) Chemical methods
(c) Biological methods
(d) All of the above

229. Food and water the indirect means of virus transmission are known as;
(a) Vehicles (b) Fomites
(c) Vectors (d) None of the above

230. Contamination of food by humans carrier falls under;
(a) Primary contamination
(b) Secondary contamination
(c) Both a and b
(d) None of the above

231. Odour and Flavour of different meats is influenced by;
(a) Muscle fibres (b) Fat
(c) Haemoglobin (d) None of the above

232. Pasteurization of milk at 72°C is done for;
(a) 15 min. (b) 30 sec
(c) 15 sec (d) 1 min

233. Cooling of milk after pasteurization is done at;
(a) 5°C or below (c) 37°C or below
(b) 10°C or below (d) 15°C or below

234. Batch holding pasteurization is done at;
(a) 63°C for 30 min (c) 72°C for 15 sec
(b) 63°C for 30 sec (d) 100°C for 1 min

235. Ultra high temperature pasteuirzation is done at;
(a) 72°C for 15 sec
(c) 135 - 150°C for a fraction of sec
(b) 100°C for sec
(d) 100°C for a fraction of sec

236. Fat % of whole milk powder is;
(a) 27.5% (c) 20.5%
(b) 35.5% (d) 40.5%

237. Protein % of whole milk powder is;
(a) 26.4% (c) 35.8%
(b) 30% (d) 50.3%

238. Protein % of skimmed milk powder is;
(a) 26.4% (c) 35.8%
(b) 30% (d) 52.3%

239. In MBRT test for milk quality the time for reductin of methyline blue is 5 min. This suggest that milk is;
(a) Very good (c) Fair
(b) Good (d) Poor

240. Heavy draft horses requir air space (ft^3);
(a) 800 (b) 1000
(c) 500 (d) 2000

241. pH of milk is ranges from;
(a) 6.0 - 6.5 (c) 6.8 - 7.2
(b) 6.6 - 6.8 (d) 7 - 7.4

242. Normal range of acidity of milk ranges between;
(a) 0.1 - 0.17 (c) 0.3 - 0.35
(b) 0.2 - 0.25 (d) 0.4 - 0.47

243. The chloride content in milk of animal suffering from mastitis is;
(a) > 0.05% (c) > 0.25%
(b) > 0.14% (d) 0.35%

244. Anthrax is a;
(a) Bacterial disease
(b) Viral Disease
(c) Mycoplasma Disease
(d) None of the above

245. Which on spreads by ticks;
(a) Bartinella (b) Anthrax
(c) Clostridium (d) All of the above

246. Which one is caused by ingestion of undercooked ground beef;
(a) Coliform infection
(b) Rabies
(c) Plague
(d) Rat bite fever.

247. Tularemia is caused by;
(a) Vibrio (b) Mycobacterium

(c) Rickettsia (d) Francisella

248. Choose the rickettsial disease;
(a) Tetanus (b) Tularemia
(c) Q-fever (d) Rat bite fever

249. Typhus is commonly seen in;
(a) Rat (b) Flying squirrel
(c) Bandicoots (d) Cattle

250. Which one spreads via ingestion of raw or partially cooked infected fresh water fish;
(a) Malaria (b) Clonorchis
(c) Anthrax (d) None of the above

251. Which one is contact zoonoses;
(a) Actinomycosis (b) Sarcocystosis
(c) Malaria (d) None of the above

252. Bite of infected Phlebotomus sandflies may spread;
(a) Anthrax (b) Clonorchis
(c) Leishmania (d) Echinostomiasis

253. Choose a fungal disease;
(a) Typhus (b) Nocardiosis
(c) Plague (d) Glanders

254. The fat soluble pigment (S) of milk is/are;
(a) Lacithin (c) Both
(b) Carotine (d) None

255. The water soluble pigment (S) of milk is/are;
(a) Riboflavin (c) Lacithin
(b) Xanthophill (d) All of the above

256. The average specific gravity for cow milk is;
(a) 1.028 - 1.030 (c) 1.030 - 1.033
(b) 1.025 - 1.028 (d) 1.032 - 1.035

257. The average specific gravity for buffalo milk is;
(a) 1.028 - 1.032 (c) 1.030 - 1.032
(b) 1.030 - 1.035 (d) 1.032 - 1.035

258. The average specific gravity of skimmed milk is;
(a) 1.028 - 1.032 (c) 1.035 - 1.037
(b) 1.030 - 1.032 (d) 1.032 - 1.035

259. The average freezing point depression of Indian cow milk is;
(a) 31.02 °F (c) 31.05 °F
(b) 31.02 °F (d) 30.60°F

260. The average freezing point depression of buffalo milk is;
(a) 31.01 °F (c) 31.05 °F
(b) 31.02 °F (d) 30.6 °F

261. The bacteria that grow at temperature 5 - 7 °C are known;
(a) Phyctrotropic (c) Mesophillic
(b) Psychophillic (d) Thermophillic

262. Bacteria that grow at temperature rarging between 20 - 40°C are called;
(a) Psychophillic (c) Thermophillic
(b) Mesophillic (d) None

263. The pasteurized milk should have the spc/ml not more than;
(a) 30,000 (c) 40000
(b) 35000 (d) 45000

264. Pasteurization of milk/cream under reduced pressure by direct steam is refered as;
(a) Stassanization (c) UHT
(b) Vacreation (d) Flash pasteurization

265. At the time of homogenization the milk should be at a temperature of above;
(a) 33°C (c) 35°C
(b) 34°C (d) 37°C

266. Tumbling motility is the characteristic of following pathogen;
(a) Pasturella (c) Bacillus
(b) Listeria (d) Leptospira

267. Fungal toxins in farage feed should not be more than;
(a) 20 ppb (c) 25 ppb
(b) 22 ppb (d) 30 ppb

268. The fungal toxins is bulk milk should not be more than;
(a) 0.5 ppb (c) .1 ppb
(b) 0.8 ppb (d) 1.2 ppb

269. Ascoli's test is used for dignosis of;
(a) Athrax (c) T.B.
(b) Buicelosis (d) Para TB

270. Starmont test is used for;
(a) Athrax (c) T.B.
(b) Buicelosis (d) Para TB

271. Kangawa phenomena is characteristics of;
(a) Leisteris (c) *E.coli*
(b) Leptospira (d) Vibiro

272. Hydatidosis is caused by;
(a) Echinococus (c) *Taenia saginata*
(b) *Taenia solium* (d) Cysticercus bovis

273. RV -10 is the selective media for;
(a) *E.coli* (c) Bacillus
(b) Salmonella (d) Leptospira

274. Hydatidosis is an example of ;
(a) Cyclozoonoses
(c) Saprozoonoses
(b) metazoonoses
(d) saproanthropozoonoses

275. Paragonimiosis is an example of;
(a) Saprozoonses (c) Metazoonses
(b) Cyclozoonoses (d) Direct zoonoses

276. Following is the example of amphixenosis;
(a) Staphylococosis (c) Both a & b
(b) Streptococosis (d) None

277. KFD is caused by;
(a) Flavivirus (c) Phlebovirus
(b) Rhabdo virus (d) Picorna virus

278. Chicken Guinya virus is;
(a) Alfavirus (c) Picornavius
(b) Beta virus (d) Fanivius

279. Hazen colour value of water should not exceed;
(a) 5 (c) 7
(b) 6 (d) 8

280. The maximum permissible limit (MPL) of fluoride in H_2O;
(a) 1 – 1.5 ug/l (c) 1.5 - 2 ug/l
(b) 0.5 – 1 ug/l (d) 2 - 2.5 ug/l

281. The MPL of sulfate in water;
(a) 200 - 400 ppm (c) 300 - 500 ppm
(b) 250 -300 ppm (d) 50 - 100 ppm

282. The amount of alum for purification of water is;
(a) 1-6 grains/gallon of H_2O
(c) 5 - 10 granis/gallon of H_2O
(b) 10 -15 grains/gallon of H_2O
(d) 15 - 20 grains/gallon of H_2O

283. Orthotoludine test determine;
(a) Free chlorine in H_2O
(c) Both a& b
(b) Bound Cl_2 in H_2O
(d) None

284. Water pollution Law was started in;
(a) 1970 (c) 1978
(b) 1974 (d) 1980

285. Requirement of air for a healthy man is;
(a) 10 - 20 m^3/day (c) 25 - 30 m^3/day
(b) 15 - 30 m^3/day (d) 30 -40 m^3/day

286. The following may be complication (S) due to used of hard H_2O;
(a) Dyspepsis (c) Both a& b
(b) Penal calculi (d) None

287. Enteroviues consists of;
(a) DNA (c) Both
(b) RNA (d) None

288. Small liquid particles showing tendency to settle down in calm condition are;
(a) Droplet (c) Aerosol
(b) Dust (d) Droplet nuclei

289. Mixture of smoke and dust is called
(a) Smut (c) Soot
(b) Smog (d) Fune

290. Mixtrue of smoke and fog is called;
(a) Smut (c) Soot
(b) Smog (d) Fune

291. Agglumeration of fine carbon particles containg hydrocarbons and mineral matter is called;
(a) Smut (c) Soot
(b) Smog (d) Fune

292. Kyoto protocal came in existance in;
(a) 1997 (c) 1996
(b) 1995 (d) 1994

293. Milker's nodule is caused by;
(a) Virus (c) Fungi
(b) Bactria (d) Protozoa

294. Which of the following is platform test for milk;
(a) Acidity test
(c) Both a & b
(b) 10 min. Reazurin test
(d) None

295. Hepatitis A is;
(a) Food born zoonoses
(c) Both
(b) Water borne disease
(d) None

296. *Brucella abortus* can infect the animal lymyh;
(a) Intact skin (c) Both a &b
(b) Conjunctiva (d) None

297. Q. Fever is caused by;
(a) *Ricketssis avis* (c) *Coxiolla burnetili*

(b) *Anaplasma ovis* (d) *Echerchia equi*

298. Which is a zoonotic diseases;
(a) Aspergillosis (c) Both
(b) Cocidioxyocosis (d) None

299. Tick borne encephalitis is caused by
(a) Group A Arbovirus
(c) Group C Arbovirus
(b) Group B Arbovirus
(d) Group D Abovirus

300. Major mycotoxin of milk is;
(a) AFM_1 (c) AFM_{12}
(b) AFM_2 (d) AFM_{13}

301. The portion of AFB1 mycotoxin ingested comes is milk is about;
(a) 1/3th (c) 1.5th
(b) 1/4th (d) 1/6th

302. For enumeration of spore flora of milk the milk is heated at;
(a) 80°C for 10 min (c) 60°C for 15 min
(b) 80°C for 30 min (d) 65°C for 20 min

303. Which of the following organism is heat resistant;
(a) *B. subtilis* (c) *B. punilus* (Bacillus)
(b) *B. cerecus* (d) *B. mycoides*

304. Sterilized milk at room temperature remain fit for human comsumption for;
(a) 2 days (c) 5 days
(b) 3 days (d) 7 days

305. Mallard reaction at the time of sterilization of milk is due to reaction between;
(a) Sugar and Protein (c) Sugar and Calcium
(b) Sugar and Fat (d) Protein and Fat

306. Carbolic taint of milk is produced by;
(a) *B. cereus* (c) *B.circulans*
(b) *B. subtilis* (d) *B. pumius*

307. Complete in bottle partiurization is done at;
(a) 100 - 105°C (c) 130 - 140°C
(b) 110 - 120°C (d) 140 - 150°C

308. Loss of vit B_{12} through sterlization of milk is about;
(a) 20% (c) 75%
(b) 50% (d) 100%

309. IgA provides which type of immunity to new born;
(a) Active (c) Both
(b) Passive (d) None

310. Head Quarter of OIE is at;
(a) Paris (c) Rome
(b) Geneva (d) Egypt

311. FAO is situated at;
(a) Paris (c) Rome
(b) Geneva (d) Egypt

312. Meat of Dear is called as;
(a) Beaf (c) Venison
(b) Chevon (d) Mutton

313. The colour of mutton is;
(a) Dark Red (c) White
(b) Pale to bright Red (d) Whitish grvey

314. The typical goaty odour in male goat is due to;
(a) Acetic acid (c) Pheromones
(b) Hydrochloric acid (d) Capric acid

315. Marbelling is the charactertics of;
(a) Muttion (c) Chevon
(b) Pork (d) Beaf

316. The refractive index of fat in Horse is;
(a) 53.5 (c) 48.3
(b) 40.5 (d) 44.9

317. The refrective index of fat of pig is
(a) 53.5 (c) < 51.9
(b) > 40 (d) > 50

318. The Iodine value of cattle meat is;
(a) 71 - 86 (c) 50 - 70
(b) 38 - 46 (d) 35 - 46

319. The Iodine value of mutton is;
(a) 71 - 86 (c) 35 - 46
(b) 38 - 46 (d) 50 - 70

320. The Biological Oxygen Demand (BOD) of strong sewage is;
(a) 300 ppm (c) > 400 ppm
(b) > 350 ppm (d) > 450 ppm

321. The BOD of weak sewage is;
(a) < 100 ppm (c) < 75 ppm
(b) < 150 ppm (d) < 50 ppm

322. Gravity type rapid sand filter is also known as;
(a) Pasteus's type (c) Candy's type
(b) Peterson's type (d) Sandy' type

323. Pressure type rapid sand filter is also known as;
(a) Pasteur's type (c) Candy's type
(b) Peterson's type (d) Sandy' type

324. Point where Cl_2 demond of water is meant and residual Cl_2 being to form is known as;
(a) Break point chlorination
(b) Highest Point chlorination
(c) Residual chlorination
(d) Joint Point chlorination

325. Streptococosis is;
(a) Antropozoonoses (b) Zooanthroponosis
(c) Amphizoonoses (d) Saprozoonoses

326. pH of water is;
(a) 6.5 - 8.5 (b) 8 - 9
(c) 4.5 - 5.4 (d) 7.8 - 9.4

327. Minimum amount of Afltoxins in food for causing food poisioning is;
(a) 20 ppm (b) 25 ppm
(c) 30 ppm (d) 40 ppm

328. Expired air consists, how much of water vapers;
(a) 6% (b) 14%
(c) 12% (d) 16%

329. Homosphere is at the level of;
(a) 100 - 120 kPa (b) 125 - 150 kPa
(c) 150 - 175 kPa (d) 175 - 200 kPa

330. Presence of ozone layer is at;
(a) Thermosphere (b) Mesosphere
(c) Stratosphere (d) Trophosphere

331. Concentration of CO_2 added to atmosphere per year is;
(a) 1 ppm (b) 2 ppm
(c) 1.5 ppm (d) 2.5 ppm

332. Area intended for providing rest to the arriving animal is know as;
(a) Abattoir (b) Lariage
(c) Stunning Pen (d) Rest Pen

333. Decapacitation is done by a swift single cut using a knife or sword in;
(a) Jewis method (b) Halal method
(c) Jhatka method (d) Sachita method

334. Temperature of water for hard scalding the poultry carcass is;
(a) 125^{0}F for 90 - 120 sec
(b) 140^{0}F for 35 - 75 seconds
(c) 160 - 180^{0}F for 30 - 60 sec
(d) 100^{0}F for 80 seconds

335. Burning the hair like apendages with flame is known as;
(a) Plucking (b) Scalding
(c) Singeing (d) Evisceration

336. Carcases yield in poultry is about;
(a) 50% (b) 70 - 75%
(c) 60% (d) 90%

337. Carcass yield of mutton is;
(a) 40% (b) 60%
(c) 50% (d) 70%

338. Carcass yield of pig meat is;
(a) 50% (b) 60%
(c) 70% (d) 80%

339. Dressing percentage of cattle meat is;
(a) 42% (b) 53%
(c) 64% (d) 69%

340. Bone taint condition is caused in meat by;
(a) *Staphylococcus aureus*
(b) *Clostridium tetani*
(c) *Clostridium perfringens*
(d) *Listeria monocytogenes*

341. Glazy Bacon is a condition in which the meat/ carcass of pig shows;
(a) DFD condition (Dark firm and Dry)
(b) PSE (pale soft exudative)
(c) Freezer burn
(d) Bile staining

342. Yellow brown or chocolate pigmentatin of carcss is;
(a) Anthrocosis (b) Ochronosis
(c) Xanthosis (d) Angiotoma

343. Dark brown colour pigmentation in teeth, lungs, kidneys and lymph nodes is known as;
(a) Xanthosis
(b) Anthracosis
(c) Osteohematochromatosis
(d) Hemotoma

344. Plum pudding condition is characteristic of;
(a) Xanthosis (b) Angiotoma
(c) Ochronosis (d) Hematoma

345. In PSE(pale soft exudative) condition the pH of the meat is approximately;
(a) 4.5 - 4.9 (b) 6 - 6.2
(c) 7 - 7.4 (d) 9 - 9.4

346. Sows air flow/hr (ft^3) is require;

(a) 300 (b) 400
(c) 700 (d) 900

347. Physiological condition seen in very young and old animals is;
(a) Emaciation (b) Poorness
(c) Suffocation (d) Oedema

348. Pathological condition seen in chronic diseases is;
(a) Poorness (b) Weakness
(c) Emaciation (d) Hematoma

349. Minimum amount of light required for PM examination or low light is;
(a) 30 foot candles (b) 50 foot candles
(c) 70 candles (d) 100 foot candles

350. Temperature of molten wax in wax picking is;
(a) 100⁰F (b) 132⁰F
(c) 142⁰F (d) 151⁰F

351. Bleeding time for poultry is:
(a) 60 sec. (b) 90 sec.
(c) 90 sec. (d) 150 sec.

352. Bleeding Time for Turkey is;
(a) 60 sec. (b) 90 sec.
(c) 120 sec. (d) 150 sec.

353. Bleeding time for cattle is;
(a) 2-3 min (b) 5-6 min
(c) 10 -12 min (d) 7-9 min

354. The yield of blood after proper bleeding in cattle is approximately;
(a) 5-10 litre (b) 10 - 15 litre
(c) 20-25 litre (d) 30 litre

355. Bleeding time and yield respectively of blood in sheep is;
(a) 2 min; 3 litre. (b) 10 min; 6 litre.
(c) 5 minute; 2 litre (d) 12 min; 4 litre.

356. Prayers are offered by person (Bismi) in which method of slaughter;
(a) Jewis (b) Jhatka
(c) Halal (d) None of the above

357. For mechanical stunnig by pithing method, the length of pithing rod should not be more than;
(a) 20 cm (b) 60 cm
(c) 100 cm (d) 120 cm

358. The space requirement for cattle and pig respectively prior to slaughter are;
(a) 4 sq. m. ; 2 sqm.
(b) 1.75 sq. m. ; 28 sqm.
(c) 3 sq. m. ; 0.9 sqm.
(d) 5 sq. m. ; 0.8 sqm.

359. The total cattle pupulation of India is about;
(a) 320 million (b) 198 million
(c) 298 million (d) 400 million

360. Rank of the India among the goat population in the world is;
(a) 1st (b) 2nd
(c) 4th (d) 6th

361. Rank of the India among the sheep population in the world is;
(a) 1st (b) 2nd
(c) 4th (d) 6th

362. Veterinary Puublic Health started with establishment of National Institute of communicable Diseases at Delhi in;
(a) 1952 (b) 1964
(c) 1968 (d) 1972

363. All India Institute of Hygine & Public Health was established in;
(a) 1963 (b) 1970
(c) 1975 (d) 1979

364. Headquarter of WHO is at;
(a) Rome (b) Paris
(c) Geneva (d) Wasington

365. The maximum amount (95%) of total meat exported from India is of;
(a) Goat meat (b) Buffalo
(c) Poultry (d) Pig

366. White fat with firm texture, lean meat with low chlolesterol & low dressing perenctage are characteristic of;
(a) Goat (b) Buffalo
(c) Pork (pig) (d) Sheep

367. Concentration of CO_2 required for stunning poultry is;
(a) 60-65% for 20 sec.
(b) 73 - 77% for 15 seconds
(c) 80 - 90% for 10 seconds.
(d) 65 -70% for 3 seconds.

368. CANPACK system is modified version of;
(a) On the Rail system

(b) Intermittent Powered system
(c) Contionuous powered system
(d) Booth system.

369. Stress to animals prior to slaughter will make the pH;
(a) Acidic (b) Alkaline
(c) Neutral (d) None of the above

370. If animal suffering from chronic type of disease & there is no acute pain to animal then such type of slaughter is called as;
(a) Delayed slaughter
(b) Casualty slaughter
(c) Emergency slaughter
(d) None of the above

371. Water soaked, loose & flabby appearance of carcass is due to;
(a) Haematoma (b) Suffocation
(c) Fevered flesh (d) Immaturity

372. Albumin portion of total egg content constitutes;
(a) 11% (b) 58%
(c) 65% (d) 32%

373. Eggyolk of total egg content constitutes;
(a) 11% (b) 40%
(c) 31% (d) 22%

374. For preservation of egg at cold storage, the temperature & Relative humidity requirement are repectively;
(a) 0^0C; 80-85% (b) 4^0C ; 80%
(c) -20^0C; 80% (d) 0^0C ; 40%

375. Marbelling is a characteristic feature of;
(a) Buffalo meat (b) Beef (cattle meat)
(c) Veal (d) Mutton

376. Deposition of subcutaneous fat is characteristic feature of;
(a) Buffalo meat (b) Mutton
(c) Deer (d) Pork

377. Vension is term given to meat of;
(a) Rabbit (b) Buffalo
(c) Deer (d) Turkey

378. Refractive index of Horse meat is;
(a) 42.4 (b) 53.5
(c) 53.5 (d) 32.1

379. Iodine value of pork is;
(a) 10 - 20 (b) 30 - 40
(c) 50 - 70 (d) 80 - 90

380. Linolenic acid and glycogne content of meat are maximum in;
(a) Goat (b) Sheep
(c) Horse (d) Buffalo

381. Protein in fish meat is.
(a) 10% (b) 19%
(c) 29% (d) 32%

382. Temperature of refrigeration of meat is;
(a) 0^0C (b) 2 - 5^0C
(c) 10 - 15^0C (d) -5^0C

383. pH of the normal meat is;
(a) 4.8 - 5.2 (b) 6.6 - 6.8
(c) 7.2 - 7.4 (d) 5 - 5.5

384. Freezing temperature for meat is;
(a) -5^0C (b) 0^0C
(c) -18^0C (d) -100^0C

385. The no. of chromosomes in riverine & swamp buffaloes are respectively;
(a) 48 ; 50 (b) 50 ; 48
(c) 54 ; 52 (d) 52 ; 54

386. Plague is transmitted by;
(a) Mite (b) Flea
(c) Fly (d) Tick

387. Q fever is transmitted by;
(a) Tick (b) Flea
(c) Mite (d) Mosquito

388. Onchocercosis is trnasmitted by;
(a) Tick (b) Mite
(c) Mosquito (d) Flea

389. Typanosomesis is transmitted by;
(a) Flea (b) Fly
(c) Tick (d) Mosquito

390. Complete removal of disease from an area is known as;
(a) Elimination (b) Eradication
(c) Control (d) Prevention

391. African sleeping sickness is spread by bite of infected;
(a) Tsetse fly
(b) Anopheles mosquito
(c) Tick
(d) Lice

392. Dwarf Tapworm of man is;

(a) *Taenia spp.* (b) *Hymenolepis nana*
(c) *Echinococcus spp.* (d) *Spirometra spp.*

393. Lyme disease is caused by;
(a) *Borvelia burgdorferi* (b) Leptospira *spp.*
(c) Listeria *spp.* (d) *Coxiella buruetti*

394. Visceral larva migrans is caused by;
(a) *Toxocara spp.* (b) *Ostertagia spp.*
(c) *Trichinella spp.* (d) *Strongyloides spp.*

395. Rockey mountain spotted fever is caused by;
(a) *Rickettsia akari*
(b) *Rickettsia rickettsii*
(c) *Rickettsia tsutsugamushi*
(d) *Rickettsia cenori*

396. Thelazia sp. is transmitted by;
(a) Fly (b) Mosquito
(c) Tick (d) Flea

397. Glander's is caused by;
(a) *Streptococcus equiperdum*
(b) *Strongylus equinus*
(c) *Typanosoma spp.*
(d) *Burkholdia mallei*

398. Micro wave used for cooking are;
(a) High frequency, non ionising electro magnetic waves
(b) Low frequency, non ionising electro magnetic waves
(c) High frequency, ionising electro magnetic waves
(d) High frequency, radio waves

399. Red spots on meat is due to;
(a) *Leuconostoc spp.* (b) *Pseudomonas spp.*
(c) Serratia marcicens (d) *Miccrococcus spp.*

399. When putrifacition sets up, the pH of the meat becomes;
(a) Acidic
(b) Alkaline
(c) Neutral
(d) May by acidic or alkaline

400. In HTST method of pasteurization, the temperature & time combination is as follows;
(a) 72°C for 15 minutes.
(b) 71 - 72°C for 15 seconds.
(c) 85°C for 15 secods.
(d) 85°C for 15 minutes.

401. Coenuriasis is caused by;
(a) *Taenia multiceps* (b) *Bartinella studeri*
(c) Fasciola (d) Diphyllobothrium

402. Herd screening test for Brucellosis is;
(a) Standard Tube Aggl. Test.
(b) Rose Bengal Test.
(c) Abortus Bang Ring Test
(d) ELISA.

403. BGA is selective media for;
(a) *Salmonella spp.*
(b) *Listeria spp.*
(c) *Corynebacterium spp.*
(d) *Staphylococcus spp.*

404. Traveller's diarrhoea is caused by;
(a) *Salmonella spp.* (b) *E. coli*
(c) *Stophylococcus sp.* (d) *Virio Cholera*

405. Dark field microscopy & silver staining are sued for defection of;
(a) *Listeria spp.* (b) *Leptospira spp.*
(c) *Pasteurella spp.* (d) *Salmonella spp.*

406. Bipolar staining is characteristic for;
(a) *Listeria spp.* (b) *Leptospira spp.*
(c) *Pasteurella spp.* (d) *Salmonella diptheria*

407. Eaton's test is performed for detection of;
(a) *Leptospira spp.* (b) *Listeria spp.*
(c) *Pasteurella spp.* (d) *Bacillus spp.*

408. Carbolic taint in milk is produced due to;
(a) *Bacillus subtalis* (b) *Bacillus circulans*
(c) *Bacillus coagulans* (d) *Bacillus anthracis*

409. Which one is usually associated with filter;
(a) *Bacillus subtalis* (b) *Bacillus circulans*
(c) *Bacillus coagulans* (d) *Bacillus anthracis*

410. Which one gives an extremily bitter taste & cause proteolysis;
(a) *Bacillus subtalis* (b) *Bacillus circulans*
(c) *Bacillus coagulans* (d) *Bacillus anthracis*

411. The amount of vitamin C and vitanim B_1 lost during sterilisation of milk are respectively;
(a) 40% ; 20% (b) 50% ; 30 - 40%
(c) 60% ; 20 - 30% (d) 30% ; 80 - 90%

412. Reduction of no. of spores to of the concentration during sterilisation of milk is known as;
(a) Rreduction time
(b) Sterilisation effect

(c) Decimal reduction
(d) None of the above

413. Hotis test is characteristic for;
(a) *Staph. aureus*
(b) *Streptococcus agalactiae*
(c) *Strept. Pyogenes*
(d) *Brucella sp.*

414. Medusa head like colonies on blod agar are characteristic for.
(a) *Bacillus anthracis* (b) *Brucella spp.*
(c) *Clostridium tetani* (d) *Pasteurella multocide*

415. For judging the efficiency of pasteurization, the best test is;
(a) MBRT test
(b) Coliform test
(c) Salt conductivity test
(d) Phosphatase Inactivation test

416. Yellow pigment on utencils is caused by;
(a) *Micrococcus candidus*
(b) *Sarcina lutea*
(c) *Micrococcus roseus*
(d) *Serratia spp.*

417. Thermophillic bacteria grow rapidly at;
(a) 40 - 50 °C (b) 55 - 70°C
(c) 70 - 80 °C (d) 80 - 90°C

418. Psychrophilic bacteria grow repidly at;
(a) 5 - 7°C (b) 1 - 4°C
(c) 15 - 20°C (d) 25 - 35 °C

419. The bacteria capable of surviving normal pasteurization tempherature are known as;
(a) Themophillic bact
(b) Thermoduric bacteria
(c) Psychrophillic bact
(d) None of the above

420. Bacillary dysentry is caused by;
(a) *Salmonella spp.* (b) *Vibrio cholera*
(c) *Shigella spp.* (d) *Listeria sp.*

421. Minimum fat & SNF recommended for toned milk are;
(a) 3 % ; 6.5% (b) 3% ; 8.5%
(c) 4%; 6% (d) 5%, 9%

422. Minimum fat and SNF recommened for double toned milk are;
(a) 3% ; 7% (b) 4%; 8%
(c) 1.5% ; 9% (d) 2%; 6%

423. Minimum fat and SNF recommeded for standardised milk are;
(a) 3% ; 7% (b) 4.5%; 8.5%
(c) 4% ; 6% (d) 5%; 9%

424. Which is responsible for sandiness defect of Ice cream?
(a) Lecithin (b) Protein
(c) Lactose (d) MIneral matter

425. Energy value of milk fat is;
(a) 4.5 calorie/gm (b) 9.1 calorie/gm.
(c) 15.6 calorie/gm (d) 22 calorie/gm.

426. Titrable acidity of cow milk is;
(a) 0.42 - 0.45 (b) 0.32 - 0.35
(c) 0.13 - 0.14 (d) 0.21 - 0.23

427. Fishy flavour in milk is due to presence of;
(a) *Pseudomonas synxantha*
(b) *Pseudomonas icthosmia*
(c) *Pseudomonas syncyanea*
(d) *Pseudomonas sapolytica*

428. Violet Red Bile Agar is growth medium for;
(a) *Staphylococcus spp.*
(b) Coliform organisms
(c) *streptococcus agalactiae*
(d) *Brucella spp.*

429. The alcohal test in milk is an indication of;
(a) Sugar balance (b) Fat balance
(c) Mineral balance (d) Water balance

430. Excessive no. of rod shaped bacteria particularly sporeformers indicate;
(a) Improperly cleaned milk utercils
(b) Improper cooling of milk
(c) Dusty & Dirty environment
(d) Mastitis infection

431. In white side test the main reagent is;
(a) NaCl (b) NaOH
(c) HCl (d) KOH

432. Differentiation of meat of different food animal can be done by;
(a) Gross observation
(b) Chemical method
(c) Serological method
(d) All

433. Highest percentage of Lysine is present among;

(a) Lamb (b) Pork
(c) Beef (d) Chevon

434. % of lysine in beef is;
(a) 7.6 (b) 7.8
(c) 8.4 (d) 9.5

435. Which one is tapeworm of dog;
(A) Diphylidium (b) Hymenolepis
(c) Taenia (d) Capillaria

436. Which of the following having highest % of Lysine, Lucine Isoleucine, Cystine and Valine;
(a) Lamb (b) Pork
(c) Beef (d) Chevan

437. What % of Tryptophan is present in Pork;
(a) 1.3 (b) 1.4
(c) 1.1 (d) 0.9

438. Highest % of phenylalanine in present in;
(a) Lamb (b) Pork
(c) Beef (d) chevan

439. Most abundant fatty acid in meat is;
(a) Oleic acid (b) Pamitic acid
(c) Stearic acid (d) None

440. Highest % of oleic acid is found in;
(a) Lamb (b) Pork
(c) Beef (d) Chevan

441. Highest % of Linoleic acid is present in;
(a) Lamb (b) Pork
(c) Beef (d) Chevan

442. Thiamine is present in lean pork;
(a) 5 to 10 times than other meat
(b) 10 to 15 times than other meat
(c) 15 to 20 times than other meat
(d) 20 to 25 times than other meat

443. Highest Ca (mg/100 gm meat) is present in;
(a) Pork (b) Lamb
(c) Beef (d) Chicken

444. Highest % of Fe (mg/100g of meat) in found in;
(a) Pork (b) Lamb
(c) Beef (d) Chicken

445. Highest % of Mg (mg/100g of meat) in found in;
(a) Pork (b) Beef
(c) Lamb (d) Chicken

446. Heighest Riboflavin (Mg/ 100 g of meat) in found in;
(a) Park (b) Lamb
(c) Lamb (d) Chicken

447. Typical colour of meat of paultry is;
(a) Light to dark red
(b) Greyish pink
(c) Gray white to dull red
(d) Cherry red.

448. Typical colour of muttan and chevan is;
(a) Light to dark red
(b) Greyish pink
(c) Gray white to dull red
(d) Cherry red.

449. Typical colour of pork is;
(a) Light to dark red
(b) Greyish pink
(c) Gray white to dull red
(d) Cherry red.

450. Typical colour of Buffalo meat and beef is;
(a) Light to dark red
(b) Greyish pink
(c) Gray white to dull red
(d) Cherry red.

451. Whole sale cuts of Lamb carcass do not contain;
(a) Neck (b) Shoulder
(c) Rack (d) Ham

452. Whole sale cuts of pork do not contain;
(a) Jwa (b) Bostan butt
(c) Ham (d) Breast

453. Chuck is the term used in whole sale cut of;
(a) Pork (b) Lamb
(c) Chicken (d) Beef carcass

454. Picnic shoulder is the term used for whole sole cut of carcass of;
(a) Pork (b) Lamb
(c) Chicken (d) Beef

455. Which is not used for grading of carcass;
(a) Carcass conformation
(b) Trimming
(c) Meat bone ration
(d) Shape

456. Which method of preservation is used for short term storage of meat;
(a) Chilling (b) Freezing
(c) Canning (d) Nano

457. What is the temperature range for chilling of meat;

(a) 2 to 5ºC (b) -10 to - 15ºC
(c) 18 to 20ºC (d) -18 to - 30ºC

458. Freezing temperature for storage is
(a) 2 to 5ºC (b) -10 to - 30ºC
(c) -90ºC (d) -196ºC

459. Storage time for chilled meat is;
(a) 5 to 7 days (b) 15 to 20 days
(c) one month (d) 6 months

460. Storage time for Freezed meat is;
(a) 5 to 7 day (b) 15 to 20 day
(c) one month (d) 6 month

461. Storage time of freezed beef is;
(a) More than that of poultry meat
(b) Less than that of poultry meat
(c) Less than that of pork meat
(d) More than that of poultry and pork

462. Storag time of cured and salted meat is;
(a) 1 month (b) 2 months
(c) 2 month (d) 6 month

463. Which is used for curing of meat;
(a) Sodium chloride (b) Sodium nitrite
(c) Both (d) None

464. Curing of meat is limited (traditionaly) to;
(a) Park (b) Beef
(c) Both a & b (d) None

465. Which is true;
(a) Smoking is followed by curing
(b) Curing is followed by smoking
(c) Both two methnods can be applied
(d) All are wrong

466. Resins is term used for smoking by;
(a) Aldehydes and phenols
(b) Aldehydes and ketone
(c) Phenols and alcohols
(d) Aldehyde and alcohols

467. In resins aldehyde acts as;
(a) Bacteriostatic (b) Bacteriocide
(c) Both (d) None

468. Phenols in resins acts are
(a) Bacteriostatic (b) Bacteriocide
(c) Both a & b (d) None

469. Thermal processing of meat can be done by;
(a) Sterilization (b) Pasteurization
(c) Both a & b (d) None

470. Sterilized meat products having canned life of;
(a) 6 months (b) 1 year
(c) 2 years (d) Life long

471. For canning which of the following steps are used;
(a) Precooking (b) Exhausting
(c) Seaming (d) All

472. Exhusting and seaming are essential steps in;
(a) Chilling (b) Freezing
(c) Curing (d) Canning

473. Dehydration of meat can be done by;
(a) Freeze and drying (b) Sundrying
(c) Both a & b (d) None

474. Which is the essential step in freez drying;
(a) Prefreezing (b) Primary drying
(c) Secondary drying (d) All

475. Water acitivty is reduced in which of the following methods of storage of meat;
(a) Chilling (b) Freezing
(c) Dehydration (d) All

476. Use of high temperature is;
(a) Essential in freez drying
(b) Can not be done in freezdrying
(c) Can not be done but of little value in freezdring
(d) None

477. Cold sterllizatin is done;
(a) At 3 to 5ºC
(b) With the hep of radiation
(c) Both
(d) None

478. Which wave is used in irradiation;
(a) Alfa (b) Lamda
(c) Beta (d) All

479. Radurization is done;
(a) With a dose of 50 to 100 k rad
(b) With a dose of 4 to 5 m rad
(c) With a dose of 4 to 5 k rad
(d) With a dose of 50 to 100 m rad

480. Radappertization is done with a dose of;
(a) 50 to 100 k rad (b) 4 to 5 m rad
(c) 4 to 5 k rad (d) 50 to 100 m rad

481. Effective food preservation can be achieved by;
(a) Chiling only (b) Canning only
(c) Irradiation only (d) Combination of

preservation factors

482. Which of the following is the source of contamination of meat;
(a) Hairs and feet
(b) Gastrointestinal contents
(c) Air born contamination
(d) All

483. Contamination of meat takes place in which step;
(a) Chilling (b) Packasing
(c) Processing (d) All

484. Micro organisms that occur in meat are;
(a) Bacteria and molds
(b) Bacteria, molds and yeast
(c) Bacteria and yeast
(d) None

485. In which phage bacteria increases in size;
(a) Lag phage (b) Log phage
(c) Stationary phage (d) Decline phage

486. In which phage bacteria increases in number;
(a) Lag phage (b) Log phage
(c) Stationary phage (d) Decline phage

487. Which phage is the largest;
(a) Lag phage (b) Log phage
(c) Stationary phage (d) Decline phage

488. The intrinsic factor for growth of bacteria in meat is;
(a) Temperature (b) Oxygen
(c) Physical state (d) pH

489. Which one is not intrinsic factor for growth of bacteria;
(a) pH (b) Water activity
(c) Temperature (d) Redox potential

490. Which of the followng requires oxygen for growth in meat;
(a) All bacteria
(b) All fungi
(c) Only molds and bacteria
(d) Only yeast and bacteria

491. In the interior of meat which kind of microflora are present;
(a) Arerobes
(b) Anaerobes
(c) Anaeorbes and yeast
(d) Anaerobes and molds

492. Bacteria can grow up to water activity of;
(a) 0.91 (b) 0.86
(c) 0.99 (d) 0.80

493. Fungi can graw up to water activity of;
(a) 0.91 (b) 0.86
(c) 0.99 (d) 0.80

494. Which pH is favourable for bacteria in meat;
(a) Basic (b) Neutral
(c) Neutral ' (d) All

495. Which pH is favourable for fungi in meat;
(a) Basic (b) Neutral
(c) Acidic (d) Less than 5.5

496. Spoilage of meat is done by;
(a) Micro organism (b) Intrinsic enzymes
(c) Insects (d) All

497. Meat decomposition is more offensive in;
(a) Aerobic condition
(b) Anaerobic condition
(c) Anaerobic condition with high temperature
(d) Aerobic condition with high temperature

498. End product of proteolysis under aerobic condition;
(a) Amino acid (b) Ammonia
(c) Aminer (d) Ketaner

499. Extract release volume can be used to determine;.
(a) Microbial spoilage of meat
(b) Water holding capacity of meat
(c) Anti biotic residue in meat
(d) Chemical spoilage of meat

500. In incipient spoilage pH of meat;
(a) Increases (b) Decreases
(c) Becomes neutral (d) Becomes acidic

501. Dogs requisite air space (ft^3)
(a) 20 (b) 40
(c) 100 (d) 300

502. Spoilage of meat can be defected by;
(a) ERV determination
(b) Rerazurin dye test
(c) Observing slime formation
(d) All

503. HACCP is a food safety sytem deals with;
(a) Packaging of meat
(b) Processing of meat
(c) Distribution of meat

(d) All

504. In which case first meat should be rejected;
(a) Total viable count < 0.5 million/gm
(b) Coliform < 500/gm
(c) Total viable count > 0.5 million/gm
(d) Caliform > 5000/gm

505. In which case coocked meat should be rejected;
(a) TVC less than 200/g
(b) TVC less than 5000/g
(c) TVC less than 10,000/g
(d) None

506. What is the recommended TVC in raw meat;
(a) 10^5 - 10^7 (b) 10^6 - 10^8
(c) 10^5 - 10^8 (d) None

507. What should be the leve log Coliforms;
(a) Absent in 0.01 in raw meat
(b) Absent in 0.1 g in precooked meat
(c) Absent in 0.01 g in cooked meat
(d) All

508. What can be the number of coliforms in frozen sea food;
(a) Absent in 1 gm
(b) Absent in 0.1 gm
(c) Not more than 10^2
(d) Not more than 10^4

509. Which of the following should be absent in frozen sea food per gram;
(a) Coliforms
(b) Enterococci
(c) *Staphyloccoccus auerus*
(d) Salmonella

510. In which of the following diseases poultry should be unfit for sloughter;
(a) Ornithosis (b) Fowl typhoid
(c) Botulism (d) All

511. Meat of ox having refractive index of;
(a) 53.5 (b) 40
(c) 51.9 (d) ·51.9

512. Iodine value of pig meat is;
(a) 71 - 86 (b) 38 - 46
(c) 35 - 46 (d) 50 – 70

513. Glycogen content is highest in meat of;
(a) Horse (b) Sheep
(c) Pig (d) Beef

514. Goaty smell from chevan comes due to;
(a) Putrifaction (b) Capric acid
(c) Arachidonic acid (d) H_2S

515. What is the method of preservation of egg;
(a) Curing (b) Oil treatment
(c) Heat sterilization (d) None

516. Thermostablization of egg in done at;
(a) 55°C 60 15 min (b) 71°C for 2 sec
(c) Both a & b (d) None

517. Candling is done;
(a) For aging of egg
(b) For presence of underirable charactercs
(c) Both a & b
(d) None

518. Water glass method is used in preservation of;
(a) Chevan (b) Beef
(c) Egg (d) Fish

519. Boar's requisite air space (ft³);
(a) 140 (ft³) (b) 190
(c) 200 (d) 250

520. Micro-organism responsible for off odder and slime formation;
(a) Pseudomonas (b) Micrococcus
(c) Micobacterium (d) All

521. Green discoloration occurs due to;
(a) *Preudomonas mephitica*
(b) *Clostridium novyi*
(c) Molds
(d) None

522. *Costridium spp.* is responsible for;
(a) Bone taint (b) Ham souring
(c) Bone stink (d) All

523. Lactobacillus causes;
(a) Green core in cooked sausage
(b) Green ring in cooked sausage
(c) Both a & b
(d) None

524. Freezer storage can do;
(a) Freezer burn (b) Bone discolouration
(c) Bone darkening (d) All

525. Green rot in egg in due to;
(a) *Pseudomonas flurenscens*
(b) Serratia
(c) *Proteus melonovagenes*

(d) All

526. Black rot is caused by (in egg);
(a) *Pseudomonas flurenscens*
(b) Serratia
(c) *Proteus melanovagenes*
(d) Moulds

527. Braising utilises which one for processing of meat;
(a) Dry heat (b) Moist heat
(c) Both a & b (d) None

528. *Diphylobothridium latum* is transmitted through;
(a) Chevan (b) Beef
(c) Chicken (d) Fish

529. Heavy draft horses air flow/hrs (ft^3) requirement is;
(a) 4000 (b) 6000
(c) 8000 (d) None

530. Venisan is meat obtained form deer is;
(a) Pink in colour
(b) Bright to dark red in colour
(c) Grey white in colour
(d) Black in colour.

531. Zoonoses term is given by;
(a) Rodolph vichow (b) Schwabc
(c) A. Jenner (d) Aristotle

532. Epiornithic term is used for epidemic in;
(a) Birds (b) Reptile
(c) Fish (d) Animal

533. Diseases transmitted from animals to man is know as;
(a) Anthropozoonoses
(b) Zooanthroponoses
(c) Amphixenosis
(d) None

534. Anthropozoonoses Includes;
(a) Anthrax (b) Brucellosis
(c) Tuberculosis (d) All the above

535. Diseases transmitted from man to animal is
(a) Zooanthroponoses
(b) Anthropozoonoses
(c) Amphixenosis
(d) None

536. Group of diseases that require more than one vertibrate host species for the perpetuation of the zoonotic agent comes under;
(a) Cyclozoonoses (b) Metazoonoses
(c) Saprozoonoses (d) None

537. The diseases Included with, this group require at least one Invertebrate host for the maintenance of the causal agent;
(a) Metazoonoses (b) Cyclozoonoses
(c) Saprozoonoses (d) None

538. Diseases which require participation of an inanimate source for their perpetuation and sprea comes under;
(a) Saprozoonses (b) Cyclozoonoses
(c) Metazoonoses (d) None

539. Diret zoonoses Includes;
(a) Influenza (b) Rabies
(c) Brucellosis (d) All the above

540. Metazoonoses includes;
(a) Plague (b) Trypanosomiasis
(c) Both a& b (d) None

541. Saprozoonoses includes;
(a) Cryptococcosis (b) Histoplasmosis
(c) Both a & b (d) None

542. African hemorrhagic fever is caused by;
(a) Marburg virus (b) *Bacillus anthracis*
(c) Arena virus (d) Junin virus

543. Looping ill is caused by an arbovirus infection transmitted by;
(a) Tick (b) Mite
(c) Both (d) None

544. Kyasanur forest disease is caued by;
(a) Flavivirus (b) Aphthavirus
(c) Herpes virus (d) Toga virus

545. Main vector of chicken guniya fever is;
(a) *Aedes aegypti* (b) *Aedes africanus*
(c) Culex sp. (d) None

546. Japanes B encephalitis is caused by;
(a) Flavivirus (b) Pox virus
(c) Alpha virus (d) Herpes virus

547. Main vector of Japanses B encephalitis is;
(a) *Culex tritaenorhynchus*
(b) *C. annulus*
(c) *C. annutirostris*
(d) None

548. Amphibian host for Japanes encephalitis is;
(a) Pig (b) Cattle

(c) Goat (d) Dogs

549. West Nile fever is caused by;
(a) Flavivirus (b) Alphavirus
(c) Merpesvirus (d) None

550. Yellow fever is caused by;
(a) Flavivirus (b) Alphavirus
(c) Herper virus (d) Poxvirus

551. Yellow fever is transmitted by;
(a) Aedes sp (b) Culere sp
(c) Anapheles sp (d) None

552. Dengue fever is caused by;
(a) Flavivirus (b) Alphavirus
(c) Herpervirus (d) None

553. Crimean - congo Haemorrhagic fever is caused by;
(a) Nairovirus (b) Flavivirus
(c) Alphavirus (d) None

554. Crimean Congo Haemorrhagic fever virus transmitted by;
(a) Tick (b) Mite
(c) Mosquito (d) None

555. Riftvalley fever is caused by;
(a) Phlebovirus (b) Flavivirus
(c) Alphavirus (d) None

556. Rabies is caused by;
(a) Rhabdovirus (b) Flavivirus
(c) Herpesvirus (d) None

557. Negri bodies are seen in the infection of (Rabies);
(a) Street virus (b) Fixed virus
(c) Both (d) None

558. Influenza is caused by;
(a) Orthomyxovirus (b) Paramyxovirus
(c) Both (d) None

559. Infuenza virus of zoonotic importance is;
(a) Influenza A virus (b) Influenza B virus
(c) Influenza C virus (d) None

560. Foot & mouth disease is caused by;
(a) Aphthovirus (b) Enterovirus
(c) Rhinovirus (d) None

561. In FMD, virus is shed in;
(a) Milk (b) Sweat & urine
(c) Sperm (d) All the above

562. Bovine spongiform encephalopathy is caused by;
(a) Prions (b) Virus
(c) Bacteria (d) None

563. Pox virus of zoonotic Importance are;
(a) Monkey pox virus
(b) Vaccinia virus
(c) Cow pox virus
(d) All the above

564. Antigenic shift of influenza virus is the cause of;
(a) Pandemic (b) Epidemics
(c) Endemics (d) None

565. Antigenic shift of FMD virus results in the occurance of;
(a) Pandemics (b) Epidemics
(c) Endemics (d) None

566. Influenza infection comes under;
(a) Direct zoonoses (b) Metazoonoses
(c) Sarozoonoses (d) None

567. Rocky mountain spotted fever is caused by;
(a) R rickettsii (b) *R. prowazekii*
(c) *R conorii* (d) *R Japonica*

568. Rocky mountain spotted fever spred through;
(a) Ticks (b) Mosquito
(c) Mite (d) None

569. Murine typhus is caused by;
(a) R. typhi (b) *R. rickettsii*
(c) *R. prowazekii* (d) *R. conorii*

570. Murine typhus spread throgh;
(a) Flea (b) Tick
(c) Mite (d) None

571. Rabies is also known as;
(a) Hydrophobia (b) Tyser
(c) Tollwat (d) All the above

572. Negri bodies in rabies are formed;
(a) Intracytoplasmic (b) Intranueclear
(c) Both (d) None

573. Important transmiter of rabies in Asias are;
(a) Mongoose ad jackal
(b) Vampire bat
(c) Both
(d) None

574. Japanese B encephaltis is also known as;
(a) Summer encephalitis
(b) Autumn encephalitis
(c) Encephalitis B

(d) All of the above

575. Scrub typhus is caused by;
(a) *R. tsutsugamushi* (b) *R. typhi*
(c) *R. rickettsii* (d) *R. conorii*

576. Colorado tick fever is caused by;
(a) Orbivirus (b) Poxvirus
(c) Herper virus (d) None

577. Ebola hemorrhagic fever is caused by;
(a) Ebolavirus (b) Alpha virus
(c) Hanta virus (d) herpes virus

578. Murray valley Ecephalitis is caused by;
(a) Flavi virus (b) Filo virus
(c) Alpha virus (d) Hanta virus

579. Serotype of dengue fever virus are;
(a) Den -1 to Den -4 (b) Den -1 to Den -5
(c) Den -1 to Den -3 (d) None

580. Amplifier host for Kyasanur forest disease virus is;
(a) Monkey (b) Pig
(c) Elephant (d) All the above

581. Most food borne viruses are transmitted through;
(a) Man to man cycle
(b) Man to animal cycle
(c) Animal to man cycle
(d) None

582. The presence of viral antigen in food can be detected by;
(a) ELISA (b) Nucleic acid probes
(c) PCR (d) All of the above

583. Food borne viruses Includes;
(a) Rotavirus
(b) Hepatitis A & E virus
(c) Norwalk virus
(d) All of the above

584. Natural cycle of Influenza transmission are;
(a) Swine to man
(b) Equine/ bird to man
(c) Bird to swine to man
(d) All the above

585. In horses major complication of influenza include;
(a) Strangle (b) Bronchopneumonia
(c) Conjunctivitis (d) All the above

586. Hydrophobia an important characteristic of Rabies is seen in;
(a) Man (b) Cow
(c) Baffalo (d) None

587. Host which play important role in maintaining the Japanese B encephalitis virus in nature are;
(a) Swine (b) Domestic wild bird
(c) Both a & b (d) None

588. Disease persisting in an area and characterized by clustering of cases in place but not in time is known as;
(a) Endemic (b) Epidemic
(c) Pendemic (d) None

589. A disease showing unusual increase in it's prevalence in a papulation at a given time and characterized by clustering of cases in place as well as time in known as;
(a) Epidemic (b) Pandemic
(c) Endemic (d) None

590. A disease affecting wide geographic teritories at a time and characterized by clustering of cases in time but not in place in know as;
(a) Pandemic (b) Epidemic
(c) Endemic (d) None

591. Occupational Anthropozonoses includes;
(a) Tetanus (b) Rabies
(c) Both a & b (d) None

592. Q-fever is also known as;
(a) Abattoir fever (b) Minemite fever
(c) Both a & b (d) None

593. Parasitic infections which are naturally trnasmissible bet ween vertebrate animal and man are;
(a) Leishmaniasis (b) Toxoplasmosis
(c) Trypanosmiasis (d) All the above

594. Helminthic infection which are naturally transmissible between vertebrate animal and man are;
(a) Clonorchiosis (b) Fasciolopsiosis
(c) Taeniosis (d) All the above

595. Meat borne parasitic dieseases are;
(a) Cysticercosis (b) Sarcocystiosis
(c) Toxoplasmosis (d) All the above

596. Disease caused by *Echinococcus granulosus* is named;
(a) Hydetidosis

(b) Echionococcus disease
(c) Unilocular echinococcosis
(d) All the above

597. Main definitive host for Echinococcus is;
(a) Dog (b) Sheep
(c) Both (d) None

598. Metacestodes stage of Echinococcus develop in;
(a) Herbivore animal (b) Canidae
(c) Fasciola (d) None

599. Casoni skin test is used for diagnosis of;
(a) Echinococosis (b) Taeniasis
(c) Fasciolopsiosis (d) Toxoplasmosis

600. Cyclozoonoses Includes;
(a) Taeniasis (b) Echinococcosis
(c) Both a & b (d) None

601. Meat Infection with cysticerci of *Taenia saginata* is known as;
(a) Measly pork (b) Measly beef
(c) Both (d) None

602. Definitive host for *Taenia solium* and *T saginata* is;
(a) Man (b) Pig
(c) Cattle (d) All the above

603. Neuro cysticercosis is caused by the infection of;
(a) *T solium* (b) *T. saginata*
(c) Both (d) None

604. Toxoplasma was first recovered from a species of rodent by;
(a) Nicolle and Manceaux
(b) Sobin and Feldman
(c) Darling
(d) None

605. *Toxoplasma gondii* causes infection by;
(a) Tachyzoite (b) Bradyzoite
(c) Sporozoite (d) All the above

606. Definite host for toxoplasmosis;
(a) Cat & other felidae
(b) Bird & man
(c) Sporozoites
(d) None

607. Trichinellosis is transmitted to man by consumption of raw or inadiquately cooked meat of;
(a) Swine (b) Sheep
(c) Goat (d) Cattle

608. Cryptosporidiosis is maintained and transmitted through;
(a) Animal to man cycle
(b) Man to animal
(c) Man to man
(d) All the above

609. Guinae worm disease is known as;
(a) Dracunculosis (b) Cryptosporidiosis
(c) Toxoplasmosis (d) None

610. Lung fluke disease is caused by;
(a) *Paragonium westernani*
(b) *Prosthogonium ovatius*
(c) *Fasciola hepatica*
(d) None

611. Man get infection of paragonimiasis by ingestion of;
(a) Crab/cray fish (b) Dragon fly
(c) Snail (d) None

612. Cutaneous larva migrans is also known as;
(a) Hook worm disease
(b) Creeping eruption
(c) Larva currens
(d) All the above

613. Visceral larva migrans is also known as;
(a) Familial eosinophilia
(b) Loeffler's syndrome
(c) Nonpatest nemtodiosis
(d) All the above

614. Schistosomosis is also known as;
(a) Snail fever (b) Cercarial dermatitis
(c) Swimmer itch (d) All the above

615. Schistosoma of zoonotic importance is;
(a) *Schistosonia japonicum*
(b) *S. bovis*
(c) Both
(d) None

616. Leishmaniosis is transmitted by;
(a) Sand fly (b) Tse Tes fly
(c) Both (d) None

617. Kalaazar/Dumdumfever/black sickness are synonyms of;
(a) Viceral leishmaniosis
(b) Cutaneous leishmaniosis
(c) Mucocutaneous leishmaniosis

(d) None

618. Oriental boil/Delhi boil/Tropical boil are synonym of;
(a) Cutaneons leichmaniosis
(b) Veiscerl leichmaniosis
(c) Mucocutaneous leichmaniosis
(d) None

619. Chagas disease is caused by;
(a) *T. cruzi* (b) *T. gambiense*
(c) *T. rhodesiense* (d) None

620. Visceral larva migrans is caured by;
(a) *Toxocara sp.* (b) *Ascaris sp.*
(c) *Capillaria sp.* (d) All the above

621. Liver fluke disease in man is caused by;
(a) *Clonorchis sp.* (b) *Opithorchis sp.*
(c) Both a & b (d) None

622. Clonorchis and Opisthorchis infection in man and animal occur due to ingestion of infected;
(a) Fish (b) Snail
(c) Crab (d) None

623. Cat scratch diseases is caused by;
(a) *Rocholimaea henselae*
(b) *Coxeiella burneti*
(c) *R typhi*
(d) None

624. Gilcrist's disease/chicago disease are synonyms of;
(a) Blastomycosis (b) Aspergillosis
(c) Candidiosis (d) None

625. Sentinel host for West Nile virus is;
(a) Swine (b) Birds
(c) Dog (d) Cattle

626. Eastern Equine Encephalitis is caused by;
(a) Alphavirus (b) Flavivirus
(c) Filovirus (d) All the above

627. Most viral zoonoses fall within the categories of
(a) Direct & metazoonoses
(b) Saprozoonoses
(c) Cyclozoonoses
(d) None

628. Food borne viruses include;
(a) Enterovirus (b) Parvovirus
(c) Adenovirus (d) All the above

629. Dengu fever is clinically characerized by;
(a) High fever
(b) Haemorrhage in most tissues
(c) Circulatory failure
(d) All the above

630. Splenic fever/wool sortes's disease/malignant pustule/malignant carbuncles/charbon/Raj picher's disease are another name of disease;
(a) Beucellosis (b) Anthrax
(c) T.B (d) J.D

631. *Bacillus anthracis*;
(a) Does not form spores
(b) Forms exoposes
(c) Form endoshpores
(d) Is gram negative organism

632. Symptoms like sphenomegaly, bleeding from natural orifices, absence of rigor mostis, absence of clotting of blood appear in;
(a) Acute fasciolosis (b) Chronic fasciolosis
(c) Enterotoxaemia (d) Anthrax

633. Which one is occupotional anthropozoonoses;
(a) Anthrax (b) Brucellosis
(c) Leptospisosis (d) All

634. Who first isolated Anthrax organism in pus culture;
(a) Luis Pasture (b) Robert koch
(c) Delofond (d) Marston

635. Sterne spore vaccine is against;
(a) Anthrax
(b) Brucellosis
(c) Pulpy kidney disease
(d) Black Quarter

636. Who first prepared vaccine against Anthrax;
(a) Luis Pasture (b) Robert Koch
(c) Delafond (d) Marston

637. Which exotoxin is released by *Bacillus anthrasis;*
(a) Oedema factor (b) Protactive Ag
(c) Lethal factor (d) All

638. *Bacillus anthrasis* is;
(a) Endospore forming organism
(b) Capsular organism
(c) Gram positive organism
(d) All

639. Spores of *Bacillus anthracis* in soil can remain alive upto;

(a) 40 - 60 years (b) 100 years
(c) 120 years (d) 140 years

640. Which transmission cycle of anthrax does not occur;
(a) Animal - Animal (b) Animal - Man
(c) Man - Animal (d) All does not occur

641. In animals fulminating form of anthrax is also called as;
(a) Peracute form (b) Acute form
(c) Subacute form (d) Chronic form

642. In man which form of anthrax occurs;
(a) Cutaneous (b) Intestinal
(c) Pulmonary (d) All

643. Ascolis test for Anthrax diagnosis is a;
(a) Allergic test (b) Molecular test
(c) Precipitation test (d) Agglutination test

644. Vaccine against Anthrax which can be used both for animals & humans is;
(a) Pasteusis vaccine (b) Sterne vaccine
(c) Cascojjo vaccine (d) Wigt vaccine

645. Epizootic abortion occurs due to;
(a) *Brucella abortus* (b) Compylobactos
(c) *Trichomonas foetus* (d) Toxoplasma

646. Undulant fever occur due to;
(a) *B. abortus* in cattle (b) *B. melitensis* in cattle
(c) *B. abortus* in man (d) *B. melitensis* in man

647. Which one of the following spp. of Brucella is not zoonotic;
(a) *B. abortus* (b) *B. melitisis*
(c) *B. suis* (d) *B. ovis*

648. *Brucella neotomae* affects;
(a) Cattle (b) Dogs
(c) Cat (d) Wood rat

649. Brucella organism is;
(a) Gm positive (b) Motile
(c) Aerobic (d) Bacilli

650. Which spp of Brucella is transmitted to man by unpasteurized milk;
(a) *B. melitansis* (b) *B. abortus*
(c) *B. suis* (d) *B. canis*

651. Biotyping of Beucella strain is done on the basis of;
(a) CO_2 requirement
(b) Urcase activity
(c) Ability to produce H_2S
(d) All

652. Bernard Bang isolated;
(a) *Breucella abortus* (b) *B. melitansis*
(c) *B. suis* (d) *B. canis*

653. David Bruce isoloted;
(a) *Brucella abortus* (b) *B. melitensis*
(c) *B. suis* (d) *B. canis*

654. Most of the Brucella infections in India are isolated from;
(a) Sheep & Goat (b) Cattle
(c) Buffalo (d) Pig

655. Which transmission cycle of Brucella does not occur;
(a) Animal - Animal (b) Animal - Man
(c) Man – man (d) None

656. I.P of Brucellosis in animals is;
(a) 1-2 weeks (b) 2 weeks - 2 months
(c) 1week - 6 months (d) > 1 year

657. In horse Brucella organism causes;
(a) Poll - evil (b) Fistulous withers
(c) Both a & b (d) None

658. Milk Ring test for Brucella diagnosis is for;
(a) Disease in animals
(b) Disease in animals
(c) Disease in young animals
(d) Herd diagnosis

659. Camli's test is for;
(a) Antheax (b) B.Q
(c) Brucellosis (d) Tetanus

660. Which vaccine (s) is/are live strain vaccine against Brrucella;
(a) B. melitansis strain Rev.1
(b) B. abortus strain -19
(c) Both A & B
(d) Brucella melitansis 53 H

661. Biphasic casteneda blood culture technique is for;
(a) Brucellosis (b) Anthrax
(c) Tetanus (d) B.Q

662. Leptospisa is a;
(a) Bacteria (b) Virus
(c) Fungi (d) Spirochaete

663. In which disease hemoglobinuria occurs;
(a) Babesiosis (b) Leptospisosis

(c) Both a & b (d) None

664. Weil's disease is also called as;
(a) Listeriosis (b) Letospisosis
(c) Tuberculosis (d) Brucellosis

665. Which group of animals/brids are not affected by Leptospira;
(a) Domestic animals (b) Wild animals
(c) Masrupials (d) Birds

666. Leptospisa organism is,
(a) Gm -ive (b) Motile
(c) Not host specific (d) All

667. Which of the following play an important role in transmision of leptospira to human;
(a) Rodents (b) Cattle
(c) Birds (d) Pigs

668. Which transmission cycle of leptospirosis does not occurs;
(a) Animal - Animal (b) Animal - Man
(c) Animal – Rodent (d) Man - Man

669. Man for Leptospira are;
(a) Dead end host (b) Accidental host
(c) Reservoir host (d) All

670. Stuttgarts's disease is;
(a) Acute Leptospisosis in Dog
(b) Chronic Leptospisosis in Dog
(c) Acute Leptospisosis in Cattle
(d) Chsonic Leptospisosis in Cattle.

671. Stuart media and Kurthop's media are for;
(a) Listeria
(b) Leptospira
(c) *Mycobocterium spp.*
(d) Yersinia spp

672. MAT (Microscopic Agglutination Test) is for;
(a) Listeria (b) Leptospira
(c) Mycobacterium (d) Yesrinia spp

673. Silver staining technique is for;
(a.) Listeria (b) Leptospira
(c) Mycobacterium (d) Yesrinia spp

674. Listeriosis is also called as;
(a) Silage disease (b) Circling disease
(c) Both a & b (d) None

675. Listeria is;
(a) Gm +ve organism (b) Short rod shaped
(c) Motile (d) All

676. Listeria organism shows tumbling motility at;
(a) 25^0C (b) 36^0C
(c) 37^0C (d) 42^0C

677. Listeriosis is a;
(a) Food borne zoonoses
(b) Vector borne Zoonoses
(c) Both a & b
(d) None

678. Which is/are anthropogoonoses;
(a) Anthrax (b) Brucellosis
(c) Listeriosis (d) All

679. Changing goonoses is shown by;
(a) Leptospirosis (b) Listeriosis
(c) FMD (d) B.Q

680. I.P for letospirosis in animals is;
(a) 1 - 3 wks (b) 5 - 6 wks
(c) 1 - 3 days (d) 5 - 6 days

681. Rufscence test for diagnosis of Letospirosis in man is;
(a) Macroscopic agglutination test
(b) Dark - field microscopy
(c) Silucus staining tecchnique
(d) MAT (Microscopic Agglutination test)

682. Carrier and reservoir for Listeria organism is;
(a) Chicken (b) Rodents
(c) Dog (d) Pigs

683. PALCAM media is for cultural examination of;
(a) Listeria (b) Leptospisa
(c) Nocardia (d) *Bacillus anthracis*

684. Anaton's test is for;
(a) Listeria (b) Leptospira
(c) Nocardia (d) *Bacillus anthrasis*

685. Toxin - antitoxin neutralization test is for the detection of;
(a) Neurotoxin of *Cl. tetani*
(b) Hemolysis of *Cl. tetani*
(c) B.Q.
(d) Pulpy kidney disease

686. Tetanus is;
(a) Lock jow;
(b) Is oocupational anthropognosis
(c) Discending infection in man
(d) All

687. Tuberculosis is also called as;

(a) Consumption disease
(b) Phthisis
(c) Pearly disease
(d) All

688. Tuberculin was first developed by;
(a) Robert Koch (b) Luis Pasture
(c) Theobald smith (d) Paul Ehrlich

689. PPD concentration in tuberculin is;
(a) 0.5 mg/ml of avian type bacilli
(b) 1 mg/ml of bovine type bacilli
(c) 2 mg/ml of human type bacilli
(d) All

690. In India T.B is a;
(a) Emerging Disease
(b) Re - emerging disease
(c) Eradicated disease
(d) None

691. Tuberculin is obtained from;
(a) *M. tuberculosis* (b) *M. bovis*
(c) *M. liparae* (d) *M. avium*

692. Third world congress on food borne infection and intoxication was held in 1992 in;
(a) Berlin (b) Paris
(c) New york (d) Tokiyo

693. Vibriosis is also known as;
(a) Brucellosis (b) Campylobacteriosis
(c) Toxoplasmosis (d) Trichomoniasis

694. Which one is/are food borne zoonoses;
(a) Campylobacteriosis
(b) Staphyloccosis
(c) *Cl. perfringins* gastroenteritis
(d) All

695. Winter dysentry in cattle is caused by;
(a) *Staphylococcus aureus*
(b) *E. coli*
(c) Giardia
(d) *Campylobocter jejuni*

696. Campylobactor is;
(a) Gm - ive organism
(b) Spirally curved rod like
(c) Motile
(d) All

697. Camplylobactor in animal causes;
(a) Enteritis
(b) Abortion
(c) Reproductive disorder
(d) All

698. I.P of Compylobacteriosis orgainism is/are;
(a) 1 - 2 days (b) 2 - 10 days
(c) 1 - 2 Wks (d) 2 -10 wks

699. Media for culture of Compylobacter orgainism is/are;
(a) Buffer's media (b) Skirrow's media
(c) Both a & b (d) None

700. *Cl. perfringens* previously was known as;
(a) *Cl. welchii* (b) *Cl. chauvoi*
(c) *Cl. septicum* (d) *Cl. novyi*

701. Which strain of *Cl. perfringins* is natural microflora of animal and human intestine;
(a) A (b) B
(c) C (d) D

702. Pulpy Kidney Disease in sheep is caused by which strain of *Cl. Perfringens*;
(a) A (b) B
(c) C (d) D

703. Which strain *of Cl. perfringens* has zoonotic importance;
(a) A (b) B
(c) C (d) D

704. I.P for *Cl. perfringens* intoxication is;
(a) 8 - 24 hrs (b) 8 - 24 days
(c) 8 - 24 wks (d) 8 - 24 month

705. *E. coli* in man causes;
(a) Haemorrhagic colitis
(b) Haemorrhagic uraemic syndrome
(c) Both a & b
(d) None

706. Sero group 0157: H7 of *E. coli* is type of;
(a) EPEC (b) ETCE
(c) EIEC (d) EHEC

707. ETEC produces;
(a) Heat labile enterotoxins
(b) Heat stable enterotoxins
(c) Both types of toxins
(d) Does not produce toxins

708. Which symptom is not characteristic of *Cl. perfringens* intoxication in man;
(a) Diarrhoea (b) Abdominal pain

(c) Dehydration (d) Vomition

709. In which animals vomition is characteristic sign of *Cl. perfringens* intoxication;
(a) Monkeys (b) Dog
(c) Cat (d) Horse

710. Ecolon, Jencine K - 99 and scour Guard are examples of vaccines of;
(a) Fimbrial vaccines of *E. coli*
(b) Somatic vaccines of *E. coli*
(c) Fimbrial vaccines of Salmonella
(d) Somatic vaccines of Salmonella

711. Swine for salmonella are;
(a) Reservoirs (b) Amplifier host
(c) Both a & b (d) None

712. I.P. of salmonellosis in man is;
(a) 1 -2 days (b) 4 -6 days
(c) 2 -4 days (d) 6 - 8 days

713. Which is/are enrichment media for salmonella;
(a) Tetrathionate broth
(b) Selenite broth
(c) Rappaport - vassiliadis broth
(d) All

714. BGA for salmonella is;
(a) Enrichment media
(b) Differential media
(c) Selective media
(d) Salmonella does not grow on BGA

715. Most suitable example of amphixenosis is;
(a) Anthrax
(b) Brucellosis
(c) Streptococcosis
(d) Staphylococcal illness

716. Staphylococcus is;
(a) Catalase +ve (b) Manitol +ve
(c) Coagulase +ve (d) All

717. In man TSS (Toxic Shock syndrome) is caused by;
(a) Streptococcus (b) Staphylococcus
(c) Micrococcus (d) *Bacillus cercus*

718. In man 'meat ball sickness' is caused by;
(a) Sterptococcus (b) Staphylococcus
(c) Micrococcus (d) *Bacillus cersus*

719. Most importan cereal for the trammission of *B. cercus* is;
(a) Rice (b) Wheat
(c) Millet (d) Jwar

720. *B. cercus* in man produces;
(a) Diarrhoeal syndrome
(b) Emetic syndrome
(c) Both a & b
(d) None

721. Most potent neurotoxin is;
(a) Rabies toxin (b) Tetanus toxin
(c) Botulinum toxin (d) Shigella toxin

722. Robertson's cooked meat media is for;
(a) *Cl. perfringens* (b) *B. cercus*
(c) Staphylococcus (d) Streptococus

723. Input botulinum in man is caused by contaminated;
(a) Milk (b) Curd
(c) Butter (d) Honey

724. Organism transmitted through sea food in man is/are;
(a) *Plesiomonas shigelloides*
(b) *Aeromonas hydrophila*
(c) *Vibrio parahemolyticus*
(d) All

725. Rice Water Diarrhoria in man is caused by;
(a) *Vibrio cholera*
(b) *Vibrio valnificus*
(c) *Vibrio parahemolyticus*
(d) *Aeromonas hydrophila*

726. Orgainis which can be transmitted to man through refrigerated milk/milk products or meat/meat product is/are;
(a) Yersinia interocolitica
(b) Listerioa monocytogenes
(c) Both a & b
(d) None

727. 'Elek test' is for the diagnosis of;
(a) *Vibrio parahaemolyticus*
(b) *Vibrio cholera*
(c) *Vibrio vulnificus*
(d) Aeromonas

728. *Aeromonas hydrophila* procuces;
(a) Cytotoxin
(b) Cytotoxic interotoxin
(c) Both a & b

(d) Not produces toxin

729. Sum total of all external condition influences affecting life and development of any living being;
(a) Enviroment (b) Climate
(c) Microclimate (d) None of these

730. Undesirable changes brought about in the natural qualitity of environment is known as;
(a) Environment hygiene
(b) Environment pollution
(c) Both
(d) None of these

731. Colouless, odourless, tasteless water without turbidity;
(a) Pure water (b) Wholesome water
(c) Both of the above (d) None

732. The water contains no pathogenic organism and poisons, chemicals beyond permissible limit;
(a) Pure water (b) Whole some water
(c) Both of the above (d) None

733. Per capita supply/person/year < 1700 m^3 in;
(a) Water stess condition
(b) Water scarse condition
(c) Both of the above
(d) None of these

734. Pollutants directly get into water are known as;
(a) Point source water pollution
(b) Non point source water pollution
(c) Both of the above
(d) None of these

735. Diseases caused by aquatic organism that spend their life in water and another part as parasite;
(a) Water based diseases
(b) Water borne diseases
(c) Water related disease
(d) None of these

736. Diseases transmitted by insects that bread or live in either polluted or non-polluted water;
(a) Water based diseases
(b) Water - borne diseases
(c) Water related diseases
(d) Water related vector diseases

737. Leprosy, diptheria, tetanus, TB, whooping cough are;
(a) Water related diseases
(b) Water related vector discases
(c) Water based diseases
(d) Water borne diseases

738. Cattle require drinking water;
(a) 55 - 68 litre (b) 40 - 50 litre
(c) 30 - 40 litre (d) 50 - 60 litre

739. For standard drinking water the value is more than 5 for;
(a) Hazen colour value
(b) Schiachen colour value
(c) Sulfer colour value
(d) All of the above

740. Odour of water is best assesed at;
(a) 20.0°C (b) 30.0°C
(c) 25.0°C (d) 40.0°C

741. H_2S like odour comes from water due to presence of;
(a) Decomposing sewage
(b) Vegetable matter
(c) Phenol
(d) None

742. Musty odour is due to presence of;
(a) Vegetable matter
(b) Decaying weeds, hay and straws
(c) Sewage
(d) None

743. Recommended value for drinking water;
(a) 6.5 - 8.5 (b) 6.8 - 9.0
(c) 5.5 - 6.5 (d) 7.0 - 7.5

744. Gastric disturbances and mucosal damages are due to;
(a) Very high alkaline medium
(b) Acidic medium
(c) Alkaline medium
(d) Neutral medium

745. Optimum temperature for drinking water;
(a) 25 - 35°C (b) 20 - 30°C
(c) 17 - 35°C (d) 50 - 60°C

746. Chemical charactertics of water is evaluated by;
(a) Organic matter (b) Metallic matter
(c) Both a & b (d) None

747. Presence of Vegetable in water indicates pollution through;
(a) Organic matter (b) Sewage

(c) Both (d) None

748. The product producced due to I[st] stage of sewage degradation is;
(a) NH_3 (b) $(NH_4)SO_4$.
(c) CO_2 (d) H_2CO_3

749. Very low amount of florides causes;
(a) Gastritis (b) Enteritis
(c) Dental caries (d) All of the above

750. Deep wells and sea water have got more amount of;
(a) Sulphate (b) Nitrates
(c) Chlorides (d) None

751. Maximum permissible limit (MPL) of chlorides;
(a) 150 - 200 mg/lit (b) 250 - 1000 mg/lit
(c) 400 - 800 mg/lit (d) None

752. Maximum permissible limit of fluorides;
(a) 1 - 1.5 ppm (b) 7 ppm
(c) 3 ppm (d) None

753. Toxicity of cyanide causes;
(a) Diarrhoea (b) Stomatitis
(c) Enterogastritis (d) None

754. Iron bacteria in water
(a) Crenothrix (b) None of these
(c) Crallionella (d) Both a & b

755. Arsenic present in water either due to;
(a) Insecticids (b) Weedicides
(c) Both of the above (d) None

756. Typical garlic odour is observed in;
(a) Cyanide (b) Nitrate
(c) Nitrite (d) Arsenic

757. Which element is generally absent in water;
(a) Co (b) Mo
(c) Fe (d) Cu

758. Slimy coating in inner wall of pipes and container is due to;
(a) Gallionella (b) Crenothrix
(c) Both of the above (d) None

759. Minamata disease is caused by;
(a) Hg (b) Co
(c) Fe (d) Mn

760. Minamata disease is caused by;
(a) Eating contaminated fish
(b) Eating snails
(c) Both
(d) None of these

761. Soil bacteria are;
(a) Nitrosomonas (b) Nitratiying bacteria
(c) Nitrobactor (d) Both a & b

762. Nitrosomonas coverts;
(a) Nitrites to Nitrates
(b) NH_3 to nitrites
(c) Nitrates to Nitrates
(d) All of these

763. For removal of viruses clorination is done at the rate of;
(a) 0.5 mg/lit (b) 0.9 mg/lit
(c) 1.4 mg/lit (d) None

764. Natural purifiers;
(a) Alage (b) Fungi
(c) Both of these (d) None

765. Fungi produces pollution due to
(a) Rife sewage (b) Raw seqage
(c) Vegatables (d) None

766. Water treatement process is classified by;
(a) Small scals processes
(b) Large scals processes
(c) Both of above
(d) None of these

767. Ultraviolet rays present in sunlight have natural;
(a) Germicidal activity
(b) Germistatic activity
(c) Both of these
(d) None

768. Bleaching powder provides;
(a) 40% free chlorine (b) 60% free chlorine
(c) 33% free chlorine (d) None of these

769. Recontamination during storage, transportation and distribution of water is charecterized by;
(a) Chlorine (b) Bleaching powder
(c) Residual Cl_2 (d) All of these

770. $KmNo_4$ acts as;
(a) Disinfectant (b) Oxidizing agent
(c) Both of these (d) All of these

771. In low pressure filters;
(a) Gravitational force is used
(b) Extrapressure is used
(c) Both of the above
(d) None of these

772. Low pressure filters;
(a) Microbes are destroyed
(b) Microbes are not destroyed
(c) Both may be destroyed
(d) None of these

773. Berkefield filters used as;
(a) Low pressure filters
(b) High pressure filters
(c) Ultra ease filters
(d) None of thses

774. In ultra ease filters filteration is in;
(a) 2 stage (b) 3 stage
(c) 5 stage (d) 6 stage

775. In superchlorination, chlorine is used at the rate of;
(a) 10 times of normal
(b) 5 times of normal
(c) 15 times of normal
(d) None of these

776. Chlorine reacts with water to from;
(a) Chloral hydrate (b) Chloral hydroside
(c) Chloramine (d) None

777. Ozone is broken down to;
(a) Two free molecules of O2
(b) Oxygen & nascent oxygen
(c) 3- nascent oxygen
(d) None

778. Slow sand filters remove;
(a) 40% of impurites (b) 70% of impurites
(c) 80% of impurites (d) 90% of impurites

779. Sterilization is done with the help of;
(a) Chlorine (b) Ozone
(c) Both of the above (d) None

780. Orthotoudine test determines;
(a) Free chlorine (b) Combired chlorine
(c) Both of a & b (d) None

781. Orthotoulidine - Arsenite test determines;
(a) Free chlorine (b) Residual chlorine
(c) Both of a & b (d) None

782. Water from the community containing liquid and solid excreta is;
(a) Sewage (b) Wastage
(c) Both a & B (d) None

783. Sewage devoid of human exreta is known as;
(a) Sullage (b) Hazen colour value
(c) Both of these (d) None of the these

784. Strength of sewage is measured by;
(a) BOD (b) COD
(c) Suspended solids (d) All of these

785. If BOD is more than 300 mg/lit, then it is;
(a) Strong sewage (b) Weak sewage
(c) Neutral sewage (d) None

786. Fungi produces pollution on which account;
(a) Pipe sewage (b) Raw sewage
(c) Vegetable (d) None

787. Bleaching powder provides the amount of chlorine;
(a) 70% free chlorine (b) 80% free chlorine
(c) 90% free chlorine (d) 33% free chlorine

788. Minamata disease is caused by;
(a) Inorganic form of Hg
(b) Methylated form of Hg
(c) Hydrated form of Hg
(d) Organic form of Hg

789. Sewage treatment is done by;
(a) Aerobic process (b) Anaerobic process
(c) Both of a & b (d) None

790. Anaerobic process is;
(a) Slower process (b) Faster process
(c) Neutral process (d) None of these

791. Sewage purification is done by;
(a) Primary stage
(b) Secondary stage
(c) Primary & secondary stage
(d) None of these

792. Fat & grease of sewage float at top known as;
(a) Sullage (b) Scum
(c) All of these (d) None of these

793. Secondary stage is aerobic which contains;
(a) Trickling filters process
(b) Activated sludge process
(c) Only trickling filters process
(d) Trickling & Activated both

794. In activated sludge treatment there is;
(a) 50% water (b) 48% water
(c) 80% water (d) > 95% water

795. Sladge disposal is done by;
(a) Sludge digestion (b) Sea disposal

(c) Land disposal (d) All above

796. Water quality criteria & standards are set by;
(a) biological aspect
(b) Chemical aspect
(c) Radiological Aspect
(d) All of these

797. Water (prevention & control of pollution) Act enforced;
(a) In 1980 (b) In 1970
(c) In 1974 (d) In 1964

798. Acceptability aspect includes;
(a) Physical parameters
(b) Inorganic parameters
(c) Organic parameters
(d) Physical & inorganic parameters

799. Substances present in larger concentration in Environment than normal are;
(a) Environment contaminants
(b) Environment pollutants
(c) Both of the above
(d) None of these

800. Maximum demand of water is in;
(a) Municipal sector (b) Agricultural sector
(c) Industrial sector (d) All of the above

801. Water needed in:
(a) Municipal sector (b) Agricultural sector
(c) Industrial sector (d) All of the above

802. On earth occean water is;
(a) 95 - 97% (b) 79%
(c) 62% (d) 40%

803. On Earth fresh wather is;
(a) 3 -5% (b) 8%
(c) 15% (d) 20%

804. Main sources of usable water is;
(a) Rain water (b) Surface water
(c) Under ground (d) All of these

805. Water requirement per capita /year is;
(a) < 100 m^3 (b) > 500 m^3
(c) > 500 m^3 (d) > 1000 m^3

806. In malta lowest avaiblitty of water in 1995 was;
(a) 72 m^3/yr/person (b) 80m^3/yr/person
(c) 82 m^3/yr/person (d) All of these

807. Sources of water pollution;
(a) Domestic (b) Agricultrural sector
(c) Industrial sector (d) All of the above

808. Diseases of water;
(a) Water borne diseases
(b) Water based diseases
(c) Water related diseases
(d) All of the above

809. Water is polluted by;
(a) Direct process (b) Indirect process
(c) Both of the above (d) None of these

810. Drinking water requirement for horses;
(a) 36 - 54 lts/day (b) 55 - 68 lts/day
(c) 9 lts/day (d) All of these

811. Water quality is evaluated by;
(a) Physical means (b) Chemical means
(c) Microbiological (d) All of these

812. Rotten egg odour of water is due to;
(a) Decomposing sewage
(b) Vegetable matter
(c) Phenol
(d) All of the these

813. Flat/incipid taste of water is due;
(a) Very soft water (b) Very hard water
(c) Neutral water (d) All of these

814. Clorides present in water as salts of;
(a) Na (b) Potassium salts
(c) Magnisium (d) All of these

815. Sea water and deep wells water contain;
(a) High amounts of chlorides
(b) Less amounts of chlorides
(c) Higher amounts of chlorides
(d) None.

816. If amount of NaCl is more than normal water, it can be;
(a) Consumed
(b) Not consumed
(c) Partialy consumsed
(d) All of these

817. Maximum permissible limit of Mg is;
(a) 50 ppm (b) 80 ppm
(c) 30 ppm (d) 40 PPm

818. Means of water pollution are;
(a) Direct process (b) Indirect process
(c) Both of these (d) None of these

819. Kind of diseases that may occur due to water

pollution;
(a) Water based diseases
(b) Water borne diseases
(c) Water related diseases
(d) All of these

820. Nitrobacter convertes;
(a) Nitrites to Nitrates
(b) NH_3 ot Nitrites
(c) Nitrites to Nitrite
(d) All of these

821. Radiological charatertics of water is measured by;
(a) Industrial disposal
(b) Nuclear reactors
(c) X- ray film disposal
(d) All of the above

822. Small scale processes includes;
(a) Boiling (b) Storage
(c) Distilation (d) All of the above

823. In activated sludge treatment, there is;
(a) 90% water (b) 48% water
(c) 80% water (d) > 95% H_2O

824. Selection of treatment of water is based on;
(a) Size of impurity
(b) Chemical reactivity of impurity
(c) Concentration of impurity
(d) All of the these

825. Water treatment is done for;
(a) Removal of objectionable odour
(b) Destruetion of all micro-organisms
(c) Removal of hardness
(d) All of these

826. $CuSo_4$ is used in treatment of water;
(a) To remove algae (b) To remove fungi
(c) To remove lime (d) All of the above

827. Highpressure filter includes;
(a) Pasture chamber land
(b) Berkfield filters
(c) Nonel of these
(d) Both of the above

828. Filteration is done by use of;
(a) Coagulants
(b) Without used of coagulants.
(c) With or without coagulants
(d) All of these

829. Pure water having character as;
(a) Taste less (b) Colour less
(c) Odour less (d) All above

830. Whole some water contains;
(a) Non pathgenic organism
(b) Pathogenic organisms
(c) Both a & b
(d) None a to b

831. On Earth having water % from ocean.
(a) 97% (b) 80%
(c) 85% (d) 75%

832. Fresh water % on earts;
(a) 3% (b) 40%
(c) 10% (d) None above

833. Fresh water source of glaciers;
(a) 85% (b) 90%
(c) 79% (d) 70%

834. Fresh water source of ground water;
(a) 50% (b) 20%
(c) 60% (d) 10%

835. Fresh water source of surface fresh water;
(a) 10% (b) 1%
(c) 20% (d) None

836. Main source of water supply;
(a) Rain water (b) Surface water
(c) Ground water (d) All above

837. Purest form of water is;
(a) Rain water (b) Surface water
(c) Ground water (d) None above

838. Which one is under ground water;
(a) Wells (b) River
(c) Both (d) None

839. Maximum demand of water is for;
(a) Agriculture (b) Municipal
(c) Industrial (d) None of above

840. Minimum demand of water is;
(a) Municipal (b) Agriculture
(c) Industrial (d) All

841. Water pollution occurs through;
(a) Point source water pollution
(b) Non point water pollution
(c) None of a to b
(d) Both a to b

842. Point source water pollution through;

(a) Industrial waste
(b) Ariculture chemical residues
(c) Both a to b
(d) None a to b

843. Non point water pollution through;
(a) Aricultural chemical residues
(b) Indusrial works
(c) Industrial consumption
(d) All above

844. Water pollution causes;
(a) Water borne disease
(b) Non water borne disease
(c) Both a to b
(d) None above

845. Water besed disease are caused by;
(a) Aquantic organism
(b) Wild animal
(c) Both a & b
(d) None

846. Some water borne viral diseases are;
(a) FMD Virus (b) R.P. Virus
(c) Both a & b (d) None above

847. Treatment of virus contaminated water may be done by;
(a) Chlorination (b) Fumigation
(c) Boiling (d) None of above

848. Fungi are present in water;
(a) Yes (b) No
(c) Both (d) All

849. Water purification is process of;
(a) Water treatment (b) Sewage water
(c) Both A to B (d) Noe

850. Removed of hardness of water is the process of;
(a) Water treatment (b) Sewage water
(c) Agriculture (d) None

851. Small scale process of water treatment is;
(a) Boiling of water (b) Add some pathogen
(c) Both (d) None

852. Water treatment is done by;
(a) Boiling (b) Storage
(c) Distillation (d) All above

853. Low pressre filter is process of;
(a) Water treatment
(b) Prevent waste water
(c) Use water in agricultrue
(d) None

854. Berk - feld filter is example of;
(a) High pressure filture
(b) Low pressure filture
(c) Both a to b
(d) None a to b

855. Ultra cone water filter is example of;
(a) Law pressure filture
(b) High pressure filture
(c) Both a & b
(d) None above

856. Chemical treatmet of water is done by;
(a) $KMNO_4$ (b) Alum
(c) $CuSO_4$ (d) All above

857. Bleaching powder is example of;
(a) Physical process (b) Chemical process
(c) Both a to b (d) None

858. Acid sodium salphate is an treatment example of;
(a) Chemical (b) Physical
(c) Biological (d) All above

859. Iodine is an example of;
(a) Physical (b) Chemical
(c) Biological (d) None

860. Water may be purification by;
(a) Storage (b) Boiling
(c) Distilation (d) All above

861. Ultraviolet Ray's present in;
(a) Sun Ray's (b) Electric light
(c) Both a to b (d) None

862. Surface water treatment is done by Ray's;
(a) Distrillation (b) Sun Ray's
(c) Stroage (d) None

863. Alum is used in water treatment @ grain/gallon of water;
(a) 1 -6 (b) 10
(c) 20 (d) None

864. $KMNO_4$ is use is water treatment @ ounce/1000 gallon;
(a) 20 (b) 1/2
(c) 2 (d) None

865. Iodine is used for water treatment @ mg/lit.
(a) 20 mg (b) 2 mg
(c) 10 mg (d) All above

866. Lime is used for water treatment @ mg/lit.
(a) 10 - 20 mg/lit. (b) 50 mg/ lit.
(c) 100 mg/ lit. (d) None

867 Filtration process is done with gravitational force as;
(a) Low pressure filter
(b) High pressure filter
(c) Both a to b
(d) None

868. Low pressure filtration is done by;
(a) Sand (b) Charcoal
(c) Stone (d) All

869. Sand is used for water treatment as;
(a) Low pressure filture
(b) High pressue filter
(c) Both a to b
(d) None

870. Pastur chamber is having;
(a) Brass chamber (b) Porcelin tube
(c) Both a to b (d) None

871. Pastur chamber having pressure lb/inch^2
(a) 50 - 60 (b) 20 - 40
(c) 0 - 10 (d) None

872. Berkfield filter is having;
(a) Porcelin candle (b) Sand
(c) Both a to b (d) None

873. Sudha microfilter is having;
(a) Cullelage membrane pad
(b) Chemical
(c) None a to b
(d) Both a to b

874. Sudha micro filter, filters water @ liter/min;
(a) 6 - 10 (b) 40
(c) 10 (d) None

875. Ultra case filter is used for;
(a) Water purification
(b) Water pollutions
(c) Both
(d) None

876. Large scale purification of water is done by;
(a) Storage tank (b) Running water
(c) Both a to b (d) None

877. Large sized particles settle down in the storage tank-botom in;
(a) 4 - 5 hrs (b) 1 -2 hrs
(c) 10 - 15 hrs (d) None

878. Organic matter settle down in the storage tank in;
(a) 10 hrs (b) 6 hrs
(c) 16 hrs (d) None

879. Impurities settle down in the stoage Tanik
(a) 90% (b) 100%
(c) Both a to b (d) None

880. Coagulants are not added in;
(a) Slow sand filter (b) Rapid sand filter
(c) Both a to b (d) None

881. Coagulants are added in;
(a) Slow sand filter (b) Rapid sand filter
(c) Both a to b (d) None

882. Rapid sand filter does not require;
(a) Extra pressure (b) Weight
(c) Both (d) None

883. Efficiency of rapid sand filter is;
(a) 15 lit/ft^2/hr (b) 11.25 lit/ft^2/hr
(c) Both a to b (d) None

884. Rapid sand filter removes the impurities (bacteria);
(a) 100% (b) 80%
(c) 99.99% (d) None

885 Rapid sand filter is not effective against;
(a) Virus (b) Bacteria
(c) Both a to b (d) None

886. Coagulation add in water as rapid sand filter is;
(a) Alum (b) Ferrous saphate
(c) Ferric sulphate (d) All above

887. Taste, colour odour of water is improved by;
(a) Rapid sand filter (b) Slow sand water
(c) Both (d) None

888. Chemical sterilization is done by;
(a) Chlorine (b) Ozone
(c) Both a & b (d) None

889. Period of chlorination is;
(a) 15 min. (b) 1 hrs
(c) 15 second (d) All above

890. Super chlorination requires dose;
(a) 20 time (b) 10 time
(c) Both (d) None

891. Dichlorination is done by;
(a) So_2

(b) Sodium thiosulphate
(c) Both a to b
(d) None

892. Chlorine reacts with ammonia in water in the form of;
(a) Cloramine (b) Cloride
(c) Both (d) None

893. Ozone oxidizes;
(a) Organic malter (b) Minerals
(c) Both (d) None

894. Widely used for sterilization of swiming pounds;
(a) Ozone (b) Chlorine
(c) Both (d) None

895. Drinking water will be treated by;
(a) Ammonia (b) Chlorine
(c) Both a to b (d) None

896. Atmospheric source of water pollution is;
(a) Acid rain (b) Dust
(c) Both (d) None

897. Cattle's requirement of water for drinking;
(a) 80 - 90 lit (b) 55 - 68 lit
(c) 40 - 50 lit (d) None

898. Horse's requirement of drinking water/day;
(a) 36 - 54 lit (b) 10 - 20 lit
(c) Both a to b (d) None

899. Sheep and goat's requirement of drinking water/day;
(a) 15 lit (b) 20 lit
(c) 9 lit (d) None

900. Liter/day drinking water requirement of camel is;
(a) 70 lit (b) 20 lit
(c) 36 lit (d) None

901. Poultry requires how much drinaking water/day;
(a) 1 lit (b) 225 ml
(c) Both (d) None

902. Dog requires how much drinaking water/day;
(a) 150 ml – 1 lit. (b) 2 lit
(c) Both a to b (d) None

903. Water quality is evaluated by;
(a) Physical method (b) Chemical method
(c) Both a & b (d) None

904. Dogs inlet outlet area (inch^2) requires;
(a) 1.0" (b) 1.8"
(c) 2.8" (d) 4.0"

905. For boars the inlet/outlet area (inch^2) is;
(a) 2.5 - 6 (b) 6 - 10
(c) 9 - 12 (d) None

906. For pig requisite air space (ft^3) is;
(a) 200 - 250 (b) 250 - 500
(c) 500 - 700 (d) 400 - 600

907. Presence of vegetation in water gives following colour;
(a) Red Colour (b) Greenigh Yellow
(c) Both (d) None

908. Presence of organic matter and iron in water gives following colour;
(a) Yellow (b) Red
(c) Orange (d) None

909. In radiation effect main organ of body affected is;
(a) Brain
(b) G.I. T. system
(c) Circulatory system
(d) Muscle

910. Vary high alkaline water causes;
(a) Mucosal damage (b) Gastric disturbance
(c) Both a to b (d) None

911. High acidic water causes;
(a) Mucosal damage (b) Gastric disturbance
(c) Both a to b (d) None

912. With high amount of minerals the water turbidity will;
(a) Increase (b) Decrease
(c) Both (d) No effect

913. Main pollutants of water are;
(a) Sewage
(b) Decomposed carcases
(c) Vegitative matters
(d) All Above

914. Presence of urea in water indicates pollution by;
(a) Carcase (b) Vegitative matter
(c) Chemicals (d) None

915. Maximum permissible limit of Ammonia in drinking water is;
(a) 0.2 ppm (b) 5 ppm
(c) 5 ppm (d) 2 ppm

916. Maximum permisable limit for chloride in drinking water is;

(a) 5 gm/lit (b) 0.25 - 1 gm/lit
(c) 15 gm/lit (d) None

917. Maximum permisable limit for sulphate in drinking water;
(a) 200 - 400 ppm (b) 800 - 1000 ppm
(c) 600 - 800 ppm (d) All Above

918 Maximum permisable limit of nitrate in drinking water is;
(a) 200 ppm (b) 45 - 100 ppm
(c) 150 ppm (d) None

919. Maximum permisable limit of nitrite in drinking water is;
(a) 3 ppm (b) 50 ppm
(c) 100 ppm (d) All

920. Maximum permisable limit for Floride in drinking water is;
(a) 4 - 10 ppm (b) 1 - 1.5 ppm
(c) 10 ppm (d) None

921. Maximum permisable limit for cyanide in drinking water is;
(a) 0.05 mg/lit (b) 1 mg/lit
(c) 2 mg/lit (d) None

922. Maximum permisable limit for iron in drinking water is;
(a) 0.3 mg/lit (b) 2 mg/lit
(c) 0.6 mg/lit (d) None

923. Maximum permisable limit for copper in drinking water is;
(a) 0.5 mg/lit (b) 1 mg/lit
(c) Both (d) None

924. Maximum permisable limit for lead in drinking water is;
(a) 5 mg/lit (b) 1 mg/lit
(c) 0.05 mg/lit (d) None

925. Maximum permisable limit for arsenic in drinking water is;
(a) 2 mg/lit (b) 0.05 mg/lit
(c) 0.5 mg/lit (d) None

926. The most contribution of gases to green house effect is;
(a) Carbondioxide (b) Methane
(c) Nitrous oxide (d) CFCS

927. Most sources of green house gases is;
(a) Combustion of fossil fuels
(b) Ruminants
(c) Agricultures
(d) Chemicals industries

928. Fossil fuel gases are;
(a) CO_2 (b) N_2O
(c) N_2O (d) All of above

929. In incinerator method the temperature for fallen animal may be rise up;
(a) 1300°C for 2 hour (b) 1200°C + 2 hour
(c) 1400°C for 3 hour (d) 1100°C for 3 hour

930. The most common practised method for fallen animal carsass is;
(a) Incineratos method
(b) Disposal of burial
(c) Disposal of burning
(d) Rendering method

931. Due to ozone depletion the percentage of ultraviolet rays on earth is;
(a) 90% (b) 96%
(c) 95% (d) 85%

932. The main disease for burring to dispose off carcass is;
(a) Anthrax (b) B.Q
(c) Tuberculosis (d) Both a & b

933. Main radiation sorce is;
(a) Natural (b) Man made
(c) Both a & b (d) None of them

934. Man made souces of radiation are;
(a) Medicinal (b) Industrial
(c) Nuclear reactors (d) All of them

935. Due to radiation conversion of organic molecules in the ionic pairs takes place in about;
(a) 10^{-13} to 10^{-14} sec (b) 10^{-10} to 10^{-12} sec
(c) 10^{-14} to 10^{-16} (d) 10^{-12} to 10^{-18} sec

936. More succeptible to radiation sources are;
(a) Youngs (b) Adult
(c) Old (d) All of above

937. Due to radition source, acute toxicity effect is produced in;
(a) 1 - 12 hourse (b) 1 -2 day
(c) 1 - 4 weks (d) 1 months

938. Death due to radiation mainly occurs because of;
(a) Vomition (b) Diarrhoea
(c) Fever (d) Dehydration

939. Du to radiation effect the hemopoeitic effect is seen in;
(a) 1-2 hrs (b) 1-2 days
(c) 5-7 days (d) 15 days after

940. One of other effect of radition effect is;
(a) Diarrhoea (b) Anaemia
(c) Fever (d) Hypersensitivity

941. Confirmative diagnosis of radition effect is done by;
(a) X - Ray (b) C-T scan
(c) M.R.I. (d) Radio tracing

942. Type of ventilation in fire clay ridge opening ventialator is ;
(a) Out let type (b) In let type
(c) Outlet- inlet type (d) Both type

943. The hight of ventilator in animal shad should be at least;
(a) Above 16 feet (b) Above 9 feet
(c) Above 14 feet (d) Above 15 feet

944. Extraction method ventilator one use in building for;
(a) Only air pass (b) CO_2 pass
(c) Fresh air (d) None of them

945. Mechanical system ventilator used in;
(a) Calf sheed
(b) Intensive poultry house
(c) Common house
(d) Pig house

946. The factor affecting the human health are;
(a) Temperature (b) Humidity
(c) Air movement (d) All of them

947. The bed ventilator most affected by;
(a) Young (b) Infants
(c) Old (d) Adult

948. With bad ventilation, the most common disease occur is;
(a) Brucellosis (b) T.B.
(c) Pneumonia (d) B.Q.

949. Commonly used inlet ventilaters are;
(a) Centinuous ridge (b) Air bricks
(c) Adjustable ridge (d) Wall window

950. Artificial ventilation is mainly;
(a) Plenum method (b) Hit + Min window
(c) Fire clay ridge (d) None of them

951. To estimate relative humidity, the instrument required is;
(a) Whirling hygrometer
(b) Room thermometer;
(c) Kata theromometer
(d) Globe Themometer

952. Ionizing radiation are;
(a) Alpha particles (b) Beta particle
(c) Gamma particles (d) Non of above

953. Naturally occurring radio isotopes are;
(a) Uranium (b) Actinium
(c) Thorium (d) All off

954. Non ionizing radiations are;
(a) Alpha (b) Beta
(c) Gama (d) U.V. rays

955. Radioactive substance on earth are;
(a) Radium Ra(226) (b) U 238
(c) Th 232 (d) All

956. Man made radioactive sources are;
(a) K^{40} (b) Th^{232}
(c) I^{31} (d) None

957. Radioactive unit of reaction is;
(a) Red (b) Erg
(c) Per gram (d) Betlian

958. Airbone radioactivity are;
(a) U^{238} (b) Th^{232}
(c) K^{40} (d) C^{14}

959. Radioisotops which is dangerous to man;
(a) 200 radio active (b) 150 radio active
(c) 250 redio active (d) 220 radio active

960. Radio isotopes used to know metabolism is;
(a) Corbon
(b) Strontium and caesium
(c) Iodine
(d) None of above

961. Type of radiotion cosmic rays produce;
(a) Natural (b) Man made
(c) Both of (d) None of these

962. Cosmic rays are passed through the;
(a) Enviroment (b) Space
(c) Atmosphere (d) None

963. Atmospheric radiation, form the radioactive gases are;
(a) Radon (b) Thoron

(c) Radon + Thoron (d) Non of all

964. Natural radition to which the average person is subjected comes to approximately;
(a) 1.0 red a year (b) 0.1 red a year
(c) 0.01 red a year (d) 10.0 red a year

965. Electromagnetic radiation are mainly;
(a) X- rays + gamma rays
(b) Only gamma X-rays
(c) Only X-rays
(d) a and b particale

966. Corpuscular radiations;
(a) X – rays
(b) a particles b particles + protein
(c) Non off them
(d) All off them

967. Minimizing radiation caused by ultraviolet, visible light, microwave radiation and;
(a) Cosmic rays (b) Radio frequency
(c) Both (d) None

968. Radiation unit is;
(a) Becqueral (B_9) (b) Milimeters
(c) Centimeters (d) Meters

969. One Becqueral is equal to;
(a) 26 Picocuries (b) 30 Picocuries
(c) 27 Picocuries (d) 25 Picocuries

970. The potency of radiation is measused in;
(a) Roentgen (b) Red
(c) Rem (d) All off above

971. Roentgen is the unit of;
(a) Exposure (b) Absorbed dose
(c) Product dose (d) None of above

972. One Roentgen is equal to;
(a) 2.5×10^{-4} c k g (b) 2.50×10^{-4} c kg
(c) 2.58×10^{-4} c kg (d) 250×10^{-4} c kg

973. One Red equal to how much roentgen;
(a) 0.006 (b) 0.01
(c) 1.0 (d) 0.02

974. Radiation protection is the youngest branch of hygiene and callded as;
(a) Brivirent of hygiene
(b) Radiotion hazard
(c) Radiation ionization
(d) Radiation hygiene

975. Organization working on protection and research in field of radiation are;
(a) WHO (b) ICRP
(c) Both a & b (d) None

976. Standard Minimal Fresh Air supply/person needed is;
(a) 300 to 350 cu ft per hours
(b) 300 to 3,000 cu ft per hours
(c) 3000 to 30000 cu ft per hours
(d) 30 to 300 cu ft per hours

977. Optimum floor space requirement/person vary from;
(a) 60 to 80 sq ft (b) 50 to 100 sq ft
(c) 50 to 150 sq ft (d) 40 to 50 sq ft

978. Type of ventilationmay be called as balanced ventilation is;
(a) Natural type ventilation
(b) Mechanical ventilation
(c) Both a & b
(d) Non of above

979. Balanced ventilation is a combination of —;
(a) Exhaust and plenum system
(b) Air conditioning
(c) Only plenum system
(d) None

980. In air conditoning type of ventilation same air should not be more then;
(a) 20 days (b) 15 days
(c) 5 days (d) 10 days

981. Which one of the following metal is more reponsible for minamata disease;
(a) Mercury (b) Cadmum
(c) Chrmium (d) Lead

982. Kidney and Brain cells are most affected by;
(a) Lead (b) Cadmium
(c) Mercury (d) None

983. Knock knee syndrome is caused by;
(a) Fluoride (b) Beriline
(c) Nitirate (d) Arsenic

984. Fluoride contant in water;
(a) 0.5 mg/lt to 1.5 mg/lt
(b) 2.0 mg/lt to 2.3 mg/lt
(c) 0.5 mg/lt to 1.0 mg/lt
(d) 3.0 mg/lt

985. Blue baby syndrome is caused by;

(a) Florides (b) Nitrate
(c) Lead (d) Mercury

986. Nitrate containts in water should be maximum upto;
(a) 45 mg/lt (b) 50 mg /lt
(c) 55 mg/lt (d) 52 mg/lt

987. The Head Quarter of United Nations Environment Programme (UNEP) is at;
(a) Nerobı (b) Tenaba
(c) Manishar (d) Japan

988. The book writtern on Ecological imbalance is by;
(a) Swear (b) Wogt
(c) Oceborm (d) All of above

989. In India first time "Ganga Safai Abhiyan" was started in;
(a) 1983 (b) 1985
(c) 1987 (d) 1984

990. The word ecology first time given by;
(a) Reiter (b) Ernest
(c) Harckel (d) Non of above

991. First environmental conference held in;
(a) 1972 (b) 1975
(c) 1982 (d) 1992

992. Noise pollution is categorised under Air Prevention and Control Act in and;
(a) 1981 (b) 1991
(c) 1982 (d) 1992

993. Normal talking of noise pollution level is;
(a) 20 d BA (b) 60 d BA
(c) 40 d BA (d) 10 d BA

994. Ambient noise standard definition in different areas is;
(a) Residential (b) Silence zone
(c) Commercial (d) All of above

995. The First International santitory conference held in;
(a) 1851 (b) 1855
(c) 1951 (d) 1900

996. World Heath Day is celebrated every year on;
(a) 5 April (b) 7 April
(c) 6 April (d) 8 March

997. Place of habitation for bovines know as;
(a) Barn (b) Pen
(c) Kennels (d) Coop

998. Place of habitation for swine;
(a) Sty (b) Pen
(c) Stable (d) Barn

999. Place of habitation for avian;
(a) Coop (b) Kannels
(c) Pen (d) Barn

1000. Ventilation requirements of domestic animal for daily cow requisite air space (ft^3);
(a) 600 - 800 (ft^3) (b) 500 - 600 (ft^3)
(c) 800 - 900 (ft^3) (d) 900 - 1000 (ft^3)

1001. Which one spreads via occupational exposure;
(a) Contagious ecthyma
(b) Pseudo cowpox
(c) Glanders
(d) All of these

1002. Principal host of Fasciolosis is;
(a). Swine (b) Dog
(c) Water buffalo (d) Rat

1003. Cattle are the principal host of;
(a) Bartinella (b) Borrelia
(c) Anthrax (d) Plague

1004. All India Institute of Public Health is situated at;
(a) Delhi (b) Calcutta
(c) Chennai (d) Lucknow

1005. Which one of the following is caused by tapeworm;
(a) Bartinellosis (b) Metagonimiasis
(c) Billharziasis (d) Paragonimiasis

1006. Ingestion of raw pork may result;
(a) Toxoplasmosis (b) Trypanosomiasis
(c) Babesiosis (d) Fasciolosis

1007. Air flow/hr requirement of a dairy cow is;
(a) 3000 (ft^3) (b) 4000 (ft^3)n
(c) 5000 (ft^3) (d) 6000 (ft^3)

1008. In a dairy cow inlet/outlet area ($inch^2$) requise;
(a) 30 ($inch^2$) (b) 34 inch
(c) 36 inch (d) 40 inch

1009. For a fattening cow requisite air space is;
(a) 300 - 500 (ft^3) (b) 500 - 600 (ft^3)
(c) 600 - 800 (ft^3) (d) 800 - 1200 (ft^3)

Write True or False as per the Statements

1. Hydatidosis is obligatory cyclozoonoses.
2. Rota viral infection is indirect anothropozoonoses

zooanthroposis.

3. All India Institute of Hygiene and Public Health is situated at Calcutta.
4. Trichinellosis spreads by ingestion of undreprocessed contaminated pork.
5. Fasciolosis is an excellent example of type I saprozoonoses, as it propagates and develops in animate object.

Answer Key

1. False 2. False 3. True 4. True 5. False

Answers

1.	(a)	2.	(a)	3.	(c)
4.	(a)	5.	(b)	6.	(a)
7.	(d)	8.	(c)	9.	(a)
10.	(b)	11.	(b)	12.	(a)
13.	(d)	14.	(d)	15.	(b)
16.	(a)	17.	(a)	18.	(a)
19.	(a)	20.	(a)	21.	(b)
22.	(b)	23.	(b)	24.	(d)
25.	(c)	26.	(c)	27.	(d)
28.	(b)	29.	(b)	30.	(a)
31.	(b)	32.	(a)	33.	(c)
34.	(a)	35.	(d)	36.	(a)
37.	(a)	38.	(a)	39.	(b)
40.	(b)	41.	(a)	42.	(b)
43.	(b)	44.	(d)	45.	(c)
46.	(c)	47.	(b)	48.	(a)
49.	(a)	50.	(b)	51.	(a)
52.	(a)	53.	(c)	54.	(a)
55.	(c)	56	(a)	57.	(a)
58.	(c)	59.	(b)	60.	(b)
61.	(a)	62.	(b)	63.	(a)
64.	(a)	65.	(c)	66.	(d)
67.	(c)	68.	(a)	69.	(b)
70.	(a)	71	(c)	72	(b)
73.	(b)	74.	(d)	75.	(c)
76.	(d)	77.	(c)	78.	(a)
79.	(a)	80.	(b)	81.	(b)
82.	(d)	83.	(c)	84.	(b)
85.	(a)	86.	(a)	87.	(d)
88.	(a)	89.	(a)	90.	(b)
91.	(d)	92.	(b)	93.	(d)
94.	(a)	95.	(b)	96.	(a)
97.	(c)	98.	(b)	99.	(c)

100.	(a)	101.	(a)	102.	(b)
103.	(a)	104.	(a)	105.	(d)
106.	(c)	107.	(a)	108.	(a)
109.	(d)	110.	(a)	111.	(c)
112.	(b)	113.	(d)	114.	(d)
115.	(d)	116.	(c)	117.	(c)
118.	(a)	119.	(d)	120.	(d)
121.	(b)	122.	(c)	123.	(a)
124.	(d)	125.	(a)	126.	(a)
127.	(a)	128.	(a)	129.	(b)
130.	(b)	131.	(d)	132.	(b)
133.	(a)	134.	(a)	135.	(b)
136.	(c)	137.	(a)	138.	(c)
139.	(a)	140.	(c)	141.	(c)
142.	(a)	143.	(d)	144	(d)
145.	(c)	146.	(d)	147.	(b)
148.	(a)	149.	(b)	150.	(b)
151.	(b)	152.	(a)	153.	(d)
154.	(d)	155.	(b)	156.	(b)
157.	(c)	158.	(d)	159	(a)
160.	(b)	161.	(c)	162.	(a)
163.	(a)	164.	(c)	165.	(a)
166.	(b)	167.	(a)	168.	(b)
169.	(a)	170.	(a)	171.	(a)
172.	(c)	173.	(c)	174.	(d)
175.	(a)	176.	(a)	177.	(d)
178.	(a)	179.	(a)	180.	(d)
181.	(a)	182.	(c)	183.	(d)
184.	(d)	185.	(d)	186.	(d)
187.	(a)	188.	(c)	189.	(a)
190.	(d)	191.	(a)	192.	(b)
193.	(d)	194.	(d)	195.	(c)
196.	(d)	197.	(a)	198.	(b)
199.	(a)	200.	(a)	201.	(c)
202.	(a)	203.	(b)	204.	(a)
205.	(d)	206.	(a)	207.	(c)
208.	(b)	209.	(a)	210.	(d)
211.	(b)	212.	(c)	213.	(c)
214.	(d)	215.	(a)	216.	(c)
217.	(b)	218.	(b)	219.	(a)
220.	(a)	221.	(a)	222.	(b)
223.	(c)	224.	(d)	225.	(b)
226.	(d)	227.	(b)	228.	(d)
229.	(a)	230.	(b)	231.	(b)
232.	(c)	233.	(a)	234.	(a)
235.	(c)	236.	(a)	237.	(a)
238.	(c)	239.	(a)	240	(a)

241.	(b)	242.	(a)	243.	(b)	382.	(b)	383.	(b)	384.	(c)
244.	(a)	245.	(a)	246.	(a)	385.	(b)	386.	(b)	387.	(a)
247.	(d)	248.	(c)	249.	(b)	388.	(c)	389.	(b)	390.	(b)
250.	(b)	251.	(a)	252.	(c)	391.	(a)	392.	(b)	393	(a)
253.	(b)	254.	(b)	255.	(a)	394.	(a)	395.	(b)	396.	(a)
256.	(a)	257.	(c)	258.	(c)	397.	(d)	398	(a)	399.	(b)
259.	(a)	260.	(a)	261.	(b)	400.	(b)	401.	(a)	402.	(c)
262.	(b)	263.	(a)	264.	(b)	403.	(a)	404	(b)	405.	(b)
265.	(a)	266.	(c)	267.	(a)	406.	(c)	407.	(b)	408	(c)
268.	(a)	269.	(a)	270.	(c)	409.	(c)	410.	(a)	411	(b)
271.	(d)	272	(a)	273.	(b)	412.	(c)	413.	(b)	414	(a)
274.	(a)	275.	(c)	276.	(c)	415.	(d)	416.	(b)	417.	(b)
277.	(a)	278.	(a)	279.	(a)	418.	(a)	419.	(b)	420.	(c)
280.	(a)	281.	(a)	282.	(a)	421.	(b)	422.	(c)	423.	(b)
283.	(c)	284.	(b)	285.	(a)	424.	(c)	425.	(b)	426.	(c)
286.	(c)	287.	(b)	288.	(a)	427.	(b)	428.	(b)	429.	(c)
289.	(a)	290.	(b)	291.	(c)	430.	(b)	431.	(b)	432.	(d)
292.	(a)	293.	(a)	294.	(c)	433.	(c)	434.	(c)	435.	(a)
295.	(b)	296.	(c)	297.	(c)	436.	(c)	437.	(b)	438.	(b)
298.	(d)	299.	(b)	300.	(a)	439.	(a)	440.	(b)	441.	(b)
301.	(c)	302.	(a)	303.	(a)	442.	(a)	443.	(c)	444.	(c)
304.	(d)	305.	(a)	306	(c)	445.	(d)	446.	(d)	447.	(c)
307.	(b)	308.	(d)	309.	(b)	448.	(a)	449.	(b)	450.	(d)
310.	(a)	311.	(c)	312.	(c)	451.	(d)	452.	(d)	453.	(d)
313.	(b)	314.	(d)	315.	(b)	454.	(a)	455.	(d)	456.	(a)
316.	(a)	317.	(c)	318.	(b)	457.	(a)	458.	(b)	459.	(a)
319.	(c)	320.	(a)	321.	(a)	460.	(d)	461.	(d)	462.	(b)
322.	(b)	323.	(c)	324.	(a)	463.	(c)	464.	(c)	465.	(b)
325.	(c)	326.	(a)	327.	(c)	466.	(a)	467.	(a)	468.	(b)
328.	(a)	329.	(a)	330.	(c)	469.	(c)	470.	(c)	471.	(d)
331.	(c)	332.	(b)	333.	(c)	472.	(d)	473.	(c)	474.	(d)
334.	(c)	335.	(c)	336.	(b)	475.	(d)	476.	(a)	477.	(b)
337.	(c)	338.	(c)	339.	(b)	478.	(b)	479.	(a)	480.	(b)
340	(c)	341.	(b)	342.	(b)	481.	(d)	482.	(d)	483.	(d)
343.	(c)	344.	(b)	345.	(a)	484.	(b)	485.	(a)	486.	(b)
346	(c)	347.	(b)	348.	(c)	487.	(b)	488.	(d)	489.	(c)
349.	(b)	350.	(b)	351.	(b)	490.	(b)	491.	(b)	492.	(a)
352.	(c)	353.	(b)	354.	(b)	493.	(b)	494.	(b)	495.	(d)
355.	(c)	356.	(c)	357.	(b)	496.	(d)	497.	(c)	498.	(a)
358.	(b)	359.	(a)	360.	(a)	499.	(a)	500.	(a)	501.	(b)
361.	(d)	362.	(b)	363.	(b)	502.	(d)	503.	(d)	504.	(c)
364.	(c)	365.	(b)	366.	(b)	505.	(d)	506.	(a)	507.	(d)
367.	(b)	368.	(c)	369.	(b)	508.	(c)	509.	(d)	510.	(d)
370.	(b)	371.	(d)	372.	(b)	511.	(b)	512.	(c)	513.	(a)
373.	(c)	374.	(a)	375.	(b)	514.	(b)	515.	(b)	516.	(c)
376.	(d)	377.	(c)	378.	(b)	517.	(c)	518.	(c)	519	(a)
379.	(c)	380.	(c)	381.	(b)	520.	(d)	521.	(a)	522.	(d)

523.	(c)	524.	(d)	525.	(a)
526.	(c)	527.	(c)	528.	(d)
529.	(c)	530.	(b)	531.	(a)
532.	(a)	533.	(a)	534.	(d)
535.	(a)	536.	(a)	537.	(a)
538.	(a)	539.	(d)	540.	(c)
541.	(c)	542.	(a)	543.	(a)
544.	(a)	545.	(a)	546.	(a)
547.	(a)	548.	(a)	549.	(a)
550.	(a)	551.	(a)	552.	(a)
553.	(a)	554.	(a)	555.	(a)
556.	(a)	557.	(a)	558.	(a)
559.	(a)	560.	(a)	561.	(d)
562.	(a)	563.	(d)	564.	(a)
565.	(b)	566.	(a)	567.	(a)
568.	(a)	569	(a)	570.	(a)
571.	(a)	572.	(a)	573.	(a)
574.	(d)	575	(a)	576.	(a)
577.	(a)	578.	(a)	579.	(a)
580.	(a)	581.	(a)	582.	(d)
583.	(d)	584.	(d)	585.	(d)
586.	(a)	587.	(c)	588.	(a)
589.	(a)	590.	(a)	591.	(c)
592.	(c)	593.	(d)	594.	(d)
595.	(d)	596.	(d)	597.	(a)
598.	(a)	599.	(a)	600.	(c)
601.	(b)	602.	(a)	603.	(a)
604.	(a)	605.	(d)	606.	(a)
607.	(a)	608.	(d)	609.	(a)
610.	(a)	611.	(a)	612.	(d)
613.	(d)	614.	(d)	615.	(a)
616.	(a)	617.	(a)	618.	(a)
619.	(a)	620.	(d)	621.	(c)
622.	(a)	623.	(a)	624.	(a)
625.	(a)	626.	(a)	627.	(a)
628.	(d)	629.	(d)	630.	(b)
631.	(c)	632.	(d)	633.	(d)
634.	(b)	635.	(a)	636.	(a)
637.	(d)	638.	(d)	639.	(a)
640.	(c)	641.	(a)	642.	(d)
643.	(c)	644.	(b)	645.	(a)
646.	(a)	647.	(d)	648.	(d)
649.	(c)	650.	(a)	651.	(d)
652.	(a)	653.	(b)	654.	(a)
655.	(c)	656.	(c)	657.	(c)
658.	(d)	659.	(c)	660.	(c)

661.	(a)	662.	(d)	663.	(c)
664.	(b)	665.	(d)	666.	(d)
667.	(a)	668.	(d)	669.	(d)
670.	(a)	671.	(b)	672.	(b)
673.	(b)	674.	(c)	675.	(d)
676.	(a)	677.	(c)	678.	(d)
679.	(a)	680.	(a)	681.	(d)
682.	(a)	683.	(a)	684.	(a)
685.	(a)	686.	(d)	687.	(d)
688.	(a)	689.	(d)	690.	(b)
691.	(b)	692.	(a)	693.	(b)
694.	(d)	695.	(d)	696.	(d)
697.	(d)	698.	(b)	699.	(c)
700	(a)	701.	(d)	702.	(d)
703.	(a)	704.	(a)	705.	(c)
706.	(d)	707.	(c)	708.	(d)
709.	(a)	710.	(a)	711.	(c)
712.	(a)	713.	(d)	714.	(c)
715.	(d)	716.	(d)	717.	(b)
718.	(d)	719.	(a)	720.	(c)
721.	(c)	722.	(a)	723.	(d)
724.	(d)	.725	(a)	726.	(c)
727	(c)	728.	(c)	729.	(a)
730.	(b)	731.	(a)	732.	(b)
733.	(a)	734.	(a)	735.	(a)
736.	(d)	737.	(a)	738.	(a)
739.	(d)	740.	(d)	741.	(a)
742.	(a)	743.	(a)	744.	(a)
745.	(a)	746.	(c)	747.	(a)
748.	(a)	749.	(c)	750.	(c)
751.	(b)	752.	(a)	753.	(a)
754.	(d)	755.	(c)	756.	(d)
757.	(d)	758.	(a)	759.	(a)
760.	(a)	761.	(d)	762.	(a)
763.	(a)	764.	(a)	765.	(b)
766.	(c)	767.	(a)	768.	(c)
769.	(c)	770.	(c)	771.	(a)
772.	(b)	773.	(b)	774.	(b)
775.	(a)	776.	(c)	777.	(b)
778.	(d)	779.	(c)	780.	(c)
781.	(c)	782.	(a)	783.	(c)
784.	(d)	785.	(a)	786.	(b)
787.	(d)	788.	(b)	789.	(c)
790.	(a)	791.	(c)	792.	(b)
793.	(d)	794.	(d)	795.	(d)
796.	(d)	797.	(c)	798.	(d)

799.	(b)	800.	(b)	801.	(d)	907.	(b)	908.	(a)	909.	(b)
802.	(a)	803.	(a)	804.	(d)	910.	(b)	911.	(a)	912.	(a)
805.	(a)	806.	(c)	807.	(d)	913.	(d)	914.	(b)	915.	(a)
808.	(d)	809.	(c)	810.	(a)	916.	(b)	917.	(a)	918.	(b)
811.	(d)	812.	(a)	813.	(a)	919.	(a)	920.	(b)	921.	(a)
814.	(d)	815.	(a)	816.	(b)	922.	(a)	923.	(a)	924.	(c)
817.	(c)	818.	(c)	819.	(d)	925.	(b)	926.	(a)	927.	(a)
820.	(a)	821.	(d)	822.	(d)	928.	(d)	929.	(a)	930.	(b)
823.	(d)	824.	(d)	825.	(d)	931.	(c)	932.	(d)	933.	(c)
826.	(a)	827.	(d)	828.	(c)	934.	(d)	935.	(a)	936.	(a)
829.	(d)	830.	(a)	831.	(a)	937.	(c)	938.	(d)	939.	(c)
832.	(a)	833.	(c)	834.	(b)	940.	(b)	941.	(d)	942.	(a)
835.	(b)	836.	(d)	837.	(a)	943.	(a)	944.	(c)	945.	(b)
838.	(a)	839.	(a)	840.	(a)	946.	(d)	947.	(b)	948.	(c)
841.	(d)	842.	(a)	843.	(a)	949.	(d)	950.	(a)	951.	(a)
844.	(a)	845.	(a)	846.	(c)	952.	(c)	953.	(d)	954.	(d)
847.	(a)	848.	(a)	849.	(a)	955.	(d)	956.	(c)	957.	(a)
850.	(a)	851.	(a)	852.	(d)	958.	(d)	959.	(a)	960.	(b)
853.	(a)	854.	(a)	855.	(b)	961.	(a)	962.	(c)	963.	(c)
856.	(d)	857.	(b)	858.	(a)	964.	(b)	965.	(a)	966.	(a)
859.	(b)	860.	(d)	861.	(a)	967.	(b)	968.	(a)	969.	(c)
862.	(b)	863.	(a)	864.	(b)	970.	(d)	971.	(a)	972.	(c)
865.	(b)	866.	(a)	867.	(a)	973.	(b)	974.	(d)	975.	(c)
868.	(d)	869.	(a)	870.	(c)	976.	(b)	977.	(b)	978.	(b)
871.	(b)	872.	(a)	873.	(a)	979.	(a)	980.	(a)	981.	(a)
874.	(a)	875.	(a)	876.	(a)	982.	(a)	983.	(a)	984.	(a)
877.	(b)	878.	(b)	879.	(a)	985.	(b)	986.	(b)	987.	(a)
880.	(a)	881.	(b)	882.	(a)	988.	(d)	989.	(b)	990.	(a)
883.	(b)	884.	(c)	885.	(a)	991.	(a)	992.	(a)	993.	(c)
886.	(d)	887.	(a)	888.	(c)	994.	(d)	995.	(a)	996.	(b)
889.	(a)	890.	(b)	891.	(c)	997.	(a)	998.	(a)	999.	(a)
892.	(a)	893.	(a)	894.	(a)	1000.	(a)	1001.	(d)	1002.	(c)
895.	(b)	896.	(a)	897.	(b)	1003.	(c)	1004.	(b)	1005.	(a)
898.	(a)	899.	(c)	900.	(c)	1006.	(a)	1007.	(b)	1008.	(b)
901.	(b)	902.	(a)	903.	(c)	1009.	(c)				
904.	(b)	905.	(a)	906.	(b)						

10 Clinical Medicine, Ethics and Jurisprudence

Salient Points

- Renatus Vegetus is father of veterinary medicine.
- Prognosis = expected outcome of disease. It is categorized as Poor / Guarded / Fair depending upon chance of survival.
- Etiology is to study cause of a disease.
- Symptom is defined as Subjective evidence of things felt by patient. It cannot be recorded. ex- Pain, Itching etc.
- Lesion = functional or morphological abnormality in tissue.
- Sign is Objective evidence of the thing observed. It can be recorded ex. Diarrhoea, Jaundice, Cardiac murmur, Anorexia.
- Adults have greater capacity for inflammation in comparison to neonates.
- Boil / furuncle is abscess on skin surface.
- Gangrenous Inflammation is seen in Degnala disease, Black Quarter, Gangrenous Myositis.
- Lymphatic Thrombus is formed due to fibrin clots and is useful in checking the spread of infection by plugging.
- Necrobiosis is programmed cell death, occurs in order to recognize the organ. Ex. RBC, skin.
- Thrombocytopaenia is one of first changes seen after endotoxin infusion.
- Disseminated intravascular coagulation (DIC) in horse characterised by petechiae/ ecchymosis on mucous membrane and sclerae with tendency to bleed.
- Fever = Syndrome with hyperthermia and toxemia by substances in blood circulations.
- Septicemia is compounded toxemia, hyperthermia and microbes in blood.
- Bubo is abscess in a lymph node.
- Allergy is state of hypersensitivity clinically recognizable. It can be detrimental to host.
- Tenting of skin is first seen at 6-8% dehydration body weight loss.
- Dehydration is characterized by an increase in packed cell volume and total serum proteins.
- Parallel loss of water and hypertonic dehydration results *isotoinc dehydration.*
- Prolonged administration of mineralocorticoids may result hypokalemia.
- Hyperorexia – increased appetite.
- Polyphagia – increased food intake.
- Inappetance – Partial absence of appetite.
- Anorexia – complete absence of appetite.
- Anophagia – decreased food intake.
- Allotriophagia – abnormal appetite (Pica).
- Osteophagia – chewing of bone.
- Infantophagia – eating of young.
- Coprophagia – eating of feces.
- Material regurgitated from esophagus is slightly alkaline while vomitus is acidic.
- Hypocuprosis or Molybdenum excess causes diarrhea.

- Total amount of feces passed per day is increased during diarrhea.
- Functional obstruction of intestine or failure of peristalsis is known as Paralytic ileus or Adynamic ileus.
- Xylazine depresses mechanism of reverse peristalsis.
- Vomiting is protective mechanism of reverse peristalsis.
- Maximum stability of foam in rumen occurs at pH of 6.
- Watery and brownish with fine mealy flakes are indicative of coliform/ Mycoplasmal mastitis.
- Biot's breathing is alternating periods of hyperpnea and apnea, of unequal length, seen in meningitis.
- Swamp fever, also known as Equine Infections Anemia; is a contagious Retro viral disease of horse and is characterized by long relapsing illness, acute anemia (due to periodic replication of virus in macrophages).
- Heavy Carbohydrate diet during rest results Azoturia.

Sl	Parameters/ Clinical signs	Small Intestine	Large Intestine
1.	Frequency of defecation	No change	Increased
2.	Fecal volume	Increased	Decreased
3.	Urgency	Absent	Present
4.	Tenesmus	Absent	Present
5.	Mucus in feces	Absent	Present
6.	Blood in feces	Dark black (Melena)	Red (Fresh)
7.	Weight loss	May be	Rare

- Littoral sands are deficient in Cobalt and Copper.

Difference between Small Intestine diarrheas from Large Intestine diarrhea

Questions

1. Trichorrhexis is an abnormality of
   (a) Skin coat (b) Hair follicle
   (c) seat gland (d) None
2. Incomplete keratinization of epithelial cells is known as
   (a) Hyperkeratosis (b) Parakeratosis
   (c) Hypokeratosis (d) Keratotis
3. Scientific term used for Dandruff is
   (a) Keratites (b) Pityriasis
   (c) Pachydermia (d) Hyperkeratosis
4. Thickening of skin affecting all the layers is known as -
   (a) Pachydermia (b) Hyperkeratosis
   (c) Pityriasis (d) Parabectosis
5. Impetigo is generally caused due to -
   (a) Parasitic infestation
   (b) Blood protozoan
   (c) Staphylococcus
   (d) Rikettsia
6. Seborrhea can be defined as -
   (a) Failure of sebaceous glands to secrete sebum
   (b) Inflammation of sweat glands
   (c) Inflammation of sebaceous glands
   (d) Excessive secretion of sebum on the skin surface
7. Degenerative & inflammatory lesions of renal tubules is known as -
   (a) Nephritis (b) Nephropathy
   (c) Nephrosis (d) All
8. The following type of nephritis is commonly known as Renal Abscess -
   (a) Glomerular nephritis
   (b) Interstitial nephritis
   (c) Embolic nephritis
   (d) None
9. Cystitis is defined as -
   (a) Presence of cyst in urinary bladder
   (b) Rupture of UB
   (c) Inflammation of UB
   (d) Obstruction in UB
10. Accumulation of water in kidney
    (a) Hydronephrosis (b) Hydronephritis
    (c) Hydrophritis (d) All of the above
11. Which of the following is a rumen function test -
    (a) Stilbamidine test
    (b) Nitrite reduction test
    (c) Glucose fermentation test
    (d) Both b) and c)
12. Moist rales at the base of lung is characteristic in case of -

(a) Right side Heart failure
(b) Left side heart failure
(c) Peripheral circulatory failure
(d) None

13. 'Sinus pause' occurs due to-
(a) Premature arterial contractions
(b) Right side heart failure
(c) Left side heart failure
(d) Failure of pacemakers.

14. Abdomen becomes of which shape in vagus indigestion -
(a) Apple shaped (b) Pear shaped
(c) Papple shaped (d) Dome shaped

15. Lactation tetany occurs due to deficiency of -
(a) Copper (b) Mg
(c) Fe (d) Cobalt

16. Pica occurs due to deficiency of -
(a) Mg (b) Phosphorus
(c) Zn (d) Co

17. Praying posture in dog is characteristic of -
(a) Cystitis (b) Gastritis
(c) Laminitis (d) Nephritis

18. Pericarditis is characterized by
(a) Audible friction rub
(b) Muffling of heart sound
(c) Adhesion
(d) All of the above

19. Father of Veterinary Medicine-
(a) Galen (b) Hippocrates
(c) Aristotle (d) Renatus Vegetius

20. Which of the statement is correct -
(a) Symptoms are subjective & signs are objective
(b) Symptoms are objective & signs are subjective
(c) Both are objective
(d) Both are subjective

21. Diagnosis made just by seeing the aural is known as-
(a) Tentative (b) Axiological
(c) Snap (d) Symptomatic

22. In cones, which of the statement is correct?
(a) Temperature is lower in morning than in evening
(b) Temperature is higher in morning than in evening
(c) It is same in morning and evening
(d) None

23. Stage of Acme is the term used for -
(a) I stage (b) II stage
(c) III stage (d) IV stage

24. Duration of Ephemeral fever is-
(a) 2-7 days (b) 1-2 days
(c) 1-2 weeks (d) 2-2 1/2 days

25. During fever, when temperature touches normal temperature sometimes in a day, it is called as
(a) Continuous fever (b) Intermittent fever
(c) Remittent fever (d) Recurrent fever

26. When temperature fluctuates but never touches normal -
(a) continuous (b) Remittent
(c) Intermittent (d) Recurrent

27. Blood present in tharacic cavity is called -
(a) Haemothroax (b) Haematorrhoea
(c) Hemophgsis (d) Haemturia

28. When there is increased amount of blood in pericardial sac, there is cardiac/ heart failure refered as.
(a) Cardic temponade (b) Hemoperitonium
(c) Hematuria (d) Melona

29. Presence of foreign body in circulatory system which may cause obstruction in blood vessel by
(a) Clump of normal cells
(b) Artifact or Gas
(c) Neoplasm
(d) All of above

30. Accumulation of extracellular fluid in interculluar space and body cavity
(a) Deficiency of protein
(b) Porin hyperemia
(c) Increased permeability
(d) All of above

31. Recording of history of a patient include -
(a) Patient data
(b) Disease history
(c) Management history
(d) All

32. After fever temperature may become subnormal

during the fall, this is known as-
(a) Effervescence (b) Resolution
(c) Decline (d) Invasion

33. Fever having no specified characters is known as -
(a) Typical fever (b) Atypical fever
(c) Remittent fever (d) None

34. In case of infectious diseases causing diarrhoea, type of dehydration is -
(a) Hypertonic (b) Hypotonic
(c) Isotonic (d) None

35. In case of simple deprivation of H_2O, type of dehydration is -
(a) Hypotonic (b) Isotonic
(c) Hypertonic (d) None

36. In case of isotonic diarrhoea, there is -
(a) More electrolyte loss
(b) More fluid loss
(c) 50% fluid & 50% electrolyte loss
(d) No electrolyte loss

37. Degree of dehydration is accessed as -
(a) % body weight loss
(b) % production loss
(c) Condition of skin coat
(d) gait of animal

38. Length of time in which animal is housed without cleaning & disinfection is known as -
(a) Cleaning time (b) Disinfection time
(c) Occupation time (d) management time

39. Demeanor is a term technically used for -
(a) Gait of animal
(b) Behaviour of animal
(c) Body wt. of animal
(d) Voice of animal

40. Ingestion of those things which are not considered as food is -
(a) Allotrophagia (b) Dysphagia
(c) Polyphagia (d) None

41. Term used for eating of soil is -
(a) Geophagia (b) Plophagia
(c) Coprophagia (d) None

42. Term used for eating of hair is -
(a) Geophagia (b) Coprophagia
(c) Pilophagia (d) None

43. Term used for eating own infants is known as -
(a) Dysphagia (b) Infantophagia
(c) Both (d) None

44. Time for which food remains in alimentary canal is known as -
(a) Sojourn (b) Occupation time
(c) Both (d) None

45. Sojourn in ruminants is of
(a) 1-4 wks. (b) 2-4 days
(c) 6-8 days (d) 1-2 wk.

46. Sojourn in carnivores is of
(a) 12-36 hr. (b) 2-4 hr
(c) 1-2 days (d) 1 wk

47. Sojourn in ruminants increases in -
(a) Abomasal displacement
(b) Vagus displacement
(c) Both
(d) None

48. Inflammation of hard palate is known as -
(a) Lampas (b) Funicalitis
(c) Palatitis (d) Stomatitis

49. Inflammation of gums are known as -
(a) Stomatitis (b) Cheilitis
(c) Gingivitis (d) None

51. Phlegmon is the term used for -
(a) Swelling of lips (b) Swelling of gums
(c) Swelling of face (d) None

52. Temperature, pulse & respiration are all normal in
(a) Ruminal acidosis (b) Tympany
(c) VAgal indigestion (d) Simple indigestion

53. % of alum used as Collutory is -
(a) 2% (b) 3%
(c) 4% (d) 5%

54. Boroglycerine contains -
(a) 31 part Boric acid + 69 part glycerin
(b) 69 part Boric acid + 31 part glycerin
(c) Any of the above (Both)
(d) None of the above

55. 1% Gentian violet is topically applied in case of -
(a) Parasitic infection (b) Mycotic infection
(c) Fungal infection (d) None

56. Which of the following is not a component of Mendal's throat point -
(a) Iodine (b) KI

(c) Glycerine (d) Alcohol

57. Choke is the term used for -
(a) Intestinal obstruction
(b) Esophageal obstruction
(c) Obstruction in stomach
(d) Obstruction in bile duct

58. When hind limb jerks into the body during walk, it is -
(a) Goose stepping gait
(b) Straddling gait
(c) Staggering gait
(d) None

59. Type of gait, pathognomic of Molybdenum toxicity in cattle -
(a) Straddling gait (b) Pacing cattle
(c) Staggering cattle (d) None

60. Double expiratory left of abdomen in horse is indicative of -
(a) Heaves
(b) Broken wind
(c) Chronic alveolar emphysema
(d) All of the above

61. When respiration is interrupted by spasm of diaphragm, it is known as -
(a) heaves (b) Thumps
(c) Hyperpnoea (d) Dysphoea

62. Eupnoea is the term used for -
(a) Normal respiration
(b) Increased respiration
(c) Decreased respiration
(d) Irregular respiration

63. Normal respiration is known as -
(a) eupnoea (b) Oligonoea
(c) Dysphoea (d) None

64. when rate of respiration decreases it is known as -
(a) Oligohoea (b) Eupnoea
(c) Dysphoea (d) None

65. When rate of respiration increases but depth decreases, it is known as -
(a) Polypnoea (b) Eupnoea
(c) Hyperpnoea (d) Dyspnoea

66. Type of esophageal obstruction more common in horse is -
(a) Cervical (b) Thoracic
(c) Both (d) None

67. Colic in horse due to ingestion of lush green feed is known as -
(a) Flatulent colic (b) Physical colic
(c) functional colic (d) All of the above

68. The term Borborygmy is used for -
(a) Intestinal mobility
(b) Intestinal obstruction
(c) Intestinal sounds
(d) None

69. Analgesia of choice in case of Equine colic is -
(a) Pethidine (b) Novalgine
(c) NSAIDS (d) All of the above

70. Increased mobility is characteristic of -
(a) Acute gastritis (b) Chronic gastritis
(c) Both (d) None

71. Cardinal signs of gastritis include -
(a) Vomiting (b) Depression
(c) Abdominal pain (d) All

72. Which of the following is not a constituent of Triple carb?
(a) Bismuth Carbonate
(b) Magnesium Carbonate
(c) NaHCO3
(d) Zinc carbonate

73. In cattle, recording of pulse can be done from -
(a) Middle coccygeal artery
(b) Transverse facial artery
(c) Both
(d) None

74. In dog the pulse is taken from -
(a) Tubular vein (b) Coccygeal artery
(c) Facial artery (d) Femoral artery

75. Pus cells in faeces in case of dysentery are -
(a) Few (b) absent
(c) Abundant (d) Less

76. Auscultation of heart in Ox is done at the level of-
(a) 3-5th Intercostal space
(b) 3-4th Intercostal space
(c) 2-4th Intercostal space
(d) 4-5th Intercostal space

77. Auscultation of heart in horse is done at the level of -
(a) 3-4th Intercostal space

(b) 3-5th Intercostal space
(c) 3rd Intercostal space
(d) 4th Intercostals space

78. Which of the statement is correct regarding heart sounds -
(a) I is systolic & II is diastolic
(b) I is diastolic & I is systolic
(c) Both are systolic
(d) Both are diastolic

79. Normal rhythm of heart sounds is -
(a) LUBB-DUP-pause
(b) DUP-LUBB-pause
(c) LUBB-DUP-LUBB
(d) pause-LUB-DUP

80. Gallop rhythm is term used for -
(a) Normal heart sound
(b) Republication of I/II sound
(c) absence of I heart sound
(d) absence of II heart sound

81. Which of the following is a synonym of rumen engorgement?
(a) Lactacidosis (b) Founder
(c) Grain overload (d) All of the above

82. Which of the following is not a synonym of rumen engorgement?
(a) Lactacidosis (b) Rumen acidosis
(c) Grain overload (d) Lactation tetany

83. Rumen engorgement occurs due to -
(a) High carbohydrate diet
(b) High fat diet
(c) High protein diet
(d) None

84. In case of 'Founder', pH of rumen -
(a) Increases (b) Decreases
(c) Normal (d) None

85. Which of the following is a primary bloat -
(a) Frothy bloat (b) Pasture bloat
(c) Feed lot bloat (d) All

86. Which one is the synonym for secondary bloat -
(a) Frothy bloat (b) Pasture bloat
(c) Grain bloat (d) Free gas bloat

87. In case of primary bloat death occurs in -
(a) 3-4 minutes (b) 3-4 hours
(c) 3-4 days (d) None

88. Arthritis in man or dog due to age & decreased immune system is known as -
(a) Rheumatic arthritis
(b) Septic arthritis
(c) Degenerative joint disease
(d) All of the above

89. Which of the following disease is related exclusively with the ingestion of sharp pointed object -
(a) Tympany (b) TRP
(c) Glossitis (d) Obstruction

90. Bamboo test is performed for the diagnosis of -
(a) Tympany (b) TRP
(c) Oesophagitis (d) Pharyngitis

91. In case of acute local peritonitis, there is
(a) Neutrophilia with shift to left
(b) Neutrophilia with shift to right
(c) Eosinophilia
(d) None

92. Right sided abomasal displacement generally occurs -
(a) during gestation
(b) Before puberty
(c) Few days after parturition
(d) Few weeks after parturition

93. During RDA, there is -
(a) Metabolic-alkalosis with hyperchloremia
(b) Metabolic-alkalosis with hypochloremia
(c) Metabolic-acidosis with hypochloremia
(d) Metabolic-acidosis with hyperchloremia

94. Torsion in case of RDA is usually of -
(a) 20-40° (b) 180-270°
(c) 150° (d) 120-130°

95. Characterstic sound during RDA heard on auscultation of right side of abdomen is -
(a) Ping sound (b) Ting sound
(c) Muffled sound (d) None

96. In case of pancreatitis, there is -
(a) Hyperglycemia (b) Hypoglycemia
(c) Hypocalcaemia (d) Hyponatremia

97. Clay coloured foul smelling faeces with undigested food is characteristic of -
(a) Cystitis (b) Enteritis
(c) Pancreatitis (d) Hepatitis

98. Synonym for toxic hepatitis is -
(a) Impactive hepatitis
(b) Jaundice
(c) Perfusion hepatitis
(d) Hepatotoxicity

99. Synonym for Nutritional hepatitis is -
(a) Jaundice
(b) Perfusion hepatitis
(c) Trophopathic hepatitis
(d) None

100. Anoxia means -
(a) No oxygen in tissues
(b) No oxygen in environment
(c) Both
(d) None

101. When tissue can not take up required amount of Oxygen, it is
(a) Anoxic anoxia (b) Anaemic anoxia
(c) Stagnant anoxia (d) Histotoxic anoxia

102. When rate of flow of blood through capillary is decreased it is -
(a) Chronic anoxia (b) Anemic anoxia
(c) Stagnant anoxia (d) Histotoxic anoxia

103. Defective oxygenation of blood because of less amount of availability is known as -
(a) Anoxic anoxia (b) Anaemic anoxia
(c) Stagnant anoxia (d) Histotoxic anoxia

104. Anoxia due to deficiency of haemoglobin per unit volume of blood is
(a) Anoxia anoxia (b) Anaemic anoxia
(c) Stagnant anoxia (d) Histotoxic anoxia

105. Hypercapnea is the term used for -
(a) O_2 retention (b) CO_2 retention
(c) NH3 retention (d) None

106. Term used for difficult or labored breathing is
(a) Dyspnoea (b) Apnoea
(c) Acapnoea (d) Hyperpnoea

107. Involuntary contraction of diaphragm with spasmodically closed glottis produces
(a) Sneezing (b) Hiccough
(c) Wheezing (d) Snoring

108. Sudden expulsion of air through squeezed nostrils to expel irritating material is
(a) Sneezing (b) Hiccough
(c) wheezing (d) Snoring

109. Wrestling sound caused by hard breathing is -
(a) Sneezing (b) Hiccough
(c) Wheezing (d) snoring

110. Breathing with rough rattling hoarse sound during sleep is -
(a) sneezing (b) Hiccough
(c) Wheezing (d) Snoring

111. Loud sound during respiration due to paralysis of intrinsic muscles of Larynx -
(a) Grunting (b) Snoring
(c) Roaring (d) Yawning

112. Epistaxis is a term used for bleeding from -
(a) Eyes (b) Ears
(c) Nostrils (d) Mouth

113. Hemoptysis is the term used for -
(a) Coughing up of blood
(b) Vomiting of blood
(c) Both
(d) None

114. Hematemesis is the term used for -
(a) Coughing up of blood
(b) Vomiting of blood
(c) Both
(d) None

115. Fluid rale is the only audible sound in case of -
(a) Pulmonary emphysema
(b) Pulmonary edema
(c) Both
(d) None

116. Anasarca is the term used for -
(a) Edema in the dependent parts
(b) General edema throughout the body
(c) Facial edema
(d) All of the above

117. Hydrocoel is the accumulation of fluid in -
(a) Testes (b) Scrotum
(c) Muscles (d) Subcutaneous tissue

118. Tickling sound on auscultation of lung is heard in case of
(a) Hydrothorax (b) Hemothorax
(c) Pneumothorax (d) None

119. Hacking cough is characteristic of -
(a) Bronchopneumonia

(b) Interstitial pneumonia
(c) Parasitic pneumonia
(d) None

120. Leucocytosis occurs in cases of
(a) Bacterial pneumonia
(b) Viral pneumonia
(c) Both
(d) None

121. Leucopoenia occurs in cases of-
(a) Bacterial pneumonia
(b) Viral pneumonia
(c) Both
(d) None

122. Health can be defined as
(a) Physical well being
(b) Mental well being
(c) Social well being
(d) all of the above

123. Acute disease is characterized by a course of -
(a) 3-14 days (b) 2 days
(c) 2-4 weeks (d) None

124. When a disease outbreak occurs in a definite area it is -
(a) Sporadic (b) Enzootic
(c) Epidemic (d) Panzootic

125. When a disease affects a large population of animals in a large area -
(a) Enzootic (b) Epizootic
(c) Epidemic (d) Panzootic

126. Disease acquired from foreign countries -
(a) Indigenous (b) Exotic
(c) Emerging (d) Exogenous

127. Milk fever is a -
(a) Production disease
(b) Metabolic disease
(c) Infectious disease
(d) Parasitic disease

128. Fatty cow syndrome is a
(a) Production disease
(b) Metabolic disease
(c) Infectious disease
(d) Parasitic disease

129. Symptoms which foretell about the equilibrium of health of an animal are -
(a) Objective symptoms
(b) Subjective symptoms
(c) Premonitory symptoms
(d) None

130. Symptoms which point directly or definitely to a particular disease
(a) Premonitoring symptoms
(b) Precursory symptoms
(c) Pathognomic symptoms
(d) None

131. Prognosis of Traumatic reticuloperitonitis with adhesion of diaphragm with abdominal wall is -
(a) Favorable (b) Doubtful
(c) Poor (d) Grave

132. When treatment is extended in case of incurable disease to prolong life span of the individual, it is known as -
(a) Empirical Rx (b) Palliative Rx
(c) Symptomatic Rx (d) Rational Rx

133. The art of treating the patient by more experience gained through a long time trial & error methods is -
(a) Palliative Rx (b) Empirical Rx
(c) Symptomatic Rx (d) Rational Rx

134. Period which lasts from discovery of 1st sign to disease the complete manifestation is known as
(a) Latent period (b) Prodromal period
(c) Prepatent period (d) None

135. Which of the following is not a sign of death?
(a) Cessation of respiration
(b) Cessation of circulation
(c) Fall of body temperature
(d) Excessive salivation

136. Bowel shaped swelling of left flank behind the rib a characteristic of
(a) Left side abomasal displacement
(b) Right side abomasal displacement
(c) Both
(d) None

137. Rounded appearance of left part of abdomen & distension of lower right abdomen
(a) LDA (b) RDA
(c) Vagus indigestion (d) Tympany

138. Cylindrical enlargement of right side of abdomen occurs in

(a) Abomasal impaction
(b) Abomasal displacement
(c) Abomasal volvulus
(d) All of the above

139. Method by which the body of animal is shaken to determine the presence of free fluid of chest or abdomen is known as
(a) Paracentasis (b) Succession
(c) Auscultation (d) Percussion

140. Pediatric diseases are the diseases of
(a) Young age group (b) Old age group
(c) Heifers (d) All of the above

141. Geriatric diseases are the diseases of
(a) Young age group (b) Old age group
(c) Heifers (d) All of the above

142. Causes of rough starring hair of animals
(a) Infectious
(b) Mineral deficiency
(c) Vitamin deficiency
(d) All of the above

143. Frog like posture in a cow with extended hind limbs is indicative of
(a) Contracture of flexor tendon
(b) Rupture of abductor muscle
(c) Obturator nerve paralysis
(d) Luxation of left hip joint

144. Contracture of flexor tendon leads to -
(a) A calf unable to extend fetlock joint
(b) Obturator nerve paralysis
(c) Luxation of left hind limb
(d) All of the above

145. Luxation of left hip joint
(a) Sinking of an intact pelvis on the left side of cow
(b) Cow stands with extended forelegs
(c) Frog like posture
(d) Preying posture

146. Cow sits on sternum and the head rests on flank in case of
(a) Downer's cow syndrome
(b) Milk fever
(c) Both
(d) None

147. Abducted elbow with extension of head & neck in a cow with brisket edema occurs in
(a) Traumatic pericarditis
(b) Tympany
(c) Both
(d) None

148. A cow stands in arched back condition with
(a) Gastritis (b) Pancreatits
(c) Cystitis (d) Peritonitis

149. A calf in lateral recumbency with head hold in opisthotonus along with tono-clonic contractions of limbs occurs in
(a) Hypomagnesemic tetany
(b) Pica
(c) Ricketts
(d) Copper deficiency

150. A horse stands with extended all the four limbs and looking at the flank in -
(a) Flatulent colic (b) Impactive colic
(c) Spasmodic colic (d) Obstructive colic

151. A horse shifting its weights from one limb to other which continuously occurs in
(a) Laminitis (b) Osteodystrophia
(c) Both (d) None

152. A horse adopts a dog sitting posture with kicking at the belly occurs in
(a) Acute gastric distension
(b) Acute intestinal obstruction
(c) Gastroenteritis
(d) Cystitis

153. A male dog urinates like a bitch
(a) Cystitis (b) Urolithiasis
(c) Both (d) None

154. A dog sits erect for a long period to relieve respiratory distress in case of -
(a) Pharyngitis (b) Laryngitis
(c) Pneumonitis (d) All

155. A dog shows arching of its back in case of
(a) Acute nephritis (b) Chronic nephritis
(c) Nephrosis (d) Renal abscess

156. A goat & sheep may adopt a posture, keeping the head in elevated direction with erect ears and listening higher sound in
(a) Lactation tetany (b) Pregnancy toxemia
(c) Tympany (d) None

157. A goat may held its head in upward direction, as

if looking at sky in case of
(a) Polyencephalomalacia
(b) Thiamine deficiency
(c) Gid
(d) All of the above

158. A sheep or goat lies in frog like posture in case of
(a) Polyencephalomalacia
(b) Pregnancy toxemia
(c) Parturient hypocalcaemia
(d) All of the above

159. Erect posture in sheep with the appearance of exaggerated alertness occurs in
(a) Scrapie
(b) Tetany
(c) Vitamin A deficiency
(d) Cu deficiency

160. Abnormal posture with abducted front legs and scapula protruding over the line of withers in sheep occurs in case of
(a) Knee joint flexion
(b) Infective arthritis
(c) Musclular dystrophy
(d) None

161. Goose stepping gait in pig occurs in case of
(a) Pantothenic acid deficiency
(b) Vitamin A deficiency
(c) Vitamin B deficiency
(d) Nicotinic acid deficiency

162. Enzootic ataxia occurs in case of
(a) Hyponatremia (b) Hypochloremia
(c) Hypocuprosis (d) Hypokalemia

163. Walking circles or circling disease occurs in case of
(a) Coenurusis (b) Otitis
(c) Listeriosis (d) All of the above

164. Stiff gait accompanied with pain occurs in
(a) Rheumatism (b) Polyarthritis
(c) Myositis (d) All of the above

165. Painful limb movement & disinclination to move occur in
(a) Laminitis (b) Pododermetis
(c) Foot rot (d) All of the above

166. Dropped hock in dog & cat occurs due to
(a) Hip dysphasia
(b) Rupture of extensors
(c) Rupture of achilles tendon
(d) Rupture of flexors

167. Normal colour of conjunctival mucus membrane in cat is
(a) Roseate (b) Pale
(c) Pale pink (d) Reddish

168. Corrosion of vessels which occurs due to ulcerative or inflammatory process or due to neoplasm is denoted by a Greek word known as
(a) Per rhexis (b) Per diabrosis
(c) Per diapedosis (d) None

169. Rupture of vascular wall is denoted by a Greek word known as
(a) Per rhexis (b) Per diabrosis
(c) both (d) None

170. Exudation of erythrocytes through the wall of vessel without any visible injury is known as
(a) Per rhexis (b) Per diabrosis
(c) Per diapedesis (d) None

171. Jaundice due to hemolytic cause is
(a) Pre-hepatic (b) Hepatic
(c) Post-hepatic (d) None

172. Jaundice due to toxic causes is-
(a) Pre-hepatic (b) Hepatic
(c) Post-hepatic (d) None

173. Jaundice due to obstruction in bile ducts is
(a) Pre-hepatic (b) Hepatic
(c) Post-hepatic (d) None

174. Animals which have no capacity to adjust their body temperature according to environmental temperature are known as
(a) Poikithermal (b) Homoeothermic
(c) Both (d) None

175. Animals which have capacity to adjust their body temperature according to environmental temperature are known as
(a) Poikithermal (b) Homoeothermic
(c) Both (d) None

176. Which of the following statements is correct?
(a) Vaginal temperature is 1°F higher than rectal temperature of healthy animal
(b) Rectal temperature is 1°C higher than vaginal temperature

(c) Both are equal
(d) None is correct

177. Graduation of thermometer meant for animal practices
(a) 90-110°F (b) 94-110°F
(c) 90-108°F (d) 94-110°F

178. Difference in temperature recorded in evening & morning hours in a healthy animal is about
(a) 1.5°F (b) 2.5°F
(c) 0.5°F (d) None

179. Degree of temperature is considered high when it ranges
(a) 1-1.5°F above normal
(b) 3°F above normal
(c) 3-6°F above normal
(d) > 6°F above normal

180. Hyperpyrexia occurs when temperature ranges
(a) 4°F above the normal
(b) 5°F above the normal
(c) 6°F above the normal
(d) 7°F above the normal

181. Special state of acute hyperthermia resulting from defects in heat regulatory mechanisms against extreme environmental hypothermia is
(a) Heat stroke (b) Hyperpyrexia
(c) Fever (d) All of the above

182. Fever caused due to injection of hypertonic saline due to osmotic disturbances is termed as
(a) Transitory fever (b) Drug fever
(c) Salt fever (d) Saline fever

183. Elevation of body temperature due to over hydration is called
(a) Transitory fever (b) Thirst fever
(c) Both (d) None

184. Elevation of temperature due to damage of brain cells
(a) Drug fever (b) Neurogenic fever
(c) Transitory fever (d) None

185. Specific fever against specific diseases is called as
(a) Idiopathic fever (b) Drug fever
(c) Transitory fever (d) None

186. Localized infection causing rise of temperature leads to
(a) Idiopathic fever
(b) Transitory fever
(c) Symptomatic fever
(d) Infectious fever

187. When there is sudden sharp elevation of body temperature to the level of 104°F or above it is
(a) Acute (b) Subacute
(c) Per acute (d) Chronic fever

188. Type of fever in which temperature doesn't exceed above 1-2°F beyond the normal range is
(a) Acute (b) Sub acute
(c) Per acute (d) Chronic

189. Daily rise & daily fall of temperature is known as
(a) Quotidian (b) Tertian
(c) Quatian (d) Hectic

190. Form of fever in which temperature appears & disappears every alternate day is
(a) Quotidian (b) Tertian
(c) Quartan (d) Hectic

191. Form of fever in which temperature comes & goes around every 4th day -
(a) Quotidian (b) Tertian
(c) Quartan (d) Hectic

192. Form of fever when there is sudden rise of temperature daily with chill or persistent for few hours & falling equally suddenly with profuse sweat is called
(a) Quatidian (b) Tertian
(c) Quartian (d) Hectic

193. When high rise of temperature is accompanied with strong bounding pulse it is
(a) Bounding fever (b) Sthenic fever
(c) Both (d) None

194. When moderate temperature is accompanied with weak but quick pulse, it is
(a) Sthenic fever (b) Asthenic fever
(c) Both (d) None

195. Severe rise of temperature occurs in cases of
(a) Acute anthrax (b) Acute rinderpest
(c) Acute peritonitis (d) All of the above

196. During the last trimester of pregnancy in cattle, pulse is
(a) 15-30% higher than normal
(b) No variation
(c) 15-30% lower than normal

(d) None

197. Bradycardia is not observed in which of the following conditions
(a) Excitements (b) Jaundice
(c) Hydrocephalus (d) Vagal indigestion

198. Bradycardia is observed in
(a) Jaundice
(b) Sinus arrhythmia
(c) Partial heart block
(d) All of the above

199. Tachycardia is not observed in
(a) Hydrocephalus (b) Jaundice
(c) Both (d) None

200. Tachycardia is observed in
(a) Atrial flutter (b) Tympany
(c) Fracture (d) All of the above

201. Irregular pulse is observed in
(a) Toxaemia (b) Atrial flutter
(c) Both (d) None

202. In which of the following, high volume pulse is observed
(a) Aortic incompetence
(b) Sinus arrest
(c) Ectopic beat
(d) None

203. Low volume pulse is characteristic in cases of
(a) Mitral stenosis
(b) Aortic stenosis
(c) Peripheral circulatory failure
(d) All of the above

204. In case of loss of excessive body fluid these is
(a) Low volume pulse
(b) High volume pulse
(c) Moderate volume pulse
(d) None

205. When each beat occupies less time then normal it is
(a) Sluggish pulse (b) Skipping pulse
(c) Full pulse (d) None

206. When each beat takes more time then normal
(a) Sluggish pulse (b) Sleeping pulse
(c) Half pulse (d) Empty pulse

207. In each pulsation, when there is extensive distension of arterial wall, it is known as
(a) Large pulse (b) Full pulse
(c) None (d) Both

208. When artery is poorly distended & remains empty
(a) Small pulse (b) Large pulse
(c) Slow pulse (d) Quick pulse

209. When amplitude of pulse is very high & the pulse cannot be resisted with digital pressure it is
(a) Sthenic pulse
(b) Asthenic pulse
(c) Strong bounding pulse
(d) None

210. When pulse is brief small & hard in nature it is
(a) Wiry pulse (b) Thready pulse
(c) Corrigen's pulse (d) None

211. Characteristic rapid rise of pulse wave with high volume until the artery is over filled followed by an equally sudden sharp collapse of arterial wall is
(a) Walter hammer pulse
(b) Corrigan's pulse
(c) Collapsing pulse
(d) All of the above

212. Groups of continuous weak waves of pulse are known as:
(a) Pulsus myurus (b) Pulsus paradoxes
(c) Pulsus anacrotic (d) Pulsus bisferiens

213. When volume of pulse decreases during deep inspiration & increases during deep expiration it is known as:
(a) Pulsus myruses (b) Pulsus paradoxes
(c) Pulsus anacrotic (d) Pulsus bisferiens

214. Pulse characterized by slow rise, low volume with prominent tidal wave is
(a) Pulsus myruses
(b) Pulsus paradoxus
(c) Pulsus anacroticus
(d) Pulsus bisferiens

215. A single pulse beat is split into two waves, it is
(a) Pulsus bisferiens (b) Pulsus myurus
(c) Pulsus paradoxus (b) Pulsus bigeminus

216. Pulse characterized by two pulse beats followed by a gap is known as
(a) Pulsus bisferiens (b) Pulsus bigeminus
(c) Pulsus paradoxus (d) None

217. When immediately after the main pulse wave a second wave followed, it is known as
(a) Dicoitic pulse (b) Double pulse
(c) Secondary pulse (d) Duplicate pulse

218. Thoracic respiration occurs in case of
(a) Ascites
(b) Pulmonary edema
(c) TRP
(d) Pharyngeal obstruction

219. Abdominal respiration occurs in case of
(a) Pulmonary edema (b) Ascites
(c) Peritonitis (d) Rupture of diaphragms

220. Prolonged inspiration occurs in case of
(a) Atypical pneumonia
(b) Peritonitis
(c)
(d) Tympany

221. Respiration characterized by pauses is:
(a) Biot's respiration
(b) Cheyne strokes respiration
(c) Syncopic respiration
(d) Kussmaul's respiration

222. In which type of respiration pause is immediately taken over by a deep breathing which successively become shallow till preceded by apnea
(a) Biot's respiration
(b) Cheyne strokes respiration
(c) Syncopic respiration
(d) None

223. When respiration is forceful & regular but expirations are unaffected it is known as
(a) Kussmaul's respiration
(b) Air hunger
(c) Both
(d) None

224. Management of periodic respiration is done by
(a) Injection of aminophylin
(b) Injection of Nikethamide
(c) Inhalation of O_2
(d) All of the above

225. In case of pneumothorax, respiration becomes
(a) Symmetrical (b) Asymmetrical
(c) Fast (d) Slow

226. Which of the following may be the cause of inspiratory dyspnea?
(a) Pleurisy (b) Bronchopneumonia
(c) Pulmonary edema (d) All of the above

227. Expiratory dyspnea occurs in cases of
(a) Pulmonary emphysema
(b) Pleural adhesions
(c) Both
(d) None

228. Intermediate dyspnea may occur due to
(a) Meningitis (b) Encephalitis
(c) Both (d) None

230. When there is inadequate power of contraction of respiratory muscles it is
(a) Restrictive disorder
(b) Hypodynamic disorder
(c) Both
(d) None

231. Cough becomes yellow and sticky in case of
(a) Parasite infections (b) Mycotic infections
(c) Fungal infections (d) Bacterial infections

232. Cough becomes putrid in case of
(a) Pulmonary abscess
(b) Pulmonary edema
(c) Pulmonary emphysema
(d) Pulmonary infarction

233. Productive & purulent cough is characteristics of
(a) Acute bronchitis
(b) Bronchopneumonia
(c) Chromic bronchitis
(d) All of the above

234. Hypodermoclysis is the term used for
(a) Dermal infusion
(b) Epidermal unfsion
(c) Intraveinus infusion
(d) Subcutancous infusion

235. Proctolysis is the term used for
(a) Renal edema (b) Vaginal edema
(c) Both (d) None

236. Which of the following is not the constituent of Ringer's solution?
(a) NaCl (b) $MgCl_2$
(c) $CaCl_2$ (d) KCl

237. This is not the constituent of Ringer's Lactate solution

(a) NaCl (b) KCl
(c) $CaCl_2$ (d) $ZnCl_2$

238. Hyperorexia is defined as
(a) Excessive appetite for liquid food
(b) Excessive appetite for solid food
(c) Excessive appetite for both
(d) Excessive appetite for none

239. Smell of faces becomes fishy in case of
(a) Decomposition of protein
(b) Decomposition of fat
(c) Decomposition of carbohydrate
(d) Decomposition of Vitamins

240. Petroleum like smell in faces comes in cases of
(a) Poisoning with mineral oil
(b) Deficiency of mineral oil
(c) Poisoning with petroleum
(d) All of the above

241. Phenolic smell in faces is characteristics of
(a) Poisoning with phenols
(b) Poisoning with alcohols
(c) Poisoning with creosote wood preservative
(d) All of the above

242. Offensive smell in faeces comes in case of
(a) Incomplete digestion
(b) Pancreatic insufficiency
(c) Both
(d) None

243. Occult test is done in case of
(a) Faeces examination
(b) Urine examination
(c) Sputum examination
(d) Skin scrapping examination

244. Following diseases cause oral lesions in ruminants
(a) FMD (b) Rinderpest
(c) Blue Tongue (d) All of the above

245. Inherited condition produced by a recessive gene causing difficulty in prehension is
(a) Prognathism (b) Pulpitis
(c) Polyodentia (d) Epulis

246. Pulpitis is
(a) Bacterial inflammation of dental pulp
(b) Viral inflammation of dental pulp
(c) Both
(d) None

247. Polyodontia is defined as
(a) Presence of extra or supernumerary teeth
(b) Presence of extra or superamammerary teat
(c) Inflammation of teeth
(d) Inflammation of teat

248. Epulis is defined as
(a) Fibrous benign tumor of gingiva
(b) Fibrous d benign tumor of tongue
(c) Both
(d) None

249. Thinning of gastric mucosa along with hyperemia is
(a) Superficial gastritis
(b) Atrophic gastritis
(c) Hypertrophic gastritis
(d) None

250. Swollen, sponge like mucosa accompanied with erosion & ulceration occur in
(a) Superficial gastritis
(b) Atrophic gastritis
(c) Hypertrophic gastritis
(d) None

251. Peptic ulcers may occur due to
(a) Excessive acid secretion
(b) Ulcerogenic drugs
(c) Genetic factors
(d) All of the above

252. Excess soil Mn levels reduce the availability of which of the following in soil.
(a) Co (b) P
(c) Zn (d) Cu

253. Relation of concentration of serum albumin to the number of services required for conception is
(a) Direct (b) Inverse
(c) Inverse (d) No relation

254. Relation of haemoblobin concentration to current milk yield in lactating cattle is
(a) Direct (b) Inverse
(c) Inverse squire (d) No relation

255. Test therapy is a method of
(a) Treatment of diseases
(b) Diagnosis of diseases
(c) Both
(d) None

256. For blood transfusion anticoagulant used
(a) EDTA (b) Sodium fluoride
(c) Sodium citrate (d) Heparin

257. Difficulty in swallowing is termed as
(a) Polyphagia (b) Dysphagia
(c) Dystrophia (d) Polydipsia

258. Ketosis is biochemically characterized by
(a) Hypoglycaemia (b) Hyperglycaemia
(c) Ketonuria (d) Both a and c

259. Rumen overload is caused by which of the following successive feeding of
(a) Urea (b) Grains like wheat
(c) Dry grasses (d) Berseem

260. Gangrene of extremities and signs of CNS stimulation are caused by the ingestion of
(a) Ergot (b) Snapdragon
(c) Reserpine (d) Nux vomica

261. pH of abomasal contents is
(a) 2 (b) 6 to 7
(c) 4 (d) None

262. Skin scrapings are treated with the following for better demonstration of manage mites
(a) 10% H_2SO_4 (b) 10% HNO_3
(c) 10% KOH (d) 10 % KH_2PO_4

263. In acute intestinal obstruction death is usually due to
(a) Severe internal haemorrhage
(b) Anoxia
(c) Respiratory failure
(d) Dehydration

264. In Co deficiency
(a) Microcytic hypochromic anaemia
(b) Normocytic normochromic anaemia
(c) Macrocytic
(d) Macrocytic

265. Liptek test is used for diagnosis of
(a) Ruminal tympany
(b) Abomasal displacement
(c) Traumatic reticuloperitonitis
(d) Diaphragmatic hernia

266. Equine acute diarrhoea syndrome is also described as
(a) Equine monocytic ehrlichosis
(b) Equine strongylosis
(c) Equine strongyloidosis
(d) None

267. Colitis X-diseases is
(a) Equine chronic diarrhoea syndrome
(b) Equine acute diarrhoea syndrome
(c) Equine colic
(d) None

268. Colic due to distension of lumen by accumulation of gases is known as
(a) Spasmodic colic (b) Tympanic colic
(c) Tympanitic colic (d) Gaseous colic

269. Alkaline vomiting containing bile occur in case of
(a) Bile duct obstruction
(b) Esophageal obstruction
(c) Intestinal obstruction
(d) Gastic obstruction

270. Concentration of dextrose given is case of colic is
(a) 5% (b) 10%
(c) 20% (d) All

271. When a portion of intestinal loop is twisted due to violent obstruction of intestine it is known as
(a) Volvulus (b) Intussusception
(c) Strangulation (d) None

272. Telescoping of one part of intestine to other part is known as
(a) Volvulus (b) Intussusception
(c) Strangulation (d) None

273. When the abdominal transudate is clean, watery fluid having a low specific gravity, it indicates
(a) Hypoproteinemia (b) Ascitis
(c) Both (d) None

274. Abdominal transudate with high specific gravity, high protein content & presence of macrophage, mesothelial cells, RBC, indicate.
(a) Passive veinous congestion
(b) Chemical irritation
(c) Penetrating wound
(d) Visceral perforation

275. Needle used for liver biopsy
(a) Tru-cut needle
(b) Vimsilverman needle
(c) Both
(d) Crazy needle

276. Vanden-Bergh test is used for
(a) Estimation of hyperbilirubinemia to conjugated bilirubin
(b) Estimation of hyperbilirubinemia unconjugated bilirubin
(c) Differentiated hyperbilirubinemia owing to conjugated bilirubin or unconjugated bilirubin
(d) None of the above

277. Presence of bilirubin in urine is indicative of
(a) Conjugated type of hyperbilirubinemia
(b) Unconjugated type of hyperbilirubinemia
(c) Both
(d) None

278. Urinobelenogen levels is urine & stool are highly elevated in case of
(a) Obstructive jaundice
(b) Hemolytic jaundice
(c) Both
(d) None

279. Icteric index of cattle is in the range of
(a) 5.8-6 (b) 8.4-9.8
(c) 6.8-10.7 (d) 7.1-9.8

280. Icteric index of dog is in the range of
(a) 5.8-6 (b) 8.4-9.8
(c) 6.8-10.7 (d) 7.1-9.8

281. Icteric index of horse is in the range of
(a) 5.8-6 (b) 8.4-9.8
(c) 15.2-18.0 (d) 7.1-9.8

282. Normal blood clotting time in case of cattle-
(a) 7 minutes (b) 11 minutes
(c) 2-3 minutes (d) 2 minutes

283. Normal clotting time in case of horse
(a) 7 minutes (b) 11 minutes
(c) 2-3 minutes (d) 2 minutes

284. Normal clotting time in case of dog and cat
(a) 7 minutes (b) 11 minutes
(c) 2-3 minutes (d) 4 minutes

285. Takata - ara test is used for
(a) Estimation of ketenes in CSF
(b) Detection lever damage
(c) Assay of hepatic enzymes
(d) Assay of hepatic cholesterol

286. Serum glutamic pyruvic transaminase is elevated in
(a) Fatty cow syndrome
(b) Azoturia in eguines
(c) White muscle disease
(d) Hepatic necrosis

287. Serum glutamic oxaloacetate transaminase is elevated in cases of
(a) Ketosis in cattle
(b) Azoturia in equines
(c) Downer's cow syndrome
(d) All of the above

288. Serum alkaline phosphatase is elevated in case of
(a) Biliary obstruction
(b) Haemolysis
(c) Liver necrosis
(d) All of the above

289. In case of hepatic necrosis
(a) SGPT is increased
(b) Serum alkaline phosphatase is increased
(c) Both
(d) None

290. Lactic dehydrogenase increases in cases of
(a) Hepatic damage (b) Renal damage
(c) Muscle damage (d) All of the above

291. Sorbitol dehydrogenase increases in cases of
(a) Aflatoxicosis (b) Muscle damage
(c) Parasitic hepatitis (d) None of the above

292. Normal level of lactic dehydrogenase in cattle is
(a) 176-135 IU/L (b) 41-104 IU/L
(c) 31-99 III U/L (d) 60-111 IU/L

293. Concentration of dextrose used in case of Jaundice is
(a) 5% (b) 10%
(c) 20% (d) 40%

294. Clay coloured faces occurs in case of
(a) Pre hepatic jaundice
(b) Hepatic jaundice
(c) Post hepatic jaundice
(d) All of the above

295. In case of Hepatic jaundice Vander Bergh reaction is
(a) Direct (b) Indirect
(c) Biphasic (d) Triphasic

296. Edema due to accumulation of fluid in an enclosed

space is termed as
(a) Encysted edema (b) False edema
(c) Tabal edema (d) Passeve edema

297. Edema due to lowered concentration of plasma protein is known as
(a) Generla edema (b) Nutritional edema
(c) Passeve edema (d) False edema

298. Somatostatin is secreted by
(a) á-cells of pancreas
(b) Delta cells of pancreas
(c)
(d) None

299. Glucagon is secreted in pancreas by
(a) á-cells (b) b-cells
(c) ä-cells (d) All

300. Insulin is secreted in pancreas by
(a) á-cells (b) b-cells
(c) ä-cells (d) All

301. Semisolid clay coloured faeces with undigested food materials indicates
(a) Hepatitis (b) Pancreatitis
(c) Gastritis (d) Gastroenteritis

302. Hypoglycemia occurs in cases of
(a) Presence of more insulin
(b) Starvation
(c) Hepatic diseases
(d) All

303. Type I diabetes is termed as
(a) Juvenile diabetes
(b) Senile diabetis
(c) Specific diabetes
(d) Non specific diabetes

304. Type II diabetes is termed as
(a) Juvenile diabetes (b) Senile diabetes
(c) Specific diabetes (d) None

305. Insulin dependent diabetes mellitus is
(a) Type I DM (b) Type II DM
(c) Type III DM (d) Type IV DM

306. Insulin independent Diabetes mellitus is
(a) Type I DM (b) Type II DM
(c) Type III DM (d) Type IV DM

307. Secondary diabetes may occur due to
(a) Hyper pituitarism
(b) Hypo thyroidism
(c) Hyper adrenalinism
(d) All of the above

308. Rumen fluid becomes milky grey in colour in cases of
(a) Acid indigestion
(b) Alkaline indigestion
(c) Impaction
(d) Bloat

309. Rumen fluid becomes dark brown in cases of
(a) Acid indigestion
(b) Alkaline indigestion
(c) Impaction
(d) Bloat

310. Rumen fluid becomes greenish black in case of
(a) Acid indigestion
(b) Alkaline indigestion
(c) Bloat
(d) Impaction

311. In case of healthy animal, the odour of rumen fluid is
(a) Aromatic, vinegar like
(b) Ammonical
(c) Fruit ester like
(d) Alcohol like

312. Porridge or gruel like consistency of rumen fluid occurs in cases of
(a) Alkalosis (b) Acidosis
(c) Impaction (d) Bloat

313. Normal pH of rumen fluid has in the range of
(a) 6.3-7 (b) 5.5-7.4
(c) 4-5.5 (d) 7.5-8.5

314. Range of pH of rumen fluid in case of simple indigestion is
(a) 6.3-7 (b) 5.6-7.4
(c) 4.5-5 (d) 7.5-8.5

315. Sedimentation rate in case of normal rumen fluid is
(a) 6 minutes (b) 3-9 minutes
(c) 6-8 minutes (d) 4-5 minutes

316. Cellulose digestion time of normal rumen fluid is
(a) 20 hours (b) 10 hours
(c) 15 hours (d) 30 hours

317. Management history involves
(a) Nutrition

(b) Breeding & parturition history
(c) Climate & housing conditions
(d) All of the above

318. Virus of dermatitis
(a) Pox (b) Adeno
(c) Parvo (d) Herpes

319. Nodule at the base of eye lash is
(a) Sty (b) Acne
(c) Both (d) Ectropion

320. Pox is associated with acne in
(a) Variola cattle pox (b) Canadian horse pox
(c) Camel pox (d) Swine pox

321. Demodectic mite may lead to
(a) Acne (b) Ptyriasis
(c) Seborrhea (d) Psoriasis

322. Rickets in calf is due to deficiency of
(a) Calcium
(b) Vitamin D
(c) Phosphorous & Vitamin D
(d) Calcium & Phosphorous

323. Joint mostly involved in rickets
(a) Knee (b) Shoulder
(c) Hip (d) Stifle

324. Osteoporosis occurs due to excess of
(a) Parthyroid hormones
(b) Calcitonin
(c) Calcium
(d) Vitamin D

325. Dental caries do not occur in
aa Sheep (b) Pig
(c) Horse (d) Dog

326. Carcinoma of mammary gland leads to decrease in level of
(a) Vitamin A (b) Vitamin B
(c) Vitamin C (d) Vitamin D

327. Excess feeding of wheat bran in horse leads to
(a) Big head disease (b) Miller disease
(c) Brain disease (d) All

328. Actinomycosis is actually
(a) Osteoporosis
(b) Osteomalacia
(c) Osteodistrophy
(d) Osteodistrophy fibrosa

329. Death of horse with azoturea occurs because of
(a) Uremia (b) Septicemia
(c) Both (d) None

330. Goiter is inherited in
(a) Mereino sheep (b) African cattle
(c) Both (d) None

331. Enzootic goiter mostly occurs in
(a) Hilly area (b) Draught area
(c) Both (d) Plain area

332. Thyroid thrill is
(a) Irregular pulsation in goiter
(b) Regular pulsation in goiter
(c) Absence of pulsation
(d) None

333. Polioencephalomalacia is
(a) Degranulation of white matter
(b) Degranulation of grey matter
(c) Both
(d) None

334. Leukoencephalomalacia is
(a) Degranulation of white matter
(b) Degranulation of grey matter
(c) Both
(d) None

335. Nitrate poisoning may lead to deficiency of
(a) Vitamin A (b) Vitamin B
(c) Vitamin C (d) Vitamin D

336. Propylene glycol is given in deficiency of
(a) Vitamin A (b) Vitamin B
(c) Vitamin C (d) Vitamin D

337. Modified forms of Vitamin A
(a) Is present in fish
(b) Can pass through placentas
(c) Both correct
(d) Both are wrong

338. Epilepsy is inherited in which
(a) Jersey (b) Hereford
(c) Brownswiss (d) All

939. Jacksoman attack is
(a) Focal felts of epilepsy
(b) Generalized of epilepsy
(c) Both
(d) None

340. Typical seizures of epilepsy of 1-2 minute in human is known as

(a) Grand-mal (b) Petit-mal
(c) Seatus (d) All

341. Tonoclonic convulsions occur in
(a) Tetanus
(b) Strychnine poisonings
(c) Ergot
(d) Epilepsy

342. Mania is
(a) Excitement of nervous system
(b) Dullness of nervous system
(c) Depression of nervous system
(d) Infection of nervous system

343. Somnolence is
(a) Excitement of nervous system
(b) Dullness of nervous system
(c) Depression of nervous system
(d) Infection of nervous system

344. Tiresome state is known as
(a) Lassitude (b) Somnolence
(c) Narcolepsy (d) Tremor

345. Uncontrollable sleep is
(a) Lassitude (b) Somnolence
(c) Narcolepsy (d) Tremor.

346. Twitching of skeletal muscle is
(a) Lassitude (b) Somnolence
(c) Narcolepsy (d) Tremor.

347. Normal CSF pressure is
(a) 10 mm of ringer lactate
(b) 120 mm of H_2O
(c) 40 mg of Hg
(d) 120 mg of Hg

348. Spastic paralysis is originated at
(a) Brain (b) Spinal cord
(c) Choroids plexus (d) Ganglia

349. Flaccid paralysis is originated at
(a) Brain (b) Spinal cord
(c) Choroids plexus (d) Ganglia

350. Bleeding from ear & nose denote injury of
(a) Brain (b) Spinal cord
(c) Choroids plexus (d) Ganglia

351. Infra red rays are used for
(a) Radiography (b) Endoscopy
(c) Ultrasonography (d) Fomentation

352. Sudden extravasations of blood up to brain is known as
(a) Epistaxis (b) Apoplexy
(c) Melena (d) Hemoptysis

353. Which of the muscle is affected in chorea?
(a) Pectoral
(b) Muscles of thorax
(c) Muscles of abdomen
(d) All

354. Hyperkinesias occurs due to lesions in
(a) Cerebrum (b) Cerebellum
(c) Spinal cord (d) Medulla oblangata

355. Forward jerky movement of forelimbs occurs in
(a) Spastic paralysis (b) Flaccid paralysis
(c) Both (d) None

356. Feed consumed/100 kg b wt is
(a) Anaphagia
(b) Feed conversion rate
(c) Dysphasia
(d) Palatability

357. Which of the following can be used as a mouth wash
(a) 2% CuSO4 (b) 2% Alum
(c) 2% KClO3 (d) All

358. Dry grain is main cause of obstruction (Choke) in
(a) Horse (b) Dog
(c) Goat (d) Sheep

359. Painful sound of sheep/goat is
(a) Groaning (b) Grunting
(c) Moaning (d) All

360. Painful sound of pig is
(a) Groaning (b) Grunting
(c) Moaning (d) All.

361. Painful sound of cow is
(a) Groaning (b) Grunting
(c) Moaning (d) All

362. Hoven is used for
(a) Ruminal acidosis (b) Tympany
(c) Vegal indigestion (d) Simple indigestion

363. Pain symptom of canine is
(a) Kicking on belly (b) Grunting
(c) Rolling of ground (d) All

364. Atropine test is used for the diagnosis of
(a) Ruminal acidosis (b) Tympany
(c) VAgal indigestion (d) Simple indigestion

365. In which type of abomasal displacement cause of death is starvation
(a) Left side displacement of abomasum
(b) Right displacement of abomasum
(c) Anterior displacement of abomasum
(d) All

366. Dark pasty faeces without blood comes in
(a) Left side displacement of abomasum
(b) Right displacement of abomasum
(c) Anterior displacement of abomasum
(d) All

367. Recovery is indicated by passage of faces in
(a) Left side displacement of abomasum
(b) Right displacement of abomasum
(c) Anterior displacement of abomasum
(d) All

368. Neruo-pathological spasm of esophagus in foal is
(a) Oesophagitis (b) Choke
(c) Impaction (d) None

369. Which of the following colic occurs in episodes
(a) Impactive (b) Spasmodic
(c) Flatulence (d) All

370. Tympany of intestine is
(a) Impactive (b) Spasmodic
(c) Flatulence (d) All

371. Septic thrombus must house in it
(a) Virus (b) Parasite
(c) Fungi (d) Bacteria

372. Presence of foreign material in blood vessels is called -
(a) Thrombus (b) Emboli
(c) Ischemia (d) Infaraction

373. Accumulation of fluid in perioteneal cavity is called
(a) Anasarca (b) Hydorpercardium
(c) Hydrothorax (d) Ascites

374. Shock is circulatory disturbance characterized by-
(a) Reduced blood volume
(b) Reduced blood flow
(c) Haemocancentration
(d) All of above

375. Active hypermia is accumitation of blood in
(a) Vein (b) Lymphatics
(c) Arteries (d) Intestine

376. Escape of all blood contents through intact blood vessels is known as
(a) Rhexis (b) Ecchymosis
(c) Petechiae (d) Diapedesis

377. Erythrophagocytosis is a feature of
(a) Congesation (b) Oedema
(c) Sludged blood (d) Infaraction

378. Ecchymoses is type of haemorrhge which diameter is
(a) More than 1 to 10 mm
(b) Less than one mm
(c) More than 10 mm
(d) All of above

379. Irregular, diffuse and flat ecchymotic surface is refered as.
(a) Suffusion (b) Ecchymosis
(c) Petechiae (d) Haemorrhage

380. On percussion water is felt in
(a) Ascites (b) Coltis-X
(c) Peretonits (d) Cystits

381. Lasix is used for treatment of
(a) Ascetis (b) Coltis-X
(c) Peretonits (d) Cystits

382. Intraperitoneal injection should be never given in
(a) Cattle (b) Buffalo
(c) Horse (d) Pig

383. Yellow tar weed seed leads to
(a) Hepatitis (b) Jaundice
(c) Liver cirrhosis (d) All

384. Prehepatic jaundice is
(a) Haematogenous (b) Hepatogenous
(c) Both (d) None

385. Toxin of jaundice is
(a) SO (b) CCl_4
(c) Both (d) None

386. Test for bile pigment in urine is
(a) Biliverdine (b) Hay sulfer test
(c) Ascoli's test (d) Alizurine test

387. Liver function test are negative in
(a) Hepatitis (b) Jaundice
(c) Cirrhosis (d) Fatty lever

388. Iatrogenic disease is caused due to
(a) Animal (b) Veterinarian
(c) Environment (d) All

389. When posterior limbs are uncontrolable & usually are extended in an abnormal position
(a) Paralysis (b) Posterior paralysis
(c) Posterior paresis (d) Paraplegia

390. Gait of pig in case of Pantothenic acid deficiency becomes
(a) Wobbling (b) Staggering
(c) Straddling (d) Goose stepping

391. Peculiar gait in case of Molybdenum toxicity in cattle
(a) Goose stepping cattle
(b) Pacing cattle
(c) Racing cattle
(d) Louping gait

392. Gait found in sheep as if it trots & with ears moving up & down
(a) Cuddie trotting
(b) Compulsive walking
(c) Jerky trotting
(d) Jerky walking

393. Ballottement is the technique used for
(a) Floating visceral masses in abdominal cavity
(b) Floating visceral masses in thoracic cavity
(c) Floating visceral masses in pelvic cavity
(d) All of the above

394. Crackles are heard in cases of
(a) Moist rales (b) Dry rales
(c) Bronchitis (d) None

395. Inflammation of eye lids in known, as
(a) Blepharitis (b) Oophorites
(c) Laucnts (d) Conjunctivitis

396. Term used for adhesions between eyelids due to blepharitis
(a) Blepharospasm (b) Blepharal adhesions
(c) Ankyloblepharon (d) Dacryoblepheritis

397. Union of conjunctiva & covering of eye ball due to adhesion is known as
(a) Ankyloblepharon (b) Symblepharon
(c) Both (d) None

398. Symblepheron is defined as
(a) Union of conjunctiva with eyelid due to adhesion
(b) Union of Sclera with eyelid due to adhesion
(c) Union of Cornea with cycled due to adhesion
(d) All of the above

399. Sinking of eyeball into orbit is known as
(a) Exophthalmia (b) Endophthalmia
(c) Dacryoadenitis (d) Orbital celluetes

400. Exophthalmia is defined as
(a) Inflammation of eyeball
(b) Protrusion of eye ball
(c) Sinking of eyeball
(d) None

401. Inflammation of lachrymal gland is known as
(a) Dacryoadenitis (b) Lacroadenitis
(c) None (d) Both

402. Opacity of eye lens leading to blindness is
(a) Glaucoma (b) Iritis
(c) Cataract (d) Epiphora

403. Excessive lachrymation is defined as
(a) Epiphora (b) Water eye
(c) Both (d) None

404. Condition in which tension of fluid contents of eyeball increases is known as
(a) Ephephora (b) Water eye
(c) Glaucoma (d) Cater act

405. Eversion of third eye lid in dog indicates
(a) Opacity of lens
(b) Inflammation of retina
(c) Edema of Harderian gland
(d) Inflammation of Harderian gland

406. Pink eye condition occurs in case of
(a) Equine influenra
(b) Equine azoturia
(c) Equine encephalitis
(d) Equine meningitis

407. Rusty coloured foul smelling nasal discharge occurs in
(a) Equine influenza
(b) Pulmonary gangrene
(c) Bovina influenza
(d) Bronchitis

408. Presence of pink coloured pus in external auditory meatus is defined as
(a) Otitis (b) Labyrinthitis

(c) Otorrhoea (d) None

409. Labyrinthitis is
(a) Inflammation of external ear
(b) Inflammation of internal ear
(c) Inflammation of middle ear
(d) All

410. Hardware disease is name given to
(a) Tympany (b) TRP
(c) Listeriosis (d) Trypanosomosis

411. Rumenocentesis is done at the level of
(a) 9th intercostals space
(b) 9-11 intercostals space
(c) 10th intercostals space
(d) 5-8 inches caudoventral to costo chondral junction of last rib

412. Omasocentesis is done at the level of
(a) 5-8 inches from last rib
(b) 5-8 inches from 2nd rib
(c) At right side of 9th intercostals space
(d) None

413. Which of the following can cause gastric distension?
(a) Torsion of stomach
(b) Intestinal obstruction
(c) Paralytic ileus
(d) All of the above

414. BSP retention test is a type of
(a) Glucose tolerance test
(b) Starch digestion test
(c) Rumen function test
(d) Liver function test

415. Which of the following is not a liver specific enzyme?
(a) Arginase
(b) Sorbitol dehydrogenase
(c) Lactic dehydrogenase
(d) None

416. Leucine test is a
(a) Liver function test
(b) Rumen function test
(c) Pancreas function test
(d) Spleen function test

417. Horse urine is turbid as compared to other animals because of the presence of
(a) Kctones (b) Bilirubin
(c) $CaCo_3$ (d) $NaHCO_3$

418. Phonocardiography is described as
(a) Graphic recording of heart beat
(b) Graphic recording of pulse
(c) Graphic recording of heart sounds
(d) All of the above

419. Which of the following is abnormality of erythrocytes?
(a) Carbot's rings
(b) Heinz bodies
(c) Basophilic stripplings
(d) All of the above

420. Muscular weakness without complete loss of sensation is known as
(a) Paresis (b) Paraplegia
(c) Paralysis (d) Hemiplegia

421. Paralysis of one side of body including fore & hind legs of that side is
(a) Paresis (b) Paraplegia
(c) Hemiplegia (d) Ataxia

422. Paralysis of all organs behind a certain level of body
(a) Paresis (b) Paraplegia
(c) Menoplegia (d) Deplegia

423. Continuous splashes as in tetanus are known as
(a) Tonic (b) Clonic
(c) Both (d) None

424. Alternate splashes as in the case of strychnine poisoning are known as
(a) Tonic (b) Clonic
(c) Both (d) None

425. Attacks of tonic splashes followed by clonic splashes of all muscles of body with loss of consciousness are
(a) Convulsions (b) Epeleptiform
(c) Ataxia (d) Nystagmus

426. Quick occurrences of clonic spasm producing shivering with out any movement of body is
(a) Convulsions (b) Tremors
(c) Nystagmus (d) Ataxia

427. Rapid rhythmical movements of eye ball are known as
(a) Nystagmus (b) Opisthotonus

(c) Both (d) None

428. Lack of functional coordination without affecting individual muscles is
(a) Opisthotonus (b) Paresis
(c) Paraplegia (d) Ataxia

429. Anosmia is defined as
(a) Absence of sleep
(b) Absence of voice
(c) Absence of sense of smell
(d) Absence of sight

430. Sensory aberrations are termed as
(a) Paraesthesia (b) Hyperaesthesia
(c) Hypoaesthesisa (d) None

431. Photophobia is defined as
(a) Decreased sensitivity to light
(b) Increased sensitivity to light
(c) Decreased sensitivity to smell
(d) Increased sensitivity to smell

432. Difficulty in closing mouth occurs due to affection of
(a) Trigeminal nerve (b) Abducent nerve
(c) Facial nerve (d) Trochler nerve

433. Paralysis & hanging of fore limbs occurs because of affection of
(a) Brachial plexus (b) Radial nerve
(c) Ulnar nerve (d) All

434. Hind legs are abducted during forward movements occurs due to affections of
(a) Femoral nerve (b) Obturator nerve
(c) Pubic nerve (d) Tibial nerve

435. Which of the following is not an excitatory mental state?
(a) Mania (b) Lassitude
(c) Frenzy (d) Aggression

436. Which of the following is a depressive mental state?
(a) Mania (b) Frenzy
(c) Syncope (d) None

437. Which of the following is not a depressive mental state?
(a) Somnolence (b) Lassitude
(c) Syncope (d) None

438. Involuntary movement of muscles includes:
(a) Excitatory mental state
(b) Depressive mental state
(c) Both
(d) None

439. Aimless wandering in animals occur as a result of
(a) Excitatory mental state
(b) Depressive mental state
(c) Both
(d) None

440. Electromyography is done
(a) To diagnose peripheral nerve injuries
(b) To determine brain disease
(c) To evaluate retinal functional
(d) None

441. Which of the following serum enzymes are elevated in case of diseases of bones & muscles?
(a) Creatinine phosphokinase
(b) Serum alkaline phosphatase
(c) l-dehydrogenase
(d) All of the above

442. Which of the following statements is correct regarding the transient bristling of hair?
(a) Produced by contraction of associated muscles
(b) It is a nervous reaction
(c) It is associated with release of adrenaline
(d) All of the above

443. Hoflund syndrome is the term used for
(a) Simple indigestion
(b) Abomasal displacement
(c) Rumen displacement
(d) Vagus indigestion

444. Apple shaped abdomen occurs in the cases of
(a) Simple indigestion
(b) Vagus indigestion
(c) Omasal transport failure
(d) All

445. Splashing or tinkling sounds are heard in case of
(a) Vagus indigestion
(b) Right side abomasal displacement
(c) Left side abomasal displacement
(d) All

446. Acute obstruction of intestine by pressure from a body situated outside that leads to blood stasis is called

(a) Volvulus (b) Intussusception
(c) Strangulation (d) None

447. In which of the following condition, tympanic sound is heard on lung
(a) Pneumo thorax (b) Dilated stomach
(c) Dilated colon (d) All

448. Dry sound produce by narrowing of larynx, trachea or bronchus is known as
(a) Stertor (b) Splashing
(c) Tympanic (d) pickling

449. Dry continuous sound produced by narrowing of either larynx or bronchi is called
(a) Splashing (b) Tympanic
(c) Tickling (d) Ronchi

450. Sound produced by presence of fluid secretions within the alveoli or bronchi is
(a) Moist rales (b) Dry rales
(c) Crepitating rales (d) None

451. Sound produced by separation of sticky walls of alveoli & bronchioles
(a) Moist rates (b) Dry rates
(c) Crepitating rales (d) All

452. Spirography is a test to measure
(a) Respiratory volume
(b) Residual air
(c) Vital capacity of lung
(d) All of the above

453. Kennel cough is a name given to
(a) Infectious tracheobronchitis
(b) Infectious rhinitis
(c) Infectious rhinotracheits
(d) Infectious tracheorhintis

454. Insufficient supply of tissues with O_2 is called
(a) Hypoxia (b) Anoxia
(c) Anemia (d) Atraxia

455. Hypoxia which occurs when arterial blood is insufficiently oxygenated is known as
(a) Anaemic hypoxia (b) Hypoxic hypoxia
(c) Stagnant hypoxia (d) Ischemic hypoxia

456. Hypoxia which occurs when circulation of blood is slow is called
(a) Stagnant hypoxia (b) Ischemic hypoxia
(c) Both (d) None

457. Anaemic anoxia occurs when
(a) Oxygen carrying capacity of blood is reduced
(b) Circulation of blood is slow
(c) Tissue loose ability to utilize oxygen
(d) Arterial blood is insufficiently oxygenated

458. Most outstanding manifestation of dry pleurisy is
(a) Dyspnea (b) Pain
(c) Increase in pulse (d) All of the above

459. Pathoghomonic symptom of pleurisy is
(a) Dyspnea during inspiration
(b) Pain in respiration
(c) Increase in temperature
(d) Increase in pulse

460. Pleural fluid becomes grey in cases of
(a) Transudes (b) Exudates
(c) Empyema (d) Chylothorax

461. Pleural fluid becomes milky in cases of
(a) Transude (b) Chylothorax
(c) Emphysema (d) Exudates

462. Neutrophils in pleural exudates are seen in case of
(a) Bacteria in pleural exudates
(b) Pulmonary imfarcs
(c) Tuberculosis
(d) Malignancy

463. Eosinophils in pleural exudates are observed in
(a) Bacterial invasion
(b) Pulmonary invasion
(c) Tuberculosis
(d) Malignancy

464. Lymphocytes in pleural exudates are observed in
(a) Bacterial invasion (b) Pulmonary imfarct
(c) Tuberculosis (d) Malgnancy

465. Mitotic cells in pleural exudates are observed in
(a) Bacterial invasion (b) Pulmonary imfarct
(c) Tuberculosis (d) Malignancy

466. Distension of lungs caused by over distension of alveoli is known as
(a) Pulmonary emphysema
(b) Broken wind
(c) Heaves
(d) All of the above

467. Ronchi & crepetations are heard in cases of
(a) Pleurisy (b) Fibrosis

(c) Emphysema (d) Pneumothorax

468. Frictional sounds are present in case of
(a) Fibrosis (b) Pneumothorax
(c) Emphysema (d) Pleurisy

469. Best preservative for acetone detection in urine is
(a) Toluene (b) Thymol
(c) Formalin (d) Formaldehyde

470. pH of urine is acidic in case of
(a) Horse (b) Cattle
(c) Dog (d) Sheep

471. In case of the following pH of urine is alkaline?
(a) Horse (b) Cattle
(c) Goat (d) All

472. Robert's test is applied for
(a) Estimation of proteins in blood
(b) Estimation of proteins in urine
(c) Estimation of proteins CSF
(d) Estimation of proteins milk

473. Physiological proteinuria occurs in cases of
(a) Excessive muscular exertions
(b) Excessive ingestion of proteins
(c) Emotional stress
(d) All of the above

474. Rothera's test is applied for the detection of
(a) Ketonuria (b) Ketonemia
(c) Ketones in CSF (d) Ketones in milk

475. Ketonurea occurs in case of
(a) Milk fever
(b) Downer's cow syndrome
(c) Fat cow syndrome
(d) Diabetes Mellitus

476. Volhard's concentration test is a
(a) Liver function test
(b) Kidney function test
(c) Rumen function test
(d) Pancreas function test

477. In Choluria, which of the following is present in the urine
(a) Oxalates (b) Ketonies
(c) Bile pigments (d) Alburinh

478. In Katurea, which of the following is present in the urine
(a) Na (b) K
(c) Cl (d) Oxalates

479. Islets of langerhan's is affected in case of
(a) Diabetes Melllitus
(b) Diabetes insipidus
(c) Both
(d) None

480. Posterior pituitary is affected in case of
(a) Diabetes mellitus (b) Diabetes insipidus
(c) Both (d) None

481. In case of interstitial nephritis, acidosis is
(a) Normochloraemic
(b) Hyperchloraemic
(c) Hypochloraemic
(d) None

482. Urolithiasis
(a) Occurs more in male
(b) Occurs more in female
(c) Occurs in both equally
(d) Has no relation with sex

483. Urolithiasis in dog may contain
(a) Triple phosphate crystals
(b) Calcium oxalates
(c) Calcium phosphate
(d) All

484. Azotemia is elevation of
(a) Proteins in blood
(b) Non protein nitrogenous compound in blood
(c) Both
(d) None

485. Kussmaul's respiration occurs in cases of
(a) pre-renal failure (b) post-renal failure
(c) pre hepatic failure (d) post hepatic failure

486. Cephalosporins should be avoided in case of renal failure as
(a) They cause nephrotoxicity
(b) They cause neurotoxicty
(c) Increase lactic acidosis
(d) Cause nausea

487. Magnesium salts should be avoided in case of renal failure, as they cause
(a) Neurotoxicity (b) Cardiotoxicity
(c) Both (d) None

488. Neomycin should be avoid with case of renal failure as it causes

(a) Ototoxicity (b) Neurotoxicity
(c) Cardiotoxicity (d) All

489. Nalidixic acid should be avoided in case of renal failure, as it causes.
(a) Nausea (b) Photosenesitivity
(c) Both (d) None

490. Biguanides should be avoided in case of renal failure, as they cause
(a) Increased risk of gastro intestinal bleeding
(b) Increased risk of lactic acidosis
(c) Nephrotoxicity
(d) All

491. Aspirin should be avoided in case of renal failure, as they cause
(a) Increased risk of gastro intestinal bleeding
(b) Increased risk of latic acidosis
(c) Nephrotoxicity
(d) All

492. Crystalluria leading to renal tubular obstruction & acute interstitial nephritis occurs due to
(a) Sulphonamides (b) Tetracycline
(c) Aspirins (d) All

493. Renal damage & increased uremia, occurs due to
(a) Sulphonamides (b) Tetracycline
(c) Aminoglycosides (d) Cephalosporines

494. Which of the drug is safe to be used during renal failure?
(a) Penicillin (b) Ampicillin
(c) Erythromycin (d) All

495. Which of the drug is not safe to be used during renal failure?
(a) Penicillin (b) Erythromycin
(c) Aspirin (d) All

496. EDTA is used as anticoagulant at the rate of
(a) 1 mg powder for 1 ml blood
(b) 4-5 drops/ml blood
(c) 5 mg/2ml blood
(d) 1 drop /ml blood

497. Blood can be collected from radial vein, in case of
(a) Dog (b) Horse
(c) Pig (d) Bull

498. Dose of heparin, used as anticoagulant is
(a) 1% soln - 0.1 ml/10 ml
(b) 2% soln - 0.1 /10ml
(c) 1% soln - 0.2 ml/10 ml
(d) 2% soln - 0.2 ml / 10 ml

499. Hayem's fluid is used as diluting fluid for
(a) Erythrocyte count (b) TLC
(c) DLC (d) All

500. Which of the fluid can be used as detecting fluid for RBC count?
(a) Hayem's fluid (b) Ganti's fluid
(c) Gower's fluid (d) All

501. Appearance of refractile bodies in RBC are known as
(a) Heinz bodies
(b) Basophilic stippling
(c) Howell Jolly body
(d) Koch's blue body

502. Appearance of small spherical eccentric nuclear remnant in young RBC is called
(a) Heinz body
(b) Howell Jolly body
(c) Basophilic stippling
(d) Koch's blue body

503. When both sides of RBC are bulged out & they appear spherical its is known as
(a) Anisocytosis (b) Poikclocytosis
(c) Spheocytosis (d) All

504. Eosinophilia occurs in cases of
(a) Allergic reactions (b) Parasitic diseases
(c) Both (d) None

505. Neutrophilia occurs in cases of
(a) Pneumonia (b) Hyper senstivity
(c) Urtrcaria (d) Filariasis

506. Lymphocytosis occurs in cases of
(a) Tuberculosis (b) Influenza
(c) Neoplasm (d) All

507. Occurrence of young forms of immature granulocytes in peripheral blood is called -
(a) Shift to left
(b) Shift to right
(c) Regenerative shift to right
(d) Degenerative shift to left

508. When peripheral blood shows abnormal number of hyper segmented cells, it is
(a) Shift to left (b) Shift to right
(c) Regenerative shift (d) Degenerative shift

509. Modified Knott technique is used for detection of
(a) Coccidia
(b) Sporulations of oocyst
(c) Microfilariae in blood
(d) Trypanosomes in blood

510. Normal PCV in case of cattle is about
(a) 33.7% (b) 43.7%
(c) 50.% (d) 25%

511. Rouleaux formation in cattle is
(a) Intense (b) Moderate
(c) Absent (d) present

512. Rouleaux formation in horse is
(a) Intense (b) Moderate
(c) Absent (d) Present

513. ESR can be measured by the use of
(a) Wintrobe tube (b) Westergren tube
(c) Both (d) None

514. Which of the following factors influence ESR?
(a) Temperature of environment
(b) Number of erythrocytes
(c) Fibrinogen concentration in a plasma
(d) All

515. Disease which increase ESR in horse
(a) Infectious equine anaemia
(b) Tuberculosis
(c) Strongyloidosis
(d) All

516. Disease which increase ESR in dog
(a) Pyometra (b) Peritonitis
(c) Neoplasma (d) All

517. Purpura haemorrhagica is a disease causes due to disorder of
(a) Platelets (b) RBC
(c) WBC (d) All

518. Hemorrhages in case of pupura haemorrhagica occur in
(a) Conjunctiva
(b) Beneath skin & mucous membrane
(c) Body orifices
(d) All

519. *Streptococcus equi* infection in horse leads to
(a) Purpura haemorrhagica
(b) Generalized edema
(c) Both
(d) None

520. Leucopoenia occurs in cases of
(a) Shock (b) Chronic nephritis
(c) Swine fever (d) All

521. Leucocytosis occurs in case of
(a) Acidosis (b) Shock
(c) Chronic nephritis (d) Swine fever

522. Eosinopenia occurs in case of
(a) Bracken fern poisoning
(b) Copper deficiency
(c) Parasitic infestations
(d) Steroids therapy

523. Erythrocytes with basophilic striplings are characteristics of
(a) Folic acid deficiency
(b) Copper poisoning
(c) Lead poisoning
(d) Molybdenum toxicity

524. Macrocytic anemia occurs in
(a) Folic acid deficiency
(b) Vitamin A deficiency
(c) Vitamin B_6 deficiency
(d) Vitamin B_{12} deficiency

525. Microcytic hypochromic anemia occurs in
(a) Folic acid deficiency
(b) Vitamin A deficiency
(c) Vitamin B_6 deficiency
(d) Vitamin b_{12} deficiency

526. Leucopenia occurs in
(a) Bracken fern poisoning
(b) Rinderpest
(c) Both
(d) None

527. In leptospirosis there is
(a) Leukocytosis with shift to left
(b) Leukocytosis with shift to right
(c) Leukocytosis with shift to left
(d) Leukocytosis with shift to left

528. Neurophilia with shift to left occurs in
(a) TRP (b) Steroid therapy
(c) Both (d) None

529. Normocytic hypochromic anaemia occur due to deficiency of
(a) Iron in diet (b) Copper in diet

(c) Vitamin C in diet (d) All

530. Microcytic normochromic anaemia occurs in
(a) Chemical poisoning
(b) Chronic interstitial nephritis
(c) Ionizing radiation
(d) All

531. Hemolysis can occur in cases of
(a) Copper deficiency
(b) Phenothiazine toxicity
(c) Babesiosis
(d) All

532. Which of the following is not present in shake venom?
(a) Haemolysin (b) Neurotoxin
(c) Cytotoxin (d) Nephrotoxin

533. Diminished intensity of heart sounds occurs in
(a) Tachycardia
(b) Mitral volve stenosis
(c) Left ventricular hypertrophy
(d) Myocarditis

534. Increased intensity of heart sounds occurs in
(a) Short P-R interval (b) Bradycardia
(c) Myocarditis (d) Emphysema

535. Any disorder that increases the flow of blood across an artrioventricular opening produces
(a) I heart sound (b) II heart sound
(c) III heart sound (d) IV heart sound

536. Normal blood pressure in case of cattle is
(a) 137.7-229 (b) 144-180
(c) 77.2-130.9 (d) 196-211

537. Difference of potential between left arm & right arm in a electrocardiogram is represented by
(a) Lead I (b) Lead II
(c) Lead III (d) Lead IV

538. Difference of potential between left leg & right arm in a electrocardiogram is represented by
(a) Lead I (b) Lead II
(c) Lead III (d) Lead IV

539. Difference of potential between left leg & left arm in a electrocardiogram is represented by
(a) Lead I (b) Lead II
(c) Lead III (d) Lead IV

540. Deflection produced by atrial depolarization is represented by
(a) P wave (b) Q wave
(c) R wave (d) S wave

541. The initial negative deflection resulting from ventricular depolarization is represented by -
(a) P wave (b) Q wave
(c) R wave (d) S wave

542. The 1st positive deflection during ventricular depolarization is represented by
(a) P wave (b) Q wave
(c) R wave (d) S wave

543. The first negative deflection of ventricular depolarization that follows first positive deflection is represented by
(a) P wave (b) Q wave
(c) R wave (d) S wave

544. The deflection produced by ventricular repolarisation is represented by
(a) Q wave (b) R wave
(c) S wave (d) T wave

545. Deflection seen following T-wave & preceding the next P wave is resented by
(a) R wave (b) S wave
(c) U wave (d) T wave

546. Atrioventicular conduction time is measured by
(a) RR interval (b) PP interval
(c) PR interval (d) None

547. Measurement of total ventricular depolarization time is
(a) RR interval (b) PP internvl
(c) PR interval (d) QRS interval

548. When the impulse generated in SA node, fails to activate atria & ventricles is called
(a) Sinus arrhythmia (b) Sinus block
(c) Incomplete block (d) Complete AV block

549. When the triggering impulses from atria are conducted very slowly through AV conduction pathway
(a) Sinus arrhythmia (b) Sinus block
(c) Incomplete block (d) Complete AV block

550. When there is no activating impulse passing from atria to ventricles, it is known as
(a) Sinus block (b) Complete AV block
(c) Incomplete Block (d) Ventricular block

551. In case of TRP

(a) There is upward displacement of ST segment
(b) T wave is inverted
(c) Both
(d) None

552. In case of myocarditis there is
(a) Prolonged PR interval
(b) Depression of ST segment
(c) Arrhythmia
(d) All

553. In case diaphragmatic hernia there is appearance of
(a) Q wave (b) P wave
(c) S wave (d) T wave

554. Shortening of QT interval occurs in
(a) Hypercalcemia (b) Hypocalcemia
(c) Hyperglycemia (d) Hypoglycemia

555. Prolonged P wave occurs in
(a) Left artial enlargement
(b) Left ventricular enlargement
(c) Right ventricular enlargement
(d) Right atrial enlargement

556. Ectopic beat is the term given to
(a) Sinus arrhythmia
(b) Extra systolic arrhythmia
(c) Atrial flutter
(d) Atrial fibrillation

557. Pulse shows runs of few beats with one equal space in
(a) Sinus arrhythmia (b) Atrial flutter
(c) Arial fibrellation (d) All

558. Dyspnea, coughing alteration of pulse & enlargement of heart occurs in case of
(a) Left side heart failure
(b) Right side heart failure
(c) Both
(d) None

559. Gallop rhythm over mitral area and apical impulse occurs in case of
(a) Left side heart failure
(b) Right side heart failure
(b) Both
(d) None

560. Monitoring & coordination of internal body functions is done by
(a) Autonomic nervous system
(b) Peripheral nervous system
(c) Central NS
(d) All

561. Musculoskeletal coordination is done under
(a) Cerebrum
(b) Cerebellum
(c) Medulla oblangata
(d) Spinal cord

562. Coordination of spinal motor movements is under
(a) Cerebrum (b) Cerebellum
(c) Both (d) Spinal cord

563. Hyperkinesias is the term given to
(a) Motor irritation (b) Sensory irritation
(c) Both (d) None

564. Involuntary contraction of group of muscles is called
(a) Tetany (b) Tremor
(c) Convulsions (d) Spasm

565. Rapidly alternating violent contraction & relaxation of muscles during which animal loses its balance are
(a) Convulsions (b) Tremor
(c) Tetany (d) Spasm

566. Fine jerky involuntary contraction of muscle or some of its fibers is
(a) Convulsions (b) Tremor
(c) Tetany (d) Spasm

567. When animal rotates in circle due to lesions or increased tension of cerebellum are known as
(a) Forced movement
(b) Involuntary movement
(c) Voluntary movement
(d) None

568. Condition characterized by involuntary fast hand irregular action of some group of muscles mainly those of face & proximal parts of extremities is
(a) Chorea (b) Spasm
(c) Tetany (d) Tremor

569. Tapping of spinal fluid in cattle & buffaloes done at
(a) Lumbosacral region
(b) 1st coccygeal region
(c) 2nd coccygeal region

(d) All

570. Cisternal puncture for tapping of spinal fluid is done in
(a) Dog & cat (b) Horse
(c) Cattle & Buffalo (d) Sheep & goat

571. Tapping of spinal fluid at sub occipital or lumbosacral region in done in
(a) Goat (b) Sheep
(c) Horse (d) All

572. CSF pressure increases in cases of
(a) Avitaminosis A
(b) Hypotension
(c) Long standing degenerative disease
(d) Shock

573. CSF pressure decreases in case of
(a) Avitaminosis A (b) Hydrocephalus
(c) Hypotension (d) Meningitis

574. Apelt test is used in chemical exam of
(a) Urine (b) Milk
(c) Blood (d) CSF

575. Pandey's method estimates presence of
(a) Albumin in CSF (b) Globulin in CSF
(c) Ketones in CSF (d) Aldehydes in CSF

576. Hypocalcemia occurs in cases of
(a) Eclampsia
(b) Hypoparathyroidisin
(c) Partureint paresis
(d) All

577. Tonoclonic convulsions in dog occur due to
(a) Calcum deficiency
(b) Magneseum deficiency
(c) Both
(d) None

578. Meningitis is the inflammation of
(a) Piamator & arachnoids
(b) Duramator & arachnoids
(c) Duramator & piamator
(d) Duramator & arachnoids
(e) All

579. Pachy meningitis is the inflammation of
(a) Piamator (b) Duramator
(c) Arachnoids (d) All

580. Meningitis in goats occurs due to
(a) Pasteurellosis (b) Hemonchosis
(c) Strongylosis (d) Salmonellosis

581. Toxic factors present in Bracken fern is
(a) Thiaminase
(b) Aplastic anemic factor
(c) Both
(d) None

582. Encephalomalacia occurs due to deficiency of
(a) Vitamin E (b) Vitamin A
(c) Vitamin B_6 (d) Vitamin B_{12}

583. Cerebral paralysis may result due to
(a) Apoplexy
(b) Inter vertebral disc protrusion
(c) Spondylopathy
(d) Ancylosis of vertebrae

584. Spinal paralysis occurs due to
(a) Apoplexy (b) Infection of CNS
(c) Encephalitis (d) Spondylopathy

585. Drug toxicity may lead to
(a) Cerebral paralysis
(b) Spinal paralysis
(c) Peripheral paralysis
(d) All

586. Calving paralysis is term given to
(a) Obturator nerve paralysis
(b) Spinal nerve paralysis
(c) Gluteal nerve paralysis
(d) Peroneal nerve paralysis

587. Which of the following is a type of general epilepsy?
(a) Grand mal
(b) Focal fits
(c) Myoclonic epilepsy
(d) All of the above

588. Which of the following is a type of focal epilepsy?
(a) Psychomotor epilepsy
(b) Myoclonic epilepsy
(c) Akinetic attack
(d) All of the above

589. Solid elevation with flat top having diameter of more than a centimeter is known as
(a) Plaque (b) Nodule
(c) Papule (d) Vesicle

590. Circumscribed semisolid elevated round or flat topped lesions are known as

(a) Plaque (b) Vesicle
(c) Nodule (d) Wart

591. Excessive accumulation of discarded keratinized debris over the skin surface is known as
(a) Scale (b) Squander
(c) Flake (d) All of the above

592. Dried discharge of exudates over the above
(a) Crust (b) Scale
(c) Squander (d) Flake

593. Superficial erosion of the skin is known as
(a) Excoriation (b) Erosion
(c) Crust (d) Scar

594. Thickening & hardening of tissues is known as
(a) Excoriation (b) Chap
(c) Lichenification (d) None

595. A small fissure extending to subcutaneous tissue is
(a) Chap (b) Sinus
(c) Fistula (d) Scar

596. Baldness associated with scarring is known as
(a) Alpeica cicatrisata
(b) Alopecia cachectica
(c) Alopecia disseminata
(d) Alopecia univesalis

597. Patchy loss of hair at different places is known as
(a) Alopecia circatrcata
(b) Alopecia disseminata
(c) Alopecia cachectica
(d) Acopecrea universalis

598. Idiopathic premature baldness is known as
(a) Alopecia simplex
(b) Alopecia universalis
(c) Alopecia follicularis
(d) Alopicia aduata

599. Uniform wheals like eruptions on cutaneous surface are known as
(a) Urticaria (b) Nettlerash
(c) Hives (d) All of the above

600. When urticaria develops due to infection or ingestion or application of certain drugs, it is
(a) Urticaria medicamentosa
(b) Urticaica perstants
(c) Serum urticaria
(d) Urticaria solaris

601. Trial diet test is a method in dermatitis is used for
(a) Diagnosis (b) Treatment
(c) Control (d) Prevention

602. Condition where animals show marked sensitivity to sunlight following ingestion of photodynamic agents
(a) Photo sensitization
(b) Slough sickness
(c) Gross poisoning
(d) All of the above

603. Dermatitis with extensive skin involvement and infiltration of inflammatory cells is
(a) Erythmatous dematitis (b) Erysepelatous dematitis
(c) Both (d) None

604. Parakeratosis occurs due to deficiency of
(a) Zn (b) Cu
(c) Ca (d) Mg

605. Which form of demodicosis is pyoderma?
(a) Papular form
(b) Squamatous form
(c) Squamopapular form
(d) Pustular form

606. Exudative epidermitis in pigs, occurs due to infection of
(a) Staphylococcus infection
(b) Streptococcus infection
(c) Proteins
(d) Cryptococcus

607. Cutaneous streptothricosis in cattle occurs due to
(a) Streptococcus (b) Staphylococcus
(c) Dermatophilus (d) Cryptococcus

608. Cushing disease in dog is name given to
(a) Hyperadrenocorticoism
(b) Hyperadrenomedullarism
(c) Hyperpituitarism
(d) All

609. Factors causing vitamin D deficiency are
(a) Large amount of carotene
(b) Diseases of liver
(c) Steatorrhoea
(d) All of the above

610. Defective calcification of bones, particularly of face & head is called

(a) Renal rickets (b) Rubber jaw
(c) Both (d) None

611. Reduced amount of bony tissue on skeleton is known as
(a) Osteopaenia (b) Osteoschlerosis
(c) Osteporosis (d) None

612. Hardening of bony spaces due to chronic inflammation & stimulation of bony cells is known as
(a) Osteopaenia (b) Osteophysis
(c) Osteomyelitis (d) Osteosclerosis

613. Rarefaction of bones is known as
(a) Osteoporsis (b) Osteoschlaerosis
(c) Osteolysis (d) All

614. Paget's disease is name given to
(a) Suppurtive osteomyelitis
(b) Non suppurative osteomyelitis
(c) Ostitis deformans
(d) All

615. Inflammation of interior of bone affecting bone marrow is
(a) Osteoschlerosis (b) Ostiolysis
(c) Osteomyelitis (d) Osteoporosis

616. Inflammation of lamina of hoofs is called
(a) Laminitis
(b) Founder
(c) Pododermatitis aseptic diffusa
(d) All of the above

617. One of the signs of Horner's syndrome is
(a) Bending of horn
(b) Tumor of horn
(c) Narrowing of palpebral fissure
(d) None

618. Tough fibrous capsule covering eyeball is
(a) Tenon's capsule (b) Toent capsule
(c) Hayeni's capsule (d) Gautis capsule

619. Vascular tunic of eyeball is
(a) Sclera (b) Cornea
(c) Uveal tract (d) Retina

620. Nervous tunic of eyeball is
(a) Sclera (b) Cornea
(c) Uveal tract (d) Retina

621. Which of the followings is fibrous tunic of eyeball?
(a) Sclera (b) Cornea
(c) Both (d) None

622. Position of vitreous humour in eyeball
(a) Anterior (b) Posterior
(c) Medial (d) Lateral

623. Position of aqueous humour in eyeball
(a) Anterior (b) Posterior
(c) Medial (d) Lateral

624. Light rays enter the eyeball through
(a) Cornea (b) Schlera
(c) Retena (d) All

625. In which of the following diseases there is corneal opacity
(a) Salmonellosis (b) Rabies
(c) Trypanosomiasis (d) All

626. When pupillary response is noted in both eyes but animal is blind, it may be due to
(a) Retero bulbar lesion
(b) Lesion at visual centre
(c) Lesions in optic nerve
(d) Lesions in at retina

627. Pupil is not constricted in both eyes when there is lesion in
(a) Retina (b) Optic nerve
(c) Visual centre (d) Oculomotor nerve

628. Techniques used to observe filtration angle of eye is
(a) Gonioscopy (b) Electoretinography
(c) Opthalmoscopy (d) Tonomerty

629. Tonometry helps to
(a) Measure filtration angle of eye
(b) Ascertain intraocular pressure
(c) Measure of pupil diameter
(d) All

630. Inversion of margin of the eyelid is known as
(a) Entropion (b) Ectropion
(c) Blepherities (d) Chemosis

631. Everson of the margin of eyelid is known as
(a) Entrpion (b) Ectropion
(c) Blepharitis (d) Chemosis

632. Edema of palpebral bulbar conjunctiva with protrusion of membranes beyond the palpebral fissure is
(a) Entropion (b) Ectropion
(c) Blepharetis (d) Chemosis

633. Tonic contractions of eye lid due to local causes or neurological lesion
(a) Blepharitis (b) Blepharospasm
(c) Blepheropathy (d) All

634. Inflammation of hair bulbs of eye is
(a) Trichitis (b) Trichiasis
(c) Districhiases (d) None

635. Condition where eye lashes on eyelids turn inward against the eye ball is
(a) Distichiasis (b) Trichitis
(c) Trichiasis (d) None

636. Retinopathy which occurs following prolonged exposure to sun light is
(a) Angiopathy
(b) Solar retinopathy
(c) Actinic retinopathy
(d) All

637. Which of the following viral infections cause ocular lesions?
(a) Scrapie (b) Blue tongue
(c) Sheep pox (d) All

638. Which of the following bacterial infection cause ocular lesions?
(a) Salmonellosis (b) Staphylococcosis
(c) Corynebacterium (d) Streptococcosis

639. Which of the following fungus cause ocular signs?
(a) Histoplasmosis (b) Cryptococcosis
(c) Both (d) None

640. Which of the following parasites cause ocular signs?
(a) Babesiosis (b) Thieleriosis
(c) Toxoplasmosis (d) All

641. Nervous form of ketosis occurs in cases of
(a) Nitrate poisoning (b) Pylonephritis
(c) Metritis (d) Peritonitis

642. Synonymous of parturient paresis include
(a) Milk fever (b) Hypocalcaemia
(c) Calving paralysis (d) All

643. Black water is the common name given to
(a) Paralytic myoglobinuria
(b) Post parturient haemoglobinuria
(c) Ketonuria
(d) Acetonuria

644. Grass staggers occurs due to deficiency of
(a) Mg (b) Ca
(c) Zn (d) Cu

645. Which of the following factors interfere with Vitamin A utilization in systems?
(a) Hypothyroidism
(b) Cathartic drug
(c) Nitrates & Nitrites
(d) All

646. Which of the following sign primary occurs in case of Vitamin A deficiency?
(a) Biot's spot (b) Night blindness
(c) Xeropthalmia (d) Corneal scar

647. Which of the following is a secondary ocular sign in Vitamin A deficiency?
(a) Xeropthalmia
(b) Biot's spot
(c) Corneal ulceration
(d) None

648. Blood urea nitrogen increases in case of
(a) Protein catabolism
(b) Renal dysfunction
(c) Nephrectomised animal
(d) All

649. BUN increases after administration of
(a) Corticosteroid (b) Tetracycline
(c) Both (d) None

650. DAM method used for estimation of
(a) Urea (b) Creatinine
(c) Ketone (d) Aldehydes

651. Normal level of BUN in mg/dl in cattle is
(a) 6-27 (b) 1.5-3
(c) 90-93 (d) 104-106

652. BUN
(a) Decreases after calving
(b) Increases after calving
(c) No change
(d) None

653. Normal ketone level in milk sample is
(a) 0.3 mg/dl (b) 3 mg/dl
(c) 13 mg/dl (d) 30 mg/dl

654. Normal ketone level in blood sample is
(a) 10 mg/dl (b) 1 mg/dl
(c) 100 mg/dl (d) None

655. Ross test is applied for estimation of

(a) Acetone
(b) â-hydroxy butyric acid
(c) Acetic acid
(d) All

656. Rothera's test is more sensitive for estimation of
(a) Acetoacetate
(b) Acetone
(c) â-hydroxy butyric acid
(d) All

657. Day blindness due to deficiency of Vitamin A is known as
(a) Nyctalopia (b) Amblyopia
(c) Myopia (d) All

658. Night blindness is known as
(a) Nyctalopia (b) Amblyopia
(c) Myopea (d) All

659. Ketosis in heavily fed high producing cows is known as
(a) Estate acetonenia (b) Bovine cetosis
(c) Feed acetonemia (d) Lactacidosis

660. Rhodopsin on exposure with light converts into
(a) Meta rhodopsin (b) Lumirhodopsin
(c) Opsin (d) None

661. Tying up syndrome in horses occurs due to deficiency of
(a) Vitamin E (b) VitaminK
(c) Vitamin A (d) Vitamin B complex

662. Deficiency of Vitamin B_1 may lead to
(a) Ataxia
(b) Polyneuretis
(c) Polioencephalomalacia
(d) All

663. Deficiency of Riboflavin may lead to
(a) Dermatitis (b) Corneal opacity
(c) Photophobia (d) All

664. Dermatitis known as Acrodyna occurs due to
(a) Mange infection
(b) Tick infestation
(c) Vitamin B_6 deficiency
(d) Mite infestation

665. Which of the following Vitamin is known as anti anaemia factor?
(a) Vitamin B_1 (b) Vitamin B_2
(c) Vitamin B_6 (d) Vitamin B_{12}

666. Scurvy occurs in human beings due to deficiency of
(a) Vitamin C (b) Vitamin A
(c) Vitamin B_6 (d) Vitamin B_{12}

667. In case of scurvy, Vitamin C is destroyed in
(a) Intestines (b) Stomach
(c) Rumen (d) Lever

668. Selenium deficiency causes
(a) White muscle disease
(b) Stiff Lamb disease
(c) Nutritional myopathy
(d) All

669. White muscle disease occurs due to def of
(a) Selenium (b) Vitamin E
(c) Both (d) None

670. Manganese deficiency may lead to
(a) Infertility (b) Limb deformities
(c) Delayed estrus (d) All

671. In Vagus indigestion abdomen becomes
(a) Apple shaped (b) Papple shaped
(c) Done shaped (d) Pear shaped

672. Prehepatic jaundice occurs in cases of
(a) Equine infections anemia
(b) Salmonellosis
(c) TB
(d) Glanders

673. Intrahepatic jaundice occurs in cases of
(a) Bacillary Haemoglobinurea
(b) Cu deficiency
(c) Snake bite
(d) TB

674. Hyperthermia after parturition occurs in
(a) Cow (b) Sow
(c) Bitch (d) Mare

675. Stertorous respiration occurs in case of
(a) Pharyngeal obstruction
(b) Pharyngitis
(c) Pharyngeal paralysis
(d) All

676. In case of diarrhoea
(a) Acidosis occurs (b) Alkalosis occurs
(c) Any (d) None

677. Which of the enzyme if increases in blood, indicate hepatitis

(a) Alkaline phosphatase
(b) ã glutamyl tranaminase
(c) Sorbitol dehydrogenase
(d) All

678. Treatment extended to prolong life span in cases of incurable diseases is called
(a) Palliatine treatment
(b) Empirical treatment
(c) Specific treatment
(d) None

679. Which of the following is not a characteristic feature of Lactation tetany of mares?
(a) Stiff gait
(b) Dilation of nostrils
(c) Thumping sound from thorax
(d) Prolapse of III eye lid

680. Which one is the choice of drug to treat hypomagnesemic tetany in case of calves?
(a) 20% $MgSO_4$ - 200 ml
(b) 12% Magnesium adipate + 5% cal gluconate
(c) 50% solution of $MgSO_4$
(d) 100 ml of 10% $MgSO_4$

681. In downer cow syndrome, which factor is not associated with disease?
(a) Hypocalcemia
(b) Hypomagnsemia
(c) Hyperphosphatemia
(d) Hypophosphataemia

682. Post parturient haemoglobinurea generally occurs after
(a) 1-2 week of calving
(b) 2-4 week of calving
(c) 3-5 week of calving
(d) 4-6 week of calving

683. Usual dose rate of calcium borogluconate for treatment of milk fever is
(a) 100-200 gm 25% solution
(b) 200-300 gm 25% solution
(c) 500-1000 gm 20-30% solution
(d) 400-800 gm 25% solution

684. Abnormal range of temperature during lactation tetany is
(a) 102-103° F (b) 104-105° F
(c) 99-100° F (d) 100-101° F

685. Which of them is not associated with occurrence of post parturient haemoglobinurea?
(a) Cruciferous plants
(b) Low selenium intake
(c) Rich protein diet
(d) Drought conditions

686. Normal value of serum magnesium in cow ranges about
(a) 1.5-4 mg/dl (b) 2.7-4 mg/dl
(c) 1.7-3 mgl/dl (d) 3-6 mg/dl

687. What should be optimum ratio of Ca & P feeding during Last month of pregnancy to avoid milk fever?
(a) 1:2 (b) 1:3.3
(c) 2:1 (d) 2.4.3

688. Frog leg attitude in animals is related with
(a) Downer's cow syndrome
(b) Milk fever
(c) Eclampsia
(d) Fat cow syndrome

689. Arched back condition occurs in
(a) Milk fever (b) Milk Tetany
(c) Both (d) None

690. Staring gaze occurs in
(a) Downer's cow syndrome
(b) Milk fever
(c) Eclampsia
(d) Fat cow syndrome

691. Which of the following is estimated in Mini profile test?
(a) Glucose (b) Albumin
(c) Urea (d) All

692. Udder inflation therapy is done for the treatment of
(a) Milk fever
(b) Fat cow syndrome
(c) Downer's cow syndrome
(d) All

693. Xylidyl blue test is applied to
(a) Estimate Mg in blood
(b) Estimate Cu in blood
(c) Estimate Mg in urine
(d) Estimate Cu in urine

694. Diseases related with thorough put of some blood

parameter are known as
(a) Production diseases
(b) Metabolic diseases
(c) Contagious diseases
(d) Infections diseases

695. Ketosis can be sometimes, self limiting in case of
(a) Sheep (b) Goat
(c) Cattle (d) All

696. High death rate in lactation tetany of cow maybe associated with increased level of serum
(a) Mg (b) Ca
(c) Mo (d) Co

697. When there is severe toxemia in cow, Ca borogluconate should be given through
(a) IV route (b) IM route
(c) I/Rumenal route (d) I/P route

698. Secondary hypomagnesaemia may occur due to high dietary intake of
(a) Ca (b) P
(c) K (d) Co

699. In downer's cow syndrome levels of Ca, P, Mg & glucose in blood are
(a) Elevated (b) Highly elevated
(c) Decreased (d) Normal

700. Which of the following is characteristics feature of Lactation tetany in mares
(a) lymphadenitis
(b) Thumping sound from thorax
(c) Fibrous udder
(d) All

701. Atropine sulfate is
(a) Anti nicotinic (b) Anti á-adrenergic
(c) Anti â-adrenergic (d) None

702. Varapamil is used as
(a) Mg channel blocker
(b) Na channel blocker
(c) Ca channel blocker
(d) Cl channel blocker

703. Which of the following is used as an anti arrhythmic?
(a) Verepamil (b) Propranolol
(c) Both (d) None

704. Sulphonamides are
(a) Bacteriostatic (b) Bacteriocidal
(c) Both (d) None

705. Biotrim contains
(a) Sulphadiazine + Trimethoprim
(b) Sulphamethoxazole + Trimethoprim
(c) Slphametholxazole only
(d) Sulphdiazine only

706. Sialoadinitis refers to inflammation of salivary glands &
(a) Lacrimal glands
(b) Sebaceous glands
(c) Cervical lymph glands
(d) Sweat glands

707. Sudden death may occur in which of the following diseases
(a) TRP
(b) Grain engorgement
(c) Primary gaseous bloat
(d) Frothy bloat

708. Incidence of dietary abomasal displacement & impaction is more in
(a) Summers (b) Winter
(c) Autumn (d) All seasons

709. Chronic recurrent tympany is characterized of
(a) TRP
(b) Diaphragmatic Hernia
(c) Rumen overload
(d) Vagus indigestion

710. Muscular dystrophy can be treated by supplementing
(a) Vitamin E (b) Protein
(c) Phosphorus (d) Calcium

711. Curled toe paralysis is caused by deficiency of
(a) Vitamin B_1 (b) Vitamin B_2
(c) Vitamin B_6 (d) Vitamin B_{12}

712. Impactive colic mostly occurs at
(a) Pelvic flexure right dorsal & small colon
(b) Cardiac end of stomach
(c) Loop of ileum
(d) Loop of jejunum

713. Lesions of which of the following conditions resemble to that of hutch burn
(a) Weepy eye (b) Burn injury
(c) Trypanosomiasis (d) Coccidiosis

714. Ketosis in guinea pigs similar to

(a) Cow (b) Dog
(c) Sheep (d) Robbet

715. Probang is used to diagnose
(a) Pharyngeal paralysis
(b) Pharyngeal obstruction
(c) Pharyngitis
(d) Parotitis

716. Diabetes mellitus is seen most commonly in
(a) Dog (b) Cow
(c) Horse (d) Pig

717. Enteroliths are most common in
(a) Dog (b) Cow
(c) Horse (d) Pig

718. Rickets is the disease of
(a) Young calves (b) Adult
(c) Old cattle (d) All

719. Deficiency of Vitamin A leads to
(a) Xerophthalmia (b) Night blindness
(c) Both (d) None

720. Trimethoprime & sulfonamides are usually available in the ratio of
(a) 1:1 (b) 1:5
(c) 5:1 (d) 2:1

721. Parturient paresis mostly occurs in
(a) Advance pregnancy
(b) First 48 hrs of parturition
(c) 10-25 days of parturition
(d) 1 month after parturition

722. Abnormal appetite in termed as
(a) Allotriophagia (b) Dysphagia
(c) Coprofagia (d) Infantophagra

723. Diaphragmatic hernia is very common in
(a) Cow (b) Buffalo
(c) Sheep (d) Goat

724. Calcium versenate acts as antidote in
(a) Pb poisoning
(b) As poisoning
(c) Cyanide poisoning
(d) Ca poisoning

725. Bestiality is punishable under which section of IPC
(a) 93 (b) 377
(c) 415 (d) 429

726. Enzootic ataxia in lamb occurs due to deficiency of
(a) Selenium (b) Copper
(c) Fe (d) Zn

727. Normal pH of bovine blood as
(a) 6.6-6.8 (b) 69.-7.1
(c) 7.2-7.4 (d) 7.5-7.7

728. Left side Displacement of Abomasum is mostly seen in
(a) Recently calved cows
(b) 1st month of pregnancy
(c) Dry cow
(d) Heifers

729. Digoxin act as
(a) Cardiac glycoside
(b) Astringent
(c) Respiratory stimulant
(d) Liver tonic

730. Excess of Molybdenum in diet leads to deficiency of
(a) Cu (b) Zn
(c) Fe (d) Pb

731. Most important specimen for diagnosis of arsenic poisoning is
(a) Liver & skin (b) Kidney, skin & hair
(c) Lymph nodes (d) Liver & Heart

732. Glander & farcy act is of the year
(a) 1899 (b) 1999
(c) 1889 (d) None

733. Bacterial stomatitis is generally caused by
(a) *Salmonella* (b) *Pasteurella*
(c) *Staphyllocous* (d) *Streptococcus*

734. Pharyngeal paralysis occurs in
(a) Tuberculosis (b) Botulism
(c) Meningitis (d) All

735. Pyelonephritis generally develops
(a) By injury
(b) Ascending infection
(c) Descending infection
(d) None

736. In cystitis urination is
(a) Normal
(b) Frequent
(c) Frequent & painful

(d) No urination

737. Which of the following may leads to shock?
(a) Trauma (b) Wound
(c) Dyspnea (d) Edema

738. Shock is manifested by
(a) Death
(b) Acute cardiac arrest
(c) Peripheral circulatory failure
(d) Respiratory arrest

739. In pleurisy there is
(a) Expiratory dyspnea
(b) Inspiratory dyspnea
(c) Both
(d) None

740. Gurgling sounds are heard in
(a) Pulmonary adenometosis
(b) Pneumonia
(c) Bronchitis
(d) Pleurisy

741. Ketosis may be confused with
(a) Abomasal displacement
(b) Lactation tetany
(c) Vagus indigestion
(d) All

742. Lipopolysaccharide of gram negative bacteria act as chemotactic force for
(a) Lymphocytes (b) RBC
(c) Monocytes (d) Eosinophilla

743. Predominant lymphocytes are small sized & they contain
(a) Ig G (b) IgM
(c) Ig A (d) IgE

744. Immunoglobulin which lead to graft rejection are present in
(a) Neutrophills (b) Lymphocytes
(c) RBC (d) Plasma

745. Migration inhibitory factors which passes from a blood donor to recipient is a
(a) Fat (b) Carbohydrate
(c) Lipid (d) Protein

746. In plasma cells, high amount of Ig are present at
(a) Cytoplasm
(b) Golgi apperatus
(c) Endoplasmic reticulum
(d) Mitochondria

747. Young & immature neutrophils in circulation indicate
(a) Uremia (b) Bacterimia
(c) Septicaemia (d) Mycotic infection

748. White velvety deposit on oral mucosa indicates
(a) Bacterial stomatitis
(b) Viral stomatitis
(c) Richettsial stomatitis
(d) Mycotic stomatitis

749. Digestive function of alimentary tract depends on
(a) Secretary function (b) Motor function
(c) Micro flora (d) All

750. Constipation is characteristic of which of the following
(a) Excitement
(b) Shock
(c) Grass sickness in horse
(d) Johne's disease

751. Which of the following is used to check hyper motility of GIT
(a) Atorpin (b) Isaverin
(c) Benzetimide (d) All

752. Ruminal atony can be caused by
(a) Histamince (b) Letanine
(c) Atropine (d) All

753. Sensitivity of occult blood test increases after faecal samples have been stored at room temperature for
(a) 5 hrs (b) 20 hrs
(c) 48 hrs (d) None

754. Which of the following neoplasm is most common?
(c) Lymphosarcoma
(b) Squamous cell carcinoma
(c) Lymphoma
(d) All

755. Blood reaches from abomasums to rectum in about
(a) 19 sec (b) 19 minutes
(c) 19 hours (d) 19 days

756. Melena occurs in
(a) Gastric ulceration (b) Intestinal ulceration
(c) Skin ulceration (d) Liver ulceration

757. Acute gastritis in dogs can be treated by
(a) Ice cubes
(b) Antacids
(c) Withhold of food & water
(d) All

758. Snoring respiration is characteristics of
(a) Pharyngeal obstruction
(b) Esophageal obstruction
(c) Laryngeal obstruction
(d) Bronchial obstruction

759. In simple indigestion of cattle, there may be
(a) Constipation (b) Diarrhoea
(c) Both (d) Either a or b

760. Simple indigestion occurs commonly in
(a) Hand-fed ruminants
(b) Pastured beef cattle
(c) Pastured beef sheep
(d) All

761. Ephemeral fever can be treated by
(a) Antacids (b) Salicylates
(c) Calcium (d) Saline

762. Polioencephalomalacia occurs due to deficiency of
(a) Vitamin B_1 (b) Vitamin B_2
(c) Vitamin B_6 (d) Vitamin B_{12}

763. Hypomagnesaemic tetany occurs due to deficiency of
(a) Mg (b) Ca
(c) Both (d) P

764. Which of the following is classified as a production disease?
(a) Rumen overload
(b) Selenium deficiency
(c) Rumen acidosis
(d) None

765. Which of the following is a metabolic disease
(a) Rumen overload
(b) Selenium deficiency
(c) Rumen acidosis
(d) None

766. Lactation tetany may result due to excessive use of which fertilizer in fodder crops
(a) Dicalcium phosphate
(b) Ammonia fertilizer
(c) Super phosphate
(d) All

767. Enteritis is accompanied by
(a) Dehydration & loss of Cl^-
(b) Dehydration & loss of alkali
(c) Dehydration & loss of acids
(d) Dehydration & loss of K+

768. Which of the following nerves are involved in swallowing reflex
(a) Glosopharyngeal (b) Trigeminal
(c) Hypoglossal (d) All

769. Projectile vomition is most common in
(a) Horse (b) Dog
(c) Both (d) None

770. Confirmatory diagnosis of esophageal obstruction in canines can be made by
(a) Hematology (b) Radiology
(c) Endoscopy (d) All

771. Jugular pulse is a unique character of
(a) Milk fever
(b) Congestive heart failure
(c) Acute heart failure
(d) TRP

772. Phenothiazine acts as potent
(a) Analgesic (a) Antihistaminic
(c) Antiemetic (d) All

773. In Nausea vomition occurs due to
(a) Gastric ulceration
(b) Intestinal ulcerations
(c) Both
(d) None

774. Fluid therapy by Ringer's Lactate is indicated in case of vomition due to
(a) Metabolic alkalosis
(b) Metabolic acidosis
(c) Poisoning
(d) All

775. Dehydration in case of gastritis is attributed to
(a) Na^+ retention
(b) Cl^- depletion
(c) Acid base imbalance
(d) Potassium expulsion

776. In case of inflammation of stomach, there is
(a) Increased motility & increased secretion

(b) Increased motility & decreased secretion
(c) Decreased motility & decreased secretion

(d) Decreased motility & increased secretion

777. In case of intestinal obstruction, there is
(a) Hemoconcentration
(b) Metabolic acidosis
(c) Hypochloremia
(d) All

778. In a horse weighing 500 kg with 20% dehydration the fluid deficit is
(a) 50 liters (b) 25 liters
(c) 100 liters (d) 200 liters

779. Jaundice, bizarre behavior, ascites & photosensitization collectively indicate
(a) Hepatic disorder (b) Renal disorder
(c) Cardiac disorder (d) Peritonitis

780. Which of the following is a liver specific enzyme in bovines?
(a) Glutamate dehydroogenase
(b) Sorbitol dehyrogenase
(c) Gamma glutamyl transferase
(d) All

781. Acute hepatitis can be treated by
(a) Maintaining blood glucose
(b) Low protein diet
(c) Water soluble vitamins
(d) All

782. Pulse rate in impactive colic in a horse may range in
(a) 100-120 or less beats /minute
(b) 90-100 or les beats/minute
(c) 40-60 or less beats/minute
(d) 50-60 or less beats/minute

783. Which of the following fluids is best suited for a horse with severe colic & dehydration
(a) Normal saline
(b) Lactate solution
(c) 25% Dextrose
(d) $NaHCO_3$ containing fluid

784. In case of paralytic ileus
(a) Alimentary transmit time increases
(b) Alimentary transmit time decreases
(c) Alimentary transmit time unaffected
(d) Alimentary transmit time stops

785. Teeth get damaged before eruption Show erosion of enamel in
(a) Flurosis
(b) Fluoride deficiency
(c) Vitamin E deficiency
(d) Selenium deficiency

786. Which form of colic is most common in foals immediatcly after birth
(a) Intestinal colic (b) Impactive colic
(c) Obstructive colic (d) None

787. Peat sours occurs due to deficiency of
(a) Co (b) Cu
(c) Mo (d) None

788. Myoglobin is present in urine of horse in
(a) Azoturia (b) Keturia
(c) Hemoglobinurea (d) Babesiosis

789. Pregnancy toxemia in ewes occurs during
(a) Early pregnancy
(b) Last month of pregnancy
(c) Mid pregnancy
(d) One month after the parturition

790. Epilepsy is very common in
(a) Sheep (b) Cattle
(c) Pig (d) Dog

791. Strong ammoniacal odour of urine occurs in
(a) Acute cystitis (b) Chronic cystitis
(c) Pyometra (d) Starvation

792. Coughing up of blood is termed as
(a) Haemturea (b) Epistaxis
(c) Haemorrhage (d) Haemoptysis

793. Corrugated appearance of skin is characteristic of death due to
(a) Drowning (b) Lightening stroke
(c) Electrocution (d) All

794. Half chewed food in mouth is characteristic of death due to
(a) Drowning (b) Lightening stroke
(c) Electrocution (d) All

795. Signs of shock with a history of damage to trees of the locality indicates
(a) Drowning (b) Lightening stroke
(c) Electrocution (d) All

796. Which of the following fodder may lead to bloat?

(a) Berseem (b) Clover
(c) Lucerne (d) All

797. Which of the following may lead to pulmonary edema?
(a) Congestive heart failure
(b) Acute anaphylaxis
(c) ANTU poisoning
(d) All

798. Prolonged ingestion of Bracken fern may lead to
(a) Enzootic ataxia
(b) Enzootic haematuria
(c) Tympany
(d) All

799. Antibiotic of choice in case of meningitis is
(a) Chloramphenicol (b) Aminoglycosides
(c) Tetracycline (d) Naladixic acid

800. Which of the following country have never experienced FMD disease?
(a) Australia (b) Newzeland
(c) Both (d) None

801. Biotypical strain when is adapted to a particular
(a) Host (b) Animal
(c) Area (d) Species

802. In which of the following death occurs due to asphyxia
(a) Rabies
(b) Strychnine poisoning
(c) Both
(d) None

803. Azoturia in horses is also called as
(a) Monday morning sickness
(b) Equine ketoses
(c) 3 day sickness
(d) None

804. Methylene blue acts as specific antidote for the poisoning of
(a) Molybdenum (b) Pb
(c) Nitrate (d) Copper

805. Because of warfarin the blood clotting in animals is
(a) Impaired (b) Increased
(c) Decreased (d) No effect

806. Which type of anoxia occurs in case of primary lung disease?
(a) Anoxic (b) Histotoxic
(c) Anemic (d) All

807. Osteodystrophic fibrosa may result due to excessive dietary intake of
(a) Ca (b) Mg
(c) P (d) Cu

808. CNS stimulation along with gangrene of extremities is characteristics of
(a) Ergot poisoning
(b) Strychnine poisoning
(c) Nitrate poisoning
(d) Nitrite poisoning

809. pH of abomasal contents is
(a) 2 (b) 1
(c) 4.0 (d) 6-7

810. Which of the following may lead to Pica?
(a) Dietary deficiency of bulk
(b) Dietary deficiency of nutrients
(c) Boredom
(d) All

811. Atropine in double doses is effective as antidote in
(a) Ergot poisoning
(b) Nitrate poisoning
(c) Nitrite poisoning
(d) Organophosphate poisoning

812. Sulfonamide of choice in large animals is
(a) Sulfamerazole (b) Sulfamezathine
(c) Surfadimidine (d) Any

813. Which of the following occur due to excessive intake of grains?
(a) Alkalin indigestion
(b) Acid indigestion
(c) Vagus indigestion
(d) Ketosis

814. Best stain for demonstration of fungi in scrapings
(a) Giemsa (b) Wrignt
(c) Methylene blue (d) Periodic acid schiff

815. Presence of immature lymphocytes with dark blue cytoplasm is characteristics of
(a) Lymphosarcoma (b) Lymphocytosis
(c) Lymphopaenia (d) Lymphomyeloma

816. Presence of Leptocytes in blood film indicate
(a) Aplastic anemia

(b) Granulocytic lukemia
(c) Pernicious anemia
(d) None

817. Examination of bone marrow smears can be helpful to diagnose
(a) Chronic bacterial infection
(b) Leukemic Leukemia
(c) Lymphatic leukemia
(d) Myeloplastic anemia

818. Rapid & asymmetric enlargement of lymph nodes occurs in
(a) Lymphadenitis (b) Leukemia
(c) Both (d) None

819. Leukemia can be confirmed by
(a) Liver biopsy
(b) Spleen biopsy
(c) Lymph node biopsy
(d) Bone marrow biopsy

820. Urethane compounds in bovines can be used for treatment of
(a) Lymphadenitis (b) Leukemia
(c) Both (d) None.

821. Haematinic mixture $CuSO_4 : CoCl_2 : Fe_2SO_4$
(a) 5 gm : 1 gm : 100 gm
(b) 1 gm : 0.5 gm : 100 gm
(c) 2 gm : 3 gm : 100 gm
(d) 3 gm : 2 gm : 100 gm

822. Absorption of Fe from GIT to blood is about
(a) 1% (b) 0.1%
(c) 10% (d) 100%

823. Excessive Fe intake may lead to deficiency of
(a) Cu (b) Co
(c) Zn (d) P

824. Which type of anemia occurs in Hemophilia?
(a) Hemolytic (b) Hemorrhagic
(c) Anoxic (d) Histotoxic

825. In cases of fatal hemorrhage there is
(a) Reduced Hematocrit value
(b) Increased clotting time
(c) Increased Prothrombim time
(d) All

826. Rate of fluid absorption through I/P route in 1st 24 hours is
(a) 100% (b) 80%
(c) 45% (d) 10%

827. A synthetic blood transfusion includes
(a) Neutral polysaccharide in saline 0.9%
(b) 6% solution of gelatin in saline
(c) 5% dextrose saline
(d) Blood plasma 50 mg/kg

828. Bovine blood can be stored safely without losing much beneficial effect
(a) at 6°C for 1 month (b) at 12°C forl week
(c) at 6°C for 1 week (d) At 12°C for 1 month

829. Safe rate of transmission of blood to a recipient after cross matching compatibility test is
(a) 100 mg/kg IV (b) 10 ml/kg IV
(c) 20 ml/kg iv (d) 30 ml/kg IV

830. Heinz bodies were first discovered in
(a) 1890 (b) 1880
(c) 1860 (d) 1870

831. Heinz bodies formation occurs in which poisoning
(a) Strychnine (b) Organophosphorus
(c) Nitrate (d) Phenothiazin

832. Viral infections lead to
(a) Leucopoenia (b) Leucocytosis
(c) Neutroplilia (d) Eosinophilia

833. Leucopoenia may be caused due to
(a) Viral infections (b) Endotoxins
(c) Anaphylaxis (d) All

834. Heinz bodies in horse after spleenectomy may be
(a) 1% (b) 5%
(c) 10% (d) 15%

835. Agranulocytopaenia may occur due to
(a) Bone marrow aplasia
(b) Irradiation
(c) Anti metabolites
(d) Hemorrhages

836. Geiger Muller counter technique is used to count exact life span of
(a) RBC (b) Platelets
(c) Leukocytes (d) Thrombocytes

837. Neutrophil haemostasis is regulated by
(a) Vinblastin sulfate (b) Nitrogen mustard
(c) Bacterial toxin (d) Viral toxin

838. H_2O_2 helps in defense of body through
(a) Erythropoisis (b) Leukocytosis

(c) Phagocytosis (d) Hb synthesis

839. Lysosomes in neutrophils contain
(a) Lectoferrin (b) Ferritin
(c) Transferrin (d) Cathopsin

840. False eosinophilia during parasitic infections may occur due to
(a) False diagnosis
(b) Dose of anthelmintics
(c) Dose of steroids
(d) All

841. *Mycobacterium tuberculosis* is a
(a) Acid fast organism
(b) Gram positive organism
(c) Gram negative organism
(d) Spiral organism

842. Braxy is caused by
(a) *Cl. chauvoei* (b) *Cl. septicum*
(c) *Cl. novyi* (d) *Cl. botulinium*

843. Struck mostly occurs in
(a) Adult sheep (b) Yong sheep
(c) Adult cattle (d) All

844. Mastitis after parturition mostly occurs due to
(a) *E. coli*
(b) *Staphylococcus*
(c) *Streptococus*
(d) *Mycoplasma agalalactiae*

845. Hotis tests is done for diagnosis of mastitis caused due to
(a) *E. coli*
(b) *Staphylococcus*
(c) *Streptococus*
(d) *Mycoplasma agalalactiae*

846. In absence of gross change in udder, type of mastitis is
(a) Acute (b) Clinical
(c) Sub clinical (d) Chronic

847. Leukocyte count increases in milk, in which type of mastitis
(a) Acute (b) Clinical
(c) Sub clinical (d) Chronic

848. Drug of choice for *Streptococcal* mastitis is
(a) Penicillin (b) Tetracycline
(c) Streptomycin (d) Sulphamerazine

849. Drug of choice for *Staphylococcal* mastitis is
(a) Penicillin (b) Tetracycline
(c) Streptomycin (d) Sulphamerazine

850. Drug of choice for *E. coli* mastitis is
(a) Penicillin (b) Tetracycline
(c) Streptomycin (d) Sulphamerazine

851. Hide bound condition & cachexia occurs in
(a) Acute disease
(b) Pe acute disease
(c) Sub clinical disease
(d) Chronic disease

852. Outcome of a disease is known as
(a) Diagnosis (b) Prognosis
(c) Anamnesis (d) None

853. Hunger arises due to
(a) Gastric contraction
(b) Esophageal contraction
(c) Ileal contraction
(d) Duodenal contraction

854. Prehension in sheep & goat occurs by
(a) Lips (b) Tongues
(c) Teeth (d) All

855. Ptaylin is
(a) Excessive secretion from Brunner's gland
(b) From salivary gland
(c) From sweat gland
(d) All

856. Antibiotics in ruminant should be given
(a) Orally (b) IV
(c) Both (d) None

857. Which of the following is a lactogenic amino acid?
(a) Acetate
(b) Propionate
(c) Acetate & butyrate
(d) Butyrate

858. Which of the following ketosis occurs in high yield cattle?
(a) Border line ketosis
(b) Spontaneous
(c) Feeding
(d) All

859. Ketosis may occur due to def of
(a) Vitamin B1 (b) Vitamin B2
(c) Vitamin B12 (d) Vitamin B5

860. Ketosis resulting due to less dietary supply than

requirement is known as
(a) Starvation ketosis (b) Diabetes ketosis
(c) Relative ketosis (d) Absolute ketosis

861. Sulkowitch test is used for
(a) Downer's cow syndrome
(b) Fat cow syndrome
(c) Milk fever
(d) Tetany

862. Eclampsia is milk fever occurs in
(a) Cow (b) Eve
(c) Sow (d) Bitch

863. Which of the following are formed in Post parturient haemoglobinurea?
(a) Heinz body (b) Howell jolly body
(c) Both (d) None

864. Which conduction occurs in creeper cow disease?
(a) Hypocalcemia (b) Hypoglycemia
(c) Hypokalemia (d) Hypophasphatema

865. Blood needed in urine in the form of clot & causes deep red to brown to urine indicates
(a) Haematuria (b) Haemoglobinurea
(c) Both (d) All

866. Tetany & Hyperesthesia disappear in which stage of milk fever
(a) I (b) II
(c) III (d) None

867. Puerperal tetany is
(a) Eclampsia (b) Milk fever
(c) Ketosis (d) lactation tetany

868. Increased heart rate count detectable is
(a) Bradycardia
(b) Paraxysmal tachycardia
(c) Both
(d) None

869. Ventricular fibrillation may result due to sudden infusion of
(a) Calcium (b) NaCl
(c) Dectrose (d) Lactate

870. Vasovagal syncope occurs due to
(a) Less stimulation of vagal nerve
(b) Over stimulation of vagal nerve
(c) Failure of stimulation of vagal nerve
(d) Contraction of atrium

871. Negative Jugular pulse results from stenosis of
(a) Bicuspid value (b) Tricuspid value
(c) Atrium (d) Ventricle

872. Positive jugular pulse
(a) Bicuspid value (b) Tricuspid value
(c) Atrium (d) Ventricle

873. Edema of conjunctiva resulting into grape like masses hanging from eye lid result from
(a) TRP (b) Endometritis
(c) Mycorditis (d) All

874. Sudden filling of pericardial sac is
(a) Cardiac tamponde
(b) Cardiac syncope
(c) Acute cardiac arrest
(d) All

875. In case of right side chronic heart failure, there is
(a) Positive jugular pulse
(b) Palpable enlarged liver
(c) Edema
(d) All

876. Left sided chronic heart failure may be manifested by
(a) Presence of murmur
(b) Moist rale
(c) Both
(d) None

877. Use of digitalis is contraindicated in
(a) Dog (b) Han
(c) Cow (d) Horse

878. Cancer of leucocytes is known as
(a) Leukemia (b) Leucoma
(c) Leucopoenia (d) Leucocytosis

879. Which of the followingis a valvular disease
(a) Endocarditis (b) Chronic heart failure
(c) Rupture of valve (d) All

880. Epistaxis in horse might indicate
(a) Endocarditis (b) Chronic heart failure
(c) Rupture of valve (d) None

881. Urine of chronic heart failure patient has high
(a) Glucose (b) Ketones
(c) Albumin (d) All

882. Which of the following is a disease of blood?

(a) Hemolytic anemia
(b) Pernicious anemia
(c) Anemic anemia
(d) All

883. Systolic murmurs present in anemia are known as
(a) Haemic murmur (b) Anaemic murmur
(c) Both (d) None

884. Which of the following is completely absorbed from glomerulor filtrate
(a) Water (b) Creatinine
(c) Phosphate (d) Glucose

885. Chronic heart failure leads to
(a) Pre renal failure (b) Renal failure
(c) Post renal failure (d) Any

886. Nephritis leads to
(a) Pre renal failure (b) Renal failure
(c) Post renal failure (d) Any

887. Which diuretic is used in urinary system diseases?
(a) Frusemide (b) Spironolactone
(c) Both (d) None

888. Cellulose digestion test is used for diagnosis of
(a) Ruminal acidosis (b) Tympany
(c) VAgal indigestion (d) Simple indigestion

889. Masturbation is a cause of pyelonephritis in
(a) Cattle (b) Camel
(c) Dog (d) Horse

890. Inflammation of urethra leads to pus, blood etc. in
(a) First portion of urine
(b) Last portion of urine
(c) Throughout urine
(d) First & last of urine

891. Inflammation of kidney leads to pus, blood etc. in
(a) First portion of urine
(b) Last portion of urine
(c) Throughout urine
(d) First & last of urine

892. Sand like precipitate with ammoniacal odour in bladder indicate
(a) Interstitial nephritis
(b) Renal insufficiency
(c) Pyelonephritis
(d) Nephrosis

893. When monoboasic N phosphate is given, urine becomes
(a) Acidic (b) Basic
(c) Neutral (d) None

894. Which of the following kind of urine is due to immunological reaction
(a) Acidic (b) Basic
(c) Neutral (d) None

895. Accumulation of H_2O in kidney is known as
(a) Hydronephrosis (b) Renal dropsy
(c) Both (d) None

896. Inbreeding in goats leads to
(a) Hydronephrosis (b) Renal dropsy
(c) Both (d) None.

897. In swine long neck of urinary bladder leads to
(a) Hydronephrosis (b) Renal dropsy
(c) Both (d) None.

898. Stage at which oliguria occurs in nephritis
(a) Initial (b) Terminal
(c) Middle (d) All

899. Stage at which polyuria occurs in nephritis
(a) Initial (b) Terminal
(c) Middle (d) All

900. Common side effect of ovariectomy in bitch is
(a) Cystitis
(b) In continuous urination
(c) Urolithiasis
(d) Urethritis

901. Excess of which Vitamin leads to urolithiasis?
(a) Vitamin A (b) Vitamin B
(c) Vitamin D (d) Vitamin C

902. Deficiency of which Vitamin leads to urolithiasis
(a) Vitamin A (b) Vitamin B
(c) Vitamin D (d) Vitamin C

903. Which of the following is not present in urolithiasis in cattle?
(a) CaPO4 (b) MgPO4
(c) NH4 PO4 (d) MgCO3

904. Which of the following is not present in urolithiasis in in horses?
(a) CaCO3 (b) CaPO4
(c) MgCO3 (d) MgPO4

905. Binding material of stone is
(a) Mucoprotein (b) Glycoprotein

(c) Chemoproein (d) Metaloprotin

906. Commonest site of stone in large animals is
(a) Ischial arch (b) Prostate gland
(c) Os Penis (d) Scrotal region

907. Commonest site for stone in dog is
(a) Ischeal arch (b) Prostate gland
(c) Os Penis (d) Scrotal region

908. Urolithiasis results from which type of diet
(a) High concentrate & high roughage
(b) Low concentrate & low roughage
(c) High concentrate & low roughage
(d) Low concentrate & high roughage

909. If tetany does not disappear after II stage of milk fever, it indicates
(a) Ca deficiency (b) Ca & Mg deficiency
(c) Mg deficiency (d) CA & P deficiency

910. Angioneurotic edema is
(a) S/c edema with plaque formation
(b) S/c edema without plaque formation
(c) Edema of leg
(d) Edema of brisket

911. Trifoleum plant is
(a) Cyanogenic (b) Phytotoxic
(c) Both (d) None

912. Nephron is
(a) Secretory unit of kidney
(b) Excretory unit of kidney
(c) Both
(d) None

913. What is correct for Polioecephalomalacia
(a) Palpabral eye reflex is positive
(b) Menace reflex is negative
(c) Occurs after prolonged acidosis
(d) All are correct

914. Ptyriasis occurs due to deficiency of
(a) Oleic acid (b) Linolenic acid
(c) Linoleic acid (d) Arachidonic acid

915. Dermatitis may further lead to
(a) Ptyriasis (b) Psoriasis
(c) Seborrhea (d) All

916. On scrapping silvery white scales are demonstrated in
(a) Ptyriasis (b) Psoriasis
(c) Seborrhea (d) All

917. Bacteria of dermatitis is
(a) *Streptococcus spp.* (b) *Staphylococcus spp.*
(c) Both (d) None

918. Weak point of alveoli extruded out & filled with air is
(a) Bullae (b) Hilus
(c) Pocket (d) Heaves

919. Expiratory phase in horse is prolonged in
(a) Rhinitis (b) Pneumonia
(c) Bronchitis (d) Heaves

920. Allergic form of rhinitis is
(a) Summer sore (b) Summer shuffle
(c) Heaves (d) Atrophic rhinitis

921. Right limb lameness is due to
(a) Kidneys disease (b) Liver disease
(c) Spleen disease (d) Heart disease

922. Diagnosis at a glance is
(a) Snap shot (b) Extensive
(c) Both (d) None

923. Sour smell of rumen fluid is characteristics of
(a) Acidosis
(b) Alkalosis
(c) Simple indigestion
(d) Vagus indigestion

924. Fishy putrefied smell of rumen fluid occur in
(a) Acidosis
(b) Alkalosis
(c) Simple indigestion
(d) Vagus indigestion

925. Abnormal sound from lungs is
(a) Pulmogenic (b) Bronchogenic
(c) Both (d) None

926. Adventitious sound from lung is
(a) Normal (b) Abnormal
(c) Irregular (d) None

927. Commonly encountered arterial thrombosis in horse is
(a) Renal (b) Jugular
(c) Mesenteric (d) Iliac

928. Mediastinum in bovine is frequent met with
(a) Lymphadenitis (b) Mesothelioma
(c) Hydrothorax (d) None

929. Common cause of venous thrombosis in calves might be

(a) Corona virus infaction
(b) Parvo virus infaction
(c) Umbilical hernia
(d) Naval ill

930. ESR is high in dog suffering from
(a) Macrocytic anemia
(b) Haemorrhagic anemia
(c) Encapsulated abscess
(d) Peritonitis

931. Polioencephalomalacia is associated with deficiency of
(a) Thiamine (b) Ascorbic acid
(c) Riboflavin (d) Vitamin D

932. Milk fever can be prevented by feeding the animal pre partum–
(a) High calcium diet
(b) High protein diet
(c) High P and low Ca diet
(d) None of above

933. Polioencephalomalacia in animals occurs due to deficiency of
(a) Thiamine (b) Vitamin – E
(c) Vitamin – D (d) All of above

934. In the complete metabolic profile test, the blood is analysed for
(a) Calcium
(b) Inorganic Phosphorus
(c) Blood urea Nitrogen
(d) Total serum protein

935. Enteritis is accompanied by
(a) Dehydration and loss of chloride ions
(b) Dehydration and loss of alkali radicals
(c) Dehydration and loss of acid radicals
(d) Dehydration only

936. Projectile vomiting is most common form of vomiting in
(a) Horses only
(b) Pigs and dogs
(c) Horses and ruminants
(d) Horses and dogs

937. Pharyngitis in cow is clinically characterized by
(a) Regurgitation through nostrils, inappetance with inability to swallow
(b) Coughing and inability to swallow
(c) Inability to swallow, vomiting and inappetance
(d) Coughing, painful swallowing and lack of appetite.

938. Jugular pulse is an important feature of the
(a) Milk fever
(b) Congestive heart failure
(c) Acute heart failure
(d) Traumatic reticulo – peritonitis

939. In vomition, due to metabolic acidosis the fluid therapy proposed is
(a) Ringers lactate (b) Normal saline
(c) Dextrose saline (d) 10 % dextrose

940. In gastritis, dehydration is caused by
(a) Sodium retention
(b) Acid base abnormality
(c) Potassium expulsion
(d) Chloride ions depletion

941. Hepatic abscesses are common cause of liver disease in
(a) Horse, dog, cat and sheep
(b) Pig and cattle
(c) Cattle
(d) Sheep and goat

942. Tenesmus is a common sign in
(a) Coccidiosis in calves
(b) Acute gastritis in canines
(c) Cystitis
(d) All

943. Urine of horse suffering from Azoturia contains
(a) Hemoglobin (b) Methaemoglobin
(c) Myoglobin (d) Uric acid

944. Pregnancy Toxemia occurs in ewes during
(a) Early pregnancy (b) Mid – pregnancy
(c) After parturition (d) Last month of pregnancy

945. The common constituents of uroliths in cattle are
(a) $CaCO_3$, $MgCO_3$ or $(NH_4)_2CO_3$
(b) Oxalates
(c) Uric acid
(d) Xanthine

946. In acute cystitis urine's odour is which of the following
(a) Sweet
(b) Sour
(c) Strong ammoniacal

(d) Normal

947. Blood in cough is termed as
(a) Haematemesis (b) Epistaxis
(c) Haemorrhage (d) Haemoptysis

948. Diaphragmatic hernia is common in
(a) Goats (b) Dogs
(c) Horses (d) Buffalo

949. The antibiotic of choice in cases of meningitis is
(a) Penicillin (b) Chloramphenicol
(c) Oxytetracycline (d) Erythromycin

950. Azoturia in horses is popularly known as
(a) Sunday sickness
(b) Monday morning sickness
(c) Myoglobinuria
(d) B & C both

951. pH of urine in horse
(a) Acidic (b) Basic
(c) Neutral (d) Depend on exercise

952. pH of urine in dogs
(a) Acidic
(b) Basic
(c) Neutral
(d) Depend on nature of feed

953. pH of urine in horse
(a) Acidic (b) Basic
(c) Neutral (d) Depend on exercise

954. Rothra's test of urine is used to detect
(a) Glucose (b) Albumin
(c) Ketone bodies (d) Haemoglobin

955. Benzidine test is used to detect in urine
(a) Glucose (b) Albumin
(c) Ketone bodies (d) Haemoglobin

956. Fouchet's test is used to detect in urine
(a) Globulins (b) Bile salts
(c) Bile pigments (d) Calcium

957. Hay's sulphur test is used to detect in urine
(a) Globulins (c) Bile salts
(c) Bile pigments (d) Calcium

958. Sulkowitch test is used to detect in urine
(a) Globulins (B) Bile salts
(c) Bile pigments (d) Calcium

959. Roberts test in used to detect in urine
(a) Glucose (b) Albumin
(c) Ketone bodies (d) Haemoglobin

960. Haematinic mixture contain which minerals
(a) Fe, Cu, Co (b) Fe, Cu, Zn
(c) Ca, Fe, Mg (d) Cu, Zn, Ca

961. Which solution is commonly known as Laal dawa
(a) Lugol's iodine
(b) $KMnO_4$
(c) Merbromin solution
(d) Acriflavin aq.

962. In a horse weighing 500 kg with 10 % dehydration, the fluid deficit is
(a) 5 litre (b) 100 litre
(c) 50 litre (d) 20 litre

963. Pesticides are common contaimnants of environment and may induce
(a) Immunosuppression
(b) Autoimmunity
(c) Hypersensitvity
(d) All of the above

964. Lead, mercury and cadmium may lead to immunosuppression by
(a) Immunotoxic (b) Nephrotoxic
(c) Hepatotoxic (d) Neurotoxic

965. Aflatoxin may cause
(a) Immunopotentiation
(b) Immunosuppression
(c) Activation of macrophges
(d) Reduction of complement

966. Aspirin decreases
(a) Antibody production
(b) Phagocytosis
(c) All of the above
(d) None of above

967. Presence of foreign material in blood vessels is called
(a) Thrombus (b) Emboli
(c) Ischemia (d) Infarction

968. Accumulation of fluid in peritoneal cavity is called
(a) Anasarca (b) Hydropericardium
(c) Hydrothorax (d) Ascites

969. Shock is circulatory disturbance characterized by
(a) Reduced blood volume
(b) Reduced blood flow
(c) Hemoconcentration
(d) All of above

970. Active hyperemia is accumultion of blood in
(a) Veins (b) Lymphatic
(c) Arteries (d) Intestines

971. Escape of all blood constituents through intact blood vessel is known as
(a) Rhexis (b) Ecchymosis
(c) Petechiae (d) Diapedesis

972. Erthrophagocytosis is characterstic of
(a) Congestion (b) Oedema
(c) Sludged blood (d) Infarction

973. Pesticides includes
(a) Insecticide (b) Rodenticide
(c) Weedicide (d) All of the above

974. Acetone, b-hydroxybutyrate and acetoacetic acid are called
(a) Ochratoxins (b) Ketone bodies
(c) Heinze bodies (d) Pyknotic bodies

975. Prolonged starvation leads to
(a) Hypertrophy of muscles
(b) Hyperplasia of muscles
(c) Atrophy of muscles
(d) Metaplasia of muscles

976. Deficiency of vitamin A casues
(a) Nutritional roup (b) Nyctalopia
(c) Calculi in urethra (d) All of the above

977. Vitamin D regulates the activity of
(a) Lymphocytes (b) Macrophages
(c) Both of the above (d) None of the above

978. Star grazing in chicks is due to deficiency of -
(a) Vitamin B_1 (b) Vitamin B_2
(c) Vitamin B_{12} (d) Vitamin B_6

979. Curled toe paralysis is due to deficiency of -
(a) Thiamine (b) Riboflavin
(c) Choline (d) Biotin

980. Crazy chick disease occur due to deficiency of -
(a) Vitamin A (b) Vitamin D
(c) Vitamin C (d) Vitamin E

981. Perosis is caused by
(a) Biotin deficiency
(b) Choline deficiency
(c) Manganeese deficiency
(d) All of the above

982. Rheumatism like syndrome is caused by deficiency of
(a) Calcium (b) Phosphorous
(c) Copper (d) Zinc

983. Hydropic degeneration of skin leads to
(a) Vesicle (b) Pustule
(c) Scab (d) Papule

984. Possible cause of ketosis in cow is
(a) Hyaline degeneration
(b) Fatty change
(c) Amyloid
(d) Cell swelling

985. Cause of mucous degenration in intestine is
(a) Rotavirus (b) *E.Coli*
(c) Ascaris (d) All of above

986. Corticosteroid therapy may lead to
(a) Fatty changes (b) Hyaline
(c) Glycogen (d) Cell swelling

987. A combination of symptom caused by altered physicological process
(a) Lesion (b) Diagnosis
(c) Syndrome (d) Sign

988. Partial loss of skin epithelium or mucocus membrane is called
(a) Abrasion (b) Erosion
(c) Laceration (d) Contusion

989. Torn area of skin remain sterile till
(a) 48 hour (b) 32 hour
(c) 20 hour (d) 24 hour

990. Epidermis and skin are destroyed leading to shock in
(a) I degree (b) II degree
(c) III degree (d) IV degree

991. Radiation affects the dividing cells
(a) Ovary (b) Testis
(c) Lymphocyte (d) All of the above

992. Transmission of disease from one generation to another
(a) Vertical (b) Horizontal
(c) Triangular (d) All of above

993. Pesticides includes
(a) Insecticide (b) Rodenticide
(c) Weedicide (d) All of above

994. Acetone, B-hydorxybutyrate and alltocltic acid are known as
(a) Oochratoxin (b) Ketone bodies

(c) Herinzlbodies (d) Pyknotic bodies

995. Prolong starvation lead to
(a) Hypertophy of muscle
(b) Atrophy of muscle
(c) Hyperplasia of muscle
(d) Metaplatia of muscle

996. Deficiency of vitamin A causes
(a) Nutritional roup (b) Hyctaplia
(c) Calculi in urettra (d) All of the above

997. Vit D regulate the activity of
(a) Lymphocyte (b) Macrophages
(c) All of above (d) None

998. Stargazing candition caused by deficency of
(a) Vit A (b) Vit B_2
(c) Vit B_5 (d) Vit B_1

999. Perosis is caused by deficency -
(a) Biotin (b) Choline
(c) Manganease (d) All of above

1000. Rheumatism like syndrome is caused by deficency of
(a) Calcium (b) Phosphorous
(c) Phosphorous (d) Zinc

1001. Each chromosome contain the DNA contents as
(a) 20% (b) 10%
(c) 70% (d) 30%n

1002. Haemorrhage appear as a linear fassion or from of clot or fold of mucocus membrane
(a) Linear haemorrhage
(b) Petechiae haemorrhage
(c) Suffusion
(d) Thrombosis

Match the following

A.

	Antibiotics		Type
1.	Penicillin	a.	Bacteriostatic
2.	Tetracycline	b.	Bactericidal
3.	Sulfonamides	c.	Fungus infection
4.	Gresiofulvin	d.	Analogue of PABA

Ans. 1.a 2. b 3. d 4. c

Write TRUE or FALSE about following sentences

1. All sulfonamides foRm crystal in urinary tract
2. Rapidly excreted sulfonamides do not produce crystalluria
3. Tissues low in protein has minimum bound sulfonamides
4. Sulfonamides readily pass through placenta
5. Sulfonamides are more soluble in blood plasma than water or saline
6. Kidney is primary organ of excretion sulfonamides
7. Sulfamethazine is rapidly absorbed and rapidly excreted (RARE) sulfonamides
8. Sulfa pyrimidine is a rapidly absorbed slowly excreted sulfonamide.
9. One unit is comparable to 0.16 microgram of penicillin
10. Food interferes with absorbtion of penicillin
11. Procaine penicillin is absorbed more rapidly than potassium penicillin
12. Highest concentration of penicillin is found in kidneys
13. Penicillin is effective against gram negative microbes only.
14. Blood dyscrasia is principal toxicity feature of Streptomycin.

Answers

1. TRUE
2. FALSE
3. TRUE
4. TRUE
5. TRUE
6. TRUE
7. TRUE
8. TRUE
9. TRUE
10. TRUE
11. FALSE
12. TRUE
13. TRUE
14. TRUE

Answers

1. (b) 2. (b) 3. (b)
4. (a) 5. (c) 6. (d)
7. (c) 8. (c) 9. (c)
10. (a) 11. (d) 12. (b)
13. (d) 14. (c) 15. (b)
16. (b) 17. (b) 18. (d)
19. (d) 20. (a) 21. (c)
22. (a) 23. (b) 24. (d)
25. (b) 26. (b) 27. (a)
28. (a) 29. (d) 30. (d)
31. (d) 32. (b) 33. (b)
34. (b) 35. (b) 36. (c)
37. (a) 38. (c) 39. (b)
40. (a) 41. (a) 42. (c)
43. (b) 44. (a) 45. (b)
46. (a) 47. (c) 48. (a)
49. (c) 51. (b) 52. (d)
53. (a) 54. (a) 55. (b)
56. (d) 57. (b) 58. (a)
59. (b) 60. (d) 61. (b)
62. (a) 63. (a) 64. (a)
65. (a) 66. (b) 67. (a)
68. (c) 69. (a) 70. (a)
71. (d) 72. (d) 73. (c)
74. (d) 75. (c) 76. (b)
77. (b) 78. (a) 79. (a)
80. (b) 81. (d) 82. (d)
83. (a) 84. (b) 85. (d)
86. (d) 87. (b) 88. (a)
89. (b) 90. (b) 91. (a)
92. (d) 93. (b) 94. (b)
95. (a) 96. (b) 97. (c)
98. (c) 99. (c) 100. (a)
101. (d) 102. (c) 103. (a)
104. (b) 105. (b) 106. (a)
107. (b) 108. (a) 109. (c)
110. (d) 111. (c) 112. (c)
113. (a) 114. (b) 115. (b)
116. (b) 117. (b) 118. (c)
119. (c) 120. (a) 121. (b)
122. (d) 123. (a) 124. (b)
125. (b) 126. (b) 127. (b)
128. (a) 129. (c) 130. (c)
131. (b) 132. (b) 133. (b)
134. (b) 135. (d) 136. (a)
137. (c) 138. (c) 139. (b)
140. (a) 141. (b) 142. (d)
143. (b) 144. (a) 145. (a)
146. (b) 147. (a) 148. (d)
149. (a) 150. (b) 151. (c)
152. (a) 153. (c) 154. (c)
155. (a) 156. (b) 157. (d)
158. (c) 159. (a) 160. (c)
161. (a) 162. (c) 163. (d)
164. (d) 165. (d) 166. (c)
167. (b) 168. (b) 169. (a)
170. (c) 171. (a) 172. (b)
173. (c) 174. (a) 175. (b)
176. (a) 177. (b) 178. (a)
179. (c) 180. (c) 181. (a)
182. (c) 183. (c) 184. (b)
185. (a) 186. (c) 187. (a)
188. (d) 189. (a) 190. (b)
191. (c) 192. (d) 193. (b)
194. (b) 195. (d) 196. (a)
197. (a) 198. (d) 199. (c)
200. (d) 201. (c) 202. (a)
203. (d) 204. (a) 205. (b)
206. (a) 207. (d) 208. (a)
209. (c) 210. (a) 211. (d)
212. (a) 213. (b) 214. (c)
215. (a) 216. (b) 217. (a)
218. (a) 219. (a) 220. (a)
221. (a) 222. (c) 223. (c)
224. (d) 225. (b) 226. (d)
227. (c) 228. (c) 230. (b)
231. (b) 232. (a) 233. (c)
234. (d) 235. (a) 236. (b)
237. (d) 238. (b) 239. (a)
240. (a) 241. (c) 242. (c)
243. (a) 244. (d) 245. (a)
246. (c) 247. (a) 248. (a)
249. (b) 250. (c) 251. (d)
252. (a) 253. (a) 254. (b)
255. (b) 256. (c) 257. (b)
258. (d) 259. (b) 260. (a)
261. (a) 262. (c) 263. (d)
264. (d) 265. (d) 266. (a)
267. (a) 268. (c) 269. (c)
270. (a) 271. (a) 272. (b)
273. (c) 274. (a) 275. (c)
276. (c) 277. (a) 278. (b)

279.	(b)	280.	(a)	281.	(c)
282.	(a)	283.	(b)	284.	(c)
285.	(b)	286.	(d)	287.	(d)
288.	(d)	289.	(c)	290.	(d)
291.	(a)	292.	(a)	293.	(b)
294.	(c)	295.	(c)	296.	(a)
297.	(b)	298.	(b)	299.	(a)
300.	(b)	301.	(b)	302.	(d)
303.	(a)	304.	(b)	305.	(a)
306.	(b)	307.	(d)	308.	(a)
309.	(b)	310.	(d)	311.	(a)
312.	(b)	313.	(a)	314.	(b)
315.	(b)	316.	(d)	317.	(d)
318.	(a)	319.	(a)	320.	(b)
321.	(c)	322.	(c)	323.	(a)
324.	(a)	325.	(a)	326.	(c)
327.	(d)	328.	(d)	329.	(c)
330.	(c)	331.	(a)	332.	(b)
333.	(b)	334.	(a)	335.	(a)
336.	(a)	337.	(c)	338.	(c)
939.	(c)	340.	(b)	341.	(d)
342.	(a)	343.	(c)	344.	(a)
345.	(c)	346.	(d)	347.	(b)
348.	(a)	349.	(b)	350.	(a)
351.	(d)	352.	(b)	353.	(d)
354.	(b)	355.	(a)	356.	(d)
357.	(d)	358.	(a)	359.	(c)
360.	(a)	361.	(b)	362.	(b)
363.	(c)	364.	(c)	365.	(a)
366.	(b)	367.	(b)	368.	(a)
369.	(b)	370.	(b)	371.	(d)
372.	(b)	373.	(d)	374.	(d)
375.	(c)	376.	(d)	377.	(c)
378.	(c)	379.	(b)	380.	(a)
381.	(a)	382.	(c)	383.	(c)
384.	(a)	385.	(c)	386.	(a)
387.	(d)	388.	(b)	389.	(d)
390.	(d)	391.	(b)	392.	(a)
393.	(a)	394.	(a)	395.	(a)
396.	(c)	397.	(b)	398.	(a)
399.	(b)	400.	(b)	401.	(a)
402.	(c)	403.	(c)	404.	(c)
405.	(c)	406.	(a)	407.	(b)
408.	(c)	409.	(b)	410.	(b)
411.	(d)	412.	(c)	413.	(d)
414.	(d)	415.	(c)	416.	(c)
417.	(c)	418.	(c)	419.	(d)

420.	(a)	421.	(c)	422.	(b)
423.	(a)	424.	(b)	425.	(b)
426.	(b)	427.	(a)	428.	(d)
429.	(c)	430.	(a)	431.	(b)
432.	(a)	433.	(a)	434.	(b)
435.	(b)	436.	(c)	437.	(d)
438.	(b)	439.	(a)	440.	(a)
441.	(d)	442.	(d)	443.	(d)
444.	(c)	445.	(c)	446.	(c)
447.	(d)	448.	(a)	449.	(d)
450.	(a)	451.	(c)	452.	(d)
453.	(a)	454.	(a)	455.	(b)
456.	(c)	457.	(a)	458.	(b)
459.	(a)	460.	(c)	461.	(b)
462.	(a)	463.	(b)	464.	(c)
465.	(d)	466.	(d)	467.	(a)
468.	(d)	469.	(a)	470.	(c)
471.	(d)	472.	(b)	473.	(d)
474.	(a)	475.	(d)	476.	(b)
477.	(c)	478.	(b)	479.	(a)
480.	(b)	481.	(b)	482.	(a)
483.	(d)	484.	(b)	485.	(b)
486.	(a)	487.	(c)	488.	(a)
489.	(c)	490.	(b)	491.	(d)
492.	(a)	493.	(b)	494.	(d)
495.	(c)	496.	(a)	497.	(a)
498.	(a)	499.	(a)	500	(d)
501.	(a)	502.	(b)	503.	(c)
504.	(c)	505.	(a)	506.	(d)
507.	(a)	508.	(b)	509.	(c)
510.	(a)	511.	(c)	512.	(a)
513.	(c)	514.	(d)	515.	(d)
516.	(d)	517.	(a)	518.	(b)
519.	(a)	520.	(d)	521.	(a)
522.	(d)	523.	(c)	524.	(a)
525.	(c)	526.	(c)	527.	(a)
528.	(a)	529.	(d)	530.	(d)
531.	(d)	532.	(d)	533.	(d)
534.	(a)	535.	(c)	536.	(a)
537.	(a)	538.	(b)	539.	(c)
540.	(a)	541.	(b)	542.	(d)
543.	(d)	544.	(d)	545.	(c)
546.	(c)	547.	(d)	548.	(b)
549.	(c)	550.	(b)	551.	(c)
552.	(d)	553.	(a)	554.	(a)
555.	(a)	556.	(b)	557.	(b)
558.	(a)	559.	(b)	560.	(a)

561.	(b)	562.	(a)	563.	(a)
564.	(d)	565.	(a)	566.	(b)
567.	(a)	568.	(a)	569.	(a)
570.	(a)	571.	(d)	572.	(a)
573.	(c)	574.	(d)	575.	(b)
576.	(d)	577.	(c)	578.	(a)
579.	(b)	580.	(a)	581.	(c)
582.	(a)	583.	(a)	584.	(d)
585.	(c)	586.	(a)	587.	(a)
588.	(d)	589.	(a)	590.	(d)
591.	(d)	592.	(a)	593.	(a)
594.	(c)	595.	(a)	596.	(a)
597.	(b)	598.	(a)	599.	(d)
600.	(a)	601.	(a)	602.	(d)
603.	(b)	604.	(a)	605.	(d)
606.	(a)	607.	(c)	608.	(a)
609.	(d)	610.	(c)	611.	(a)
612.	(d)	613.	(a)	614.	(c)
615.	(c)	616.	(d)	617.	(c)
618.	(a)	619.	(c)	620.	(d)
621.	(c)	622.	(b)	623.	(a)
624.	(a)	625.	(c)	626.	(b)
627.	(a)	628.	(a)	629.	(b)
630.	(a)	631.	(b)	632.	(d)
633.	(b)	634.	(a)	635.	(a)
636.	(c)	637.	(d)	638.	(a)
639.	(c)	640.	(d)	641.	(a)
642.	(d)	643.	(a)	644.	(a)
645.	(d)	646.	(a)	647.	(a)
648.	(d)	649.	(c)	650.	(a)
651.	(a)	652.	(a)	653.	(b)
654.	(a)	655.	(a)	656.	(a)
657.	(b)	658.	(a)	659.	(a)
660.	(b)	661.	(a)	662.	(d)
663	(d)	664.	(c)	665.	(d)
666.	(a)	667.	(c)	668.	(d)
669.	(c)	670.	(d)	671.	(b)
672.	(a)	673.	(d)	674.	(b)
675.	(a)	676.	(a)	677.	(d)
678.	(a)	679.	(d)	680.	(d)
681.	(c)	682.	(b)	683.	(a)
684.	(b)	685.	(c)	686.	(c)
687.	(b)	688.	(a)	689.	(b)
690.	(d)	691.	(d)	692.	(a)
693.	(c)	694.	(a)	695.	(c)
696.	(a)	697.	(d)	698.	(c)

699.	(c)	700	(b)	701.	(d)
702.	(c)	703.	(c)	704.	(a)
705.	(a)	706.	(a)	707.	(c)
708.	(b)	709.	(b)	710.	(a)
711.	(b)	712.	(a)	713.	(c)
714.	(c)	715.	(b)	716.	(a)
717.	(c)	718.	(a)	719.	(c)
720.	(b)	721.	(b)	722.	(a)
723.	(b)	724.	(a)	725.	(b)
726.	(b)	727.	(c)	728.	(a)
729.	(a)	730.	(a)	731.	(d)
732.	(a)	733.	(d)	734.	(b)
735.	(b)	736.	(c)	737.	(a)
738.	(c)	739.	(b)	740.	(d)
741.	(a)	742.	(c)	743.	(c)
744.	(c)	745.	(b)	746.	(c)
747.	(b)	748.	(d)	749.	(d)
750.	(c)	751.	(d)	752.	(a)
753.	(c)	754.	(b)	755.	(c)
756.	(b)	757.	(d)	758.	(a)
759.	(c)	760.	(a)	761.	(b)
762.	(a)	763.	(a)	764.	(d)
765.	(d)	766.	(b)	767.	(a)
768.	(d)	769.	(b)	770.	(c)
771.	(d)	772.	(c)	773.	(c)
774.	(b)	775.	(c)	776.	(a)
777.	(d)	778.	(c)	779.	(a)
780.	(d)	781.	(d)	782.	(c)
783.	(d)	784.	(a)	785.	(a)
786.	(a)	787.	(c)	788.	(a)
789.	(b)	790.	(d)	791.	(a)
792.	(d)	793.	(a)	794.	(c)
795.	(b)	796.	(d)	797.	(d)
798.	(b)	799.	(a)	800.	(c)
801.	(d)	802.	(c)	803.	(a)
804.	(c)	805.	(a)	806.	(b)
807.	(c)	808.	(a)	809.	(a)
810.	(b)	811.	(d)	812.	(c)
813.	(b)	814.	(d)	815.	(a)
816.	(a)	817.	(b)	818.	(a)
819.	(d)	820.	(b)	821.	(b)
822.	(a)	823.	(d)	824.	(b)
825.	(d)	826.	(b)	827.	(b)
828.	(c)	829.	(c)	830.	(a)
831.	(a)	832.	(a)	833.	(d)
834.	(d)	835.	(c)	836.	(c)

837.	(b)	838.	(c)	839.	(c)	921.	(a)	922.	(a)	923.	(a)
840.	(c)	841.	(a)	842.	(b)	924.	(c)	925.	(c)	926.	(c)
843.	(a)	844.	(a)	845.	(c)	927.	(c)	928.	(b)	929.	(d)
846.	(c)	847.	(b)	848.	(a)	930.	(b)	931.	(a)	932.	(c)
849.	(c)	850.	(d)	851.	(d)	933.	(a)	934.	(d)	935.	(a)
852.	(b)	853.	(a)	854.	(a)	936.	(d)	937.	(d)	938.	(d)
855.	(b)	856.	(b)	857.	(b)	939.	(a)	940.	(b)	941.	(c)
858.	(d)	859.	(c)	860.	(c)	942.	(a)	943.	(c)	944.	(d)
861.	(c)	862.	(d)	863.	(c)	945.	(a)	946.	(c)	947.	(d)
864.	(c)	865.	(a)	866.	(b)	948.	(d)	949.	(b)	950.	(d)
867.	(a)	868.	(b)	869.	(a)	951.	(b)	952	(d)	953.	(b)
870.	(b)	871.	(b)	872.	(b)	954.	(c)	955.	(d)	956.	(c)
873.	(a)	874.	(a)	875.	(d)	957.	(b)	958.	(d)	959.	(b)
876.	(c)	877.	(c)	878.	(a)	960.	(a)	961.	(b)	962.	(c)
879.	(d)	880.	(d)	881.	(c)	963.	(d)	964.	(a)	965.	(b)
882.	(b)	883.	(a)	884.	(d)	966.	(c)	967.	(b)	968.	(d)
885.	(d)	886.	(b)	887.	(d)	969.	(d)	970	(c)	971.	(d)
888.	(d)	889.	(b)	890.	(a)	972.	(c)	973.	(d)	974.	(b)
891.	(c)	892.	(c)	893.	(a)	975.	(c)	976.	(d)	977.	(c)
894.	(b)	895.	(c)	896.	(c)	978.	(a)	979.	(b)	980.	(d)
897.	(c)	898.	(a)	899.	(b)	981.	(a)	982.	(a)	983.	(a)
900.	(b)	901.	(c)	902.	(a)	984.	(b)	985.	(d)	986.	(a)
903.	(d)	904.	(d)	905.	(a)	987.	(c)	988.	(a)	989.	(c)
906.	(a)	907.	(c)	908.	(d)	990.	(c)	991.	(d)	992.	(a)
909.	(b)	910.	(b)	911.	(c)	993.	(d)	994.	(b)	995.	(b)
912.	(b)	913.	(d)	914.	(b)	996.	(d)	997	(c)	998.	(d)
915.	(c)	916.	(b)	917.	(a)	999.	(d)	1000.	(a)	1001.	(c)
918.	(a)	919.	(d)	920.	(a)	1002.	(a)				

11 Epidemiology & Preventive Medicine

Salient Points

- Veterinary Epidemiology deals with diseases in population and factors affecting them include productivity.
- National Institute of Epidemiology is situated in Chennai.
- OIE stands for *Office International des Epizooties.*
- OIE (France) and Centre for Disease Control (USA) are international organizations to deal with epidemic.
- National Institute of Communicable Diseases (NICD) now renamed as NCDC, New Delhi is premier organization of India to deal with communicable diseases.
- Peat Soil is characterized by Copper deficiency and Molybdenum excess.
- Parturient paresis is generally seen in milking cows.
- Enterotoxaemia is most common in Finishing lambs and Pigs.
- Excess grain feeding results *Osteodysptrophia fibrosa* in horses.
- Age is a variable factor.
- Sex is an attribute.
- Disease occurrence is contributed by various factors like season, age, sex, species, breed.
- Climate is a permanent feature of a place.
- Weather is temporary feature of a place.
- Disease Model is mathematical simulation of a disease. May be used for disease prediction & study.
- Disease distribution in population may be according to time frame, space frame.
- Elimination, eradication are two methods for disease control.

Questions

1. Aphteuse in french & Affta epizoothica in Italian are names for
   (a) FMD (b) Ranikhet disease
   (c) HS (d) BQ
2. FMD is also known as
   (a) Panzootica Aptha (b) Apthous fever
   (c) Contageous aptha (d) All
3. Most common mode of spread of FMD is
   (a) Ingestion (b) Skin penetration
   (c) Direct contact (d) Droplet infection
4. Maintenance host of FMD virus according to seller & parker is
   (a) Cattle (b) Buffalo
   (c) Sheep (d) Goat
5. Amplifier host of FMD virus is
   (a) Cattle (b) Buffalo
   (c) Goat (d) Pig
6. Tiger heart appearance occurs in case of
   (a) FMD (b) HS
   (c) BQ (d) Toxoplasmosis
7. Rise in temperature in case of FMD may range from
   (a) 102-183^{0}F (b) 103-104^{0}F
   (c) 104-105^{0}F (d) 104-106^{0}F

8. FMD does not occur in
(a) Pig (b) Sheep
(c) Goat (d) Horse

9. Experimental inoculation of FMD virus in Guinea pig is done in
(a) Stomach (b) Conjunctiva
(c) Mouth (d) Foot pad

10. Polyvalent vaccine for FMD contains strains as
(a) O, A, C (b) O,A,C Asia 1
(c) A,C Asia 1 (d) O.A. Asia 1

11. Number of strains in polyvalent vaccine for FMD is
(a) 3 (b) 4
(c) 5 (d) 6

12. Raksha FMD vaccine contains following strains
(a) O, A, C, Asia 1 (b) O, C, Asia 1, A_{22}
(c) O, A, C. A_{22} (d) OA A_{22} Asia 1

13. Diagnosis of FMD can be confirmed within 3-4 hours by
(a) Neutralization test
(b) Complement fixation test
(c) Flourcescent anibody test
(d) Tissue culture

14. FMD virus belongs to ———— tissue group
(a) Corona (b) Picorna
(c) Morbilli (d) Toga

15. Synonym for Rinderpest
(a) Cattle plague (b) Bovine typhus
(c) Pste bovine (d) All

16. Rinderpest is a disease of
(a) Even toed ungulates (b) Cloven footed animals
(c) Both (d) None

17. Rinderpest virus belongs to group
(a) Picona (b) Corona
(c) Morbilli (d) Toga

18. Zebra markings in intestine are present in
(a) FMD (b) Rinderpest
(c) HS (d) Cowpox

19. Rinderpest virus shows intimate antigenic relationship C -
(a) FMD virsus (b) Corona virus
(c) Pox virus (d) Measles virus

20. For Rinderpest
(a) Young cattle are more susceptible
(b) Pure bred cattle are more susceptible
(c) Hill cattle are more susceptible
(d) All of the above

21. Rinderpest also occurs in
(a) Giraffe (b) Wart hogs
(c) Goat (d) All

22. Natural infection of Rinderpest occurs through
(a) Direct contact (b) Aerosol route
(c) Both (d) None

23. High rise of temperature seldom present for more than 5-6 days & drops suddenly with production of lesions & diarrhoea in
(a) Rinderpest (b) FMD
(c) Cow pox (d) HS

24. Bran like deposit in oral mucosa occurs in
(a) FMD (b) Rinderpest
(c) Hog cholera (d) Cow pox

25. Incubation period of Rinderpest in natural condition is
(a) 2-15 days (b) 2-6 days
(c) 12-15 days (d) 12-16 days

26. Cardinal signs of Rinderpest are eminent in which stage
(a) Incubation stage (b) Mucosal stage
(c) Prodromal stage (d) Convalescent stage

27. Raised, grayish white pin head punctate necroses of epithelium of oral mucosa occurs in
(a) FMD (b) Stomatitis
(c) Rinderpest (d) Cow pox

28. Zebra markings or Tiger stripping are characteristic of
(a) Rinderpest (b) FMD
(c) Stomatitis (d) Cowpea

29. In case of rinderpest there is presence of
(a) Eosinophilic intranuclear inclusions bodies
(b) Basophilic intracytoplasmic inclusions bodies
(c) Both
(d) None

30. Epidemic form is name given to which form of BVD?
(a) Acute (b) Mild
(c) Sub acute (d) Chronic

31. Synonyms for malignant catarrhal fever are
(a) Snotsiekte (b) Gangrenous coryza
(c) Epetheliosis (d) All

32. Malignant catarrhal fever is caused by
(a) Bovine Herpes virus 1
(b) BHV-2
(c) BHV-3
(d) BHV-4

33. In case of malignant catarrhal fever, virus remains strictly adhered to
(a) Lymph nodes (b) WBC or RBC
(c) Platelets (d) CSF

34. Mucosal disease is the name given to
(a) Bovine viral diarrhoea (BVD)
(b) FMD
(c) Rinderpest
(d) HS

35. Virus causing BVD belong to
(a) Picorna (b) Morbilli
(c) Corona (d) Pesti virus

36. BVD virus has got antigen relationship with
(a) Swine fever virus of pig
(b) Border disease virus of sheep
(c) Both
(d) None

37. BVD occurs mostly in cattle of age
(a) 6-24 months (b) 2 years
(c) > 5 years (d) None

38. Elementary bodies in case of malignant catarrhal fever can be detected in
(a) Spleen (b) Lymph glands
(c) Lungs (d) All

39. Malignant catarrhal fever is transmitted through
(a) Domestic animals (b) Wild beast
(c) Ticks (d) All

40. Incubation period of malignant catarrhal fever disease ranges from
(a) 2-8 wks (b) 2-8 hours
(c) 2-8 days (d) 2-4 months

41. Offensive odour from mouth is characteristic feature of
(a) Malignant catarrhal fever
(b) BVD
(c) HS
(d) BQ

42. In case of malignant catarrhal fever inclusion bodies are
(a) Acidophilic intranuclear
(b) Basophilic intranuclear
(c) Basophilic intra ytoplasmic
(d) Acidophilic intracytoplasmic

43. Pathognomonic changes in case of malignant catarrhal ever are observed in
(a) Wall of small blood vessels
(b) Lymphoid tissues
(c) Both
(d) None

44. Blue tongue is also known as
(a) Sore mouth
(b) Range stiffness in lamb
(c) Pseudo FMD
(d) All

45. Sore mouth is the other name for
(a) FMD (b) Hog cholera
(c) Blue tongue (d) All

46. Blue tongue is caused by
(a) Arbo virus (b) Toga virus
(c) Pesti virus (d) Morbilli virus

47. Blue tongue virus spread through
(a) Mosquitoes (b) Biting flies
(c) Sheep ked (d) All of the above

48. Blue tongue virus multiplies in
(a) Intestine of vectors
(b) Ovary of vectors
(c) Stomach of vectors
(d) Salivary glands of vectors

49. Appearance of brown streak down the hoof, congestion & hemorrhage on coronary band occurs in
(a) Blue tongue (b) FMD
(c) Rinderpest (d) BVD

50. Synonyms for vesicular Stomatitis
(a) Sporadic aptha (b) Sore nose
(c) Mouth thrush (d) All

51. Vesicular Stomatitis occurs in
(a) Dog (b) Sheep
(c) Goat (d) Pig

52. First outbreak of vesicular Stomatitis was recorded

from
(a) Sheep (b) Horse
(c) Pig (d) Cattle

53. Vesicular Stomatitis is caused by
(a) Rheo virus (b) Rhabdo virus
(c) Morbilli virus (d) Picorna

54. Most virulent strain of vesicular Stomatitis virus is
(a) New jersey strain (b) Indiana strain
(c) Eocoal strain (d) Trinidad strain

55. Vesicular Stomatitis virus is
(a) Cigar shaped (b) Diamond shaped
(c) Bullet shaped (d) None of the above

56. Which of the following is resistant to Vesicular Stomatitis?
(a) Horse (b) Pig
(c) Cattle (d) Sheep

57. Synonyms for ephemeral fever are
(a) Three day sickness
(b) Stiff sickness
(c) Bovine epizootic fever
(d) All

58. Ephemeral fever virus belongs to
(a) Rhabdo virus (b) Reo virus
(c) Morbili virus (d) Corona virus

59. Ephemeral fever virus has got similarly in chemical & physical properties with that of
(a) FMD virus
(b) Blue tongue virus
(c) Vesicular Stomatitis virus
(d) All

60. Ephemeral fever virus is related to
(a) FMD in cattle
(b) Blue tongue in sheep
(c) Dengue fever in man
(d) None

61. Ephemeral fever virus remains associated with
(a) WBC (d) RBC
(c) Platelets (d) Thrombocytes

62. Ephemeral fever does not occur in
(a) Goat (b) Pig
(c) Dog (d) All

63. Ephemeral fever is transmitted by
(a) Sand fly (b) Biting midges
(c) Sheep ked (d) All

64. Which of the following diseases is never transmitted by direct contact from animal to animal?
(a) FMD (b) Vesicular Stomatitis
(c) Blue Tongue (d) Ephemeral fever

65. Ephemeral fever virus localizes in
(a) Liver (b) Spleen
(c) Blood (d) Mesodermal tissues

66. Polysinovitis, valovaginitis & periarthritis may be associated with
(a) Ephemeral fever (b) FMD
(c) HS (d) BQ

67. Red nose is the name given to
(a) Infectious Rhinitis
(b) Infection tracheitis
(c) Infectious bovine bronchitis
(d) Infectious bovine rhinotracheitis

68. Abortion storm in a herd may occur following infection of
(a) BVD virus (b) IBR virus
(c) FMD virus (d) HS virus

69. Pseudorabies is also known as
(a) Aujesky's disease (b) Mad itch
(c) None (d) Both

70. The term Infectious bulbar paralysis was attributed for pseudorabies in
(a) Dog (b) Pigs
(c) Guinea (d) Rabbit

71 Pseudorabies is caused by
(a) Rhabdo virus (b) Reo virus
(c) Toga virus (d) Herpes virus

72. Pseudorabies primarily occurs in
(a) Horses (b) Pigs
(c) Dogs (d) Rabbit

73. Reservoir host for pseudorabies
(a) Cattle (b) Sheep
(c) Horse (d) Pigs

74. Natural way of entry of Pseudorabies virus is
(a) Breach in continuity of skin
(b) Ingestion
(c) Inhalation
(d) Droplet infection

75. Pseudo rabies virus is
(a) Epitheliotropic (b) Pantropic

(c) Both (d) None

76. Pseudorabies virus multiples in
(a) Spinal ganglia
(b) Brain
(c) Respiratory tract epithelia
(d) Intestinal villi

77. Pseudorabies is fatal in case of
(a) Dog (b) Sheep
(c) Goat (d) None

78. Intranuclear inclusion bodies in Pseudo rabies are found in
(a) Epithelial cells of alveoli
(b) Epithelial cells of intestine
(c) Epithelial cells of skin
(d) Epithelial cells of lever

79. Cow dry type A inclusion bodies in degenerated nervous are observed in
(a) Rabies (b) Pseudorabies
(c) Both (d) None

80. Variola vaccinia is a synonym for
(a) Cow pox (b) Sheep pox
(c) Goat pox (d) Fowl pox

81. Cow pox is caused by
(a) Herpes virus (b) Pesti virus
(c) Toga virus (d) Vaccinia virus

82. Cow pox virus is in closely related with
(a) Sheep pox (b) Goat pox
(c) Horse pox (d) All

83. Haemorrhage pock lesions on chorjo allantoic membrane of developing check embryo are produced due to
(a) Cow pox (b) Sheep pox
(c) goat pox (d) All

84. Cow pox is prevalent in which region?
(a) Hind limbs (b) Oral mucosa
(c) Perianal area (d) Udder & teat

85. Typical pock lesions in cowpox are found on
(a) Hind links (b) Oral mucosa
(c) Pereanal aera (d) Udder & teat

86. Milker's nodules are formed in case of
(a) Cow pox (b) Pseudocow pox
(c) Small pox (d) Chicken pox

87. Buffalo pox mostly occurs in
(a) Dry buffaloes (b) Lactating buffaloes
(c) Heifers (d) All

88. Ring shaped or horse shoe pattern scab is found in
(a) Buffalo pox (b) Pseudobuffalo pox
(c) Cow pox (d) Pseudo cowpox

89. Diameter of skin pustules in goat pox is
(a) 0.5-1 cm (b) 0.5-2 mm
(c) 2 mm (d) 5 mm

90. In case of goat pox inclusion bodies are
(a) Intracytoplasmic (b) Intranuclear
(c) Both (d) None

91. Laclavelec is the name given to
(a) Sheep pox (b) Goat pox
(c) Chicken pox (d) Horse pox

92. To protect lumpy skin disease in cattle, as vaccine one may use
(a) Sheep pox virus (b) Goat pox virus
(c) Horse pox virus (d) Small pox virus

93. Sheep pox is closely related with
(a) Contagious pustuler dermatitis
(b) Lumpy skin disease
(c) Bovine pustuler dermatitis
(d) All

94. Physical address of an organism in an ecosystem is
(a) Niche (b) Bcome
(c) Biotope (d) Biocenosis

95. Carriers is
(a) An inapparently infected individual which is transmitter of a disease
(b) An apparently infected individual which transmits disease
(c) A maintenance site of the infectious agent
(d) A host species which harbors infection without propagating

96. Reservoir is
(a) An in apparently infected individual which is transmitter of a disease
(b) An apparently infected individual which transmits disease
(c) A maintenance site of the infectious agent
(d) A host species which harbors infection without propagating

97. Sensitivity of a test is
(a) Ability to detect diseased animals

(b) Ability to detect non diseased animals
(c) Ability to detect exposed animals
(d) Ability to detect unexposed animal

98. Specificity of a test is
(a) Ability to detect diseased animals
(b) Ability to detect non diseased animals
(c) Ability to detect exposed animals
(d) Ability to detect unexposed animal

99. Natural home of a disease is called
(a) Nidus
(b) Niche
(c) Nosogenic territory
(d) Biotope

100. Epidemiological triad is
(a) Host, agent & environment interaction
(b) Host, agent & management interaction
(c) Host, agent & climate interaction
(d) None

101. Rinderpest virus is antigenically identical to
(a) Rota virus
(b) Corona virus
(c) Canine distemper virus
(d) Rift valley fever virus

102. Clinical and pathological signs of one of the following diseases closely resemble that of rinderpest.
(a) I.B.R. (b) Rift valley fever
(c) Virus diarhoea (d) Salmonellosis

103. Infection pustular vulvo-vaginitis is caused by a
(a) Pesti virus (b) Herpes virus
(c) Morbilli virus (d) Picorna virusa

104. Which of the following is caused by a Herpes virus?
(a) BVD
(b) FMD
(c) Mucosal disease
(d) Enzootic bovine leucosis

105. Which of the following clinical sign may be seen in an animal suffering from B.V.D.?
(a) Conjunctivitis (b) Dyspnea
(c) Tenesmus (d) Pyrexia

106. Which of the following is invariably fatal?
(a) Rinderpest
(b) Foot and mouth disease
(c) Blue tongue
(d) Bovine virus diarrhoea

107. Intra nuclear basophilic inclusion bodies in brain tissue are present in:
(a) Rabis (b) Pseudorabies
(c) Canine distenper (d) None

108. Acidophilic intra cytoplasmic inclusion bodies in dog gall-bladder are present in:
(a) Rabies (b) Pseudorabies
(c) Canine distemper (d) None

109. Cheesy pus discharge from lesions occurs in
(a) Glanders (b) Strangles
(c) Bovine fancy (d) Bovine artaritis

110. Actinomycosis is effectively treated by:
(a) Potassium iodide orally
(b) Sodium iodide intravenously
(c) Sulfonamide
(d) Sulfamethazine

111. The fibrosis in Actinomycosis can be controlled by
(a) Sulpha drugs
(b) Sodium iodide orally
(c) Sodium iodide intravenously
(d) Antibiotics

112. In glanders primarily organisms are localized in
(a) Lymph nodes (b) Lungs
(c) Kidney (d) Liver

113. Acute myocardial failure may occur in
(a) FMD (b) RP
(c) Mucosal disease (d) None

114. Mallein test is useful in
(a) Strangles
(b) Glanders
(c) Vesicular Stomatitis
(d) BVD

115. Pseudo rabies in swine must be differentiated from:
(a) Swine erysipelas (b) Swine fever
(c) Swine influenza (d) Leptospirosis

116. Which rabies vaccine is used as post bite and pre bite both in dogs?
(a) Samples vaccine (b) LEP vaccine
(c) Both (d) None

117. The symptoms observed in Pseudo rabies in pigs are :
(a) Encephalitis alone

(b) Encephalitis and itching
(c) Dermatitis
(d) None

118. Brucella K45/20A strain
(a) Ineffective when given before 6 months of age
(b) Produces high titers of CFT antibodies
(c) Produces severe reactions at the site of infection
(d) Is expensive

119. The Brucella organism normally found in
(a) Placental fluid
(b) Fetal fluid
(c) Placental or fetal fluid
(d) Placental and fetal fluid

120. The Brucella strain 19 vaccine produces immunity for
(a) 3 months (b) 6 months
(c) 12 months (d) Life long

121. The *Brucella abortus* in cattle may cause
(a) Fistula of withers
(b) Hygroma of knee
(c) Arthritis
(d) Abscess in the region of sternum and fetlock

122. Death of fetus affected with Brucella is caused because of
(a) Toxemia
(b) Asphyxia
(c) Nervous breakdown
(d) Fatiqueness of muscles due to excessive convulsions

123. Ascoli's test is used for the diagnosis of
(a) Para tuberculosis (b) Anthrax
(c) FMD (d) Barbone

124. *Pasteurella multocida* can easily be destroyed by
(a) Heat treatment at 100°C for 10 minutes.
(b) 0.2% cresol solution
(c) Heat treatment at 150°C for 30 minutes
(d) All of the above

125. In cases of HS mortality occurs due to
(a) Renal failure
(b) Cardiac arrest
(c) Respiratory distress
(d) None of the above

126. Outbreaks of shipping fever pneumonia occur commonly during
(a) Winters (b) Summers
(c) Rainy season (d) Any time of year

127. In calves the most enterotoxic *E. colli* strain is one that produces
(a) K 88$^+$ antigen (b) 987 P$^+$ antigen
(c) K 99$^+$ antigen (d) All of them

128. Of three biotypes of *Fusobacterium necrophorum* type A is mainly associated with
(a) Rumenitis (b) Pneumonia
(c) Endocarditis (d) Liver abscess

129. Expiratory dyspnea is more common in bovines in
(a) RP
(b) BQ
(c) Tetanus
(d) Pneumonic Pasteurellosis

130. Septicemic colibacillosis is more common in
(a) First three days of life
(b) After one week
(c) After one month
(d) After two month

131. *Erysipelothrix rhusiopathiae* organisms have following number of strains
(a) 5 (b) 8
(c) 22 (d) 31

132. Erysipelas in pigs is caused by
(a) Rough strains
(b) Smooth strains
(c) Both types of strains
(d) None

133. The young cultures of *Streptococcus equi* are more pathogenic as they have
(a) Less surface electric charge
(b) More surface area occupied by young culture
(c) More acidity
(d) More surface electric charge

134. Strangles occurs in case of
(a) Equines (b) Bovines
(c) Canines (d) All of them

135. In pigs endocarditis and arthritis are symptoms in
(a) Semilunar valves (b) Mitral valves

(c) Aortic valve (d) All of them

136. For diagnosis of tuberculosis in unknown herd, we inject tuberculin intradermaly
(a) 0.1 ml (b) 0.5 ml
(c) 1.0 ml (d) 0.2 ml

137. Recently parturated animals may be tested for tuberculosis by
(a) SID
(b) I/V test
(c) DID test
(d) Stormont tuberculin test

138. Abortions in Leptospirosis can occur during
(a) First three months
(b) During last three months
(c) At any time pregnancy
(d) None

139. Occurrence of anthrax is low in
(a) Goats (b) Sheep
(c) Buffalo (d) Cow

140. *Mycobacterium bovis* organisms are
(a) Non sporulating
(b) Sporulating non miltile
(c) Non spourlatign non motile
(d) Sporulating motile

141. Wool sorter disease is caused by
(a) *Brucella abortus*
(b) *Bacillus anthracis*
(c) *Listeria monocytogenes*
(d) *Mycobacterium avium*

142. H.S. is mainly caused by *Pasteurella multocida* type
(a) A (b) B
(c) C (d) D

143. Immunoglobulin in piglets can be absorbed from Intestine up to
(a) 24 hrs (b) 48 hrs
(c) 96 hrs (d) One week

144. BUN is increased in cases of colibacillosis due to
(a) Diarrhoea
(b) Toxaemia
(c) Pulmonary effusion
(d) Renal perfusion

145. Symptoms of para tuberculosis commonly occur in animals of
(a) One week age
(b) One month age
(c) One year age
(d) Above two years of age

146. The most common strain of FMD to produce disease in a Indian cattle is
(a) O (b) A
(c) C (d) Asia I

147. Acute myocardial failure may occurs in
(a) Colibacillosis (b) FMD
(c) RP (d) Actinomycosis

148. The fibrosis in actinomycosis can be controlled by
(a) Potassium Iodide orally
(b) Sodium iodide orally
(c) Potassium Iodide Intravenously and sodium Iodide orally
(d) All of the above

149. *Actinomyces bovis* is a
(a) Gram negative organism
(b) Acid fast organism
(c) Spore forming organism
(d) Gram positive organism

150. Mastitis occurs because of
(a) Chemical change in milk and microbiological change in glandular tissue
(b) Physical change in milk and microbiological change in glandular tissue
(c) Microbiological change in milk and physical change in glandular tissue
(d) Physical, chemical microbiological change in milk and pathological change in glandular tissue

151. C.B.P.P. occurs because of
(a) Contaminated feed
(b) Contaminated water
(c) Inhalation of infected droplets
(d) All above means

152. Foot Rot can be prevented by keeping the animals on
(a) Muddy soil
(b) Rocky soil
(c) Dry and smooth surface
(d) Rough ground

153. Colibacillosis can be prevented by feeding
(a) Ad-libitum milk

(b) Ad-libitum colostrums
(c) Colostrums 50 ml/kg body weight per day
(d) Colostrums 50 ml/kg body weight /day

154. Which sentence is incorrect?
(a) Mastitis is a disease of economic concern
(b) Mastitis is a management born diseases
(c) Mastitis is primarily a new infection disease
(d) Mastitis is a multiple etiology disease

155. National control programme so far have failed to eradicate
(a) FMD (b) PPR disease
(c) Colibacillosis (d) All of the above

156. Highest number of Mastitis is observed out of
(a) *Staphylococcus spp.*
(b) *Streptococcus spp.*
(c) *Corynibacterium spp.*
(d) *Klebsiella spp.*

157. Incubation period for C.B.P.P. is
(a) 24-48 hrs (b) 24-48 days
(c) 10-260 days (d) 1- 7 days

158. FMD is still prevalent because
(a) Virus is highly resistant for environmental influences.
(b) It is a natural habitat of soil
(c) It can change its antigenic structure
(d) It can change it nucleic acid sequence very fast

159. R.P. virus is having affinity to
(a) R.E. system (b) Lymphoid tissue
(c) Lever (d) Kidney

160. Small spatial unit in ecosystem is known as
(a) Niche (b) Biome
(c) Nidus (d) Biotope

161. Collection of living organism in a biotope is called as
(a) Biogenesis (b) Population
(c) Living sphere (d) Biocenosis

162. As per De crandlle classification, megatherms include
(a) Tropical rain forest
(b) Temperate deciduous
(c) Boreal forest
(d) None

163. Diagnostic survey is called as
(a) Monitoring (b) Surveillance
(c) survey (d) Screening

164. Which route for Mallein test is used for the diagnosis of Glanders?
(a) Cutaneous
(b) Subcutaneous
(c) Intradermo paapebral
(d) Any one of above

165. Which of the following diseases is clinically characterized by pneumonia, neonatal mortality & abortions?
(a) Toxocariosis (b) Coccidiosis
(c) Toxoplasmosis (d) Theileriosis

166. Laminitis, coronitis with erosive lesions in cavity are characteristic signs of
(a) Ephemeral fever
(b) Vascular Stomatitis
(d) Bovine viral diarrhoea
(d) Blue tongue

167. In sheep how long is the life cycle of pathogenic coccidia?
(a) 3-4 days (b) 1-2 week
(c) 3-4 week (d) 2-3 months

168. Which of the following diseases is likely to cause abortion during 1st 1/2 gestation in cows
(a) IBR
(b) BVD
(c) Epizootic bovine abortion
(d) Leptospirosis

169. Which class of commercial poultry is most susceptible to aflatoxicosis
(a) Broilers (b) Turkeys
(c) Japanese quells (d) Ducklings

170. Niclosamide in case of immature amiphistomosis, @ 90 mg/kg body weight has high efficacy in
(a) Sheep but not cattle
(b) Cattle but not in sheep
(c) Both cattle & sheep
(d) Neither cattle nor sheep

171. Recommended dose of Niclosamide in very young lamb is
(a) 75 mg /kg body weight
(b) 7.5 mg/kg body weight

(c) 1 gm/kg body weight
(d) 1 gm irrespective of wt

172. Most important parasitic disease of horses in which verminous arteritis & colic are observed
(a) Strongylosis (b) Fasciolosis
(c) Amphistomosis (d) Strogyloidosis

173. Chronic parasitic disease in which Hypoalbuminemia, normochromic anaemia & sub mandibular edema is seen is
(a) Strongylosis (b) Fasciolosis
(c) Ascariosis (d) Strongyloidosis

174. Edema of head & temporal fossa can be seen in
(a) African horse sickness
(b) Epizootic lymphangitis
(c) Infectious equine encephalitis
(d) Glanders

175. The causative agent of Bovine viral diarrhoea is closely related to the causative agent of
(a) African swine fever
(b) Ephemeral fever
(c) Hog cholera
(d) Bovine inalignant catarrh

176. Eggs of Stephenurus can be collected from
(a) Faeces
(b) Urine
(c) Ephemeral fever
(d) Bovine malignant catarrh

177. *Stephanurus dentatus* may remain as facultative parasite in
(a) Earthworm (b) Ant
(c) Snail (d) Mosquito

178. Which of the following is not a scour worm?
(a) *Trichostrongylous spp.*
(b) *Oesophagostomum spp.*
(c) *Cooperia spp.*
(d) *Nematodirus spp.*

179. Eggs of *Bunostomum phlebotum* are having
(a) Rounded ends & thick wall
(b) Blunt ends & pigmented embryonic mass
(c) Blunt ends with pitted surface
(d) Thick wall, pigmented as well as pitted

180. Life cycle of red worm is
(a) Direct in horses
(b) Indirect in mule
(c) Indirect in horse but direct in mule
(d) Direct in horse but direct in mule

181. For vaccination of lung worm infection
(a) 1000 irradiated larvae are used
(b) 10000 irradiated larvae are used
(c) 20000 irradiated larvae are used
(d) 100 irradiated larvae are used

182. Worm nodule disease is also called as
(a) Esophagostomosis
(b) Pimply gut
(c) Both
(d) None

183. Adult of *Chabertia ovina* lays eggs in
(a) Abomasum (b) Duodenum
(c) Colon (d) Rectum

184. Eggs of *Ascaris vitulorum* are
(a) Thin walled having
(b) Thick walled with a pitted surface
(c) Thick walled having transverse line
(d) None

185. *Oxyuris equi* is inhabitant of
(a) Perianal area (b) Rectum
(c) Caecum & colon (d) Abomasum

186. *Rhabditis strongyloides*
(a) May cause dermatitis
(b) Is a facultative parasite
(c) Can lead a part of life cycle as free living
(d) All of the above

187. Whip worm inhabits the
(a) Caecum (b) Duodenum
(c) Rectum (d) Abomasum

188. Dourine in horses occurs through
(a) Contaminated feed
(b) Inhalation
(c) Skin penetration
(d) Coitus

189. The prepatent period for *Fasciola gigantica* is
(a) 9-11 weeks (b) 13-14 weeks
(c) 15-17 weeks (d) 19-21 weeks

190. Anemia in Fasciolosis occurs due to
(a) Hepatic insufficiency
(b) Sucking of blood by mature parasite
(c) Proline secretion
(d) All of the above

191. Nitroxynil is used in Fasciolosis @
(a) 10 mg/kg s/c (b) 10 mg/kg orally
(c) 100 mg/kg s/c (d) 100 mg/kg orally

192. Amphistomosis caused by immature parasite is
(a) More severe than caused by mature parasite
(b) Less severe than caused by mature parasite
(c) Shows no clinical signs
(d) Can't be treated

193. Toxoplasmosis in cat is transmitted by ingestion of
(a) Infective meat
(b) Contaminated feed
(c) Contaminated H_2O
(d) Unsporulated oocyst

194. In *Babesia bovis* infection there is profound hypertension due to production of kallikrein which is
(a) A kinin (b) A vasoactive amine
(c) Both (d) None

195. Survey is a
(a) Study
(b) Examination of units
(c) Both
(d) None

196. Nosogenic territory is
(a) An area that supports a disease
(b) An area where disease is absent
(c) An area where occurrence of disease is sporadic
(d) None

197. Disease evoking capacity of an infectious agent in a particular host is called as
(a) Virulence (b) Pathogenecity
(c) Susceptibility (d) None

198. Predisposing factors
(a) Increases the susceptibility of host
(b) Facilitate disease manifestations
(c) Are associated with definite on set of disease
(d) Increases the probability of infection

199. Enabling factors
(a) Increase the susceptibility of host
(b) Facilitate disease manifestation
(c) Are associated with definite of set of disease
(d) Increase the probability of infection

200. Precipitating factors
(a) Increase the susceptibility of host
(b) Facilitate disease manifestation
(c) Are associated with definite of set of disease
(d) Increase the probability of infection

201. Risk factors
(a) Increase the susceptibility of host
(b) Facilitate disease manifestation
(c) Are associated with definite of set of disease
(d) Increase the probability of infestation

202. Mastitis is caused by
(a) Chemical agents
(b) Physical agents
(c) Microbiological agents
(d) All of above

203. For animal inoculation in FMD, one should inject suspected material
(a) Intradermaly (b) Intraperitonially
(c) Intralingualy (d) Intraveinously

204. In case of F.M.D.
(a) Endocrine exhaustion is considered more important
(b) Clinical form of disease is more important
(c) None of the form is important as there is very low mortality in FMD
(d) FMD is not at all economically important disease

205. Which route of administration does not produces Vesicular Stomatitis in cattle
(a) i/p (b) i/v
(c) i/m (d) s/c

206. Course of Vesicular Stomatitis is
(a) Longer then FMD
(b) Shorter then FMD
(c) Depends upon rate of administration
(d) Can't be compared with FMD

207. In case of peste des petits
(a) All the dairy animals of India are equally susceptible
(b) Cross bread sheep are most susceptible
(c) Goat is most susceptible
(d) Buffalos are most susceptible

208. Caprinised vaccine in case of Rinderpest is
(a) Not at all effective in hill cattle
(b) Can be used in hill cattle but produces less immunity
(c) Can't be used as it is virulent for hill cattle
(d) cannot be used in cross bred.

208. Bovine viral diarrhoea and mucosal diseases are
(a) Etiologically different but epidemiologically similar
(b) Epidemiologically and clinically different
(c) Etiologically and epidemilogically similar
(d) Etiologically and epidemiologically different

209. Which statement is incorrect?
(a) Measles virus can be used as protective vaccine against RP
(b) RP virus can be used to protect pups from CD
(c) BVD virus can be used to protect swine fever
(d) R.P. virus can be used to product from B.M.C.

210. Constant exposure of any infective agent to a particular herd leads to carrier stage or sub clinical form of disease because
(a) Constant exposure can reduce the virulence
(b) Constant mutation of virus may occur which may lead to development of less virulent strain
(c) Resistant may develop in the host to the causative agent
(d) All of the above

211. Which statement is wrong about ephemeral fever?
(a) It is insect born retrovirus infection
(b) It is self cure disease
(c) It is inflammation of mesoderm tissue
(d) It can't be cured

212. Which statement is wrong as far as susceptibility for ephemeral fever is concern?
(a) Buffalo are highly susceptible for ephemeral fever
(b) They can be experimentally affected
(c) They act as reservoir
(d) Buffaloes are mildly susceptible

213. The Number of antigenic strains of African horse sickness virus
(a) 30 (b) 22
(c) 42 (d) 7

214. Which one may not be reservoir of African Horse Sickness?
(a) Donkey (b) Dog
(c) Elephant (d) Zebra

215. On necropsy, pharynx, trachea and bronchi are filled with yellow serous fluid and froth in
(a) Equine Infectious anaemia (EIA)
(b) Equine Arteritis
(c) African horse sickness
(d) Glanders

216. Degeneration and necrosis of small blood vessels can be seen in
(a) Equine viral arteritis
(b) Equine viral abortion
(c) Equine viral anaemia
(d) African horse sickness

217. Intermittent diarrhoea and cachexia can be seen in
(a) Johne's disease
(b) Bovine viral diarrhoea (BVD)
(c) Enerotoxaema
(d) Rinderpest (RD)

218. Severe pruritis and staggering gait can be seen in
(a) Louping ill (b) Scrapie
(c) Rabies (d) Pseudorabies

219. Erythematic patechial hemorrhages on lower part of abdomen occur in
(a) Swine erysipelas (b) Hog cholera
(c) Both (d) None

220. Asepsis can be defined as
(a) Absence of bacteria
(b) Absence of virus
(c) Absence of both
(d) Absence of septic matter

221. Fixed virus of Rabies can
(a) Produce disease
(b) Have longer incubation period
(c) Have shorter incubation period
(d) Can be converted in street virus

222. Cathartics are drugs which
(a) Cause irritation in intestine

(b) Cause constipation
(c) Increase salivation

223. Colostrum is the
(a) Fluid which is secreted by mammary glands
(b) Fluid which is secreted by mammary glands few days before and after parturition
(c) Fluid which is secreted by mammary glands first after parturition
(d) None

224. Endotoxins are
(a) Toxin produced inside the body
(b) Produced and remain within the bacterial cell and liberated only after the death or disintegration of the organism
(c) Any toxin produced by micro organism present in intestine
(d) Produced within the bacteria but can be liberated by live cells

225. *Brucella Abortus* has a predilection for
(a) Pregnant uterus only
(b) Uterus and udder only
(c) Uterus, testicles and udder not for accessory male sex glands
(d) Pregnant uterus, udder, testicles, accessory male sex glands, lymph nodes and joint capsule

226. Transmission of Brucella organism occurs
(a) By ingestion of contaminated food and water
(b) By bull which discharge semen containing organism
(c) During AI
(d) All above

227. Which sentence is wrong?
(a) *Brucella abortus* is an intra cellular organism
(b) It can survive in host up to 5 years
(c) It shows transitory titer during bacterimia, which disappears in latent period
(d) 6 months after abortion antibody titer can be observed

228. Which test can be used as herd test in case of Brucellosis?
(a) Card test
(b) Bang's ring test
(c) Compliment fixation test
(d) Serum neutralization test

229. Why commonly used antibiotics like tetracycline & sulfonamides are not effective in tuberculosis
(a) Because they cannot penetrate giant cell
(b) Because they cannot penetrate mycolic acid, which is present in bacterial cell wall
(c) Because they cannot penetrate calcification around lesions
(d) None of the above

230. Which one descending order is correct as for as susceptibility for TB is concern
(a) Cattle-goat-horse (b) Goat-cattle-horse
(c) Horse-goat-cattle (d) Goat-horse-cattle

231. Clinical cases of paratuberculosis are more common in adults because
(a) Only adult is susceptible for disease and not young
(b) Young are susceptible but organism multiplies very slowly to exert its clinical effect
(c) Organism growth is some how related with puberty and so effects at adult hood
(d) It only multiply in adult and exert its effect

232. Actinomycosis can be diagnosed by
(a) Gram's staining
(b) Acid fast staining
(c) Serum neutralization
(d) All of above

233. One dose of tuberculin contains
(a) 5000 tuberculin unit
(b) 1000 and 1500 tuberculin unit
(c) 1000 and 5000 tuberculin unit
(d) None of the above

234. Which statement is wrong?
(a) Leptospirosis is a zoonotic disease
(b) Leptospirosis cause abortion in most of the animals
(c) Leptospirosis cause interstitial nephritis, hemolytic anemia and abortions
(d) Leptospirosis is a disease of animal which occasionally occurs in human beings

235. In Anthrax,
(a) Blood immediately clots
(b) Rigor mortis occurs

(c) Gaseous decomposition takes place
(d) Hair loss occurs

236. Adult worm of this disease inhabits cysts around the renal pelvis and wall of ureter. The cyst communicate with urinary passage and eggs are passed out into the urine of the host
(a) Bunostomiasis (b) Strongylosis
(c) Lung worm (d) Stephenuriasis

237. Eggs of this parasite have blunt ends and contain deeply pigmented embryonic cells and worms are strong blood suckers
(a) *Bunostomum spp.* (b) *Strongylosus spp.*
(c) Lungworm (d) *Trichuris spp.*

238. Larvae of which penetrate the glands of Abomasum forming white, raised, umbilicate nodules which when confluent give morocco leather appearance
(a) *Bunostomum spp.* (b) *Strongylosus spp.*
(c) Lungworm (d) *Trichuris spp.*

239. Diagnosis of this parasite depends mainly on detection of yellow oval eggs, which have a transparent plug at each end
(a) *Bunostomum spp.* (b) *Strongylosus spp.*
(c) Lungworm (d) *Trichuris spp.*

240. Diagnosis of this disease can be achieved by radiography of chest, apart from identifying larvae.
(a) Bunostomiasis (b) Strongylosis
(c) Lung worm (d) Trichuriases

241. Which one is not a use of Epidemiology?
(a) Investigation and control of diseases
(b) Acquisition of information on the ecology
(c) Formulation of the line of treatment
(d) Cost analysis of disease

242. The aggregate of all facts related to animals and plants are their
(a) Natural history (b) Ecology
(c) Epidemiology (d) Niche

243. Representation of disease using mathematical models that attempt to simulate patterns of disease occurrence is
(a) Analytical Epidemiology
(b) Theoretical Epidemiology
(c) Landscape Epidemiology
(d) Clinical Epidemiology

244. Comparison of a group of diseased animals with a group of healthy animals with respect to exposure to hypothesized causal factors is
(a) Case control study
(b) Cohort study
(c) Cross sectional study
(d) Clinical trial

245. Commensal are
(a) Microbes, which can produce disease in animals of several species
(b) Microbes found on skin or within the body that do not usually cause the disease
(c) Microbes found inside the body that can cause disease
(d) Microbes find outside the body unable to cause disease

246. Monitoring is routine collection of information on
(a) Disease (b) Productivity
(c) Health (d) All of the above

247. Outbreak of disease is
(a) Sudden appearance of disease
(b) Sudden appearance of known disease with expected frequencies
(c) An identified occurrence of disease involving one ore more animals
(d) Occurrence of disease in more than one herd

248. Point source epidemic is
(a) An Epidemic resulting from exposure of animals to a single common cause
(b) Epidemic resulting from exposure of animals to a single diseased animal
(c) An Epidemic resulting from exposure of animals to a single herd
(d) An Epidemic resulting in single animal

249. Mortality is number of deaths in
(a) Population (b) Unexposed animals
(c) Diseased animals (d) Healthy animals

250. Retrospective study is
(a) A case control study
(b) Any study that collects and utilizes historical data
(c) Study on previously collected data
(d) All of above

251. Attack rate is actuality proportion of new disease cases
(a) In a long line
(b) In a brief period of risk
(c) That develops outside the range of incubation period
(d) That develops outside the range of incubation period

252. The ability of agent to infect host is related to
(a) Susceptibility of host
(b) Virulence of agent
(c) Suitable environment
(d) All of the above

253. Paratenic host is that
(a) In which an agent is transferred mechanically without further development
(b) In which an agent increases its number in heavy amount to infect others
(c) In which an agent undergoes some development
(d) In which an agent normally lives and multiplies

254. Deciduous forests are described as formation of
(a) Megatherm (b) Mesotherm
(c) Xerophils (d) None of the above

255. Home range for animals is
(a) Area where they make home
(b) Area where they roam
(c) Area where they prefer to live
(d) All of the above

256. Nidality is the characteristics of an Infectious agent associated with particular
(a) Geographic condition
(b) Climatic condition
(c) Ecological condition
(d) All of the above

257. Which one is not conveying the same meaning of the landscape epidemiology?
(a) Medical Epidemiology
(b) Medical Ecology
(c) Horizontal Epidemiology
(d) Medical Geography

258. Functional position in a community of animals is also known as
(a) Niche (b) Biome
(c) Nidis (d) Biotope

259. Eradication is
(a) Complete elimination of an infectious agent
(b) Reduction of infectious disease prevalence in a specified area to a level at which transmission does not occur
(c) Reduction in the incidence of an infectious disease where no cases occur, although the infectious agent may be allowed to persist

260. Territoriality is
(a) Animal's house range
(b) Animals' behavioral to territory
(c) Animal's choice of neighborhood
(d) Area that animals defend aggressively

261. Nidality is the characteristic of an Infectious agent associated with particular
(a) Geographic condition
(b) Climatic condition
(c) Ecological condition
(d) All of the above

262. Selenium toxicity may occur after top dressing in
(a) White clone. (b) Maize
(c) Brown top (d) None

263. Junction of two ecosystems are called as
(a) Ecological interface
(b) Ecological joint
(c) Ecological interaction
(d) Ecological conjunction

264. Zoonotic disease caused by coccidian parasite, which is clinically characterized by pneumonia, neonatal mortality and abortions
(a) Toxoplasmosis (b) Theilariosis
(c) Fasciolosis (d) Toxocariosis

265. A parasitic or protozoea disease where high fever appears along with peripheral lymph node swelling and conjunctival hemorrhage
(a) Anaplasmosis (b) Theilariosis
(c) Fasciolosis (d) Toxocariosis

266. It is usually a chronic parasitic disease in which hypoalbuminemea/ normochromic anaemia and submandibular edema can be seen
(a) Toxoplasmosis (b) Theilariosis
(c) Fasciolosis (d) Toxocariosis

267. Parasitic disease in which transplacental transmis-

sion occurs and egg of which are thick celled
(a) Toxoplasmosis (b) Theilariosis
(c) Fasciolosis (d) Toxocariosis

268. Most important parasitic disease of horses in which verminous arteritis and colic are common
(a) Toxoplasmosis (b) Strongylosis
(c) Fasciolosis (d) Amphistomosis

269. R.P. virus has affinity to
(a) R.E. System (b) Lymphoid tissue
(c) Livei (d) Oral cavity

270. Which serological test is most accepted in diagnosis of glanders
(a) ELISA (b) CFT
(c) FAT (d) AGPT

271. Feeding can present colibacillosis
(a) Ad-libidum milk
(b) Ad-libidum colostrums
(c) Colostrums @ 50 ml/kg b.w.l./day
(d) Colostrums @ 5.0 ml/kg b.w.t./day

272. In white side test, milk drops are stirred with
(a) NaOH (b) $NaHCO_3$
(c) HCl (d) None

273. Which of the following is more affected by pox?
(a) Indigenous sheep (b) Merino sheep
(c) Both (d) None

274. Insects are primary host in case of
(a) African horse sickness
(b) Swamp fever
(c) Infectious equine influenza
(d) Infectious equine arteritis

275. Eyes become blue in
(a) CD (b) Rabies
(c) ICH (d) Leptospirosis

276. Negribodies can be seen in impression smear of
(a) Medulle oblungata
(b) Whitc matter
(c) Pituitary
(d) Hippocampus

277. White side test is used for
(a) Mastitis (b) Brucellosis
(c) Salmonellosis (d) None

278. Mastitis is also known as
(a) Garget (b) Marmites
(c) Caked udder (d) All of above

279. Most potential route of infection in neonatal calf is
(a) Naval (b) Mouth
(c) Nostrils (d) None

280. Rate of absorption of Sulfonamides in sick animal is, as compared to healthy animal
(a) Slower (b) Higher
(c) No charge (d) Variable

281. Prolong administration of Sulfonamides may produce
(a) Vitamin K deficiency
(b) Vitamin A deficiency
(c) Vitamin B complex deficiency
(d) None

282. Which one neutralizes sulfonamide action?
(a) Blood (b) Pus
(c) Tissue waste (d) All of above

283. Drug of choice for trypanosoma infection is
(a) Sulphadimidine sulphate (b) Quinapyramine
(c) Penicillin (d) None of the above

284. Loss of heat tolerance in cattle is seen as sequelae of which disease:
(a) Parasitic disease (b) FMD
(c) Anthrax (d) None of the above

285. Negri bodies are characteristic of
(a) Canine distemper
(b) Rabies
(c) Infection canine hepatitis
(d) Parvovirus infection

286. Saddle curve temperature is characteristic of:
(a) C. D. (b) Rabies
(c) ICH (d) Parvovirus

287. Pericarditis is clinically characteristic by:
(a) Muffling of heart sound
(b) Frictional sound
(c) Inflammatory leucopenia
(d) Tachycardia

288. Haemorhage leads to which of the following
(a) Toxic shock
(b) Cardiogenic shock
(c) Vasogenic shock
(d) Hypovolumic shock

289. Tibersa is the term used for surra in

(a) Cattle (b) Buffalo
(c) Camel (d) Goat

290. Caecal Coccidiosis is caused by
(a) *E. necatrix* (b) *E. tenella*
(c) *E. maxima* (d) All

291. Acaricides are the drugs act on
(a) Mites (b) Ticks
(c) Fleas (d) Protozoa

292. First antibiotics discovered is
(a) Penicillin (b) Sulfonamides
(c) Cephalosporin (d) None

293. Most wasteful use of antimicrobial drugs for systemic Infectious is
(a) Oral (b) I/M
(c) I/V (d) None

294. Fastest achievement of maximum blood plasma level of drug observed in
(a) I/M route (b) I/ V route
(c) Topical route (d) Oral route

295. What will be the effect of acidification of urine on Sulfonamide level in plasma
(a) Increase (b) Decreased
(c) No effect (d) First increase than decrease

295. Elimination is
(a) Complete elimination of the infectious agents
(b) Regional elimination of an infectious agent
(c) Reduction of infectious disease prevalence in a specified area to a level at which transmission does not occur
(d) Reduction in the incidence of infectious disease where no cases occur, although the infectious agent may be allowed to persist

296. In elimination incidence of disease becomes
(a) Below the level achieved by control
(b) Very few case may occur
(c) None of the case occurs
(d) All of the above

297. Which of the following is list A disease
(a) Himonchosis (b) Rinderpest
(c) Ring worm (d) Amphistomosis

298. Horizontal epidemiology may be same as
(a) Landscape epidemiology
(b) Computational Epidemiology
(c) Clinical Epidemiology
(d) Experimental Epidemiology

299. Which of the following is quantitative data?
(a) Discrete data (b) Continuous data
(c) Both (d) None

300. Transmission of diseases may take place with the help of transmission factors in case of
(a) Aerosol transmission
(b) Contact transmission
(c) Vector transmission
(d) Ingestion

301. Convalescent carriers are animals which transmit disease during
(a) Incubation period
(b) Clinical disease
(c) Recovery
(d) Latent phase of infection

302. Which one may be intrinsic determinant of any disease?
(a) Calcium metabolism
(b) Virus
(c) Climate
(d) Anaplasma

303. One of the important characterstics of Evan's postulates is that the hypothesized causal factor should be
(a) Statistically insignificant
(b) Statistically significant
(c) Non-statistically associated
(d) Non-statistically variable

304. In a cohort study we compare
(a) Hypothesized causal factors with health related factors in a specified population
(b) A group of diseased animals with a group of healthy animals in relation to hypothesized causal factor
(c) A group of animals exposed to casual factors with respect to development of a disease
(d) None of the above

305. In Epizootiological studies proportions and rates are expressed in
(a) Crude farms
(b) Specific farms

(c) Adjusted farms
(d) All of the above farms

306. Contagious pustular stomatitis is the name given to
(a) Swine pox (b) Horse pox
(c) Goat pox (d) Sheep pox

307. Jenner's horse pox is
(a) Leg form of pox
(b) Flank form of pox
(c) Pox C lesions on mane & tail
(d) None

308. In case of Jenner's horse pox lesions appear on
(a) Backs portion of hock
(b) Back portion of pastern
(c) Back portion of elbow
(d) Back portion of knee

309. For Horse pox
(a) Young animals are more susceptible
(b) Older animals are more susceptible
(c) Both are equally susceptible
(d) No relation with age

310. Milker's nodules are formed due to
(a) Parapox virus (b) Swine pox virus
(c) Orthopox virus (d) Capripox virus

311. Course of pseudo cow pox is about
(a) 21 hours (b) 21 days
(c) 21 weeks (d) 21 months

312. Capri pox virus is a
(a) DNA virus (b) RNA virus
(c) Both (d) None

313. For sheep pox
(a) Younger sheep are more susceptible over older
(b) Marine breeds are more prone than indigenous breeds
(c) Both and correct
(d) Both are wrong

314. Transmission of sheep pox may occur through
(a) Direct contact
(b) Droplet infection
(c) Through placental blood
(d) All

315. In sheep pox ovination is a method of
(a) Immunization (b) Treatment
(c) Control (d) Diagnosis

316. Ring sore is the name given to
(a) Pseudocowpox (b) Cowpox
(c) Swine pox (d) Horse pox

317. Ring sore is a lesion which is
(a) a chromic purulent vesicle
(b) Scab falling off leaving a small horse shoe shaped ring like lesion
(c) Circular lesion with pus in it
(d) None of the above

318. Udder impetigo is caused by infection of
(a) *Staphylococcus auereus*
(b) *Streptococcus bovis*
(c) *Borellia spp.*
(d) *Yersinia spp.*

319. Bovine ulcerative mammillitis is caused by
(a) Bacterial infection
(b) Parapox virus
(c) Ricketlseal infection
(d) Herpes virus

320. Inc case of swine fever abortion & still birth of pregnant sows occur in
(a) Acute form of disease
(b) Chronic form
(c) Both
(d) None

321. Swine fever is caused by
(a) Pantropic RNA virus - Toga virus
(b) Pantropic DNA virus - Toga virus
(c) Epethiliotropic DNA virus - Toga virus
(d) Epethiliotropic RNA virus - Toga virus

322. For toga virus causing Hog cholera there are
(a) Many antigenic type but only one strain
(b) Many strains but only one antigenic type
(c) Only 1 antigenic type & 1 strain
(d) Many antigenic types & strains

323. Swine fever virus shows strong correlation with
(a) *Staphyllococus*
(b) *Streptococcus*
(c) *Salmonella choleraesuis*
(d) All

324. Swine fiver virus can be propagated most suitably in
(a) Suckling white mice

(b) Chick embryo
(c) Both
(d) None

325. Swine fever virus can be transmitted through
(a) Larvae of lung worm
(b) Blood protozoa
(c) Arthropods
(d) *Gigantocotyle explanatum*

326. Biphasic temperature, diarrhoea & death are characteristic feature of
(a) Swine pox (b) Swine erysipelas
(c) Swine fever (d) All

327. Turkey egg appearance of kidney due to petechiae in cortex is characteristic feature of
(a) Swine pox (b) Swine erysipelas
(c) Swine fever (d) All

328. Button ulcer appearance in caecum & colon occur in
(a) Swine pox (b) Swine erysipelas
(c) Swine fever (d) All

329. In case of swine fever, following type of inclusion bodies may be observed in reticular cells of lymph nodes, spleen & other organs
(a) Acidophilic intra cytoplasmic inclusion bodies
(b) Acidophilic intra nuclear inclusion bodies
(c) Basophilic intra nuclear inclusion bodies
(d) Basophilic intra cytoplasmic inclusion bodies

330. Mulberry heart disease mostly affects
(a) Weak and emaciated pigs
(b) Piglets
(c) Best, healthy pigs
(d) Pregnant sows

331. In cause of Aujesky's disease, nervous manifestations occurs in
(a) Young suckling piglets
(b) Pregnant sows
(c) Pigs > 5 years of age
(d) Pigs of all ages

332. In cases of salt poisoning ———— estimation of brain is most useful aid of diagnosis
(a) Sodium (b) Chloride
(c) Potessium (d) All of the above

333. Vesicular stomatitis now occurs in
(a) Only in week animals
(b) Cloven footed animals
(c) Both a & b
(d) All kind of animals

334. Number of antigenic strains of Vesicular exanthema virus
(a) 3 (b) 13
(c) 33 (d) 100

335. Vesicular exanthema occurs mostly in
(a) Piglets
(b) Pregnant sows
(c) Pigs < 5 years of age
(d) Pigs of all ages

336. Vesicular exanthema can be produced through which route of inoculation of infected viscera or muscle
(a) Dermal (b) Intramuscular
(c) Both (d) None

337. Wart hog disease is the name given to
(a) Hog cholera
(b) Swine fever
(c) African swine fever
(d) Vesicular exanthema

338. African swine fever is caused by virus belonging to
(a) Calci virus ssp. (b) Toga virus ssp.
(c) Irido virus ssp. (d) Pox virus ssp.

339. African swine fever virus remains attached with
(a) RBC (b) WBC
(c) Platelets (d) Lymphocytes

340. African swine fever virus can be transmitted through
(a) *Orthodorus moubata*
(b) *Hematopinus suis*
(c) Indirect contact
(d) All

341. Renal hemorrhages are characteristics of
(a) Swine pox
(b) Hog cholera
(c) African swine fever
(d) Swine fever

342. When cell cultures consisting of bone marrow Leucocytes are inoculated with blood suspected

for Africa swine fever
(a) Virus infects Lymphocytes then adsorbs with RBC
(b) Virus infects macrophages then adsorbs with RBC
(c) Virus infects RBC then adsorbs with Lymphocytes
(d) Virus infects RBC then adsorbs with macrophages

343. Corona virus infection in pigs causes
(a) Swine fever
(b) Hog cholera
(c) Transmissible gastroenteritis
(d) None

344. Which of the following virus does not affect any laboratory animal
(a) Calci virus (b) Toga virus
(c) Corona virus (d) Piconia virus

345. Dehydrated carcass with presence of curdled milk in milk veins are characteristics of
(a) Parasitic gastroenteritis
(b) Transmissible gastroenteritis
(c) Bacterial gastroenteritis
(d) Viral gastroenteritis

346. Japanese encephalitis is caused by
(a) Arbo virus of Type B
(b) Flavi virus
(c) Virus of sub group Togaviridae
(d) All of the above

347. Which of the following is a zoonotic disease?
(a) Swine fever
(b) Vesicular stomatitis
(c) Japanese encephalitis
(d) None

348. Natural reservoir of Japanese encephalitis virus is
(a) Arthropods
(b) Snails
(c) Swamp dwelling birds
(d) All

349. Amplifier host for Japanese encephalitis are
(a) Pig (b) Horse
(c) Cattle (d) Dog

350. Presence of focal & punched out areas of necrosis in grey matter are characteristics of
(a) Swine fever
(b) Swine pox
(c) Rabies
(d) Japanese encephalitis

351. Contagious ecthyma of sheep & goat is known as
(a) Orf (b) Sore mouth
(c) Scabby mouth (d) All

352. Contagious ecthyma of sheep & goat occurs due to
(a) Parapox virus (b) Orthopox virus
(c) Flavi virus (d) Calci virus

353. Contagious pustular disease virus is antigenically related to
(a) Sheep pox (b) Goat pox
(c) Cow pox (d) Swine pox

354. Virus causing contagious ecthyma of sheep is
(a) Epethiliotropic (b) Pantropic
(c) Nemotropic (d) None

355. Ballooning degeneration of cells of rate-malphigii & infiltration with polymorph nuclear cells occurs in
(a) Japanese encephalitis
(b) Contagious ecthyma
(c) Rabies
(d) Trypanosomosis

356. Maedi disease of sheep is called by
(a) Pulmonary adenomatosis
(b) Driving disease
(c) Both
(d) None

357. Maedi & Visna is not
(a) Synonyms
(b) Antigenicaly different
(c) Closely related
(d) Occur differently

358. Jaagsiekte devotes
(a) Pulmonary adenomatosis
(b) Driving disease
(c) Both
(d) None

359. Pulmonary adenomatosis mostly occurs in
(a) Younger age group animals
(b) Infants
(c) Older age group animals
(d) Animals of all ages

360. Incubation period of pulmonary adenomatosis ranges from
(a) 1-3 days (b) 1-3 months
(c) 1-3 wks (d) 1-3 years

361. Equine viral rhinopneumonitis is caused by
(a) Equine Herpes virus -1
(b) EHV-2
(c) Calci virus
(d) Flavi virus

362. Equine Herpes virus 1 shows antigenic relationship with .
(a) Human Herpes simplex virus
(b) Pseudo rabies virus
(c) Both
(d) None

363. Abortion storm in mares may occur due to
(a) Japanese encephatitis virus
(b) Equine viral arteitis virus
(c) Equine viral Rhinopneunonitis virus
(d) All

364. Hard pad disease is the name given to
(a) Canine parvo virus infection
(b) Canine rabies
(c) ICH
(d) Canine distemper

365. Canine distemper is
(a) RNA virus of para myxo group
(b) RNA virus of ortho myxo group
(c) DNA virus of ortho myxo group
(d) DNA virus of para myxo group

366. Canine distemper virus is closely related to
(a) Pox virus (b) Exanthema virus
(c) Measles virus (d) All

367. Rinderpest virus shows relationship with
(a) Rabies virus
(b) Pseudo rabies virus
(c) Canine distemper virus
(d) ICH virus

368. Canine distemper is a
(a) Air borne disease
(b) Water borne disease
(c) Feed borne disease
(d) All of the above

369. Canine distemper virus is
(a) Epetheliotropic (b) Mesotheliotropic
(c) Pantropic (d) Neurotropic

370. Characteristics disphasic temperature reaction is seen in
(a) Trypanosomes (b) Babesiosis
(c) Canine distemper (d) ICH

371. A coryza like syndrome characterized by occulonasal discharge, pharyngitis & bronchitis are seen in
(a) Equine viral pneumonia
(b) Pseudo rabies
(c) Pulmonary adenomatosis
(d) Canine distemper

372. Which of the following vaccine is used to prevent canine distemper?
(a) Pox virus vaccine
(b) ICH vaccine
(c) Measles virus vaccine
(d) All of the above

373. Rubarth's disease is the name given to
(a) Rabies (b) Pseudo rabies
(c) Canine distemper (d) ICH

374. Infectious canine hepatitis is also known as
(a) Contagious hepatitis
(b) Fox encephalitis
(c) Rubarth's disease
(d) All

375. ICH is caused by
(a) Adeno virus (b) Herpes virus
(c) Calci virus (d) Flavi virus

376. ICH virus has affinity for
(a) Epithelial cells (b) Mesothelial cells
(c) Hepatic cells (d) All

377. Which of the following is not transmitted through droplets?
(a) Pulmonary adenomatosis
(b) Canine distemper
(c) Equine viral peumonitis
(d) ICH

378. Saddle shaped temp curve is characteristics of
(a) Canine distemper (b) ICH
(c) Rabies (d) Pseudo rabies

379. ICH most commonly occurs in
(a) Acute form (b) Per acute form

(c) inapparent form (d) Chronic form

380. Rabies is also known as
(a) Lyssa (b) Tollwat
(c) Mad dog (d) All

381. Rabies is caused by
(a) RNA virus
(b) Few virus of family Rhabdoviridae
(c) Lyssa virus
(d) All

382. Rabies virus is
(a) Epetheliotrpic (b) Pantopic
(c) Neuroptropic (d) Mesotropic

383. Fixed virus is prepared by
(a) Serial intra spinal passage in laboratory animals
(b) Serial intra cranial passage in laboratory animals
(c) Serial intra CSF passage in laboratory animals
(d) None

384. In fixed virus of rabies infection, there is
(a) Short incubation period
(b) Absence of Negri's bodies
(c) Absence of virus in salivary glands
(d) All are corrects

385. Incubation period of fixed virus of rabies is about
(a) 11-47 days (b) 6-7 days
(c) 13-14 days (d) 9 weeks

386. Which of the viruses is used for rabies vaccine preparations?
(a) Street virus (b) Fixed virus
(c) Both (d) None

387. Which of the following is incorrect about fixed virus?
(a) Has short incubation period
(b) Does not produces negri's bodies
(c) Absence of affinity for salivary glands
(d) It is not self limiting

388. Incubation period of street virus under laboratory conditions is about
(a) 11-47 days (b) 6-7 days
(c) 13-14 days (d) 9 wks

389. Street virus is
(a) Always self limiting
(b) Not self limiting
(c) May be self limiting
(d) May or may not be self limiting

390. Rabies mostly occurs in
(a) Young dogs
(b) Older dogs
(c) Dogs < 5 years of age
(d) No relation with age

391. Which of the following is considered as dead end host for rabies of virus?
(a) Cattle (b) Horse
(c) Both (d) None

392. A bite by rabid animal on the face of animal has a contagion index of
(a) 2% (b) 10%
(c) 15% (d) 100%

393. A bite on body or leg by rabid animal has contagion index of
(a) 1% (b) 2%
(c) 10% (d) 100%

394. Rabies virus is excreted in saliva at about
(a) 3-8 days after manifestation of clinical symptoms
(b) 3-8 days before manifestation of clinical symptoms
(c) Same day of manifestation of clinical symptoms
(d) No relation with manifestation of clinical symptoms

395. Incubation period of rabies virus is
(a) Shorter in younger animals
(b) Shorter in older animals
(c) No relation with age
(d) Equal in both

396. Stage of melancholy occurs in which form of rabies?
(a) Furious form (b) Dumb form
(c) Acute form (d) Chronic form

397. Which form of rabies is also known as paralytic form?
(a) Furious form (b) Dumb form
(c) acute form (d) Chronic form

398. Rabies in cat is
(a) More furious than in dog

(b) Less furious than in dog
(c) Equally furious to dog
(d) Not furious

399. Paralysis of muscles with excessive salivation & grinding of teeth occurs in cattle in
(a) Rabies (b) Pseudo rabies
(c) Babesiosis (d) FMD

400. For the first time on the basis of histological studies rabies was diagnosed by observing
(a) Negri's bodies
(b) Babe's nodules
(c) Mouse inoculation test
(d) CFT

401. Negri's bodies in rabies are found in
(a) Gasserian ganglion
(b) Hippocampus
(c) Medulla oblangata
(d) All

402. In a dog died, suspected of rabies which part of body should be sent for lab investigations
(a) Heart (b) Liver
(c) Brain (d) Spinal cord

403. Absence of Negri's bodies in brain cells indicates
(a) Presence of rabies
(b) Absence of rabies
(c) Rabies may be preent or absent
(d) No indication

404. For detection of Negri's bodies, impression smears of brain should be stained with
(a) Leishmain's stain (b) Wright's stain
(c) Seller's stain (d) Any alcoholic stain

405. What is the concentration of the suspension used for mouse inoculation test for rabies?
(a) 1% (b) 0.1%
(c) 5% (d) 0.05%

406. Most reliable & rapid test for diagnosis of rabies is
(a) Mouse inoculation test
(b) ELISA
(c) Immunoperoxidase test
(d) FAT

407. For a dog of body weight less than 15 kg, post bite treatment should be
(a) 2ml daily x 1 week
(b) 1 ml daily x 2 week
(c) 2 ml daily x 2 week
(d) 1 ml on 0,3,7,14,28 & 90 days

408. Smallest known DNA virus infecting dogs is
(a) Corona virus (b) Parvo virus
(c) Calci virus (d) Flavi virus

409. Why young dogs in the process of growth are specially victimized with parvo virus infection
(a) Because young dogs are given good nutrition
(b) Because young dogs have less immunity
(c) Because young dogs are healthy
(d) Virus multiplies in cells which are undergoing multiplication

410. What are the causes of failure of active immunization with parvo virus infection?
(a) Presence of natural infection
(b) Maternal antibodies which hinder the immunization
(c) Both
(d) None

411. When parvo virus infection occurs
(a) Ist IgM is produced then IgG
(b) Ist IgG is produed them IgM
(c) Both are produced at the same time
(d) Both are never produced

412. Parvo virus has got affinity for
(a) Macrophages (b) Monocytes
(c) Lymphocytes (d) All

413. Parvo virus infection in dogs leads to
(a) Enteritis (b) Myocarditis
(c) Both (d) None

414. Feline Panleucopenia is the name given to
(a) Feline infectious enteritis
(b) Feline distemper
(c) Cat plague
(d) all

415. Cat plague virus is antigenically identical to
(a) Human pox virus
(b) Human measles virus
(c) Rinderpest virus
(d) Mink enteritis virus

416. Which of the following is a synonym for anthrax?
(a) Spleenic fever

(b) Charbon
(c) Wool sorter's disease
(d) All

417. Carcass should never be opened in a suspected case of
(a) Anthrax (b) Salmonellosis
(c) Tuberculosis (d) JD

418. Spores of *Bacillus anthracis* may remain viable in infected tissue for
(a) 10 days (b) 10 weeks
(c) 10 months (d) 10 years

419. Medusa head colonies are produced by
(a) Rough form of *Bacillus anthracis*
(b) Smooth form of *Bacillus anthracis*
(c) Both form of *Bacillus anthacis*
(d) None

420. Factor I toxin of *Bacillus anthracis* denotes
(a) Edema toxin (b) Protecting Antigen
(c) Lethal factor (d) None

421. Factor II toxin of *Bacillus anthracis* denotes
(a) Edema toxin (b) Protecting Antigen
(c) Lethal factor (d) None

422. Factor III toxin of *Bacillus anthracis* denotes
(a) Edema toxin (b) Protecting Antigen
(c) Lethal factor (d) None

423. Vegetative form of *Bacillus athracis* can be killed by heating at
(a) 60° C for30 minutes
(b) 30° C for 30 minutes
(c) 60° C for 1 hour
(d) 30°for 1 hour

424. Animals most susceptible for anthrax are
(a) Cattle & sheep
(b) Horse & pig
(c) Dog & cat
(d) All animals are equally susceptible

425. Which form of anthrax predominantly occurs in cattle & buffalo
(a) Acute form (b) Per acute form
(c) Sub acute form (d) Chronic form

426. Anthrax can be characterized by
(a) Spleenomegaly
(b) Oozing out of blood from all the natural orifices
(c) Absence of rigor mortis
(d) All

427. Which of the following active agent is found in snake venom
(a) Haemolytic factor (b) Cardiotoxin
(c) Coagulating factor (d) All of the above

428. Acute Leptospirosis is characterized by
(a) Oliguria (b) Proteinuria
(c) Hemoglobunuria (d) All

429. Sterne vaccine for anthrax is a
(a) Avirulent spore vaccine
(b) Virulent spore vaccine
(c) Virulent vegetative vaccine
(d) Avirulent vegetative vaccine

430. Which of the following vaccines is used against Anthrax?
(a) Sterne vaccine (b) Pastur vaccine
(c) Spore vaccine (d) All

431. Hemorrhagic septicemia is also known as
(a) Stockyard disease (b) Shipping fever
(c) barbone disease (d) All

432. Hemorrhagic septicemia is caused by
(a) *Pasteurella multocida* type I organism
(b) *Pasteurella multocida* type II organism
(c) *Pasteurella multocida* type III organism
(d) *Pasteurella multocida* type IV organism

433. *Pasteurella multocida* doese not produce
(a) Exotoxin (b) Endotoxin
(c) Both (d) Any toxin

434. Most affected age group of cattle by *Pasteurella multocida* is
(a) 6 years (b) < 6 months
(c) 6 months - 2 years (d) > 2 years

435. *Pasteurella multocida* can not invade lung due to
(a) Pulmonary defense mechanism
(b) Cilia in trachea
(c) It's anaerobic nature
(d) All of the above

436. Death in Hemorrhagic septicemia occurs due to
(a) Hypoxia (b) Toxemia
(c) Both (d) None

437. Incubation period of Hemorrhagic septicemia in cattle & buffalo is
(a) 2-5 days (b) 2-5 week

(c) 2-5 months (d) 2-5 years

438. In pigs pasteurellosis occurs usually secondary to
(a) Enzootic pneumonia virus
(b) Swine fever
(c) Swine erysipelas
(d) African swine fever

439. Which of the following usually remains as symptom less carrier of Hemorrhagic septicemia
(a) Cattle (b) Goat
(c) Pig (d) Dog

440. Non hemolytic dew drop like colonies are characteristic of
(a) *Bacillus anthracis*
(b) *Bordetella bronchoceptica*
(c) *Pasturella multocida*
(d) *Brucella abortus*

441. Brucellosis is also known as
(a) Bang's disease (b) Infectious abortion
(c) Enzootic abortion (d) All

442. Brucellosis in cattle & buffalo is usually due to
(a) *B. abortus* (b) *B. melitenis*
(c) *B. suis* (d) *B. ovis*

443. No of biotypes recorded in bovine brucellosis is
(a) 6 (b) 7
(c) 8 (d) 9

444. Precursor from which all biotypes of Brucella organism in cattle have evolved is
(a) *Burcella abortus* type I
(b) *Burcella abortus* type II
(c) *Burcella abortus* type III
(d) *Burcella abortus* type IV

445. Brucella organisms are
(a) Aerobic but may required added CO_2 for its growth
(b) Aerobic & may never require added CO_2 for its growth
(c) Anaerobic & may never required added CO_2 for its growth
(d) Anaerobic but may added CO_2 for its growth

446. Which of the following Brucella never requires CO_2 for its growth?
(a) *B. abortus* (b) *B. suis*
(c) *B. melitancis* (d) *B. ovis*

447. *B. abortus* is communicable from
(a) Cattle to sheep (b) Sheep to cattle
(c) Sheep to sheep (d) All

448. *B. abortus* can survive for about
(a) 30 days in manure
(b) 60 days in manure
(c) 120 days in manure
(d) Infinite days in manure

449. *B. abortus* can survive for about
(a) 60 days in foetal tissues
(b) 120 days in foetal tissues
(c) 180 days in foetal tissues
(d) Infinite period foetal tissues

450. Susceptibility of cattle to *Brucella abortus* is
(a) Less before sexual maturity
(b) More before sexual maturity
(c) Absent before sexual maturity
(d) Equal before & after sexual maturity

451. Brucella infection leads to fistulous wither when it is in association with
(a) *Streptococcus felcalis*
(b) *Actinomycies bovis*
(c) *Yeirsenia spp.*
(d) *Staphylococcus aureous*

452. Best & most common mode of transmission of Brucella infection is
(a) Ingestion (b) Inhalation
(c) Droplet (d) Transplacental

453. Experimental transmission of Brucella is possible by deposition of organism in susceptible host
(a) S/C route
(b) I/M route
(c) Intra mammary route
(d) I/P

454. Deposition of Brucella in which organ/can never produce infection
(a) Uterus (b) Vagina
(c) Muscle (d) Subcutaneous tissue

455. *B. abortus* has affinity to invade
(a) Lymphnodis (b) Joints
(c) Testes (d) All

456. *B. abortus* shows great affinity towards foetus due to the production of
(a) Erythritol (b) Phenol

(c) Kalikrein (d) All

457. Abortion due to Brucclla occur in
(a) 1st trimester of pregnancy
(b) Mid trimester of pregnancy
(c) Advance stage of pregnancy
(d) Any trimester of pregnancy

458. Retention of foetal membranes is a characteristic of abortions caused by
(a) Brucculloıs (b) Listeriosis
(c) Leptospirosis (d) All

459. Animal of choice for pathogenicity test of Brucella is
(a) Guinea pig (b) Rabbit
(c) Mice (d) Hamster

460. Which test is used for screening of heard for Brucellosis?
(a) Milk ring test
(b) CFT
(c) Rose Bengal plate test
(d) All

461. Rose Bengal plate test is type of
(a) Agglutination (b) Precipitation
(c) Oxidation (d) Reduction

462. False negative reaction in Rose Bengal plate may occur due to
(a) Early incubation of disease
(b) Immediately after abortion
(c) Both
(d) none

463. Which immunoglobulin are produced in response to S_{19} vaccination of Brucellosis
(a) Ig G1 (b) Ig G2
(c) Ig M (d) All

464. Which of the following may be a cause of false positive reaction in Rose Bengal plate test?
(a) Early incubation of disease
(b) Immodeficiency after abortion
(c) Cross reactivity with vaccine IgM
(d) All of the above

465. Which test can differentiate antibodies of S_{19} vaccinated animals & infected animals with Brucella
(a) ELISA (b) FAT
(c) CFT (d) Immunoperoxidase

466. Which stained is used with suspension of killed *B. abortus* antigen for detection of antibodies in milk
(a) Hematoxylin (b) Eosine
(c) Negrosin (d) Haymistain

467. The cotyledons appear yellowish brown in case of abortion due to
(a) Leptospira (b) Listeria
(c) Trichomonas (b) Brucella

468. Abortion caused by *Trichomonas fetus* occurs at about
(a) 6 months of gestation
(b) 2-4 months of gestation
(c) Later half of gestation
(d) Any time

469. Abortions caused by *Campylobactor foetus* occurs at about
(a) 2-4 months of gestation
(b) 5-6 months of gestation
(c) First 2 months of gestation
(d) Last 2 months of gestation

470. Placenta shows pin point haemorrhage, edema & plague in case of abortion due to
(a) Listeriosis (b) Leptospirosis
(c) Brucellosis (d) Vibriosis

471. Placenta shows necrosis at intercotyledonary areas and leathery appearance of placenta in case of abortions due to
(a) Mycotic abortions
(b) Bacterial abortions
(c) Viral abortions
(d) Parasitic abortions

472. Tuberculosis is also known as
(a) Pearl's disease (b) Pthisis
(c) Scrofula (d) All

473. Tuberculosis occur in India as
(a) Endemic (b) Pandemic
(c) Epidemic (d) Sporadic

474. Vole bacillus type of Mycobacterium affects
(a) Animals (b) Birds
(c) Man (d) Marines

475. TB in horse is caused mainly by
(a) *M. bovis* (b) *M. tuberculosis*
(c) *M. avium* (d) None

476. Acid fast character of mycobacterium is due to

(a) Mycolic acid (b) Succinic acid
(c) Glycine (d) Aspartate

477. Dorset's egg media is a selective media for
(a) Succinic acid (b) Streptococcus
(c) Mycobacterium (d) Brucella

478. Which domestic animal is most susceptible for TB
(a) Cattle (b) Buffalo
(c) Horse (d) Dog

479. Most pathogenic strain of mycobacterium is
(a) *M. tuberculosis* (b) *M. canis*
(c) *M. bovis* (d) *M. avium*

480. Incidence of TB is lesser in
(a) Pure bred cattle (b) Cross bred cattle
(c) Zebu cattle (d) None

481. Which of the statement is incorrect about TB?
(a) Young age group animals are less susceptible
(b) Young age group human are more susceptible
(c) Malnourished animal and human are more susceptible
(d) None of the above

482. Johne's disease is the name given to
(a) Chronic specific enteritis of cattle
(b) Chronic bacillary dysentery
(c) Paratuberculosis
(d) All

483. A specific growth factor called mycobactin is required for growing this organism on artificial media
(a) *Mycobacterium tuberculosis*
(b) *M. paratuberculosis*
(c) *M. bovis*
(d) *M. avium*

484. Which stain is used to demonstrate M. paratuberculosis organism in tissue sections
(a) Eosin (b) Nigrosin
(c) Hematoxylin (d) Z-N stain

485. Which age group of animal is most susceptible for Jonhe's disease?
(a) > 2 months (b) < 1 months
(c) > 2 years (d) < 2years

486. For Johne's disease
(a) High yielding dairy cattle are more susceptible
(b) Low yielding dairy cattle are more susceptible
(c) Dry dairy cattle are more susceptible
(d) All dairy cattle equally susceptible

487. In John's disease plasma leakage into GIT leads to how much % of total nitrogen loss compared to 2-3% in normal cattle?
(a) 2-3% (b) 11-21%
(c) 21-31% (d) 94%

488. The most cardinal sign of Johnes' disease is
(a) Diarrhoea (b) Vomition
(c) Straggling gait (d) Anorexia

489. Loose skin in intermandibular space, dewlap & brisket simulating edema is characteristic of
(a) TB (b) Paratuberculosis
(c) Fasciolosis (d) None

490. Corrugated thickening of the intestinal wall occurs in
(a) Johne's disease
(b) Parasitic gastroenteritis in pig
(d) All

491. By which route Johnin test is more accurate
(a) IM (b) IV
(c) I/Dermal (d) I/conjunctival

492. Which media is specific for culture of *M. paratuberculosis?*
(a) Dorset egg media
(b) Blood agar
(c) Harold's egg yolk media
(d) SM-110

493. False positive cases in Johnin test may appear because of
(a) Cross reactivity with mammalian tuberculin
(b) Resistance to with *M. paratuberculosis*
(c) Both
(d) None

494. False negative reaction in Johnin test occur due to
(a) Terminal stage of disease
(b) Tolerance
(c) Antigen matching factors
(d) All

495. Which of the following Infectious is named as stuff gart disease
(a) Brucellosis (b) Leptospirosis
(c) Listeriosis (d) Borelliasis

496. Leptospirosis is also known as
(a) Rice field worker's disease
(b) Canine typhus
(c) sugar cane worker's disease
(d) All

497. Most common bacterial infection in swine handlers is
(a) Brucella (b) Listeria
(c) Leptospira (d) Staphylococcus

498. Transmission of Leptospirosis occurs
(a) Direct contact with infected faces
(b) Direct contact with infected urine
(c) Direct contact with infected sputum
(d) Direct contact with infected blood

499. If the feed & water of a herd are grossly contaminated with urine of another herd showing symptoms of anaemia, Haemoglobinurea & jaundice the most probable bacterial infection to occur is
(a) Listeriosis (b) Leptospirosis
(c) Borelliosis (d) Brucellosis

500. Hemolytic & cytotoxic reaction of Leptospirosis is due to the release of
(a) Lipase (b) Amylase
(c) Proline (d) Lysine

501. Most characteristic lesions of Leptospirosis are seen in
(a) Liver (b) Kidney
(c) Heart (d) Gall bladder

502. Mastitis with yellow clotted milk followed by agalactia persisting for a few days to weeks with no swelling of udder is known as
(a) Hot mastitis (b) Cold mastitis
(c) True mastitis (d) False mastitis

503. Carcass showing jaundice & multiple widespread haemorrhagic spots below mucus & serous membrane indicates
(a) Listeriosis (b) Leptospirosis
(c) Staphylococcusi (d) None

504. Listeriosis is also known as
(a) Circling disease
(b) Meningoencephalitis
(c) Silage disease
(d) All

505. Most common infection transmitted through silage is
(a) Listeriosis (b) Leptosprosis
(c) Borelliosis (d) Yersiniosis

506. Unilateral facial paralysis with drooling of saliva occurs in
(a) Listeriosis (b) Leptospirosis
(c) Borelliosis (d) Yersiniosis

507. Abortion in bitch showing partially opened cervix & brown vulvar discharge is charge of
(a) Listeriosis (b) Leptospirosis
(c) Borelliosis (d) Yersiniosis

508. Listerial abortion is rare feature in
(a) Cow (b) Sow
(c) Sheep (d) Goat

509. CSF shows cloudiness due to presence of excess globulin & leukocytes in
(a) Cow (b) Sow
(c) Sheep (d) Goat

510. Colibacillosis is known as
(a) Calf scour
(b) White diarrhoea
(c) Septicemia of calves
(d) All

511. *E. coli* shows
(a) Enterotoxic effect
(b) Enterotoxaemic effect
(c) Septicemic effect
(d) All

512. Virulent strain of *E. coli* in pigs is
(a) K^{88+} (b) K^{99+}
(c) Both (d) None

513. Virulent strain of *E. coli* in calf is
(a) K^{99+} (b) K^{88+}
(c) Both (d) None

514. Heat labile toxin of *E. coli* is activated by
(a) Adenylate cyclase (b) Guanylate cyclase
(c) Butylate cyclase (d) None

515. Heat stable toxin of *E. coli* is activated by
(a) Adenylate cyclase (b) Guanylate cyclase
(c) Butylate cyclase (d) None

516. Duration of action of LT toxin of *E. coli* is
(a) Longer than ST (b) Shorter then ST
(c) Equal to ST (d) Variable

517. Onset of action of ST toxin of *E. coli* is
(a) Delayed (b) Very slow
(c) Relatively quick (d) None

518. Colibacillosis mostly occurs in calves of age
(a) 12 hours - 14 days (b) 12 weeks-14 weeks
(c) 12 days - 14 days (d) 12 months

519. *E. coli* endotoxin produces
(a) Hypoglycemia (b) Lactic acidosis
(c) Both (d) Hyperglycemia

520. Characteristic colour of faeces varying from yellowish brown to grayish white occurs in calves in
(a) Parvo virus infection
(b) Colibacillosis
(c) Parasitism
(d) None

521. Salmonella causes
(a) Typhoid (b) Paratyphoid
(c) Typhus (d) All

522. Lumpy jaw occurs due to
(a) *Actinomyces bovis*
(b) *Actinobacillus ligneresi*
(c) *Streptococcus aureus*
(d) All

523. Rarefying osteomyelitis of bone of skull occurs in cattle by
(a) *Actinomyces bovis*
(b) *Actinobacillus ligneresi*
(c) Japanese encephalitis
(d) Listeriosis

524. Involvement of bursa of ligamentum nuchae in Actinomycosis occurs in
(a) Cow (b) Dog
(c) Horse (d) Pig

525. Study of diseases especially on animal population is known as
(a) Epizootiology (b) Epidemiology
(c) Both (d) None

526. Occurrence of disease involving many continents & countries is
(a) Pandemic (b) Epidemic
(c) Endemic (d) Sporadic

527. Occurrence of disease in a large area but limited in one country is
(a) Pandemic (b) Epidemic
(c) Endemic (d) Sporadic

528. Occurrence of disease with expected frequency is
(a) Pandemic (b) Epidemic
(c) Endemic (d) Sporadic

529. Disease which has come from other country is
(a) Epidemic (b) Exotic
(c) Exzootic (d) Pandemic

530. Any disease which has been removed from a country completely is
(a) Epidemic (b) Exotic
(c) Exzootic (d) Pandemic

531. When the disease has been removed but the causal agent may still present in a country, it is called
(a) Eradication (b) Elimination
(c) Removal (d) Controlled

532. Data base is defined as
(a) Base on which data is collected
(b) Structured collection of data
(c) Both
(d) none

533. Study based on past records is termed as
(a) Perspective study (b) Retrospective study
(c) Record study (d) All

534. Study in which one group is exposed to the hypothetic cause & then the presence or absence of disease in two groups is studied is
(a) Case control study
(b) Cohort study
(c) Prospective study
(d) Retrospective study

535. Survey conducted on a particular point of time (date) is
(a) Cross sectional survey
(b) Longitudinal survey
(c) Case control survey
(d) Cohort survey

536. Survey conducted over a period of time
(a) Cross sectional survey
(b) Longitudinal survey
(c) Case control survey
(d) Cohort survey

537. If there is constant interval between two successive variables it is known as
(a) Continuous variable
(b) Discrete variable
(c) Distinct variable
(d) Correlated variables

538. If there is continuous variation between two successive variables it is known as
(a) Continuous variable
(b) Disecrete variable
(c) Distinct variable
(d) Correlated variables

539. Graph plotted between numbers of new cases against time is
(a) Endemic curve (b) Incidence curve
(c) Prevalence curve (d) Epidemic curve

540. Number of new cases that occur over a specific period of time is
(a) Incidence (b) Prevalence
(c) Epidemics (d) Pandemics

541. Total numbers of cases occurring at a particular time
(a) Incidence (b) Prevalence
(c) Epidemics (d) Pandemic

542. Routine collection of information about the disease & associated factors
(a) Study (b) Survey
(c) Surveillance (d) Monitoring

543. Which of the following is not a component of epidemiology
(a) Data collection (b) Data analysis
(c) Information (d) Conclusion

544. Ecology of a disease includes
(a) Distribution of disease
(b) Mode of transmission of disease
(c) Maintenance of disease
(d) All of the above

545. When we study the presence or absence of the hypothetic cause in diseased & non diseased groups, it is
(a) Case control study
(b) Cohort study
(c) Cross sectional study
(d) Perspective study

546. Case control study is a
(a) Perspective study
(b) Retrospective study
(c) Both
(d) Cross sectional study

547. Cohort study is a
(a) Prospective study
(b) Retrospective study
(c) Both
(d) Cross sectional study

548. Which of the following is not an observational study?
(a) Cohort (b) Case control
(c) Cross sectional (d) Experimental

549. Which the following is observational study
(a) Cohort (b) Case control
(c) Cross sectional (d) All

550. Which of the following is not a quantitative study?
(a) Survey (b) Monitoring
(c) Surveillance (d) Causal hypothesis

551. Which of the following is a qualitative study?
(a) Survey (b) Monitoring
(c) Surveillance (d) Causal hypothesis

552. Ecosystem developed by nature is
(a) Autochthonous (b) Anthropurgic
(c) Synanthropic (d) All

553. Ecosystem developed by man is
(a) Autochthons (b) Anthropurgic
(c) Synanthropic (d) All

554. Ecosystem not made by man purposefully but made experimentally due to ignorance is
(a) Autochthons (b) Anthropurgic
(c) Synanthropic (d) All

555. Modified patch of vegetation developed by human
(a) Ecological interface
(b) Ecoloigcal mosaic
(c) Biocenosis
(d) Nosogenic territory

556. Predisposing factors helping the occurrence of disease are
(a) Primary determinants
(b) Secondary determinants
(c) Intrinsic determinants

(d) Extrinsic determinants

557. Intrinsic determinants are
(a) Factors Intrinsic to host
(b) Factors Intrinsic to causal agent
(c) Factors Intrinsic to environment
(d) Factors Intrinsic to Location

558. Gradient of infection comes under
(a) Host determinants
(b) Agent determinents
(c) Environment determinents
(d) Virulence determinants

559. Per acute disease establishes in
(a) First few hours (b) First few days
(c) Up to 2 weeks (d) More than 2 weeks

560. Acute disease establishes in
(a) First few hours (b) First few days
(c) Up to 2 weeks (d) More than 2 weeks

561. Sub acute disease establishes in
(a) Few hours
(b) Few hours - 2-4 days
(c) Up to 2 weeks
(d) More than 2 weeks

562. Chronic is disease establishes in
(a) Few hours
(b) Few hours - 2-4 days
(c) Up to 2 weeks
(d) More than 2 weeks

563. When large number of cases occur within a short period of time its
(a) Point epidemics
(b) Propagative epidemics
(c) Period epidemics
(d) Continuous epidemics

564. When large number of cases occur with the passage of time its is
(a) Point epidemics
(b) Propagative epidemics
(c) Period epidemics
(d) Continuous epidemics

565. Hyper endemic disease means
(a) Disease involves all species of animals
(b) Disease involves all breeds of a species
(c) Disease involves all age group of animals
(d) Disease involves all animals

566. Organism uses reservoir for its
(a) Maintainence (b) Multiplication
(c) Transmission (d) All

567. Inanimate transmitter of infection are called
(a) Fomites (b) Vectors
(c) Transmitters (d) All

568. When there is development of infectious agent in the vector, it is
(a) Developmental biological vector
(b) Propagative biological vector
(c) Cyclopropagative biological vector
(d) Transmitter biological vector

569. When there is multiplication of Infectious agent in the vector, it is
(a) Developmental biological vector
(b) Propagative biological vector
(c) Cyclopropagative biological vector
(d) Transmitter biological vector

570. When there is multiplication as well as development of infectious agent in the vector, it is
(a) Developmental biological vector
(b) Propagative biological vector
(c) Cyclopropagative biological vector
(d) Transmitter biological vector

571. Infectiousness of host refers to
(a) Susceptibility of host
(b) Virulence of organism in that host
(c) Duration of illness
(d) All of above

572. Period between entry of pathogen in host & appearance of 1st clinical signs is
(a) Incubation period (b) Generation period
(c) Prepatent period (d) None

573. Period between infection & maximum infectiousness in the host
(a) Incubation period
(b) Generation period
(c) Prepatent period
(d) Extensic incubation period

574. Entry of causal agent to the release of causal agent from host
(a) Incubation period
(b) Generation period
(c) Prepatent period
(d) Extensic incubation period

575. Period from entry of agent in host to availability of agent in arthropod vector
(a) Incubation period
(b) Generation period
(c) Prepatent period
(d) Extrinsic incubation period

576. Period from entry of agent in host to availability of agent in arthropod vector
(a) Eclipse period (b) Latent period
(c) Prepatent period (d) All above

577. Amount of organism required to initiate the process of infection is host is
(a) Infectivity (b) Stability
(c) Pathogenicity (d) Virulence

578. Period during which organism can remain stable & infective
(a) Infectivity (b) Stability
(c) Pathogenicity (d) Virulence

579. Which of the following is a strategy adopted by an organism to become resistant?
(a) Avoid coming in external environment
(b) Development of resistance form
(c) Rapidly in & rapidly out strategy
(d) All of above

580. Discrete values generate
(a) Counts (b) Measurement
(c) Both (d) None

581. Continuous values generate
(a) Counts (b) Measurement
(c) both (d) none

582. Which of the following scales is used to classify qualitative data into specific codes?
(a) Normal scale (b) Ordinal scale
(c) Interval scale (d) Ratio scale

583. Which of the following scales is used to compare one group of animals with other?
(a) Normal scale (b) Ordinal scale
(c) Interval scale (d) Ratio scale

584. Which of the following scales is used to calculate distance between the ranked values?
(a) Normal scale (b) Ordinal scale
(c) Interval scale (d) Ratio scale

585. A type of interval scale where initial value start with zero
(a) Normal scale (b) Ordinal scale
(c) Internal scale (d) Ratio scale

586. Which of the following is a classificatory scale?
(a) Normal scale (b) Ordinal scale
(c) Interval scale (d) Ratio scale

587. Which of the following is a ranking scale?
(a) Normal scale (b) Ordinal scale
(c) Interval scale (d) Ratio scale

588. Which of the following is simple & non invasive?
(a) Ordinal scale
(b) Visual analogue scale
(c) Both
(d) None

589. Degree of detail of data that being recorded is
(a) Accuracy (b) Refinement
(c) Sensitivity (d) Specificity

590. Term used statistically to indicate consistency of a series of measurements
(a) Refinement (b) Accuracy
(c) Precision (d) Reliability

591. Which of the following is not an advantage of case control study?
(a) Can be used for diseases where incidence is low
(b) Past records can be used
(c) No risk to the subjects
(d) Incidence of disease in exposed & unexposed populations can be calculated

592. Which of the following is not true for cross sectional study?
(a) Requires less time
(b) No risk to subjects
(c) Cost is less
(d) Suitable for rare diseases

593. Census is defined as survey conducted on
(a) Exposed population
(b) Unexposed population
(c) Whole of the population
(d) Sample of the population

594. Population of which information is required is
(a) Target population (b) Sample population
(c) Elementary unit (d) Primary unit

595. Which of the following is a variable?
(a) Sex (b) Age

(c) Species (d) None

596. Smallest unit of study population is
(a) Target unit (b) Sample unit
(c) Elementary unit (d) Primary unit

597. Group of elementary units classified according to specific character is
(a) Stratum (b) Sampling frame
(c) Sampling unit (d) Sampling fraction

598. Ratio of sample size to the study population is
(a) Stratum (b) Sampling frame
(c) Sampling unit (d) Sampling fraction

599. Each member of sampling frame is
(a) Stratum (b) Sampling frame
(c) Sampling unit (d) Sampling fraction

600. Sampling done as per the choice of the investigator is
(a) Non probability sampling
(b) Probability sampling
(c) Random sampling
(d) None

601. Sampling done as per the ideas, which are to be met
(a) convenience sampling
(b) purposive Sampling
(c) stratified Sampling
(d) Sampling fraction

602. When one sample is selected randomly & successive samples after fixed interval it is called
(a) Simple random sampling
(b) Stratified sampling
(c) Cluster sampling
(d) Systematic sampling

603. When first the categorization of animals is done on some criteria & then sampling is done from different groups, it is
(a) Simple random sampling
(b) Stratified sampling
(c) Cluster sampling
(d) Systematic sampling

604. When first categorization is done on the basis of geographical area & then sampling is done
(a) Simple random sampling
(b) Stratified sampling
(c) Cluster sampling
(d) Systematic sampling

605. When determinants are modified so that occurrence of disease is delayed it is known as
(a) Primary prevention
(b) Secondary prevention
(c) Tertiary prevention
(d) Specific prevention

606. When the disease is determined in the preclinical stage & treated immediately it is
(a) Primary prevention
(b) Secondary prevention
(c) Tertiary prevention
(d) Specific prevention

607. When disease is treated by giving lower doses of drugs for longer periods it is
(a) Primary prevention
(b) Secondary prevention
(c) Tertiary prevention
(d) Specific prevention

608. Relationship between resources that produce input & resources that comprise output is
(a) Production function
(b) Demand function
(c) Cost benefit analysis
(d) Supply function

609. Value of stream of discounted benefits less cost over time period is known as
(a) Net present value
(b) Cost benefit ratio
(c) Interval rate of return
(d) Internal benefit

610. Ratio of present value to benefits to that of cost is
(a) Net present value
(b) Cost benefit ratio
(c) Interval rate of return
(d) Internal benefit

611. Rate of discount that equates a present value of costs with the value of benefits is
(a) Net present value
(b) Cost benefit ratio
(c) Interval rate of return
(d) Internal benefit

612. Cost or benefit which directly add to the cost or benefit of the disease is
(a) Net present value
(b) Cost benefit ratio

(c) Interval rate of return
(d) Internal benefit

613. Communicable diseases which have potential for very serious & rapid spread irrespective of national boundaries are grouped under
(a) List A (b) List B
(c) List C (d) List D

614. Communicable diseases which are not potential from socio-economic or public health view in a country are
(a) List A (b) List B
(c) List C (d) List D

615. Communicable diseases which are socio economically important & have public health importance at local level are
(a) List A (b) List B
(c) List C (d) List D

616. Actinobacillosis is also known as
(a) Wooden tongue (b) Timber tongue
(c) Big head (d) All

617. Big head is the name given to
(a) Rabies (b) Actinobacillosis
(c) Actinomycosis (d) Japanese encephalitis

618. Most susceptible age group of cattle for wooden tongue is
(a) 2-5 days of age (b) 2-5 weeks of age
(c) 2-5 months of age (d) 2-5 years of age

619. Reaction occurs in guinea pigs due to intra peritoneal inoculation of
(a) *Actinomycies ssp.* (b) *Actinobacillus ssp.*
(c) *Listiria ssp.* (d) *Leptospira ssp.*

620. Foot rot is known as
(a) Swine erysipelas
(b) Exudative epidermitis
(c) Infectious keratoconjunctivitis
(d) Infectious pododermatitis

621. Diameter of lesions formed in lumpy wool of sheep is
(a) 2.5 mm (b) 2.5 cm
(c) 2 mm (d) 1.5 cm

622. Strawberry foot rot in sheep occurs due to
(a) Actinobacillosis (b) Actiomycosis
(c) Yersiniasis (d) Dermatophillus infection

623. Which of the following is known as Diamond skin disease in pigs
(a) Swine fever (b) African swine fever
(c) Swine erysipelas (d) Swine pox

624. For swine erysipelas
(a) Indigenous breeds of pig are more susceptible
(b) Pure breeds of pig are more susceptible
(c) Both are equally susceptible
(d) Both are not susceptible

625. Epizootic abortions occur due to
(a) Vibriosis (b) Staphylococcus
(c) Leptospirosis (d) Listeriosis

626. *Vibrio foetus* multiplies in
(a) Uterus (b) Vagina
(c) Cervix (d) Fallopian tubes

627. Abortions due to *Vibrio cholera* occur during
(a) 4-7 months of pregnancy
(b) 1-2 months of pregnancy
(c) 8-9 months of pregnancy
(d) 1st month of pregnancy

628. Which of the following does not help to detect vibriosis
(a) Demonstration of organism from stomach of aborted calf
(b) Demonstration of organism from vaginal mucus
(c) Rectal examination of uterus
(d) Isolation & identification of organism

629. Glanders is caused by
(a) *Actinobacillus lignersi*
(b) *Burkholderia maleii*
(c) *Actinomyces bovis*
(d) *Streptococcus equi*

630. Which of the following species is mot susceptible for Glanders?
(a) Horse (b) Sheep
(c) Dog (d) Cat

631. Formation of small, grey or yellowish nodules about the size of millet seed on mucosa of upper respiratory tract occurs in
(a) Pulmonary adenomatosis
(b) Equine viral arteritis

(c) Strangles
(d) Glanders

632. Strangles is also known as
(a) equine Distemper
(b) Infectious viral arteritis
(c) Both
(d) None

633. Strangles is caused by
(a) *Streptococcus equi*
(b) Infectious viral arteritis
(c) Both
(d) None

634. Most susceptible age group for strangles is
(a) 6 months-36 months
(b) Less than 6 months
(c) More than 36 months
(d) All ages

635. Incubation period of strangles ranges from
(a) 2-5 years (b) 2-5 weeks
(c) 2-5 months (d) 2-5 years

636. Exudative epidermitis is
(a) Seborrhea oleosa
(b) Greasy pig disease
(c) Impetigo contagiosa suis
(d) All

637. Impetigo of udder of cattle, sheep & goat is caused by
(a) *Staphylococcus hyicus*
(b) *Staphylococcus aureus*
(c) Both
(d) None

638. Glasser's disease is known as
(a) Infectious polyarthritis
(b) Porcine polyserositis
(c) Both
(d) None

639. Sever pain & affection of joints is characteristics of
(a) Strangles (b) Glanders
(c) FMD (d) Glasser's disease

640. Ulcerative lymphangitis primarily occurs in
(a) Horse (b) Cattle
(c) Pig (d) Dog

641. Transmission of which of the following diseases is related to soil contamination
(a) Infectious anaemia
(b) FMD
(c) Ulcerative lymphangitis
(d) Scabies

642. Thick greenish exudate mixed with blood appear from ulcers in
(a) FMD
(b) Ulcerative lymplangitis
(c) Hog cholera
(d) Vesicular stomatitis

643. Foot rot is also known as
(a) Infectious pododemitis
(b) Foul in the foot
(c) Both
(d) None

644. Foot rot occurs due to
(a) *Shperophorus necrophorus*
(b) *Fusiformis necrophorus*
(c) Both
(d) Both as the are synonyms

645. Infectious keretoconjunctivitis leads to
(a) Pink eye
(b) Blight
(c) Infectious ophthalmia
(d) All

646. Pink eye disease occurs more in
(a) Cattle (b) Young calves
(c) Heifers (d) Dry cows

647. Infectious keretoconjunctivitis can be transmitted by
(a) Ticks (b) Mites
(c) Mosquito (d) Flies

648. Appearance of a clear line on the face below the inner canthus of eyes occurs in
(a) Infection keretoconjunctivitis
(b) Pink eye
(c) Infectious opthalmia
(d) All

649. Black quarter is also known as
(a) Quarter Ill
(b) Symptomatic anthrax
(c) Emphysematous gangrene
(d) All

650. Symptomatic anthrax is name given to
(a) BQ (b) HS
(c) FMD (d) Hog cholera

651. False BQ is caused by
(a) *Clostridium perfringens*
(b) *Cl. novyi*
(c) *Cl septicum*
(d) All

652. Most susceptible species for occurrence of BQ is
(a) Cattle (b) Horse
(c) Pig (d) Sheep

653. Incubation period in cattle for BQ ranges from
(a) 2-5 days (b) 2-5 weeks
(c) 2-5 months (d) 2-5 years

654. In case of BQ muscles of which region are affected
(a) Shoulder (b) leg
(c) Neck (d) All

655. Lock jaw condition occurs in
(a) BQ (b) Vesicular stomatitis
(c) Trypanosomes (d) Tetanus

656. Which of the following toxin is produced by *Cl. tetani*
(a) Neurotoxin (b) Hemolysin
(c) Fibrinolysin (d) All

657. Which of the following antigen of *Cl. tetani* is heat labile?
(a) H (b) O
(c) Both (d) None

658. Which of the following antigen of *Cl. tetani* is heat stable?
(a) H (b) O
(c) Both (d) None

659. Which of the following antigen of *Cl. tetani* is responsible for tetanospasms
(a) H (b) O
(c) Both (d) None

660. Spores of *Cl. tetani* can be destroyed by boiling at
(a) 115°C for 30-60 minutes
(b) 200°C for 0.3 minutes
(c) 75°C for 60 minutes
(d) 30°C for 60 minutes

661. Susceptibility of different species for tetanus is
(a) Man>Horse>Sheep>Cattle
(b) Cattle>Horse>Sheep>Man
(c) Sheep>Horse>Man>Cattle
(d) Horse>Sheep>Man>Cattle

662. Spastic paralysis in tetanus occurs due to
(a) Distribution of toxin in the blood stream
(b) Local invasion of nerves
(c) Both
(d) None

663. Flaccid paralysis in tetanus occurs due to
(a) Distribution of toxin in the blood stream
(b) Local invasion of nerves
(c) Both
(d) None

664. Tetanospasmin inhibits
(a) Acetyl choline (b) Succinyl choline
(c) Adenytyl cyclae (d) Gnanylyl cyclase

665. Death in tetanus occurs due to
(a) Asphyxia
(b) Muscle contractions
(c) Tetanus toximia
(d) Septicimia

666. Which of the following act as symptoms less carrier of rabies
(a) Raccoons (b) Bats
(c) Dog (d) Mongoose

667. Babesiosis is also known as
(a) Tick fever (b) Red water disease
(c) Piroplasmosis (d) All

668. In case of Murine respiratory mycoplasmosis which part of eye is inflammed
(a) Conjunctiva (b) Cornea
(c) Schlera (d) Iris

669. Infectious ictromelia is name given to
(a) Small pox (b) Sheep pox
(c) Rabbit pox (d) Mouse pox

670. Rinderpest mostly occurs in
(a) Young animals (b) Adult animals
(c) Both (d) None

671. Blood stained saliva is characteritics of
(a) FMD (b) BMC
(c) RP (d) HS

672. Thymus atrophy is a consistent PM finding in
(a) CD
(b) ICH
(c) Parvo virus infection

(d) All

673. Blue tongue is
(a) Infectious (b) Contagious
(c) Non infection (d) Non contagious

674. Parvo virus can be isolated from
(a) Blood (b) Serum
(c) Plasma (d) Faeces

675. Thymus edema is a constant PM finding in
(a) CD (b) ICH
(c) Canine filariasis (d) All

676. Mematiasis is a
(a) Bacterial infection (b) Viral infection
(c) Yeast infection (d) Mould infection

677. Safest & best vaccine for Rinderpest is
(a) Goat adapted vaccine
(b) Oil adjuvant vaccine
(c) Cell culture vaccine
(d) Chick embryo vaccine

678. Rabies may leads to
(a) Death (b) Recumbencey
(c) Paralysis (d) All of the above

679. Which of the following nerve is involved in migration of rabies virus?
(a) Olfactory nerve
(b) Optic nerve
(c) Occulomotor nerve
(d) Facial nerve

680. Fiberoptiscope in horses helps in examination of
(a) Fibrous tissue (b) Muscles
(c) Pharynix (d) Lung parenchyma

781. Premilking can reduce level of Immunoglobin up to
(a) 60 g/l (b) 30 g/l
(c) 120 g/l (d) 15 g/dl

682. Which of the following is clinical pathology of Downer's cow syndrome?
(a) Hyperglycemia
(b) Hypomagnesaemia
(c) Increase level of CP
(d) None

683. Hemonchosis in sheep leads to
(a) Rumenitis (b) Reticutitis
(c) Oesophagitis (d) Abomasitis

683. Anthelmintics of choice for treatment of Ascariosis in dog is
(a) Piperazine (b) Triclebendazole
(c) Closental (d) All

684. Which of the following is used for dissolving skin scrapings for better demonstration of mango mites?
(a) 10% KOH (b) 100% KOH
(c) 1% KOH (d) 5% KOH

685. In Trypanosomiasis, anemia occurs due to
(a) Destruction of RBC
(b) Ag-Ab complex reaction
(c) Intravenous haemolysis
(d) All

686. Feline erythrocytes appear pitted on outer surface in
(a) Anaplasmiosis
(b) Hemobartonellosis
(c) Eperythrozoonosis
(d) Feline panleucopoenia

687. Anisocytosis polychromiasis & basophilic striplings of RBC in sheep indicate
(a) Hemonchosis (b) Coccidiosis
(c) Fasciolosis (d) Amphistomosis

688. Toxic granules in acute bacterial infection seen in neutrophils are known as
(a) Heinz bodies
(b) Koch's blue bodies
(c) Basophilic neutrophils
(d) Dohle bodies

689. In which disease, bacteria though phagocytes by leukocytes helps to proliferate the disease due to protection by humoral defense factors
(a) Trypanosomiosis (b) Brucellosis
(c) Babesioses (d) Yersiniosis

690. Which of the following diseases is caused by *Pasteurella Species?*
(a) Barbone
(b) Pneumonic pasteurellosis
(c) Atrophic rhinitis of swine
(d) both a and b

691. Lamb dysentery mostly occurs in
(a) Young sheep (b) Old sheep
(c) Adult sheep (d) All

692. Necrotic edema is caused by

(a) *Cl. perfringens* (b) *Cl. novyi*
(c) *Cl. septicum* (d) Mixed *Clostridia ssp.* infection

693. Enterotoxaemia mainly occur in
(a) Cow (b) Calf
(c) Sheep (d) Lamb

694. Enterotoxaemia is also known as
(a) Over eating diseases
(b) Pulpy kidney disease
(c) Both
(d) None

695. Etiology of paratyphoid is
(a) *Actinobacillus mallei*
(b) *Actinomyces bovis*
(c) *Salmonella typhimurium*
(d) *Streptococcus equi*

696. Salmonella in sheep & goat is caused by
(a) *S. dublin* (b) *S. typhimurium*
(c) *S. anatum* (d) All

697. Salmonella affecting man is
(a) *S. paratyphi* (b) *S. typhi*
(c) Both (d) None

698. Which of the following occurs in horses?
(a) Distemper (b) Farcy
(c) Glanders (d) All

699. Which mycobacterium can cause mastitis
(a) *M. Lactiocola* (b) *M. bovis*
(c) *M. raprae* (d) M. paratuberculosis

700. Skin TB is caused by
(a) Pathogenic acid fast organism
(b) Non pathogenic acid fast organism
(c) Both
(d) None

701. Serovars of Listeria are identified on the basis of
(a) Somatic antigen (b) Flagellar antigen
(c) Both (d) None

702. Leptospirosis of cattle is caused by
(a) *L. hardzo* (b) *L beateslava*
(c) *L. pomona* (d) All

703. Leptospirosis of Horse is
(a) *L. hardzo* (b) *L beateslava*
(c) *L. pomona* (d) All

704. *Morexella bovis* leads to
(a) Impetigo
(b) Ephemeral fever
(c) Infectious keretoconjunctivitis
(d) None

705. Wooden tongue is a disease of
(a) Dog, cat sheep
(b) Cattle, buffalo, sheep
(c) Sheep, goat, horse
(d) Horse, dog, pig

706. Environmental mastitis can be caused by
(a) *E. coli*
(b) *Streptococcus dysgalatae*
(c) *St. uberis*
(d) All

707. Koch has discovered
(a) TB (b) FMD
(c) HS (d) BQ

708. Tarry coloured blood from all the natural orifices is characteristic of
(a) Babesiosis (b) Theileriosis
(c) FMD (d) Anthrax

709. For HS
(a) Buffalo is 3 times more susceptible than cattle
(b) Cattle is 3 times more susceptible than buffalo
(c) Both are equally susceptible
(d) Both are not susceptible

710. Nagoic is belt area for
(a) FMD (b) Rinderpest
(c) PPR (d) Anthrax

711. In HS death occurs due to
(a) Hypoxia (b) Toxaemia
(c) Both (d) None

712. Purpura haemorrhagica is chronic form of
(a) Anthrax (b) Strangle
(c) Glanders (d) Farcy

713. Chronic edema of throat & lip in horse & pig occur is
(a) Anthrax (b) Strangle
(c) Glanders (d) Farcy

714. First discovered bacterial disease is
(a) Anthrax (b) Strangle
(c) Glanders (d) Farcy

715. Pearl's disease is
(a) FMD (b) Swine erysipelas
(c) TB (d) HS

716. Persistent painful dry hacking cough in characteristic of
(a) FMD (b) Swine erysipelas
(c) TB (d) HS

717. Animal most susceptible for anthrax is
(a) Cattle (b) Horse
(c) Pig (d) Sheep

718. Animal most susceptible for TB is.
(a) Cross bred cattle (b) Zebu cattle
(c) Goat (d) Pig

719. Animal most resistant for TB is
(a) Zebu cattle (b) Cross bred cattle
(c) European cattle (d) None

720. Which organ is never affected in TB?
(a) Lung (b) Lever
(c) Smooth muscle (d) Skeletal muscle

721. Acid fast staining of Mycobacterium is due to
(a) DABA (b) Mysolin
(c) Mycolic acid (d) All

722. Dose & site of SID for TB is
(a) 0.5 ml I/D at neck
(b) 4 ml S/c at neck
(c) 0.1 I/D at neck
(d) any

723. Diagnostic test of TB used in case of mammals only is
(a) Thermal test (b) SID
(c) DID (d) All

724. Diagnostic test of TB can be used in both mammals & avian
(a) Thermal test (b) SID
(c) DID (d) All

725. Frothy blood discharge which clots from anus & nostrils is character of
(a) Anthrax (b) Babesiosis
(c) BQ (d) Tetanus

726. Lacked jaw condition with prolapsed third eyelid is characteristic of
(a) Anthrax (b) Babesiosis
(c) BQ (d) Tetanus

727. Rapidly fatal motor nerve paralysis occurs in
(a) Tetanus (b) Botulism
(c) BQ (d) Braxy

728. Bradsot is also known as
(a) Tetanus (b) Botulism
(c) BQ (d) Braxy

729. Abomasal lesions are seen in
(a) Tetanus (b) Botulism
(c) BQ (d) Braxy

730. BQ organism produces
(a) Exotoxin (b) Endotoxin
(c) Neuotoxin (d) All

731. Species resistant to botulism is
(a) Dog (b) Horse
(c) Cattle (d) Sheep

732. Animal most susceptible to tetanus is
(a) Cattle (b) Sheep
(c) Horse (d) Dog

733. Animal least susceptible to tetanus
(a) Cattle (b) Sheep
(c) Horse (d) Dog

734. Idiopathic tetanus is characteristic by
(a) History of wound
(b) Absence of history of wound
(c) Disruption of skin
(d) All

735. Congestive heart failure in dogs can occur in –
(a) Toxocara infection
(b) Dirofilariasis
(c) Ancylostomiasis
(d) Trypanosomiasis

736. Settling of early Rigor mortis is characteristic of
(a) Enterotoxaemia (b) Tetanus
(c) Anthrax (d) Strangle

737. Maximum fatality in goat occurs due to
(a) Enterotoxaemia (b) Tetanus
(c) Anthrax (d) Strangle

738. In case of Enterotoxaemia, the toxin present is
(a) Epsilon toxin (b) â-toxin
(c) á-toxin (d) All

739. Guttural pouch empyema is evident in
(a) Enterotoxaemia (b) Tetanus

(c) Anthrax (d) Strangle

740. Nodule & ulcer formation of respiratory tract & skin is present in
(a) Glanders
(b) BQ
(c) Strangle
(d) Infectious canine hepatitis

741. Which of the following is an acute disease?
(a) Glanders (b) BQ
(c) Strangle (d) Infectious canine hepatitis

742. Tubercle like lung lesion is evident in
(a) Glanders
(b) BQ
(c) Strangle
(d) Infectious canine hepatitis

743. Ophthalmic test & Strauss reaction can be used to identify
(a) Glanders
(b) BQ
(c) Strangle
(d) Infectious canine hepatitis

744. Strauss reaction is identified by
(a) Painful cystitis (b) Painful orchitis
(c) Skin ecthyma (d) Brisket edema

745. Thick yellowish creamy pus from Lymph nodes is characterstic of
(a) Painful cystitis (b) Painful orchitis
(c) Skin ecthyma (d) Brisket edema

746. Summer mastitis is caused by
(a) Staphylococcus (b) Streptococus
(c) Mycoplasma (d) Corynebacterium

747. Faulty milking may lead to mastitis due to
(a) Staphylococcus (b) Streptococus
(c) Mycoplasma (d) Corynebacteium

748. Mastitic milk appears
(a) Yellowish (b) Reddish
(c) Brownish (d) Bluish

749. pH of mastitis milk is
(a) 7.4 (b) 6
(c) 6.4 (d) 7

750. Most cases of TRP occurs during
(a) Early pregnancy
(b) Late pregnancy
(c) Just after parturition
(d) Mid pregnancy

751. Stuart's flecher media is used for growth of
(a) Leptospira (b) Listiria
(c) Salmonella (d) All

752. Leptospirosis leads to
(a) Dog urinating in bitch sitting position
(b) Periodic opthalmia in horse
(c) Renal failure
(d) All

753. Listeriosis leads to
(a) Unilateral facial paralysis
(b) Abortion
(c) Retention of placenta
(d) All

754. In which of the following infection lesion at nasal septum takes star shape after healing
(a) Listeriosis (b) Leptospirosis
(c) Glanders (d) Strangle

755. Button shaped ulcer in iliocecal value in pig occur in
(a) Salmonellosis (b) Hog cholera
(c) Swine fever (d) African swine fever

756. *Clostridium novyi* produces
(a) Haemoglobinurea
(b) Myoglobinurea
(c) Enzootic haematuria
(d) All

757. Salmonella produces
(a) Exotoxin (b) Endotoxin
(b) Both (d) None

758. In young animals salmonellosis mostly occurs in following form
(a) Septicemic (b) Pneumonic
(c) Enteric (d) None

759. In adult animals salmonellosis mostly occurs in following form
(a) Septicemic (b) Pneumonic
(c) Enteric (d) None

760. Auto immune hemolytic anemia can be diagnosed by
(a) Ascoli's test
(b) Serum neutralization test
(c) Coomb's test

(d) CFT

761. Jaw & skull bones are affected in
(a) Actinomycosis (b) Actimobacillosis
(c) Staphylococcosis (d) Tetanus

762. Tongue & soft tissue are affected in
(a) Actinomycosis (b) Actimobacillosis
(c) Staphylococcosis (d) Tetanus

763. Johne's disease can be diagnosed by
(a) Intradermal Johnin test
(b) Rectal pinch biopsy test
(c) Both
(d) None

764. Limber neck is the name given to
(a) Botulism (b) Braxy
(c) BQ (d) Enterotoxaemia

765. Braxy mostly affects
(a) Adult sheep (b) Old sheep
(c) 1 year age lamb (d) 4 months age lamb

766. For which of the following diseases farcy act is applicable
(a) HS (b) Glanders
(c) Strangle (d) BQ

767. BUN incrases in
(a) Listeriosis (b) Leptospirosis
(c) BQ (d) HS

768. Disease which has causal organism species is icterohaemorrhagica
(a) Listeriosis (b) Leptospirosis
(c) BQ (d) HS

769. Disease characterized by encephalitis & repeat breeding
(a) Listeriosis (b) Leptospirosis
(c) BQ (d) HS

770. Campylobacteriosis leads to abortion in
(a) Early pregnancy
(b) Mid of pregnancy
(c) Late pregnancy
(d) Any Trimester of pregnancy

771. A venereal disease of cattle is
(a) Lesteriosis (b) Leptospirosis
(c) Vibriosis (d) All

772. Large sulfur granules are produced in
(a) Actinomycosis (b) Actimobacillosis
(c) Both (d) None

773. Small sulfur granules are produced in
(a) Actinomycosis (b) Actimobacillosis
(c) Both (d) None

774. Poll evil disease in horse is associated with
(a) Actinomycosis (b) Actimobacillosis
(c) Both (d) None

775. Ligamentum nuchae in sheep is affected in
(a) Actinomycosis (b) Actimobacillosis
(c) Both (d) None

776. Sulfur granules show rosettes of radiating club like body under microscopic in
(a) Actinomycosis (b) Actimobacillosis
(c) Both (d) None

777. Tongue is not affected in Actinobacillosis in
(a) Cattle (b) Sheep
(c) Horse (d) Pig

778. Causal organism of which disease produces toxin
(a) Actinomycosis (b) Actimobacillosis
(c) brucellosis (d) salmonellosis

779. Rhomboidal urticarial lesions in swine erysipelas may be observed in
(a) Acute form (b) Chronic form
(c) Both (d) None

780. Suppurative & vegetative endocarditis in swine erysipelas is seen in
(a) Acute form (b) Chronic form
(c) Both (d) None

781. Preservative used for ruminal fluid is
(a) $Ca(OH)_2$ (b) NaCl
(c) K_2SO_4 (d) $HgCl_2$

782. Red water disease is
(a) Babesiosis
(b) Bacillary Haemoglobenuia
(c) Both
(d) None

783. Red water fever is
(a) Babesiosis
(b) Bacillary Haemoglobenuia
(c) Both
(d) None

784. Haemoglobenurica occurs in
(a) Babesiosis
(b) Bacillary Hemoglobenuia
(c) Both

(d) None

785. Lecithinase toxin is produced in
(a) Babesiosis
(b) Bacillary Hemoglobinuria
(c) Both
(d) None

786. Dose of tetanus toxoid in small animal is
(a) 1-2 ml (b) 2-7 ml
(c) 5 ml (d) 10 ml

787. 1 ml Tetanus Toxoid contain
(a) 4 lyophilised flocule
(b) 6 lyophilised flocule
(c) 8 lyophilised flocule
(d) 10 lyophilised flocule

788. Anthrax vaccine contains
(a) Live spore (b) Dead spore
(c) Attenuated spore (d) None

789. Drug of choice for Listeriosis
(a) Streptomycin (b) Erythromycin
(c) Penicillin (d) Tetracycline

790. Infectious coryza in poultry is caused by
(a) Mycoplasma (b) Hemophillus
(c) Borrelia (d) Fowl pox virus

791. Air sacculitis in poultry is caused by
(a) Mycoplasma (b) Hemophillus
(c) Borrelia (d) Fowl pox virus

792. *Borrelia ssp.* in poultry leads to
(a) Spirochaetosis (b) Tick fever
(c) Tick paralysis (d) All

793. Eggs are normal but their production is decreased in
(a) Infectious coryza
(b) Tick paralysis
(c) Chronic respiratory disease
(d) Ranikhet disease

794. Ruffled feathers, dropping of wings, torticolis & fall in egg production occurs in
(a) Infectious coryza
(b) Tick paralysis
(c) Chronic respiratory disease
(d) Ranikhet disease

795. Greenish diarrhoea with cyanosis of comb & enlarged spleen occur in
(a) Infectious coryza
(b) Tick paralysis
(c) Chronic respiratory disease
(d) Ranikhet disease

796. F_1, R_2b & Lasota strain belong to
(a) Infectious coryza
(b) Tick paralysis
(c) Chronic respiratory disease
(d) Ranikhet disease

797. Causal agent of this disease is demonstrated by Fontana's silver strain
(a) Infectious coryza
(b) Tick paralysis
(c) Chronic respiratory disease
(d) Ranikhet disease

798. Which of the following is caused by Adeno virus
(a) CD (b) ICH
(c) Rabies (d) Rinderpest

799. Orbi virus causes
(a) African horse sickness
(b) Blue Tongue
(c) Both
(d) None

800. Bovine viral diarrhoea is caused by a virus of family
(a) Rheoviridae (b) Flaviviridae
(c) Togaviridae (d) Retroviridae

801. Louping ill is caused by a virus of family
(a) Rheoviridae (b) Flaviviridae
(c) Togaviridae (d) Retroviridae

802. Maedi is caused by a virus of family
(a) Rheoviridae (b) Flaviviridae
(c) Togaviridae (d) Retroviridae

803. Hemorrhagic enteritis in dog is caused by
(a) Parvo virus (b) Morbilli virus
(c) Herpes (d) All

804. PPR is caused by
(a) Parvo virus (b) Morbilli virus
(c) Herpes (d) All

805. Herpes virus causes
(a) Bovine malignant catarrh
(b) Marek's disease
(c) Both
(d) None

806. Equine influenza as caused by

(a) Orthomyxo virus
(b) Paramyxo virus
(c) Myxovirus type A
(d) Myxovirus type B

807. Scrapie in sheep & goat is caused by
(a) Herpes virus (b) Paramyo virus
(c) Prion particle (d) None

808. Kuru disease occurs in
(a) Cow (b) Sheep
(c) Goat (d) Man

809. Prion particle are
(a) Protein particle (b) Nucleic acid
(c) Both (d) Bacteria

810. East coast fever in Africa is caused by
(a) *Theileria annulata* (b) *T. parva*
(c) *T. mutans* (d) All

811. Tropical Theileriosis in India is caused by
(a) *Theileria annulata* (b) *T. parva*
(c) *T. mutans* (d) All

812. Which of the following may lead to Chorea?
(a) ICH (b) CD
(c) Parvovirus (d) Rabies

813. Which of the following is transmitted by urine?
(a) ICH (b) CD
(c) Parvovirus (d) Rabies

814. Hepatitis blue eye is found in
(a) ICH (b) CD
(c) Parvovirus (d) Rabies

815. Bilateral systolic murmur occur in
(a) ICH (b) CD
(c) Parvovirus (d) Rabies

816. Acute myocarditis is cause of death in
(a) ICH (b) CD
(c) Parvovirus (d) Rabies

817. In case of ICH
(a) Blood clotting is disturbed
(b) Forming of immune complex
(c) Droplet infection occur
(d) All are correct

818. Mad cow disease is
(a) Scrapie
(b) Bovine spongiform encephalomyelitis
(c) Both
(d) None

819. Intra cytoplasmic vacoulation of neurons in brain occur in
(a) Scrapie
(b) Bovine spongiform encephalomyelitis
(c) Both
(d) None

820. In Scrapie, lesions in brain are
(a) Unilaterally symmetrical
(b) Bilaterally symmetrical
(c) Asymmetrical
(d) Irregular

821. Necrotic lesions & bubbly salivations occur in
(a) PPR (b) RP
(c) FMD (d) HS

822. Cattle plague is
(a) PPR (b) RP
(c) FMD (d) HS

823. Goat plague is
(a) PPR (b) RP
(c) FMD (d) HS

824. Picorna virus leads to
(a) PPR (b) RP
(c) FMD (d) HS

825. Nature of cough in equine influenza
(a) Severe persistent dry
(b) Severe intermittent dry
(c) Acute dry
(d) Acute moist

826. Nucleus of epithelial cells show pycnotic changes in
(a) PPR (b) RP
(c) FMD (d) HS

827. African horse sickness is transmitted by
(a) Arthropod (b) Snail
(c) Fomite (d) None

828. Which form of African horse sickness is most common?
(a) Dunkop (b) Dikkop
(c) Both (d) None

829. Pseudo FMD is
(a) Ephemeral fever (b) Blue tongue
(c) HS (d) BQ

830. Virus is present in all secretions in
(a) FMD (b) Rabies

(c) Swine erysipelas (d) Swine fever

831. Which of the following is zoonotic?
(a) Shigellosis (b) Tularemia
(c) Both (d) None

832. Tetanus not often occur in
(a) Cattle (b) Goat
(c) Horse (d) Sheep

833. Which animal is most susceptible to ephemeral fever?
(a) Cattle (b) Goat
(c) Horse (d) Sheep

834. In which of the following tuberculosis does not cause calcification
(a) Cattle (b) Horse
(c) Dog (d) Birds

835. Botulism is a
(a) Febrile diease
(b) Non febrile disease
(c) Sometimes febrile and sometimes none febrile
(d) None

836. Pink lesion over coronet & Lameness occur in
(a) FMD (b) BQ
(c) Blue tongue (d) HS

837. Lesions occur in oral cavity & foot in
(a) FMD (b) Blue tongue
(c) Both (d) None

838. Animal most susceptible to Jaagsiekte is
(a) Horse (b) Cattle
(c) Sheep (d) Dog

839. Lung becomes rubbery in sheep in
(a) Maedi (b) Jaggsiekte
(c) Both (d) None

840. Benign form of pox affects
(a) Skin
(b) Digestive & respiratory system
(c) Respiratory system
(d) Skull

841. In adult animals which form of pox occurs?
(a) Benign (b) Malignant
(c) Both (d) None

842. Malignant form of pox affects
(a) Skin
(b) Digestive & respiratory system
(c) Respiratory system
(d) Skull

843. Concept of immunization was given by
(a) Lewis (b) Clintock
(c) Jenner (d) Robert hook

844. Pox lesions on eye, nose & face occur in
(a) Cattle (b) Buffalo
(c) Both (d) None

845. Pustule stage does not occur in
(a) Swine pox (b) Goat pox
(c) Small pox (d) Fowl pox

846. Both benign & malignant form of pox occur in
(a) Camel (b) Swine
(c) Horse (d) Cattle

847. Pox virus does not infect
(a) Horse (b) Cattle
(c) Camel (d) Dog

848. Bovine lumpy skin virus is included in
(a) Capri pox (b) Cattle pox (cow)
(c) Buffalo pox (d) All

849. Orf virus causes
(a) FMD
(b) Vesicular stomatitis
(c) Vesicular exanthema
(d) Contagious ecthyma

850. In horse which forms of pox occur
(a) Leg form (b) Jenner's horse pox
(c) Buccal form (d) All

851. Guarnieri's body occur in
(a) Sheep pox (b) Goat pox
(c) Swine pox (d) cow pox

852. Spleenomegaly & Hepatomegaly occur in
(a) Anthrax (b) Babesiosis
(c) Swamp fever (d) Blue tongue

853. Which species suffering form rabies start biting it's own body
(a) Swine (b) Cattle
(c) Dog (d) Horse

854. Which type of rabies is transmitted through Dog
(a) Sylvatic (b) Urban
(c) Both (d) None

855. Schedule of post bite rabies vaccine is
(a) 0, 3, 9, 18, 28, 90 days
(b) 0, 9, 18, 28, 90 days

(c) 0, 3, 7, 28, 90 days
(d) 0, 3, 7, 14, 28, 90 days

856. Which virus is used for producing rabies vaccine?
(a) Fixed virus (b) Rabies virus
(c) Both (d) Any

857. Vector for Rabies virus is
(a) Monkey (b) Dog
(c) Bat (d) All

858. Howl voice in rabid dog is produced in
(a) Dumb form (b) Furious form
(c) Both (d) None

859. For diagnosis of rabies, brain should be preserved in
(a) 10% glycerine (b) 20% glycerine
(c) 30% glycerine (d) 50% glycerine

860. Hygroma & abscess occur in African cattle due to
(a) Listeriosis (b) Staphylococcuosis
(c) Brucellosis (d) None

861. Vaccine of Brucella used in calf
(a) Strain 19 (b) 45/20 vaccine
(c) Both (d) None

862. Theileriosis is also known as
(a) East cost fever
(b) Red water
(c) Roclesian tick fever
(d) All

863. Which of the following is a fly borne disease?
(a) Babesiosis (b) Bacillary haemoglobinurea
(c) Theileriosis (d) Surra

864. Which of the 2 is a tick born disease?
(a) Babesiosis (b) Theileriosis
(c) Both (d) None

865. Necrotic changes in placenta & bursitis may occur due to
(a) *Brucella ssp.* (b) *Babesia ssp.*
(c) *Theileria ssp.* (d) All

866. Punched necked necrotic ulcers in abdomen occur in
(a) *Brucella ssp.* (b) *Babesia ssp.*
(c) *Theileria ssp.* (d) All

867. Raksha vac T is used for
(a) *Brucella ssp.* (b) *Babesia ssp.*
(c) *Theileria ssp.* (d) All

868. In Theileriosis, signet ring stages is present in
(a) RBC (b) Lymphocyte
(c) Platelet (d) Plasma

869. Koch's blue body is found in
(a) Theileriosis (b) Babesiosis
(c) Trypanosomiasis (d) Toxoplasmosis

870. Koch's blue bodes are found in
(a) RBC (b) Lymphocyte
(c) Platelet (d) Plasma

871. Gamet of Theileria is present
(a) RBC (b) Lymphocyte
(c) Platelet (d) Plasma

872. Macroschizont of Theileria is present in
(a) RBC (b) Lymphocyte
(c) Platelet (d) Plasma

873. Microschizont of Theileria is present in
(a) RBC (b) Lymphocyte
(c) Platelet (d) Plasma

874. *Babesia divergens* causes
(a) Spasm of anal sphincter
(b) Pipe stems faeces
(c) Both
(d) None

875. *Babesia bovis* causes
(a) Nervous form of disease
(b) Pulmonary form of disease
(c) Both
(d) None

876. Which of the following is ring shaped?
(a) *Theileria parva* (b) *Theileria annulata*
(c) Both (d) None

877. *Leishmania donovani* causes
(a) Dum Dum fever
(b) Visceral form of diease
(c) Kalazar
(d) All

878. Oriental sore is caused by
(a) Babesia (b) Theileria
(c) Trypanosome (d) Leishmania

879. Nagana disease is caused by
(a) Babesia (b) Theileria
(c) Trypanosome (d) Leishmania

880. Which of the following protozoa can be found in plasma?

(a) Babesia (b) Theileria
(c) Trypanosome (d) Leishmania

881. Which stage of leishmania occur in sand fly
(a) Amastigote (b) Epimastigote
(c) Promastigote (d) Trypinastigote

882. Which stage of Leishmania occurs in macrophage?
(a) Amastigote (b) Epimastigote
(c) Promastigote (d) Trypinastigote

883. Mal-de- cadras is caused by
(a) Amastigote (b) Epimastigote
(c) Promastigote (d) Trypinastigote

884. Silver dollar spot on skin is formed in which disease
(a) Dourine (b) Nagana
(c) Surra (d) All

885. *Eimeria maxima* affect which part of intestine
(a) Upper (b) Middle
(c) Terminal (d) All

886. *E. tenella* is present in
(a) Duodenum (b) Cecum
(c) Abomasum (d) Colon

887. In a sporulated oocyst of coccidia there are
(a) 2 sporocyst & 4 sporozoites
(b) 4 sporocyst & 2 sporozoites
(c) 4 sporocyst & 8 sporozoites
(d) 4 sporocyst & 4 sporozoites

888. In case of sporulated occyst of Isospora
(a) 2 sporocyst & 4 sporozoites
(b) 4 sporocyst & 2 sporozoites
(c) 4 sporocyst & 8 sporozoites
(d) 4 sporocyst & 4 sporozoites

889. Heart water disease is cased by
(a) *Cowdria ruminantium*
(b) *Moraxella bovis*
(c) Equine influenza
(d) *Babesia begemia*

890. Pink eye of sheep & goat is a
(a) Bacterial disease (b) Viral disease
(c) Rickettsial disease (d) Magot disease

891. *Coxiella burnetti* causes
(a) Q fever (b) Swine fever
(c) Red water fever (d) X fever

892. South African gall sickness is
(a) Babesiosis (b) Theileriosis
(c) Anaplasmosis (d) None

893. Potomac horse fever occurs due to
(a) Babesiosis (b) Theileriosis
(c) Ehrlichiosis (d) None

894. Canine Ehrlichiosis lead to
(a) Lahore disease
(b) Nairobi bleeding disease
(c) Both
(d) None

895. Bitch sitting posture of male dog during urination in
(a) Strangle (b) H.S.
(c) Listeriosis (d) Leptospirosis

896. Ornithosis in poultry is caused by
(a) *Pasteularlla ssp.*
(b) *Salmonella pullorum*
(c) *Salmonella gllinarum*
(d) *Chlamydia ssp.*

897. RNA virus infection in poultry is
(a) Infectious bursitis
(b) Gumboro disease
(c) Avian leucosis complex
(d) All

898. Synonym of Marek's disease is
(a) Range paralysis (b) Skin leucosis
(c) Neural leucosis (d) all

899. In Marek's disease
(a) Young birds are more susceptible
(b) Split leg stance occurs
(c) HVT vaccine is used
(d) All are correct

900. Swelling of bursa is a characteristic feature in
(a) Gumboro disease (b) Marek's disease
(c) Ornithosis (d) New castle disease

901. Bollinger bodies are produced in
(a) Fowl pox (b) Small pox
(c) Cow pox (d) Goat pox

902. Profuse greenish diarrhoea is characteristic of
(a) Fowl cholera (b) Avian leucosis
(c) Shigellosis (d) Fowl typhoid

903. Streaky brick red appearance of liver is characteristic of
(a) Fowl cholera (b) Avian leucosis
(c) Shigellosis (d) Fowl typhoid

904. Ratting noise during breathing is characteristic of
(a) Fowl cholera (b) Avian leucosis
(c) Shigellosis (d) Fowl typhoid

905. Takata is test used for diagnosis of
(a) MD (b) RD
(c) Avian leucosis (d) Fowl typhoid

906. Which of the following is known as Doyle's diseases?
(a) MD (b) RD
(c) Avian leucosis (d) Fowl typhoid

907. Which fungal infection involves lungs?
(a) Aspergillosis (b) Coccidiomycosis
(c) Blastomycosis (d) Dermatomycosis

908. Tropical Actinomycosis is
(a) Aspergillosis (b) Coccidiomycosis
(c) Nocardiosis (d) Dermatomycosis

909. Which of the following is systemic fungal infection?
(a) Aspergillosis (b) Blastomycosis
(c) Histoplasmosis (d) All

910. *Candida albicans* causes
(a) Thrush (b) Favus
(c) Bed sore (d) Summer sore

911. Hebronema leads to
(a) Thrush (b) Favus
(c) Bed sore (d) Summer sore

912. On post mortem crop shows Turkish Towel appearance in
(a) Thrush (b) Favus
(c) Bed sore (d) Summer sore

913. Ovary of poultry becomes cauliflower like in
(a) Avion leucois complex
(b) Gumboro
(c) Blastomycosis
(d) Histoplasmosis

914. Buparvaquinone is drug of choice in
(a) Babesiosis (b) Theileriosis
(c) Anaplasmosis (d) All

915. Drug of choice for treatment of stomach flukes is
(a) Oxyclosanide (b) Berenil
(c) Clasantel (d) Piperazine

916. Parental pamoate can be used for the treatment of
(a) Stomach flukes (b) Ring worm
(c) Hook worm (d) Tapeworm

917. Anaplasmosis occurs in
(a) 1-2 month age animals
(b) Only adults
(c) Only young
(d) All ages

918. In swine erysipelas, cauliflower like growth occurs on
(a) Mitral valve of heart
(b) Tricuspid value of heart
(c) Lung
(d) Lever

919. Glanders is
(a) Infectious disease (b) Contagious disease
(c) Both (d) None

920. Incidence and prevalence of infectious disease of is studied under
(a) Preventive medicine
(b) Clinical medicine
(c) Pathology
(d) Toxicology

921. Forensic medicine deals with which branch of medicine
(a) Jurisprudence (b) Toxicology
(c) Ethics (d) All

922. Prognosis of rabies is
(a) Good (b) Guarded
(c) Grave (d) All

923. Haemoglobinurea occurs in
(a) Babesiosis
(b) Phenothiazine toxicity
(c) Rape poisoning
(d) All

924. Pharyngeal edema occurs in
(a) Haemonchosis (b) Fasciolosis
(c) Amphistomosis (d) Schistosomiasis

925. Histoplasma causes
(a) Epizootic lymphangitis
(b) Ulcecerative lymphangitis
(c) Farcy
(d) Lymphadenitis

926. Corynebacterium pseudotuberculosis causes
(a) Epizootic lymphangitis
(b) Ulcerative lymphangitis
(c) Farcy

(d) Lymphadenitis

927. In horse farcy occurs due to
(a) Pseudomonas maleii
(b) *Mycobacterium tuberculois*
(c) *Nocardia facinicus*
(d) None

928. In cattle, farcy occurs due to
(a) Pseudomonas maleii
(b) *Mycobacterium tuberculois*
(c) *Nocardia facinicus* (d) None

929. Lymphadenitis occurs in
(a) Babesiosis (b) Theileriosis
(c) Lishmoniasis (d) Anaplasmosis

930. Cutaneous mycosis is caused by
(a) Blue worm maggots
(b) Screw worm
(c) Both
(d) None

931. Viral encephalomyelitis in horse occur due to
(a) Adeno virus
(b) Rhabdo virus
(c) Arbo virus
(d) Toga virus

932. Most virulent strain of arbo virus is
(a) Eastern (b) Western
(c) Venezuelan (d) All

933. Temperature in Rabies may rise up to
(a) 102°F
(b) 105°F
(c) 107°F
(d) There is no effect on temperature

934. Which type of stomatitis occurs in Rinderpest?
(a) Catarrhal (b) Vesicular
(c) Ulcerative (d) None

935. Which of the following is clone disease?
(a) Allergic stomatitis
(b) Catarrhal stomatitis
(c) Vesicular stomatitis
(d) Ulcerative stomatitis

936. Pipe stem lever is characteristic of
(a) Ascariasis (b) Amphistomiasis
(c) Fasciolosis (d) Schistosomiasis

937. In Horse jaundice is caused by
(a) Babesia (b) Theileria
(c) Trypanosoma (d) Eimeria

938. Congestive heart failure in dog can occur in
(a) Toxocara infection
(b) Dirofilarasis
(c) Ancylostomiasis
(d) None

939. In sheep pericarditis occurs due to
(a) Staphanurea (b) Pateurella
(c) Mycoplasma (d) All

940. Which of the following is a fly born disease?
(a) Babesiosis (b) Theileriosis
(c) Anaplasmosis (d) Trypanosomiasis

941. Trypanosomiasis is
(a) Mosquito born (b) Tick born
(c) Fly born (d) Flea born

942. Babesiosis is
(a) Mosquito born (b) Tick born
(c) Fly born (d) Flea born

943. Clostridium produces
(a) Endotoxin (b) Exotoxin
(c) Both (d) None

944. Pasteuella produces
(a) Endotoxin (b) Exotoxin
(c) Both (d) None

945. Which one is used for the prevention of tetanus
(a) Antitetanus serum (ATS)
(b) Tetanus toxoid (TT)
(c) Oil adjuvant tetanus vaccine
(d) Oxytetracycline in high dose

946. Drug of choice for Salmonellosis
(a) Oxytetiacycline (b) Chloitetiacycline
(c) Sulpha (d) Penicillin

947. Drug of choice for Listeriosis
(a) Oxytetiacycline (b) Chloitetiacycline
(c) Sulpha (d) Penicillin

948. Prophylactic dose of Tetanus antitoxic serum in cattle & horse is
(a) 1500-3000 IU i/m or s/c
(b) 5000 IU i/m
(c) 1 Lac IU i/m or s/c
(d) 10 Lac IU i/m

949. Foot rot is known as
(a) Swine erysipelas
(b) Bacillary Haemoglobinurea

(c) Infectious keretoconjunctivitis
(d) Infectious pododormitis

950. Lecithinase toxin is produced in
(a) Swine erysipelas
(b) Bacillary Haemoglobinurea
(c) Infectious keretoconjunctivitis
(d) Infectious pododormitis

951. Causal agent of Listeriosis in ruminants particularly in sheep is
(a) *Listeria monocytogens*
(b) *Listeria icterohemorrhagica*
(c) Both
(d) All

952. Salmonella affecting all species of animals
(a) *S. dublin* (b) *S. typhimurium*
(c) *S. newport* (d) *S. anatum*

953. Hypoxia & toxemia is the cause of death in
(a) Strangle (b) Anthrax
(c) HS (d) TB

954. Mycolic acid is present in the cell wall of
(a) Salmonella (b) Pasteunella
(c) Streptococcus (d) Mycobacterium

955. Most affected organ in TB is
(a) Liver & lymph node
(b) Lung & Lymph node
(c) Liver & lung
(d) Liver lump & Heart

956. Risky season for HS is
(a) Monsoon (b) Heavy each
(c) Hot & humid (d) All

957. Which of the following is characterized by hemorrhagic enteritis
(a) Brucellosis (b) Authrax
(c) Coccidiosis (d) Dourine

958. Which of the following is a self limiting disease?
(a) Brucellosis (b) Authrax
(c) Coccidiosis (d) Dourine

959. Which Anaplasma is more pathogenic?
(a) *Anaplasma marginale*
(b) *A. centrale*
(c) Both
(d) None

960. Anapalsma is found in
(a) RBC (b) Lymphocyte
(c) Platelet (d) Plasma

961. Digitalization is indicated by which of the following
(a) Reduction in heart rate pulse rate
(b) Polyurea and increased coughing
(c) Severity of edema is reduced
(d) All of the above

962. Cattle pink eye is caused by
(a) *Cowdria ssp.*
(b) *Moraxella bovis*
(c) Equine influenza virus
(d) All

963. Equine pink eye is caused by
(a) *Cowdria ssp.*
(b) *Moragella bovis*
(c) Equine influenza virus
(d) All

964. Which of the following is a bacterium?
(a) *Morexella bovis*
(b) *Coxiella burnette*
(c) *Rickettsia conjunctivae*
(d) None

965. The split leg stance is a usual feature of
(a) Avian Leucosis Complex
(b) Marek's diease
(c) Both
(d) None

966. Nerve paralysis occurs in
(a) Avian Leucosis Complex
(b) Marek's diease
(c) Both
(d) None

967. Tumor are formed in
(a) Avian Leucosis Complex
(b) Marek's diease
(c) Both
(d) None

968. Visceral form of disease in more common in
(a) Avian Leucosis Complex
(b) Marek's disease
(c) Both
(d) None

969. In which of the following disease of bird, cutaneous, diphtheric, ocular & nasal forms are seen

(a) Gumboro (b) Fowl pox
(c) Pigeon pox (d) Marek's disease

970. In which disease lesion is flat & reddish grey in colour & diffuse in nature
(a) Gumboro (b) Fow pox
(c) Pigeon pox (d) Marek's disease

971. In which disease lesion is pale yellow to white in colour & focal in nature
(a) Gumboro (b) Fow pox
(c) Pigeon pox (d) Marek's disease

972. Profuse greenish diarrhoea occurs in
(a) Fowl cholera (b) Coccidiosis
(c) Fowl typhoid (d) Pullorum

973. Breast blister is
(a) Large abscess diaphragm
(b) Large abscess on apex of sternam
(c) Abscess on ligamentum nuchie
(d) Abscess on bursa

974. Large abscess on apex of sternum is
(a) Breast blister (b) Thoracic blister
(c) Sternum blister (d) All

975. *Coccidioides immitis* causes
(a) Coccidiosis
(b) Coccidioidosis
(c) Coccidioidomycosis
(d) All

976. Drug of choice for Babesia
(a) Berenil (b) Butalex
(c) Amprolium (d) All of the above

977. Drug of choice for Theileriosis
(a) Berenil (b) Butalex
(c) Amprolium (d) All of the above

978. Drug of choice for Leptospirosis
(a) Berenil (b) Butalex
(c) Tetracyclin (d) Amprolium

979. Drug used in case of Coccidiosis
(a) Berenil (b) Butalex
(c) Both (d) Amprolium

980. Hide bound condition & Cachexia indicate that animal is suffering from
(a) Acute disease (b) Chronic disease
(c) Healthy (d) Sub clinical

981. Examination of any organ by fingers is
(a) Auscultation (b) Percussion
(c) Palpation (d) All

982. Examination of any organ by stethoscope
(a) Auscultation (b) Percussion
(c) Palpation (d) All

983. Prognosis of gangrene is always
(a) Good (b) Grave
(c) Poor (d) Guarded

984. Disease in which CFR is 100%
(a) Fowl plaque
(b) BQ
(c) Bovine Spongiform Encephalomyelitis
(d) All

985. CFR is not 100% in
(a) BQ (b) HS
(c) Scrapie (d) Surra

986. Drug contraindicated in cat
(a) Digitoxin (b) Caffine
(c) Amitraz (d) All

987. Trichophyton causes
(a) Favus (c) Thrush
(c) Dermatitis (d) All

988. Favus is a disease of
(a) Dog (b) Cat
(c) Sheep (d) Fowl

989. *Blastomyces dermititidis* infects
(a) Dog (b) Cat
(c) Sheep (d) Fowl

990. Ondiri disease is caused by
(a) *Ehrlichia canis* (b) *Ehrlichia ondiri*
(c) *Babesia bigenina* (d) *Cytoecetes ondiri*

991. Ondiri disease occurs in
(a) Cattle (b) Sheep
(c) Horse (d) Dog

992. Disease caused by prion particle
(a) Scrapie
(b) Kuru
(c) Bovine Spongiform encephalomyelitis
(d) All

993. Para pox virus infects
(a) Dry cows (b) Pregnant cows
(c) Lactating cows (d) Heifers

994. Causal agent of which of the following produces neuraminidase enzyme
(a) Swine fever
(b) Fowl cholera
(c) African swine fever
(d) Swine erysipelas

995. Abortion occurs in mid gestation in
(a) Brucellosis (b) Campylobacteriosis
(c) Both (d) None

996. Disease of zoonotic importance
(a) Anthrax (b) TB
(c) Both (d) None

997. Causal agent of which disease produce toxin
(a) Anthrax (b) TB
(c) Both (d) None

Match the following

A.

1.	Brucellosis	a	Clostridium perfringens type C
2	Braxy	b	Clostridium chauvoei
3.	Lamb dysentery	c.	Clostridium perfringens type D
4.	Struck	d	Clostridium septicum
5.	B. Q.	e	Brucella abortus
6.	Enterotoxaemia	f.	Clostridium perfringens type B

Answers

1. e 2. d 3. F 4. a 5. b 6. c

B.

1.	Limber neck	a.	Enterotxaemia
2.	Lion disease	b.	Botulism
3.	Bad sore		
4.	Pulpy kidney disease		

Answers

1. b 2. b 3. b 4. a

C.

	Organism		Drug of choice
1.	Clostridia	A.	Sulphadimidine
2.	Salmonella	B.	Diaminazine aceturate
3.	Listeria	C.	Penicillin
4.	Babesia	D.	Quinapyramine

Answers

1. c 2. a 3. c 4. d

Answers

1.	(a)	2.	(d)	3.	(c)
4.	(c)	5.	(d)	6.	(a)
7.	(d)	8.	(d)	9.	(d)
10.	(b)	11.	(b)	12.	(b)
13.	(b)	14.	(b)	15.	(d)
16.	(a)	17.	(c)	18.	(b)
19.	(d)	20.	(d)	21.	(d)
22.	(c)	23.	(a)	24.	(b)
25.	(a)	26.	(b)	27.	(c)
28.	(a)	29.	(c)	30.	(a)
31.	(d)	32.	(c)	33.	(b)
34.	(a)	35.	(d)	36.	(c)
37.	(a)	38.	(d)	39.	(b)
40.	(a)	41.	(a)	42.	(d)
43.	(c)	44.	(d)	45.	(c)
46.	(a)	47.	(d)	48.	(d)
49.	(a)	50.	(d)	51.	(d)
52.	(b)	53.	(b)	54.	(a)
55.	(c)	56.	(d)	57.	(d)
58.	(a)	59.	(a)	60.	(c)
61.	(c)	62.	(d)	63.	(a)
64.	(d)	65.	(d)	66.	(a)
67.	(d)	68.	(b)	69.	(d)
70.	(d)	71.	(d)	72.	(b)
73.	(d)	74.	(a)	75.	(b)
76.	(c)	77.	(a)	78.	(a)
79.	(b)	80.	(a)	81.	(d)
82.	(c)	83.	(a)	84.	(d)
85.	(d)	86.	(b)	87.	(b)
88.	(b)	89.	(a)	90.	(a)
91.	(a)	92.	(a)	93.	(d)
94.	(c)	95.	(a)	96.	(c)
97.	(a)	98.	(b)	99.	(a)
100.	(a)	101.	(c)	102.	(a)

103.	(b)	104.	(d)	105.	(d)	243.	(c)	244.	(a)	245.	(b)
106.	(a)	107.	(d)	108.	(a)	246.	(d)	247.	(a)	248.	(a)
109.	(a)	110.	(a)	111.	(c)	249.	(c)	250.	(d)	251.	(b)
112.	(b)	113.	(a)	114.	(b)	252.	(d)	253.	(a)	254.	(a)
115.	(a)	116.	(b)	117.	(b)	255.	(d)	256.	(d)	257.	(d)
118.	(b)	119.	(d)	120.	(d)	258.	(a)	259.	(d)	260.	(b)
121.	(b)	122.	(b)	123.	(b)	261.	(d)	262.	(c)	263.	(a)
124.	(d)	125.	(c)	126.	(c)	264.	(a)	265.	(b)	266.	(c)
127.	(c)	128.	(d)	129.	(a)	267.	(d)	268.	(b)	269.	(b)
130.	(a)	131.	(c)	132.	(b)	270.	(b)	271.	(c)	272.	(a)
133.	(d)	134.	(a)	135.	(b)	273.	(b)	274.	(a)	275.	(c)
136.	(a)	137.	(d)	138.	(b)	276.	(d)	277.	(a)	278.	(d)
139.	(a)	140.	(c)	141.	(b)	279.	(a)	280.	(a)	281.	(a)
142.	(b)	143.	(b)	144.	(d)	282.	(d)	283.	(b)	284.	(b)
145.	(d)	146.	(a)	147.	(b)	285.	(b)	286.	(c)	287.	(a)
148.	(c)	149.	(d)	150.	(d)	288.	(d)	289.	(c)	290.	(b)
151.	(d)	152.	(c)	153.	(d)	291.	(b)	292.	(a)	293.	(a)
154.	(c)	155	(a)	156.	(b)	294.	(b)	295.	(b)	295.	(c)
157.	(c)	158.	(c)	159.	(b)	296.	(a)	297.	(b)	298.	(a)
160.	(b)	161.	(d)	162	(c)	299.	(c)	300.	(c)	301.	(c)
163.	(d)	164.	(c)	165.	(c)	302.	(a)	303.	(b)	304.	(a)
166.	(d)	167.	(c)	168.	(b)	305.	(d)	306.	(d)	307.	(a)
169.	(d)	170.	(a)	171.	(d)	308.	(d)	309.	(a)	310.	(a)
172.	(a)	173.	(b)	174.	(a)	311.	(b)	312.	(a)	313.	(c)
175.	(c)	176.	(b)	177.	(a)	314.	(d)	315.	(a)	316.	(a)
178.	(b)	179.	(b)	180.	(a)	317.	(b)	318.	(a)	319.	(d)
181.	(a)	182.	(d)	183.	(c)	320.	(b)	321.	(a)	322.	(b)
184.	(b)	185.	(c)	186.	(d)	323.	(c)	324.	(a)	325.	(a)
187.	(a)	188.	(d)	189.	(b)	326.	(c)	327.	(c)	328.	(c)
190.	(d)	191.	(a)	192.	(a)	329.	(b)	330.	(c)	331.	(a)
193.	(a)	194.	(c)	195.	(c)	332.	(b)	333.	(b)	334.	(b)
196.	(a)	197.	(a)	198.	(a)	335.	(d)	336.	(c)	337.	(c)
199.	(b)	200.	(c)	201.	(d)	338.	(b)	339.	(a)	340.	(a)
202.	(d)	203.	(b)	204.	(a)	341.	(c)	342.	(b)	343.	(c)
205.	(d)	206.	(b)	207.	(c)	344.	(c)	345.	(b)	346.	(d)
208.	(c)	208.	(c)	209.	(d)	347.	(c)	348.	(c)	349.	(a)
210.	(d)	211.	(d)	212.	(d)	350.	(d)	351.	(d)	352.	(a)
213.	(b)	214.	(c)	215.	(c)	353.	(b)	354.	(a)	355.	(b)
216.	(a)	217.	(a)	218.	(b)	356.	(d)	357.	(a)	358.	(c)
219.	(c)	220.	(d)	221.	(c)	359.	(c)	360.	(d)	361.	(a)
222.	(b)	223.	(b)	224.	(b)	362.	(c)	363.	(d)	364.	(d)
225.	(d)	226.	(a)	227.	(d)	365.	(a)	366.	(c)	367.	(c)
228.	(a)	229.	(b)	230.	(a)	368.	(a)	369.	(a)	370.	(c)
231.	(b)	232.	(d)	233.	(b)	371.	(d)	372.	(c)	373.	(d)
234.	(b)	235.	(c)	236.	(d)	374.	(d)	375.	(a)	376.	(d)
237.	(a)	238.	(a)	239.	(d)	377.	(d)	378.	(b)	379.	(c)
240.	(c)	241.	(c)	242.	(a)	380.	(d)	381.	(d)	382.	(c)

383.	(b)	384.	(d)	385.	(b)	524.	(c)	525.	(a)	526.	(a)
386.	(b)	387.	(d)	388.	(a)	527.	(b)	528.	(c)	529.	(b)
389.	(b)	390.	(d)	391.	(c)	530.	(c)	531.	(a)	532.	(b)
392.	(d)	393.	(b)	394.	(b)	533.	(b)	534.	(b)	535.	(a)
395.	(c)	396.	(b)	397.	(b)	536.	(b)	537.	(b)	538.	(a)
398.	(a)	399.	(a)	400.	(b)	539.	(d)	540.	(a)	541.	(b)
401.	(b)	402.	(c)	403.	(c)	542.	(d)	543.	(c)	544.	(d)
404.	(c)	405.	(c)	406.	(d)	545.	(a)	546.	(b)	547.	(a)
407.	(d)	408.	(b)	409.	(d)	548.	(d)	549.	(d)	550.	(d)
410.	(c)	411.	(a)	412.	(c)	551.	(d)	552.	(a)	553.	(b)
413.	(c)	414.	(d)	415.	(d)	554.	(c)	555.	(b)	556.	(b)
416.	(d)	417.	(a)	418.	(d)	557.	(a)	558.	(b)	559.	(a)
419.	(a)	420.	(a)	421.	(b)	560.	(b)	561.	(c)	562.	(d)
422.	(c)	423.	(a)	424.	(a)	563.	(a)	564.	(b)	565.	(c)
425.	(a)	426.	(d)	427.	(d)	566.	(d)	567.	(a)	568.	(a)
428.	(d)	429.	(a)	430.	(d)	569.	(b)	570.	(c)	571.	(c)
431.	(d)	432.	(a)	433.	(a)	572.	(a)	573.	(b)	574.	(c)
434.	(c)	435.	(a)	436.	(c)	575.	(d)	576.	(c)	577.	(a)
437.	(a)	438.	(a)	439.	(d)	578.	(b)	579.	(d)	580.	(a)
440.	(c)	441.	(d)	442.	(a)	581.	(b)	582.	(a)	583.	(b)
443.	(d)	444.	(b)	445.	(a)	584.	(c)	585.	(d)	586.	(a)
446.	(b)	447.	(a)	448.	(b)	587.	(b)	588.	(c)	589.	(b)
449.	(c)	450.	(a)	451.	(b)	590.	(c)	591.	(d)	592.	(d)
452.	(a)	453.	(a)	454.	(b)	593.	(c)	594.	(c)	595.	(b)
455.	(d)	456.	(a)	457.	(c)	596.	(c)	597.	(a)	598.	(d)
458.	(a)	459.	(a)	460.	(a)	599.	(c)	600.	(a)	601.	(b)
461.	(a)	462.	(c)	463.	(c)	602.	(d)	603.	(b)	604.	(c)
464.	(c)	465.	(c)	466.	(a)	605.	(a)	606.	(b)	607.	(c)
467.	(a)	468.	(b)	469.	(b)	608.	(a)	609.	(a)	610.	(b)
470.	(d)	471.	(a)	472.	(d)	611.	(c)	612.	(d)	613.	(a)
473.	(a)	474.	(d)	475.	(a)	614.	(b)	615.	(d)	616.	(d)
476.	(a)	477.	(c)	478.	(a)	617.	(b)	618.	(d)	619.	(b)
479.	(c)	480.	(c)	481.	(d)	620.	(d)	621.	(b)	622.	(d)
482.	(d)	483.	(b)	484.	(d)	623.	(c)	624.	(b)	625.	(a)
485.	(b)	486.	(a)	487.	(b)	626.	(c)	627.	(a)	628.	(c)
488.	(a)	489.	(b)	490.	(a)	629.	(d)	630.	(a)	631.	(d)
491.	(b)	492.	(c)	493.	(c)	632.	(a)	633.	(a)	634.	(a)
494.	(d)	495.	(b)	496.	(d)	635.	(a)	636.	(d)	637.	(b)
497.	(c)	498.	(b)	499.	(b)	638.	(c)	639.	(d)	640.	(a)
500.	(a)	501.	(b)	502.	(b)	641.	(c)	642.	(b)	643.	(c)
503.	(b)	504.	(d)	505.	(a)	644.	(d)	645.	(d)	646.	(b)
506.	(a)	507.	(a)	508.	(b)	647.	(d)	648.	(d)	649.	(d)
509.	(a)	510.	(d)	511.	(d)	650.	(a)	651.	(c)	652.	(a)
512.	(c)	513.	(a)	514.	(a)	653.	(a)	654.	(d)	655.	(d)
515.	(b)	516.	(a)	517.	(c)	656.	(d)	657.	(b)	658.	(a)
518.	(a)	519.	(c)	520.	(b)	659.	(b)	660.	(a)	661.	(d)
521.	(d)	522.	(a)	523.	(a)	662.	(a)	663.	(b)	664.	(a)

665.	(a)	666.	(b)	667.	(d)	802.	(d)	803.	(a)	804.	(d)
668.	(a)	669.	(d)	670.	(c)	805.	(c)	806.	(c)	807.	(c)
671.	(c)	672.	(a)	673.	(a)	808.	(d)	809.	(c)	810.	(b)
674.	(d)	675.	(b)	676.	(c)	811.	(a)	812.	(b)	813.	(a)
677.	(c)	678.	(a)	679.	(a)	814.	(a)	815.	(c)	816.	(c)
680.	(c)	781.	(b)	682.	(c)	817.	(d)	818.	(c)	819.	(c)
683.	(d)	683.	(a)	684.	(a)	820.	(b)	821.	(b)	822.	(b)
685.	(d)	686.	(b)	687.	(a)	823.	(a)	824.	(c)	825.	(a)
688.	(d)	689.	(b)	690.	(d)	826.	(c)	827.	(a)	828.	(a)
691.	(a)	692.	(d)	693	(d)	829.	(b)	830.	(c)	831.	(c)
694.	(d)	695.	(c)	696.	(d)	832.	(a)	833.	(a)	834.	(d)
697.	(c)	698.	(d)	699.	(a)	835.	(b)	836.	(c)	837.	(c)
700.	(b)	701.	(c)	702.	(a)	838.	(c)	839.	(c)	840.	(a)
703.	(b)	704.	(c)	705.	(b)	841.	(b)	842.	(b)	843.	(c)
706.	(d)	707.	(a)	708.	(d)	844.	(b)	845.	(a)	846.	(a)
709.	(a)	710.	(d)	711.	(c)	847.	(d)	848.	(a)	849.	(d)
712.	(b)	713.	(a)	714.	(a)	850.	(d)	851.	(d)	852.	(c)
715.	(c)	716.	(c)	717.	(a)	853.	(d)	854.	(b)	855.	(d)
718.	(a)	719.	(a)	720.	(d)	856.	(a)	857.	(c)	858.	(b)
721.	(c)	722.	(c)	723.	(b)	859.	(d)	860.	(c)	861.	(a)
724.	(c)	725.	(c)	726.	(d)	862.	(d)	863.	(d)	864.	(c)
727.	(b)	728.	(d)	729.	(d)	865.	(a)	866.	(c)	867.	(c)
730.	(a)	731.	(a)	732.	(c)	868.	(a)	869.	(a)	870.	(b)
733.	(a)	734.	(b)	735.	(b)	871.	(b)	872.	(b)	873.	(b)
736.	(c)	737.	(a)	738.	(a)	874.	(c)	875.	(b)	876.	(b)
739.	(d)	740.	(a)	741.	(c)	877.	(d)	878.	(d)	879.	(c)
742.	(a)	743.	(a)	744.	(b)	880.	(c)	881.	(c)	882.	(a)
745.	(c)	746.	(d)	747.	(a)	883.	(c)	884.	(a)	885.	(a)
748.	(a)	749.	(a)	750.	(c)	886.	(b)	887.	(c)	888.	(a)
751.	(a)	752.	(d)	753.	(d)	889.	(a)	890.	(c)	891.	(a)
754.	(d)	756.	(a)	755.	(b)	892.	(c)	893.	(c)	894.	(c)
757.	(b)	758.	(c)	759.	(a)	895.	(d)	896.	(d)	897.	(d)
760.	(c)	761.	(a)	762.	(b)	898.	(d)	899.	(d)	900.	(a)
763.	(c)	764.	(a)	765.	(d)	901.	(a)	902.	(d)	903.	(d)
766.	(b)	767.	(b)	768.	(b)	904.	(a)	905.	(c)	906.	(b)
769.	(a)	770.	(b)	771.	(c)	907.	(b)	908.	(c)	909.	(d)
772.	(a)	773.	(b)	774.	(a)	910.	(a)	911.	(d)	912.	(a)
775.	(a)	776.	(c)	777.	(b)	913.	(a)	914.	(b)	915.	(a)
778.	(d)	779.	(a)	780.	(b)	916.	(c)	917.	(b)	918.	(a)
781.	(d)	782.	(b)	783.	(a)	919.	(c)	920.	(a)	921.	(d)
784.	(c)	785.	(b)	786.	(a)	922.	(c)	923.	(d)	924.	(a)
787	(c)	788.	(a)	789.	(c)	925.	(a)	926.	(b)	927.	(a)
790.	(b)	791.	(a)	792.	(a)	928.	(c)	929.	(b)	930.	(c)
793.	(c)	794.	(d)	795.	(c)	931.	(c)	932.	(a)	933	(a)
796.	(d)	797.	(b)	798.	(b)	934.	(b)	935.	(a)	936.	(c)
799.	(c)	800.	(c)	801.	(b)	937.	(a)	938.	(b)	939.	(d)

940.	(d)	941.	(c)	942.	(b)	970.	(b)	971.	(c)	972.	(b)
943.	(b)	944.	(a)	945.	(b)	973.	(b)	974.	(a)	975.	(a)
946.	(c)	947.	(d)	948.	(a)	976.	(a)	977.	(b)	978.	(c)
949.	(d)	950.	(b)	951.	(b)	979.	(d)	980.	(b)	981.	(c)
952.	(b)	953.	(c)	954.	(d)	982.	(a)	983.	(d)	984.	(d)
955.	(b)	956.	(d)	957.	(c)	985.	(b)	986.	(d)	987.	(a)
958.	(c)	959.	(a)	960.	(a)	988.	(d)	989.	(c)	990.	(d)
961.	(d)	962.	(b)	963.	(c)	991.	(a)	992.	(d)	993.	(c)
964.	(a)	965.	(b)	966.	(c)	994.	(d)	995.	(b)	996.	(c)
967.	(a)	968.	(a)	969.	(b)	997.	(c)				

12 Animal Reproduction

Salient Points

- Testis consists of several crypts, enclosed in a serous layer called tunica vaginalis.
- Wall of seminiferous tubules has two types of cells namely germ cells and sertoli cells.
- Leydig cells produce male hormone.
- Many seminiferous tubules join to form rete testis.
- Vas efferentia emerge from rete testis.
- Epididymis is 115 feet long in bull.
- Spermatic cord consists of vas deferens, spermatic arteries, veins, nerves and cremaster muscle.
- Vas deferens is involved in ejaculation.
- Scrotum provides for testes an environment that is 1- 8 ^{0}F cooler than the body cavity.
- Infundibulum receives ova, discharged from ovary.
- Caruncles develop into cotyledons during pregnancy.
- Cervix is also known as neck of womb.
- Spermiogenesis is also known as spermateliosis.
- Period of start of heat in animal is known as proestrum.
- Period of desire is called as oestrum. It lasts for 12-24 hours in cow: -2 days in ewe: 4-5 days in mare: 2-3 days in sow.
- Diestrum is longest phase of oestrus cycle and is characterized by fully developed corpus luteum.
- Movement of spermatozoa from sertoli cells is known as spermeation.
- In cow, implantation actually begins from 11 to 40th day post coitum.
- Uterine milk is composed of protein, fat, and glycogen.
- Between 21st and 22nd day, heart begins to beat in cattle.
- Rosette inhibition test is used for diagnosis of pregnancy (Early pregnancy factor). It has 72 % sensitivity.
- Free martin is a sterile female with underdeveloped reproductive organs having male characteristics, occurs when female is born along with male as a twin.

Types of placentation in animals:

Sl No.	Placenta	Gross shape	Example
1	Epitheliochorial	Diffuse	Pig, horse, donkey
2	Syndesmochorial	Cotyledonary	Sheep, goat, cow.
3	Endotheliochorial	Zonary or discoid	Cat, dog, ferret
4	Hemochorial	Zonary or discoid	Primates
5	Hemoendothelial	Spheroidal or discoid	Rat, rabbit

Questions

1. Normal, safe, easy, natural or physiological parturition.
   (a) Eutocia (b) Dystocia
   (c) Both (d) None

2. Difficult birth comes under.
(a) Eutocia (b) Dystocia
(c) Both (d) None

3. Relationship at long axis of fetus to long axis of dam and portion at the Fetus entering in birth canal signifies.
(a) Presentation (b) Position
(c) Posture (d) None

4. Relation ship of dorsum of fetus in longitudinal presentation has possible position.
(a) Dorso sacral
(b) Right & Left dorsoilial
(c) Dorsopubic
(d) All of the above

5. Different possible position in transverse presentation is
(a) Right cephaloilial (b) Left cephaloilial
(c) Both (d) None

6. Relationship at the movables appendages of the fetus to the body of the fetus signifies.
(a) Presentation (b) Position
(c) Posture (d) None

7. Sterno abdominal presentation also called as
(a) Anterior longitudinal presentation
(b) Posterior longitudinal presentation
(c) Transverse dorsal presentation
(d) Transverse ventral presentation

8. In Normal case following are present.
(a) Anterior longitudinal presentation
(b) Dorso sacral position
(c) Head of fetus rest of metacarpal bone & knees of the fore limb extended in the birth canal
(d) All of the above

9. Normal birth also occur, if fetus is in
(a) Posterior longitudinal presentation
(b) Dorso sacral position
(c) Both
(d) None

10. Transverse presentation seen in
(a) Mare (b) Ruminants
(c) Ewes (d) All

11. Posterior longitudinal presentation, dorso sacral position with limb retained or extended beneath the body is.
(a) Breech presentation
(b) Vertex presentation
(c) Poll presentation
(d) Nape presentation

12. Anterior longitudinal presentation, dorso sacral position with slight down ward deviation of fetal head between the fore limbs in which only nose of fetus is caught on the brim at the pelvis.
(a) Breech presentation
(b) Vertex presentation
(c) Poll presentation
(d) Nape presentation

13. Anterior longitudinal presentation dorso sacral position with more severe flexion of the head & neck of fetus between the fore limbs is.
(a) Breech presentation
(b) Vertex presentation
(c) Poll presentation
(d) Nape presentation

14. Anterior – longitudinal presentation, dorso sacral position with most severe flexion of the head and neck of the fetus between the fore limb in such a way that the head is against the fetal sternum or abdomen is.
(a) Breech presentation
(b) Nape presentation
(c) Poll presentation
(d) Vertex presentation

15. Anterior longitudinal presentation, dorso sacral position occurs in.
(a) Nape presentation
(b) Poll presentation
(c) Vertex presentation
(d) All of the above

16. Posterior longitudinal presentation, dorso sacral position occurs in.
(a) Breech presentation
(b) Vertex presentation
(c) Poll presentation
(d) Nape presentation

17. The gestation period of Rhinoceros is
a. 550 days b. 330 days
c. 90-93 days d. 105-113 days

18. Primary uterine inertia is due to

(a) Deficiency in contractile potential of myometrium
(b) Due to exhaustion
(c) Both
(d) None

19. Signs of primary uterine inertia are.
(a) Mammary development during pregnancy
(b) Discharge of mucus from valva
(c) Ligamentous relaxation of pelvis
(d) All of above

20. Bandl's ring is
(a) Contraction of uterus around the fetus
(b) Type at ring present in fetus
(c) Both
(d) None

21. Prognosis in secondary uterine inertia is
(a) Good (b) Poor
(c) Guarded (d) None

22. If live fetus is in the birth canal then what may be the signs
(a) Foots grasped & pinched then movement
(b) Eye ball pinched movement of fetal head
(c) Post presentation – contraction at anal sphincter
(d) All of the above

23. Bandl's rings are present, the prognosis.
(a) Grave (b) Good
(c) Poor (d) None of them

24. In mare, at what time fetus may die with in onset of labour?
(a) 30-40 minutes (b) 3-12 hours
(c) 6-8 hours (d) None of the above

25. Fetus dies and emphysema develops within time respectively.
(a) Cow – 3-12 hours, 24-36 hours
(b) Bitch – 6-8 hours, 24-36 hours
(c) Both
(d) None

26. Epidural anesthesia helps in.
(a) Stopping straining
(b) Stopping pain
(c) Performing obstetrical operation in standing animal
(d) All

27. Which of the following are more prone to vagino cervical prolepses?
(a) Pluripara (b) Primipara
(c) Both (d) None

28. Causes of vagino cervical prolapse
(a) Secretion of large amount of estrogen during last 2-3 months
(b) Injuries & stretching at preceding parturition
(c) Low level of serum calcium & phosphorus
(d) All

29. Sings of vagino cervical prolapse are
(a) Edematous & inflamed mucus membranes
(b) None return of organs on pressure
(c) Both
(d) None

30. To handle vulvar torsion, following are used.
(a) Rope (b) Leather
(c) Both (d) None

31. What are the various obstetrical operations?
(a) Mutation
(b) Forced extraction
(c) Fetotomy & Cesarean section
(d) All

32. Mutation is done by
(a) Repulsion (b) Rotation
(c) Version (d) All

33. Mutation includes those operations through which the fetus is brought into normal.
(a) Presentation (b) Position
(c) Posture (d) All

34. Repulsion can be done by
(a) Operators arm (b) Arms of helper
(c) Crutch repeller (d) All

35. Rotation is the turning of the fetus on its long axis to bring it into the
(a) Dorso sacral position
(b) Sterno abdominal position
(c) Both
(d) None

36. Version is the rotation of fetus on its
(a) Long axis (b) Transverse axis
(c) Both (d) None

37. Extension & adjustment of the extremities is the correction of abnormalities in

(a) Presentation (b) Position
(c) Posture (d) None

38. What are the contra indications of the forced extraction?
(a) Abnormal presentation, position & posture
(b) Cervical stenosis
(c) Obturator paralysis
(d) All

39. Fetotomy operation in anterior presentation includes.
(a) Decaptitation
(b) Cephalotomy
(c) Amputation of head, neck and forelimbs
(d) All

40. Fetotomy operation in posterior presentation, includes
(a) Embryotomy
(b) Bisection of pelvis in breech presentation
(c) Amputation of rear limb at the tarsus
(d) All

41. Decapitation or Amputation of head done when
(a) Both limbs are retained & head is present in vulva
(b) Swollen fetus
(c) Emphysematous fetus
(d) All

42. Cephalotomy done during
(a) Hydrocephalous (b) Extensive head size
(c) Both (d) None

43. Dog sitting posture indicates.
(a) Anterior presentation
(b) Posterior presentation
(c) Both
(d) None

44. In mare site of cesarean section.
(a) Upper left flank (b) Lower left flank
(c) Right lower flank (d) None

45. In cow, site of cesarean section
(a) Upper left flank (b) Upper right flank
(c) Both (d) None

46. In bitches during whelping, the body temperature.
(a) Increases (b) Decreases
(c) None (d) Both

47. Follicular phase is
(a) Pro estrum (b) Estrum
(c) Both (d) None

48. Estrogenic phase is
(a) Pro estrum (b) Estrum
(c) Both (d) None

49. Luteal phase is
(a) Met estrum (b) Diestrum
(c) Both (d) None

50. Estrum cycle is controlled by interaction between
(a) FSH, hypothalamus
(b) Pituitary gland, ovary
(c) Uterus
(d) All

51. Bleeding is seen in bitch during
(a) Pro estrus (b) Estrus
(c) Met estrum (d) Diestrum

52. Cow, Sow and Queen are
(a) Polyestrus (b) Monoestrus
(c) Both (d) None

53. Estrus in cow is about
(a) 12-24 hrs (b) 4-7 days
(c) 2-4 days (d) None

54. Queen ovulates.
(a) Spontaneously (b) After induction
(c) Both (d) None

55. Time of ovulation in cow is about.
(a) 1-2 days before end of estrum
(b) 10-15 hrs after end of estrum
(c) 25-40 hrs after and of estrum
(d) None

56. Which species is most sensitive to PGF_2a?
(A) Bovine (B) Equines
(C) Canine (D) Feline

57. Steroid hormones having nucleus of
(a) amino acid
(b) Cyclopentanoperhydro phenanthrene
(c) Both
(d) None

58. Relaxin is secreted by
(a) Ovary (b) Uterus
(c) Placenta (d) All

59. Protein hormones are administered.
(a) Orally (b) Parenterally

(c) Both (d) None

60. Inhibiting hormone released by hypothalamus is
(a) STIH (b) PRH
(c) PIF (d) All

61. Anterior pituitary contain 3 parts.
(a) Pars tuberalis (b) Pars intermedia
(c) Pars distalis (d) All

62. Pars intermedia produces.
(a) STH (b) ACTH
(c) MSH (d) None

63. Posterior pituitary stores.
(a) Oxytocin (b) Vasopressin
(c) Both (d) None

64. Oxytocin & Vasopressin are produced from
(a) Hypothalamus (b) Pituitary
(c) Both (d) None

65. Acidophil cells of pituitary are producer of
(a) Somatotrophs (b) Lactotrophs
(c) Both (d) None

66. The gestation period of Seal is
a. 550 days **b.** 330 days
c. 90-93 days d. 105-113 days

67. Which of the following are glycoproteins?
(a) FSH (b) L H
(c) TSH (d) All

68. Hormones of polypeptide nature are
(a) ACTH (b) STH
(c) LTH (d) All

69. FSH acts on the
(a) Ovary
(b) Seminiferous tubules
(c) Both
(d) None

70. LH acts on the
(a) Ovary
(b) Seminiferous tubules
(c) Both
(d) None

71. TSH acts on
(a) Thyroid gland (b) Soma
(c) Adrenal cortex (d) None

72. LTH acts on
(a) Ovary (b) Mammary gland
(c) Both (d) None

73. Gn RH stimulates synthesis and secretion of
(a) LH (b) FSH
(c) Both (d) None

74. Prolactin inhibiting hormone, inhibits release of
(a) LTH (b) TSH
(c) ACTH (d) None

75. Oxytocin helps in
(a) Uterine contraction
(b) Milk led down
(c) Both
(d) None

76. Oxytocin helps in
(a) Parturition
(b) Sperm & egg transport
(c) Both
(d) None

77. Androgen is released from
(a) Testis (b) Adrenal cortex
(c) Ovary (d) All

78. Progesterone is released from
(a) Ovary (b) Placenta
(c) Adrenal cortex (d) All

79. Adrenalin is releases from
(a) Ovary (b) Uterus
(c) Placenta (d) None

80. Hormones released from ovary are
(a) Testosterone (b) Estrogen
(c) Progesterone (d) All

81. Hormones released from placenta are
(a) Estrogen (b) Relaxin
(c) Placenta (d) All

82. FSH causes
(a) Growth of ovary
(b) Maturation of ovary
(c) Both
(d) None

83. Puberty is a coordinated process governed by
(a) CNS (b) Hypothalamus
(c) Ovary (d) All

84. Average age at puberty in cattle
(a) 24-34 months (b) 8-12 months
(c) 6-15 months (d) None

85. Boney pelvis is composed of.

(a) Sacrum (b) Os coxae
(c) Both (d) None

86. Haunch is the
(a) Upper most segment at hind limb
(b) Lower most segment of hind limb
(c) Both
(d) None

87. Os coxae comprising of
(a) Ilium (b) Ischium
(c) Pubis (d) All

88. Dorsal wall of bony pelvis composed of
(a) Sacrum
(b) First 2-3 coccigeal vertebra
(c) Both
(d) None

89. Ventral wall is formed by
(a) Pubis (b) Ischial bone
(c) Both (d) None

90. Sacrum is consist at following number of vertebra in cattle
(a) 5 (b) 6
(c) 7 (d) 9

91. Medial portion of the wing, articulating with sacrum is called.
(a) Tuber sacrale (b) Tuber coxae
(c) Both (d) None

92. Lateral external portion of the wing is called
(a) Tuber coxae (b) Tuber sacrale
(c) Both (d) None

93. Tuber ischii in cow bears following tuberosities.
(a) Dorsal (b) Ventral
(c) Lateral (d) All

94. Acetabulum is formed by the fusion of
(a) Ilium (b) Ischium
(c) Pubis (d) All

95. The pelvic ligaments are
(a) Dorsal and lateral sacro iliac ligament (paired)
(b) Sacro sciatic ligament (paired)
(c) Prepubic tendon
(d) All

96. Diameter of the pelvic inlet is
aa 5 cm (b) 6 cm
(c) 7 cm (d) 8 cm

97. Diameters of the pelvic outlet is
(a) 2 cm (b) 3 cm
(c) 4 cm (d) 5 cm

98. Cow & Sow have
(a) Elliptical pelvic inlet
(b) Round pelvic inlet
(c) Square pelvic inlet
(d) None

99. Female reproductive organs consist of
(a) Ovaries (b) Tubular portion
(c) Both (d) None

100. Broad ligament supports
(a) Ovary (b) Oviduct
(c) Uterus (d) All

101. Broad ligament consists of
(a) Mesovarium (b) Mesosalpinx
(c) Mesometrium (d) All

102. In early life nephric & genital regions are formed from
(a) Mesodermal tissue
(b) Ectodermal tissue
(c) Endodeimal tissue
(d) None

103. Which duct develops into tubular & ducts in male.
(a) Mesonephric (b) Wolffian tubules
(c) Both (d) None

104. Paramesonephric or mullerian ducts develops in female on
(a) Ovary (b) Ducts
(c) Tubular portion (d) None

105. Indifferent stage signifies.
(a) Male embryo (b) Female
(c) Both (d) None

106. Gonads are present in
(a) Indifferent stage (b) Male
(c) Female (d) None

107. Origin of the primary germ cell is
(a) Extra gonadal
(b) From the wall of yolk sac
(c) Both
(d) None

108. During development, in mare follicle are distributed
(a) Throughout the ovary

(b) Cortical region
(c) Both
(d) None

109. Tunica albuginea does not develop in the
(a) Male (b) Female
(c) Both (d) None

110. Tunica albuginea is the first histological evidence that the developing gonad is
(a) Testis (b) Ovary
(c) Duct (d) None

111. Ovary of cow is
(a) Almond shaped
(b) Bean shaped
(c) Grape cluster shape
(d) Oval

112. Ovary of mare is
(a) Almond shaped
(b) Bean shaped
(c) Grape cluster shape
(d) Oval

113. Ovary of bitch is
(a) Almond shaped
(b) Bean shaped
(c) Grape cluster shape
(d) Oval

114. Which of the following hormones is secreted by ovary?
(a) Estrogen (b) Progesteron
(c) Oxytocin (d) All

115. Site of ovulation in ruminants is
(a) Any point
(b) Any point except hiatus
(c) Ovulation fossa
(d) None

116. Site of ovulation in mare is
(a) Any point
(b) Any point except hiatus
(c) Ovulation fossa
(d) None

117. Site of ovulation in sow is
(a) Any point
(b) any point except hiatus
(c) Ovulation fossa
(d) None

118. Animals which give single offspring at parturition are
(a) Unipara (b) Monotochus
(c) Both (d) Premipara

119. Animals which experience first parturition are
(a) Umpare (b) Monotochus
(c) Both (d) Premipara

120. Animal pregnant for the second or more time
(a) Unipara (b) Multipera
(c) Premipara (d) Pleuripara

121. Time of sex differentiation in Fetus of cattle is
(a) 1 month (b) 2 months
(c) 3months (d) 4 months

122. Embryo is
(a) Unisexual (b) Bisexual
(c) Asexual (d) Haploid

123. Male genital organs develop from
(a) Mullerean duct (b) Wolffian duct
(c) Both (d) None

124. Female genital organs develop from
(a) Mullerean duct (b) Wolffian duct
(c) Both (d) None

125. Medulla of gonad develops into
(a) Testes in male (b) Ovary in female
(c) Both (d) Any

126. Cortex of gonad develops into
(a) Testes in male (b) Ovary in female
(c) both (d) any

127. Which part of oviduct receives ovum
(a) Infundibulum (b) Ampulla
(c) Both (d) None

128. Site of fertilization is
(a) Infundibulum (b) Ampulla
(c) Both (d) None

129. Connector between oviduct & uterus is
(a) Testes in male (b) Ovary in female
(c) both (d) any

130. Which part of uterus are 2 in numbers
(a) Horn (b) Body
(c) Cervix (d) All

131. Bandl's rings are formed in case of
(a) Uterine torsion (b) Veginal torsion
(c) Pyometra (d) Metritis

132. Germ cells develop from
(a) Yolk sac endoderm
(b) Yolk sac epithelium
(c) Mesoderm
(d) Yolk sac mesothelium

133. In corpus luteum & placenta depended animals ovary can be
(a) Removed after 1 month of pregnancy
(b) Removed after 6 months of pregnancy
(c) Removed after 5 months of pregnancy
(d) Can't be removed

134. Relaxin is secreted from
(a) Gonads (b) Foetal membrane
(c) Both (d) None

135. Melanocyte stimulating hormone is secreted from
(a) Pars tuberalis (b) Pass intermedia
(c) Pars distalis (d) All

136. For handling live Fetus which kind of tools are used
(a) Sharp (b) Blunt
(c) Both (d) None

137. For handling dead Fetus
(a) Sharp (b) Blunt
(c) Both (d) None

138. Estrous cycle in cow is of
(a) 21 days (b) 21 weeks
(c) 1 month (d) 18 days

139. Estrous cycle in multiparous cow is
(a) 21 days (b) 21 weeks
(c) 1 month (d) 18 days

140. Preovulatory follicles release
(a) Estrogen (b) Progestérone
(c) Oxytocin (d) Prostaglandine

141. Leutiolysis occurs due to
(a) Estrogène (b) Progestérone
(c) Oxytocin (d) Prostaglandins

142. Follicular maturation occurs in influence of
(a) FSH (b) LH
(c) Inhibin (d) Progesterone

143. Ovum remain in fallopian tubes for
(a) 1 day (b) 15 hours
(c) 5-6 days (d) 5-6 hours

144. Ovum floats in a uterus of sheep/goat for
(a) 17-20 days (b) 25 days
(c) 1 month (d) 1 week

145. Ovum floats in a uterus of cow for
(a) 17-20 days (b) 25 days
(c) 1 month (d) 1 week

146. Effect of progesterone during pregnancy
(a) Decreases myometreal contraction ability
(b) Decrease growth of uterine glands
(c) Decrease effect on estrogen
(d) All

147. Concentration of progesterone differs after how many days in pregnant & non pregnant animal
(a) 17 days (b) 1 month
(c) 25 days (d) 20 days

148. Pregnancy maintaining hormone is
(a) Oxytocin (b) Estrogen
(c) Progesterone (d) All

149. Bovine trophoblast protein I is produced by
(a) Uterine glands (b) Endrometrium
(c) Placenta (d) Fetus

150. Erythritol is present in
(a) Pregnant uterus
(b) Non pregnant uterus
(c) Both
(d) None

151. CL dependent species is
(a) Goat (b) Mare
(c) Ewe (d) All

152. Corpus luteum independent species is
(a) Mare (b) Goat
(c) Sow (d) All

153. At the end of gestation, estrogen level
(a) Increases (b) Decreases
(c) Disappears (d) No change

154. Relaxin is secreted by
(a) Placenta (b) Ovary
(c) Uterus (d) All

155. Synthesis of actin & myosin for myometrial contractions occurs under influence of
(a) Placenta (b) Ovary
(c) Uterus (d) All

156. Post parturient anestrous occurs more in
(a) Low yielding cows (b) Heifers
(c) High yielding cows (d) All

157. Effect of suckling, on post parturient anestrous

(a) Increases (b) Decreases
(c) No effect (d) All

158. Corpus luteum disappears after how many days of parturition
(a) 4 (b) 10
(c) 14 (d) 24

159. Corpus luteum spurium is present in
(a) Estrus (b) Pregnancy
(c) As scar (d) None

160. Corpus luteum verum is present in
(a) Estrus (b) Pregnancy
(c) As scar (d) None

161. Corpus luteum albicans is present in
(a) Estrus (b) Pregnancy
(c) As scar (d) None

162. Numbers of caruncles in cattle is
(a) 70-120 (b) 100-120
(c) 80-90 (d) 130

163. Numbers of caruncles in buffalo
(a) 70-120 (b) 100-120
(c) 80-90 (d) 130

164. Numbers of caruncles in sheep/goat
(a) 70-120 (b) 100-120
(c) 80-90 (d) 130

165. Caruncles in goat is
(a) Concave (b) Convex
(c) Both (d) Round

166. Caruncle in cow is
(a) Concave (b) Convex
(c) Both (d) Round

167. Glands which seal cervix are
(a) Cervical glands
(b) Vaginal glands
(c) Bulbo urethral gland
(d) Goblet glands

168. Clean discharge during estrus comes due to
(a) Cervical glands
(b) Vaginal glands
(c) Bulbo urethral gland
(d) Goblet glands

169. Estrus cycle is
(a) Cyclic rhythm of reproductive pattern
(b) Cyclic rhythm of uterine sloughing
(c) Cyclic rhythm of vaginal sloughing
(d) All are correct

170. Which is the follicular phase?
(a) Proestrus (b) Metestrus
(c) Diestrus (d) Anestrus

171. Which of the following is luteal phase?
(a) Proestrus (b) Metestrus
(c) Estrus (d) Anestrus

172. Luteal phase is absent in
(a) Cow (b) Mare
(c) Ewe (d) Bitch

173. Diestrus is absent in
(a) Dog (b) Cat
(c) Both (d) None

174. Greek work OISTROS means
(a) Madness (b) Reproduction
(c) Offspring (d) Pregnancy

175. Cervical folds are transverse in
(a) Cow (b) Mare
(c) Both (d) None

176. Steroid secreted by ovary is
(a) P_4 (b) Inhibin
(c) Oxytocin (d) All

177. Hormone secreted by ovary is
(a) P4 (b) E3
(c) PGF2á (d) All

178. Secretion of FSH from pituitary is inhibited by
(a) Inhibin (b) Esteradiol
(c) Progesteron (d) Oxytocin

179. FSH secretion, by the influence of Melatonin
(a) Increases (b) Decreases
(c) No effect (d) All

180. Regulation on number of ovulations is done by
(a) Inhibin (b) Estradiol
(c) Progesteron (d) Oxytocin

181. Which of the following is seasonal breeder?
(a) Cow (b) Mare
(c) Sheep (d) b & c

182. In induced ovulators, which one is must for LH surge?
(a) Light (b) Vitamin B6
d(c) Coitus (d) Cold environment

183. Leutilization occurs when
(a) Cells that produces estrogen, start

producing progesterone
(b) Cells that produces Progesterone, start producing estrogen
(c) All cells produce estrogen
(d) all cells produce progesterone

184. Length of estrus cycle is decided by
(a) Estrogen (b) Progesterone
(c) Inhibin (d) Oxytocin

185. Leydig cells have
(a) LH receptors (b) FSH receptors
(c) Both (d) None

186. Granulosa cells have
(a) LH receptors (b) FSH reception
(c) Both (d) None

187. Estrogen progesterone ratio is responsible for secretion of following from luteal cells
(a) Estrogen (b) Progesterone
(c) Inhibin (d) Oxytocin

188. Length of estrus in cow is
(a) 18 hours (b) 30 hour
(c) 48-72 hours (d) 4-8 days

189. Length of estrus in ewe is
(a) 18 hours (b) 30 hours
(c) 48-72 hours (d) 4-8 days

190. Length of estrus sow is
(a) 18 hours (b) 30 hours
(c) 48-72 hours (d) 4-8 days

190. Length of estrus mare is
(a) 18 hours (b) 30 hours
(c) 48-72 hours (d) 4-8 days

191. Gestation length of cow is about
(a) 282 days (b) 305 days
(c) 148 days (d) 215 days

192. Length of gestation in buffalo is about
(a) 282 days (b) 305 days
(c) 148 days (d) 215 days

193. Length of gestation in ewe is about
(a) 282 days (b) 305 days
(c) 148 days (d) 114 days

194. Length of gestation in sow is about
(a) 282 days (b) 305 days
(c) 148 days (d) 215 days

195. Length of gestation in mare is about
(a) 335 days (b) 285 days
(c) 60-65 days (d) 305 days

196. Length of gestation in bitch is about
(a) 335 days (b) 285 days
(c) 60-65 days (d) 305 days

197. Which of the following is seasonal polyestrus?
(a) Mare (b) Bitch
(c) Goat (d) Sow

198. Which of the following in seasonal monoetrus
(a) Mare (b) Bitch
(c) Goat (d) Sow

199. Ovulation in cow occurs
(a) 12 hours after estrus
(b) Near end of estrus
(c) 35-45 hours after onset of estrus
(d) 1-2 days before end of estrus

200. Ovulation in ewe occurs
(a) 12 hours after estrus
(b) Near end of estrus
(c) 35-45 hr after onset of estrus
(d) 1-2 days before end of estrus

201. Temperature of artificial vagina used for semen collection in horse is –
(a) 40-42°C (b) 45-50°C
(c) 50-55°C (d) 60°C

202. Temperature of artificial vagina used for semen collection in dog is –
(a) 40-42°C (b) 45-50°C
(c) 50-55°C (d) 60°C

203. Osmotic pressure of semen prior to A1 should be –
(a) 100 m osmoles (b) 200 m osmoles
(c) 300 m osmoles (d) 400 m osmoles

204. Which of the following diluents is used for preservation of semen at room temperature?
(a) Coconut milk extender
(b) Egg yolk citrate
(c) Both
(d) None

205. Which of the following diluents is used for preservation of semen at refrigeration temp?
(a) Coconut milk extender
(b) Egg yolk tris
(c) Egg yolk citrate
(d) All

206. Which of the following diluents is used for preservation of semen at – 79 to – 196°C
(a) Coconut milk extender
(b) Egg yolk tris
(c) Egg yolk citrate
(d) All

207. Sulfadimedine can't be added in which of the following semen diluters –
(a) Coconut milk extender
(b) Egg yolk tris
(c) Egg yolk citrate
(d) All

208. During semen dilution, temperature of diluter should be –
(a) Slightly more than that of semen
(b) Slightly less than that of semen
(c) Equal to semen
(d) Any temperature

209. Glycerol is added in semen diluter as –
(a) Antiseptic
(b) Base
(c) Nutrient
(d) Cryoprotectant

210. Equilibration period is time required by sperm prior to
(a) Capacitating (b) Freezing
(c) Fertilization (d) None

211. After equilibration, the membrane of sperm becomes
(a) More permeable (b) Semi permeable
(c) Less permeable (d) Impermeable

212. French mini straws for semen storage are sealed by
(a) Polyvinyl alcohol (b) Glass balls
(c) Both (d) None

213. Continental straws for semen storage are sealed by
(a) Polyvinyl alcohol powder
(b) Glass balls
(c) Both
(d) None

214. At first service minimum body weight of cattle should not be less than –
(a) 250 kg (b) 300 kg
(c) 100 kg (d) 350 kg

215. At first service minimum body weight of buffalo should not be less than –
(a) 250 kg (b) 300 kg
(c) 100 kg (d) 350 kg

216. Service after normal calving in cattle, should be done at interval of –
(a) 60 days (b) 90 days
(c) 120 days (d) 100 days

217. AI after dystocia, should be done at interval of –
(a) 60 days (b) 90 days
(c) 120 days (d) 100 days

218. Maximum limit of exotic blood in cross breed progeny is –
(a) 25% (b) 40%
(c) 62.5% (d) 70.5%

219. AI gun should be passed in vagina at an angle of –
(a) 20° (b) 90°
(c) 45° (d) 180°

220. Semen may be deposited in cervix in cases of –
(a) Cow (b) Buffalo
(c) Sheep (d) All

221. Semen may be deposited in uterus in cases of –
(a) Mare (b) Cow
(c) Both (d) None

222. Rapid thawing of stored frozen semen is done at –
(a) 37°C for 30 sec (b) 70°C for 30sec
(c) 37°C for 5 sec (d) 70°C for 5 sec

223. Slow thawing of stored frozen semen is done at –
(a) 37°C for 30 sec (b) 70°C for 30sec
(c) 37°C for 5 sec (d) 70°C for 5 sec

224. Breeding bulls should be preferably exercised during –
(a) Morning hours (b) Evening
(c) None (d) Late night

225. Libido refers to
(a) Masturbation (b) Consciousness
(c) Sexual desire (d) Slugging breeding

226. Volume of semen in French medi straw is –
(a) 0.5ml (b) 0.25ml
(c) 1ml (d) 0.75ml

227. Volume of semen in French mini straw is –
(a) 0.5ml (b) 0.25ml
(c) 1ml (d) 0.75ml

228. Volume of semen in continental straw is –
(a) 0.5ml (b) 0.25ml
(c) 1ml (d) 0.75ml

229. Per vaginal technique for AI is adopted in
(a) Mare (b) Cow
(c) Buffalo (d) Sow

230. Equilibration of sperms prior to freezing is done at.
(a) 5°C (b) 10°C
(c) 5°C (d) 15°C

231. Ejaculation time in case of Stallion is
(a) 15-20 seconds (b) 15-20 minutes
(c) 5 minutes (d) 10 seconds

232. Ejaculation time in case of Dog is
(a) 15-20 sec (b) 15-20 minutes
(c) 5 minutes (d) 10 sec

233. Ejaculation time in case of Boar is
(a) 15-20 sec (b) 15-20 minutes
(c) 5 minutes (d) 10 sec

234. Ejaculation time in case of Buck is.
(a) 15-20 sec (b) 15-20 minutes
(c) 5 minutes (d) 10 sec

235. Gloved hand method for semen collection is used in.
(a) Dog (b) Boar
(c) Buck (d) Bull

236. Best method for semen collection in routine is
(a) Natural service
(b) Artificial vagina
(c) Electro ejaculation
(d) Directly from vagina

237. Prostate hyperplasia occurs due to increased level of
(a) Testosteron (b) Estrogen
(c) Progesteion (d) All

238. Fructose in semen is derived from –
(a) Seminal vesicle (b) Prostate
(c) Both (d) None

239. pH of semen is –
(a) Acidic (b) Alkaline
(c) Neutral (d) Depends on season

240. Milk diluted semen is stored at
(a) 5°C (b) 18°C
(c) 79°C (d) 196°C

241. Coconut milk is which type of semen diluter
(a) Ambient temperature diluter
(b) Refrigeration temperature diluter
(c) Freezing temperature diluter
(d) None

242. Milk is which type of semen diluter
(a) Ambient temperature diluter
(b) Refrigeration temperature diluter
(c) Freezing temperature diluter
(d) None

243. Egg yolk tris is which type of semen diluter
(a) Ambient temperature diluter
(b) Refrigeration temperature diluter
(c) Freezing temperature diluter
(d) None

244. Crystal formation is prevented in deep frozen semen by addition of –
(a) Glycerol (b) Sulfonamide
(c) Phosphoric acid (d) Tri hydroxymethyl

245. Which of the following antibiotics in absent in Egg yolk tris diluter
(a) Sulphonamide
(b) Phényle haxen B
(c) Penicillin & Sodium
(d) Dihydro streptomycin

246. Which antibiotic is never added in diluter at deep freezing temperature?
(a) Sulphonamide
(b) Phényle haxen B
(c) Penicillin & Sodium
(d) Dihydro streptomycin

247. Which of the following crystallizes in freezing process in deep frozen semen storage?
(a) Sulphonamide
(b) Polymixen B
(c) Penicillin & Sodium
(d) Dehydrostreptomycin

248. Which straw is best suited for storage of deep frozen semen?
(a) French mini (b) Conventional
(c) French medium (d) Continental

249. During electro ejaculation which gland is stimulated?
(a) Ampullae (b) Seminal
(c) Prostat (d) a & b

250. Glycerol is added in semen diluters at the rate of
(a) 10% (b) 14%
(c) 24% (d) 25%

251. Lack of sexual desire & ability to copulate is
(a) Impotentia generandi
(b) Impotentia coeundi
(c) Both
(d) None

252. Inability or reduced ability to fertilize –
(a) Impotentia generandi
(b) Impotentia coeundi
(c) Both
(d) None

253. Fertile of high libido males may be
(a) More (b) Less
(c) Absent (d) No relation

254. Forked configuration of penis occurs in –
(a) Phimosis (b) Paraphimosis
(c) Phallocampsis (d) Diphallus

255. Rainbow deviation refers to, which side deviation of penis?
(a) Dorsal (b) Ventral
(c) Medial (d) Lateral

256. Which side rapture of penis generally occurs with the attachment of retractor penis muscle?
(a) Anterior (b) Behind
(c) Ventrally (d) Dorsally

257. Which nerve blockage is done for operation for tumors of penis & prepuce?
(a) Pudendal (b) Peroneal
(c) Internal obturator (d) All

258. Chronic prolapses of prepuces is common in –
(a) Indian milch breeds
(b) Indian draught breeds
(c) Both
(d) None

259. Animal suffering with which type of hernia should not be used for breeding
(a) Umbilical (b) Inguinal
(c) Both (d) None

260. Cork screening of penis occurs in
(a) Premature full erection
(b) Retraction
(c) Incomplete protrusion
(d) None

261. Normal motility & concentration of sperms is evident in
(a) Deadem (b) Dag deffect
(c) Both (d) None

262. Feulgen stain helps in revealing which defect of spermatozoa?
(a) Deadem effect
(b) Knobbed spermatozoa
(c) Chromosomal defects
(d) All

263. Eocin B stain helps in revealing which defect of spermatozoa?
(a) Deadem effect
(b) Knobbed spermatozoa
(c) Chromosomal defects
(d) All

264. Which one is a sex linked defect related to Golgi apparatus –
(a) Deadem effect
(b) Knobbed spermatozoa
(c) Chromosomal defects
(d) All

265. Acrosome is accentrically placed in case of –
(a) Deadem effect
(b) Knobbed spermatozoa
(c) Chromosomal defects
(d) All

266. High flankers has
(a) One testicle in inguinal canal
(b) Both testicles in inguinal canal
(c) Both a or b
(d) None

267. When testes lie in inguinal region they are known as –
(a) High flankers (b) Cryptorchids
(c) Both (d) None

268. Incidence of testicular hypoplasia among testicular pathology cases –
(a) 23% (b) 75-80%
(c) 100% (d) 50%

269. Incidence of testicular degeneration is
(a) 23% (b) 75-80%
(c) 100% (d) 50%

270. Incidence of left side testicular hypoplasia is

(a) 66.7% (b) 23.3%
(c) 50% (d) 100%

271. Incidence of right side testicular hypoplasia is
(a) 66.7% (b) 23.3%
(c) 50% (d) 100%

272. Sertoli cell tumors increase secretion of
(a) Estrogen (b) Testosterone
(c) Both (d) None

273. Leydig cell tumors produce
(a) Estrogen (b) Testosterone
(c) Both (d) None

274. Testicular tumors an more common in.
(a) Old dogs (b) Young dogs
(c) Infant (d) All

275. Summer infertility is common is –
(a) Exotic bulls (b) Rams
(c) Both (d) None

276. Which cells are most sensitive to irradiation?
(a) Spermatocytes (b) Spermatogonia
(c) Leydig cells (d) Spermatids

277. Which cells are least sensitive to irradiation?
(a) Spermatocytes (b) Spermatogonia
(c) Leydig cells (d) Spermatids

278. Which cells are most resistant to trauma & stress?
(a) Spermatocytes (b) Spermatogonia
(c) Leydig cells (d) Spermatids

279. Dystrophia adiposo genitalis is associated with tumors of
(a) Dog (b) Bull
(c) Horse (d) All

280. Dystrophia adiposo genitalis is associated with tumors of
(a) Testes (b) Uterus
(c) Ovary (d) Vagina

281. Arsenic solutions cause testicular degeneration in
(a) Boar (b) Ram
(c) Bull (d) Dog

282. Antimony compounds cause temporary infertility in –
(a) Boar (b) Ram
(c) Bull (d) Dog

283. Chlorinated naphthalenes produce testicular degeneration in –
(a) Bulls (b) Boars
(c) Both (d) None

284. Testicular degeneration in animal occurs due to –
(a) Ethylating agents (b) Amphetericin B
(c) Cadmium chloride (d) All

285. Testicular tumors are not common in
(a) Bulls (b) Dogs
(c) Both (d) None

286. Testicular tumors originated from
(a) Sertoli cells
(b) Leydig cells
(c) Germinal epithelium
(d) All

287. 80% of testes are composed of –
(a) Leydig cells
(b) Sertoli cells
(c) Seminiferous tubules
(d) All

288. Reduced volume of semen is called –
(a) Hypospermia (b) Hypozoospermia
(c) Both (d) None

289. Increased volume of semen is termed as –
(a) Oligozoospermia (b) Azoospermia
(c) Asepermia (d) Hyperspermia

290. Zero concentration of sperm in semen is termed as –
(a) Oligozoospermia (b) Azoospermia
(c) Asepermia (d) Hyperspermia

291. No volume of semen is –
(a) Oligozoospermia (b) Azoospermia
(c) Asepermia (d) Hyperspermia

292. Reduced concentration of sperms in semen
(a) Oligozoospermia (b) Azoospermia
(c) Asepermia (d) Hyperspermia

293. Increased concentration of sperms in semen
(a) Hyperspermia (b) Asthenospermia
(c) Polyspermia (d) Polyzoospermia

294. Increased motility of sperms is known as –
(a) Oligozoospeimia (b) Azoospermia
(c) Asepermia (d) Hyperspermia

295. All dead sperms in semen is known as –
(a) Aspermia (b) Necrospermia
(c) Teratozoospermia (d) Necrozoospermia

296. High percent of abnormal sperms is known as –
(a) Aspermia (b) Necrospermia

(c) Teratozoospermia (d) Necrozoospermia

297. Testicular degeneration increases number of
(a) Primary abnormalities
(b) Secondary abnormalities
(c) Both
(d) None

298. Testicular degeneration can be managed by which vitamin
(a) Vitamin A (b) Vitamin D
(c) Vitamin E (d) Vitamin K

299. Use of heat or counter irritants in case of testicular degeneration is
(a) Indicated (b) Contraindicated
(c) Not so effective (d) Very effective

300. Use of gonadotropin hormones in case of testicular degeneration is
(a) Indicated (b) Contraindicated
(c) Not so effective (d) Very effective

301. Spermatic granuloma can be formed due to high concentration of
(a) Lipids (b) Nucleic acid
(c) Both (d) None

302. Spermiostasis occurs in
(a) Blind rudimentary mesonephric tubules
(b) Ductile aberrances
(c) Defective afferent tubules
(d) All

303. Spermiostasis is common in
(a) Bucks (b) Horses
(c) Swine (d) Dog

304. Segmental aplacia of mesonephric duct occurs most commonly in –
(a) Bulls (b) Bucks
(c) Dogs (d) Pigs

305. Most common cause of seminal vesiculitis is –
(a) *Brucella abortus* (b) *Campylobacterium*
(c) *E. coli* (d) None

306. Prostate infection is most common in –
(a) Brucella (b) Campylobacterium
(c) Trichomonas (d) *E. coli*

307. Prostate infection is common in dogs of
(a) More than 5 years age
(b) Less than 5 years age
(c) More than 10 years age
(d) Less than 1 year age

308. Leukocytes are frequently found in urine & at prepuce orifice in
(a) Prostatitis (b) Ampullitis
(c) Both (d) None

309. Prostate hyperplasia is more common in –
(a) Castrated dog
(b) None castrated dogs
(c) Very young dog
(d) Dog of less than 5 years age

310. Which condition occurs due to abnormal androgen estrogen ratio?
(a) Diadem effect (b) Knobbed sperm
(c) Dag defect (d) Decapitated sperm

311. Nuclear pouch formation defect is seen in
(a) Castrated dog
(b) None castrated dogs
(c) Very young dog
(d) Dog of less than 5yr age

312. Defect in nuclear membrane of sperms occurs in–
(a) Diadem effect (b) Knobbed sperm
(c) Dag defect (d) Decapitated sperm

313. Fast green stain can reveal which sperm defect –
(a) Diadem effect (b) Knobbed sperm
(c) Dag defect (d) Decapitated sperm

314. When sperm disintegrates into head & tail in the epididymis it is known as
(a) Diadem effect (b) Knobbed sperm
(c) Dag defect (d) Decapitated sperm

315. Main piece of sperm is strongly pooled over mid piece in case of
(a) Diadem effect (b) Knobbed sperm
(c) Dag defect (d) Decapitated sperm

316. Instead of actual tail there is a short tail in case of
(a) Dag defect
(b) Sterilizing tail stump
(c) Pseudo droplet effect
(d) Cork screw defect

317. Sperms have rounded or elongated thickened on mid piece in –
(a) Dag defect
(b) Sterilizing tail stump
(c) Pseudo droplet effect
(d) Cork screw defect

318. Which sperm defect occurs due to irregular distribution of mitochondrial sheath?
(a) Dag defect
(b) Sterilizing tail stump
(c) Pseudo droplet effect
(d) Cork screw defect

319. Returned tail & narrow head is common in which breed of cattle –
(a) Jersey (b) Sahiwal
(c) Holstein Frisian (d) Brown Swiss

320. Cross of Horse & Ass produces mule which is –
(a) Fertile
(b) Unfertile
(c) Sterile
(d) May be sterile or fertile

321. When goat & sheep are crossed–
(a) No conception occurs
(b) Conception occurs but all embryos die
(c) Conception occurs & embryo service
(d) Can't be crossed

322. When Bison & domestic cattle are crossed, bull produced is –
(a) No conception occurs
(b) Conception occurs but all embryos die
(c) Conception occurs & embryo service
(d) Can't be crossed

323. In case of pseudo hermaphrodites, there in discrepancy between external genitalia and
(a) Hormones (b) Gonads
(c) Both (d) None

324. Male pseudo hermaphrodites have.
(a) Testes & male genitalia
(b) Testes & female genitalia
(c) Ovary & female genitalia
(d) Ovary & male genitalia

325. Female hermaphrodites have –
(a) Testes & male genitalia
(b) Testes & female genitalia
(c) Ovary & female genitalia
(d) Ovary & male genitalia

326. Cryptorchidism is rare in
(a) Dog (b) Stallion
(c) Boar (d) Cat

327. Which type of cryptorchidism is more common?
(a) Unilateral (b) Bilateral
(c) Both (d) None

328. Which type of cryptorchidism distort much with fertility
(a) Unilateral (b) Bilateral
(c) Both (d) None

329. Lazzaro spallanzani first discovered –
(a) Egg counting chamber
(b) AI technique
(c) Pregnancy diagnosis
(d) None

330. Kumaran in India first performed –
(a) Egg counting chamber
(b) AI technique
(c) Pregnancy diagnosis
(d) None

331. Rush of venereal diseases after Al has
(a) Reduced
(b) Increased
(c) Vanished
(d) All under circumstances

332. Spread of genetic abnormalities after Al is
(a) Reduced (b) Increased
(c) Vanished (d) Any

333. PMSG is detected is the blood of pregnant mare during:
(A) 20-3 0 days (B) 40-150 days
(C) 160-200 days (D) 200-340 days

334. Al in mare is done –
(a) Second to fourth day of estrus
(b) First day of estrus
(c) Last day of estrus
(d) Any day of estrus

335. Cervical fold are horizontal in –
(a) Cow (b) Mare
(c) Both (d) None

336. Cervical folds are longitudinal in
(a) Cow (b) Mare
(c) Both (d) None

337. Exotic bull do not perform well for semen collection during
(a) Summers (b) Winter
(c) Spring (d) All

338. Which cells are least affected by heat stress

(a) Spermatogonia (b) Spermatocytes
(c) Spermatids (d) Spermatozoa

339. Which species bulls have less sensitive thermoregulatory mechanism?
(a) Cattle (b) Buffalo
(c) Boar (d) Dog

340. Which vitamin is necessary for normal spermatogenesis –
(a) Vitamin A (b) Vitamin B
(c) Vitamin C (d) Vitamin D

341. pH of bull semen is –
(a) 6.8 (b) 7.4
(c) 6.7 (d) 8

342. pH of stallion semen is
(a) 6.8 (b) 7.4
(c) 6.7 (d) 8

143. pH of dog semen is
(a) 6.8 (b) 7.4
(c) 6.7 (d) 8

344. A repeat breeder can also be called as
(a) Cyclic non breeder
(b) Acyclic breeder
(c) Non recurrent breeder
(d) Recurrent breeder

345. Which of the following can be a cause of repeat breeder?
(a) Segmental aplasia of female genital tract
(b) Low amount of Iodine and other mineral supplementation
(c) Pyometra
(d) All of the above

346. A case of right uterine torsion must be rolled on?
(a) Right side, right side
(b) Right side, left side
(c) Left side, right side
(d) Left side, left side

347. Placentome can be palpated at how many days of pregnancy?
(a) 10 20 days (b) 40 50 days
(c) 80 95 days (d) 90 100 days

348. Pyometra can be differentially diagnosed with?
(a) Pregnant uterus (b) Mummified Fetus
(c) Both (d) None

349. The ratio of FSH : LH in Normocyclic animal is?
(a) 1 : 3 (b) 2 : 1
(c) 3 : 1 (d) 1 : 2

350. Which of the following progesterone compound in not given orally?
(a) MAP (b) Norgestomet
(c) CAP (d) Melengestrol acetate

351. 'SOBESTRUS' is a synonym for which of the following term?
(a) Silent estrus (b) Quiet estrus
(c) Weak estrus (d) All of the above

352. At which month of pregnancy chances of Vagino cervical prolapse are more common in cow?
(a) Last 2-3 months (b) First 2 months
(c) Mid gestation (d) None of the above

353. Mesovarium holds
(a) Testes (b) Ovary
(c) Cutes (d) Penis

354. Scrotum is placed vertically in
(a) Bull (b) Ram
(c) Buck (d) All

355. Scrotum is horizontal in
(a) Bull (b) Ram
(c) Buck (d) Stallion

356. Testes is exactly oral in
(a) Bull (b) Ram
(c) Buck (d) Stallion

357. Tests is placed obliquely in
(a) Horse (b) Bull
(c) Ram (d) Boar

358. Vaginal process is an extension of
(a) Peritoneum (b) Vagina
(c) Mesoreluim (d) None

359. Medeastinum testes is absent in
(a) Bull (b) Stallion
(c) Ram (d) Buck

360. Which layer forms medeastinum testes?
(a) Tunica albugenia (b) Vaginal process
(c) Tunica daetus (d) None

361. How many sperms are approximately produced per gram of testicular mass daily in bull?
(a) 10 million (b) 12-17 million
(c) 17-25 m (d) 50 m

362. Approximate length of epididymis of Bull

(a) 30 meter (b) 50 meter
(c) 20 meter (d) 100 meter

363. Approximate length of epididymis of Ram.
(a) 30 meter (b) 50 meter
(c) 20 meter (d) 100 meter

364. Approximate length of epididymis of Horse
(a) 30 meter (b) 50 meter
(c) 20 meter (d) 100 meter

365. Knocelea in epididymis is present in which segment
(a) Proximal (b) Meddle
(c) Terminal (d) All

366. Sperm suspension is highly concentrated in
(a) Caput epididymis (b) Body of epididymis
(c) Cauda epididymis (d) None

367. Which of the following is considered as Gonadotrophin:
(a) FSH (b) LH
(c) Prolactin (d) All

368. Which hormone is responsible for ovulation?
(a) FSH (b) LH
(c) Prolactin (d) All

369. Which hormone is mainly responsible for maintenance of pregnancy:
(a) Progesterone (b) Estrogen
(c) LH (d) Oxytocin

370. Which of the following steroid hormone has widest range of physiologic function:
(a) Progesterone (b) Estrogen
(c) Testosterone (d) None

371. Steroids are though to pass through cell membrane by:
(a) Simple diffusion
(b) Blood mediated transport
(c) Osmosis
(d) None

372. Ferguson's reflex at the time of parturition is related with release of hormones:
(a) PGF_2 (b) Estrogen
(c) Oxytocin (d) Cortisol

373. Syncro Mate B used for induction and synchronization of oestrus contains:
(a) Prostaglandin
(b) MCG
(c) Norgestomet and estradiol
(d) Norgestomet and PMSG

374. PMSG is less preferred for super ovulation in comparison to FSH due to:
(a) Large half life
(b) Higher LH content
(c) Premature ovulation
(d) All

375. Sexual behaviours and ovulatory surge depend on:
(a) Hypothalamic hormone
(b) Gonadotrophin
(c) Steroids
(d) All

376. In animals secretion of Gonadotrophin and their releasing factors begins:
(a) Before foetal life (b) During foetal life
(c) After foetal life (d) None

377. Female reproductive organs undergoes a rapid growth under the influence of:
(a) Progesterone (b) Estrogen
(c) Oxytocin (d) GnRH

378. First embryo transfer in Buffalo was done by:
(a) Nicholas (b) Warwick Berry
(c) Drost (d) None

379. In cattle, blastocyst develops:
(a) 3-4 days after ovulation
(b) 2-6 days after ovulation
(c) 6-8 days after ovulation
(d) None of the above

380. Best results by non surgical technique is obtained when embryo transfer is done at:
(a) Morula stage
(b) Early blastocyst stage
(c) Hatched blastocyst stage
(d) None

381. Dose of PMSG required for follicular growth in a cow weighing 400 kg is:
(a) 1000 – 1200 IU (b) 1500 – 3000 IU
(c) 750 – 1000 IU (d) 2000 – 3000 IU

382. Dose of LH for ovulation in cattle is:
(A) 10-20 mg (B) 15-25 mg
(C) 25-50 mg (D) 75-100 mg

383. PGF_2a, the luteolytic hormone, is secreted from:
(A) Perimetrium (B) Myometrium

(C) Endometrium (D) None

384. Nymphomaniac condition is associated with:
(A) Luteal cyst (B) Paraovarian cyst
(C) Follicular cyst (D) All

385. Ovulation in cow occurs:
(A) Within the heat period
(B) After termination of heat
(C) Both a and b
(D) None

386. For behavioral sign of heat, the hormonal profile of the cow should be:
(A) Low progesterone and low estrogen
(B) High progesterone and light estrogen
(C) Low progesterone and high estrogen
(D) None

387. Interval between two successive heat is:
(A) Calving interval
(B) Mean inter service interval
(C) Inter estrus interval
(D) Submission rate

388. "Days open" or "Open interval" is:
(A) Calving interval
(B) Mean calving to conception interval
(C) Submission rate
(D) None

389. Which of the following can be the best remedial measure in 180 degree right uterine torsion in buffalo:
(A) Ceasarian section (B) Oxytocin
(C) Velosin (D) Rolling of the dam

390. Early pregnancy factor can be determined by:
(A) Cuboni test
(B) Rosette inhibition test
(C) Vaginal biopsy
(D) None

391. Rise in cortisol level at the time of parturition is related to:
(A) Manual removal (B) Placental origin
(C) Prostaglandin F_2a (D) Oestradiol

392. Tapping of the cyst is done per:
(A) Rectum (B) Vagina
(C) Left flank (D) Right flank

393. Treatment of choice for persistent corpus luteum is:
(A) Manual removal
(B) Removal of fluid by needle
(C) Prostaglandin F_2 a
(D) Oestradiol

394. Trichomonal abortion is commonly noticed at:
(A) Early pregnancy
(B) Late pregnancy
(C) 6-9 month pregnancy
(D) None

395. Mostly embryonic mortality is noticed during:
(A) 16 – 34 days of gestation
(B) 34-60 days of gestation
(C) 60-85 days of gestation
(D) 85-120 days of gestation

396. In true anoestrous condition, the ovarian examination may reveal:
(A) Multiple small ovarian cyst
(B) Single large ovarian cyst
(C) Cyclic corpus luteum
(D) Small round smooth ovaries

397. Greatest incidence of abortion associated with vibriosis is observed during:
(A) 1-2 month of gestation
(B) 2-4 month of gestation
(C) 4-7 month of gestation
(D) 709 month of gestation

398. Potato soup like pus from uterus is characterized of:
(A) Brucellosis (B) Vibriosis
(C) Trichomoniasis (D) IBR – IVP

399. Which of the following is most effective in treatment of luteal cyst:
(A) PGF_2 a (B) Estrogen
(C) Prolactin (D) LH

400. The length of estrous cycle in cow is:
(A) 16-17 day (B) 10-15 day
(C) 20-21 day (D) 25-27 day

401. Pre ovulatory endocrine surge in cows occurs at:
(A) Onset of estrous
(B) At mid estrus
(C) At the end of estrus
(D) At pro estrus

402. Endocrine basis of post partum anoestrous is:
(A) Failure of resumption of episodic pattern

of FSH release
(B) Failure of resumption of episodic pattern of LH release
(C) Failure of resumption of episodic pattern of FSH and LH surge.
(D) None

403. Fish look vulva condition of female is:
(A) Inter sex
(B) Free martin
(C) White heifer disease
(D) None

404. Three common organisms associated with bovine pyometra are:
(A) Trichomonas, Pseudomonas and Vibrio
(B) Trichomonas, Vibrio and Staphylococcus
(C) Trichomonas, Vibrio and Corynebacterium
(D) Trichomonas, Vibrio and Streptococci

405. In Trichomoniasis:
(A) Fetus gests macerated
(B) Fetus gets mummified
(C) There is retention of placenta
(D) None

406. Breach presentation is:
(A) Bilateral hock flexion
(B) Bilateral shoulder flexor
(C) Complete retention of rear limbs beneath body
(D) None

407. Best method for pregnancy diagnosis in cow at 3 months of gestation is:
(A) RIA
(B) ELISA
(C) Per Rectal examination
(D) All

408. Enucleation of corpus luteum will result in termination of pregnancy in cow:
(A) Before day 200 of pregnancy
(B) After day 200 day of pregnancy
(C) Both
(D) None

409. Corpus luteum of pregnancy is also known as:
(A) Corpus luteum spurium
(B) Corpus luteum verum
(C) Corpus haemorhagicum
(D) Corpus albicans

410. Corpus luteum of estrous cycle i.e. also known as:
(A) Corpus luteum spurium
(B) Corpus luteum verum
(C) Corpus haemorrhagicum
(D) Corpus albicans

411. Sex differentiation in embryonic development in goat occurs at:
(A) 40 day of gestation
(B) 60 day of gestation
(C) 75 day of gestation
(D) 90 day of gestation

412. Ovaries arise from:
(A) Mullerian duct (B) Wolffian duct
(C) Germinal ridge (D) Phallus

413. Best time to breed a cow is:
(A) Early estrous (B) Mid estrous
(C) Late estrous (D) 2nd day of estrurs

414. Average time of ovulation in cattle is:
(A) Mid estrous
(B) Late estrous
(C) 4-10 hours after end of estrous
(D) 20 hours after end of estrus

415. In dairy cattle, the ovulation from right ovary are about:
(A) 20 % (B) 40 %
(C) 60% (D) 80%

416. Maternal recognition of pregnancy in cows occurs on:
(A) 12th day (B) 14-16th days
(C) 16-17 day (D) None

417. Physiological expulsion time limit for fetal membrane is:
(A) Within 6 liter after delivery of Fetus
(B) Within 18 hour after delivery of Fetus
(C) Within 24 hours after delivery of Fetus
(D) Within 12 hours after delivery of Fetus

418. Bovine pyometra occurs most commonly during:
(A) Early post parturient period
(B) Mid lactation period
(C) Dry period
(D) Mid pregnancy

419. In camel, the copulation takes place while:

(A) Standing (B) Sitting
(C) Lying (D) None

420. Maternal behavior of licking is characteristic of:
(A) Sheep (B). Goat
(C) Horse (D) Cattle

421. Retention of placenta is most common in:
(A) Cattle (B) Horse
(C) Sheep (D) Goat

422. In cow the placenta is considered to be retained if it does not fall:
(A) Within 1 hour (B) Within 2-3 hour
(C) Within 8-12 hour (D) In 20-24 hour

423. If the hanging placenta in cow is to be cut, it should be cut:
(A) Close to cervix (B) At the level of hock
(C) Close to vulva (D) Close to ground

424. In replacing prolapsed uterus in cattle, it should be held:
(A) Hanging position as such
(B) Lifted as up as possible
(C) Above the level of floor of the pelvis
(D) None

425. After replacement of prolapsed uterus in cows, the units of oxytocin should be given:
(A) 1-2 unit (B) 20-40 unit
(C) 75-100 unit (D) 100-500 unit

426. Uterine caruncles in case of cow are:
(A) Convex in shape (B) Concave in shape
(C) Both in shape (D) None

427. Follicular cyst is clinically characterized by:
(A) Large interval of estrus cycle
(B) Frequent irregular estrus
(C) Estrus at regular interval but of short development
(D) None

428. The important herd diagnosis of Brucellosis cattle is:
(A) Milk ring test
(B) Serum Agglutination test
(C) Mucus Agglutination test
(D) None

429. In Fetal mummification, fetal membrane is:
(A) Unaffected
(B) Shriveled and dried
(C) Separated from fetus
(D) None

430. The most important Vitamin deficiency which results in infertility is:
(A) Vitamin A (B) Vitamin B complex
(C) Vitamin D (D) None

431. In Trichomoniasis of cow, death of Fetus occurs in:
(A) First trimester (B) 2nd trimester
(C) 3rd trimester (D) None

432. In Vibriosis of cow, abortion occurs in:
(A) First trimester (B) 2nd trimester
(C) 3rd trimester (D) None

433. In brucellosis of cow, abortion occur in:
(A) Ist trimester (B) 2nd trimester
(C) 3rd trimester (D) None

434. Enzymes which help sperms to penetrate ovum:
(A) Hyaluronidase (B) Acrocin
(C) Both (D) None

435. Part of Pelvis that forms the angle of Lourch:
(A) Tuber coxas (B) Tuber socrale
(C) Tuber ischi (D) None

436. Part of Pelvic girdle form angle of croup:
(A) Tuber coxas (B) Tuber socrale
(C) Tuber ischi (D) None

437. Tuber coxes is trifed in:
(A) Cow (B) Mare
(C) Bitch (D) Sheep

438. Puberty in female is characterized by:
(A) Development of vulva
(B) Development of uterus
(C) Ability of gonads to start steroidogenic and gametogenic function
(D) None

439. Estrus period is characterized by:
(A) Secretion of progesterone from C. L.
(B) Secretion of LH from Ant pituitary
(C) High estrogen secretion from preovulatory graffian follicle
(D) None

440. Uterus of cow is:
(A) Bipartite type (B) Bicornuate type
(C) Both (D) None

441. Increased frequency of urination is most impor-

tant characteristic of estrus in:
(A) Cow (B) Buffalo
(C) Horse (D) Goat

442. Interval from first insemination to conception depend on:
(A) Correct timing of insemination
(B) Uterine involution
(C) Post partum infection
(D) All of the above

443. Reasons for failure of normal behavioral sign of estrus may be:
(A) Insufficient production of Gonadotropin
(B) Insufficient release of Gonadotropin
(C) Failure of gonads to response to Gonadotrpins
(D) All of above

444. Uterine torsion is a complication of:
(A) Late 1st stage of labour
(B) Early second stage of labour
(C) 3rd stage of labour
(D) None

445. Retained placenta is a complication of:
(A) 1st stage of labour (B) 2nd stage of labour
(C) 3rd stage of labour (D) None

446. Expulsion of Fetus occur in:
(A) Ist stage of labour (B) 2nd stage of labour
(C) 3rd stage of labour (D) None

447. Polyspermy is checked by:
(A) Zona reaction (B) Vitelline block
(C) Both (D) None

448. Cervix of the cow is:
(A) 1-2 cm long (B) 5-10 cm long
(C) 15-20 cm long (D) 25-30 cm long

449. Gestation period of male calves is:
(A) Longer than female calves
(B) Shorter than female calves
(C) Some as female calve
(D) None

450. Genital system is formed by:
(A) Ectodermal tissue
(B) Mesodermal tissue
(C) Endeodermal tissue
(D) All

451. Female reproductive organs are developed from:
(A) Mesonephric duct
(B) Paramesonephric duct
(C) Both
(D) None

452. Ovaries of cows are:
(A) Oval shaped (B) Almond shape
(C) Both (D) None

453. Ovaries are drawn forward in abdominal cavity and out of react of hand on rectal palpation in:
(A) Ist / 2nd month of gestation
(B) 2nd – 3rd month of gestation
(C) 4th and 5th month of gestation
(D) 7th and 8th month of gestation

454. Fertilization of ova occurs in:
(A) Ovary (B) Oviduct
(C) Uterus (D) Vagina

455. Implantation of embryo occurs in:
(A) Ovary (B) Oviduct
(C) Uterus (D) Vulva

456. Functions of uterus are:
(A) Reception of fertilized ovum
(B) Site of implementation
(C) Provide nutrition and protection to Fetus.
(D) All of above

457. The structure that form sufficient placental attachment to result in normal: development of embryo is:
(A) Perimetrium of uterus
(B) Myometriun of uterus
(C) Endometrium
(D) All

458. Fetus can usually be balloted after:
(A) 3 months of gestation
(B) 4 months of gestation
(C) 6 months of gestation
(D) None

459. Site of fertilization in oviduct is:
(A) Fimbrae
(B) Isthmus
(C) Infundibulum
(D) Ampullary Isthmus junction

460. In which period of gestation, major tissue organs and systems of body are formed:
(A) Period of ovum

(B) Period of embryo
(C) Period of Fetus
(D) All

461. Period of embryo in cow extends for:
(A) Fertilization to 10-12 days
(B) 12 days to 45 days
(C) 45 days to term
(D) None

462. Branch of science dealing with abnormal development and malformation of prenatal individual is:
(A) Gynaecology (B) Obstetrics
(C) Teratology (D) Theriogenology

463. Principal carbohydrate in bovine fetal blood is:
(A) Glucose (B) Fructose
(C) Galactose (D) None

464. Animals in which normally one ovum is released at ovulation and one Fetus develops in uterus are known as:
(A) Primipara
(B) Nullipra
(C) Unipara
(D) Pleuripara

465. Females that have never conceived or carried young are called:
(A) Primipara (B) Nullipara
(C) Unipara (D) Pleuripara

466. The relation of the spinal axis of the fetus to that of the dam is:
(A) Presentation (B) Position
(C) Posture (D) None

467. The normal presentation in uniparous animal is:
(A) Anterior longitudinal
(B) Posterior longitudinal
(C) Transverse presentation
(D) All

468. Natural and physiological parturition is:
(A) Dystocia (B) Eutocia
(C) Paratocia (D) None

469. Which type pf mummification is found in cattle:
(A) Hematinic (B) Papyraceous
(C) Both A & B (D) None

470. Mummification of fetus is most common in:
(A) Bovine (B) Swine
(C) Equine (D) Ovine

471. Uterine torsion is most common in:
(A) Bovine (B) Equine
(C) Swine (D) Canine

472. Uterine torsion is observed most commonly in:
(A) Advanced pregnancy
(B) At time of parturition
(C) After parturition
(D) None

473. Uterine torsion is most common in:
(A) Primipara (B) Pleuripara
(C) Both A & B (D) None

474. Dystocia is more common in:
(A) Primipara (B) Pleuripara
(C) Both A & B (D) None

475. Trichomonal pyometra is always:
(A) Post service (B) Post partum
(C) Both A & B (D) None

476. Retained placenta is most commonly observed in:
(A) Trichomonas abortion
(B) Vibrio abortion
(C) Brucella abortion
(D) All

477. Which is not a venereal disease:
(A) Brucellosis (B) Campylobacteriosis
(C) IBR – IPV (D) None

478. Frequent irregular estrous / nymphomania is found in:
(A) Follicular cyst (B) Luteal cyst
(C) Both A & B (D) None

479. Which is the most common cystic condition affecting bovine ovary:
(a) Follicular cyst (b) Cystic corpora lutea
(c) Luteal cyst (d) All

480. Cystic ovary is principally a disease of:
(a) Dairy cattle (b) Beef cattle
(c) Both A & B (d) None

481. Which is on abnormality of ovulation:
(a) Cystic ovary (b) Twinning
(c) Both A & B (d) None

482. In nymphomania, which hormone is present at peak level:
(a) Progesterone (b) Estrogen
(c) PGF_2a (d) None

483. Swiss cheese appearance of uterus and advanced virilism are associated with:
(a) Cervico vaginal prolepses
(b) Uterine inertia
(c) Retained placenta
(d) Cystic ovary

484. Progesterone in milk is higher in:
(a) Follicular cyst (b) Luteal cyst
(c) Both A & B (d) None

485. Which of the following statement for buffalo is true:
(a) Estrus behavior is more pronounce
(b) Ovaries are more developed.
(c) Uterine horn are smaller + more coiled in buffalo than cow:
(d) All

486. Number of follicles in buffalo ovaries are about:
(a) 10,000 – 20,000 (b) 25,000 – 50,000
(c) 50,000 – 1,00000 (d) None

487. Average age of puberty in riverine buffalo is:
(a) 9-12 month (b) 15-18 month
(c) 20-24 month (d) None

488. Average age of puberty in swamp buffalo is:
(a) 9-12 month (b) 15-18 month
(c) 20-24 month (d) None

489. Most reliable sign of estrus in HF cow is:
(a) Standing to be mounted by bull
(b) Clear mucoid vulvar discharge
(c) Bellowing
(d) Frequent urination

490. Gestation period of buffalo is:
(a) 284 days –2 90 days
(b) 305-320 days
(c) 335-340 days
(d) None

491. Type of placenta of buffalo is:
(a) Zonary (b) Diffused
(c) Cotyledonary (d) None

492. Fertile life of cattle sperm is
(a) 30-48 hours (b) 72-120 hours
(c) 30-35 hours (d) 24-72 hours

493. Fertile life of cattle ovum is:
(a) 20-24 hours (b) 6-8 hours
(c) 6-10 hours (d) 16-18 hours

494. Maternal recognition of pregnancy occurs in cattle at:
(a) 12 days (b) 16-17 days
(c) 20 days (d) None

495. Corpus luteum is somewhat embedded in:
(a) Cow (b) Buffalo
(c) Mare (d) None

496. Molecular weight of equine LH is:
(A) 13,000 (B) 23,500
(C) 33,500 (D) 40,000

497. Molecular weight of equine FSH is:
(A) 12,000 (B) 28,000
(C) 33,200 (D) 40,000

498. Normal expulsion of fetal membrane in mare takes about:
(A) 180 minutes (B) 60 minutes
(C) 120 minutes (D) 30 minutes

499. Which of the following animals do not eat their after birth?
(A) Cow (B) Sow
(C) Bitch (D) Mare

500. The main estrogen in mare during pregnancy is:
(A) Estradiol – 17 b
(B) Estradiol – 17 a
(C) Equine
(D) Oestrane and equiline

501. eCG is also a synonym for:
(A) hCG (B) hMG
(C) Progesterone (D) None

502. Accessory corpus luteum is formed in mare during:
(A) Pregnancy (B) Prolonged diestrus
(C) Uterine pathology (D) None

503. A first coccygeal vertebra is fused to last sacral vertebrae in:
(A) Cow (B) Mare
(C) Sheep (D) None

504. Young one of this species is not susceptible to chilling:
(A) Sheep (B) Goat
(C) Horse (D) Cattle

505. Ovaries of mare are:
(A) Oval shaped (B) Rounded
(C) Bean shaped (D) Almond shaped

506. Duration of estrous cycle in mare is:
(A) 6-17 days (B) 19-24 days
(C) 18-20 days (D) None

507. Duration of estrus period in mare is:
(A) 1-2 days (B) 2-4 days
(C) 5 days (D) 4-9 days

508. Type of placenta in mare:
(A) Diffused (B) Cotyledonary
(C) Oval (D) Discoid

509. Waxing of teat, before parturition is a characteristic symptom in:
(A) Cow (B) Sheep
(C) Goat (D) Mare

510. Foot nape posture is quite common in:
(A) Cow (B) Sheep
(C) Goat (D) Mare

511. Ovulation takes place from a specific part of ovary called "Ovulation fossa" in:
(A) Cow (B) Sheep
(C) Mare (D) Swine

512. Uterus is cruciform or T shaped having horn perpendicular to body of uterus in:
(A) Cow (B) Mare
(C) Sheep (D) Dog

513. Vagina of cow is:
(A) 5 -10 cm long (B) 10-20 cm long
(C) 25-30 cm long (D) 35-40 cm. long

514. Most practical and accurate method of pregnancy diagnosis in cow is:
(A) Rectal examination
(B) Ultrasonography
(C) Radiography
(D) Vaginal biopsy

515. Males at birth are larger and heavier than females in all animals except:
(A) Cattle (B) Horse
(C) Sheep (D) Goat

516. Wry neck is most common in:
(A) Bovine (B) Equine
(C) Ovine (D) Canine

517. Largest corpora haemorrhagica is found in:
(A) Cow (B) Swine
(C) Mare (D) Sheep

518. Split heat is most common in:
(A) Bovine (B) Equine
(C) Canine (D) d. Feline

519. Which of the following is associated with Dolly?
(A) Wilkins (B) Wilmut
(C) Watson (D) Drost

520. Rupture of prepubic tendon or prepubic desmorrhexis of pregnancy is most common in:
(A) Bovine (B) Canine
(C) Equine (D) Ovine

521. Barium Chloride test for pregnancy diagnosis not reliable in animals:
(A) Fed primarily on pasture
(B) Fed mainly on concentrates
(C) Fed pelleted feeds
(D) None

522. Cuboni test is a chemical method for pregnancy diagnosis in:
(A) Cattle (B) Mare
(C) Sheep (D) None

523. A hormone detected in the blood of pregnant mare which can be used for Pregnancy Diagnosis by injection into immature rates is:
(A) Oxytocin (B) Relaxin
(C) eCG (D) None

524. Age of puberty in mare is:
(A) 5-15 months (B) 15-25 months
(C) 20-30 months (D) 30-40 months

525. In which species, unfertilized ova retained in the oviduct for several months:
(A) Bovine (B) Equine
(C) Swine (D) Ovine

526. In which species, PGF_2á secreted from uterus reaches ovary via general circulation:
(A) Bovine (B) Equine
(C) Both (D) None

527. Ovulation in mare occurs:
(A) 12-24 hrs before end of estrus
(B) 24-48 hrs before end of estrus
(C) 24-48 hrs after end of estrus
(D) None

528. Enucleation of C. L. will not cause abortion in mare after:
(A) 2 month (B) 3 month
(C) 4 month (D) 6 month

529. Fetus of equine can be balloted at:
(A) 100 days (B) 200 days
(C) 300 days (D) None

530. Which of the following ultrasonographic method is used extensively in mare for Pregnancy Diagnosis?
(A) Doppler method
(B) A mode ultrasonography
(C) b mode ultrasonography
(D) None

531. Endometrial cups are temporary endocrine organs during pregnancy in:
(A) Cow (B) Mare
(C) Sheep (D) Sow

532. At birth the average number of primary or primordial follicles in the ovary of a heifer calf is:
(A) 50,000 (B) 50,0000
(C) 1,50,000 (D) 20,0000

533. Age of puberty of mare is:
(A) 24 – 36 months (B) 12-24 months
(C) 7-18 months (D) 28-32 months

534. Age of puberty of queen cat is:
(A) 7-12 months (B) 10-24 months
(C) 2-6 months (D) 16-24 months

535. In heifer around how many number of growing follicles are present on the ovary at puberty:
(A) 1000 (B) 50
(C) 5000 (D) 200

536. The hormone primarily responsible for onset of ovarian activity, and hence puberty is:
(A) LH (B) FSH
(C) Oestradiol (D) GnRH

537. A fully functional corpus luteum is present during:
(A) Metestrus (B) Diestrus
(C) Proestrus (D)

538. Which animal species do not ovulate spontaneously?
(A) Cow (B) Mare
(C) Camel (D) None of the above

539. In dairy breeds the average body weight at puberty should be:
(A) 35 % of mature body weight
(B) 50 % of the mature body weight
(C) 350 kg
(D) None of the above

540. In beef breeds of cattle the average body weight at puberty should be:
(A) 50% of the mature body weight
(B) 400 kg
(C) 30 of mature body weight
(D) All of the above

541. Oocytes are capable of fertilization upto:
(A) 8 12 hrs after ovulation
(B) 6 hours after ovulation
(C) 20 hrs after ovulation
(D) None of the above

542. The diameter of mature Graffian follicle is:
(A) 5-6 cm. (B) 1.5 – 2.2 cm.
(C) 2-2.5 cm. (D) 2.35-4.2 cm.

543. Corona radiata in the ruminants of cell of:
(A) Cumulus Oophorus
(B) Granulosa cells
(C) Theca externa
(D) Vitelline membrane

544. At ovulation the follicle ruptures through a breach in:
(A) Tunica albuginea
(B) Zona pellucida
(C) Cumulus Oophorus
(D) All of the above

545. In a mature Graffian follicle the Oocyte is surrounded by:
(A) Granulosa cells
(B) Theca interna
(C) Cumulus Oophorus
(D) None of the above

546. The time of ovulation in cows is:
(A) 12-18h after the end of estrus
(B) 24 h after the end of estrus
(C) 24-36 h after the end of estrus
(D) 6-8 h after the end of estrus

547. The degenerating, avascular, nonfunctional corpus luteum is called:
(A) Corpus haemorrhagicum
(B) Corpus luteum verum
(C) Corpus luteum spurium
(D) Corpus luteum albicans

548. Corpus luteum of pregnancy is called:
(A) Corpus luteum albicans
(B) Corpus haemorrhagicum
(C) Corpus luteum verum
(D) Corpus luteum spurium

549. Corpus luteum in cycling non pregnant animals is called:
(A) Corpus luteum verum
(B) Corpus luteum spurium
(C) Corpus haemorrhagicum
(D) Corpus luteum albicans

550. The opening of the infundibulum is called:
(A) Fimbriae
(B) Ostium abdominalis
(C) Ostium infundibulum
(D) None of the above

551. In swine, the uterus is:
(A) Bicornuate (B) Bipartite
(C) Both (A) & (B) (D) None of the above

552. The transport time of ova in the oviduct is following hours after ovulation in cattle:
(A) 10-12 hours (B) 5-10 hours
(C) 20-36 hours (D) 72-90 hours

553. The ovum reaches ampulla of the domestic animals in about:
(A) 5 - 8 hours (B) 9-12 hours
(C) 12-16 hours (D) 16-24 hours

554. The ova remain viable for 12 to 24 hours in domestic animals except where it remains viable for about four days:
(A) Sow (B) Mare
(C) Bitch (D) Queen cat

555. LH stimulates:
(A) Theca cells (B) Granulosa cells
(C) Both of the above (D) None of the above

556. Determination of live % by eosin nigrosin staining is based on:
(A) Penetration of eosin into dead sperm membrane
(B) Penetration of eosin into live sperm membrane
(C) Binding of sperm to zona pellucida
(D) None of the above

557. Organogenesis in bovine Fetus is completed in:
(A) 30 days (B) 90 days
(C) 120 days (D) 45 days

558. The placenta in cow is:
(A) Syndesmochorial (B) Cotyledonary
(C) Haemochorial (D) None of the above

559. After how many days of gestation, corpus luteum is not necessary for the maintenance of pregnancy in cow:
(A) 120 days (B) 240 days
(C) 150 days (D) 190 days

560. Gestation period of camel is:
(A) 406 days (B) 442 days
(C) 360 days (D) 306 days

561. The normal time taken for shedding of placenta in cattle is:
(A) 10 hours (B) 14 hours
(C) 6 hours (D) 10 hours

562. The embryo of dogs and cats reaches uterus after:
(A) 2 – 4 days (B) 1-2 days
(C) 8-10 days (D) 5-8 days

563. Embryonic attachment to uterus occurs in cow at:
(A) 12th day (B) 21st day
(C) 18th day (D) 30th day

564. Which of the following hormones inhibits FSH release?
(A) LH (B) Estrogen
(C) Inhibin (D) All of the above

565. Which of the following hormones, directly or indirectly, do not affect reproduction?
(A) TRH (B) Prolactin
(C) Oxytocin (D) None of the above

566. Which of the following species have Kidney shaped ovary?
(A) Cow (B) Ewe
(C) Sow (D) Mare

567. Almond shaped ovary is found in:
(A) Cow (B) Ewe
(C) Both a and b (D) None of the above

568. Pear shaped corpus luteum is common in:
A. Mare B. Sow
C. Cow D. Goat

569. The longer half life of PMSG is due to the presence of:
A. Higher amount of organic carbon
B. Sialic acid
C. Greater LN activity
D. None of the above

570. Mean of calving to next conception interval is called:
A. Calving interval B. Days open
C. Submission rate D. None of the above

571. Nymphomania is a condition associated with:
A. Follicular cyst
B. Luteal cyst
C. Increased FSH concentration
D. None of the above

572. BA strain 19 is:
A. Live attenuated B. Live
C. Killed D. None of the above

573. Transuterine migration of Zygotes is common in:
A. Multiparous B. Uniparous
C. Primiparous D. Pluriparous

574. The superstitious belief that offspring from one sire may derive characteristics from a sire to which the same dam has previous borne offspring is called:
A. Super fetation B. Super fecundation
C. Telegony D. None of the above

575. When a female ovulate two or more ova during one estrum and copulate with two or more males during that estrum with ova being fertilized by spermatozoa from each male, the condition is called:
A. Super fetation B. Super fecundation
C. Telegony D. None of the above

576. When a second conception occurs in uterus already containing atleast one live Fetus, the condition is called:
A. Telegony
B. Super fecundation
C. Multiple pregnancies
D. Super fetation

577. The following is / are comparatively more common in multiparous animals:
A. Super fetation and super fecundation
B. Super fetation, super fecudnation and telegrony
C. Twins and super fecundation
D. All of the above

578. Cyesiognosis is the term used for:
A. Diagnosis by per rectal examination
B. Pregnancy diagnosis by per rectal examination
C. Pregnancy diagnosis
D. Pregnancy diagnosis by ultrasonography

579. In pregnant cow amniotic vesicles can be palpated as early as:
A. 30 days B. 20 days
C. 60 days D. 65-70 days

580. Middle uterine artery is a branch of:
A. Utero – ovarian artery
B. Internal iliac artery
C. Caudal uterine artery
D. None of the above

581. Fremitus can be felt in:
A. Middle uterine artery
B. Iliac artery
C. Utero – ovarian artery
D. None of the above

582. The gravid uterus descends to abdomen in cows at:
A. 5-6 months B. 2-3 months
C. 3-5 months D. None of the above

583. Which of the following is not a confirmatory sign of pregnancy?
(A) Fetal membrane slip
(B) Palpation of placentomes
(C) Palpation of amniotic vesicles
(D) Enlargement of uterine horn

584. Which of the following methods can be used for pregnancy diagnosis in ewe:
(A) Rectal palpation
(B) Recto – abdominal method
(C) Abdominal palpation
(D) Both (B) and (C)

585. Which of the following is not a method of pregnancy diagnosis?
A. Vaginal biopsy examination
B. Uterine biopsy examination
C. Progesterone assay
D. Rossette inhibition test

586. Cuboni's test relies upon the estimation of which of the following hormones:
A. Progesterone B. Estrogen
C. eCG D. ECG

587. Endometrial cups, formed due to invasion of fetal trophoblast cells into: Endometrium, appears in mare during
A. Third month of pregnancy
B. Seventh month of pregnancy
C. Earlier part of second month of pregnancy
D. Late par of fifth month of pregnancy

588. The following hormone is produced by the endometrial cups:
A. HCG B. HMG
C. Progesterone D. eCG

589. Aschein zondek test and Friedmoat test for pregnancy diagnosis in mare are based on:
A. Identification of PMSG in blood/ Serum
B. Identification of progesterone in blood
C. Both of the above
D. None of the above

590. Females that have never conceived or carried young are called:
A. Primiparous B. Pluriparous
C. Monotocous D. Nullipara

591. Unipara is synonyms to:
A. Primipara B. Pluripara
C. Monotocous D. Polytocous

592. In contrast to uniparaous animal the multiparous animals usually have:
A. Well developed cervix
B. Poorly developed cervix
C. Well developed uterine horns
D. Poorly developed uterine horns

593. The weight of Fetus at birth in unipara should be how much % of the weight of post partum dam:
A. 20 B. 10
C. 5 D. 3

594. The weight of Fetus in multipara at the time of birth should how much % of weight of post partum dam
A. 1-3 B. 3-6
C. 6-9 D. 9-10

595. A sow normally bears:
A. 3-4 Fetuses B. 20-22 Fetuses
C. 3-8 Fetuses D. 6-12 Fetuses

596. A queen cat normally bears:
A. 4-8 Fetuses B. 3-5 Fetuses
C. 1-3 Fetuses D. 2-8 Fetuses

597. In cows, the Vaginocervical prolapse in more common in which of the following stages:
A. Last 2-3 months of gestation
B. First two months of pregnancy
C. Diestrus
D. Proestrus

598. The duration of gestation period in Tiger is:
A. 60-80 days B. 90-100 days
C. 105-113 days D. 123 – 141 days

599. The gestation of Rhinoceros is:
A. 213 – 315 days B. 530 – 548 days
C. 312 – 390 days D. 630 – 651 days

600. The gestation period of Indian Elephant is:
A. 615 – 650 days B. 420-436 days
C. 510-523 days D. 496-513 days

601. The occurrence in an individual of two or more cell populations or tissues each with a different chromosome complement derived from a single Zygote is called
A. Chimerism B. Mosaicism
C. All of the above D. None of the above

602. The relation of the dorsum of the fetus in longitudinal presentation, or the head in transverse presentation, to the quadrants (Sacrum, right ileum, lift ileum and pubis) of the maternal pelvis is called:
A. Presentation B. Posture
C. Position D. None of the above

603. The relation of the extremities, on the head, neck and limbs to the body of the Fetus is called:
A. Presentation B. Posture
C. Position D. None of the above

604. The normal position of Fetus in uniparous animals is:
A. Dorsoilial B. Dorsopubic
C. Left celphaloilial D. Dorso – sacral

605. Transverse presentation is comparatively more common in which of the following species:
A. Cattle B. Buffalo
C. Mare D. Goat

606. The posterior longitudinal presentation, dorso sacral position, with the hind limbs retained or extended beneath the body is called:
A. Breech presentation
B. Dog sitting posture
C. Hip lock in posterior presentation
D. None of the above

607. The average pH of bull semen is:
A. 7.4 B. 5.6
C. 6.8 D. 8.2

608. The volume of oxygen used by 10^8 spermatozoa in 1 hour at 37^{0}C is called:
A. Fructolysis index
B. Respiratory coefficient
C. O_2 index
D. None of the above

609. IVT diluents are used for preservation of semen at:
A. Cryopreserved state
B. Refrigeration temperature
C. Room temperature
D. All of the above

610. The temperature of liquid nitrogen is:
A. 79^0 C B. 129^0 C
C. 146^0 C D. 196^0 C

611. The site of insemination in Goat is:
A. Body of the uterus B. Deep cervix
C. Internal os cervix D. External os cervix

612. Which of the following has the highest ejaculate volume?
A. Buffalo bull B. Bull
C. Boar D. Stallion

613. The best method of semen collection in bull is:
A. Artificial vagina method
B. Massage method
C. Electro ejaculation method
D. Vaginal aspiration method

614. The pH of semen in cock is:
A. 6.0 6.8 B. 6.2 – 6.8
C. 6.7 – 6.8 D. 7.0 – 7.4

615. Number of semen collections per week in a bull should ideally be:
A. Two to three B. Five times
C. Seven D. None of the above

616. If discoloration of dye, in methylene blue reduction test, takes 30 minutes the semen sample will be of:
A. Poor quality B. Excellent quality
C. Good quality D. Fair

617. Respiratory coefficient is lowest in semen of which of the following species:
A. Ram B. Cock
C. Rabbit D. Bull

618. The ideal intercalving period in cross bred cows should be:
(A) 28 months (B) 21 months
(C) 12 months (D) 26 months

619. Hypo osmotic swelling test is based on which of the following principle:
A. Intact sperm membrane will respond to hypo osmotic stress
B. Intact sperm membrane will resist hypo osmotic stress
C. Live spermatozoa will not allow the entry of the solvent through the membrane
D. Greater response to hypo osmotic stress significance decreased fertility

620. Spermateliosis is the process in which:
A. Spermatogonium developes into primary spermatocyte
B. Primary spermatocyte divides into two secondary spermatocytes
C. Segregation of x and y takes place
D. Secondary spermatocytes are transformed into spermatids

621. The bull semen should be thawed at:
(A) 37 ^{0}C for 30 seconds
(B) 28 ^{0}C for 30 seconds
(C) 40 ^{0}C for 1 minute
(D) 04 ^{0}C for 1 minute

622. Giemsa staining is used for:
(A) Acrosome reaction test
(B) Hypo osmotic swelling test
(C) Live dead count
(D) All of the above

623. Which of the following antibiotics are used in routine used TRIS diluter:
(A) Gentamicin
(B) Chloramphenicol

(C) Ampicillin
(D) Streptomycin sulphate

624. Cytoplasm of the sperm cells is located at:
(A) Head (B) Mid piece
(C) Tail (D) All of the above

625. Optimum time to inseminate in ewe is:
(A) Mid estrus or end of estrus
(B) Third day of estrus
(C) Towards the end of estrus
(D) Start of estrus

626. Optimum time to inseminate swine is:
(A) First or second day of estrus
(B) Met estrus
(C) Late estrus
(D) End of the estrus

627. Site of semen deposition in mare:
(A) Vagina (B) Cervix
(C) External os cervix (D) Uterus

628. Approximate number of females which can be bred by one ejaculate of bull is:
(A) 700 (B) 100
(C) 30 (D) 12

629. Liquid semen of bull can be stored for:
(A) 1 day (B) 12 hours
(C) 2 days (D) 4 days

630. In goats AI is done at which of the following sites:
(A) Oviduct (B) Body of uterus
(C) Internal os cervix (D) External os cervix

631. Pre estral bleeding is seen in:
(A) Mare (B) Ewe
(C) Sow (D) Bitch

632. Post estral bleeding is seen in:
(A) Mare (B) Cow
(C) Sow (D) Bitch

633. During what time uterine glands undergo atrophy:
(A) Proestrus (B) Estrus
(C) Diestrus (D) Met estrus

634. The casual organism of EBA is:
(A) Psittacosia lymphogranuloma
(B) Trichomonas
(C) Herpes virus
(D) None of the above

635. The vector of EBA is:
(A) Mite (B) Tick
(C) Flea (D) Fly

636. Major symptom of Bovine Trichomoniasis is:
(A) Short estrus cycle
(B) Prolonged estrus cycle
(C) Pyometra
(D) All of the above

637. Long estrus cycles (27-53 days) in bovine can be caused by:
(A) Trichomonas fetus
(B) Streptococci ssp.
(C) Brucella abortus
(D) Pseudomonas aeruginosa

638. Which of the following is an anomaly of trunk?
(A) Spastic paresis
(B) Schistosomus reflexus
(C) Hydrocephalus
(D) Syndactylion

639. Condition characterized by birth of dummy or bawler's calves is known as:
(A) Epitheliogenesis imperfecta
(B) Ichthyosis congenita
(C) Hypotrichosis
(D) None of the above

640. Recessive defects characterized by degree of hairlessness is known as:
(A) Hydrocephalus
(B) Ichthyosis congenita
(C) Hypotrichosis congenital
(D) Epitheliogensis Imperfecta

641. Epizootic bovine abortion is transmitted through which of the following vector:
(A) Argus persicus
(B) Ornithodoros spp.
(C) Glossina morsitaus
(D) *Diaemus youngi*

642. The normal progesterone concentration in the midluteal phase of cow is:
(A) 4-20 n g / ml (B) 4-20 i g / ml
(C) 4-20 mg / ml (D) 4-20 pg / ml

643. The active form of testosterone in the accessory sex glands is:
(A) Androgen
(B) Dihydrotestosterone
(C) Estradiol

(D) None of the above

644. Which of the following is used as flushing medium for embryo collection?
(A) Dulbucco's phosphate buffer saline
(B) TALP
(C) Hank's medium
(D) Normal saline solution

645. The first successful embryo transfer was performed by:
(A) Wilmut and Rowson
(B) Walter Heape
(C) Drost
(D) Casida

646. Which of the following hormones are used for super ovulation?
(A) Equine chorionic gonadotropin
(B) Luteinising hormone
(C) Estradiol valerate
(D) None of the above

647. The dose of PMSG for super ovulation in cattle is:
(A) 3000 – 4000 IU (B) 1000 – 2000 IU
(C) 500 – 1000 IU (D) 2000 – 3000 IU

648. The following is the disadvantage of use of PMSG:
(A) Short biological half life
(B) Continuous production of prostaglandins
(C) Long biological half life
(D) None of the above

649. The total dose of FSH for super ovulation in large animals varies from:
(A) 200-400 mg (B) 400 – 600 mg
(C) 600-800 mg (D) 800-1000 mg

650. The pH of the flushing medium for embryo flushing should be:
(A) 7.2 – 7.6 (B) 7.8 – 8.2
(C) 6.5 – 6.8 (D) 6.7- 7.1

651. The holding medium for embryo contains:
(A) 1 % BSA (B) 4 % BSA
(C) 0.1 %BSA (D) 0.4% BSA

652. The flushing medium for embryo flushing contains:
(A) 0.1 % BSA (B) 0.2 %BSA
(C) 0.4 % BSA (D) 1 % BSA

653. Embryo collection is done on which days after the onset of super ovulatory heat in buffaloes:
(A) 6-7 (B) 6.5-7.5
(C) 5.5 – 6.5 (D) 7.5 – 8

654. What is the approximate number of cells in morula?
(A) 43 (B) 32
(C) 48 (D) 64

655. The hatching of blastocyst in bovines normally occurs at:
(A) day 5-6 (B) day 6-7
(C) day 4-8 (D) day 8-10

656. The embryonic cells are called:
(A) Blastocyst (B) Germ cells
(C) Blastomeres (D) Blastocoele

657. Blastomere is surrounded by:
(A) Blastomere (B) Trophoblast
(C) Inner cell mass (D) None of the above

658. Prostaglandins are derivatives of:
(A) Melonic acid (B) Arachidonic acid
(C) Benzoic acid (D) None of the above

659. Early abortion is evident in which of the following:
(A) Tuberculosis (B) Brucellosis
(C) Vibriosis (D) None of the above

660. Which of the following conditions are not associated with infection?
(A) Abortion (B) Repeat breeding
(C) Maceration (D) Mummification

661. Estrumate is an analogue of:
(A) Prostaglandin F_2 Alfa
(B) FSH
(C) PMSG
(D) Estrogen

662. Palace dairy farms, Mysore is associated with:
(A) First embryo transfer in dairy cattle in India
(B) First artificial insemination performed in India
(C) First progeny testing programme launched in India.
(D) None of the above

663. Which of the following is used in estrus synchronization?
(A) Folligon

(B) Norgestomate and Estradiol valerate
(C) Stilbesterol
(D) Follitropin

664. Which of the following can he used for super ovulation:
(A) PMSG (B) HCG
(C) Estrogen (D) All of the above

665. Progesterone therapy is used in which once of the following conditions:
(A) Cystic ovary
(B) Increasing conception rate
(C) Estrus synchronization
(D) All of the above

666. Which hormone is mainly responsible for development of female secondary sexual characters:
(a) Progesterone (b) Estrogen
(c) FSH (d) All

667. In cats and dogs which type of placenta is formed?
(A) Haemochorial (B) Endotheliochorial
(C) Epitheliochorial (D) Syndesmochorial

668. Average time taken for methylene blue reduction by superior quality semen is:
A. 3-6 minute B. 7-9 minute
C. 10 minute D. None

669. "Citric acid whey" semen dilution was developed by:
A. Thecker B. IVRI
C. NDRI D. NBRI

670. Citric acid whey dilutor is most suitable for:
A. Buffalo B. Bull
D. Buck D. Ram

671. F_2 dilutor contains:
A. 25% egg yolk B. 5 % egg yolk
C. 50 % egg yolk D. 10 % egg yolk

672. Amount of fructose solution (5%) present in E_5 dilution is:
A. 5 % B. 10 %
C. 20 % D. 30 %

673. Dilutor used for storing semen at room temperature is:
A. IVT dilutor B. EYC dilutor
C. D_2 dilutor D. Tris dilutor

674. IVT dilutor was developed by:
A. U. D. Sharma B. Thecker
C. Marshall D. Wilmut

675. Amount of Penicillin (I. U.) used in IVT dilutor:
A. 10^5 B. 10^{10}
C. 10^1 D. 10^9

676. Ovisinch is a:
A. Estrus synchronization protocol
B. Repeat breeding treatment
C. Drug used to treat cystic ovary
D. None

677. Which one is used to induce fertile estrus in bitches?
A. FSH B. GnRH
C. eCG D. All of above

678. Ovaries can be directly palpated through rectum in:
A. Cow B. Mare
C. Both a & b D. Bitch

679. Which type of semen is best in terms of color and concentration?
A. Thick creamy B. Thick milky
C. Watery D. Thin creamy

680. Yellow colour of bovine semen indicates presence of:
A. Pus B. Blood
C. Bile D. None

681. Optimum fructolysis index in bull semen is:
A. 1-2 B. 3-4
C. 0-1 D. 5-6

682. Cystic ovary in cows causes:
A. Nymphomania B. Anoestrus
C. Mucous discharge D. All of above

683. A dairy cow should ideally be bred:
(A) 45-60 days after parturition
(B) 30 days after parturition
(C) 25 days after parturition
(D) None

684. Average normal heart rate for calf is:
(A) 200 / minute (B) 120 / minute
(C) 20 / minute (D) 40 / minute

685. Epoophoron in adult female develops from:
a. Genital ridge
b. Genital fold
c. Mesonephric tubule
d. Urogenital sinus

686. Seminal Vesicles in adult male develops from:
a. Genital ridge
b. Genital fold
c. Mesonephric duct
d. Urogenital sinus

687. Bulbourethral gland develops from:
a. Genital ridge
b. Genital fold
c. Mesonephric tubule
d. Urogenital sinus

688. Prepuce develops from:
a. Genital ridge
b. Genital fold
c. Mesonephric tubule
d. Urogenital sinus

689. Penis develops from:
a. Genital ridge
b. Genital fold
c. Mesonephric tubule
d. Urogenital sinus

690. The pH of semen of Ram is:
a. Acidic b. Alkaline
c. Neutral d. Any

691. The pH of semen of cock is:
a. Acidic b. Alkaline
c. Neutral d. Any

692. The pH of semen of Buck is:
a. Acidic b. Alkaline
c. Neutral d. Any

693. Cystic ovary can be treated by using:
a. Estrogen
b. Oxytocin
c. Chorionic gonadotropin
d. Testosterone

694. Milk let down can be induced by using:
a. Estrogen
b. Oxytocin
c. Chorionic gonadotropin
d. Testosterone

695. Mismatching in bitch can be treated by using:
a. Estrogen
b. Oxytocin
c. Chorionic gonadotropin
d. Testosterone

696. Pyometra can be treated by using:
a. Estrogen b. Oxytocin
c. Lutalyse d. Testosterone

697. Cryptorchidism can be prevented by using:
a. Estrogen b. Oxytocin
c. Testosterone d. Testosterone

698. Cervical ripening can be prevented by using:
a. Estrogen
b. Oxytocin
c. Chorionic gonadotropin
d. Testosterone

699. Repeat breeders can be treated by using:
a. Estrogen
b. Oxytocin
c. Chorionic gonadotropin
d. Testosterone

700. Threatened Abortion can be treated by using:
a. Estrogen b. Oxytocin
c. Duraprogen d. Testosterone

701. Duration of estrus in Sow is:
a. 9 days b. 1-2 days
c. 2-4 days d. 4-7 days

702. Conception percentage on 1st insemination in case of cattle through AI is
(a) 65% (b) 70 %
(c) 90 % (d) 95 %

703. Duration of estrus in Bitch is:
a. 9 days b. 1-2 days
c. 2-4 days d. 4-7 days

704. The gestation period of Tigress is
a. 550 days b. 330 days
c. 90-93 days d. 105-113 days

705. Bactericidal component of semen is
(A) Acid (B) Spermin and Zn
(C) Lysozyme (D) None

706. Which one is the cause of abortion in cattle?
(a) Bacteria (b) Virus
(c) Chlameydia (d) Spirochaete

707. The gestation period of panther is
a. 550 days b. 330 days
c. 90-93 days d. 105-113 days

708. Function of ovary is
(a) Oogensis (b) Steroidogenesis
(c) Both (d) None

709. Type of oterus in sow is
(a) Bipartite uterus (b) Duplex utreus
(c) Bicoruate utreus (d) Simplex utreus

710. C.L. of pregnancy is called
(a) Corpus luteum (b) Corpus albicans
(c) Corpus uirum (d) All

711. Mulbery shaped ovary is present in
(a) Cow (b) Horse
(c) Sow (d) Dog

712. Ovulatory fossa is present in ovary of which animal
(a) Dog (b) Sow
(c) Mare (d) Cow

713. Which animal exhibit metestrus bleeding?
(a) Zebu cattle (b) Buffalo
(c) Cross breed cattle (d) Mare

714. Lardosis is found in
(a) Cattle (b) Horse
(c) Sow (d) Dog

715. Assymetry in sizes of horns occurs in which month?
(a) 15 days (b) 25 days
(c) 21 days (d) 35 days

716. Uterus moved to abdominal floor in which month?
(a) 2nd month (b) 4th month
(c) 5th month (d) 7th month

717. Fetal bones can be felt at which month
(a) 1st month (b) 4th month
(c) 6th month (d) 3th month

718. Fremitus is very clear at
(a) 5th month (b) 4th month
(c) 7th month (d) 8th month

719. Uterus is present in abdominal cavity between
(a) 4th 5th month (b) 6th – 5th month
(c) 5th – 7th month (d) 8th – 9th month

720. Ultrasound by trans cutaneous scanning is done in
(a) Cattle (b) Buffalo
(c) Dog (d) Goat

721. Progesterone level declines by which day in non preg. ani
(a) 10th – 11th day (b) 20th – 21st day
(c) 16th – 17th day (d) 6th – 7th day

722. Raised level of progesterone occurs in
(a) Pyometra (b) Mummification
(c) Both (d) None

723. Spaying hook is used for
(a) Removal of testes
(b) Removal of uterus
(c) Removal of ovaries
(d) None

724. Which instrument is used for taking biopsy of endometrium
(a) Vaginal speculum
(b) Vaginoscope
(c) Nelson's biopsy punch
(d) Obel's apparatus

725. Inflammation of oviduct is
(a) Metritis (b) Mastitis
(c) Salpingitis (d) Funiculitis

726. Thick cyst wall present in
(a) Folicular cyst (b) Perimetrial cyst
(c) Luteal cyst (d) All

727. Pyometra is infectious condition of
(a) Urinary bladder (b) Ovary
(c) Uterus (d) Vagina

728. Ovulation occurs under influence of
(a) FSH (b) Progesteron
(c) LH (d) Estogen

729. Nymphomania is a condition due to
(a) Luteal cyst
(b) Cystic corpus luteum
(c) Follicular cyst
(d) All

730. Deficiency of which vitamin causes abortion
(a) Vit. B (b) Vit. B_2
(c) Vit. A (d) Vit. D

731. Premature and dead faetus is due to deficiency of
(a) Phosphorus (b) Manganese
(c) Iodine (d) Sulphur

732. Trichomoniasis causes abortion during
(a) Last trimester (b) Middle trimester
(c) First trimester (d) At any time

733. Abortion in mid trimester is caused by
(a) Brucellosis
(b) Trichomoniasis
(c) Campylobacteriosis
(d) None

734. Abortion in last trimester occurs due to
(a) Campylobacteriosis
(b) Trichomoniasis
(c) Burcellosis
(d) None

735. Leathery placenta is seen in
(a) Trichomoniasis (b) Vibriosis
(c) Brucellosis (d) Campylobacteriosis

736. Pyometra occurs in
(a) Brucellosis (b) Campylobacteriosis
(c) Trichomoniasis (d) None

737. ABRT is done for diagnosis of
(a) Campylobacteriosis
(b) Trichomoniasis
(c) Brucellosis
(d) Aspergillosis

738. Diagonosis of Brucellosis is done by
(a) Milk ring test
(b) Rapid plate agglutination test
(c) Both
(d) None

739. Pin bone is related to
(a) Ilium (b) Pubis
(c) Ischium (d) None

740. Hip bone is related to
(a) Ischium (b) Pubis
(c) Ilium (d) None

741. Largest bone of os coxae is
(a) Pubis (b) Ischium
(c) Ilium (d) All

742. Acetabulum is formed by
(a) Ischium & Pubis
(b) Ilium & Pubis
(c) Ilium, ischium & pubis
(d) Ilium & ischium

743. Ilium bone is
(a) Quadrilateral (b) Rectangular
(c) Triangular (d) Square

744. Medial portion of wing of ilium is
(a) Tuber coxal (b) Tuber lochi
(c) Tuber sacrale (d) None

745. Pelvic inlet of cow is
(a) Round (b) Spherical
(c) Elliptical (d) Triangular

746. Round pelvic inlet is present in
(a) Cow (b) Sow
(c) Mare (d) All

747. Which instrument is used for repulsion of foetus
(a) Cammerer's detorsion fork
(b) Frey berger's hook
(c) Kuhn's crutch repeller
(d) Obermayer's hook

748. What is the presentation in Breech Presentation?
(a) Anterio longitudinal
(b) Transverse
(c) Posterio longitudinal
(d) None

749. Schaffer's plank method is used to correct
(a) Pyometra (b) Metritis
(c) Uterine torsion (d) Prolapse

750. Cervico-vaginal prolepse can be corrected by
(a) Rope truss method
(b) Vulver sturing
(c) Both
(d) None

751. Plasma extenders
(a) Dextran (b) Normal saline
(c) Both (d) None

752. Total no. of cotyledons in cows
(a) 80-90 (b) 70-90
(c) 70-120 (d) 90-100

753. Concave caruncles present in
(a) Cow (b) Buffalo
(c) Sheep (d) Dog

754. Type of placenta in Ruminants
(a) Zonary (b) Discoidal
(c) Cotyledonary (d) None

755. First faeces of calf is called as
(a) Stool (b) Dung
(c) Meconium (d) None

756. Umblical cord, from umbli lices is cut at about
(a) 5 inches (b) 1 inches
(c) 2 inches (d) 10 inches

757. External genitalia includes
(a) Scrotum (b) Testes
(c) Both (d) None

758. Which is unpaired gland?
(a) Seminal vesicle (b) Cowper's gland

(c) Prostate gland (d) None

759. Which of the following is communicable disease?
(a) Brucellosis (b) Campylobacteriosis
(c) Both (d) None

760. Semen evaluation includes
(a) External genitalia examination
(b) Internal genitalia examination
(c) Progressive motility
(d) Serological examination

761. Fructolytic index in semen evaluation test is
(a) Macroscopic parameter
(b) Microscopic parameter
(c) Biochemical test
(d) Serological test

762. Staining of sperms is done by
(a) Crystal violet (b) Malachite green
(c) Eosin-nigrosin (d) $CuSO_4$

763. Eosin gives this colour to death sperms
(a) Blue (b) Yellow
(c) Pink (d) Violet

764. Blue background in sperm counting is provided by
(a) Eosin (b) Methylene blue
(c) Nigrosin (d) Crystal violet

765. Chromic acid contains
(a) Potassium dicromate
(b) Conc. H_2SO_4
(c) Both
(d) None

766. Innermost laryer of testes is
(a) Tunica vaginalis
(b) Dartos layer
(c) Tunica albuginea
(d) loose connective tissue

767. Tail of epididymis is formed by
(a) Caput (b) Corpus
(c) Cauda (d) All

768. Sperm maturition occurs in
(a) Caput (b) Corpus
(c) Cauda (d) None

769. Sperms are stored in
(a) Rete testis
(b) Seminiferous tubules
(c) Epididymis
(d) Seminal vesicle

770. Capacity of graduated semen collection tube is
(a) 5 ml (b) 10 ml
(c) 15 ml (d) 20 ml

771. Inner temperature of A.V. should be
(a) 30-40°C (b) 50-60°C
(c) 40-45°C (d) 50-55°C

772. Which is not a part of A.V.?
(a) Hard rubber cylinder
(b) Latex cone & liver
(c) Pump for filling air
(d) Insulation bag

773. Too cold temperature causes
(a) Primary abnormality
(b) Secondary abnormality
(c) Tertiary abnormality
(d) All

774. Pressure is important factor in A.V. for
(a) Ram (b) Bull
(c) Boar (d) Buck

775. Glove hand method is used in semen collection in
(a) Bull (b) Ram
(c) Boar (d) Stallion

776. Color of semen in Orchitis
(a) Red (b) Yellowish green
(c) Greenish (d) Creamy white

777. In pseudomonas infection, color of semen is
(a) Red (b) Brownish
(c) Greenish (d) Creamy white

778. Red color of semen indicates
(a) Orchitis
(b) Pseudomonas infection
(c) Haemorrhage
(d) None

779. Most important parameter of microscopic examination of semen
(a) Mass motility
(b) Sperm conc.
(c) Progressive motility
(d) Live & dead spermatozoa

780. Max. acceptable limit of abnormal spermatozoa is
(a) 5-10% (b) 10-15%
(c) 15-20% (d) 20-25%

781. Diadem defect is
(a) Tertiary abnormility
(b) Secondary
(c) Primary
(d) None

782. Free heads & free tails is which type of abnormality
(a) Primary (b) Tertiary
(c) Secondary (d) None

783. Proximal protoplasmic droplet is which type of abnormality
(a) Tertiary (b) Primary
(c) Secondary (d) Congenital

784. Loosened galea capitis is which type of abnormality
(a) Heriditary (b) Primary
(c) Secondary (d) Tertiary

785. Pyriform head is which type of abnormality
(a) Secondary (b) Tertiary
(c) Primary (d) All

786. Cells found in semen
(a) Medusa cell
(b) Squamous epithelial cells
(c) Both
(d) None

787. Which of the following is inherited defect?
(a) Broken head
(b) Broken tail
(c) Dag defect
(d) Protoplasmic droplets

788. In MBRT for semen evaluation, blue color change to
(a) Red (b) Pink
(c) White (d) Green

789. Normal pH of bull semen is
(a) 4.8 (b) 5.8
(c) 6.8 (d) 7.8

790. Preservation of semen at ambient temperature is done for
(a) 1-2 days (b) 5-6 days
(c) 2-3 days (d) 4-5 days

791. For preservation of semen at ambient temperature, temperature is
(a) 3-5°C (b) -196 °C
(c) 18-30 °C (d) -79 °C

792. Dilutors used for preservation of semen at 18-30 °C
(a) CME (b) IVT
(c) Both above (d) D_2 dilutor

793. Milovanov's Dilutor is of which type of temperature
(a) Refrigerator temperature
(b) Deep freeze
(c) Ambient
(d) None

794. CO_2 gas is passed in which dilutor, to maintain pH
(a) D_2 (b) CME
(c) IVT (d) EYC

795. Preservation of bovine semen at refrigerator temperature is done for
(a) 1-2 d (b) 2-3 d
(c) 3-4 d (d) 5-6d

796. Preservation of semen at refrigerator temperature done at what °C
(a) 18-30 °C (b) -196 °C
(c) 3-5 °C (d) -80 °C

797. Example of refrigerator temperature dilutor(s) is/are
(a) Egg yolk littrate (b) D_2
(c) Both above (d) IVT

798. D_2 dilutor is used to reserve sperm at which temperature
(a) Deep freezed (b) Ambient
(c) Refrigerated (d) None

799. Which chemical disperses fat globules in EYC dilutor?
(a) Sulphanilamide (b) Peucillin
(c) Sodium citrate (d) Egg yolk

800. Ice crystal formation during preservation of semen prevented by
(a) Glycogen (b) Glucose
(c) Glycerol (d) Sodium citrate

801. 0.5 ml is the volume of which type of show
(a) French mini (b) Continental
(c) Both (d) None

802. 0.25 ml is the volume of
(a) French mini (b) Continental
(c) Both (d) None

803. Thawing of deep frozen semen is done at 35-37°C for how many seconds
(a) 70 sec (b) 5 sec
(c) 30-60 sec (d) 1-2 sec

804. Rapid thawing is done at
(a) 35-37°C (b) 40°C
(c) 70°C (d) 100°C

805. The elevated tail heat in case of nymphomania is called as
(a) Sterility head (b) Sterility hump
(c) Both a and b (d) None of them

806. Whihc oestrum is classified under class I with functional corpus luteum
(a) Apparant anestrum
(b) Cystic ovary
(c) Free martinism
(d) Silent heat

807. Corupus luteum is not regress in condition of
(a) Before parturition
(b) In case of pyometra
(c) In uterine unicornis
(d) All of the above

808. In which condition corpus luteum is absent
(a) Pyometra (b) Uterine unicornis
(c) Mucometra (d) Pregnancy

809. In unobserved estrum
(a) Estrus is silent
(b) Estrus period is shorten
(c) CL is retained
(d) Mucometra

810. Sign of pregnency in cow is
(a) Absence of placentome
(b) Enlarged horn
(c) Slipping of fetal membrane
(d) All of the above

811. Palpation of walled whirring uterine arteries is also known as
(a) Placentome (b) Fetatome
(c) Fremitus (d) All of the above

812. Semen collection from bulls should be made during
(a) Early evening (b) Early morning
(c) Late evening (d) Afternoon

813. Slipping of fetal membrane is best performed at
(a) 90 days of pregnancy
(b) 35-90 days of pregnancy
(c) 120 days of pregnancy
(d) 30 days of pregnancy

814. The location of pregnancy utreus at 5th to 6th month of pregnancy at
(a) Pelvic cavity
(b) Brim of pelvis
(c) Forward and downward in abdominal cavity
(d) All of the above

815. At which stage only cervix & uterine artery can be palpated
(a) 1-2 month of pregnancy
(b) 3-4 month of pregnancy
(c) 5-6 month of pregnancy
(d) After 8th month of pregnancy

816. To find out the mouth of pregnancy, we use
(a) (2 x C-R length) (b) (3 x C-R length)
(c) (2 x C-R length) (d) Ö (2 x C-R length)

817. Palpation of placentome should be done at what age of pregnancy
(a) 30-60 days (b) 75-80 days
(c) 15-30 days (d) 90-120 days

818. Fremitus is felt at
(a) 30-60 days of pregnancy
(b) 60-70 days of pregnancy
(c) 80-120 days of pregnancy
(d) 30-40 days of pregnancy

819. Fetal heart rate at 6 months of pregnancy is
(a) 150/min (b) 140/min
(c) 120/min (d) 100/min

820. Fetal heart rate at 9 months of pregnancy is
(a) 150/min (b) 140/min
(c) 120/min (d) 100/min

821. In diagnosing pregnancy in mare which test should be performed
(a) Cobal test (b) Roberts test
(c) Salkowitch test (d) Cuboni test

822. Which is used in cuboni test?
(a) Urine of pregnant mare
(b) Serum of pregnancy
(c) Epithelium of pregnant mare
(d) All of the above

823. Mesentry of testes of Embryo is differentiated in adult male as
(a) Mesorvarium (b) Mesochrium
(c) Cervix (d) Oviduct

824. Severe chronic metritis with complete destruction of endomentrium and fibrotic changes of the uterine wall is called
(a) Pyometra (b) Schlerotic metritis
(c) Atresia of cervix (d) Catarrhal endometritis

825. After birth is detached because
(a) Blood supply is reduced
(b) Contraction of uterus
(c) Caruncle reduced in size
(d) All of the above

826. Which of the following may cause retained placenta?
(a) Hyperkeratosis (b) Lack of Iodine
(c) Both a & b (d) None of them

827. Which of the following is correct about retained placenta in beef breeds than in dairy breeds?
(a) Less common (b) More common
(c) Not common (d) All of the above

828. Which symptoms is seen in deficiency of progesterone
(a) Sterility (b) Anoestrus
(c) Irregular estrus (d) Abortion

829. Which is seen in excess of progesterone?
(a) Abortion
(b) Failure of the fertilized ova to get implant
(c) Irregular oestrus
(d) All of the above

830. The various physiological processes all together involved in the birth of young ones are known as
(a) Abortion (b) Gestation
(c) Parturition (d) None of the above

831. Oozing of colostrums from test before 2 days of parturition in the horse is known as
(a) Puberty (b) Waxing
(c) Weaning (d) Both a & c

832. An additional symptom which is seen in bitch approaching at parturition in contrast to cow is
(a) Enlargement of mammary gland
(b) Oedematous vulva
(c) Vulvar discharge
(d) Panting

833. Which is a sign of approaching parturition in cow?
(a) Enlargement of mammary gland
(b) Tenacious, White mucus discharge from vagina
(c) 2-6 times enlarged valva
(d) All of the above

834. In 1st stage of parturition contraction occur in utreus for
(a) 3 to 5 min (b) 10 to 15 min
(c) 15 to 30 sec (d) 40 to 60 sec

835. Which is a multiparous animal?
(a) Bitch (b) Cow
(c) Mare (d) Buffalo

836. In mare which position is acquired by
(a) Dorso- Ventral (b) Dorso- Sacral
(c) Dorso Lateral (d) None of them

837. Brownish colour semen probably indicates
(a) Degenerative
(b) Pus and cells
(c) Fresh blood
(d) Purulent degeneration

838. Yellow colour semen is indicative of
(a) Degenerative blood tissue
(b) Pus and cells
(c) Fresh blood
(d) Purulent degeneration

839. Pinkish or reddish colour is indication of
(a) Degenerative blood tissue
(b) Pus and cells
(c) Fresh blood
(d) Purulent degeneration

840. Proportion of foetuses delivered posteriorly is high in
(a) Cow (b) Bitch
(c) Both a & b (d) None of them

841. Which is known as 4th stage of parturition?
(a) Involution
(b) Rotation
(c) Explusion of foetus
(d) Expulsion of foetal membrane

842. Time required for involution in cow is
(a) Thirteen to twenty-five days

(b) Ten days
(c) Nine days
(d) Thirty days

843. Time required for involution in sow is
(a) Thirteen to twenty-five days
(b) Ten days
(c) Nine days
(d) Thirty days

844. Time required for involution in ewe is
(a) Thirteen to twenty-five days
(b) Ten days
(c) Nine days
(d) Thirty days

845. Time required for involution in mare is
(a) Thirteen to twenty-five days
(b) Ten days
(c) Nine days
(d) Thirty days

846. Time required for expulsion of foetus in mare is
(a) Half to two hours
(b) Ten to Thirty min
(c) Half to three hours
(d) One to four hours

847. Time required for expulsion of foetus in cow is
(a) Half to two hours
(b) Ten to Thirty min
(c) Half to three hours
(d) One to four hours

848. Time required for expulsion of foetus in sow is
(a) Half to two hours
(b) Ten to thirty min
(c) Half to three hours
(d) One to four hours

849. Time required for expulsion of foetus in ewe is
(a) Half to two hours
(b) Ten to Thirty min
(c) Half to three hours
(d) One to four hours

850. Time required for preparatory stage in cow is
(a) Half to twenty-four hours
(b) Two to twelve hours
(c) One to four hours
(d) One to two hours

851. Time required for preparatory stage in sow is
(a) Half to twenty-four hours
(b) Two to twelve hours
(c) One to four hours
(d) One to two hours

852. Time required for preparatory stage in mare is
(a) Half to twenty-four hours
(b) Two to twelve hours
(c) One to four hours
(d) One to two hours

853. Normal time required for expulsion of placenta in the sow is
(a) One to four hours
(b) Half to eight hours
(c) Eight to twenty hours
(d) Twenty to twenty-five hours

854. Normal time required for expulsion of placenta in the cow, mare and ewe is
(a) One to four hours
(b) Half to eight hours
(c) Eighty to twenty hours
(d) Twenty to twenty five hours

855. In cows mostly vagino-cervical prolapse occur in
(a) Early gestation (b) Advanced gestation
(c) Mid gestation (d) None of them

856. Vagino-cervical prolapse in more commonly used in
(a) Primipara (b) Pleuripara
(c) Both a & b (d) None of them

857. In which breed of cow, vagino-cervical prolepse is common
(a) Holestein (b) Hereford
(c) Jersey (d) Brown swiss

858. In dogs vagino-cervical prolepse is occur at during
(a) Advanced gestation
(b) Mid gestation
(c) Proestrus
(d) None of them

859. Vagino-cervical prolepse in often spoken of by the farmer as
(a) Casting of weathers
(b) Casting
(c) Advenal virilism
(d) Sterility hump

860. For treating the case of vagino-cervical prolepse what should be done
(a) Rear part elevated

(b) Injection progesterone
(c) Replacing the prolapsed part
(d) All of the above

861. Expulsion of dead foetus of recognisable size at any stage of the gestation is known as
(a) Mummification (b) Stillbirth
(c) Infertility (d) Abortion

862. Expulsion of dead foetus at completion of gestation period is known as
(a) Mummification (b) Stillbirth
(c) Infertility (d) Abortion

863. If there is early embryonic death then fertilized ova, early embryo or foetus may abort without being seen is
(a) Mummification (b) Stillbirth
(c) Infertility (d) Abortion

864. If foestus died after 3-4 month and corpus luteum is maintained then it will not expelled but retained in uterus and undergo autolytic changes known as
(a) Mummification (b) Stillbirth
(c) Infertility (d) Abortion

865. If there is presence of infection then foetus may undergo heterolytic degeneration which is known as
(a) Mummification (b) Maceration
(c) Infertility (d) Abortion

866. Which change occur within 12 hour of death of foetus in uterus
(a) Foetal color cloudy
(b) Skin color changes
(c) Discharge is Reddish, cloudy & mucoid
(d) All of the above

867. Non infectious cause of abortion is
(a) IBR (b) BVD
(c) PPR (d) Genetic

868. Which infection is caused by virus?
(a) IBR (b) BVD
(c) PPR (d) All of the above

869. Which is known as "Bang Disease?"
(a) Trichomoniasis (b) Brucellosis
(c) Leptospirosis (d) Vibriosis

870. In humen, brucella causes which of the following
(a) Undulating fever (b) Malta fever
(c) Both a & b (d) None of them

871. Which strain of brucella affects sheep & goat?
(a) *Brucella abortus* (b) *Brucella suis*
(c) *Brucella canis* (d) *Brucella malitensis*

872. In bull brucella infection is manifested by
(a) Orchitis (b) Abortion
(c) Both a & b (d) None of them

873. In cow symptom of brucellosis is
(a) Enlargement of supra mammalian lymph node
(b) Hygroma of joint
(c) Swelling of vulva
(d) All of the above

874. Abortion occur due to brucellosis in the cow at
(a) Early pregnancy (b) Last trimester
(c) Second trimester (d) Any stage

875. Which is a dead vaccine of brucella
(a) Cotton strain 19 (b) *B. melitensis* vaccine
(c) K 45/20 (d) All of the above

876. Which test should be performed in diagnosing brucellosis?
(a) Plate agglutination
(b) Rose bengal plate test
(c) Tube agglutination
(d) All of the above

877. Which test is performed with milk to diagnose the brucella organism?
(a) MRT
(b) Plate agglutination
(c) Rose Bengal plate test
(d) All of the above

878. In ABR test if blue ring is at top & milk is seen, the diagnosis is
(a) Negative (b) Positive
(c) ++ (d) +++

879. Greenish coloured semen is indicates of
(a) Degenerative blood tissue
(b) Pus and cells
(c) Fresh blood
(d) Purulent degeneration

880. The average specific gravity of whole semen in dogs is
(a) 1.028 (b) 1.011
(c) 1.035 (d) 1.040

881. For motility test 0 is indicative of
(a) No motility (b) 20-40 % motility
(c) 40-60 % motility (d) 60-80 % motility

882. Which type of semen is recommended for artificial insemination?
(a) ++ (b) 0
(c) +++ or more (d) +

883. Hypothalamic hormones are small molecules of
(a) Arachidonic acid (b) Peptide
(c) Starch (d) Cellulose

884. In case of Trichomoniasis abortion occur at
(a) 4 month of gestation
(b) 6 month of gestation
(c) 7 month of gestation
(d) None of them

885. Trichomonas foetus infection is propagated by
(a) Inhalation (b) Ingestion
(c) Coitus (d) All of above

886. Potato soup" like pus is seen in case of
(a) Brucella (b) Trichomonas
(c) IBR- IPV (d) All of above

887. IBR – IPV infection is caused by
(a) Adenovirus (b) Parvo virus
(c) Herpes virus (d) None of them

888. In IBR – IPV infection abortion occur at the
(a) Early pregnancy (b) IInd trimester
(c) IIIrd trimester (d) In all trimester

889. In aborted foetus due to IBR – IPV virus which sign is seen
(a) Patechial heart (b) Placentitis
(c) Hepatitis (d) All of the above

890. In vibriosis occur in which stage of pregnancy
(a) Early stage (b) Last stage
(c) Second half (d) In all stages

891. Which disease is transmitted by coitus?
(a) Vibriosis (b) Tuberculosis
(c) Trypanosomiasis (d) Leptospirosis

892. Isonicotinic acid is the drug of choice in which disease
(a) Leptospirosis (b) Vibriosis
(c) AIDs (d) Tuberculosis

893. In tuberculosis affected animal, the abortion occur in
(a) Early stage of pregnancy
(b) Last trimester of pregnancy
(c) Second half of pregnancy
(d) All of the above

894. In which condition corpus luteum persists
(a) Mummification (b) Oestrus
(c) Aborted foetus (d) All of the above

895. In polytoccus animals which type of mummification is present?
(a) Haematinic type (b) Papyraceous type
(c) Both a & b (d) None of them

896. In cattle which type of mummification is present?
(a) Haematinic (b) Papyraceous type
(c) Both a & b (d) None of them

897. In papyraceous type mummification foetus is felt as
(a) Hard & graveled
(b) Dry, firm & leather fit
(c) Spongy mass
(d) Normal

898. In haematinic mummification foetus is felt as
(a) Hard & graveled
(b) Dry, firm & leather fit
(c) Spongy mass
(d) Normal

899. In which condition external infection is get entered
(a) Mummification (b) Maceration
(c) Both a & b (d) Abortion

900. Heterolysis is occur in which condition
(a) Mummification (b) Maceration
(c) Both a & b (d) None of the above

901. Heterolysis is occur in which condition
(a) Difficult acceptance
(b) Difficult breathing
(c) Difficult birth
(d) None of them

902. Dystocia is more common in which of the following
(a) Pleuripara (b) Primipara
(c) Both a & b (d) None of them

903. Traumatic cause of dystocia is categorized as
(a) Basic caused of dystocia
(b) Immediate cause of dystocia
(c) Both a & b
(d) None of them

904. Mainly dystocia is caused in cow by
(a) Abnormal position, presentation & posture

of foetus
(b) Disproportion between foetal size & pelvis
(c) Postural abonormality plus twins & triplet dystocia
(d) All of the above

905. Wry neck is most commonly found in
(a) Mare (b) Cow
(c) Ewe (d) Goat

906. Uterine torsion is common in
(a) Mare (b) Cow
(c) Ewe (d) Goat

907. Both gravid and non gravid horn are involved in torsion in which of the following
(a) Unipara (b) Multipara
(c) Both a & b (d) None of them

908. In multipara
(a) Both horns are involved in torsion
(b) Both horns are not involved in torsion
(c) Both a & b
(d) All of the above

909. Which is a cause of torsion?
(a) Sudden slip or fall
(b) Confinement in stables
(c) Lack of tone pregnant uterus
(d) All of the above

910. Intercornual ligament is strong in
(a) Cow (b) Dog
(c) Cat (d) All of above

911. Intercornual ligament is absent in
(a) Cow (b) Dog
(c) Cat (d) Both a & b

912. Treatment of torsion of uterus is
(a) Rolling on the earth
(b) Laparotomy
(c) Caesarean section
(d) All of the above

913. If right side uterine torsion is occur then rolling of animal on earth is done in
(a) Same direction (b) Opposite direction
(c) Any of the two (d) None of them

914. In case of the left torsion, through laparotomy is rotated to which side
(a) Right & downward
(b) Left & downward
(c) Both a & b
(d) None of them

915. In artificial vagina for bulls, the length of cylinder is
(a) 6 cm (b) 20 cm
(c) 30-40 cm (d) 50-55 cm

916. In AV for bulls, the length of inner sleeve is
(a) 6 cm (b) 20 cm
(c) 30-40 cm (d) 50-55 cm

917. In AV for bulls, the width of cylinder is
(a) 6 cm (b) 20 cm
(c) 30-40 cm (d) 50-55 cm

918. If the inner sleeve used in AV is too thin then
(a) It bulges at ends of cylinder
(b) It is inflexible
(c) Both a & b
(d) None of them

919. If the inner sleeve used in AV is thick then which of the following is correct?
(a) It bulges at ends of cylinder
(b) It is inflexible
(c) Both a & b
(d) None of them

920. The width of inner sleeve used in AV for bulls is
(a) 7-8 cm (b) 20-25 cm
(c) 25-30 cm (d) 30-35 cm

921. The length of cone used in AV for bulls is which of the following
(a) 7-8 cm (b) 20-25 cm
(c) 25-30 cm (d) 30-35 cm

922. The capacity of collecting tube used in AV for bulls is
(a) 5 ml (b) 7 ml
(c) 10 ml (d) 13 ml

923. The movements of sperm may be which of the following
(a) Progressive (b) Rotatory
(c) Oscillatory (d) All of the above

924. The range of temperature in AV for bulls is
(a) 34-40 ^{0}C (b) 42-46 ^{0}C
(c) 46-50 ^{0}C (d) 50-56 ^{0}C

925. If length of AV is more than size of penis of bull then which of the following occur
(a) Bull gets hurt by hitting the collection tube

(b) Through off the collection vial
(c) Deposition of semen in cylinder
(d) Both a & b

926. If length of AV is less than size of penis of bull then which of the following occur
(a) Bull get hurt by hitting the collection tube
(b) Through off the collection vial
(c) Deposition of semen in cylinder
(d) Both a & b

927. Generally how many times semen is collected from bull in a week
(a) Once/twice a week
(b) Thrice a week
(c) Many times
(d) None of them

928. The characteristics of semen collected from electro ejaculation method is
(a) Less in volume and more concentrated
(b) More in volume and less concentrated
(c) Both a & b
(d) None of them

929. Which one is correct for electric source for electro ejaculation?
(a) AC/200 volts/single phase/100 cycles
(b) AC/ 200-250 volts/single phase/50 cycles
(c) DC/200 volts/double phase/50 cycles
(d) DC/200/single phase/50 cycles

930. The length of cylinder used in AV for Ram is
(a) 10 cm (b) 15 cm
(c) 20 cm (d) 25 cm

931. The length of cylinder used in AV for buck is
(a) 10 cm (b) 15 cm
(c) 20 cm (d) 25 cm

932. The length of inner sleeve used in AV for Ram is
(a) 5-8 cm long then cylinder
(b) 5-8 cm short then cylinder
(c) 10-20 cm long then cylinder
(d) 10-20 cm short then cylinder

933. Prostaglandins cause luteolysis in cycling cows between
(a) 3-5 days of cycle
(b) 5-16 days of pregnancy
(c) Both of the above
(d) None of the above

934. Which on of the following is disadvantage of electro ejaculation?
(a) Contaminated semen with urine
(b) Highly technical method
(c) Some males resist
(d) All of the above

935. Penis locks into curvature of uterus in the case of
(a) Ram (b) Bull
(c) Stallion (d) Boar

936. Quantity of sperm rich fraction of semen of boar is
(a) 10 ml (b) 40-80 ml
(c) 150-200 ml (d) None of them

937. Quantity of pre sperm fraction of semen of boar is
(a) 10 ml (b) 40-80 ml
(c) 150-200 ml (d) None of them

938. Quantity of low sperm fraction of sperm of boar is
(a) 10 ml (b) 40-80 ml
(c) 150-200 ml (d) None of them

939. The post sperm fraction which is gelatinous is secreted by
(a) Scortum
(b) Epididymis
(c) Bulbourethral gland
(d) Prostate gland

940. Two inner tubes are used in AV of which animal
(a) Bull (b) Ram
(c) Stallion (d) Boar

941. Which type of AV is used for boar?
(a) Norweigian type
(b) Holland type
(c) Missouri type
(d) Mississippi model

942. Mississippi model of AV is used for
(a) Bull (b) Ram
(c) Stallion (d) Boar

943. Air pump is used in AV of which of the following animal
(a) Bull (b) Ram
(c) Stallion (d) Boar

944. Ejaculation is occur by digital pressure in case of
(a) Bull (b) Ram
(c) Stallion (d) Boar

945. The length of AV is used for stallion is
(a) 20-30 cm
(b) 22.5-36.6 cm
(c) 91.5-122 cm
(d) 65.2- 69.8 cm

946. Which fraction of semen is milky and contains high concentration of sperm in case of stallion
(a) I fraction (b) II fraction
(c) III fraction (d) None of them

947. The shape of hole of AV for boar is
(a) L-like (b) W-like
(c) C-like (d) Y-like

948. Volume of ejaculate for bull is
(a) 5-8 ml (b) 152 ml
(c) 1 ml (d) 215 ml

949. Volume of ejaculate in ml for boar is
(a) 3-5 ml (b) 1 ml
(c) 125 ml (d) 215 ml

950. Volume of ejaculate in ml for boar is
(a) 3-5 ml (b) 1 ml
(c) 125 ml (d) 215 ml

951. Recommended diluent for semen of horse is
(a) Yolk-citrate modification
(b) Yolk- glucose bicarbonate
(c) Glucose-gelatine
(d) Yolk – glucose citrate

952. Recommended diluent for semen of horse is
(a) Yolk-citrate modification
(b) Yolk- glucose bicarbonate
(c) Glucose-gelatine
(d) Yolk – glucose citrate

953. Recommended diluent for semen of swine is
(a) Yolk-citrate modification
(b) Yolk- glucose bicarbonate
(c) Glucose-gelatin
(d) Yolk – glucose citrate

954. Recommended diluent for semen of bull is
(a) Yolk-citrate modification
(b) Yolk- glucose bicarbonate
(c) Glucose-gelatin
(d) Yolk – glucose citrate

955. Storage temperature for semen of bull is
(a) 5 ^{0}C (b) 15 ^{0}C
(c) 25^{0}C-30 ^{0}C (d) None of them

956. Storage temperature for semen of horse is
(a) 5 ^{0}C (b) 15 ^{0}C
(c) 25^{0}C-30 ^{0}C (d) None of them

957. Rate of dilution of house's semen is
(a) 1 : 5 (b) 1 : 9
(c) 1 : 4 (d) 1 : 2

958. Rate of dilution of boar's semen is
(a) 1 : 5 (b) 1 : 9
(c) 1 : 4 (d) 1 : 2

959. For live and dead count method living spermatozoa appear
(a) Unstained
(b) Stained pink
(c) Stained brownish
(d) Stained black

960. In normal bull semen the percentage of abnormal forms should not exceed
(a) 15-20 % (b) 25-30%
(c) 35-40% (d) 35-50 %

961. The main objective of dilution of semen is
(a) To increase the volume of ejaculate
(b) To preserve fertility capacity of sperm
(c) Both of the above
(d) None

962. Which bacteria is not completely eliminated
(a) Corynebacterium pyogenes
(b) Brucella
(c) Mycobacterium
(d) All of the above

963. The use of fructose in dilution as
(a) Nutrient
(b) Buffer
(c) Prevent sperm agglutination
(d) All of the above

964. The mode of action of glycerol is
(a) It modify size and shape of ice crystal
(b) Binds water and decrease freezing point
(c) Prevents denaturation of proteins
(d) All of t he above

965. How many parts of egg yolk is used in sodium citrate dilution
(a) 30 Parts (b) 40 Parts
(c) 50 Parts (d) 60 Parts

966. The main anaerobic source of energy in bull and

Ram semen is
(a) Glucose (b) Fructose
(c) Galactose (d) Mannose

967. Fructose is not utilized by
(a) Azospermic semen
(b) Necrospermic semen
(c) Both of the above
(d) None of them

968. Azoospermia means
(a) Devoid of sperms
(b) Immotile sperms
(c) Both of the above
(d) None of them

969. Necrospermia means
(a) Devoid of sperms
(b) Immotile sperms
(c) Both of the above
(d) None of them

970. Which type of diluents is used if we want to preserve active sperm for 7 to 10 days at room temperature?
(a) Sodium citrate dilutor
(b) CUE
(c) IVT
(d) Coconut based

971. In preparing egg yolk fresh han's egg is wiped with
(a) Whey
(b) 50 % alcohol
(c) 60 % alcohol
(d) 70 % alcohol

972. IF cold diluent is mixed in semen then what will happen
(a) No effect on semen
(b) Cold shock to semen
(c) Both of the above
(d) None

973. Who accidentally added 20% glycerol to fowl sperm solution?
(a) Polge (b) Smith
(c) Parks (d) All of above

974. First insemination was done with deep frozen semen by
(a) 1941 (b) 1951
(c) 1961 (d) 1991

975. First insemination was done with deep frozen semen by
(a) Steward (b) Johnal
(c) Smith (d) Park

976. Semen is stored in liquid N_2 at which of the following temperature
(a) -196 ^{0}C (b) 196 ^{0}C
(c) 0 ^{0}C (d) 4 ^{0}C

977. Non-flagellar sperm are found in
(a) Mammals (b) Primates
(c) Artiodactyls (d) Crustacean

978. Nutritional deficiency causing bovine infertility is of
(a) Single entity nature
(b) Multiple one
(c) Lack of grass
(d) Lack of hay

979. The anterior part of the nucleus is covered by a cap like structure is known as
(a) Acroinen (b) Acrocarp
(c) Acrosome (d) All of above

980. A loose protoplasmic structure which envelops the apical part of the sperm head is known as
(a) Acrosome (b) Galea capitis
(c) Centrosome (d) All of above

981. For bull spermatozoa, the numerical pattern of fibril is
(a) 9+9+2 (b) 8+8+3
(c) 7+7+8 (c) 9+0+9

982. Compared with prostatic fluid the seminal vesicle secretion is usually
(a) More acidic (b) Less acidic
(c) Neutral (d) None of them

983. Seminal vesicles are absent in
(a) Cat (b) Dog
(c) Bull (d) Both a and b

984. In higher mammals the main sources of fructose are
(a) Prostate (b) Seminal vesicles
(c) Testicals (d) All of the above

985. At which age a nose ring is fixed in bull
(a) 9 months (b) 9 weeks
(c) 9 yrs. (d) 9 days

986. At 12 months of age the bulls will be screened of freedom from

(a) Vibriosis (b) Brucellosis
(c) Trichomoniasis (d) All of the above

987. At which age bull should be trained for semen collection
(a) 9 months (b) 15 months
(c) 18 months (d) 36 months

988. Total sperm ejaculation (million) for bull semen is
(a) Nine thousand and six hundred
(b) Three thousand
(c) Fifteen thousand
(d) Fifteen thousand
(d) Fifty eight thousand

989. Total sperm ejaculation (million) for swine semen is
(a) Nine thousand and six hundred
(b) Three thousand
(c) Fifteen thousand
(d) Fifteen thousand

990. Total sperm ejaculation (million) for horse semen is
(a) Nine thousand and six hundred
(b) Three thousand
(c) Fifteen thousand
(d) Fifteen thousand

991. Total sperm ejaculation (million) for sheep semen is
(a) Nine thousand and six hundred
(b) Three thousand
(c) Fifteen thousand
(d) Fifteen thousand

992. Motile sperm percentage for bull semen is
(a) 70 (b) 75
(c) 60 (d) 90

993. Motile sperm percentage for stallion semen is
(a) 70 (b) 75
(c) 60 (d) 90

994. Motile sperm percentage for sheep (Ram) semen is
(a) 70 (b) 75
(c) 60 (d) 90

995. Motile sperm percentage for swine semen is
(a) 60 (b) 75
(c) 90 (d) 80

996. Morphological normal sperm percentage for swine semen is
(a) 70 (b) 70
(c) 60 (d) 90

997. Morphological normal sperm percentage for bull semen is
(a) 60 (b) 70
(c) 90 (d) 80

998. Morphological normal sperm percentage for horse semen is
(a) 60 (b) 70
(c) 90 (d) 80

999. Morphological normal sperm percentage for Ram semen is
(a) 80 (b) 90
(c) 100 (d) 60

1000. Which is storage time of liquid semen for bulls in days?
(a) 4 days (b) 1 or 2 days
(c) 3 days (c) 5 days

1001. Which is storage time of liquid semen for Ram in days?
(a) 4 days (b) 1 or 2 days
(c) 3 days (c) 5 days

1002. Optimum time to inseminate cow is
(a) Middle or end of estrus
(b) Towards end of estrus
(c) Third days of estrus
(d) First and second day of estrus

1003. Optimum time to inseminate ewe is
(a) Middle or end of estrus
(b) Towards end of estrus
(c) Third days of estrus
(d) First and second day of estrus

1004. Optimum time to inseminate swine is
(a) Middle or end of estrus
(b) Towards end of estrus
(c) Third days of estrus
(d) First and second day of estrus

1005. Optimum time to inseminate cow is
(a) Middle or end of estrus
(b) Towards end of estrus
(c) Third days of estrus
(d) First and second day of estrus

1006. Site of deposition of semen in cow is
(a) Cervix
(b) Uterus
(c) Both of the above
(d) None of them

1007. Site of deposition of semen in mare is
(a) Cervix (b) Uterus
(c) Vagina (d) Vulva

1008. Dose of insemination for bull semen is
(a) 1 ml (b) 50 ml
(c) 20-40 ml (d) 0.2 ml

1009. Dose of insemination for Ram semen is
(a) 1 ml (b) 50 ml
(c) 20-40 ml (d) 0.2 ml

1010. Dose of insemination for swine semen is
(a) 1 ml (b) 50 ml
(c) 20-40 ml (d) 0.2 ml

1011. Dose of insemination for stallion semen is
(a) 1 ml (b) 50 ml
(c) 20-40 ml (d) 0.2 ml

1012. Number of possible female bred/ejaculate for bull is
(a) 800 (b) 17
(c) 40 (d) 7

1013. Conception percentage on 1st insemination in case of swine through Al is
(a) 65% (b) 70 %
(c) 90 % (d) 95 %

1014. At which of the following temperature frozen semen may be stored by using solid CO_2 and alcohol
(a) -79 °C (b) -190 °C
(c) -196 °C (d) -296 °C

1015. Number of possible female bred/ejaculate in case of stallion is
(a) 800 (b) 17
(c) 40 (d) 7

1016. Number of possible females bred/week by one bull's semen through Al is
(a) Thirty two thousand
(b) Six hundred
(c) Eighty
(d) Sixty

1017. Number of possible females bred/week by one Ram's semen through Al is which of the following
(a) Thirty two thousand
(b) Six hundred
(c) Eighty
(d) Sixty

1018. Frequency of semen collection/ week for sheep is
(a) Three to five times
(b) Seven to ten times
(c) Seven to twenty –five days
(d) None of them

1019. ZO_2 value for rabbit semen is
(a) 21 (b) 7
(c) 11 (d) 22

MATCH THE COLUM

A. Match the species with their semen pH

	Animal Species		Semen pH
1.	Buck	A.	Neutral
2.	Ram	B.	Alkaline
3.	Cock	C.	Acidic

Ans. 1 –B, 2-C, 3 – A

B. Match the commercial names of Hormones with their active compound

i.	Epidosin	a.	Busarelin acetate
ii.	Prosowin	b.	Gonadorelin
iii.	Progynon Depot	c.	Dinoprost
iv.	Prolutone Depot	d.	Valethamiate valerate
v.	Receptal	e.	Progesterone
vi.	Folligon	f.	Estradiol valerate
vii.	Chorulon	g.	Oxytocin
viii.	Lutalyse	h.	PMSG
ix.	Syntocinon	i.	HCG
x.	Fertagyl	j.	Luprostiol

Ans. i. d, ii – j, iii – f, iv – e, v – a, vi – h, vii – I, viii – c, ix – g, x -b

C. Match the reproductive problems with their hormonal remedies

i.	Cystic ovaries	a.	Duraprogen
ii.	Estrus synchronization	b.	Cortisol and prostaglandin
iii.	Threatened Abortion	c.	Estrogen
iv.	Repeat breeder	d.	Oxytocin
v.	Super ovulation	e.	Chorionic gonadotropin
vi.	Cervical ripening	f.	Testosterone
vii.	Cryptorchidism	g.	Chorulon
viii.	Pyometra	h.	Lutalyse
ix.	Mismatching in bitch	i.	Follpropis
x.	Milk let down	j.	Crestar

Ans. I – e/g. ii – j, iii – a, iv. – e/g/ a, v – I, vi – b, vii – f, viii – h, ix – c, x- d

D. Match the reproductive organs with their origin:

i.	Epoophoron in adult female	a.	Genital ridge
ii.	Seminal Vesicles in adult male	b.	Genital fold
iii.	Bulbourethral gland	c.	Mesonephric tubule
iv.	Prepuce	d.	Urogenital sinus
v.	Penis	e.	Mesonephric duct

Ans. i. – c, ii – e, iii – d iv. b, v – a

E. Match the species with their estrus duration:

i.	Mare	a.	9 days
ii.	Cow	b.	1-2 days
iii.	Bitch	c.	2-4 days
iv.	Sow	d.	4-7 days

Ans. i. – d, ii – e , iii – a, iv – c, v – b

F. Match the animal species with their gestation period

1.	Tiger	A.	550
2.	Panther	B.	330
3.	Seal	C.	90 93
4.	Rhinoceros	D.	105 113

Ans. 1 –D, 2 – C, 3 – B, 4 – A

G. Match the following

	Animal Species		Average Semen Volume (ml)
1.	Bull	A.	10
2.	Canine	B.	100.00
3.	Stallion	C.	0.60
4.	Cock	D.	5.00

Ans. 1 – D, 2 – A, 3 – B, 4 – C

H. Choose the correct chromosome number for the animal species in first column:

	Animal species		Chromosome no.
1.	Bovine	A.	54
2.	Equine	B.	64
3.	Swine	C.	60
4.	Sheep	D.	38

Ans. 1 – C, 2 – B, 3 – D, 4 – A

FILL IN THE BLANKS

1. The two types of cells of epithelium of the Seminiferous tubules are ——— and ———.
2. The least potent estrogen hormone is ——— .
3. The undetached protoplasmic droplet of spermatozoa contains the reminants of ———.
4. The ——— is a fetal part, the ——— is the maternal part and the combined name is placentome.
5. In cattle the diameter of ova without zona pellucida is ——— and with zona pellucida is ———.
6. By the time the fertilized ovum reaches the uterus, the Endometrium is under the influence of hormone ———.
7. The duration of the ova transport the oviduct in cattle is ——— of which nearly ——— part of time is spent in the isthmus.
8. The spermatozoa in all the domestic species take about ——— minute to pass through the uterus. This movement of spermatozoa in the uterine lumen is due to ——— and ——— hormones.
9. The testicular degeneration along with obesity is called ———.
10. The length of Seminiferous tubules in bulls is ———.
11. The color of testicular Parenchyma in bull is ———.
12. The growth of follicle before cell stage in under ——— control.
13. The second and third stage of labour is interspersed in ———.

14. Ovary of sow is ————.
15. Best result is obtained when embryo transfer is done by non surgical techniques at ———— stage.
16. Specific gravity of the cryoprotectant glycerol is ————.
17. For optimum result the recipients should be in estrus in the ———— hours of donors estrus.
18. Mean calving to conception interval is called ————.
19. For use in semen diluter, the milk must be heated at ———— temperature for ———— time to destroy spermicidal factor present in it.
20. Semen volume is contributed by the secretions from ————.
21. Site of semen deposition in AI of mare with frozen semen is ————.
22. ———— and ———— present in egg yolk protects the sperm cells during semen dilution.
23. In massage method of semen collection, the semen may contain more of ———— secretion.
24. Cellular theory of freemartins refers to the transfer of ———— from male fetus to female fetus in early pregnancy.
25. The yellow colour of Guernsey bull semen is due to the present of ————.
26. The dog defect is grouped as ———— sperm abnormalities.
27. Annular folds are found in the cervix of ————.
28. Female reproductive system develops from ————.
29. Screw shaped cervix is found in ————.
30. Ewe has ———— shaped ovary.
31. ———— is not found in isthmus but is found in Ampulla of oviduct.
32. The yellowish colour in the CL of cow and mare is due to the presence of ————.
33. Wolfian duct gives rise to ———— reproductive system.
34. ————is the functional unit of the testes.
35. Collecting tubules located in mediastinum in testes are called ————.
36. ———— Accessory genital gland is absent in Ram.
37. Highly developed Cowper's gland is found in ————.
38. Ram has ———— type of penis.
39. Stallion has ———— type of penis.
40. Swiss cheese appearance is seen in endometrial glands in ————.
41. Expulsion of fetus occurs in ———— stage of labour.
42. Cuboni test is used for ———— in mare.
43. Various physiological processes involved in the birth of young one are combinally known as ————.
44. Oozing of colostrums from teats before two days of foaling in mare is called ————.
45. Expulsion of foetal membranes takes place in ———— stage.
46. Potato Soup like pus is seen in ————.
47. Abortion due to ————is also know as foot hill abortion.
48. If patechial heart, placentitis and hepatitis is seen in abortion occurring at all the trimesters of pregnancy, ———— infection should be suspected.
49. Wry neck is lonely seen in ————.
50. The range of temperature in bull AV should be ————.

Answer -

1. Normal cells,
2. 2 Estriole,
3. Golgi apparatus,
4. Cotyledon,caruncle
5. 185-188 um, 200 um
6. Progesterone
7. 90 hrs., 2/3rd
8. 15 min., Oxytocin & prostaglandin

9. Dystrophia adipogenitalis
10. 5000 m
11. Yellow
12. Intraovarian
13. Bitch
14. Mulberry shaped
15. Early blastocyst stage
16. 1.25
17. 12
18. Days open
19. 92 95^0 C, 10 min.
20. Seminal vesicles
21. Intrauterine
22. Phosphotidyl choline and Phosphotidyl serine
23. Seminal vesicle
24. Primordial germ cells
25. Riboflavin
26. primary
27. Ewe
28. Mullerian duct
29. Sow
30. Spheroid
31. Secondary folds
32. Lutein
33. Male
34. Seminiferous tubules
35. Rete testes
36. Prostate
37. Boar
38. Fibro – elastic
39. Vasculo muscular
40. Nymphomaniac cows
41. Second
42. Pregnancy diagnosis
43. Parturition
44. Waxing
45. Third
46. Trichomoniasis
47. EBA
48. IBR – IPV
49. Mare
50. 42 – 46^0 C

CHOOSE THE CORRECT STATEMENT

1. In boar the testicles are located in between thighs.
2. For optimum semen production the temperature of the testes should be 101.4^0 F in bull.
3. Both seminal vesicles and Bulbourethral glands are absent in dogs.
4. The sigmoid flexure is prescrotal in boar.
5. Acidophils of Neurohypophysis produce STH.
6. The structural integrity of Adrenal medulla is maintained by A. C. T. H.
7. Estrogen can be used successfully in are estrus cows to induce estrus and ovulation.
8. Estradiol – 17 alfa is more potent than Estradiol 17 B.
9. Met estrum is the building up phase of the estrus cycle.
10. Indian cattle breeds have short estrous periods.
11. In bulls, the storage period of sperm in the epididymis is 60 days.
12. Flehman reaction is particular to bulls only.
13. Implantation in cows occurs at about day 35 following service and before implantation the embryo draws nutrition only by uterine secretions.
14. Umbilical arteries carry oxygenated blood from placenta to the fetus.
15. The testis is both mesodermal and endodermal in origin.
16. Accessory glands are mesodermal in origin.
17. Sustentacular cells are responsible for the production of testosterone hormone.
18. Maturation of spermatozoa takes place in female genital tract.
19. Acquaintance of horse and mare is necessary for mating.
20. Vesicular glands are paired in dog.
21. In bull the relationship of pituitary gonadotropin and testes is cyclic.

22. Thiouracil would cause increase in sperm production.
23. Vocalization of bull during courtship is frequently observed.
24. Stretching of head and neck is a general post coital reaction in bull and ram.
25. Penis develops from the genital ridge.
26. Duration of heat in cows is 4-5 hours.

Answer : **4, 10, 15, 25 are correct**

Answers

1.	(a)	2.	(b)	3.	(a)
4.	(d)	5.	(c)	6.	(c)
7.	(d)	8.	(d)	9.	(c)
10.	(d)	11.	(a)	12.	(b)
13.	(c)	14.	(b)	15.	(d)
16.	(a)	17.	(a)	18.	(a)
19.	(a)	20.	(a)	21.	(c)
22.	(d)	23.	(a)	24.	(a)
25.	(c)	26.	(d)	27.	(a)
28.	(d)	29.	(c)	30.	(c)
31.	(d)	32.	(d)	33.	(d)
34.	(d)	35.	(a)	36.	(b)
37.	(c)	38.	(d)	39.	(d)
40.	(d)	41.	(d)	42.	(c)
43.	(a)	44.	(a)	45.	(b)
46.	(b)	47.	(b)	48.	(c)
49.	(c)	50.	(d)	51.	(a)
52.	(a)	53.	(a)	54.	(b)
55.	(b)	56.	(d)	57.	(b)
58.	(d)	59.	(b)	60.	(d)
61.	(d)	62.	(c)	63.	(c)
64.	(a)	65.	(c)	66.	(b)
67.	(d)	68.	(d)	69.	(c)
70.	(c)	71.	(a)	72.	(c)
73.	(c)	74.	(a)	75.	(c)
76.	(a)	77.	(d)	78.	(d)
79.	(d)	80.	(d)	81.	(d)
82.	(d)	83.	(d)	84.	(a)
85.	(c)	86.	(a)	87.	(d)
88.	(c)	89.	(a)	90.	(a)
91.	(a)	92.	(a)	93.	(d)
94.	(d)	95.	(d)	96.	(a)
97.	(a)	98.	(a)	99.	(c)
100.	(d)	101.	(d)	102.	(a)

103.	(c)	104.	(c)	105.	(d)
106.	(a)	107.	(c)	108.	(a)
109.	(b)	110.	(a)	111.	(a)
112.	(b)	113.	(d)	114.	(d)
115.	(d)	116.	(c)	117.	(a)
118.	(d)	119.	(d)	120.	(d)
121.	(a)	122.	(d)	123.	(b)
124.	(a)	125.	(a)	126.	(b)
127.	(a)	128.	(b)	129.	(c)
130.	(a)	131.	(a)	132.	(a)
133.	(b)	134.	(c)	135.	(b)
136.	(b)	137.	(c)	138.	(a)
139.	(d)	140.	(a)	141.	(d)
142.	(a)	143.	(c)	144.	(a)
145.	(b)	146.	(d)	147.	(a)
148.	(c)	149.	(c)	150.	(a)
151.	(a)	152.	(a)	153.	(a)
154.	(d)	155.	(b)	156.	(c)
157.	(a)	158.	(c)	159.	(a)
160.	(b)	161.	(c)	162.	(a)
163.	(b)	164.	(c)	165.	(a)
166.	(b)	167.	(c)	168.	(d)
169.	(a)	170.	(a)	171.	(b)
172.	(d)	173.	(c)	174.	(a)
175.	(a)	176.	(d)	177.	(c)
178.	(a)	179.	(b)	180.	(a)
181.	(d)	182.	(c)	183.	(a)
184.	(b)	185.	(a)	186.	(b)
187.	(b)	188.	(a)	189.	(b)
190.	(c)	190.	(d)	191.	(a)
192.	(b)	193.	(c)	194.	(d)
195.	(a)	196.	(c)	197.	(a)
198.	(b)	199.	(a)	200.	(b)
201.	(b)	202.	(a)	203.	(c)
204.	(a)	205.	(c)	206.	(b)
207.	(b)	208.	(c)	209.	(d)
210.	(b)	211.	(a)	212.	(a)
213.	(b)	214.	(a)	215.	(b)
216.	(a)	217.	(b)	218.	(c)
219.	(c)	220.	(d)	221.	(c)
222.	(d)	223.	(a)	224.	(a)
225.	(c)	226.	(a)	227.	(b)
228.	(b)	229.	(a)	230.	(a)
231.	(a)	232.	(c)	233.	(b)
234.	(d)	235.	(b)	236.	(b)
237.	(a)	238.	(a)	239.	(c)
240.	(a)	241.	(a)	242.	(b)

243. (c) 244. (a) 245. (a)
246. (a) 247. (a) 248. (a)
249. (d) 250. (b) 251. (b)
252. (a) 253. (d) 254. (d)
255. (b) 256. (b) 257. (a)
258. (a) 259. (a) 260. (a)
261. (a) 262. (a) 263. (b)
264. (b) 265. (b) 266. (c)
267. (c) 268. (a) 269. (b)
270. (a) 271. (b) 272. (a)
273. (c) 274. (a) 275. (c)
276. (a) 277. (c) 278. (c)
279. (a) 280. (a) 281. (b)
282. (d) 283. (c) 284. (d)
285. (a) 286. (d) 287. (c)
288. (a) 289. (d) 290. (b)
291. (c) 292. (a) 293. (d)
294. (d) 295. (d) 296. (c)
297. (a) 298. (a) 299. (b)
300. (a) 301. (c) 302. (d)
303. (a) 304. (a) 305. (a)
306. (c) 307. (a) 308. (c)
309. (b) 310. (a) 311. (b)
312. (a) 313. (b) 314. (d)
315. (c) 316. (b) 317. (c)
318. (d) 319. (a) 320. (c)
321. (b) 322. (c) 323. (b)
324. (b) 325. (d) 326. (d)
327. (a) 328. (b) 329. (b)
330. (b) 331. (a) 132. (b)
333. (b) 334. (a) 335. (b)
336. (a) 337. (d) 338. (a)
339. (b) 340. (a) 341. (a)
342. (b) 143. (c) 344. (a)
345. (d) 346. (a) 347. (d)
348. (c) 349. (a) 350. (b)
351. (d) 352. (a) 353. (b)
354. (d) 355. (d) 356. (d)
357. (d) 358. (a) 359. (b)
360. (c) 361. (b) 362. (a)
363. (b) 364. (c) 365. (d)
366. (c) 367. (d) 368. (b)
369. (a) 370. (b) 371. (c)
372. (c) 373. (c) 374. (d)
375. (d) 376. (b) 377. (c)
378. (c) 379. (c) 380. (b)
381. (b) 382. (d) 383. (c)

384. (c) 385. (c) 386. (c)
387. (b) 388. (d) 389. (b)
390. (d) 391. (b) 392. (c)
393. (a) 394. (a) 395. (a)
396. (c) 397. (d) 398. (d)
399. (c) 400. (a) 401. (c)
402. (c) 403. (a) 404. (a)
405. (c) 406. (a) 407. (b)
408. (c) 409. (a) 410. (a)
411. (c) 412. (b) 413. (c)
414. (c) 415. (c) 416. (c)
417. (c) 418. (b) 419. (a)
420. (a) 421. (c) 422. (b)
423. (b) 424. (c) 425. (a)
426. (a) 427. (b) 428. (b)
429. (a) 430. (a) 431. (b)
432. (c) 433. (b) 434. (c)
435. (c) 436. (a) 437. (b)
438. (c) 439. (a) 440. (b)
441. (a) 442. (d) 443. (c)
444. (d) 445. (b) 446. (c)
447. (b) 448. (a) 449. (b)
450. (b) 451. (b) 452. (c)
453. (b) 454. (c) 455. (d)
456. (c) 457. (a) 458. (d)
459. (b) 460. (d) 461. (c)
462. (b) 463. (c) 464. (b)
465. (a) 466. (a) 467. (b)
468. (a) 469. (b) 470. (a)
471. (b) 472. (a) 473. (a)
474. (b) 475. (c) 476. (a)
477. (c) 478. (b) 479. (a)
480. (c) 481. (b) 482. (c)
483. (b) 484. (d) 485. (b)
486. (c) 487. (b) 488. (a)
489. (b) 490. (c) 491. (b)
492. (a) 493. (b) 494. (a)
496. (b) 497. (c) 498. (c)
499. (d) 500. (d) 501. (d)
502. (a) 503. (b) 504. (c)
505. (c) 506. (c) 507. (d)
508. (a) 509. (d) 510. (c)
511. (c) 512. (b) 513. (c)
514. (a) 515. (b) 516. (b)
517. (c) 518. (b) 519. (b)
520. (c) 521. (a) 522. (b)
523. (c) 524. (b) 525. (b)

526.	(c)	527.	(b)	528.	(b)
529.	(a)	530.	(c)	531.	(b)
532.	(c)	533.	(b)	534.	(a)
535.	(d)	536.	(a)	537.	(b)
538.	(c)	539.	(a)	540.	(a)
541.	(a)	542.	(c)	543.	(a)
544.	(a)	545.	(c)	546.	(a)
547.	(d)	548.	(c)	549.	(b)
550.	(b)	551.	(a)	552.	(d)
553.	(a)	554.	(c)	555.	(c)
556.	(a)	557.	(d)	558.	(b)
559.	(c)	560.	(a)	561.	(c)
562.	(d)	563.	(a)	564.	(c)
565.	(d)	566.	(d)	567.	(c)
568.	(a)	569.	(b)	570.	(b)
571.	(a)	572.	(a)	573.	(a)
574.	(c)	575.	(b)	576.	(d)
577.	(a)	578.	(c)	579.	(a)
580.	(b)	581.	(a)	582.	(a)
583.	(d)	584.	(d)	585.	(b)
586.	(b)	587.	(c)	588.	(d)
589.	(a)	590.	(d)	591.	(c)
592.	(b)	593.	(b)	594.	(a)
595.	(d)	596.	(b)	597.	(a)
598.	(c)	599.	(b)	600.	(a)
601.	(b)	602.	(c)	603.	(b)
604.	(d)	605.	(c)	606.	(a)
607.	(c)	608.	(b)	609.	(c)
610.	(d)	611.	(d)	612.	(c)
613.	(a)	614.	(d)	615.	a)
616.	(a)	617.	(b)	618.	(c)
619.	(a)	620.	(d)	621.	(a)
622.	(a)	623.	(d)	624.	(b)
625.	(c)	626.	(a)	627.	(d)
628.	(a)	629.	(d)	630.	(d)
631.	(d)	632.	(b)	633.	(c)
634.	(a)	635.	(b)	636.	(d)
637.	(a)	638.	(b)	639.	(d)
640.	(c)	641.	(b)	642.	(a)
643.	(b)	644.	(a)	645.	(b)
646.	(a)	647.	(d)	648.	(c)
649.	(b)	650.	(a)	651.	(d)
652.	(a)	653.	(a)	654.	(b)
655.	(b)	656.	(c)	657.	(b)
658.	(b)	659.	(c)	660.	(d)
661.	(a)	662.	(b)	663.	(b)
664.	(a)	665.	(c)	666.	(a)

667.	(b)	668.	(a)	669.	(c)
670.	(a)	671.	(b)	672.	(c)
673.	(a)	674.	(a)	675.	(a)
676.	(a)	677.	(d)	678.	(c)
679.	(a)	680.	(a)	681.	(a)
682.	(d)	684.	(b)	685.	(c)
686.	(c)	687.	(d)	688.	(b)
689.	(a)	690.	(a)	691.	(c)
692.	(a)	693.	(c)	694.	(b)
695.	(a)	696.	(c)	697.	(c)
698.	(a)	699.	(c)	700.	(c)
701.	(c)	702.	(a)	703.	(a)
704.	(c)	705.	(b)	706.	(a)
708.	(c)	709.	(c)	710.	(a)
711.	(c)	712.	(c)	713.	(c)
714.	(c)	715.	(d)	716.	(b)
717.	(c)	718.	(c)	719.	(c)
720.	(c)	721.	(c)	722.	(c)
723.	(c)	724.	(c)	725.	(c)
726.	(c)	727.	(c)	728.	(c)
729.	(c)	730.	(c)	731.	(c)
732.	(c)	733.	(c)	734.	(c)
735.	(c)	736.	(c)	737.	(c)
738.	(c)	739.	(c)	740.	(b)
741.	(c)	742.	(c)	743.	(a)
744.	(c)	745.	(d)	746.	(b)
747.	(c)	748.	(c)	749.	(c)
750.	(c)	751.	(a)	752.	(c)
753.	(c)	754.	(c)	755.	(c)
756.	(a)	757.	(c)	758.	(c)
759.	(c)	760.	(c)	761.	(c)
762.	(c)	763.	(c)	764.	(c)
765.	(c)	766.	(c)	767.	(c)
768.	(c)	769.	(c)	770.	(c)
771.	(c)	772.	(c)	773.	(c)
774.	(c)	775.	(c)	776.	(c)
777.	(c)	778.	(c)	779.	(c)
780.	(c)	781.	(c)	782.	(c)
783.	(c)	784.	(c)	785.	(c)
786.	(c)	787.	(c)	788.	(c)
789.	(c)	790.	(c)	791.	(c)
792.	(c)	793.	(c)	794.	(c)
795.	(c)	796.	(c)	797.	(c)
798.	(c)	799.	(c)	800.	(c)
801.	(d)	802.	(c)	803.	(c)
804.	(c)	805.	(b)	806.	(d)
807.	(d)	808.	(c)	809.	(b)

810.	(d)	811.	(c)	812.	(b)	915.	(c)	916.	(d)	917.	(a)
813.	(b)	814.	(c)	815.	(c)	918.	(a)	919.	(b)	920.	(a)
816.	(d)	817.	(b)	818.	(c)	921.	(b)	922.	(c)	923.	(d)
819.	(a)	820.	(c)	821.	(d)	924.	(b)	925.	(c)	926.	(d)
822.	(a)	823.	(a)	824.	(b)	927.	(a)	928.	(b)	929.	(b)
825.	(d)	826.	(c)	827.	(a)	930.	(c)	931.	(b)	932.	(a)
828.	(d)	829.	(c)	830.	(c)	933.	(c)	934.	(d)	935.	(d)
831.	(b)	832.	(d)	833.	(d)	936.	(b)	937.	(a)	938.	(c)
834.	(c)	835.	(a)	836.	(b)	939.	(c)	940.	(d)	941.	(a)
837.	(a)	838.	(b)	839.	(c)	942.	(c)	943.	(d)	944.	(d)
840.	(b)	841.	(a)	842.	(c)	945.	(c)	946.	(b)	947.	(d)
843.	(b)	844.	(d)	845.	(a)	948.	(a)	949.	(c)	950.	(d)
846.	(b)	847.	(c)	848.	(d)	951.	(c)	952.	(b)	953.	(d)
849.	(a)	850.	(a)	851.	(b)	954.	(a)	955.	(a)	956.	(b)
852.	(c)	853.	(a)	854.	(b)	957.	(d)	958.	(c)	959.	(a)
855.	(b)	856.	(b)	857.	(b)	960.	(a)	961.	(c)	962.	(d)
858.	(c)	859.	(a)	860.	(d)	963.	(c)	964.	(d)	965.	(c)
861.	(d)	862.	(b)	863.	(c)	966.	(b)	967.	(c)	968.	(a)
864.	(a)	865.	(b)	866.	(a)	969.	(b)	970.	(d)	971.	(d)
867.	(d)	868.	(d)	869.	(b)	972.	(b)	973.	(d)	974.	(b)
870.	(c)	871.	(d)	872.	(a)	975.	(a)	976.	(a)	977.	(d)
873.	(d)	874.	(b)	875.	(c)	978.	(b)	979.	(c)	980.	(b)
876.	(d)	877.	(a)	878.	(d)	981.	(a)	982.	(b)	983.	(d)
879.	(d)	880.	(b)	881.	(a)	984.	(b)	985.	(d)	986.	(d)
882.	(c)	883.	(b)	884.	(a)	987.	(c)	988.	(a)	989.	(d)
885.	(c)	886.	(b)	887.	(c)	990.	(c)	991.	(b)	992.	(a)
888.	(d)	889.	(d)	890.	(a)	993.	(a)	994.	(b)	995.	(c)
891.	(a)	892.	(b)	893.	(b)	996.	(a)	997.	(d)	998.	(b)
894.	(a)	895.	(b)	896.	(a)	999.	(b)	1000.	(a)	1001.	(b)
897.	(a)	898.	(b)	899.	(b)	1002.	(a)	1003.	(b)	1004.	(d)
900.	(b)	901.	(c)	902.	(a)	1005.	(c)	1006.	(a)	1007.	(b)
903.	(a)	904.	(b)	905.	(a)	1008.	(a)	1009.	(d)	1010.	(b)
906.	(b)	907.	(a)	908.	(b)	1011.	(c)	1012.	(a)	1013.	(b)
909.	(d)	910.	(a)	911.	(d)	1014.	(a)	1015.	(d)	1016.	(a)
912.	(d)	913.	(a)	914.	(a)	1017.	(b)	1018.	(c)	1019.	(c)

13 Surgery and Radiology

Salient Points

- Acupuncture and acupressure deal with non-chemical therapeutic approach for various disorders.
- X-rays were discovered by Roentgen.
- Repeated exposure to X-rays delays healing process.
- Minimal invasive surgery aims at minimum loss of blood during operation.
- COLIC – means abdominal pain.
- Main etiology of colic includes abrupt decrease in diameter, junction between left ventral colon and pelvic flexure is most common location for impaction.
- Right dorsal colon (RDC) is closely attached to the right ventral clone (RVC) by intercolic fold and to body wall by mesentery with the base of the cecum. While neither the left ventral (LVC) nor the left dorsal colons (LDC) are attached directly to the body wall that is why these portions of colon to be displaced or twisted.
- Celiac artery supplies to stomach, pancreas, liver, spleen, first part of duodenum.
- Cranial artery goes to remaining duodenum, jejunum, ileum, caecum, large colon and transverse colon, initial part of descending colon, pelvic flexure.
- Volvulus of large colon near the junction of colon Cecum impedes the flow of blood to left colon.
- Inguinal hernia is common in foals.
- Epiploic foramen is site of intestinal strangulation/ incarceration (constriction).
- Natural space between dorsal side of spleen and left kidney, bounded by nephrospleenic ligament, which provides a shelf over which large colon can be displaced.
- ABSCESS - circumscribed aggregation of bacterial debris & necrotic tissues finely walled off a dense fibrotic wall.
- Aseptic surgery was introduced by J. Lister.
- Thick yellow pus indicates involvement of Staphylococci.
- *Fusobacterium necrophorum* infection results foul smell of pus and presence of gas.
- Bog Spavin / Serous tarsitis/ Puffy hock is characterized by free soft fluctuating swellings b/w ligaments of femorotarsal joint, without pain.
- Cataracts refers to opacity of lens or its capsule.
- Navicular disease is also known as podotrochlosis/ podotrochlitis and is defined as chronic degenerative condition of naviculor bursa and navicular bone that involves damage to flexor surface of bone and overlying deep digital flexor tendon with osteocyte formation on lateral and proximal borders of bone. Most common cause of chronic forelimb lameness in horses.
- Sweeny, also known as Shoulder atrophy/ slipped shoulder refers to neurogenic atrophy of supraspinatus and infraspinatus muscles.
- Entropion and ectropion are surgical interventions for eye lids' defects.
- Hysterectomy refers to removal of uterus.

- Gastrotomy refers to surgical intervention in stomach.
- Aspiration pneumonia is common complication of cricopharyngeal achalasia.
- Lumbo-sacral stenosis is most common in German shepherds.
- Diskospondylitis is the inflammation of intervertebral disk and adjacent vertebral bodies.

Questions

1. Inclusion any where in abdomen is known as
(a) Ceilotoning (b) Lapaiotony
(c) Both (d) None
2. Inclusion is flank region is known as
(a) Clouting (b) Laparoting
(c) Both (d) None
3. Protrusion of contents of body cavity through a normal or abnormal opening to the beneath the intact skin is known as
(a) Prolapse (b) Hernia
(c) Atrangulation (d) None
4. Contents of Hernia include
(a) Herrnial sac (b) Hernial content
(c) Hernial ring (d) All of the above
5. When the hernia is of acquired opening
(a) Muscular layer is present
(b) Peritoneal layers is present
(c) Peritoneal layer is present but muscular layer is absent
(d) Both are present
6. Term used for scrotal hernia is
(a) Omphalocoele (b) Oscheocoele
(c) Bubonocele (d) Exomphalocoele
7. Term used for inguinal hernia is
(a) Omphalocoele (b) Oscheocoele
(c) Bubenocoele (d) Exomphalocoelc
8. Hernia of omentum is termed as
(a) Oscheocoele (b) Epiplocoele
(c) Both (d) None
9. Vesicocele is the term used for Hernia of
(a) Rectum (b) Ureter
(c) Urinary bladder (d) All
10. When tissue grafts are used to make the hernial ring lips opposable it is known as
(a) Hermiography (b) Hermorrhaphy
(a) Both (d) None
11. Gastroduodenostomy is done in operation named as
(a) Billruth type I (b) Billruth type II
(c) Billruth type III (d) Bellruth type IV
12 Gastro jejunotomy is done in operation named a
(a) Bellruth type I (b) Bellruth II
(c) Bellruth type III (d) Bellruth type IV
13. In case of supporting of Lameness, symptoms are seen during
(a) Mention (b) Rest
(c) Both (d) Never
14. Type of lameness in which symptoms are seen when animal is moving is known as
(a) Supporting (b) Sweeping
(c) Mixed (d) Complementary
15. When the lamb showing caneners is not actually affected, it is known as
(a) Supporting (b) Swinging
(c) Mixed (d) Complementary
16. Angle of scapula with body of animal is
(a) 50-75^0 (b) 85-110^0
(c) 128-132^0 (d) 125-135^0
17. Angle between dorsal walls of hoof to ground in case of formula is
(a) 45-50^0 (b) 50-55^0
(c) 55-60^0 (d) 60-65^0
18. Angle between dorsal walls of hoof to ground in case of hind limb is
(a) 45-50^0 (b) 50-55^0
(c) 55-60^0 (d) 60-65^0
19. In case of Toe in condition of Limit
(a) Padding occurs (b) Winging occurs
(c) Plating occurs (d) Swinging occurs
20. In case of splay footed condition
(a) Padding occurs (b) Winging occurs
(c) Plating occurs (d) Swinging occurs
21. Which of the following is formed deviation?
(a) Bucked knee (b) Knee spring
(c) Goat knee (d) All
22. Over in the knee is, which type of deviation limb
(a) Formed (b) Backward
(c) Lateral (d) Material

23. Which of the following is Medial deviation of limb?
(a) Knock knees (b) Carpus valgus
(c) Narrow knees (d) All

24. Which type of deviation of limb is carpus valgus
(a) Formed (b) Backward
(c) Lateral (d) Medial

25. Which of the following is backward deviation?
(a) Calf knee (b) Sheep knee
(c) Both (d) None

26. Open knee condition occurs because of irregular profile of
(a) Elbow (b) Humerus
(c) Radius (d) Carpals

27. Which of the following is lateral deviation of knee?
(a) Offset knee (b) bench knee
(c) Both (d) None

28. Capmed infront is abnormal confirmation of
(a) Carpals (b) Toe
(c) Knee (d) Elbow

29. Which type of peritonitis is common in ruminants?
(a) Diffuse (b) Local
(c) Generalized (d) None

30. Which type of peritonitis is common in non ruminants?
(a) Diffuse (b) Local
(c) Generalized (d) None

31. When strangulation of abdominal organ occurs during estuation in horse it as known as
(a) Sehrrous coid (b) Guttie
(c) Both (d) None

32. Hyper alimentation refers to
(a) Prolonged ingestion
(b) Operating
(c) Both
(d) Long term parental nutrition

33. Planting is common in
(a) Base narrow toe out
(b) Base made toe out
(c) Base made toe in
(d) Base narrow toe in

1046. Wound in which superficial layer of skin is destroyed by friction is known as
A. Contusion B. Abrasion
C. Erosion D. Both B and C

35. In case of artheritis which phase of stride is reduced
(a) Anterior (b) Posterior
(c) Both (d) None

36. In case of affection of posterior aspect of limb which phase of stride is reduced
(a) Anterior (b) Posterior
(b) Both (d) None

37. Forelimb of horse bears what % of b. wt'
(a) 40% (b) 50%
(c) 60% (d) 10%

38. When foot of a forelimb strikes with elbow of same unit it is
(a) Elbow getting (b) Interference
(c) Knee hitting (d) None

39. When knee of limb is hit by sole of same limb it is
(a) Elbow getting (b) Interference
(c) Knee hitting (d) None

40. Abnormal contact of fore & hind limb of same side is
(a) Scalping (b) Cross ferring
(c) forging (d) Overreaching

41. When hind limb strikes bulb of heal of forelimb of same side
(a) Scalping (b) Cross ferring
(c) Forging (d) Overreaching

42. When hind limb strikes bulb of heal of forelimb of opposites
(a) Scalping (b) Cross ferring
(c) Forging (d) Overreaching

43. When toe of hind limb strikes forelimb at the sole it is known as
(a) Scalping (b) Cross ferring
(c) Forging (d) Overreaching

44. Which limb comes in content of ground 1st in horse?
(a) Forelimb (b) Hind limb
(c) Both

45. When lameness is not observed during walk but seen during trot it is
(a) Grade I (b) Grade II

(c) Grade III (d) Grade IV

46. When lameness is observed during walk but movement of head is not associated with it
(a) Grade I (b) Grade II
(c) Grade III (d) Grade IV

47. Lameness at walk & trot both with Nodding as special character is
(a) Grade I (b) Grade II
(c) Grade III (d) Grade IV

48. When animal is unable to bear weight of affected limb lameness of grade
(a) Grade I (b) Grade II
(c) Grade III (d) Grade IV

49. Which is the method for diagnosis of lameness
(a) No of testing technique (b) Nerve block
(c) Radiography (d) All

50. How many types of striated muscles are?
(a) 1 (b) 2
(c) 3 (d) 4

51. Extent of twitching in type 1 striated muscles is
(a) Low (b) fast
(c) High (d) None

52. Extent of twitching in type type 2astriated muscles is
(a) Low (b) Fast
(c) High (d) None

53. Degree of oxidation process in type I 5 m is
(a) Low (b) fast
(c) High (d) None

54. Which of the following muscles get fatigue easily & are not suitable for race?
(a) Type 1 (b) Type 2
(c) Both (d) none

55. Which type of stated muscles is stable for race?
(a) Type 1 (b) Type 2
(c) Both (d) none

56. Myosin ATDase activity determines which character of muscles
(a) Twitching ability (b) Oxidative ability
(c) Glycogen content (d) None

57. Succinic dehydrogenase
(a) Twitching ability (b) Oxidative ability
(c) Glycogen content (d) None

58. Periodic acid stiff method is for
(a) Twitching ability (b) Oxidative ability
(c) Glycogen content (d) None

59. Which of the following acts as response to inflammation in muscle?
(a) Cloudy swelling
(b) Alkaline degeneration
(c) Fatty degeneration
(d) All

60. Growth of muscle per day is about
(a) 1 mm (b) 5 mm
(c) 10 mm (d) 1 mm

61. Muscle atrophy is defined as
(a) Loss in volume of muscle
(b) Lose in toxicity of muscle
(c) Muscle paralysis
(d) Degeneration of muscle

62. Muscle autophagy is known as Sweeny occurs in
(a) Horse (b) Goat
(c) Bull (d) Calves

63. Sweeny in horse occur in muscle of
(a) Heart (b) flank
(c) Shoulder (d) Hip

64. Which is incorrect in case of muscle atrophy?
(a) Affected side appear flat
(b) Loss in volume of muscle
(c) Intense pain
(d) All

65. Normal texture of muscle is test & they become hard in case of
(a) Fibers
(b) Myopathy
(c) Fibrotic myopathy
(d) Muscler atrophy

66. Muscles involved in case of fibrotic myopathy are
(a) Semi membranous
(b) Semi tendons
(c) Biceps femoris
(d) All

67. When limb jerks towards anterior before touching ground it is
(a) Stringhalt (b) Fibrotic myopathy
(c) Both (d) None

68. When limb jerks towards posterior side before touching ground it is
(a) Stringhalt (b) Fibretic myopathy
(c) Both (d) None

69. Largest endocrine organ in body is
(a) Liver (b) Spleen
(c) Pancreas (d) Intestine

70. Intestinal obstruction is classified as strangulated when
(a) Lymph nodes are involved
(b) Mesentery nodes are involved
(c) Vascular atrophy of mesentery is involved
(d) None

71. Saliva produced/day/cattle is about
(a) 120-130 liter (b) 60 liter
(c) 50 liter (d) 100 liter

72. Choking is always more serious in
(a) Dogs (b) Ruminants
(c) Non ruminants (d) All

73. Choking is more severe in ruminants because of
(a) Excess salivation (b) Cape rumen
(c) Narrow lumen (d) All

74. Liptek test is used for judgment of
(a) pH (b) Urine
(c) Specific gravity (d) All

75. Litpek test helps in diagnosis of
(a) Omasal displacement
(b) Abomasal displacement
(c) Vagus indigestion
(d) All

76. Which species is affected least with mammary affections
(a) Cow (b) Buffalo
(c) Mare (d) Sheep

77. Congenital affection of udder & test
(a) Agenesis of teat (b) Supramammary teat
(c) Both (d) None

78. Supramammary teat become prominent
(a) Before calving (b) After calving
(c) Before puberty (d) After puberty

79. What is best for cleaning a fresh wound?
(a) Any corrosive material
(b) Soap
(c) Shampoo
(d) Savlon

80. Fracture of Os penis is common in
(a) Dog (b) Cat
(c) Horse (d) Bull

81. When animal is unable to protrude its penis from prepuce due to construction of prepucial orifice it is as
(a) Phimosis (b) Paraphimosis
(c) Persistent ferulum (d) Phalocampsis

82. When animal is unable to retract back the penis it is
(a) Phimosis (b) Paraphimosis
(c) Persistent ferulum (d) Phalocampsis

83. When peins déviâtes ventrally
(a) Phimosis (b) Paraphimosis
(c) Persistent fermium (d) Phalocampsis

84. Deviation of penis on either side is known as
(a) Phimosis
(b) Paraphinosis
(c) Perustant firemlum
(d) Phalocampsis

85. Which type of milking should be done when teat mucosa is injured?
(a) Free hand (b) Knuckling
(c) Both (d) None

86. Teat spider is
(a) Acquired (b) Congenital
(c) Both (d) None

87. Membranous obstruction in teat canal is known as
(a) Teat web (b) Fibrosis
(c) Membrosa udder (d) Teat spider

88. Persistent erection of penis without any sexual urge is known as
(a) Phimosis (b) Paraphimosis
(c) Phalocampsis (d) Preapism

89. Which tissue can be used as graft to surgically increase the length of a tendon?
(a) Teusor fasealata
(b) Ligamentum nuchae
(c) Sacro coccygeal ligament
(d) All

90. Jet plasty is a technique used to increase length of
(a) Arteries (b) Veines
(c) Intestines (d) Tendon

91. Knuckling refers to
(a) Contraction of flexors
(b) Contraction of extensors
(c) Contraction of intestine
(d) Contraction of heart

92. Inflammation of carpal joint is known as
(a) Capped knee (b) Omarthritis
(c) Gonitis (d) Coxitis

93. Inflammation of shoulder joint is known as
(a) Capped knee (b) Omarthritis
(c) Gonitis (d) Coxitis

94. Inflammation of hip joint is known as
(a) Capped knee (b) Omarthritis
(c) Gonitis (d) Coxitis

95. Inflammation of stifle joint is known as
(a) Capped knee (b) Omarthritis
(c) Gonitis (d) Coxitis

96. Pedal arthritis refers to inflammation of
(a) Coffin joint (b) Fetlock
(c) Pastern (d) knee

97. Hygroma of knee is
(a) Inflammation of knee
(b) Degeneration of knee
(c) Tumerous growth
(d) None

98. When elbow joint appears at lower level than normal it is
(a) Capped elbow (b) Dropped elbow
(c) Fallen elbow (d) None

99. Activity of extensors is abolished because of paralysis of
(a) Median nerve (b) Radial nerve
(c) Both (d) None

100. Brachial plexus does not involve
(a) C_5 (b) T_1
(c) C_6 (d) T_3

101. Tying up condition is found in
(a) Monday morning sickness
(b) Muscular dystrophy
(c) Myopathy
(d) Spastic paresis

102. In case of Monday morning sickness, azoturea occurs due to
(a) High carbohydrate diet
(b) High protein diet
(c) High fat diet
(d) High mineral diet

103. Myoglobin released after muscle destruction proves toxic for
(a) Liver (b) Kidney
(c) Spleen (d) Lymph nodes

104. Congenital shortening of gastrocnemius muscle & superficial digital flexor & contraction of achilles tendon is known as
(a) Spastic paresis (b) Myopathy
(c) Muscle dystrophy (d) Muscle spasm

105. In case of spastic paresis which type of lameness occurs?
(a) Swinging (b) Complementary
(c) Mixed (d) Supporting

106. Inflammation of Olecrenon bursa leads to clinical condition known as
(a) Capped elbow (b) Capped knee
(c) Capped hock (d) All

107. Olecranon bursa is which type of bursa
(a) Subcutaneous & natural
(b) Subcutaneous & acquired
(c) Subtandenous & acquired
(d) Subtendenous & natural

108. Bicipital bursa is
(a) Semitendenous type
(b) Subtendaneous type
(c) Both
(d) None

109. Site for pleurocentesis is at the level of
(a) 5th intercostals space
(b) 7th intercostals space
(c) 4-6th intercostals space
(d) 8th intercostals space

110. Site for cardiocentesis is
(a) 5th intercostals space
(b) 7th intercostals space
(c) 4-6th intercostals space
(d) 8th intercostals space

111. Site for spleenactomy is

(a) Upper 10-11 intercostals space left para costal incision
(b) Upper 10-11 intercostals space right para costal incision
(c) Lower 10-11 intercostals space left para costal incision
(d) Lower 10-11 intercostals space right para costal incision

112. Quittor can be defined as
(a) Chronic inflammation of achilles tendon
(b) Chronic inflammation of Collateral cartilage
(c) Chronic inflammation of Bicepital bursa
(d) Chronic inflammation of Olecrenon bursa

113. Quitter is more in
(a) Forelimb (b) Hind limb
(c) Both (d) None

114. When there is calcification of collateral cartilage, it is known as
(a) Quitter (b) Sand crack
(c) Side bone (d) None

115. Grooving of quarters proves useful for the treatment of
(a) Quitter (b) Side bone
(c) sand crack (d) All

116. Which of the following acts as landmark for perineal diaphragm?
(a) Sacrotuberous ligament
(b) Sacro sciatic ligament
(c) Both
(d) None

117. Perineal hernia is more common in
(a) Pups (b) Adult dogs
(c) Old dogs (d) All

118. Muscle lying medial to Ischiorectal border
(a) Gluteus medius (b) Coccygeus
(c) Levator (d) Both b & c

119. Rectococcygeus muscle forms which floor of ischeorectal border?
(a) Dorsal (b) Mental
(c) Medial (d) Lateral

120. Internal obturator muscle forms which floor of ischeorectal border?
(a) Dorsal (b) Ventral
(c) Medial (d) Lateral

121. Anoplasty refers to
(a) Preparation of artificial anus
(b) Cutaneous membrane of anus is excise
(c) Both
(d) None

122. Lollipop method is used for operation of
(a) Aural haematoma (b) Anal sacs
(c) Udder (d) Scrotum

123. Affection of anal sac is least in
(a) German shepherd (b) Spittz
(c) Doberman (d) All

124. Affection of anal sac is most common in
(a) German shepherd (b) Spittz
(c) Doberman (d) All

125. Idiopathic colitis is
(a) Colitis X (b) Colitis Y
(c) Colitis Z (d) Colitis I

126. Affection of anal sac is common in
(a) Males
(b) Nude base tailed animals
(c) Dogs whose tail is dissected downward
(d) All

127. Pseudocyesis refers to
(a) Pseudo pregnancy (b) Pseudo abortion
(c) Pseudo cyanosis (d) None

128. Idiopathic colitis is common in
(a) Horse (b) Cat
(c) Both (d) None

129. Dyschezia refers to
(a) Painful ingestion (b) Painful urination
(c) Painful defecation (d) painful insertion of penis

130. CURB occurs due to inflammation of
(a) Collateral ligament
(b) Planter ligament
(c) Sacrosciatic ligament
(d) Sacroiliac ligament

131. In CURB, there is swelling on posterior aspect of
(a) Radio-ulner bone (b) Tebio-tarsal bone
(c) Carpals (d) Humerus

132. Which of the following is True spavin?
(a) Bone spavin (b) Jack spavin
(c) High spavin (d) All spavins

133. Term used for sideway stoppage of heart's action

is
(a) Cardiac arrest (b) Syncope
(c) Cardiac failure (d) AV block

134. Continuance for an abnormal length at time of pain caused by injury is
(a) Primary neuralgia
(b) Secondary neuralgia
(c) Complicated neuralgia
(d) Specific neuralgia

135. Lesions occurring on cow's knee or on elbow of large breeds of dogs from repeated injury by contact with ground are known as
(a) Collositis (b) Honey indurations
(c) Both (d) None

136. Formation of vesicles associated with arrhythmia on the course of a sensory nerve is known as
(a) Cracked Heels (b) Herpes Zoster
(c) Honey indications (d) None

137. Contagious acne is
(a) Contagious non pruritic purulent dermatitis of horse
(b) Contagious non pruritic purulent dermatitis of cow
(c) Contagious non pruritic purulent dermatitis sheep
(d) Contagious non pruritic purulent dermatitis of dog

138. Fibrotic hypertrophic dermatitis with sclerosis of skin & subcutaneous connective tissue is termed as
(a) Elephantiasis
(b) Chronic purulent dermatitis
(c) Contagious acne
(d) Herpes zoster

139. Congenital generalized hypertrophy of epidermis, forming a sort of cover which conceals the hairs & resembles the skin of crocodile is
(a) Elephantiasis (b) Ichthyiosis
(c) Swamp cancer (d) Chronic purulent dermatitis

140. Affection of skin & subcutaneous connective tissue of horse met within mashy districts of Australia is
(a) Swamp dermatitis (b) Swamp fever
(c) Swamp cancer (d) None

141. Mycosis of skin characterized by purulent nodules in ox is known as
(a) Bursattee (b) Lecches
(c) Both (d) None

142. Adenomata usually appear in perennial region
(a) Dog (b) Horse
(c) Swine (d) Cow

143. Which of the following is not a true spavin?
(a) Bone spavin (b) Jack spavin
(c) High spavin (d) Bog spavin

144. Distension of joint capsule occurs in
(a) Bone (b) Jack
(c) High (d) Bog spavin

145. How many swellings are formed in case of bog spavin
(a) 1 (b) 2
(c) 3 (d) 4

146. When there is distension of saphanus vein passing through joint it is
(a) Blood spavin (b) Occult spavin
(c) Both (d) None

147. When animal is spavin positive but no gross lesions are present & joint appears normal it is
(a) Blood spavin (b) Occult spavin
(c) Both (d) None

148. An animal giving spavin test positive is
(a) Certainly positive for spavin
(b) Certainly negative for spavin
(c) May be positive or negative
(d) Never positive

149. Spavin is a disease of
(a) Hock joint (b) Fetlock
(c) Knee (d) Slip

150. Hock joint is formed by
(a) Tibiotarsal joint
(b) Intertarsal joint
(c) Tarsometalical joint
(d) All

151. Spavin is ostitis & periostitis of
(a) Carpals (b) Tarsals
(c) Metacarpals (d) Long bones

152. Spavin leads to
(a) Periostisis (b) Ostitis
(c) Degeneration (d) both a & b

153. Point where achilles tendon attaches is known as
(a) Point of hip (b) Point of hip
(c) point of shoulder (d) point of neither

154. Inflammation of cecum is
(a) Typhilitis (b) Typholotomy
(c) Typhlectoncy (d) All

155. Incision on cecum is
(a) Typhilitis (b) Typholotomy
(c) Typhlectoncy (d) All

156. Removal of cecum is
(a) Typhilitis (b) Typholotomy
(c) Typhlectoncy (d) All

157. Which of the following are flexors of colon?
(a) Sternal flexure (b) Diaphragmatic flexure
(c) Pelvic flexure (d) All

158. Rectal prolapse in which only mucosal & submucosal layer is protruded outside anus is
(a) Type I (b) Type II
(c) Type III (d) Type IV

159. When all 4 layers of rectum are protruded outside anus it is
(a) Type I (b) Type II
(c) Type III (d) Type IV

160. When there is some portion of intussusceptions of colon into rectum during rectal prolapse, it is
(a) Type I (b) Type II
(c) Type III (d) Type IV

161. When a total loop of cranial part of colon is protruded along with rectal prolapse it is
(a) Type I (b) Type II
(c) Type III (d) Type IV

162. Hypospadia refers to
(a) Rudimentary urethral opening
(b) Rudimentary urethral process
(c) Opening of urethra in penile sheath
(d) All

163. Epesiotomy is an incision on
(a) Vulva (b) Vagina
(c) Fallopean tube (d) Vesicular

164. No development of anal opening in foetal life is
(a) Atresia ani (b) Atresia ani rectreti
(b) Both (d) None

165. No development of anal as well as rectal opening during foetal life is
(a) Atresia ani (b) Atresia ani rectreti
(b) Both (d) None

166. When wall of hoof is affected it is known as
(a) Sand crack (b) Side bone
(c) Quittor (d) None

167. Sand crack may occur because of
(a) Changes in climate (b) Moisture
(c) Deficiency of nutrients(d) All

168. When sensitive lamina is exposed, sand crack is
(a) Deep (b) Superficial
(c) True (d) False

169. Pin point firing is done for the treatment of
(a) Ring bone (b) Sand crack
(c) Side bone (d) Quittor

170. When extension process of III phalynx is exposed, hard swelling at anterior aspect of hoof is known as
(a) Buttress foot (b) Pyramidal disease
(c) Both (d) None

171. When bony growth remain restricted to periarticular surface
(a) True ring bone (b) False ring bone
(c) Both (d) None

172. When bony growth involves articular surface it is
(a) True ring bone (b) False ring bone
(c) Both (d) None

173. True ring bone involves
(a) Articular surface
(b) Periarticular surface
(c) Both
(d) None

174. False ring bone involves
(a) Articular surface
(b) Periarticular surface
(c) Both
(d) none

175. When distal end of I & proximal and of III phalanx is involved it is
(a) High ring bone (b) Low ring bone
(c) Both (d) None

176. When distal end of II & proximal end of III phalanx is involved it is
(a) High ring bone (b) Low ring bone

(c) both (d) None

177. High ring bone is
(a) Proximal (b) Distal
(c) True (d) False

178. Low ring bone is
(a) Proximal (b) Distal
(c) True (d) False

179. Navicular bone is which sesamoid bone
(a) Proximal (b) Distal
(c) true (d) False

180. Navicular bone is a sesamoid bone between
(a) I & II phalanx (b) II & III P
(c) III & I P (d) all

181. Pain occurs in which joint during navicular disease
(a) Coffin (b) Fetlock
(c) Pastern (d) All

182. Cheirourgia is the Greek term used for
(a) Surgery (b) Operation
(c) Death (d) Hemorrhage

183. Father of surgery
(a) Floureus (b) William TG
(c) Hippocrates (d) John Hunter

185. Surgery intended to increase life span of patient is
(a) Emergency (b) Extirpative
(c) Reconstructive (d) Prosthetic

186. When part is replaced by artificial surgery it is
(a) Emergency (b) Extirpative
(c) Reconstructive (d) Prosthetic

187. Surgery intended to improve life of patient
(a) Emergency (b) Extirpative
(c) Reconstructive (d) Prosthetic

188. Surgery intended to save life of patient
(a) Emergency (b) Extirpative
(c) Reconstructive (d) Prosthetic

189. Antiseptic principle of surgery can be sometimes overlooked in which type of surgery
(a) Emergency (b) Extirpative
(c) Reconstructive (d) Prosthetic

190. Surgery intended to increase economics value of patient
(a) Elective (b) Explorative
(c) Experimental (d) All

191. Surgery for diagnosis of some disease
(a) Elective (b) Explorative
(c) Experimental (d) All

192. Surgery done for creating an experimental modal is
(a) Elective (b) Explorative
(c) Experimental (d) All

193. General surgical principles were propagated by
(a) Wiliam Steward Halsted
(b) Wiliam TG
(c) Flourcem
(d) Hippocrates

194. Which type of animals require more drug during an aesthesia
(a) Hide bound animals
(b) Younger an
(c) Older an
(d) Fatty animals

195. Direction of incision should be to which direction of muscle fibers
(a) Parallel (b) Median
(c) Opposite (d) Transverse

196. Direction of sutures should be to which line of incision P
(a) Parallel (b) Transverse
(c) Any (d) None

197. Tensile strength of suture should be
(a) Less than tensile strength of tissue
(b) More than tensile strength of tissue
(c) Equal to tensile strength of tissue
(d) Any

198. Transport of fluid from one end of thread to other by virtue of osmosis
(a) Capillary action (b) Suture action
(c) Tissue action (d) Thread diffusion

199. Demerit(s) of capillary actions
(a) Invasion of microorganism
(b) Loss of electrolytes
(c) Both
(d) None

200. Capillary action is more in
(a) Monofilament suture
(b) Multifilament suture
(c) Both

(d) None

201. Maximum Suture holding power is in
(a) Bone (b) Adipose tissue
(c) Muscles (d) Visceral organs

202. Mainimum Suture holding power is in
(a) Bone (b) Adipose tissue
(c) Muscles (d) Visceral organs

203. Distance between two suture in ideal conditions should be about
(a) 1 cm (b) 1/2 cm
(c) 2 cm (d) 10 mm

204. Sutures are never applied in case of
(a) Lacerated wound (b) Aseptic wound
(c) Infections wound (d) All

205. Which of the following is a natural absorbable suture?
(a) Catgut (b) Polyglycolic acid
(c) Nylon (d) Both b & c

206. ____________ non absorbable suture
(a) Catgut (b) Polyglycolic acid
(c) Nylon (d) b & c

207. Collagen fiber is
(a) Absorbable suture (b) Non absorbable
(c) Synthetic (d) Metallic

208. Absorption of PGA starts & completed in how many days respectively
(a) 14 and120 (b) 10 and 30
(c) 20 and 50 (d) 5 and 100

209. Bovine flexor tendon is treated with which one to act as natural absorbable suture
(a) HCHO (b) Chromium
(c) Both (d) None

210. Catgut is prepared from
(a) Cat-gut (b) Sheep
(c) Bovine (d) Both b+c

211. Catgut is prepared from which layer
(a) Mucosal (b) Sub mucosal
(c) Serosal (d) Muscularis

212. Which one is natural non absorbable suture?
(a) Silk (b) Cotton
(c) Both (d) None

213. Which of the following is not a synthetic non absorbable suture?
(a) Polyamide (b) Polyester
(c) Polyethylene (d) Nylon

214. Which catgut dissolves in longer duration?
(a) Chromic catgut (b) Plane catgut
(c) Both (d) none

215. Smallest size of suture is
(a) 14/0 (b) 7
(c) 0 (d) 00

216. Longest introduced as suture natural in
(a) 14/0 (b) 7
(c) 0 (d) 00

217. Which one leads to best knot?
(a) 1939 (b) 1949
(c) 1955 (d) 1959

218. Which was introduced as suture material?
(a) Nylon (b) Silk
(c) Stainless steel (d) Cotton

219. Clinking of thread is maximum in
(a) Nylon (b) Silk
(c) Stainless steel (d) Cotton

220. Theodar koucher used which one as suture for the 1st time
(a) Silk (b) Cotton
(c) Nylon (d) Stainless steel

221. Which one is never used in case of hollow organs?
(a) Silk (b) Cotton
(c) Nylon (d) Stainless steel

222. Which one is best for suturing bone, tendon & ligaments?
(a) Silk (b) Cotton
(c) Nylon (d) Stainless steel

223. Which one is biologically inert?
(a) Silk (b) Cotton
(c) Nylon (d) Stainless steel

224. Capillary action is absent in case of
(a) Silk (b) cotton
(c) Nylon (d) Stainless steel

225. Suture with highest tensile strength is
(a) Silk (b) Cotton
(c) Nylon (d) Stainless steel

226. Suture with can be used in case of infections case
(a) Silk (b) Cotton

(c) Nylon (d) Stainless steel

227. Which suture is best for Herniorrhaphy?
(a) Steel (b) Nylon
(c) Catgut (d) Tantalum

228. Nylon is derived from
(a) Hexamethylenediamine
(b) Adipic acid
(c) Both
(d) None

229. Which of the following is not used for suturing hollow organ?
(a) Steel (b) Nylon
(c) Catgut (d) Tantalum

230. Polybutester is composed of
(a) Poly glycol triphthalate
(b) Poly butyline triphthalate
(c) Both
(d) None

231. Absorption time is more in case of
(a) Chromic catgut (b) Plane catgut
(c) Both (d) None

232. Tissue reaction is severe in case of
(a) Chromic catgut (b) Plane catgut
(c) Both (d) None

233. Loss of tensile strength is rapid in case of
(a) Chromic catgut (b) Plane catgut
(c) Both (d) None

234. Collagen is available as
(a) Monofilament (b) Multifilament
(c) Both (d) None

235. PGA is a polymer of
(a) Glycolic acid (b) Hydroxy acetic acid
(c) Both (d) None

236. Absorption of PGA in urine is
(a) Decreased (b) Increases
(c) Vanished (d) Not affected

237. Polygalactin 910 is a breaded fiber of
(a) Glycolic acid (b) Lactic acid
(c) Both (d) None

238. Which one has greatest flexibility?
(a) PGA (b) Polyglactin 910
(c) Poydioxanon (d) Polyglycolate

239. Blunt edges are present in
(a) Incased wound (b) Lacerated wound
(c) Inflections would (d) All

240. Sharp edges are present in
(a) Incised wound (b) Lacerated wound
(c) Inflections would (d) All

241. Most serious wound among the following
(a) Lacerated wound (b) Infections wound
(c) Punctured wound (d) Septic wound

242. Gun shot wound is a type of
(a) Lacerated wound (b) Infections wound
(c) Punctured wound (d) Septic wound

243. Basement membrane is involved in
(a) Ulcerative wound (b) Erosive wound
(c) Both (d) Contusion

244. Shallow area of necrosis involving on epidermis is
(a) Ulcerative wound (b) Erosive wound
(c) Both (d) Contusion

245. Injury is not seen on skin in case of
(a) Ulcerative wound (b) Erosive wound
(c) Both (d) Contusion

246. Ecchymosed hemorrhages are seen in which type of contusions
(a) 1st degree (b) 2nd degree
(c) 3rd degree (d) All

247. Haematoma formation is seen in which type of contusions
(a) 1st degree (b) 2nd degree
(c) 3rd degree (d) All

248. Gangrene formation is seen in which type of contusions
(a) 1st degree (b) 2nd degree
(c) 3rd degree (d) All

249. Shock might be a sequel of which type of contusions
(a) 1st degree (b) 2nd degree
(c) 3rd degree (d) All

250. Local symptoms of wound include
(a) Hemorrhage (b) Pain
(c) Both (d) Ischemia

251. Remote symptom of wound includes
(a) Ischemia (b) Abscess
(c) Paralysis (d) All

252. General symptom of wound includes
(a) Neuritis (b) Paralysis

(c) Abcess (d) Fever

253. Gapping is more in case of
(a) Transverse wound
(b) Longitudinal include
(c) Both
(d) None

254. Local secondary symptoms of a wound include
(a) Inflammation (b) Repair
(c) Cicatrisation (d) All

255. Hemorrhage immediately after wound is
(a) Primary (b) Secondary
(c) Curative (d) Preventive

256. Hemorrhage after sometime of the formation of clot
(a) Primary (b) Secondary
(c) Curative (d) Preventive

257. Hemorrhages after incision are known as
(a) Primary (b) Secondary
(c) Curative (d) Preventive

258. Hemorrhages before incision are known as
(a) Primary (b) Secondary
(c) Curative (d) Preventive

259. Pus is never present in case of
(a) Ulcerative wound (b) Lacerated wound
(c) Septic wound (d) Maggot wound

260. Which one can be used to check hemorrhage from a wound?
(a) Thermocautery (b) Ice packs
(c) Colloidal iodine (d) All

261. Running down pulse is a characteristic of
(a) Acute hemorrhage
(b) Chromic H
(c) Both
(d) None

262. Prolonged pain after injury is characteristic of
(a) Primary Neuralgia
(b) Secondary Neuralgia
(c) Both
(d) None

263. Pain occurs during cauterization in case of a
(a) Primary Neuralgia
(b) Secondary Neuralgia
(c) Both
(d) None

264. Emphysema is infiltration of gas in
(a) Lungs (b) Subcutaneous tissue
(c) Connective tissue (d) Muscle

265. Gas gangrene in a wound generally forms due to
(a) *Bacillus septicus*
(b) *Corynebacterium spp.*
(c) *Straphylococcus spp.*
(d) All

266. Healing of a wound occurs by
(a) Fibroblastic healing
(b) Epithelial regenerations
(c) Both
(d) None

267. Epithelial regeneration occurs by
(a) Contraction phase (b) Remodeling phase
(c) Both (d) None

268. Which of the following is not a phase of fibroblastic healing?
(a) Exudative phase (b) Collagen phase
(c) Maturation phase (d) Remodeling phase

269. Which of the following is phase of fibroblastic healing?
(a) Exudative phase (b) Collagen phase
(c) Maturation phase (d) Remodeling phase

270. Inflammatory signs during fibroblastic healing are due to
(a) Increased vascularity
(b) Lymphatic drainage
(c) Pressure over nerve fibers
(d) All

271. Connective tissue formation during wound healing occurs during
(a) Exudative phase (b) Contraction phase
(c) Collagen phase (d) All

272. During wound healing collagen in synthesized by fibroblast from
(a) Hydroxyproline (b) Hydroxylysine
(c) Both (d) None

273. Inflammatory phase in wound healing last for
(a) 1- 5 days (b) 2-4 weeks
(c) Months to years (d) Indefinite period

274. Fibroblastic phase in wound healing last for
(a) 1- 5 days (b) 2-4 weeks
(c) Months to years (d) Indefinite period

275. Maturation phase in wound healing last for
(a) 1- 5 days (b) 2-4 wks
(c) Months to years (d) Indefinite period

276. Migration of epithelial cells during wound healing occurs by
(a) Sliding over (b) Rolling over
(c) Both (d) None

277. Inspissated pus in an abscess occurs when
(a) Liquid portion of pus is absorbed
(b) Solid portion is coasted
(c) Tendency to calcify
(d) All

278. Inflammation of hair follicle is
(a) Furuncle (b) Carbuncle
(c) Abscess (d) Fistuta

279. Painful inflammation of sub cutaneous tissue is
(a) Furuncle (b) Carbuncle
(c) Abscess (d) Fistula

280. Injury by dry heat is known as
(a) Burn (b) Scald
(c) Both (d) None

281. Injury by moist heat is known as
(a) Burn (b) Scald
(c) Both (d) None

282. Decreased blood circulation to extreme points is
(a) Burn (b) Scald
(c) Both (d) None

283. Increased blood circulation to extreme points
(a) Ischemia (b) Shock
(c) Both (d) None

284. Inadequate perfusion of superficial tissues
(a) Ischemia (b) Shock
(c) Both (d) None

285. Shock occurring due to production & ingestion of toxins is
(a) Septic (b) Anaphylactic
(c) Traumatic (d) All

286. Shock occurring due to some foreign protein injected in the body is
(a) Septic (b) Anaphylactic
(c) Traumatic (d) All

287. Shock due to hemorrhage, contusion, crushing etc is
(a) Septic (b) Anaphylactic
(c) Traumatic (d) All

288. Which of the following may lead to surgical shock?
(a) Epidural analgesia
(b) Incision
(c) Forceful extraction of foetus
(d) All

289. In shock patient Oligouria occurs due to release of
(a) ADH (b) Angiotensin
(c) Rennin (d) Conticosteroids

290. Which of the following is released during shock?
(a) Ferretin (b) Serrotonin
(c) Angiotensin (d) All

291. Effect of shock on capillary refilling time
(a) It increases
(b) It decreases
(c) It may increase or decreases
(d) No effect

292. Effect of shock on heart rate
(a) It increases
(b) It decreases
(c) It may increase or decreases
(d) No effect

293. Effect of shock on respiration rate
(a) It increases
(b) It decreases
(c) It may increase or decreases
(d) No effect

294. Effect of shock on body temperature
(a) It increases
(b) It decreases
(c) It may increase or decreases
(d) No effect

295. on cential venous pressure
(a) It increases
(b) It decreases
(c) It may increase or decreases
(d) No effect

296. PCV decreases in which type of shock
(a) Traumatic (b) Septic
(c) Hemorrhagic (d) Neurogenic

297. What % of total volume of blood can be taken out safely without producing shock?

(a) 5% (b) 10%
(c) 20% (d) 2%

298. Which of the following are sub cutenious wounds
(a) Abrasions (b) Contusions
(c) Front bite (d) All

299. Shock due to extreme cold is
(a) Frost bite (b) Scald
(c) Contusion (d) None

300. Shock due to moist heat
(a) Front bite (b) Scald
(c) Contusion (d) None

301. Gangrenous dermatitis many occur after
(a) Frost bite (b) Scald
(c) Contusion (d) None

302. Which layer of bone has osteogenic activities?
(a) Outer protective layer
(b) Periosteum
(c) Canibus layer
(d) All

303. Dense cortical, hard part of bone is
(a) Diphysis (b) Epiphysis
(c) Metaphysis (d) All

304. Spongy porous cancellous bone is
(a) Diphysis (b) Epiphysis
(c) Metaphysis (d) All

305. Medullary cavity of bone is lined by
(a) Periosteum (b) Endosteum
(c) Mesostcum (d) All

306. Blood supply through medullary cavity in bone is about
(a) 70% (b) 20%
(c) 10% (d) 50%

307. Percosteal blood supply of bone contributes about
(a) 70% (b) 20%
(c) 10% (d) 50%

308. Metaphysial and epiphysial blood supply in bone contributes about
(a) 70% (b) 70%
(c) 10% (d) 50%

309. The fracture in which discontinuity of bone is not complete
(a) Green stick fracture
(b) Comminuted fracture
(c) Avulsion fracture
(d) Stable fracture

310. When there are at least 3 fracture segment & they unit at a point it is
(a) Green stick fracture
(b) Comminuted fracture
(c) Avulsion fracture
(d) Stable fracture

311. When a part may be detached due to excessive force it is
(a) Green stick fracture
(b) Comminuted fracture
(c) Avulsion fracture
(d) Stable fracture

312. Fracture which has less tendency of dislodgement is
(a) Green stick fracture
(b) Comminuted fracture
(c) Avulsion fracture
(d) Stable fracture

313. When three or more fracture segments unit at a point, it is
(a) Comminuted fracture
(b) Multiple fractures
(c) Both
(d) None

314. When three or more fracture segments do not unit at a point, it is
(a) Comminuted fracture
(b) Multiple fractures
(c) Both
(d) None

315. Spiral fracture generally occurs in
(a) Radius (b) Ulna
(c) Humerus (d) Scapula

316. Spiral fracture can never occur in
(a) Radius (b) Ulna
(c) Humerus (d) Scapula

317. Which of the following may lead to fracture of bone?
(a) Trauma
(b) pathological conditions
(c) Mineral imbalance
(d) All

318. Which layer of bone provides attachment for tendon & ligaments?

(a) Fibrous layer (b) Conibus layer
(c) Periosteum (b) Endosteium

319. In Haversean canal, how many osteocytes are supplied by one blood vessel?
(a) 1 (b) 10
(c) 100 (d) Infinite

320. Bone forming cells are
(a) Osteoblasts (b) Osteocytes
(c) Osteoclasts (d) All

321. Mature bone cells are
(a) Osteoblasts (b) Osteocytes
(c) Osteoclasts (d) All

322. Bone cleaving cells are
(a) Osteoblasts (b) Osteocytes
(c) Osteoclasts (d) All

323. Bone forming cells are provided by
(a) Endosteum (b) Periosteum
(c) Epiphyseal plate (d) All

324. Which of the following is an advantage of haematoma formation?
(a) Reduction in pain
(b) Reduction in inflammation
(c) Reduction in swelling
(d) Reduction in wound gap

325. Which one is the 1st stage of fracture healing?
(a) Haematoma formation
(b) Callus formation
(c) Calcificaiton
(d) Clinical union

326. 2nd stage of fracture healing is
(a) Haematoma formation
(b) Callus formation
(c) Calcification
(d) Clinical union

327. 3rd stage
(a) Haematoma formation
(b) Callus formation
(c) Calcification
(d) Clinical union

328. Cinical union of fracture refers to stage when strength of bony has be regained to the extent of
(a) 50% (b) 60%
(c) 70% (d) 90%

329. More amount of callus is formed during fracture healing when there is
(a) Less immobilization
(b) More immobilization
(c) Absolute immobilization
(d) None

330. More amount of callus is formed during fracture healing when there is
(a) Use of bone plates (b) Use of bone pins
(c) Both (d) None

331. Diagnosis of clinical union of fracture can be made on the basis of
(a) Absence of pain
(b) Absolute rigidity
(c) Presence of bony callus
(d) All

332. Maximum number of osterblasts is present in
(a) Epiphyseal cartilage
(b) Canecellous bone
(c) Cortical bońe
(d) All

333. Minimum number of osterblasts is present in
(a) Epiphyseal cartilage
(b) Canecellous bone
(c) Cortical bone
(d) All

334. In case of delayed union, ability of osteogenesis is
(a) Increased (b) Decreased
(c) Lost (d) No affected

335. In case of non union, ability of ostcogenesis is
(a) Increased (b) Decreased
(c) Lost (d) No affected

336. Which cells are used in cases of seed grafts?
(a) Osteocytes (b) Osteoblasts
(c) Ostcoclasts (d) All

337. Seed graft for bone can be taken from
(a) Ileum (b) Scapula
(c) Floating ribs (d) All

338. In case of autogenous skin grafts
(a) Same individual (b) Same breed
(c) Different species (d) Different species

339. In case of homogenous skin grafts
(a) Same individual (b) Same breed
(c) Different species (d) Different species

340. In case of heterogeneous skin grafts
(a) Same individual (b) Same breed
(c) Different species (d) Different species

341. Pre anesthetics are used for
(a) Increasing secretions
(b) Blocking vagal reflex
(c) Maintain free airflow
(d) All

342. Animal sleeps of reacts to stimuli in case of
(a) Sédation (b) Narcosis
(c) Hypnoses (d) All

343. UV light used for therapeutics is of weave length
(a) 10^{-10} m (b) 10^{-12} m
(c) 10^{-8} m (d) 10^{-15} m

344. Soft X-rays are in the wave length range of
(a) $100A^0$-$1A^0$ (b) $1A^0$-$0.1\ A^0$
(c) $0.1A^0$-$10^{-4}A^0$ (d) $10^1\ A^0$

345. Diagnostic X-rays are in the wave length range of
(a) $100A^0$-$1A^0$ (b) $1A^0$-$0.1\ A^0$
(c) $0.1A^0$-$10^{-4}A^0$ (d) $10^1\ A^0$

346. Therapeutic hard X-rays are in the wave length range of
(a) $100A^0$-$1A^0$ (b) $1A^0$-$0.1\ A^0$
(c) $0.1A^0$-$10^{-4}A^0$ (d) $10^1\ A^0$

347. Energy is transmitted through vacuum in case of
(a) Particulate radiation
(b) Electromagnetic radiation
(c) Both
(d) None

348. X-rays are generated from
(a) Nucleus (b) Orbital electron
(c) Both (d) None

349. Father of Radiology is
(a) W C Roentgen (b) R Eberlin
(c) John Hunter (d) None

350. Father of Veterinary radiology is
(a) W C Roentgen (b) R Eberlin
(c) John Hunter (d) None

351. Which of the following is used as source of electrons for X-rays?
(a) Copper (b) Molybdate
(c) Iron (d) Tungsten

352. Upto what temperature filament must be raised for release of electrons
(a) 2100^0C (b) 1100^0C
(c) 1150^0C (d) 2200^0C

353. Process of generation of electrons by use of heat is known as
(a) Thermo ionic emission
(b) Edison's effect
(c) Both
(d) None

354. Space charge effect of electrons refers to
(a) Accumulation of electrons around electrode
(b) Repulsions of electrons around electrode
(c) Release of electrons around electrode
(d) None

355. Anode is kept positive in X-ray tube by use of
(a) AC (b) DC
(c) Both (d) None

356. Flow of electrons in X-ray tube is
(a) Cathode to anode (b) Anode to cathode
(c) Both ways (d) Any way

357. Place on anode where electrons strike in X-ray tube is
(a) Focus (b) Locus
(c) Target (d) Window

358. Amount of heat generated in X-ray tube is product of
(a) Voltage X current
(b) No of electrons X Voltage
(c) Voltage X KE of electrons
(d) Velocity X KE of electrons

359. To dissipate heat, the anode is kept at
(a) Copper (b) Iron
(c) Tungsten (d) None

360. Place on tube from where X-ray emerge out is
(a) Copper (b) Iron
(c) Tungsten (d) None

361. Focal spot in X ray tube should be
(a) Small (b) Large
(c) Any size (d) only one

362. KVP & MAS values with X ray machine has to be operated is indicated by
(a) Tube rating chart
(b) Cooling chart
(c) Measurement chart

(d) None

363. Safe limit of various exposure & amount of heart generated in X-ray tube is indicated by
(a) Tube rating chart
(b) Cooling chart
(c) Measurement chart
(d) None

364. Angle of tilt of anode in X ray tube is
(a) 10^0 (b) 15^0
(c) 20^0 (d) 25^0

365. Which of the following is smaller?
(a) Effective focal spot
(b) Actual focal spot
(c) Both are same
(d) None

366. Which of the following is imaginary?
(a) Effective focal spot
(b) Actual focal spot
(c) Both are same
(d) None

367. Fibrous layer of eye is formed by
(a) Cornea (b) Schelera
(c) Conjunctiva (d) All

368. Layer of eye in cornea is
(a) Fibrous (b) Vascular
(c) Neuroectodermal (d) Neural

369. Layer of eye in Ubeal tract is
(a) Fibrous (b) Vascular
(c) Neuroectodermal (d) Neural

370. Layer of eye in Retina is
(a) Fibrous (b) Vascular
(c) Neuroectodermal (d) Neural

371. Ubeal tract is formed by
(a) Iris (b) Choroid
(c) Both (d) None

372. Complete absence of eye ball but presence of cyclids is in as
(a) Anopthalmia (b) Crypotpthalmia
(c) Cylopia (d) Expohthalmia

373. Incomplete development of eye ball with or without palpebral fissure is
(a) Anopthalmia (b) Crypotpthalmia
(c) Cylopia (d) Expohthalmia

374. Presence of one eye in the centre of head is
(a) Anopthalmia (b) Crypotpthalmia
(c) Cylopia (d) Expohthalmia

375. Protrusion of eye ball from socket is
(a) Anopthalmia (b) Crypotpthalmia
(c) Cylopia (d) Expohthalmia

376. Retraction of eyeball in orbet is
(a) Anopthalmia (b) Crypotpthalmia
(c) Cylopia (d) Endophalmia

377. Ephephoria is defined as production of
(a) Saliva (b) Semen
(c) Mucus (d) Tears

378. Additional uvea emerging from opening of mebo via gland
(a) Destichiasis (b) Ectopic celia
(c) Trichiasis (d) None

379. Additional uvea arising in gland & emerging through palperbral conjunctions
(a) Destichiasis (b) Ectopic celia
(c) Trichiasis (d) None

380. Outer cilia & adjacent skin hairs pointing in an abnormal direction towards cornea is known as
(a) Destichiasis (b) Ectopic celia
(c) Trichiasis (d) None

381. Blepharospasm is pain in
(a) Eye (b) Ear
(c) Nose (d) Spinal cord

382. Trichiasis can be treated by
(a) Electro epilating
(b) Removal of unwanted hair
(c) Everson of eye lids
(d) All

383. Paralysis of orbicularis muscle occurs due to injury on which nerve
(a) Facial (b) Trigeminal
(c) Obturator (d) Occulomotor

384. Due of paralysis of orbiculais muscle animals is unable to
(a) Blink eyes (b) Open eyes
(c) Close eyes (d) All

385. Ptosis occurs to tension in which nerve
(a) Blink eyes (b) Open eyes
(c) Close eyes (d) All

386. Dropping of upper eyelid is known as
(a) Ptosis (b) Entropion

(c) Ectropion (d) None

387. Inward rolling of eyelid margin is known as
(a) Ptosis (b) Entropion
(c) Ectropion (d) None

388. Outward turning of eyelid margins is known as
(a) Ptosis (b) Entropion
(c) Ectropion (d) None

389. Which one can be treated by a an elliptical incision
(a) Ptosis (b) Entropion
(c) Ectropion (d) None

390. 'V' or 'Y' shaped inclusion is given to treat
(a) Ptosis (b) Entropeon
(c) Ectropoid (d) None

391. Tumor of eyelid particular to cats & bovines is
(a) Squamous cell adenoma
(b) Squamous cell carcinoma
(c) Sebaceous carcinoma
(d) Benign carcinoma

392. Which nerve block is done for the removal of eye ball?
(a) Facial
(b) Cranial
(c) Auriculopalpebral
(d) Retro bulbar

393. Dacrocystitis is inflammation of
(a) Urinary bladder (b) Anal sacs
(c) Lachrymal sac (d) None

394. Abnormal dryness of cornea is known as
(a) Xerotis
(b) Keratitis
(c) Keratoconjunctivitis
(d) All

395. Xerotis is most common in
(a) Dog (b) Cat
(c) Sheep (d) Pig

396. Most powerful optical refraction surface of eye is
(a) Lens (b) Retina
(c) Cornea (d) Sclera

397. Transparent layers in eye is
(a) Lens (b) Retina
(c) Cornea (d) Sclera

398. Congenital abnormalities of cornea include
(a) Micro cornea (b) Dermoids
(c) Corneal opacity (d) All

399. Inflammation fo cornea is
(a) Microcornea (b) Dermoids
(c) Corneal opacity (d) All

400. Transplant of cornea is known as
(a) Superficial keratectomy
(b) Keratoplasty
(c) Keratopathy
(d) Keratotomy

401. Transplant of half thickness of cornea is
(a) Lamellar transplantation
(b) Penetration transplantation
(c) Both
(d) None

402. Transplant of full thickness of cornea is
(a) Lamellar transplantation
(b) Penetration transplantation
(c) Both
(d) None

403. Lipid keratopathy occurs due to
(a) Elevated serum level of lipid
(b) Metabolic lipid imbalances
(c) Injury to cornea
(d) All

404. Hyphema is bleeding in
(a) Anterior chamber of eye
(b) Cornea of eye
(c) Conjunctiva
(d) Retina

405. Glaucoma is defined as
(a) Increased intra ocular pressure
(b) Decreased intra ocular pressure
(c) Both
(d) None

406. Cataract is defined as
(a) Inflammation of lens
(b) Degeneration of lens
(c) Absence of lens
(d) Opacity of lens

407. Removal of anterior lens capsule is
(a) Extracapsular extraction
(b) Intracapsular extraction
(c) Both
(d) None

408. Removal of entire lens is
(a) Extracapusulars extraction
(b) Intracapeular extraction
(c) Both
(d) None

409. General anesthesia is least preferred in
(a) Dog (b) Goat
(c) Horse (d) Ruminants

410. In case of grid iron technique incision on a muscle is made through
(a) Parallel to muscle
(b) Across the muscle
(c) Away from muscle
(d) Any direction

411. No. of electrons generated at cathode is calculated by
(a) $\frac{mAS \times e}{C}$ (b) mas
(c) mas/N (d) mASxC/e

412. 1 mA current ejects about how many electrons
(a) 3X 10^{-9} (b) 4.77 x 10^{-10}
(c) 6.25 x 10^{18} (d) 6.25 x 10^{15}

413. Electric charge on an electron is
(a) 3X 10^{-9} (b) 4.77 x 10^{-10}
(c) 6.25 x 10^{18} (d) 6.25 x 10^{15}

414. Energy of electron is measured by equation
(a) $\frac{12.407}{KVP} A^{0}$ (b) $\frac{12.407}{ev} A^{0}$
(c) Both (d) None

415. Efficiency of X-ray tube is calculated by
(a) ZV x 10^{-9} (b) ZV 10^{-10}
(c) ZV 10^{10} (d) ZV 10^{9}

416. Scattered radiation is
(a) Primary X-rays
(b) Secondary X-rays
(c) Non specific X-rays
(d) Colliding X-rays

417. Large size of primary X-rays beam leads to production of more
(a) Primary X-rays
(b) Secondary X-rays
(c) Non specific X-rays
(d). Colliding X-rays

418. Primary X-ray beam is always
(a) Homogenous (b) Hetrogenous
(c) Antogenous (d) All

419. Quantity of X-rays is determined by
(a) mA (b) KVP
(c) Both (d) None

420. Quality of X rays is determined by
(a) mA (b) KVP
(c) Both (d) None

421. Density of a radiograph is defined by
(a) mA (b) KVP
(c) Both (d) None

422. Detail of a radiograph is defined by
(a) mA (b) KVP
(c) Both (d) None

423. Energy & wavelength of X-rays are
(a) Directly related (b) Inversely related
(c) Not related (d) None

424. Energy & penetrating power of electron are
(a) Directly related (b) Inversely related
(c) Not related (d) None

425. Relation between intensity & Distance (D) is
(a) I=D (b) Ix 1/D2
(c) IxI/D (d) I xD2

426. Inverse square law stages that
(a) I = D (b) I x 1/D2
(c) I x /D (d) I x D2

427. To prevent scatting of X-rays, glass envelop of X-ray tube is covered by
(a) Pb (b) Cu
(c) Fe (d) Tungsten

428. Bending energy of a K shell electron is
(a) 70 kcv (b) 11 kcv
(c) 2.5 kcv (d) 100 kcv

429. Bending energy of a L shell electron is
(a) 70 kcv (b) 11 kcv
(c) 2.5 kcv (d) 100 kcv

430. Bending energy of a M shell electron is
(a) 70 kcv (b) 11 kcv
(c) 2.5 kcv (d) 100 kcv

431. 1 KVP produces
(a) 1 electron (b) 10
(c) 100 (d) Infinite

432. X-ray machine should always be operated at
(a) KVP mAS (b) KVP mAS
(c) KVP mAS (d) KVP mAS

433. Characteristic radiation is produced by
(a) Collision interaction
(b) Radiation interaction
(c) Both
(d) None

434. Radiation formed by radioactive interaction is
(a) Characteristic radiation
(b) Breaking radiation
(c) Bremsstrahlung radiation
(d) b & c

435. Radiation formed by collisional radiation are
(a) Characteristic radiation
(b) Breaking radiation
(c) Bremsstrahlung radiation
(d) b & c

436. Each electron generate how many X-rays
(a) 1 (b) 10
(c) 100 (d) Infinite

437. Intensity of X-ray beam depends on
(a) mAS (b) Ma
(c) S (d) KVP

438. Which of the following anodes is more advantageous?
(a) Stationary (b) Fixed
(c) Rotation (d) None

439. Multiple targets belong to which anode
(a) Stationary (b) Fixed
(c) Rotation (d) None

440. Lengenital effects of ear include
(a) Microtea (b) Macrotea
(c) Anotia (d) All

441. Ear extending from acoustic canal to tympanic membrane is
(a) Internal (b) Middle
(c) External (d) None

442. Zepp's technique is sued for
(a) Cropping of ears
(b) Transplant of cornea
(c) Transplant of retina
(d) Opening of ear canal

443. When Ootitis media occurs through auditory tube it is
(a) Primary (b) Secondary
(c) Both (d) None

444. Myringotomy is incision on
(a) External ear
(b) Ear canal
(c) Tympanic membrane
(d) Nictitanus membrane

445. Main site of detoxification of non inhalant anesthetics is
A. Liver B. Blood
C. Kidney D. All of these

446. Labyrynthetis refers to inflammation of
(a) External ear (b) Middle ear
(c) Internal ear (d) All

447. Cellulose nitrate can be used for preparation of which layer of X-ray film
(a) Base (b) Adhesive layer
(c) Emulsion (d) Protective layer

448. Which layer binds emulsion with base?
(a) Base (b) Adhesive layer
(c) Emulsion (d) Protective layer

449. AgBr is used in preparation of
(a) Base (b) Adhesive layer
(c) Emulsion (d) Protective layer

450. Which layer covers emulsion of X-ray film?
(a) Base (b) Adhesive layer
(c) Emulsion (d) Protective layer

451. % of Ag I & Ag Br added in emulsion of X-ray film
(a) 10:90 (b) 1:10
(c) 50:50 (d) 90:10

452. Ag I is added in emulsion of X-ray film
(a) to volume of emulsion
(b) to stability of emulsion
(c) to sensitivity of emulsion
(d) all

453. Thickness of base of X ray film is about
(a) 0.008" (b) 0.001"
(c) 0.08" (d) 0.01"

454. Thickness of emulsion
(a) 0.008" (b) 0.001"
(c) 0.08" (d) 0.01"

455. Direct exposure of milk occurs in which X-ray

film
(a) Screen type (b) Non screen type
(c) Both (d) None

456. Which type of Dental film is used of X-ray of root of teeth?
(a) Periapceal (b) Interproximal
(c) Occlusal (d) All

457. Which type of Dental film is used of X-ray of cavities in teeth?
(a) Periapceal (b) Interproximal
(c) Occlusal (d) All

458. Which type of Dental film is used of X-ray of larger dental area?
(a) Periapceal (b) Interproximal
(c) Occlusal (d) All

459. Which of the following film is sensitive to light by fluoroscopic screen?
(a) Gnoflurogaphy film
(b) Photofluorography film
(c) Both
(d) None

460. Which film has emulsion on side only?
(a) Photographic film (b) Polaroid film
(c) Both (d) None

461. Which film gives positive image on an organ?
(a) Photographic film (b) Polaroid film
(c) both (d) None

462. Processed film should be stored at temperature of
(a) 40-60^{0}F (b) 50-80^{0}F
(c) 20^{0}F (c) 90-100^{0}F

463. Unexposed film should be stored at temperature of
(a) 40-60^{0}F (b) 50-80^{0}F
(c) 20^{0}F (c) 90-100^{0}F

464. How many layers are present in intensifying screen?
(a) 2 (b) 3
(c) 4 (d) 5

465. Reflecting layer of intensifying screen is made up of
(a) Titanium dioxide (b) Iron di sulphide
(c) ZnO (d) $CaCO_3$

466. Thickness of plastic protective layer of intensifying screen is
(a) 0.11 mm (b) 0.016 mm
(c) 0.017 m (d) 0.0017 mm

467. Thickness of phosphor layer of intensifying screen is
(a) 0.11 mm (b) 0.016mm
(c) 0.017 m (d) 0.0017mm

468. Phosphor layer belongs to
(a) X-ray film (b) Dental film
(c) Intensifying screen (d) All

469. Intensifying screen converts X-rays into
(a) Electrons (b) UV rays
(c) Infra red rays (d) Visible light

470. Reflecting layer of intensifying screen can be made up of
(a) TiO2 (b) MgO
(c) Both (d) None

471. Material used in phosphor layer of intensifying screen
(a) Calcium tungstate (b) Barium lead sulfate
(c) Zinc cadmium sulfite (d) All

472. Most preferred material for intensifying screen
(a) Calcium tungstate
(b) Barium lead sulfate
(c) Zinc cadmium sulfite
(d) All

473. Effect of intensifying screen on exposure factors
(a) Increased
(b) Decreased
(c) Either increased or decreased
(d) Not affected

474. Effect of intensifying screen on radiation dose
(a) Increased
(b) Decreased
(c) Either increased or decreased
(d) Not affected

475. Disadvantage of using intensifying screen is
(a) Increases exposure factors
(b) Increases radiation dose
(c) Loss of detail
(d) All

476. Relationship
(a) Direct (b) Indirect
(c) Inverse square (d) Not affected

477. Sensitivity of screen to given amount of radiation

is
(a) Screen rate
(b) Specificity of screen
(c) Speed of screen
(d) Energy of screen

478. Which screen (speed wise) is preferred in veterinary radiography?
(a) High speed (b) Medium speed
(c) Low speed (d) All

479. Exposure time is less in which type of screen
(a) High speed (b) Medium speed
(c) Low speed (d) All

480. Which of the following act as collimators?
(a) Cone (b) Diaphragm
(c) Both (d) None

481. Collimators are used to
(a) Restrict beam
(b) Absorb secondary radiation
(c) Release of electrons
(d) Dissipation of heat

482. Grid are used to
(a) Restrict beam (b) Absorb secondary radiation
(c) Release of electrons (d) Dissipation of heat

843. Gustov Bucky discovered
(a) X ray film (b) Intensifying screen
(c) Grid (d) Cone

484. X ray absorbing material used in grid is
(a) Cu (b) Fe
(c) Pb (d) All

485. X ray transparent material used in grid is
(a) Cu (b) Fe
(c) Pb (d) All

486. Grid ratio is defined as ratio of
(a) No. of Pb strips & Al strips
(b) Height of Pb strips & Al strips
(c) Highest of Pb strips & distance between them
(d) None

487. Lead strips are placed parallel to each other in
(a) Linear grid (b) Crossed grid
(c) Focused grid (d) All

488. Grid made of two superimposed parallel
(a) Linear grid (b) Crossed grid
(c) Focused grid (d) All

489. Pre anesthetic chemicals are used to
A. Increase the effect of anesthetic drug
B. Decrease the effect of the anesthetic drug
C. Decrease the dose of anesthetic drug.
D. Both A and C

490. Grid in which strips are at angle increasing towards the edge is
(a) Linear grid (b) Crossed grid
(c) Focused grid (d) All

491. Which one is true for grids?
(a) Improve contrast (b) Exposure factors
(c) Radiation dose (d) All

492. Effect of grid on exposure factors
(a) Increased
(b) Decreased
(c) Either increased or decreased
(d) Not affected

493. Petter Bucky diaphragm is a
(a) Moving collimator
(b) Static grid
(c) Moving gird
(d) None

494. When a heterogeneous X rays beam is passed through a filter it's energy is
(a) Moving collimator
(b) Static grid
(c) Moving gird
(d) None

495. Filters are placed between
(a) Patient & X ray tube
(b) Patient & film
(c) Film & screen
(d) patient & screen

496. Filtration of X ray beam practically occurs at how many places
(a) 1 (b) 2
(c) 3 (d) 4

497. Which one is free for use of filters?
(a) Intensity of X ray beam
(b) Exposure factor
(c) Both
(d) None

498. Which filters are used to filter low energy radiation?
(a) Cu (b) Al
(c) Both (d) None

499. Which filters are used for high energy radiation?
(a) Cu (b) Al
(c) Both (d) None

500. Effect of filters on exposure factors is
(a) Increased
(b) Decreased
(c) Either increased or decreased
(d) Not affected

501. Latent image is
(a) Final image after processing of X ray film
(b) In visual image before processing of X ray film
(c) Both
(d) None

502. Hydro quinone in developing solution acts as
(a) Acceleration (b) Reducer
(c) Restrainer (d) Antioxidant

503. NaOH in developing solution acts as
(a) Acceleration (b) Reducer
(c) Restrainer (d) Antioxidant

504. KI in developing solution acts as
(a) Acceleration (b) Reducer
(c) Restrainer (d) Antioxidant

505. Sodium sulfite
(a) Acceleration (b) Reducer
(c) Restrainer (d) Antioxidant

506. NaOH is used as accelerator in which form of developer
(a) Powder (b) Liquid
(c) Both (d) None

507. Na_2CO_3 is used as accelerator in which form of developer
(a) Powder (b) Liquid
(c) Both (d) None

508. Acetic acid solution is used in X ray film processing for
(a) Developing (b) Rinsing
(c) Fixing (d) Preservative

509. Sodium thiosulfate is used in fixer solution as
(a) Cleaning agent (b) Acidifier
(c) Hardener (d) Preservative

510. Any salt of Al can be used in fixer as
(a) Cleaning agent (b) Acidifier
(c) Hardener (d) Preservative

511. Cheilitis is most common in which breed of dog
(a) Doberman (b) GSD
(c) Cocker spanial (d) All

512. Epulis is defined as
(a) Tumor of dental margin gingival
(b) Out growth of periodontal membrane
(c) Both
(d) None

513. The only calcified epithelial tissue in the body is
(a) Enamel (b) Dentine
(c) Cement (d) Both b & c

514. Which one is mesoderm in origin?
(a) Enamel (b) Dentine
(c) Cement (d) Both b & c

515. Dental tartar is a mixture of
(a) Calcium phosphate & CaCO3
(b) Calcium phosphate & $MgCO_3$
(c) Magnesium phosphate & $CalO_3$
(d) Magnesium phosphate & $MgCO_3$

516. Alveolar periostitis is also known as
(a) Periodonitis (b) Perecementitis
(c) Both (d) None

517. Dental carries form due to progressive disintegration of
(a) Dentine (b) Cement
(c) Pulp (d) All

518. Fixing time of X ray film is
(a) ½ of developing time
(b) Twice of developing time
(c) Thrice of developing time
(d) 1/4 of developing time

519. Ideal temperature of developing of X ray film is
(a) 60^0F (b) 65^0F
(c) 68^0F (d) 75^0F

520. Fog on X ray film is due to
(a) Radiation fog (b) Physical fog
(c) Chemical fog (d) All

521. Fog on over aged film is due to
(a) Radiation fog (b) Physical fog
(c) Chemical fog (d) All

522. Minimum temperature for developing of X ray film is
(a) 60^0F (b) 65^0F
(c) 68^0F (d) 75^0F

523. Maximum temperature for developing of X ray film is
(a) 60^0F (b) 65^0F
(c) 68^0F (d) 75^0F

524. If temperature of developing X ray film increases by 2^0F, developing time should
(a) by 1 minute (b) by 2 minute
(c) by 1 min (d) by 2 min

525. Maximum time set for developing X ray film is
(a) 2 minutes (b) 5 minutes
(c) 9 minutes (d) 3 minutes

526. Minimum time set for developing X ray film is
(a) 2 minutes (b) 5 minutes
(c) 9 minutes (d) 3 minutes

527. Which of the following is responsible for early X ray tube failure
(a) Overheating of tube
(b) Damage to filament
(c) Insulation failure
(d) All

528. Life of X ray tube can be prolonged by
(a) Roughening of anode surface
(b) Thinning of filament
(c) Anode breaking
(d) All

529. Last choice for restraining of animal for radiography is
(a) Physical (b) Chemical
(c) Psychic (d) All

530. Most suitable method for restraining of dogs for radiography is
(a) Physical (b) Chemical
(c) Psychic (d) All

531. Radiography is a presentation of
(a) 2D object in 3D (b) 3D object in 2D
(c) 2D object in 2D (d) 3D object in 3D

532. A technique, of using combination of two or more anesthetic agents to anaesthetize, is known as
A Light anesthesia
B Basal anesthesia
C Balanced anesthesia
D None

533. Which view in best for radiography of esophagus?
(a) Dorsoventral (b) Ventrodorsal
(c) Oblique (d) Any

534. Cranial aspect of abdomen should be place towards which side during radiography
(a) Cathode side (b) Anode side
(c) Any side (d) No relation

535. Thicker part of object should be placed towards cathode side this is
(a) Crompton effect
(b) Heel's effect
(c) Radiographic effect
(d) All

536. Which incumbency is best sited for the radiography of abdomen
(a) Dorsovental (b) Ventrodosal
(c) Lateral (d) None

537. In case of ventrodorsal exposure, the central X ray beam should fall on
(a) Umbilicus
(b) 3rd Lumber vertèbrae
(c) Centre of flank
(d) Any where

538. In case of dorsoventral exposure, the central X ray beam should fall on
(a) Umbilicus
(b) 3rd Lumber vertebrae
(c) Centre of flank
(d) Any where

539. In case of Lateral exposure, the central X ray beam should fall on
(a) Umbilicus
(b) 3rd Lumber vertebrae
(c) Centre of flank
(d) Any where

540. When animal is restrained on it's sternum it is
(a) Pron position (b) Frog position
(c) Both a & b (d) Supine position

541. When animal is restrained on it's spine it is
(a) Pron position (b) Frog position
(c) Both a & b (d) Supine position

542. In case of radiography of thoracic cavity the cen-

tral ray falls on
(a) 1st Rib
(b) Last Rib
(c) 3rd inter costal space
(d) 5th inter costal space

543. Air provides which Type of contrast in radiography
(a) Negative (b) Positive
(c) Both (d) None

544. Which of following is used as IV contrast agent in radiography?
(a) Barium sulfate (b) Iodinated contrast
(c) Both (d) None

545. Which one is contra indicated in case of intestinal perforations?
(a) Barium sulfate (b) Iodinated contrast
(c) Both (d) None

546. Myelography is radiograph of
(a) Brain (b) Menenges
(c) Spinal cord (d) All

547. Which type of peritoneal reaction is seen in case of pulmonary osteopathy?
(a) Laminar (b) Smooth
(c) Palisade (d) Sunburst

548. Which type of peritoneal reaction is seen in case of benign tumors
(a) Laminar (b) Smooth
(c) Palisade (d) Sunburst

549. Sympathetic supply to salivary glands is from
(a) Glossopharyngial (b) Facial
(c) Lingual (d) All

550. Which of the following glands is more prone to trauma?
(a) Parotid (b) Buccal
(c) Mandibular (d) Maxillary

551. Ranula is defined as the rupture of
(a) Mandibular duct (b) Sublingual duct
(c) Both (d) Lachrymal duct

552. Empyema is defined as the inflammation of
(a) Eustachian tube
(b) Guttural pouch
(c) Lachrymal system
(d) Mandibular duct

553. Uibrog's triangle is used for the drainage of
(a) Eustachian tube
(b) Guttural pouch
(c) Lachrymal system
(d) Mandibular duct

554. The type pus in guttural pouch becomes hard & dry, it is known as
(a) Empyema (b) Chondiods
(c) Hemorrhoid (d) Alherome

555. Sebaceous cyst formed in posture portion of false nostul in horse is
(a) Empyema (b) Chondiods
(c) Hemorrhoid (d) Alherome

556. Epiphysis is irregular in case of
(a) Young animals (b) Mature animals
(c) Female (d) Male

557. Physis is always translucent in cases of
(a) Young animals (b) Mature animals
(c) Female (d) Male

558. Nutrient foramen is located in
(a) Epiphysis (b) Diphysis
(c) Metaphysis (d) All

559. Bony growth at right angle to the surface of cortex occur in which type of periosteal reaction
(a) Sunburst (b) Palisade
(c) Laminated (d) All

560. Codman's triangle is observed in cases of
(a) Benign tumors (b) Bone lyses
(c) Bone cyst (d) all

561. Which of the following periosteal reaction is aggressive in nature?
(a) Sunburst (b) Codman's triangle
(c) Both (d) None

562. Bone destruction in which general appearance of bone is lost & is non aggressive in nature is
(a) Geographic (b) Moth-eaten
(c) Permiative (d) None

563. Aggressive bony destruction with loss of cortical density & uneven surface is known as
(a) Geographic (b) Moth-eaten
(c) Permiative (d) None

564. Highly aggressive bone destruction involving large area & finally dead ding to pathological fracture is
(a) Geographic (b) Moth-eaten
(c) Permiative (d) None

565. Which one might be a reason for non visualization of fracture
(a) Poor radiographic density
(b) Early cortical stress fracture
(c) Fracture line not tangential to X ray beam
(d) All

566. Normal structures that may simulate fracture are
(a) Open physis
(b) Syndosmosis
(c) Ectopic nutrient foramen
(d) All

567. Primary bone healing is by
(a) Bone formation
(b) Connective tissue
(c) Fibrocartelogenous cartilage
(d) Both b & c

568. Secondary bone healing occurs by
(a) Bone formation
(b) Connective tissue
(c) Fibrocartelogenous cartilage
(d) Both b & c

569. Salter fracture in growing bone is the fracture of
(a) Metaphysis (b) Physis
(c) Epiphysis (d) All

570. There is always delayed healing of esophagus due to
(a) Lack of serosa
(b) Lack of omentum
(c) Poor suture holding capacity
(d) All

571. Odinophagia is defined as pain during
(a) Mastication (b) Defecation
(c) Micturation (d) Swallowing

572. Dyschezia is pain during
(a) Mastication (b) Defecation
(c) Micturation (d) Swallowing

573. Esophageal achalasis is
(a) Congenital default of esophagus
(b) Inflammation of esophagus
(c) Tumor in esophagus
(d) Extramural lesion of esophagus

574. Ramp retina is oval in case of
(a) Horse (b) Cattle
(c) Both (d) None

575. Ramp retina is spherical in case of
(a) Horse (b) Cattle
(c) Both (d) None

576. Colour of eye is determined by
(a) Corne (b) Conjunctiva
(c) Iris (d) Pupil

577. Which of the following is refractory surface of eye?
(a) Corne (b) Conjunctiva
(c) Iris (d) Pupil

578. Amount of light passing to retina is controlled by
(a) Corne (b) Conjunctiva
(c) Iris (d) Pupil

579. Accommodation is ability of
(a) Cornea to change shape
(b) Iris to change shape
(c) Pupil to change shape
(d) Lens to change shape

580. Anterior chamber of eye
(a) Cornea to iris
(b) Cornea to retina
(c) Iris to anterior surface of lens
(d) Iris to posterior surface of lens

581. Posterior chamber of eye is extended from
(a) Cornea to iris
(b) Cornea to retina
(c) Iris to anterior surface of lens
(d) Iris to posterior surface of lens

582. Aqueous humour is filled in which chamber of eye
(a) Anterior (b) Posterior
(c) Both (d) None

583. Vitrous Humour is filled in which chamber of eye
(a) Anterior (b) Posterior
(c) Both (d) None

584. First Image in eye is formed at
(a) Cornea
(b) Auterior surface of lens
(c) Posterior surface of lens
(d) None

585. Which image in eye is bright large & erect?
(a) First (b) Second
(c) Third (d) Fourth

586. Geiger Muller counter is used to trace

A. Radioisotope in body
B. Non radioactive elements in body
C. Both A and B
D. Useless in radioisotope search

587. Which one is first aid for acute inflammation?
A. Ice pack application
B. Anodyne preparation
C. Warm application
D. Rubbing and pressure

588. Which image in eye is dull, hazy & erect?
(a) First (b) Second
(c) Third (d) Fourth

589. Which image is dull, hazy & inverted?
(a) First (b) Second
(c) Third (d) Fourth

590. In which image of eye there is no refractory error?
(a) Enemetropic eye (b) Ammetropic eye
(c) Metropic eye (d) Myopic eye

591. Refractory error is present in case of
(a) Enemetropic eye (b) Ammetropic eye
(c) Metropic eye (d) Myopic eye

592. Which of the following is short sightedness?
(a) Myopia (b) Hypermetropia
(c) Hyperopia (d) Both b & c

593. Which of the following is long sightedness?
(a) Myopia (b) Hypermetropia
(c) Hyperopia (d) Both b & c

594. Angle of refraction increases in case of
(a) Myopia (b) Hypermetropia
(c) Hyperopia (d) Both b & c

595. Angle of refraction decreases in case of
(a) Myopia (b) Hypermetropia
(c) Hyperopia (d) Both b & c

596. Blind area in case of cattle & horse is
(a) 120^0 (b) 3^0
(c) 65^0 (d) 146^0

597. Blind area in case of cat is
(a) 120^0 (b) 3^0
(c) 65^0 (d) 146^0

598. Binocular vision in case of cattle & horse is
(a) 120^0 (b) 3^0
(c) 65^0 (d) 146^0

599. Binocular vision in case of cat is
(a) 120^0 (b) 3^0
(c) 65^0 (d) 146^0

600. Eyes are more frontally placed in
(a) Cat (b) Horse
(c) Cattle (d) Bovines

601. Which side deviation of vertebral column is known as Scholiosis?
(a) Lateral (b) Medial
(c) Dorsal (d) Ventral

602. Which side deviation of vertebral column is known as Kyphosis?
(a) Lateral (b) Medial
(c) Dorsal (d) Ventral

603. Which side deviation of vertebral column is known as Lordosis?
(a) Lateral (b) Medial
(c) Dorsal (d) Ventral

604. Barbiturates are derivatives of
A. Picric acid B. Benzoic acid
C. Barbituric acid D. Phenol

605. Torticollis is most common in
(a) Cow (b) Pig
(c) Dog (d) Poultry

606. Which of the following type of sutures cause least reduction in the lumen of intestine?
(a) Inversion (b) Everson
(c) Hoft croft plug (d) None

607. For a perfect intestinal anastamosis which layer should be essential in opposition?
(a) Serosae (b) Muscularis
(c) Submucosal (d) All

608. Most dangerous type of hernia among the following is
(a) Gastrocaele
(b) Omphalocaele
(c) Strangulated hernia
(d) None

609. Size of catgut used for cuterstomy in canines
(a) 5 (b) 2
(c) 00 (d) 00000

610. Inguinal hernia is also known as
(a) Omphalocoele (b) Bubanocoele
(c) Oscheocoele (d) All

611. Umbilical hernia is also known as

(a) Omphalocoele (b) Bubanocoele
(c) Oscheocoele (d) All

612. Scrotal hernia is also known as
(a) Omphalocoele (b) Bubanocoele
(c) Oscheocoele (d) All

613. Most common site for gastrotomy in dog is
(a) Left paracostal (b) Right paracostal
(c) Left flank (d) Right flank

614. Which of the following is used in ultra sound transducer?
(a) Lead ferroziroconate
(b) Cupper ferroziroconate
(c) Lead ferrotitianate
(d) Lead zirconate titanate

615. Which of the following are non ionizing radiations?
(a) X rays (b) ã rays
(c) Ultra sound (d) â rays

616. Which of the following tumor is most radiosensitive?
(a) Osteo sarcoma
(b) Cupper firrozuoconate
(c) Vaginal tumors
(d) Lympho sarcoma

617. Unit of radiation dose in Ram, it is calculated by multiplying relative biological effective uses of particular radiation to dose of radiation in
(a) Roentgen (b) Rad
(c) Ram (d) Curie

618. Computerized toniographic value for H_2O is
(a) -20 (b) -100
(c) +100 (d) -20

619. ECG reads which information of heart
(a) Force of contraction
(b) Pace maker activity
(c) Electrical activity
(d) Cardiac output

620. Electrical potential between left rear leg & right foreleg is measured by
(a) Lead I (b) Lead II
(c) Lead III (d) Lead IV

621. Which wave indicates depolarization of ventricles?
(a) ST segment (b) T wave
(c) P wave (d) QRS complex

622. Wandering base line in ECG occurs due to
(a) Fluctuation In electricity
(b) Movement of the patient
(c) Poor electrode contact
(d) All

623. Clinical signs of fluid deficit appear after body weight loss exceeds about
(a) 10% (b) 4%
(c) 5% (d) 0.6%

624. Mild clinical signs of fluid defect indicate a fluid deficit of
(a) 4% (b) 6%
(c) 8% (d) 10%

625. Which of the following contains higher concentration of sodium?
(a) Extra cellular fluid
(b) Intra cellular fluid
(c) Both
(d) None

626. Which of the following contains higher concentration of Potassium
(a) Extra cellular fluid
(b) Intra cellular fluid
(c) Both
(d) None

627. Osmotic pressure of blood plasma is because of
(a) Globulin (b) Albumine
(c) Fibrenogen (d) Thrombin

628. Cardiac activity is least affected because of
(a) Calcium ions (b) Oxygen
(c) Adrenaline (d) Hemoglobin

629. Cardiac activity is most affected because of
(a) Calcium ions (b) Oxygen
(c) Adrenaline (d) Hemoglobin

630. Blood for transfusion later should be stored at
(a) 10^0C (b) 1^0C
(c) -10^0C (d) 4^0C

631. Maximum safe amount of blood collection from a horse is about
(a) 2 liter (b) 4 liter
(c) 6 liter (d) 8 liter

632. Loso of Nitrogen from body occurs via
(a) Lungs (b) Skin

(c) Faeces (d) All

633. Biomaterial used in cardio vascular surgery has least affinity with
(a) Albumine (b) Globulin
(c) Fibrinogen (d) All

634. Desmitis is defined as the inflammation of
(a) Bone (b) Muscle
(c) Ligament (d) None

635. Cold application proves useful in which case of inflammation
(a) Acute (b) Sub acute
(c) Chronic (d) All

636. Angioma is the tumor of
(a) Blood vessels (b) Lymphatics
(c) Both (d) None

637. Abnormal large amount of granulation tissue is known as
(a) Proud flesh (b) Callus
(c) Sarcoma (d) None

638. Optimum environmental temperature for wound healing is
(a) 20⁰C (b) 25⁰C
(c) 30⁰C (d) 35⁰C

639. Capacity of drugs to penetrate CNS increases at
(a) Normal body temp
(b) Hypothermia
(c) Hyperthermia
(d) All

640. For operation in case of TRP, which block is conducted
(a) T_{13}, L_1, L_2 (b) T_{12}, L_3, L_4
(c) T_{12}, L_1, L_2 (d) T_{13}, L_3, L_4

641. In case of TRP incision is given
(a) Parallel to last rib
(b) Between Last 2 ribs
(c) In 5th Inter costal space
(d) In 3rd Inter costal space

642. Weengirth rumenotomy set is used in cases of
(a) TRP
(b) Diaphragmatic hernia
(c) LDA
(d) All

643. Which type of sutures is suitable in cases of rumenotomy
(a) Lambert (b) Lock stitch
(c) Vertical mattress (d) Horizontal mattess

644. Which type of sutures is suitable for abomasoplexy
(a) Lambert (b) Lock stitch
(c) Vertical mattress (d) Horizontal mattress

645. General anesthesia is seldom given in cases of
(a) Horse (b) Pig
(c) Ruminants (d) None

646. In case of atresia, which type of inclusion is given?
(a) Criss cross (b) Semi lunar
(c) Elliptical (d) Y shape

647. In case of diaphragmatic hernia, which type of inclusion is given?
(a) Criss cross (b) Semi lunar
(c) Elliptical (d) Y shape

648. Triangle shaped inclusion is given in case of
(a) Atresia ani
(b) Diaphragmatic hernia
(c) Phemosis
(d) Preputeal prolapse

649. Circum scribe inclusion is given in case of
(a) Atresia ani
(b) Diaphiagmatic hernia
(c) Phemosis
(d) Preputeal prolapse

650. Lock stitch sutures are required in
(a) Atresia ani
(b) Diaphragmatic hernia
(c) Phemosis
(d) Preputeal prolapse

651. Which approach is useful for Cystorrhaphy
(a) Pre publc paramedian
(b) Post pubic paramedian
(c) Mid line Incision
(d) All

652. Which approach is useful for Urethrotomy
(a) Ischial approach (b) Right paramedian
(c) Left paramedian (d) Median

653. Epidural anesthesia is used is cases of
(a) 5th rib dissection (b) Urethrotomy
(c) Gastrotomy (d) Spleenectomy

654. Which nerve block is done in treatment of horn cancer?
(a) Auriculopalpebral

(b) Trigeminal
(c) Retrobulbar
(d) Cornual

655. Cricothyroid ligament is severed in which operation
(a) Horn cancer
(b) Operation for esophageal obstruction
(c) Tracheotomy
(d) Laryngeal hemiplagia

656. Roaring is a synonym for
(a) Horn cancer
(b) Operation for esophageal obstruction
(c) Tracheotomy
(d) Laryngeal hemiplagia

657. Poll evil is also known as
(a) Fistulous abscess (b) Fistulous neither
(c) Fistulous mane (d) Fistulous thorax

658. Which anesthetic technique is used in operation for wind sucking?
(a) Local infiltration liner
(b) Inverted L block
(c) Inverted T block
(d) General anesthesia

659. Inclusion from one jugular furrow to another is conducted in case of
(a) Collapsed trachea
(b) Pharyngeal paralysis
(c) Esophageal obstruction
(d) Wind sucking

660. Schamedeal suture technique is used in case of
(a) Intestinal obstruction
(b) End to end intestinal anastomosis
(c) Gastric obstruction
(d) Urinary bladder

661. Inflammation of hard palate is
(a) Lampas (b) Ganthitis
(c) Gingivitis (d) Ranula

662. Inflammation of Interdental space
(a) Lampas (b) Ganthitis
(c) Gingivitis (d) Ranula

663. Retention cyst under tongue is called
(a) Lampas (b) Ganthitis
(c) Gingivitis (d) Ranula

664. Frontal sinus is divided by a thin bony septum in
(a) Ox (b) Horse
(c) Both (d) None

665. When upper jaw is longer than lower jaw it is known as
(a) Lumpy jaw (b) Extended jaw
(c) Parrot jaw (d) All

666. Term used when upper jaw is longer than lower jaws is
(a) Brachynethism (b) Tachynathism
(c) Prognethism (d) Bradynethism

667. When 2 layers of eyelashes are present condition is called
(a) Entropian (b) Trichiasis
(c) Entropian (d) Districhiasis

668. Cystic swelling beneath the tongue is known as
(a) Raphe (b) Ranula
(c) Canula (d) None

669. Vascular thickening of conjunctiva towards median canthus
(a) Cyclops equi (b) Ptery divum
(c) Dermoid (d) None

670. Skin & hair growth at dermosclerojunction is
(a) Cyclops equi (b) Ptery divum
(c) Demoid (d) None

671. Wound over cornea with no tendency to heal is
(a) Corneal ulcer (b) Corneal opacity
(c) Cataract (d) Glaucoma

672. Apron type Keratoplasty is used in treatment of
(a) Corneal ulcer (b) Corneal opacity
(c) Cataract (d) Glaucoma

673. Glaucoma can be treated by
(a) Cyclodialysis technique
(b) Iridendeisis technique
(c) Both
(d) None

674. Enucleation of eye ball is known as
(a) Exterpation (b) Extraction
(c) Evesceration (d) All

675. Posterior X-phoid laparotomy is conducted for
(a) Intestinal obstruction
(b) Diaphragmatic hernia
(c) Inguinal hernia
(d) All

676. Purse string sutures are applied in case of

(a) Intestinal anastomosis
(b) Rectal prolapse
(c) Anal fistula
(d) Anal sacuilectomy

677. For suturing hernial ring which sutures are made
(a) Matters horizontal
(b) Vertical mattres
(c) Overlapping sutures
(d) Quill sutures

678. After replacement of prolapse vagina & uterus which types of sutures are applied
(a) Mattres horizontal
(b) Vertical mattres
(c) Overlapping sutures
(d) Quill sutures

679. Utrecht method is used for
(a) Left omasoplexy (b) Right omasoplexy
(c) Abomasoplexy (d) TRP

680. Shift to left test is used for
(a) Left omasopexy (b) Rght omasopexy
(c) Abomasoplexy (d) TRP

681. Jugular vein is raised in cases of
(a) LDA (b) RDA
(c) Gastritis (d) Vagas indigestion

682. Liptek test is used in case of
(a) LDA (b) RDA
(c) Gastritis (d) Vagas indigestion

683. Which of the following is internal hernia?
(a) Ventral (b) Inguinal
(c) Umbilical (d) Diaphragmatic

684. During a kick on abdomen which hernia is most probable?
(a) Ventral (b) Inguinal
(c) Umbilical (d) Diaphragmatic

685. Soft non nucleated masses arising from nasal granuloma are known as
(a) Polyps (b) Granuloma
(c) Neoplasm (d) Nodule

686. Site of incision for pneumonectomy
(a) 5th rib (b) 8th rib
(c) 7th rib (d) 5-7th intercostals space

687. Site of incision for thoracocentesis
(a) 5th rib
(b) 8th rib
(c) 7th rib
(d) 5-7th intercostals space

688. Site of incision for drainage of pericardial sac
(a) 5th rib
(b) 8th rib
(c) 7th rib
(d) 5-7th intercostals space

689. Site of incision for lobectomy of Left side lobe of lung
(a) 5th rib
(b) 8th rib
(c) 7th rib
(d) 5-7th intercostals space

690. Site of incision for diaphragmatic hernia
(a) 5th rib
(b) 8th rib
(c) 7th rib
(d) 5-7th intercostals space

691. Site of incision for of transthoracic esophagotomy
(a) 5th rib
(b) 8th rib
(c) 7th rib
(d) 5-7th intercostals space

692. Ectopia cardis is defined as
(a) Placement of heart outside of thoracic cavity
(b) Blood from heart
(c) Lateral deviation of heat
(d) Medial deviation of heart

693. Post scrotal sigmoid flexure is found in
(a) Ox (b) Horse
(c) Pig (d) Camel

694. Sigmoid flexure parallel to scrotum is found in
(a) Ox (b) Horse
(c) Pig (d) Camel

695. Sigmoid flexure is absent in
(a) Ox (b) Horse
(c) Pig (d) Camel

696. Most common site of urethral obstruction in camel is
(a) Sigmoid flexure
(b) Terminal part of urethra
(c) Urethral process

(d) Os penis

697. Most common site of urethral obstruction in Ram is
(a) Sigmoid flexure
(b) Terminal part of urethra
(c) Urethral process
(d) Os penis

698. Most common site of urethral obstruction in dog is
(a) Sigmoid flexure
(b) Terminal part of urethra
(c) Urethral process
(d) Os penis

699. Water belly condition appears in
(a) Obstructive urolithiasis
(b) TRP
(c) Rupture of urethra
(d) Pervious urachus

700. Brisket edema is seen in
(a) Obstructive urolithiasis
(b) TRP
(c) Rupture of urethra
(d) Pervious urachus

701. Extensive subcutaneous infiltration of urine occurs in
(a) Obstructive urolithiasis
(b) TRP
(c) Rupture of urethra
(d) Pervious urachus

702. Multiple stab incision is given in case of
(a) Obstructive urolithiasis
(b) TRP
(c) Rupture of urethra
(d) Pervious urachus

703. Paracentesis abdominis is conducted for confirmation of
(a) Obstructive urolithiasis
(b) TRP
(c) Rupture of urethra
(d) Pervious urachus

704. Which condition occurs in camel due to urethritis
(a) Obstructive urolithiasis
(b) TRP
(c) Rupture of urethra
(d) Pervious urachus

705. Urine dribbles from urethra & area remains wet in
(a) Obstructive urolithiasis
(b) TRP
(c) Rupture of urethra
(d) Pervious urachus

706. 90% phenol is used for treatment of
(a) Obstructive urolithiasis
(b) TRP
(c) Rupture of urethra
(d) Pervious urachus

707. Which of the following is a congenital abnormality?
(a) Obstructive urolithiasis
(b) TRP
(c) Rupture of urethra
(d) Pervious urachus

708. Drawer's syndrome refers to abnormal movement of which joint during locomotion
(a) Hip (b) Knee
(c) Shoulder (d) Stifle

709. Drawer syndrome occur due to rupture of
(a) Sacrosceative ligament
(b) Achillus tendon
(c) Cruciate legament
(d) None

710. Cruciate ligament binds which two bones
(a) Radius - ulna (b) Tibia - femur
(c) Femur - patella (d) Tibia - metatarsal

711. Leg parther's ds refers to
(a) Hip dislocation (b) Shoulder dysplasea
(c) Hip dysplasea (d) None

712. Avascular necrosis of femoral head occurs in case of
(a) Hip dislocation (b) Shoulder dysplasea
(c) Hip dysplasea (d) None

713. Splint bone refers to
(a) I & II rudimentary metatarsal / carpal
(b) II & III rudimentary metatarsal / carpal
(c) II & IV rudimentary metatarsal / carpal
(d) I & III rudimentary metatarsal / carpal

714. Radial nerve paralysis leads to
(a) Dropped elbow (b) Dropped knee

(c) Shoulder (d) Dropped sole

715. Animal can not lift limb in radial nerve paralysis due to paralysis of
(a) Extensor (b) Flexors
(c) Both (d) None

716. Laminitis leads to
(a) Extensors (b) Flexors
(c) Both (d) None

717. Which statement is incorrect for Jet plasty
(a) Increase length of ligament
(b) Increase trength of ligament
(c) Tendon transplants are used
(d) Bunnel Mayer technique is used

718. Horse kicks
(a) Laterally (b) Caudally
(c) Laterocaudally (d) All

719. Cattle kick
(a) Laterally (b) Caudally
(c) Laterocaudally (d) All

720. Horse can not kick, if it is hold at
(a) Metatarsal (b) Hoof
(c) Achilles tendon (d) Entire hind limb

721. Bacteria leading to interdigital hygroma are
(a) Anaerobic (b) Aerobic
(c) Thermophillic (d) All

722. Burley method is best for restraining
(a) Bulls (b) Lactating cows
(c) Dry cones (d) All

723. Burley method should not be used in casting of
(a) Bulls (b) Lactating cows
(c) Dry cones (d) All

724. Most common direction of hip dislocation in cattle
(a) Craniodosral
(b) Craniodorsal ventral
(c) Caudodorsal
(d) Caudoventral

725. Gallamine is classified under
A. Depolarizing agent
B. Non depolarizing agent
C. Dual blocking agent
D. None of the above

726. Popped knee refers to
(a) Arthritis (b) Carpitis
(c) Pedal ostitis (d) None

727. Operation done for production of Teaser include
(a) Vasectomy (b) Epideydectomy
(c) Phimosis (d) Castration

728. Condition which glans penis is fused with penile section of prepuce
(a) Persistent frenulum
(b) Monorchid
(c) Ectopictestis
(d) Priapsim

729. Condition in which one testis is descended in scrotum
(a) Persistent frenulum
(b) Monorchid
(c) Ectopictestis
(d) Priapsim

730. Condition in which testis is found other than scrotal sac is
(a) Persistent frenulum
(b) Monorchid
(c) Ectopictestis
(d) Priapsim

731. Episiotomy refers to inclusion on
(a) Vulva (b) Vagena
(c) Cervix (d) Fallopian tube

732. Incision on uterus is
(a) Hystereotomy (b) Hysterectomy
(c) Episiotomy (d) None

733. Removal of uterus is
(a) Hysterotomy (b) Hysterectomy
(c) Episiotomy (d) None

734. Removal of testes is
(a) Orchiotomy (b) Orchidectomy
(c) Orchiectomy (d) Both b & c

735. Bunnal sutures are applied for healing of
(a) Bone (b) Tendon
(c) Muscle (d) Ligament

736. When ligament of joint are ruptured, it is known as
(a) Sprain (b) Strain
(c) Bursitis (d) Tenosynovitis

737. Injury of Tendon
(a) Sprain (b) Strain
(c) Bursitis (d) Tenosynovitis

738. Inflammation of synovial sheath with enclosed tendon is known as
(a) Sprain (b) Strain
(c) Bursitis (d) Tenosynovitis

739. Upward fixation of patella is common in
(a) Bullock (b) Horse
(c) Camel (d) Pig

740. Upward fixation of patella is known as stringhalt in
(a) Bullock (b) Horse
(c) Camel (d) Pig

741. Medial patellar ligament is absent in
(a) Bullock (b) Horse
(c) Camel (d) Pig

742. Synovial hernia is defined as
(a) Protrusion of joint capsule
(b) Out pouching of synovial membrane
(c) Out pouching of articular point from synovial membrane
(d) Exudation from synovial membrane

743. Keratitis is the inflammation of
(a) Hair (b) Nair
(c) Cornea (d) Schlera

744. When fracture site does not communicate with environment it is known as
(a) Simple fracture
(b) Complete fracture
(c) Incomplete fracture
(d) Compound fracture

745. When skin is also broken along with fracture of bone, it is known as
(a) Simple fracture
(b) Complete fracture
(c) Incomplete fracture
(d) Compound fracture

746. When bone has not completely last it's continuity, the fracture is known as a
(a) Simple fracture
(b) Complete fracture
(c) Incomplete fracture
(d) Compound fracture

747. When there is complete loss of continuity of bone it is
(a) Simple fracture
(b) Complete fracture
(c) Incomplete fracture
(d) Compound fracture

748. When only simple crack is present on bone the fracture is known as
(a) Fissure fracture (b) Dépression fracture
(c) Avulsion fracture (d) Green stick fracture

749. When small portion of bone is depressed than fracture it is in as
(a) Fissure fracture (b) Depression fracture
(c) Avulsion fracture (d) Green stick fracture

750. When cortical end of fracture bone is forced into cancellous bone than fracture is known as
(a) Impacted fracture
(b) Communicated fracture
(c) Multiple fracture
(d) Compression fractures

751. When two or more fracture lines interconnect each other at one point it is
(a) Impacted fracture
(b) Communicated fracture
(c) Multiple fracture
(d) Compression fractures

752. When cancellous bone collapses & compresses upon itself the fracture is known as
(a) Impacted fracture
(b) Communicated fracture
(c) Multiple fracture
(d) Compression fractures

753. External immobilization of bone can be done by the use of
(a) Splint (b) Cast
(c) Thomas splint (d) All

754. Internal immobilization of bone is done by
(a) Intramedullary pin
(b) Intramedullry plates
(c) Screw
(d) All

755. If eye is excessively large without any fluid it is called
(a) Endopthalme (b) Megalopthalmus
(c) Nanopthalmia (d) Sliabismus

756. Restricted development of eye in all demensions is called

(a) Endoplthalme (b) Megalopthalmus
(c) Nanopthalmia (d) Sliabismus

757. Involuntary movement of eye ball resulting from unequal tones in two antagonistic muscle of eye is called
(a) Strabismus (b) Chemosis
(c) Nystagmus (d) Chalazion

758. Deviation of globe from normal axis due to excessive tension is known as
(a) Strabismus (b) Chemosis
(c) Nystagmus (d) Chalazion

759. Enlargement of tarsal gland is known as
(a) Strabismus (b) Chemosis
(c) Nystagmus (d) Chalazion

760. Extensive edematous condition of conjunctiva is known as
(a) Strabismus (b) Chemosis
(c) Nystagmus (d) Chalazion

761. Collection of blood in anterior chamber of eye is called
(a) Hyphaemia (b) Hypopion
(c) Aniridea (d) Iridocyclitis

762. Collection pus in anterior chamber of eye is called
(a) Hyphaemia (b) Hypopion
(c) Aniridea (d) Iridocyclitis

763. Absence of iris is called
(a) Hyphaemia (b) Hypopion
(c) Aniridea (d) Iridocyclitis

764. Inflammation of iris & uteacy body is
(a) Hyphaemia (b) Hypopion
(c) Aniridea (d) Iridocyclitis

765. Horn cancer is a
(a) Papilloma
(b) Melanoma
(c) Squamous cell carcinoma
(d) Lymphosarcoma

766. Luomyosarcoma is
(a) Benign neoplasm of smooth muscle
(b) Malignant neoplasm of smooth muscle
(c) Malignant neoplasm of skeletal muscle
(d) Benign neoplasm of smooth muscle

767. Benign tumor of striated muscle is
(a) Luo myoma (b) Luo sarcoma
(c) Rhabdomyoma (d) Chondroma

768. Benign tumor of cartilage is
(a) Luo myoma (b) Luo sarcoma
(c) Rhabdomyoma (d) Chondroma

769. Gonitis is the inflammation of
(a) Stifle joint (b) Hip joint
(c) Hock joint (d) Coffin joint

770. Coxetis is the inflammation of
(a) Stifle joint (b) Hip joint
(c) Hock joint (d) Coffin joint

771. Spavin is the arthritis of
(a) Stifle joint (b) Hip joint
(c) Hock joint (d) Coffin joint

772. Pedal ostitis is the inflammation of
(a) Stifle joint (b) Hip joint
(c) Hock joint (d) Coffin joint

773. Instrument used to limit the primary X-ray beam to size of film in X-ray machine
(a) Collemater (b) Grid
(c) Filter (d) Cassettes

774. Instrument used for absorbing scattered radiation
(a) Collemater (b) Grid
(c) Filter (d) Cassettes

775. Equipment used to keep an X-ray film for part being radiograph
(a) Collemater (b) Grid
(c) Filter (d) Cassettes

776. Equipment used to harmful and non penetrating X-rays
(a) Collemater (b) Grid
(c) Filter (d) Cassettes

777. Which of the defect is produced by secondary radiation in X-ray film?
(a) Grey non contrast radiograph
(b) Dark spot
(c) White spot
(d) Fog film

778. Weak & old developer produces
(a) Grey non contrast radiograph
(b) Dark spot
(c) White spot
(d) Fog film

779. Spilling drop of developer on X ray film during loading into cassette produces the following
(a) Grey non contrast radiograph

(b) Dark spot
(c) White spot
(d) Fog film

780. Metallic base containing medicine pasted on animal body during radiography produces
(a) Grey non contrast radiograph
(b) Dark spot
(c) White spot
(d) Fog film

781. Contrast radiography using $BaSO_4$ is used for
(a) Bronchography (b) Oesophagography
(c) IV phylography (d) Myelography

782. After $BaSO_4$ meal X ray is taken for esophagus
(a) Immediately (b) After 30 minutes
(c) 3 hours (d) 5 hours

783. After $BaSO_4$ meal X ray is taken for reticulum
(a) Immediately (b) After 30 minutes
(c) 3 hours (d) 5 hours

784. After $BaSO_4$ meal X ray is taken for colon
(a) Immediately (b) After 30 minutes
(c) 3 hours (d) 5 hours

785. After $BaSO_4$ meal X ray is taken for rectum
(a) Immediately (b) After 30 minutes
(c) 3 hours (d) 5 hrous

786. Swelling surrounding tissue of sesamoid bone is
(a) Sesamoditis (b) Osselets
(c) Bone spavin (d) Thoroughpin

787. Arthritis of fetlock joint is
(a) Sesamoditis (b) Osselets
(c) Bone spavin (d) Thoroughpin

788. Periostitis of third metatarsal is
(a) Sesamoditis (b) Osselets
(c) Bone spavin (d) Thoroughpin

789. Tendosynovitis of tarsal shealth is
(a) Sesamoditis (b) Osselets
(c) Bone spavin (d) Thoroughpin

790. Hygroma of carpus is a
(a) Congenital bursitis at point of elbow
(b) Acquired bursitis at point of elbow
(c) acquired bursitis at point of knee
(d) conginital bursitis at point of elbow

791. Hard cement to floor leads to which condition in animals
(a) Supra scapular nerve paralysis
(b) Hygrom of corpus
(c) Both
(d) None

792. Paralysis of pectoral nerve leads to
(a) Outward blowing of limb
(b) Inward blowing of limb
(c) Inward rotation of digit
(d) Both a & c

793. Knuckling at corpus & fetlock occurs due to
(a) Contraction of flexor tendon
(b) Paralysis of flexor tendon
(c) Relaxation of flexor tendon
(d) Breaking up of flexor tendon

794. Bowed tendon refers to
(a) Low tendovagenitis
(b) High tendovagenitis
(c) True tendovagenitis
(d) False tendovagenitis

795. Adhesions between superficial & deep digital flexor tendon with volar ligament is known as
(a) Splint (b) Bowed tendon
(c) Joint mouse (d) Buttress foot

796. Ashcean operation is conducted for
(a) Splint (b) Bowed tendon
(c) Joint mouse (d) Buttress foot

797. Cobalt 60 therapy is used for
(a) Splint (b) Bowed tendon
(c) Joint mouse (d) Buttress foot

798. Firing is best treatment for
(a) Splint (b) Bowed tendon
(c) Joint mouse (d) Buttress foot

799. Pyramidal disease is also known as
(a) Splint (b) Bowed tendon
(c) Joint mouse (d) Buttress foot

800. Which of one is true for Buttress Foot?
(a) Occurs due to concussion.
(b) Swelling of coronary band
(c) Pyramidal disease
(d) All

801. Chronic hypertrophy of fog of third phalanx is
(a) Thrush (b) Canker
(c) Wind puff (d) Founder

802. Lack of proper frog pressure leads to
(a) Thrush (b) Canker

(c) Wind puff (d) Founder

803. Unhygienic bedding & muddy ground leads to
(a) Thrush (b) Canker
(c) Wind puff (d) Founder

804. $CuSO_4$ & Zn O are used as cauterizing agent for treatment of
(a) Thrush (b) Canker
(c) Wind puff (d) Founder

805. 10% phenol, Tincture of Iodine & 10% formalin are used for
(a) Thrush (b) Canker
(c) Wind puff (d) Founder

806. Synovial swelling of joint capsule & tendon sheath is
(a) Thrush (b) Canker
(c) Wind puff (d) Founder

807. There is no lameness in case of
(a) Thrush (b) Canker
(c) Wind puff (d) Founder

808. Condition due to poor nutritional status
(a) Thrush (b) Canker
(c) Wind puff (d) Founder

809. Other name of laminitis is
(a) Thrush (b) Canker
(c) Wind puff (d) Founder

810. Aseptic spontaneous inflammation of sensitive lamina
(a) Thrush (b) Canker
(c) Wind puff (d) Founder

811. Seedy toe condition develops in case of
(a) Thrush (b) Canker
(c) Wind puff (d) Founder

812. High amount of histamine secretion occurs in case of
(a) Thrush (b) Canker
(c) Wind puff (d) Founder

813. Obesity & ingestion of grass leads to
(a) Thrush (b) Canker
(c) Wind puff (d) Founder

814. Animal showing sign as hind limb under the body & fore limb forward in
(a) Thrush (b) Canker
(c) Wind puff (d) Founder

815. A technique in which two or more anesthetic agents are combinely used to achieve anesthesia is known as
(a) Light anesthesia
(b) Desiccative anesthesia
(c) Balanced anesthesia
(d) Mixed anesthesia

816. Loss of sensation of whole body due to functional disruption by marked stimulation rather than depression is
(a) Light anesthesia
(b) Desiccative anesthesia
(c) Balanced anesthesia
(d) Mixed anesthesia

817. Dose of anesthesia needed in small animal in comparison to large animal is
(a) High (b) Low
(c) Equal (d) Not related with age

818. Anesthetic is deposited around the nerve trunk in
(a) Nerve block (b) Epidural anesthesia
(c) Spinal anesthesia (d) Inverted & block

819. Drug is injected with subarachnoid space in
(a) Nerve block (b) Epidural anesthesia
(c) Spinal anesthesia (d) Inverted & block

820. More dose of anesthesia is required in
(a) Mature animal (b) Old animal
(c) Obese animal (d) Lean & then animal

821. Recovery from anesthesia occurs latest in
(a) Mature animal (b) Old animal
(c) Obese animal (d) Lean & then animal

822. Dose of anesthesia in male as compared to female is
(a) High (b) Low
(c) Equal (d) Not related

823. Dose of anesthesia in active animal as compared to less active animals is
(a) High (b) Low
(c) Equal (d) Not related

824. Dose of anesthesia in pregnant female as compared to non pregnant female is
(a) High (b) Low
(c) Equal (d) Not related

825. Atropine is obtained from
(a) *Atropa nirger* (b) *Atropa belladona*

(c) *Hyocine nirger* (d) None

826. Dose of atropine in dog
(a) 2mg/lb wt (b) 4 mg/lb wt
(c) 0.2 mg/lb wt (d) 0.2 wg/lb wt

827. Which of the following is more potent?
(a) Atropine sulfate (b) Scopolomine
(c) None (d) Equal

828. Which one is a phenothazine derivative?
(a) Chlorpromazine (b) Xylazine
(c) Both (d) None

829. IV chlorpromazine is contraindicated in
(a) Ruminant (b) Cat
(d) Dog (d) All

830. Xlyazine in cat produces
(a) Heart block (b) Respiratory failure
(c) Emesis (d) Coma

831. Reserpine is a
(a) Tranquilzer (b) Antihypertensive
(c) Both (d) None

832. Atropine and Xylazine are
(a) Synonym (b) Substitute
(c) Antagonist (d) Partial agonist

833. Lavallorphane and Meperidine HCL
(a) Synonym (b) Substitute
(c) Antagonist (d) Partial agonist

834. Which one is known as Innovar vet?
(a) Droperidol
(b) Fentanyl
(c) Combination of a & b
(d) None

835. Narcotic in Innovar Vet is
(a) Droperidol
(b) Fentanyl
(c) Combination of a & b
(d) None

836. Swelling reflex is lost in which stage of anesthesia
(a) Stage I (b) Stage II
(c) stage III (d) Stage IV

837. Stage of anesthesia in which animal enters in shock
(a) Stage I (b) Stage II
(c) stage III (d) Stage IV

838. Cough reflex is totally absent in which stage
(a) Stage I (b) Stage II
(c) stage III (d) Stage IV

839. Respiration becomes thoraco-abdominal in which stage
(a) Stage I (b) Stage II
(c) stage III (d) Stage IV

840. Mucus membrane become pale in which stage
(a) Stage I (b) Stage II
(c) stage III (d) Stage IV

841. Gasping type of respiration occurs in which stage
(a) Stage I (b) Stage II
(c) stage III (d) Stage IV

842. Hypertension occurs in which stage
(a) Stage I (b) Stage II
(c) stage III (d) Stage IV

843. Eye ball position is normal in which stage
(a) Stage I (b) Stage II
(c) stage III (d) Stage IV

844. Which anesthesia is contra indicated in case of respiratory infection
(a) Ether (b) Barbiturate
(c) Xylazine (d) All

845. Cocaine is an ester of
(a) Benozinc acid (b) Succinic acid
(c) Malonic acid (d) PABA

846. Procaine is an ester of
(a) Benozinc acid (b) Succinic acid
(c) Malonic acid (d) PABA

847. Which statement is true about lignocaine comparison to procaine?
(a) Double potent
(b) Rapid onset of action
(c) Both
(d) None

848. The term spray anesthesia is used for
(a) Procaine (h) Xylocaine
(c) Ethylchloride (d) None

849. Ketamin is mainly used in
(a) Ruminant (b) Dog
(c) Cat (d) Horse

850. GP of drugs which paralyze voluntary muscle tone
(a) Anesthetic (b) Muscle relaxants
(c) (d) All

851. Muscle relaxants act on
(a) Neuromuscular function

(b) Synapsis in spinal cord
(c) Both
(d) None

852. Decamethonium is classified under
(a) Depolarizing agent
(b) Non polarizing agent
(c) Dual blocking agent
(d) Miscellaneous agent

853. Succenyl choline is a
(a) Depolarizing agent
(b) Non polarizing agent
(c) Dual blocking agent
(d) Miscellaneous agent

854. Hexabis carbacholine is classified under
(a) Depolarizing agent
(b) Non polarizing agent
(c) Dual blocking agent
(d) Miscellaneous agent

855. Gallamine is classified under
(a) Depolarizing agent
(b) Non polarizing agent
(c) Dual blocking agent
(d) Miscellaneous agent

856. D - tubocurarine chloride is classified under
(a) Depolarizing agent
(b) Non polarizing agent
(c) Dual blocking agent
(d) Miscellaneous agent

857. Neostygmine methyl sulfate is the antidote of
(a) Gallamine
(b) D - tubocurarine
(c) Hexabis carbacholine
(d) Succinyl choline

858. The word surgery is derived from Greek word
(a) Cheer & gery (b) Cheer & ourgose
(c) Sur & gery (d) Sur & Ourgose

859. Haematoma is characterized under which degree of contusion
(a) I (b) II
(c) III (d) IV

860. Actual loss of tissue occurs in cases of
(a) Abrasion (b) Contusin
(c) Avulsion (d) Laceration

861. Which of the wounds is caused by flies?
(a) Insect bite (b) Maggot wound
(c) Punctured wound (d) Gram native wound

862. Phosphatase activity of cells is seen during
(a) Bone formation (b) Bone resorption
(c) Both a & b (d) Inactive stage

863. pH of haematoma at the site of fracture is
(a) Alkaline (b) Highly alkaline
(c) Acidic (d) Neutral

864. Primary callus during bone healing is formed by which bone
(a) Lamellar (b) Cancellous
(c) Woven (d) Medullary

865. Bone most susceptible for spiral fracture is
(a) Radius (b) Ulna
(c) Humerus (d) Tibia

866. Periosteum is absent from
(a) Diaphysis (b) Metaphysis
(c) Surface of patella (d) Epiphysis line

867. Use of Bone curette is
(a) To elevate periosteum
(b) To check point of fracture
(c) To remove creative bone
(d) All

868. Asepsis can be defined as
(a) Absence of pathogenic microbes
(b) Killing of all microorganisms
(c) Killing of pathogenic organisms
(d) All

869. Principle of steam sterilization involves
(a) Coagulation of cellular proteins(b) Destruction of all exogenous material
(b) Both
(d) None

870. Boiling water at atmospheric pressure is
(a) Disinfecting agent (b) Sterilizing agent
(c) Both (d) None

871. Which of the following alcohols is used for cold sterilization?
(a) Methanol (b) Ethanol
(c) Glycerol (d) Glycol

872. Which % of HCHO in water is used in cold sterilization?
(a) 20% (b) 100%
(c) 40% (d) 37%

873. Antiseptic agent present in Tincture is
(a) Formaldehyde (b) Chlorhexidine
(c) Inorganic iodine (d) Carbolic acid

874. Oldest known germicidal agent is
(a) Founaldeliyede (b) Chlorhexidine
(c) Inorganic codine (d) Carbolic acid

875. Which of the following are used as general disinfectants on environmental surfaces?
(a) Phenols (b) Cresols
(c) Bisphenols (d) All

876. Which of the following cant be sterilized by autoclaving
(a) Suture material
(b) Surgical electro cautery
(c) Instruments
(d) Microscope

877. Which suture is best used in cases of prolapse of vagina or uterus?
(a) Umbilical tape (b) Horse hair
(c) Linen (d) Skin

878. Which one is non capillary in nature?
(a) Umbilical tape (b) Horse hair
(c) Linen (d) Skin

879. Which of the following produces more tissue reaction than cotton?
(a) Umbilical tape (b) Horse hair
(c) Linen (d) Skin

880. Which suture becomes ionized in tissues?
(a) Tantalum (b) Silver
(c) Copper (d) Aluminum

881. Which one is commercially available as Novafil?
(a) Polycstufibre (b) Surgilene
(c) Polybutester (d) Tereline

882. Which one is incorrect for suture material?
(a) Should have tensile strength
(b) Should be non capillary in action
(c) Should be easily knottable
(d) Should alter healing

883. Which of the suture is recommended for cardiac muscle?
(a) Polypropyline (b) Silk
(c) Cotton (d) Surgilline

884. Rupture of underlying tissue without separation of skin is known as
A. Abrasion B. Contusion
C. Erosion D. All

885. Periosteum material for suturing tendon is
(a) Ovary (b) Uterus
(c) Both (d) Oviduct

886. Which is the common suture size used for skin suturing in small animals?
(a) 4-0 to 3-0 (b) 3-0 to 0
(c) 6-0 to 5-0 (d) 4-0 to 2-0

887. Which is the common suture size used for muscle
(a) 4-0 to 3-0 (b) 3-0 to 0
(c) 6-0 to 5-0 (d) 4-0 to 2-0

888. Which is the common suture size used for ligatiure of vessel
(a) 4-0 to 3-0 (b) 3-0 to 0
(c) 6-0 to 5-0 (d) 4-0 to 2-0

889. Which is the common suture size used for suturing nerve
(a) 4-0 to 3-0 (b) 3-0 to 0
(c) 6-0 to 5-0 (d) 4-0 to 2-0

890. Which of the following are not apposition suture?
(a) Simple interrupted
(b) Sub cuticular
(c) Pin suture
(d) Lambert

891. Lumber suture are of which type?
(a) Apposition (b) Everson
(c) Inversion (d) Relaxation

892. Suture technique used to suture cut end of vessels is
(a) Apposition (b) Everson
(c) Inversion (d) Relaxation

893. Halsted suture are of which type?
(a) Apposition (b) Everson
(c) Inversion (d) Relaxation

894. Sub cuticular suture are of which type?
(a) Apposition (b) Everson
(c) Inversion (d) Relaxation

895. Best suturing material for suturing tendon is
A. Silk B. Cotton
C. Catgut D. Stainless steel wire

896. Suture line is parallel to line of incision case of
(a) Cushing (b) Lembert
(c) Both (d) None

897. Suture line is perpendicular to line of inclusion in
(a) Cushing (b) Lembert
(c) Both (d) None

898. Needle penetrates all layers except mucus layer in
(a) Cushing (b) Connell
(c) both (d) None

899. Needle penetrates all layers including mucus layer in
(a) Cushing (b) Connell
(c) both (d) None

900. Quill sutures are
(a) Vertical mattress (b) Horizontal mattress
(c) Halsted mattress (d) Not mattress

901. Bunell Mayer technique is used for repair of
(a) Tendon (b) Nerve
(c) Bone (d) Intestine

902. Gambee is a suture technique related to
(a) Tendon (b) Nerve
(c) Bone (d) Intestine

903. Spaying strictly means removal of
A. Ovary B. Uterus
C. Both D. Oviduct

904. Non traumatic needle should not be used in case of
(a) Parenchymatous organs
(b) Fat muscles
(c) Ligament
(d) All

905. Which of the following is known as KHUNTA knot?
(a) Clove hitch (b) Grany knot
(c) Halter (d) Twitch

906. Which of the following is known as MOHARA?
(a) Clove hitch (b) Grany knot
(c) Halter (d) Twitch

907. A new borne foal should never be restrained by
(a) Ear (b) Mane
(c) Tail (d) All

908. Easiest method for casting a horse is
(a) Double side line method
(b) Hobble method
(c) Burley method
(d) Rope square method

909. Method useful for casting powerful & heavy horses within a confined area
(a) Double side line method
(b) Hobble method
(c) Burley method
(d) Rope square method

910. A bandage has how many layers
(a) 1 (b) 2
(c) 3 (d) 10

911. Which type of bandage should not be used during late stages of wound healing?
(a) Adherent type (b) Non adherent type
(c) Both (d) None

912. Which type of bandages are used for treatment of acute wounds?
(a) Adherent type (b) Non adherent type
(c) Both (d) None

913. Which type of adherent bandages is preferred in amount of fluid?
(a) Dry to dry (b) Wet to dry
(c) Wet to wet (d) Any

914. Which type of adherent bandages is preferred in wounds with high viscosity exudates & loose debris?
(a) Dry to dry (b) Wet to dry
(c) Wet to wet (d) Any

915. Which type of adherent bandages is preferred in wounds that have an abundant of viscous exudates?
(a) Dry to dry (b) Wet to dry
(c) Wet to wet (d) Any

916. Which type of following bandaging is permeable to wound fluids?
(a) Occlusive (b) Semiocclusive
(c) Both (d) None

917. Which bandages are impermeable to wound fluids but permeable to gases?
(a) Occlusive (b) Semiocclusive
(c) Both (d) none

918. Which of the following can be used for preparing intermediate layer of bandage?
(a) Cast padding (b) Disposable diapers
(c) Absorptive pads (d) All

919. Which catheter is made up of gum elastic?

(a) Mare catheter (b) Cow catheter
(c) Dog catheter (d) Both a & c

920. Which catheter is made of metal?
(a) Mare catheter (b) Cow catheter
(c) Dog catheter (d) Both a & c

921. Which one is a metallic catheter?
(a) Uterine catheter (b) Vascular catheter
(c) Foley's catheter (d) All

922. Which one is radio opaque catheter?
(a) Uterine catheter (b) Vascular catheter
(c) Foley's catheter (d) All

923. Which catheter is used as an indwelling catheter to drain bladder?
(a) Uterine catheter (b) Vascular catheter
(c) Foley's catheter (d) All

924. Probang in cattle are used to clear
(a) Esophageal passage
(b) Respiratory passage
(c) Urinary passage
(d) Uterine passage

925. Operation for umbilical hernia is not done in
(a) Very old animals (b) Very young animals
(c) Obese animals (d) Thin animals

926. Technique to break the continuity of a part is
(a) Dieresis (b) Excision
(c) Resection (d) Ablation

927. Act of removal of a part from body is
(a) Dieresis (b) Excision
(c) Resection (d) Ablation

928. Removal of a lobe of liver or lung comes under
(a) Dieresis (b) Excision
(c) Resection (d) Ablation

929. Technique which uses excision, amputation & resection is
(a) Dieresis (b) Excision
(c) Resection (d) Ablation

930. Which one is not used during Ablation?
(a) Excision (b) Amputation
(c) Résection (d) Inclusion

931. Which of the following is not a type of curative haemostasis?
(a) Torniquet (b) Ligation
(c) Torsion (d) Compression

932. In Boyle's apparatus oxygen cylinder is of which colour?
(a) Green (b) Blue
(c) Orange (d) Red

933. Nitrous oxide cylinder of which colour?
(a) Green (b) Blue
(c) Orange (d) Red

934. Cyclopropane cylinder is of which colour?
(a) Green (b) Blue
(c) Orange (d) Red

935. Ethylene cylinder is of which colour?
(a) Green (b) Blue
(c) Orange (d) Red

936. Which cylinder is grey in colour?
(a) O_2 (b) Co_2
(c) Helum (d) None

937. Which cylinder is Brown in colour?
(a) O_2 (b) Co_2
(c) Helium (d) None

938. Drugs which increase heart rate & reduce venous pooling are
(a) l-adrenergic (b) b-adrenergic
(c) l-blockers (d) b-blockers

939. Drugs used as cardiac stimulants are
(a) l-adrenergic (b) b-adrenergic
(c) l-blockers (d) b-blockers

940. The drugs which reduce arterial BP & increase venous return are
(a) l-adrenergic (b) b-adrenergic
(c) l-blockers (d) b-blockers

941. Drugs which reduce heart rate & increase peripheral resistance are
(a) l-adrenergic (b) b-adrenergic
(c) l-blockers (d) b-blockers

942. Levarterenol is a
(a) l-adrenergic (b) b-adrenergic
(c) l-blockers (d) b-blockers

943. Isoproterenol is a
(a) l-adrenergic (b) b-adrenergic
(c) l-blockers (d) b-blockers

944. Phenothiazine tranquilizers are
(a) l-adrenergic (b) b-adrenergic
(c) l-blockers (d) b-blockers

945. Propranol & Amphetamine is

(a) l-adrenergic (b) b-adrenergic
(c) l-blockers (d) b-blockers

946. What % of $NaHCO_3$ can aid to treat cardiac arrest?
(a) 2.5% (b) 5%
(c) 7.5% (d) 10%

947. Which drug is used to give anesthesia by open method?
(a) Ether (b) Xylazine
(c) Barbiturate (d) All

948. Which anesthesia is used for desensitizing superficial layers of skin?
(a) Infiltration anesthesia
(b) Surface anesthesia
(c) Field block
(d) Regional anesthesia

949. In which technique the anesthetic is deposited in the close vicinity of nerve endings
(a) Infiltration anesthesia
(b) Surface anesthesia
(c) Field block
(d) Regional anesthesia

950. Anesthetic is deposited in certain planes of body along the course of all nerves which cross these planes in
(a) Infiltration anesthesia
(b) Surface anesthesia
(c) Field block
(d) Regional anesthesia

951. Which anesthesia is achieved by blocking conduction of sensory nerve of the region?
(a) Infiltration anesthesia
(b) Surface anesthesia
(c) Field block
(d) Regional anesthesia

952. Which technique is also known as conduction block?
(a) Infiltration anesthesia
(b) Surface anesthesia
(c) Field block
(d) Regional anesthesia

953. Anesthetic is deposited in sub cutaneous space in
(a) Infiltration anesthesia
(b) Surface anesthesia
(c) Field block
(d) Regional anesthesia

954. In case of intravenous retrograde regional analgesic anesthetic is deposed
(a) Parallel to direction of vein
(b) Longitudinal
(c) Close vicinity of vein
(d) Directly in the vein

955. Effect of epinephrine on direction of local anesthetic
(a) Prolonged (b) Decreased
(c) May or (d) No effect

956. Effect of Hyaluronidase
(a) Prolonged (b) Decreased
(c) May or (d) No effect

957. Hyaluronidase is
(a) Lepolylic (b) Neurolytic
(c) Histotoxic (d) Mucolytic

958. In case of Hyaluronidase, the diffusion of anesthetic agent into the tissue
(a) Increases
(b) Decreases
(c) Either increases or decreases
(d) No effect

959. For complete analgesia & akinesia of tongue which nerve should be blocked
(a) Lingual (b) Hypoglossal
(c) Both (d) None

960. Lingual nerve block in cattle is done at the level of
(a) 4-5th lower check tooth
(b) 4-5th upper check tooth
(c) 3rd upper check tooth
(d) 3rd lower check tooth

961. Which nerve block desensitizers lower jaw in Paresis?
(a) Mandibuloalveolar
(b) Mental
(c) Both
(d) None

962. Mental nerve bock in cow is done at the level of
(a) 4th incisor (b) 1st molar
(c) 6th incisor (d) Last molar

963. Mental nerve bock in dog & cat is done at the

level of
(a) 4th incisor (b) 1st molar
(c) 6th incisor (d) Last molar

964. For Trephining of facial sinuses which nerve block is preferred?
(a) Infraorbital (b) Supraorbital
(c) Both (d) None

965. Which nerve block is done for trephining of frontal skins?
(a) Infraorbital (b) Supraorbital
(c) Both (d) None

966. Which nerve block is done in pterygopaletine fossa?
(a) Maxillary (b) Mandibular
(c) Mental (d) Cornual

967. Which nerve block is done in temporal fossa?
(a) Maxillry (b) Mandibeilar
(c) Mental (d) Cornual

968. Cornual nerve lies about 4 cm deep in case of
(a) Cow (b) Buffalo
(c) Sheep (d) Goat

969. Which nerve block is done in horse to relieve the spasm of eye lids?
(a) Auriculopalpebral
(b) Retrobulbar
(c) Cornual
(d) Both a & c

970. For treatment of horn cancer in goat which nerve block is done?
(a) Auriculopalpebral
(b) Retrobulbar
(c) Cornual
(d) Both a & c

971. For management of conditions of nictitating membrane which nerve block is done?
(a) Auriculopcolppebral
(b) Retrobulbar
(c) Cornual
(d) Both a & c

972. Which nerve block is done about 3 cm below the highest point of the dossal border of Zygomatic arch?
(a) Auriculopalpebral
(b) Retrobulbar
(c) Cornual
(d) Both a & c

973. Which nerve block is done about 2 cm behind the middle of supraorbital process parallel to the roof of bony orbit?
(a) Auriculopalpebral
(b) Retrobulbar
(c) Cornual
(d) Both a & c

974. Peterson nerve block desensitizes which cranial nerves?
(a) III (b) IV
(c) VI (d) All

975. Site for caudal epidural anesthesia in horse is
(a) Sacrococcygeal space
(b) Between I & II inter coccygeal space
(c) Both
(d) None

976. Site for caudal epidural anesthesia in cattle is
(a) Sacrococcygeal space
(b) Between I & II inter coccygeal space
(c) Both
(d) None

977. Lumbosacral space is chosen for injection in
(a) Posterior epidural anesthesia
(b) Anterior epidural anesthesia
(c) Both
(d) None

978. Which anesthesia is preferred for operations like castration vasectomy etc.?
(a) Posterior epidural anesthesia
(b) Anterior epidural anesthesia
(c) Both
(d) None

979. Which anesthesia is preferred for operations like amputation of tail?
(a) Posterior epidural anesthesia
(b) Anterior epidural anesthesia
(c) Both
(d) None

980. Which operation should not be done with posterior epidural analgesia?
(a) Urethrotomy (b) Amputation of tail
(c) Caudal myectomy (d) Vasectomy

981. Which operation should not be done with anterior epidural analgesia
(a) Amputation of tail
(b) Castration
(c) Vasectomy
(d) All

982. Site of injection in Lumber segmental epidural analgesia is
(a) Sacro coccygial (b) Lumbosacral
(c) Between L1 & L2 (d) Between L2 & L3

983. Which one is not an advantage of Epidural analgesia?
(a) No respiratory assistances required
(b) Easy restraining of animal
(c) No effect on fetus
(d) Achieved in shorter time as compared to IV

984. Which waves are blocked in case of paravertebral analgesia?
(a) Spinal (b) Cranial
(c) Both (d) None

985. Which thoracic nerves are required to be blocked for median & paramedian incision in abdominal wall anterior to umbilicus?
(a) 9th to 12 th (b) 8th to 12 th
(c) 9th to 11th (d) 8th to 11th

986. Which nerves should be blocked for mid flank Laparotomy?
(a) T13, L1, L2 (b) T12, T13, L1
(c) T13, L1 & L2, L3 (d) T12, T13, L1, L2

987. Which nerve blocks are necessary for paramedian Laparotomy in caudal half of the abdominal wall?
(a) T12, T13, L1, L2 (b) T12, T13, L1
(c) T13, L1, L2 (d) T13, L1, L2, L3

988. Which nerve block is performed to do surgery on penis of bull in standing position?
(a) Peroneal (b) Obturator
(c) Proximal dorsal (d) Pudendal

989. Any operation on volar aspect of lower leg can be done by which nerve block?
(a) Radial (b) Ulnar
(c) Volar (d) Musculocutaneous

990. Which nerve block is done for operations on medial & dorsal anterior of the carpus?
(a) Radial (b) Ulnar
(c) Volar (d) Musculocutaneous

991. Which nerve block is done for diagnosis of laminitis & to relieve pain originating from distal part of limb?
(a) Radial (b) Ulnar
(c) Volar (d) Musculocutaneous

992. Which nerve block is done in flexed limb first above the lateral extensor?
(a) Peroneal (b) Tibial
(c) Saphenus (d) Digital

993. Which nerve block is done between achilles tendon & digital extensor on medial aspect of limb
(a) Radial (b) Ulnar
(c) Volar (d) Musculocutaneous

994. Which nerve supplies posterior aspect to hoof in both fore & hind limbs?
(a) Radial (b) Ulnar
(c) Volar (d) Musculocutaneous

995. The sensitivity of respiratory centre to Co_2 during barbiturate anesthesia is
(a) Increased (b) Decreased
(c) Unchanged (d) Any

996. Pupil of eye under ketamine anesthesia remains
(a) Dilated (b) Constricted
(c) Open (d) Closed

997. In case of intervertebral disc protrusion, knee jerk reflex is
(a) Exaggerated (b) Absent
(c) Not affected (d) Present

998. Sensitivity of cells to radiations is increased during
(a) Hypoxia (b) Oxygenation
(c) Normal condition (d) All

999. Which of the following cells are most radiosensitive?
(a) Muscle cells (b) Lymphoid cells
(c) Nerve cells (d) Osteocytes

1000. Tendon surrounded by sheath heals by
(a) Regeneration of proximal severed end
(b) Regeneration of distal severed end
(c) Elognation of do dy
(d) Proliferation of tissue from deeper layer of surrounding facial sheath

1001. Objective of pre anesthetic medication is
A. Minimize pain
B. Increase reflex autonomic activity
C. Facilitate handling
D. Both A and C

1002. Which action is not shown by phenothiazine tranquilizers on nervous system –
A. Antiemetic
B. Sympathomimetic
C. Sedation
D. All of the above

1003. Choose the correct one
A. Atropine is longer acting than glycopyrrolate
B. Atropine has same site of action as glycopyrrolate
C. Atropine causes more increase in heart rate than glycopyrrolate
D. None of above

1004. Opiate induced respiratory depression is antagonized by
A. Yohimbine B. Naloxone
C. Ephedrine D. Etorpine

1005. Choose most potent opioid agent
A. Meperidine B. Morphine
C. Oxymorphone D. Butorphanol

1006. Most potent inhalation agent is
A. Halothane B. Isoflurane
C. Methoxy flurane D. Nitrous oxide

1007. Choose the gas liquefied by pressure applied at room temperature –
A. Oxygen B. Carbon Dioxide
C. Nitrous oxide D. Both B and C

1008. Anatomic dead space during anesthesia
A. Can not change
B. Is greater than tidal volume
C. Can increase
D. Can decrease

1009. Blood contains which protein in highest concentration?
A. Hemoglobin B. Albumin
C. Transferrin D. Fibrinogen

1010. Choose the correct one
A. Diazepam is centrally acting muscle relaxant
B. Ketamine is non – dissociative agent
C. Phenothiazine causes vasoconstriction
D. Dopamine is sympatholytic

1011. Anatomic dead space is an area
A. Involved in gas exchange
B. Not involved in gas exchange
C. Equal to tidal volume
D. None of the above

1012. Anesthesia results in
A. Increased arterial CO_2 level
B. Decreased arterial CO_2 level
C. No change in arterial CO_2 level
D. Either increased or decreased CO_2 level

1013. In case of cattle, Xylazine administration results
A. Bradycardia B. Slow respiration
C. Diarrhea D. All of above

1014. Epinephrine causes
A. Premature ventricular contraction
B. Mature atrial contraction
C. Ventricular dilatation
D. None of the above

1015. White line disease is characterized by separation of fibrous junction between the sole and the wall on
A. Abaxial border of sole
B. Adaxial border of sole
C. Lateral side.
D. None of the above.

1016. Pododermatitis circumscripta is also known as
A. Whit line disease B. Sole ulcer
C. Toe ulcer D. Double sole

1017. Type One vertical fissure is confined to
A. Coronary band B. Middle of claw
C. Middle of wall D. None of the above

1018. Pathophysiologic disturbance of microvasculature of the corium is known as
A. Slipper foot B. Laminitis
C. Lameness D. Corkscrew claw

1019. Serous tarsitis is also known as
A. Bog spavin B. Puffy hock
C. Laminitis D. Both A and B

1020. Reaction of living tissue to injury is
A. Wound B. Infection

C. Bleeding D. Inflammation

1021. Condition characterized by three soft fluctuating swellings between the ligaments of the femorotarsal joint and is often seen in related animals is known as:
A. Serous bursitis B. Puffy hock
C. Bog spavin D. All of the above

1022. Progressive unilateral or bilateral hyperextension of the hind limb is known as
A. Spastic paresis B. Elso heel
C. Frost bite D. Both A and B

1023. Tendonitis occurs generally in race horses after fast exercise. Which tendon is involved in such cases most frequently?
A. Superficial flexor B. Extensor
C. Deep flexor D. None of the above.

1024. Tendonitis is also known as
A. Bog spavin B. Bowed tendon
C. Puffy hock D. Tenosynovitis

1025. Fistulous withers also has infectious etiology and caused by
A. *Brucella abotus* B. *Staphylococcus spp.*
C. *Bacillus anthracis* D. None of the above

1026. Nature of surgery involved in removal of a part of body
A. Extirpative surgery
B. Replacement surgery
C. Plastic surgery
D. General surgery

1027. Site for liver biopsy in cattle is
A. 11-12 Inter Costal space, right side
B. 7-8 Inter Costal space, right side
C. 11-12 Inter Costal space, left side
D. 7-8 Inter Costal space, right side

1028. Nerve block used for eye examination is
A. Infraorbital B. Mental
C. Retrobulbar D. auriculopalpebral

1029. Inguinal hernia is also known as
A. Omphalocele B. Bubnocele
C. Oscheocele D. None of these

1030. The pupil of eye under ketamine anesthesia remains
A. Dilated B. Open
C. Constricted D. Half open

1031. Which one is most radio-sensitive?
A. Muscle cells B. Nerve cells
C. Lymphoid cells D. Osteocytes

1032. Which technique is most suitable to brain scanning?
A. MRI B. CAT
C. DSA D. NONE

1033. SIALOGRAPHY is used for
A. Adrenal gland B. Axillary gland
C. Salivary gland D. Lymph gland

1034. In cushing suture, the needle –
A. Passes parallel to the incision
B. Does not enter the lumen
C. Causes inversion of margins
D. All of the above

Answers

1.	(a)	2.	(b)	3.	(b)	4.	(d)
5.	(c)	6.	(b)	7.	(c)	8.	(b)
9.	(c)	10.	(b)	11.	(a)	12.	(b)
13.	(b)	14.	(b)	15.	(d)	16.	(a)
17.	(a)	18.	(a)	19.	(a)	20.	(b)
21.	(d)	22.	(a)	23.	(d)	24.	(d)
25.	(c)	26.	(d)	27.	(c)	28.	(c)
29.	(b)	30.	(a)	31.	(c)	32.	(d)
33.	(a)	34.	(d)	35.	(a)	36.	(b)
37.	(c)	38.	(a)	39.	(c)	40.	(a)
41.	(d)	42.	(b)	43.	(c)	44.	(a)
45.	(a)	46.	(b)	47.	(c)	48.	(d)
49.	(d)	50.	(b)	51.	(a)	52.	(b)
53.	(a)	54.	(a)	55.	(b)	56.	(a)
57.	(b)	58.	(c)	59.	(d)	60.	(a)
61.	(a)	62.	(a)	63.	(c)	64.	(c)
65.	(c)	66.	(d)	67.	(a)	68.	(b)
69.	(d)	70.	(c)	71.	(a)	72.	(b)
73.	(a)	74.	(a)	75.	(b)	76.	(c)
77.	(c)	78.	(b)	79.	(d)	80.	(a)
81.	(a)	82.	(b)	83.	(c)	84.	(d)
85.	(a)	86.	(c)	87.	(d)	88.	(d)
89.	(d)	90.	(d)	91.	(a)	92.	(a)
93.	(b)	94.	(c)	95.	(d)	96.	(a)
97.	(c)	98.	(b)	99.	(c)	100.	(d)
101.	(a)	102.	(a)	103.	(b)	104.	(a)
105.	(d)	106.	(a)	107.	(b)	108.	(a)
109.	(d)	110.	(c)	111.	(a)	112.	(b)
113.	(a)	114.	(c)	115.	(b)	116.	(a)

117.	(c)	118.	(d)	119.	(a)
120.	(b)	121.	(b)	122.	(b)
123.	(c)	124.	(a)	125.	(a)
126.	(d)	127.	(a)	128.	(c)
129.	(c)	130.	(b)	131.	(b)
132.	(d)	133.	(b)	134.	(c)
135.	(c)	136.	(b)	137.	(a)
138.	(a)	139.	(b)	140.	(c)
141.	(c)	142.	(a)	143.	(d)
144.	(d)	145.	(c)	146.	(a)
147.	(b)	148.	(c)	149.	(a)
150.	(a)	151.	(b)	152.	(d)
153.	(b)	154.	(a)	155.	(b)
156.	(c)	157.	(d)	158.	(a)
159.	(b)	160.	(c)	161.	(d)
162.	(d)	163.	(a)	164.	(a)
165.	(b)	166.	(a)	167.	(d)
168.	(a)	169.	(a)	170.	(c)
171.	(b)	172.	(a)	173.	(a)
174.	(b)	175.	(a)	176.	(b)
177.	(a)	178.	(b)	179.	(b)
180.	(b)	181.	(a)	182.	(a)
183.	(d)	185.	(b)	186.	(d)
187.	(c)	188.	(a)	189.	(a)
190.	(a)	191.	(b)	192.	(c)
193.	(a)	194.	(d)	195.	(a)
196.	(b)	197.	(b)	198.	(a)
199.	(c)	200.	(b)	201.	(a)
202.	(b)	203.	(b)	204.	(c)
205.	(a)	206.	(d)	207.	(a)
208.	(a)	209.	(c)	210.	(d)
211.	(b)	212.	(c)	213.	(d)
214.	(a)	215.	(a)	216.	(b)
217.	(a)	218.	(d)	219.	(d)
220.	(a)	221.	(a)	222.	(d)
223.	(d)	224.	(d)	225.	(d)
226.	(c)	227.	(d)	228.	(c)
229.	(b)	230.	(c)	231.	(a)
232.	(b)	233.	(b)	234.	(b)
235.	(c)	236.	(a)	237.	(c)
238.	(c)	239.	(b)	240.	(a)
241.	(c)	242.	(c)	243.	(a)
244.	(a)	245.	(a)	246.	(a)
247.	(b)	248.	(c)	249.	(c)
250.	(c)	251.	(d)	252.	(d)
253.	(a)	254.	(d)	255.	(a)
256.	(b)	257.	(c)	258.	(d)

259.	(d)	260.	(d)	261.	(a)
262.	(a)	263.	(b)	264.	(c)
265.	(a)	266.	(c)	267.	(c)
268.	(d)	269.	(d)	270.	(d)
271.	(c)	272.	(c)	273.	(a)
274.	(b)	275.	(c)	276.	(c)
277.	(d)	278.	(a)	279.	(b)
280.	(a)	281.	(b)	282.	(b)
283.	(a)	284.	(b)	285.	(a)
286.	(b)	287.	(c)	288.	(d)
289.	(a)	290.	(d)	291.	(a)
292.	(a)	293.	(a)	294.	(b)
295.	(b)	296.	(c)	297.	(b)
298.	(b)	299.	(a)	300.	(b)
301.	(a)	302.	(c)	303.	(a)
304.	(b)	305.	(b)	306.	(a)
307.	(c)	308.	(b)	309.	(a)
310.	(b)	311.	(c)	312.	(d)
313.	(a)	314.	(b)	315.	(c)
316.	(d)	317.	(d)	318.	(a)
319.	(a)	320.	(a)	321.	(b)
322.	(c)	323.	(d)	324.	(d)
325.	(a)	326.	(b)	327.	(c)
328.	(c)	329.	(a)	330.	(b)
331.	(d)	332.	(a)	333.	(b)
334.	(b)	335.	(c)	336.	(b)
337.	(d)	338.	(a)	339.	(c)
340.	(c)	341.	(d)	342.	(a)
343.	(a)	344.	(a)	345.	(b)
346.	(c)	347.	(b)	348.	(b)
349.	(a)	350.	(b)	351.	(d)
352.	(d)	353.	(c)	354.	(a)
355.	(b)	356.	(a)	357.	(c)
358.	(a)	359.	(a)	360.	(b)
361.	(a)	362.	(a)	363.	(b)
364.	(b)	365.	(a)	366.	(a)
367.	(d)	368.	(a)	369.	(b)
370.	(c)	371.	(d)	372.	(a)
373.	(b)	374.	(c)	375.	(d)
376.	(d)	377.	(d)	378.	(a)
379.	(b)	380.	(c)	381.	(a)
382.	(d)	383.	(a)	384.	(c)
385.	(d)	386.	(a)	387.	(b)
388.	(c)	389.	(b)	390.	(c)
391.	(b)	392.	(d)	393.	(c)
394.	(a)	395.	(b)	396.	(c)
397.	(d)	398.	(d)	399.	(b)

400.	(b)	401.	(a)	402.	(b)
403.	(b)	404.	(d)	405.	(a)
406.	(d)	407.	(a)	408.	(b)
409.	(d)	410.	(a)	411.	(d)
412.	(d)	413.	(b)	414.	(c)
415.	(a)	416.	(b)	417.	(b)
418.	(b)	419.	(a)	420.	(b)
421.	(a)	422.	(b)	423.	(b)
424.	(a)	425.	(b)	426.	(b)
427.	(a)	428.	(a)	429.	(b)
430.	(c)	431.	(a)	432.	(c)
433.	(a)	434.	(d)	435.	(a)
436.	(a)	437.	(a)	438.	(c)
439.	(c)	440.	(d)	441.	(b)
442.	(d)	443.	(a)	444.	(c)
445.	(a)	446.	(c)	447.	(a)
448.	(b)	449.	(c)	450.	(d)
451.	(a)	452.	(c)	453.	(a)
454.	(a)	455.	(b)	456.	(a)
457.	(b)	458.	(c)	459.	(c)
460.	(a)	461.	(b)	462.	(b)
463.	(a)	464.	(c)	465.	(a)
466.	(c)	467.	(a)	468.	(c)
469.	(d)	470.	(c)	471.	(d)
472.	(d)	473.	(a)	474.	(b)
475.	(c)	476.	(a)	477.	(c)
478.	(a)	479.	(a)	480.	(c)
481.	(a)	482.	(a)	843.	(c)
484.	(c)	485.	(a)	486.	(c)
487.	(a)	488.	(b)	489.	(d)
490.	(c)	491.	(a)	492.	(a)
493.	(c)	494.	(a)	495.	(a)
496.	(c)	497.	(c)	498.	(b)
499.	(a)	500.	(a)	501.	(b)
502.	(b)	503.	(a)	504.	(c)
505.	(d)	506.	(a)	507.	(a)
508.	(b)	509.	(a)	510.	(a)
511.	(c)	512.	(c)	513.	(a)
514.	(a)	515.	(a)	516.	(c)
517.	(a)	518.	(b)	519.	(c)
520.	(a)	521.	(b)	522.	(a)
523.	(d)	524.	(a)	525.	(c)
526.	(c)	527.	(d)	528.	(d)
529.	(b)	530.	(d)	531.	(b)
532.	(c)	533.	(c)	534.	(a)
535.	(b)	536.	(c)	537.	(a)
538.	(b)	539.	(d)	540.	(c)

541.	(d)	542.	(d)	543.	(a)
544.	(b)	545.	(b)	546.	(c)
547.	(a)	548.	(b)	549.	(d)
550.	(a)	551.	(c)	552.	(b)
553.	(c)	554.	(b)	555.	(d)
556.	(a)	557.	(a)	558.	(b)
559.	(b)	560.	(d)	561.	(a)
562.	(a)	563.	(b)	564.	(c)
565.	(d)	566.	(d)	567.	(a)
568.	(d)	569.	(d)	570.	(d)
571.	(d)	572.	(b)	573.	(a)
574.	(a)	575.	(b)	576.	(c)
577.	(a)	578.	(d)	579.	(d)
580.	(a)	581.	(c)	582.	(c)
583.	(d)	584.	(a)	585.	(a)
586.	(a)	587.	(a)	588.	(b)
589.	(c)	590.	(a)	591.	(b)
592.	(a)	593.	(c)	594.	(a)
595.	(d)	596.	(b)	597.	(a)
598.	(c)	599.	(a)	600.	(a)
601.	(a)	602.	(c)	603.	(d)
604.	(c)	605.	(c)	606.	(b)
607.	(c)	608.	(c)	609.	(c)
610.	(b)	611.	(a)	612.	(c)
613.	(a)	614.	(d)	615.	(c)
616.	(d)	617.	(b)	618.	(c)
619.	(c)	620.	(b)	621.	(d)
622.	(c)	623.	(c)	624.	(a)
625.	(a)	626.	(b)	627.	(b)
628.	(d)	629.	(b)	630.	(d)
631.	(c)	632.	(d)	633.	(a)
634.	(c)	635.	(a)	636.	(c)
637.	(b)	638.	(b)	639.	(c)
640.	(a)	641.	(a)	642.	(a)
643.	(a)	644.	(b)	645.	(c)
646.	(a)	647.	(b)	648.	(c)
649.	(d)	650.	(b)	651.	(a)
652.	(a)	653.	(b)	654.	(a)
655.	(d)	656.	(d)	657.	(b)
658.	(d)	659.	(d)	660.	(a)
661.	(a)	662.	(b)	663.	(d)
664.	(a)	665.	(c)	666.	(a)
667.	(d)	668.	(b)	669.	(b)
670.	(c)	671.	(a)	672.	(a)
673.	(c)	674.	(a)	675.	(b)
676.	(b)	677.	(c)	678.	(d)
679.	(a)	680.	(d)	681.	(d)

682.	(a)	683.	(d)	684.	(a)
685.	(a)	686.	(a)	687.	(d)
688.	(a)	689.	(a)	690.	(a)
691.	(b)	692.	(a)	693.	(a)
694.	(d)	695.	(b)	696.	(b)
697.	(c)	698.	(c)	699.	(a)
700.	(b)	701.	(c)	702.	(c)
703.	(a)	704.	(c)	705.	(d)
706.	(d)	707.	(d)	708.	(d)
709.	(c)	710.	(b)	711.	(c)
712.	(c)	713.	(c)	714.	(a)
715.	(a)	716.	(d)	717.	(b)
718.	(b)	719.	(c)	720.	(a)
721.	(a)	722.	(a)	723.	(b)
724.	(a)	725.	(b)	726.	(b)
727.	(a)	728.	(a)	729.	(b)
730.	(c)	731.	(a)	732.	(a)
733.	(b)	734.	(d)	735.	(b)
736.	(a)	737.	(b)	738.	(d)
739.	(a)	740.	(b)	741.	(c)
742.	(b)	743.	(c)	744.	(a)
745.	(d)	746.	(c)	747.	(b)
748.	(a)	749.	(b)	750.	(a)
751.	(b)	752.	(c)	753.	(d)
754.	(d)	755.	(b)	756.	(c)
757.	(c)	758.	(a)	759.	(d)
760.	(b)	761.	(a)	762.	(b)
763.	(c)	764.	(d)	765.	(c)
766.	(b)	767.	(c)	768.	(d)
769.	(a)	770.	(b)	771.	(c)
772.	(d)	773.	(a)	774.	(b)
775.	(d)	776.	(c)	777.	(a)
778.	(d)	779.	(b)	780.	(c)
781.	(b)	782.	(a)	783.	(b)
784.	(c)	785.	(d)	786.	(a)
787.	(b)	788.	(c)	789.	(d)
790.	(b)	791.	(b)	792.	(d)
793.	(a)	794.	(a)	795.	(c)
796.	(b)	797.	(b)	798.	(a)
799.	(d)	800.	(d)	801.	(b)
802.	(b)	803.	(a)	804.	(b)
805.	(a)	806.	(c)	807.	(c)
808.	(c)	809.	(d)	810.	(d)
811.	(d)	812.	(d)	813.	(d)
814.	(d)	815.	(c)	816.	(b)
817.	(a)	818.	(a)	819.	(c)
820.	(c)	821.	(c)	822.	(a)

823.	(a)	824.	(a)	825.	(b)
826.	(d)	827.	(a)	828.	(c)
829.	(a)	830.	(c)	831.	(c)
832.	(c)	833.	(c)	834.	(c)
835.	(b)	836.	(c)	837.	(d)
838.	(d)	839.	(b)	840.	(d)
841.	(d)	842.	(c)	843.	(a)
844.	(a)	845.	(a)	846.	(d)
847.	(c)	848.	(c)	849.	(c)
850.	(b)	851.	(c)	852.	(a)
853.	(a)	854.	(c)	855.	(b)
856.	(b)	857.	(b)	858.	(b)
859.	(b)	860.	(d)	861.	(b)
862.	(c)	863.	(c)	864.	(c)
865.	(c)	866.	(c)	867.	(c)
868.	(a)	869.	(a)	870.	(a)
871.	(b)	872.	(d)	873.	(b)
874.	(d)	875.	(d)	876.	(d)
877.	(a)	878.	(b)	879.	(c)
880.	(b)	881.	(c)	882.	(d)
883.	(a)	884.	(b)	885.	(c)
886.	(a)	887.	(b)	888.	(d)
889.	(c)	890.	(d)	891.	(c)
892.	(b)	893.	(d)	894.	(a)
895.	(d)	896.	(a)	897.	(b)
898.	(a)	899.	(b)	900.	(a)
901.	(a)	902.	(d)	903.	(a)
904.	(c)	905.	(a)	906.	(c)
907.	(d)	908.	(a)	909.	(b)
910.	(c)	911.	(a)	912.	(b)
913.	(a)	914.	(b)	915.	(c)
916.	(b)	917.	(a)	918.	(d)
919.	(d)	920.	(b)	921.	(a)
922.	(b)	923.	(c)	924.	(a)
925.	(b)	926.	(a)	927.	(b)
928.	(c)	929.	(d)	930.	(d)
931.	(a)	932.	(a)	933.	(b)
934.	(c)	935.	(d)	936.	(b)
937.	(c)	938.	(b)	939.	(a)
940.	(c)	941.	(d)	942.	(a)
943.	(b)	944.	(c)	945.	(d)
946.	(c)	947.	(a)	948.	(b)
949.	(a)	950.	(c)	951.	(d)
952.	(d)	953.	(a)	954.	(d)
955.	(a)	956.	(b)	957.	(d)
958.	(a)	959.	(c)	960.	(a)
961.	(c)	962.	(a)	963.	(b)

964.	(a)	965.	(b)	966.	(a)
967.	(d)	968.	(b)	969.	(a)
970.	(d)	971.	(b)	972.	(a)
973.	(b)	974.	(d)	975.	(b)
976.	(b)	977.	(b)	978.	(b)
979.	(a)	980.	(d)	981.	(a)
982.	(c)	983.	(d)	984.	(a)
985.	(a)	986.	(a)	987.	(a)
988.	(d)	989.	(b)	990.	(d)
991.	(c)	992.	(a)	993.	(b)
994.	(d)	995.	(b)	996.	(a)
997.	(b)	998.	(b)	999.	(b)

1000.	(d)	1001.	(d)	1002.	(b)
1003.	(c)	1004.	(b)	1005.	(d)
1006.	(c)	1007.	(d)	1008.	(c)
1009.	(a)	1010.	(a)	1011.	(b)
1012.	(a)	1013.	(d)	1014.	(a)
1015.	(a)	1016.	(b)	1017.	(a)
1018.	(b)	1019.	(d)	1020.	(c)
1021.	(d)	1022.	(d)	1023.	(a)
1024.	(b)	1025.	(a)	1026.	(a)
1027.	(a)	1028.	(d)	1029.	(b)
1030.	(a)	1031.	(c)	1032.	(a)
1033.	(c)	1034.	(d)		